GOVERNOR REAGAN

GOVERNOR REAGAN

HIS RISE TO POWER

Lou Cannon

PublicAffairs
New York

BOOK DESIGN AND COMPOSITION BY JENNY DOSSIN. TEXT SET IN ADOBE JANSON.

Library of Congress Cataloging-in-Publication Data
Cannon, Lou, 1933–.
Governor Reagan: his rise to power / Lou Cannon.
p. cm.
Includes bibliographical references and index.
ISBN 1–58648–030–8
1. Reagan, Ronald.
2. Governors—California—Biography.
3. California—Politics and government—1951–
I. Title.
F866.4.R43C36 2003
979.4'053'092—dc21
[B]
2003047053

FIRST EDITION
1 3 5 7 9 10 8 6 4 2

To Mary, with love and appreciation,
and for Carl, David, Judy, and Jack,
and Nicholas, Kelly, Grace, Tiffany, Stephanie, and Nathan,
and with special thanks to Bill Clark, Ike Livermore,
Tom Reed, Stuart Spencer, and George Steffes

Contents

ACKNOWLEDGMENTS

THE IDEA FOR A COMPREHENSIVE examination of Ronald Reagan's governorship of California was conceived in a series of conversations with my publisher Peter Osnos, my editor Robert Kimzey, my agent Kristine Dahl, and my wife and researcher, Mary Cannon. Our premise was that the governorship and its influence on Reagan's presidency had been unduly neglected. Although I wrote extensively about the early governorship in my first book, *Ronnie and Jesse: A Political Odyssey*, published in 1969, it covered only two and a half years of Reagan's eight-year governorship. While I examined later aspects of his governorship in a 1982 book, *Reagan*, this biography focused on Reagan's pursuit of the presidency. So we conceived of a new book that would stand on the shoulders of my earlier works but make use of material that has become available since they were written.

Fortunately, Governor Reagan's first cabinet secretary, William P. Clark, made available to me the complete minutes of the cabinet meetings of the early governorship taken at his direction by his secretary, the meticulous Helene von Damm. I had utilized a few of these revealing minutes in *Ronnie and Jesse*; Clark supplied all of them for this book. Clark, who subsequently served as Reagan's chief of staff in Sacramento, also provided a key interview and helped on many details. Later cabinet minutes, which are stored at the Ronald Reagan Presidential Library in Simi Valley, California, were made available by the Ronald Reagan Presidential Foundation through the courtesy of Nancy Reagan and Joanne Drake. I have examined all of these minutes.

Thomas C. Reed, Reagan's first appointments secretary as governor, provided another treasure trove. Reed, who managed Reagan's successful reelection campaign in 1970, kept a diary that sheds light on the inner workings of this campaign and on a crucial staff shakeup in 1967. Reed made material from this diary and his valuable insights about Reagan available for this book.

Contemporaneous records were also kept by Norman ("Ike") Livermore, Reagan's secretary of resources, and the only cabinet member to serve the entire eight years of Reagan's governorship. Drawing upon these records, Livermore shared his recollections. They provide important new information about Reagan's environmental record.

Edwin Meese III, Reagan's chief of staff in Sacramento for six years, contributed a vital interview and many follow-up details. Lyn Nofziger, Reagan's press secretary in the 1966 campaign and his first communications director as governor, contributed an important interview. His memoir, *Nofziger* (1992), was also helpful.

For political background, I am especially grateful to Stuart K. Spencer, who played a major role in every one of Reagan's successful campaigns for governor and president. He has helped me with all of my five books on Reagan, none more so than this one. The same is true for George Steffes, Reagan's legislative liaison in Sacramento and now a prominent lobbyist there. Steffes provided information, anecdotes, and the benefit of his analysis on a dozen occasions. His predecessor, Jack B. Lindsey, provided a useful interview and an unpublished collection of stories and analysis: "Ronald Reagan: The First Year."

Verne Orr, who started out as director of motor vehicles for Governor Reagan and served in the key post of director of finance for five years, was another vital source of information. I thank him for his interview and for the information he provided in follow-up telephone conversations.

Several other key figures in Reagan's governorship gave useful interviews that contained new information, in particular Michael Deaver, Paul Haerle, Gordon Luce, Gordon Paul Smith, and Kirk West.

Retired legislative analyst A. Alan Post, Sacramento's premier institutional memory, provided a thoughtful interview that framed significant fiscal issues of the Reagan era.

A number of former state legislators were helpful, especially Anthony Beilenson, a state senator who sponsored pioneer abortion-rights legislation in 1967 and played a major role in the welfare-reform bill of 1971. I am grateful for the insights of William Bagley, who led the way in preserving the Rumford Fair Housing Act; Robert Monagan, the speaker of the Assembly in 1969–1970; and George Deukmejian, who carried Governor Reagan's fiscal package in 1967 and was later a two-term governor of California.

This book also draws upon more than 400 interviews that I conducted for my first two books on Reagan, the most important of which were 30 interviews and conversations with Reagan. He and Nancy Reagan were generous with their time and accessibility.

It would take a chapter to list the names and titles of those who helped me in earlier books and articles about Reagan, but a few need to be mentioned here. Among Democrats, I'm appreciative of the interviews provided by two former Assembly speakers, now deceased: Bob Moretti and Jesse Unruh. Moretti's chief of staff, Bill Hauck, subsequently an aide to other leading California politicians, was particularly helpful. So was Fred Dutton, a longtime adviser to Governor Edmund G. ("Pat") Brown.

On the Republican side, the words and insights of two deceased members of the Reagan team live in this book: Bill Roberts, who with Spencer managed Reagan's 1966 campaign for governor, and Rus Walton, a premier idea man for the "Creative Society."

I am in considerable debt to my readers and researchers. Mary Cannon annotated the cabinet minutes and checked notes and quotations with her customary thoroughness, while also serving as my editor of first resort. My reliable Sacramento-based researcher Lark Park scoured the microfilm of old copies of *The Sacramento Bee*, the *Los Angeles Times*, the *San Francisco Chronicle*, and the *San Jose Mercury-News*. The conscientious Gregory Cumming, archivist at the Ronald Reagan Presidential Library, delved into numerous historical records. Others at the Reagan Presidential Library who provided useful assistance were Meghan Lee, Mike Duggan, and Steve Branch, the audiovisual archivist.

A. G. Block, publisher of *California Journal*, to which I am a contributing editor, made available to me all copies of the magazine from its inception in 1970 through the end of the Reagan governorship in 1974. These issues provide a more detailed record of public policy events and California politics in this period than any other publication.

Block is also one of five persons, all friends, who took time from their busy lives to read this manuscript and make useful suggestions. The others are Mary Cannon, Carl Cannon, Judson Clark, and William Lee Miller. Carl Cannon, my eldest son, is White House correspondent for *National Journal*. Clark, a founder of *California Journal*, is chief operating officer of the Sacramento public information firm State Net and a former legislative aide. Miller, a distinguished historian at the Miller Center at the University of Virginia and the author, most recently, of *Lincoln's Virtues* (2002), has helped me with manuscripts of six of my seven previous books.

Michael Barone, the nation's premier resource on election data and demographics, took time from writing the latest edition of *The Almanac of American Politics* and his column at *U.S. News and World Report* to check statistics and share his insights, as he has done for many of my books. So did Mervin D. Field, California's leading political pollster for more than half a century.

Hugh Heclo, Robinson Professor of Public Affairs at George Mason University, shared his interesting paper, "Ronald Reagan and the American Public Philosophy," prepared for the Conference on the Reagan Presidency at the University of California at Santa Barbara.

Sherry Bebitch Jeffe, a well-known political scientist and writer in Southern California and a friend, contributed a useful interview of Bob Moretti conducted for the California Speakership Project.

Gary Kurutz, director of special collections at the California State Library, helped find useful documents of the Reagan era. I appreciate his efforts and thank Jenny Hoye in the California history room of the library for copying them.

For material on Reagan's activities in the Screen Actors Guild, I am thankful to Valerie Yaros, the Guild archivist. She also made it possible for me to interview Jack Dales, the longtime executive officer of the Guild, a few weeks before his death.

Others who helped in various ways include Terri Bimes, Bill Boyarsky, Wilson Elliot Brownlee, William F. Buckley Jr., David Doerr, John Douglass, Albert Eisele, Scott Hadly, Peter Hannaford, Steven Hayward, Al Hyam, Jay Nordlinger, Lou Papan, Ethan Rarick, Phil Schott, Kathleen Sharp, George Skelton, Adam Sofen, John Van de Kamp, and Sander Vanocur.

Our family physician, Dr. Thomas Allyn, kept my blood pressure within manageable bounds and gave good counsel when I needed it.

My peerless agent, Kristine Dahl of ICM, has represented and encouraged me for twenty years. As always, my thanks.

At PublicAffairs there are many people to thank, starting with publisher Peter Osnos, a onetime colleague at *The Washington Post*, and my patient and capable editor, Robert Kimzey. His assistant, Melanie Johnstone, and Gene Taft, director of publicity, provided cheerful assistance. Thanks also to photo researcher Melissa Goldstein, copy editor Katherine H. Streckfus, book designer Jenny Dossin, and jacket designer Nina D'Amario.

The four concluding chapters in this book on Reagan's 1976 and 1980 campaigns for the presidency contain a smattering of new material but are otherwise drawn from *Reagan*.

It should go without saying, but I will say it anyway: While the efforts of many people made this book possible, any errors or misperceptions are my responsibility alone.

Lou Cannon

Summerland, California
June 3, 2003

I

THE RISE OF
RONALD REAGAN

1

CALIFORNIA

W HEN RONALD REAGAN began his quest for the governorship
in 1965, California epitomized the American dream that
William Faulkner had described as "sanctuary on earth for
individual man."[1] Since the Gold Rush of 1849, the state had been a
magnet for American dreamers; in World War II it became the em-
barkation point for servicemen en route to war in the South Pacific and
an arsenal for the ships, planes, and guns that destroyed the imperial
forces of Japan. The GIs who returned from the war were dazzled by
the blue skies and easy ways of California, which seemed to them a land
of limitless possibilities. Many settled there and raised families, as did
even more of the defense workers who had flocked to the state during
the war. In the next twenty years, California attracted more than a thousand new residents a day, doubled in population to 18 million, and (in
1964) surpassed New York as the nation's most populous state. The
pace of growth was intoxicating; the only constant in California, said
social historian Carey McWilliams, was "rapid, revolutionary change."[2]

To provide a good life for the newcomers, while enriching themselves in the process, developers changed the California landscape.
They uprooted orange groves and orchards in Los Angeles, Orange,
and San Diego counties in the south and Santa Clara, Alameda, and
Contra Costa counties in the north, replacing them with subdivisions,
roads, and shopping centers. The state government helped finance
thousands of new schools and poured vast sums of money into a community college system that made higher education widely accessible
and into a university system that educated the scientists and engineers
who manned the aerospace barricades during the Cold War. During the
eight years of Edmund G. ("Pat") Brown's governorship, beginning in
1959, California completed a thousand miles of freeways and con-

structed a gigantic aqueduct, "the eighth wonder of the world,"[3] to move water from the wetter and less populous northern sections of California to drier and more populous Southern California. By the mid-1960s, California had become a font of technological and cultural innovation so global and diverse in its outlook that it became fashionable to describe it as a "nation-state." Indeed, in its economic output, California was exceeded by only six nations in the world: the United States, the Soviet Union, West Germany, Great Britain, France, and Japan. Its per capita income, was greater than any of these nations, indeed of all the countries in the world.

This prosperity was deceptive. To those on the outside looking in, California seemed to be an attractive dreamland when Reagan began the political journey that would one day take him to the White House, but insiders were reeling from two decades of unrestrained growth. Southern California, where public transportation was scarce, choked on this growth as its vaunted freeway system was overwhelmed by traffic flows that made commuting a nightmare and polluted the skies of the Los Angeles basin. In the north, developers were gradually filling in San Francisco Bay. Property taxes soared as local governments struggled frantically to meet demands for new schools and services. As cities sprawled far beyond their original boundaries, nearby agricultural areas were assessed at their "highest and best use," a premise that forced farmers, willing or not, to sell their land, which was promptly converted into new subdivisions far from city centers. The loss of open space spurred a nascent environmental movement, but the continual need for new revenues committed local governments to constant growth and promoted a breathtaking boosterism. Explaining his newspaper's enthusiasm for a housing boom that had wiped out the orchards of Santa Clara Valley—"the valley of heart's delight"—the circulation manager of the *San Jose Mercury-News* told a reporter: "Trees don't read newspapers."

Governor Brown, however, did read the papers, and he realized that Californians were becoming resistant to higher tax burdens. Brown, a classic tax-and-spend Democrat, was one of California's most pragmatic and successful politicians. Decent and honorable in both personal and public life, he had begun his career as a Republican in San Francisco and switched parties when the city became Democratic during the New Deal era. In 1939, in his third try for public office, he defeated an incumbent district attorney whom he had accused of being tolerant of vice. Brown's honesty was his biggest asset. In 1950, he was elected state attorney general after his Republican opponent (who had defeated Brown four years earlier) became entangled in a bribery scandal. Brown was now the only statewide Democratic official in California. In 1958, he exploited a Republican schism and was elected governor.

Brown believed that government existed to do good. He financed ambitious programs of ever more costly state services, first by spending the remnant of the "rainy day" funds accumulated by Governor Earl Warren during the prosperous World War II years, and then by imposing new taxes and accelerating collections of existing taxes. By 1965, when Brown was about to seek a third term as governor, the state's coffers were nearly bare. While reluctant to cut state spending, Brown realized that a tax increase would doom his chances of reelection. Since the California Constitution required a balanced budget, he seized upon the creative brainchild of state finance director and political adviser Hale Champion, who proposed a shift to "accrual accounting," in which the state counted revenues when they became due instead of when they were collected. The accounting changeover was not in itself novel, but Champion proposed making the change without funding it. As a result, the state in a single year spent its entire 1966 revenues in addition to revenues it was accruing for 1967, thus avoiding a tax increase before the election and guaranteeing one afterward. Republicans howled and nonpartisan legislative analyst Alan Post, the state's most reliable and vigilant watchdog, described the Champion-Brown plan as irresponsible. Brown ignored Post and plunged the state into deficit financing.[4]

While fiscally unsound, Brown's resort to an accounting gimmick was politically understandable in view of his multitudinous problems. After seven years as governor, he suffered from the inevitable erosion of incumbency and the ambitions of Democratic rivals who wanted his job. On the Right, there was Sam Yorty, the erratic mayor of Los Angeles, who opposed Brown's commitment to racially integrated housing. On the Left, he was badgered by the volunteer California Democratic Council, which considered Brown insufficiently liberal and was becoming uneasy over the growing U.S. involvement in Vietnam. In Sacramento, he was undermined by the independence of Assembly Speaker Jesse ("Big Daddy") Unruh, a powerful Democrat who wanted to be governor and resented Brown for refusing to step aside at the end of his second term. Unruh, who had once described Brown as "a tower of Jell-O," repeatedly assailed the governor for alleged indecisiveness. Brown also suffered from association as a national Democrat with President Lyndon B. Johnson's Great Society and the civil rights revolution, which had begun to stir a backlash among white working-class Democrats. And long before campus protests became a staple of the 1960s, there was trouble at the verdant Berkeley campus of the University of

California.

The Berkeley protests began in the late summer of 1964 after university officials discovered that the university owned the 26-foot Bancroft Strip outside the Sather Gate main entrance, long used by political activists to pass out leaflets that university rules banned them from distributing on campus. Egged on by the conservative *Oakland Tribune*, which objected to the long hair and scruffy appearance of activists who supported civil rights causes and the Democratic ticket, university administrators applied the leaflet ban to the strip as students returned from their summer vacations in September.

This decision set in motion a chain of events. Students picketed Sproul Hall, the university administration center, and negotiated with administrators to overturn the ban. Radicals and liberal Democratic students were in the majority, as is often the case with campus protests, but conservatives and student supporters of Republican presidential candidate Barry Goldwater also opposed this provocative and unnecessary restriction on political discourse. Nonetheless the peaceful efforts to overturn the ban on leaflet distribution in the Bancroft Strip were rejected by the university.

In response, the students predictably became more militant. They banded together and formed the Free Speech Movement under the firebrand leadership of Mario Savio, a physics student, former civil rights worker, and effective agitator. As the university held firm, the movement grew and rallies and demonstrations jammed the campus. After a police officer arrested an activist who was not a student, a sit-in trapped them both in a police car. On December 2, 1964, Savio gave an impassioned speech, and students occupied Sproul Hall and bedded down for the night. Governor Brown, torn between sympathy for the students and a desire to restore order, hesitated—"dithered," said his critics. He consulted with Edwin Meese III, a deputy district attorney in Alameda County whom Brown had known when Meese was a law enforcement lobbyist in Sacramento. Meese had been told—inaccurately, as it turned out—that the students were tearing up Sproul Hall, and he passed this information on to Brown. The governor decided to remove the students. He sent in the California Highway Patrol (CHP), which arrested 773 students who had refused to leave the building.[5]

Worse was to come in Los Angeles, 500 miles to the south, where blacks chafed at the rough-handed style of the Los Angeles Police Department (LAPD). California had been spared the riots that engulfed Harlem, Philadelphia, Chicago, and Jacksonville in the summer of 1964. But during a torrid Southern California heat wave on August 11, 1965, while Governor Brown was vacationing in Greece, violence exploded in the small, mostly black community of Watts in south Los Angeles. It began when a black motorist flagged down a CHP officer to point out a car that was being driven recklessly. The officer, a white man, pursued the car, and the driver, a black man, pulled over at an intersection just outside of Watts. Marquette Frye, the twenty-one-year-old driver, had been drinking. He flunked a sobriety test, and the officer arrested him and called for a tow truck to impound his car.

In the meantime, the driver's younger brother and passenger sprinted two blocks to his home to tell his mother what was going on. She ran to the scene and berated her son for drinking. Frye, cooperative until then, became obstreperous. His cries attracted the attention of residents who had been quietly watching the arrest in the heat of the late afternoon. They poured off their porches and joined others who were coming home from work to form a crowd around the police car. The officer radioed for help, and LAPD officers responded. Two of them dove into the growing crowd to arrest a woman in a barber's smock who had spit at them, and a rumor spread that police were abusing a pregnant woman. Police cars were stoned, and the Watts riot erupted. Before it ended six days later, 34 persons, most of them blacks, had died, and another 1,032 had been injured. The central business district of Watts was burned to the ground. In the riot's aftermath, blame was heaped on rioters and police—but also on Brown's lieutenant governor, Glenn Anderson, for being slow to call out the National Guard. Some of the political fallout inevitably drifted over Brown, although there was little he could have done from Greece.

In that protest-minded summer of 1965, another challenge to the old order with political implications for Governor Brown arose in the lush agricultural cornucopia of the San Joaquin Valley. This challenge, more peaceful and profound than any riot, was the work of faceless farm workers who risked their meager livelihoods to defy an alliance of the valley's most powerful grape growers. They followed Cesar Chavez, who became a mystical folk hero to Mexican Americans, but, as Chavez would have said, they were led by their own sense of justice and fair play.

Chavez had been a farm worker in childhood, attending forty schools as his parents followed the crops from state to state. He dropped out in the seventh grade. In 1961, at age thirty-four, after several years of working for the slow-paced Los Angeles–based Community Service Organization, Chavez moved with his wife and eight children to the town of Delano in the San Joaquin Valley, where he worked for a dollar an hour in the vineyards. Here, he created the fledgling union he called the National Farm Workers Association (NFWA). The family lived in a four-room house that doubled as union headquarters. During the next three years, Chavez built a tiny, loyal union with 1,200 members, set up an insurance plan, and began a credit union. Although he won a small strike against local rose growers, the grape growers did not at first take Chavez and his union seriously.

Then, in 1964, Congress heeded pleas from organized labor and Mexican American organizations and ended the *bracero* program, which since 1942 had provided growers with guaranteed cheap contract farm labor from Mexico. The reduced supply of farm workers, and hence of potential strikebreakers, helped the previously ineffective Agricultural Workers Organizing Committee (AWOC), affiliated with the AFL-CIO, to win wage increases to $1.40 an hour for grape pickers in the Coachella Valley. But when the union moved north into the San Joaquin Valley, grape growers refused to pay more than a dollar an hour or to negotiate with the union. On September 8, 1965, hundreds of AWOC members walked out of the San Joaquin vineyards.

Larry Itliong, the head of AWOC, and most of his union members were Filipinos. When they abandoned the vineyards, growers turned to a time-tested tactic of pitting ethnic groups against one another and tried to hire Mexican Americans as replacements. Itliong appealed to Chavez for help. Would the NFWA join the strike? Chavez, who was worried about keeping his fledgling union intact, put the question to his membership in a meeting at Our Lady of Guadalupe Church in Delano on September 16, Mexican Independence Day. The walls of the church were hung with the black eagle Aztec flag of the union, a picture of the Mexican peasant revolutionary hero Emiliano Zapata, and a poster of Jack London's "Definition of a Strikebreaker." Chavez made a motion to support AWOC, and the crowd responded with a roar of *"Huelga!"*— the Spanish word for "strike." It was the beginning of the great grape strike and a national boycott of table grapes that would in time force growers to recognize the union.[6]

The strike posed another difficult test for Pat Brown. The San Joaquin Valley and adjoining Sacramento Valley were bastions of support for the Democratic Party and had voted heavily for Brown in previous elections. Chavez was unpopular with all but farm workers in these agricultural areas, and most NFWA members were not even U.S. citizens, let alone voters. Six months after the strike began, Chavez, by now supported by organized labor and a broad coalition of liberal and religious activists, led a twenty-five-day, 300-mile march from Delano to Sacramento that ended on the steps of the State Capitol. Two of the major grape growers in the San Joaquin Valley capitulated along the way and signed contracts with the NFWA. But Governor Brown would not meet with Chavez. He spent Easter weekend at Frank Sinatra's home in Palm Springs.

As isolated events, neither the revolt of the farm workers nor the Watts riot nor the campus disorders that Ronald Reagan called "the mess at Berkeley" would have changed the political direction of California. But the events came piled one on top of another in the context of rising crime rates, increased congestion and pollution, and heavy tax burdens. Nationally, it was also a time of discontent. In late 1965, after a brief pause during the Christmas holiday season, President Johnson resumed heavy bombing raids of North Vietnam, and in February 1966 he agreed to increase U.S. military forces in Vietnam from 184,000 to 429,000 by the end of the year. Protests erupted again on college campuses, none of them more loudly than in California.

By 1966, a state that had given Johnson a million-vote margin of victory over Barry Goldwater two years earlier was no longer secure for the Democrats. By then, many Californians who had previously voted Democratic blamed their grievances on government and no longer believed that they lived in the Golden State of their dreams and memories. California was a nation-state, to be sure, but a nation-state on the brink, a state hungering for reform and a new sense of direction. Few in the press or in the political community, least of all Governor Brown, recognized the depth of the discontent in the early months of 1966, but California was ripe for a change.

As a leading Democratic legislator would say in hindsight, California was ripe for Ronald Reagan.[7]

2

OPTIMIST

R<small>ONALD</small> R<small>EAGAN</small> <small>PREPARED</small> for public life by writing his memoirs
and making the only movie of his life in which he played a vil-
lain. The movie was *The Killers*, vaguely inspired by the classic
Ernest Hemingway story of the same name, and a 1964 remake of a
more compelling 1946 film. Reagan was cast as a murderous crime boss
who in one scene slaps Angie Dickinson, the female lead. The film was
made for television but released instead in theaters because it was regarded as too violent for the home screen. The movie was not a hit, and
Reagan was unhappy that he'd made it. Despite a plausible performance
as the crime boss, Jack Browning, Reagan said he disliked being cast as a
heavy and regretted that he had allowed Lew Wasserman, the head of
Universal and his former agent, to talk him into taking the role.[1]

The filming of *The Killers* coincided with a request from Barry Goldwater to Reagan to make speeches in behalf of his presidential candidacy. Although Reagan would speak powerfully for Goldwater late in
1964, he was too busy to do so early in the year. Instead, he sent his
brother, Neil, to join Goldwater while he focused on completing his
memoirs, which were published in April 1965 as *Where's the Rest of Me?*
The book had a dual political purpose. For general readers, it asserted
the continuity of a life that Reagan believed had prepared him for public service. For Republicans, it explained Reagan's rationale for leaving
the Democratic Party and becoming one of them.

Strictly speaking, Reagan did not "write" these memoirs. Although
he wrote his own speeches until he became governor in 1967 and continued writing many of them until he became president in 1981, Reagan
found it easier to tell stories than to write a book. He dictated the autobiography to Richard C. Hubler, a jack-of-all-trades Hollywood writer
who had written screenplays, novels, and "as-told-to" books, including

one for songwriter Cole Porter that was also published in 1965. The Reagan book is of this genre. It is unclear how much influence, if any, Hubler had over its final form, but the first-person voice sounds authentically Reagan, if by authenticity we mean the story of Reagan's life as he remembered it. Memory fades and becomes ever more selective; long before he dictated this book, Reagan had reconstructed the events and emotions of his life into entertaining stories that simplified the complications. There is nothing unusual about that, but Reagan was a gifted and frequent storyteller, and most of the stories he told and retold had acquired for him the power of truth. Although several of the incidents described in the autobiography are inaccurate or unverifiable, as we shall see, Reagan thought of the book as his true life story. When I interviewed him in 1968 for my first book, Reagan often repeated passages of *Where's the Rest of Me?* nearly verbatim in response to my questions.[2]

In his autobiography, Reagan at once romanticizes and confronts his nomadic boyhood in small-town Illinois, where he was born on February 6, 1911, in the front bedroom of a five-room flat above the general store and bakery where his father worked. The store was on Main Street in Tampico. In Ronald Reagan's version of events, Tampico, with a population of 849, lacked a doctor, but a midwife told Nelle Wilson Reagan that she would have a hard delivery and needed medical assistance.[3] By luck, the midwife found a physician named Harry Terry who had been stranded in Tampico by an unexpected blizzard. Even with Terry in attendance, the delivery was so difficult that the doctor advised Nelle not to have more children. So Ronald Wilson Reagan became the second and last Reagan child. Neil, not quite two and a half years old, had been expecting a sister and refused to look at his baby brother.

Ronald Reagan was, from the beginning, the joy of his soft-voiced and pietistic mother, who gave him her maternal name and a supportive, nurturing foundation that lasted into adulthood. He was also an immediate source of pride to his father, John Edward Reagan, a muscular, handsome Irish American known as Jack. The week after Ronald was born, Jack gave customers at the Pitney Store thirty-seven inches for a yard and seventeen ounces for a pound on their purchases.

Tampico was too small for Jack Reagan, a dapper orphan who had been raised by an aunt. He was at once a drinker and a dreamer who, much like Willy Loman in *Death of a Salesman*, pursued the big sale or the unlikely deal with a shoeshine and a smile. Although he spent much of his life as a clerk and was selling general goods when Ronald was born, Jack fancied himself a premier shoe salesman, having learned his trade at something called the American School of Proctipedics. One of his dreams was owning a fancy shoe store, but he didn't have the money to do it. So Jack moved from town to town in Illinois, always hoping that success was in the store ahead. He had a gift of gab and a cheerful way with customers. But long before it happened to the fictional Loman, the customers stopped smiling back at Jack.

Ronald Reagan at first knew none of this. He was three years old when the Reagans left Tampico for Chicago, where Jack worked as a clerk in the Fair Store, the city's first gigantic department store. He was four when they moved to Galesburg, where Abraham Lincoln once debated Stephen Douglas. He was seven when they moved to Monmouth, eight when they moved back to Tampico, and nine when they settled uncertainly in Dixon, where they moved five times. As a consequence of this nomadic boyhood, Ronald formed few friendships except with Neil, who as an adult remembered his brother as a quiet boy, "not one you would suspect would wind up an actor or a politician."[4] This quiet boy depended on himself and realized, as children of alcoholics often do, that life can change in a twinkling. While rarely downcast, Reagan never lost that understanding or allowed others to intrude into his inner life. Years later, explaining her husband's inwardness to me, Nancy Reagan focused on these early years and his "never feeling any roots anywhere and never having an old friend, for a long, long time."[5]

Neil Reagan had hard memories of early boyhood. He remembered, better than his brother, the specifics of family itinerancy and poverty, much of it attributable to their father's drinking. He remembered sharing a cramped bed with Ronald which both boys wet. He remembered his Saturday morning chore in Chicago when he was six years old and Ronald three and a half:

> I was given a dime and went down to the meat market on Cottage Grove Avenue and Sixty-Third Street to buy a ten-cent soup bone. In those days the medical profession hadn't gotten to the point where they felt there was much value to liver. When I went down to buy the ten-cent soup bone, I was also told to ask the butcher for liver for the cat. We didn't have a cat. Our big meal on Sunday was always fried liver. We ate on the soup bone all the rest of the week. My mother would put it in the pot and keep on adding potatoes and slices of carrots and more water, and we ate on the soup bone until it was Saturday again.[6]

Ronald Reagan had no similarly compelling recollections of early poverty, or, if he did, they were subsumed by nostalgia. "We were poor, but we didn't know we were poor," he often said as an adult. In *Where's the Rest of Me?* Reagan described his boyhood as "one of those rare Tom

Sawyer–Huck Finn idylls" in which he discovered butterflies and birds' nests, explored the dark mysteries of woods and water in the gently rolling hill country of northwestern Illinois, and enjoyed a series of friendships and escapades in a sheltered and happy land. Like Voltaire's Professor Pangloss, Reagan believed he inhabited "the best of all possible worlds." But Pangloss would seem a sourpuss compared to Reagan, who despite the dark cloud cast by his father's drinking, developed a relentless optimism that became a dominant characteristic of his personality. Later in life, in the bleak days for Republicans after the culmination of the Watergate scandal, Reagan often began his political speeches with a story about two little boys, one a pessimist and the other an optimist, who were taken by their parents to a psychiatrist. The parents hoped to make the pessimist more cheerful and the optimist more conscious of life's obstacles. So they lock the pessimistic child in a room with shiny new toys and the optimistic child in a room with a shovel and a pile of horse manure. When the parents return, the pessimistic child is crying, refusing to play with the toys because he fears that they might break. The optimistic child is cheerfully shoveling through the manure. He tells his parents, "With this much manure around, I know there's a pony in here someplace."

Ronald Reagan was the boy who hoped to find the pony, the child who believed with greater confidence than his father that success would surely come his way. From early days, he learned to subordinate bad memories to good ones and to end stories on a happy note. The description in *Where's the Rest of Me?* of his supposedly idyllic boyhood follows a passage describing his mother's near-fatal brush with influenza and precedes a sentence relating how children drowned in the swift waters of the canals near Tampico.[7] Reagan softened his portrayal of his father as an unsuccessful drunk by picturing him as a fierce foe of racial and religious intolerance and "a sentimental Democrat who believed fervently in the rights of the working-man."[8]

But there are limits to the bounds of even Ronald Reagan's optimism. As diligently as he promoted light amidst the shadows, Reagan's recollections of Jack Reagan's drinking bouts were far more dramatic and convincing than the anecdotes he told to demonstrate his father's virtues. "I was eleven years old the first time I came home to find my father flat on his back on the front porch and no one there to lend a hand but me," Reagan wrote. "He was drunk, dead to the world." Jack's arms were spread out as if he were crucified, "as indeed he was." Ronald Reagan, a small boy slight of build, dragged his father, "his hair soaked with melting snow," off the porch and into bed.[9] The boy did not tell his mother what he had done, but the memory never left him. Even Neil, with less need or aptitude for rose-colored recall, was uncomfortable when he reflected on his father's drinking bouts. "Sometimes," Neil told me, "I'd be asked, 'Does your father drink?' and I'd say, 'Hell, yes.' What else would I say? There were times when he didn't open the screen door, he just walked through it."[10]

In discussing his mother, Ronald Reagan had no need to perform a balancing act. When I asked him in 1968 to tell me about his parents, he talked nonstop about her sterling qualities and said nothing about his father until the question was put to him again. He believed, with good reason, that his mother was a remarkable human being. Nelle Reagan was a deeply religious woman with bright blue eyes who, in Reagan's words in *Where's the Rest of Me?* "had the conviction everyone loved her just because she loved them. My father's cynicism never made the slightest impression on her, while I suspect her sweetness often undermined his practical viewpoint of the world. Neither she nor my father had ever graduated from any school but the elementary grades. No diploma was needed for kindness, in her opinion, just as my father believed energy and hard work were the only ingredients needed for success."[11]

Ronald Reagan and most of his biographers have assumed, as I wrote in an earlier book, that she was "a lifelong member" of the Christian Church (Disciples of Christ). Nelle's piety is undisputed, but Garry Wills has made a persuasive circumstantial case that her religious awakening and induction into the Christian Church occurred less than a year before Ronald Reagan was born. For one thing, Nelle was an accomplished dancer, an unlikely skill if she had spent her life in a church that disapproved of dancing. For another, Nelle was baptized as a Disciple of Christ by total immersion in Tampico on March 27, 1910. If she already had been a Disciple, the customary method of joining a new church would have been by a letter of transfer.[12] We also know that Nelle insisted on baptizing Ronald as a Disciple after permitting Neil (his Christian name was "John Neil Reagan") to be baptized in the Roman Catholic faith of his father.

If Nelle, as seems probable, was a new member of the church at the time of Ronald's birth, she had the ardor of the recent convert. Indeed, she plunged into church activities with joy and devotion, serving as song director for the choir. For eighteen years, Nelle taught the True Blue Class, composed of adult women, in Sunday school. Ronald cleaned up at the church and, beginning when he was only five, performed in his mother's skits. In his autobiography, Ronald said his mother was "the dean of dramatic recitals for the countryside" and "a frustrated actress." Reagan believed that his own "dramatic yen" derived from early performances with Nelle, a number of them centering on the evils of Demon Rum, for the Disciples were in the forefront of the growing Prohibition movement. In Dixon, Nelle wrote a temperance play in which the daughter of the drunkard says, "I love you, Daddy, except when you have that old bottle."[13]

Tampico had outlawed liquor licensing in 1907, a year after Jack and Nelle arrived in the town. In 1919, the National Prohibition Act, commonly known as the Volstead Act, passed over the veto of President Woodrow Wilson. Nelle joined other Disciples in cheering its passage, but Prohibition did not prevent Jack Reagan from finding intoxicants—the traumatic episode when Ronald dragged his unconscious father in from the snowy porch probably occurred in the winter of 1920–1921. Ronald Reagan adored his mother and accepted her teachings. "I was raised to believe that God has a plan for everyone and that seemingly random twists of fate are all a part of His plan," Reagan later wrote.[14] He credited his mother for this instruction and said that Nelle had taught him that "even the most disheartening setbacks"[15] were also part of this divine plan. On May 6, 1920, in church, he recited a sentimental tribute to Nelle, "About Mother." Two years later, mother and son entertained patients at Dixon State Hospital with what the local newspaper called a "short and enjoyable program" that featured Nelle on the banjo and two readings by Ronald. Both of the Reagan boys remember Nelle becoming so involved with the rehabilitation of ex-convicts that she brought them home and fed them at a time when the family had little to share.

Nelle was also determined that her boys would be better educated than their parents. The same could be said of many mothers, then and now, but education had a special resonance with the Disciples of Christ, which built schools and colleges all over the South and Midwest. Nelle taught Ronald to read before he started school. When Ronald was five, he read aloud to his parents a newspaper account of a notorious bombing in San Francisco on July 22, 1916, which occurred at Preparedness Day ceremonies sponsored by advocates of U.S. entry into World War I.[16] Jack called in the neighbors to show off his younger son's precocity by having him read the story again. This is one of the relatively few childhood remembrances recounted by Ronald that Neil, who learned more slowly and may have resented the attention given his brother, specifically verified. But Jack's reaction to Ronald's performance suggests that he, as much as Nelle, valued his younger son's gifts. Within the Reagan household, and perhaps in Ronald Reagan's heart, there was an early sense that he was a child of destiny.

The Reagan boys recognized early in life that Ronald, in behavior and attitudes, resembled his mother and Neil his father. Neil thought that Nelle favored Ronald, and he may have been showing his displeasure with her when, at nineteen, he left the Disciples of Christ, into which his mother had rebaptized him five years earlier, and proclaimed himself a Catholic like his father. But it would be a mistake to overdraw the descriptions of Ronald as "Nelle's boy" and of Neil as Jack's. Both parents influenced both boys. Nelle's insistence on education rubbed off on Neil, although it took more time than it did with Ronald. Jack taught Ronald to work with his hands, and his stories of the evils of the Ku Klux Klan and intolerance had a lasting influence. As devoted as he was to his mother, Ronald displayed a large measure of Jack's Irish charm and salesmanship.

In time, he would make bigger sales than Jack had ever dreamed of.

3

LIFEGUARD

IXON, WHERE Ronald Reagan lived from the age of nine until he went off to college at the age of seventeen, was a peaceful dairy town with martial memories. An arch spanned Main Street in honor of those who had fought and died in Europe during the Great War, as Americans then knew World War I. The arch was at once a reminder of recent conflict and a mirror to the past. When Reagan was a boy, veterans of the Grand Army of the Republic survived in every town and hamlet of northern Illinois. Ulysses S. Grant had left his brothers' harness-making shop in Galena, two counties to the northwest, at the outset of the Civil War to rejoin the Army, eventually becoming its most successful general. A veteran who had served as an eighteen-year-old in 1863 under Grant in the bloody fighting at Missionary Ridge, where the 104th Illinois regiment distinguished itself, would have been seventy-five years old in 1920.

Reagan felt connected to this military past. As a young child, he fought solitary battles for hours with lead Civil War soldiers, shutting out the outside world while his brother played games with other boys. His heroes were always heroes: generals and presidents and captains of industry who had arisen from the ranks. "I'm a sucker for hero worship," he said years later,[1] and it is not surprising that this would be so. Heroes, dead and alive, were all around him.

Dixon may have sent its young men off to fight, but war had never come to Dixon, nor would it. The Great War had been "the war to end all wars," it was then believed, and no one in that self-contained corner of Illinois disputed it. Dixon in 1920 had a population of 8,191, and Lee County, of which it is the county seat, 28,004. Lee was an agricultural county in a farming state, and the principal business of Dixon was servicing farmers, especially dairymen. Dixon was home to a large milk-condensing plant, owned by Borden's, and the Grand Detour Plow Company, established in 1837. There was also a train depot, a public library, a teachers college, several churches, a YMCA, and, in 1922, a new theater for vaudeville and silent movies. It was, in all, a useful town, secure in place and purpose.

Not everyone thought well of such small towns. The popular Sinclair Lewis novel *Main Street*, published in 1920 when the Reagans moved to Dixon, satirized the insularity and drabness of small-town life. Lewis, who was raised in a small town in Minnesota, couldn't wait to leave. But others who absorbed the dependable rhythms of such towns thought of them later as Reagan remembered Dixon, as "the place to go back to,"[2] the place where he discovered himself. Three small-town Illinois boys who as adults observed President Reagan from various vantage points at *The Washington Post* had similar feelings. "Growing up in small-town Illinois gave one a sense of great freedom and security," said David S. Broder, whose hometown was Chicago Heights.[3] "[You had] the feeling that people are basically good and will treat you right if you're good to them," said Dan Balz, who grew up in Freeport.[4] "You'd get on your bike and go anywhere," said George F. Will, who was raised in Champaign. "As soon as you left town, there were cornfields."[5]

Reagan, who didn't have a bicycle, wandered the wooded south bank of the Rock River that bisected Dixon. All his life, even when he occupied center stage in Hollywood or Sacramento or Washington, he would feel a need to withdraw to the solitude of nature on foot or, later, on horseback. He liked open country, and the openness of Dixon encouraged what Will called Reagan's "talent for happiness." School came easily to him, perhaps too easily, because he could do numbers and memorized written material readily and well. He liked to draw and began a lifelong habit of doodling that made him briefly flirt with a career as a cartoonist. He liked to read, too. On December 27, 1920, six weeks before his tenth birthday, he took out a card at the public library, and walked to what he called this "house of magic" once or twice a week after dinner. But he was not, for all that, a bookish person. His cheerfulness commended him to adults and children alike, although he had few close friends. Neil noticed that he did not seem in need of them. Ronald was a pleasant boy who liked going to church on Sunday (as Neil did not) and acting in his mother's skits and plays. He knew that life was good in Dixon, and he did not fret about his future. Ronald knew that everything would turn out all right. As his mother often said, everything was part of God's plan.

His reading revealed an adventurous turn of mind. Based on his recollections and the record of books he checked out from the library, Reagan plowed through stories about King Arthur and the Knights of the Round Table and several books about the exploits of the Rover Boys. He read *Northern Trails*, which contributed to his fantasy of living as a trapper along the Rock River, where the banks and surrounding woods abounded in muskrats, rabbits, and other small game. Indeed, he briefly participated in a scheme of Neil's to raise rabbits and poultry to sell for meat. Ronald withdrew because he was unwilling to kill rabbits that he had fed. He was a reader, not a trapper. His adventure reading included *The Last of the Mohicans, The Count of Monte Cristo*, and Zane Grey's novels. He had a preference for the less-famous books of well-known writers: Sir Arthur Conan Doyle's *The White Company*, instead of the Sherlock Holmes stories (which he also read), and the Edgar Rice Burroughs books about John Carter, an imaginary explorer of an imaginary Mars, instead of *Tarzan.*[6] The Carter books ignited an interest in science fiction that never waned; Reagan would read such fantasies as president. He also read the Horatio Alger stories, but he preferred a now-forgotten 1902 novel called *That Printer of Udell's: A Story of the Middle West*, by Harold Bell Wright. The hero, Dick Falkner, works by day as a printer, attends night school, and marries a beautiful socialite whom he saves from a life of prostitution. Falkner blends Christian and business principles to uplift a midwestern town, valuing the principles more than he does the organized church or the business community. At the end, he is off to Congress. "All in all, as I look back I realize that my reading left an abiding belief in the triumph of good over evil," Reagan wrote when he was sixty-six. "There were heroes who lived by standards of morality and fair play."[7]

Away from books, young Ronald was limited by sight and size. He was nearsighted, as his parents discovered on a drive when he could not read the highway signs. They outfitted him with horn-rimmed glasses, which he detested and avoided wearing whenever possible. Boys want to be liked by other boys, and the glasses did not help. Neither did Ronald's given name. As a boy, Ronald asked to be called "Dutch," a nickname he said in his autobiography had been bestowed at birth by his father, who thought he resembled a "fat, little Dutchman." In fact, Ronald seems to have insisted upon its use because he thought that it sounded more masculine than his real name. Neil, too, preferred a nickname. His was "Moon," because he was bulky and full of face.

Moon was bigger and stronger than his younger brother. Dutch was more agile and coordinated but small for his age. Then, as now, boys set store in athletic prowess, and Dutch was at a disadvantage. His nearsightedness made it impossible for him to hit a baseball, and he was usually the last boy chosen at neighborhood pickup games. Basketballs and footballs were also troublesome; a ball passed or thrown to Dutch was apt to go in and out of his hands before he knew it was there. But he was not reluctant to mix it up, and he learned to block and tackle in rough-and-tumble neighborhood football games with his brother and older boys. In *Where's the Rest of Me?* Reagan called these "the happiest times in my life."[8] He might have been an outstanding football lineman except for his size. When he played tackle on the 135-pound team during his first year in high school, he weighed only 108 pounds and couldn't find a uniform that fit him. But his spunk impressed his teammates, who chose him captain.

Dutch's best sport by far was swimming, where agility helped and eyesight was less of an issue. He had no fear of water and was soon swimming in the Rock River, a treacherous tributary of the Mississippi in which drownings have occurred with frightful regularity since the early nineteenth century. Swimming appealed to Reagan because it was at once competitive and solitary. Moon, a dominant older brother in other sports, could not keep up with him in the water.

In Dutch's first year in high school, the Reagan family moved from a rented house on the south side of town to a rented house on the north side. Dixon High fielded single athletic teams, but the school had separate Northside and Southside campuses. Moon, then a junior, continued attending Southside, while his brother went to classes at Northside nearer to home. Dutch welcomed the move because he had a crush on Margaret ("Mugs") Cleaver, the pretty and witty daughter of Ben Cleaver, the minister at the local Christian Church, of which Nelle Reagan was a pillar. Mugs was one of the brightest pupils at Northside, which, despite the supposed social equality of Dixon, was known to be the "better" school. The Northside crowd, especially the boys, was too genteel for Southside, where the favorite hangout for Moon and his friends was a pool hall. Northsiders, boys and girls alike, preferred an ice cream store as their chosen meeting ground. The difference was more than a matter of taste. Southsiders were expected to find work after high school. This would be the fate of most Northsiders as well, but some of them, including Mugs Cleaver, knew they had the option of college.

Away from his brother, Dutch blossomed at Northside. The scholastic separation gave him running room in which he could make new friends and pursue his interests. Dutch was less exhibitionist than Moon. The older brother was a leader of his crowd and excelled in elaborate pranks, such as disassembling a manure spreader and reassembling it on the roof of the high school. Dutch's method of attracting attention was (in his junior year) to try out for and win the lead male role in the Philip Barry play *You and I*, where the female lead was the desirable Mugs Cleaver.

Dutch was also beginning to grow. He filled out in his junior year and then, as a senior, shot up to his adult height of six feet. In his pleasant, cheerful way, Dutch was now a big man on the Northside campus. He was helped by his height and handsomeness and also by the acceptance that achievement at athletics gives boys in high school. Reagan wasn't all that good a player, but he was a courageous one on a marginal football team. In 1926, Moon's last year, the Dixon team went undefeated, winning eight games and tying one. Moon was a star end. In 1928, when Dutch played both end and tackle, the team won two games and lost seven.

By this time, however, Dutch had emerged as the winner in other competitions. He had gained Mugs Cleaver's affections as her steady boyfriend, winning out over a friend, Dick McNicol, the team quarterback. And in his senior year, Dutch was elected student body president at Northside. His class photo shows a good-looking young man in a bow tie, the hint of a smile on his face, and both his given name and his nickname under the photograph. It was the custom of school yearbooks in those days to include a motto, usually written by the student, which was supposed to describe his attributes or outlook. The motto beneath Reagan's nickname reads: "Life is just one grand sweet song, so start the music." Those words were almost surely written by Dutch, the art editor of the yearbook, for they are taken from a poem he had written earlier in high school. The poem, entitled "Life," was a ballad of youthful optimism.

Dutch, who remained active in the Christian Church throughout high school, had reason to be optimistic. He had a loyal girlfriend and the implicit support of the Reverend Cleaver, who liked him, counseled him, and taught him to drive. He also held a coveted job as lifeguard at Lowell Park, 3 miles north of Dixon on a lovely, wooded section of the Rock River where the water is both inviting and dangerous. Dutch had landed this job in the summer of 1927, when he was still so slender that the park concessionaires, Edward and Ruth Graybill, were uncertain about hiring him, even though Mrs. Graybill was a member of the Christian Church who knew the Cleavers and thought well of young Reagan. Because of the danger of swimming in the river, as Garry Wills observed, "a competent and careful lifeguard was necessary for the Graybills to keep their license and maintain their insurance rates."[9] Mrs. Graybill told Wills that they consulted with Reagan's father about his son's skills in the water, and Jack had assured them that Dutch had taken a lifesaving course at the YMCA.

So Dutch began six summers as a lifeguard at Lowell Park, where he started out at $15 a week. In his fifth year, the pay was raised to $18, and in his final summer at Lowell to $20. He worked hard for the money. Each morning he went to the Graybills' house and used their van to pick up food supplies and a 300-pound block of ice at the icehouse. At the park, he broke the ice into three pieces and put them in as many coolers. In busy times, he would double or triple the order of ice. The park, which was floodlit, did not close until 10 P.M. (sometimes later), and Reagan stayed afterward to clean up. He worked twelve hours a day, seven days a week, while many of his friends were enjoying summer vacations. Later in life, Reagan developed (and to some degree cultivated) a reputation for relaxed work habits. "It's true hard work never killed anybody, but I figure, why take the chance," he joked at a Gridiron Dinner when he was president. But the truth was that he rarely shrunk from work.

Most biographers of Reagan's early life have focused on the more dramatic part of his lifeguard duties.[10] When I first started writing about Reagan in the 1960s, it was widely assumed within the political and journalistic communities in Sacramento that he had exaggerated in *Where's the Rest of Me?* when he said he had rescued seventy-seven people from drowning. In fact, at his father's suggestion, Reagan had kept a record of these rescues by making notches on a log, and most of them were documented in the local newspaper in details more vivid than the ones Reagan provided in a modest, four-paragraph account in his autobiography. The *Dixon Daily Telegraph* reported in a page-one story on August 3, 1928, that Reagan had rescued a drowning man in the darkness after another rescue attempt had failed—a notable feat considering Reagan's poor eyesight. On July 3, 1931, an article in the *Telegraph* praised Reagan's "fine mark" as a lifeguard, reporting that he had (until then) rescued seventy-one persons and lost no one even though he sometimes had 1,000 bathers to watch and never had an assistant.

Reagan's six years as a lifeguard were decisive in his transition from boy to man. At Lowell Park, he learned the responsibility of work and the rewards that come from public service. He also learned to save, putting aside most of his summertime earnings, which were augmented by money he received for giving swimming lessons to the children of affluent parents who vacationed on the Rock River. He never bragged about his exploits as a lifeguard, and his only complaint, recorded in his autobiography and repeated to biographers, was that people never thanked or rewarded him for saving their lives, with the sole exception of a man who gave him $10 for pulling his dental plate from the river.

Rewards aside, Reagan enjoyed being a lifeguard. Being the solitary figure on the shore who swam to the rescue when danger threatened was an appealing role, and he performed it well. Later, after he had become famous, a legend arose that he had rescued pretty girls who were in no danger of drowning. Reagan smilingly denied it. "I never got my suit wet unless there was a need for it," he said.[11] I believed him, but he seemed to rather like the legend.

4

STORYTELLER

O N A WARM SEPTEMBER afternoon in 1928, Ronald Reagan tossed
his steamer trunk into the rumble seat of Margaret Cleaver's
coupe, and he and his steady girlfriend made the 95-mile drive
from Dixon to Eureka College, 20 miles east of Peoria in the heartland
of Illinois. Margaret, the youngest of three daughters, looked forward
to this change in her life; her oldest sister had graduated from Eureka
and another sister was attending college there. Reagan was less assured.
He had $400 accumulated from his summers of work at Lowell Park,
but this would not cover the full cost of tuition, room, and board at Eureka. After spending the night at the Tau Kappa Epsilon ("Teke") fraternity house, Reagan discussed his predicament with Dean Samuel
Harrod, a Princeton-educated professor of classics who, among other
duties, was also college registrar. Harrod took him to see the football
coach, Ralph ("Mac") McKinzie, who reluctantly agreed to recommend
a half athletic scholarship of $90 a year, based as much on Reagan's
swimming prowess as on his football ability.[1]

Harrod then helped Reagan obtain a job washing dishes at the Teke
house, which paid for his meals. This job and the scholarship made it
possible for Reagan to attend Eureka. In his freshman year, Reagan paid
$270 for his room at the fraternity house, $90 for the other half of his
college tuition, and a $5 enrollment fee, leaving him only $35 of the
$400 he had saved. But his precarious financial position was not unusual
in this time and place. Although the stock market crash was still a year
away, the Great Depression hovered over the farm belt before it arrived
on Wall Street, and many of Eureka's 220 students scraped to make
ends meet.

Eureka College's administrators scraped, too. The elm-shrouded
college, the first in Illinois to admit men and women students on an

equal basis, had been founded in 1855 by a Disciple of Christ and at first specialized in training students for the ministry and teaching. By 1928, when Reagan arrived, Eureka was a liberal arts college where only a small minority of students was preparing for the ministry. Eureka was nonetheless dependent on Disciples churches in Illinois for most of its annual endowment of $658,000 and was, as Reagan observed, "perpetually broke."[2] As he and Margaret Cleaver looked ahead to four years at college, Eureka's trustees were debating whether to close its doors.

Eureka's financial instability plunged Reagan into the first political activity of his life. His involvement, foreshadowing an aspect of his campaign for governor of California, was directed against the unpopular policies of a college administration. The president of Eureka at the time was Bert Wilson, as devoted to a balanced budget as Reagan would proclaim he was as governor. As Reagan recalled events in *Where's the Rest of Me?* Wilson "tripped over the panic button" and proposed to make Eureka solvent by eliminating courses he considered marginal and laying off the faculty members who taught them. "He favored a plan," Reagan wrote, "which called for such a drastic cutback academically that many juniors and seniors would have been cut off without the courses needed for graduation in their chosen majors. Needless to say, the faculty would have been decimated and Eureka would have lost its high academic rating."[3]

Reagan asserted that Wilson, who had an authoritarian reputation, persuaded the trustees to go along with the plan without consulting with students or faculty. Students presented a counterplan to the board, which was rejected, and then petitioned for Wilson's resignation. The board was scheduled to meet on Saturday, November 17. As Reagan described events in his autobiography, students had discussed striking if Wilson's plan was approved but took time off that day to attend a football game between Eureka and Illinois College, a bigger school with a better team. In the second half of the game, newsboys arrived in the stands with papers headlining the rejection of the student-faculty appeal to save the threatened classes. The stories attracted more attention than the game. "The win over Illinois was the least-celebrated victory a hungry Eureka would ever know," Reagan wrote.[4]

That night, the students remained on campus as the board of trustees met. The trustees accepted Wilson's plan for consolidating classes, and the students met at midnight in the chapel. Reagan said he had been chosen to make the strike motion because he was a freshman and "the charge could be made that upper classmen had a selfish interest." He gave a speech at once detailed and emotional recounting the grievances of the students. "When I came to actually presenting the motion there was no need for parliamentary procedure; they came to their feet with a roar—even the faculty members present voted by acclamation," Reagan wrote. "It was heady wine. Hell, with two more lines, I could have had them riding through 'every Middlesex village and farm'—without horses yet."[5]

After Thanksgiving, the students struck. They skipped all classes but attended athletic practices and chapel and held a dance every afternoon. The faculty members marked the striking students present, and the students (according to Reagan) kept up a study regimen outside of class. After two weeks, Wilson resigned and "Eureka got back into the business of education, with the faculty agreeing to withhold any salary demands for an indefinite period." As a result of the strike, said Reagan, students and faculty developed a "remarkably close bond."[6]

Reagan's account and chronology of the strike is inaccurate, as Garry Wills has demonstrated.[7] Wilson actually offered his resignation on Friday, November 16, the day before the trustees met. He did so, as he made clear in a statement to the board, because he was convinced his consolidation plan was necessary to save Eureka and did not want a debate about his own future to cloud the issue. It was also on this Friday, "Dad's Day" at Eureka, that Illinois College and Eureka met on the football field. The result was not the stirring "least-celebrated victory" that Reagan described but a crushing 19–0 defeat.

Students and faculty soon became aware of Wilson's resignation offer, and they realized that the trustees were unlikely to accept it. Backed by resident alumni (according to the school newspaper), they shifted tactics and attacked Wilson for hurting Eureka by saying it was "confronted with a dark future." On Tuesday, November 27, the trustees met most of the day and well into the night. They rejected Wilson's resignation, provoking the midnight meeting in the chapel that Reagan misremembered as having occurred the previous week. At the meeting, the assembled students and faculty debated several proposals, including a plan to leave Eureka en masse at the end of the semester. The discussion became so heated, according to the student newspaper, that at one point a Eureka music teacher took it upon himself to quiet the crowd by singing spirituals. Reagan apparently gave an effective speech, but the newspaper account does not suggest it was a turning point of the evening. Nor did the upper-class members stay on the sidelines, as Reagan remembers. One of them chaired the meeting.

When the meeting broke up at 2:30 A.M. Wednesday, everyone involved was exhausted. The students went home for a Thanksgiving holiday. After they returned and went on strike, the trustees and the faculty maneuvered in an attempt to reach a settlement before the next board meeting on December 4. The trustees were unwilling to let Wilson go under fire. The faculty members were concerned about reprisals against two anti-Wilson teachers and three student ringleaders. (Reagan was not among them.) Aware of the attitude of the board, the students withdrew their demand for Wilson's resignation. Even so, there were those on the board who were not inclined to accept it. They finally did, after another long meeting, but they also reprimanded Dean Harrod for allegedly fomenting the strike. The counterplan from the students that Reagan said had been rejected by the board before they petitioned for Wilson's removal actually was submitted after his resignation was accepted. It did not amount to much, consisting largely of a student pledge to recruit more freshmen the following year.

The most significant omission in Reagan's version of events is the fact that the trustees agreed with Wilson on the necessity of consolidating classes to save money. Indeed, they went him one better, reducing the number of departments to eight instead of the nine that Wilson had recommended. Upper-class students who had felt threatened by the Wilson plan lost every one of their demands that had made them seek his resignation. The winners were the anti-Wilson faculty members, who had used the students in their campaign to oust the Eureka president.

How was it that Reagan so misrepresented the outcome of the strike? And why, in a book where he was often modest about genuine achievements such as saving people from drowning, did he exaggerate his role? There are three probable explanations for Reagan's self-serving account, none of them mutually exclusive. The first is that *Where's the Rest of Me?* was an autobiography intended as a campaign document. Reagan dictated it before the troubles erupted at Berkeley, but he wanted to distinguish the Eureka strike from what he called the "fevered picketing" already occurring on some campuses in the 1960s. In the process, in his book he gave extra weight to any public activity in which he had engaged, anticipating that his political inexperience would become an issue when he ran for office.

A second reason for Reagan's misrepresentation is that he had more at stake in the movement to remove Wilson than he acknowledged. Dean Harrod was a ringleader of the anti-Wilson forces, as the board's reprimand of him suggests. This is the same Harrod who had talked Coach McKinzie into granting Reagan a partial scholarship and who then arranged the dishwashing job for him in the Teke house. Together, these favors made it possible for Reagan to attend Eureka. In his autobiography, Reagan identifies neither Harrod nor Wilson by name (he calls the latter, a bit inaccurately, "the new president"), and, after the passage of thirty-seven years, he may have forgotten their names. But at the time of the strike, he was loyal to Harrod, his benefactor, and would have opposed any proposal to remove him as registrar, as Wilson wanted to do. For Reagan, the "close bond" that the strike supposedly engendered between faculty and students existed before the strike began.

The third reason for Reagan's self-serving account is that he was a storyteller recreating his political debut, which had indeed been "heady wine" for him. Reagan was usually the hero of his early stories, which were typically rescued from self-righteousness by self-deprecating humor. The inspirations for Reagan's storytelling were the sermons preached by the Reverend Cleaver in the Christian Church in Dixon, or, even more, the church skits in which he had participated with his mother. These sermons and skits were rooted in the teachings of the Christian Gospels and had a purpose of moral uplift, to which was assigned a higher value than literal truth. Reagan was, in Wills' phrase, an "unembarrassed moralist."[8] In an expression of the time, he was also "a muscular Christian" who lived his beliefs and drew clear distinctions between good and evil. Nuanced understanding was never a Reagan strong point. His misremembering of what happened in the strike, if indeed he understood it at the time, reflects Reagan's confidence that one could always draw a bright line between right and wrong.

In making such distinctions, Reagan usually, if not always, saw his opponents as misguided but sincere. This is a concession he made retrospectively to Wilson and would often make in his criticisms of "liberals" after he became a conservative political advocate. Reagan did not hate his adversaries or compile an enemy's list. As class president addressing the graduating class of Dixon High School, Reagan had taken as his text a variation of the affirmation of John 10:10, "I have come that they have life in all its abundance." His God was his mother's God, a deity who offered solace instead of vengeance and who promised salvation to all who believed in Him. Reagan's preference for happy endings began in Sunday school, not in Hollywood. His confidence that everything would turn out for the best may explain why he remembered Eureka's resounding defeat at the hands of Illinois College as a glorious victory. In Reagan's world, the good guys always won.

From the outset, Reagan was a narrative storyteller. His strike speech in the chapel anticipated his political speeches in relying on an accumulation of memorized detail (later punctuated with statistics and bizarre anecdotes) to make his case but concluded, as Reagan speeches almost always did, with an emotional peroration. Reagan was proud of the speech at the time, and it seemed even better to him in retrospect. Once he told a story, he would commit it to memory, calling upon it when it served his purpose and sometimes adding new details. Through constant repetition, Reagan's stories acquired—for him, at least—the power of truth.

Reagan always had a rosy glow when he talked about his college days. In his autobiography, he wrote that he "fell head over heels in love with Eureka" at first sight. It was a love that would last. He returned to Eureka ten times after his graduation, most notably on the night of October 17, 1980, when in the midst of his campaign for president he visited Eureka and accepted the gift of a football jersey from retired Coach McKinzie, then eighty-six. I had never seen Reagan happier. In a nostalgic speech in the gymnasium, Reagan assured students that they were better off at Eureka than at a big, well-endowed major university. "Those big assembly-line diploma mills may teach, but with all due respect to them, you will have memories, you will have friendships that are impossible on those great campuses and that are just peculiar to this place," Reagan told the students. "As far as I am concerned, everything good that has happened to me—everything—started here on this campus in those four years that still are such a part of my life."9

Reagan had a basis for this romantic view. Not only did Eureka give Reagan his first taste of political oratory, and the satisfaction of hearing the plaudits of the crowd, but it honed the dramatic skills that would lead to his successful careers as a radio announcer and movie actor. On a vacation during his freshman year at Eureka, the Cleavers drove Ronald and Margaret to Rockford to see a touring London play, *Journey's End*, set on the Western Front. Reagan identified with the major character, war-weary Captain Stanhope, saying, "In some strange way, I was also on stage." Looking back on this evening in his autobiography, Reagan described it as an epiphany that revealed to him his career. But he may have suspected even before then what he would do with much of his life. When I asked him decades later if *Journey's End* had kindled his ambition to become an actor, he replied: "I knew then that I wanted to be an actor, but it wasn't considered a way to make a living."10

From that time on, however, Reagan missed few opportunities to go on stage. He joined Alpha Epsilon Sigma, the student dramatic society. He appeared in a comedy loosely based on *Pygmalion* called *The Brat*. And he excelled in Edna St. Vincent Millay's play *Aria da Capo*, in which he played a shepherd who is strangled to death. The Eureka drama department entered the play, which also featured Margaret Cleaver, in a prestigious one-act competition at Northwestern University, where it finished third. Reagan won an individual acting award.

Reagan was always influenced by his roles. *Aria da Capo*, an antiwar play, touched a pacifist sensibility, common at the time in the Midwest, which would become a bedrock of resistance to U.S. entry into World War II. "I went through a period in college, in the aftermath of World War I, where I became a pacifist and thought the whole thing was a frame-up," Reagan told me years later.[11] He did not mention this in his autobiography, when he was militantly anti-Soviet and committed to the Cold War, but there is no doubt that he harbored pacifist sentiments while in college. Reagan was a sophomore when he appeared in *Aria da Capo*. The following year, he wrote a short story, "Killed in Action," set on the Western Front, in which the hero says that the war will be worth fighting for only when it ends. The hero, who is gassed in the war, loses all purpose in life. Thirteen years later, while "bumming his way" to a veterans hospital for treatment, he slips while trying to board a freight train and is crushed beneath the wheels.

Reagan was as interested in football as he was in dramatics, but he was not the natural on the gridiron that he was on stage. Coach McKinzie, the most successful athlete in Eureka's history, observed that Reagan was slow and overimpressed by his high school football credentials. As a consequence, McKinzie kept him on the bench during his freshman year. Reagan resented this treatment, but he did not quit. His consolation, which seemed small to him at the time, was swimming. It took him awhile to master the art of competitive swimming in a pool after years of swimming in a river. Once he did, he won five of six events in a freshman meet at Eureka and earned his varsity letter the following year.

But Reagan took swimming for granted. He wanted to be a football player and was pleased when McKinzie looked upon him more favorably as a sophomore. What the coach had come to appreciate was Reagan's spunk and his ability to block and tackle. McKinzie called Reagan "a plugger" and made him a starting guard midway through his sophomore season. During the next two and a half years, Reagan played his heart out for the coach and the team, although the Eureka Golden Tornadoes never had a winning season during his playing years. Reagan's teammates valued him more for his effort and his high spirits than for his athletic ability. On the way back to the gym after practice, recalled former teammate Garrard Camp, Reagan would pretend to be a sports announcer. Using a broomstick as a microphone, he created entire imaginary football games.

One of Reagan's football friends was William Franklin Burghardt, known as "Burgie," the center in Reagan's senior year, playing next to him in the line. Burghardt was one of Eureka's best players and became captain of the team two years after Dutch had graduated. Reagan had helped recruit him from Greenfield, Illinois, where Burghardt's father, grandfather, and uncle worked as barbers. They were black in a state where public accommodations were segregated by custom rather than by law. Reagan had been raised to believe that prejudice was abhorrent, but only a dozen black families lived in Dixon, and Reagan lacked first-hand knowledge of racial discrimination.

In 1931, the Eureka team traveled by bus to play undefeated Elmhurst. McKinzie left the bus and went inside to check the team into a hotel. This took so long that Reagan left the bus to find out what was happening. He found the coach arguing with the hotel manager, who told McKinzie that the hotel wouldn't accommodate Burghardt and the team's other "colored" player—and neither would any other hotel in town. McKinzie didn't know what to do. The coach thought the entire team should sleep in the bus, but Reagan said that would embarrass the black players because everyone would be discomforted. He had a better idea. Dixon was nearby, Reagan told McKinzie, and Burghardt and Jim Rattan, the other black player, could come home with him. "Are you sure?" McKinzie asked. Reagan insisted that the players would be welcome at his home, and McKinzie provided cab fare to Dixon.*

Reagan naively believed for years that the cover story he and McKinzie devised fooled Burghardt and Rattan. They told the black players that Reagan was taking them to his home in Dixon because the hotel didn't have enough room for everyone. In any case, Nelle Reagan warmly welcomed her younger son and his teammates. "I just don't think he was conscious of race at all," Burghardt said in 1981. "If you listened to the [President Jimmy] Carter debate during the campaign, Reagan said that when he was growing up they didn't know they had a race problem. It was the dumbest thing a grown person could say, but he'd never seen it. I believe that hotel was his first experience of that sort."[12] Burghardt and Reagan were friends for the rest of Burghardt's life. He voted for Reagan in 1980 and said that they had "a mutual respect and admiration."

Burghardt's memory of Reagan at Eureka was that he had "a personality that would sweep you off your feet." He also recalled Reagan as a practical joker who once electronically wired the front row of seats at the college chapel. This irreverence would have suited the Tekes, who

---

*There is no dispute about the essentials of this story, but there are discrepancies about the details. McKinzie said it occurred in Aurora, 68 miles from Dixon, and that Reagan and the players went home by bus. Reagan, in *Where's the Rest of Me?* and Burghardt in an interview with *The Washington Post*, said the incident took place in an unnamed town 10 to 15 miles from Dixon and that McKinzie gave them cab fare. In his postpresidential memoir *An American Life*, Reagan said the incident occurred in Dixon but did not say how he and the two black players reached his home.

honored in the breach the school's taboos on gambling, drinking, smoking, sex, and dancing. A leading participant in the Teke high jinks was Moon Reagan, who to the dismay of his mother had spent three years working in a cement plant after graduating from Dixon High. Nelle did everything she could to convince him that he ought to go to college, and Dutch made it possible by landing Moon a job in the Teke house and a partial scholarship, then convincing the college to defer its tuition until after graduation. With the help of Margaret Cleaver, Dutch had already made a similar deal for himself, but he had reservations about going out on a limb for his brother. He recalled in his autobiography that Neil had never paid him back a loan, "and I didn't like to think he might someday treat Eureka the same way." Dutch put aside his reservations and reached out to his brother because he wanted, as always, to please his mother. Neil, who in later life was sometimes reluctant to give full credit to his famous brother, always acknowledged that his intervention had made it possible for him to attend Eureka, where his superior speed enabled him to outshine Dutch on the football field.

No memories of scholarship intrude on Ronald Reagan's recollections of his college days. He worked at several jobs, participated repeatedly in plays (seven in four years), played football, swam and coached the swimming team, won a letter in track as a member of the 440-yard relay team, organized the basketball cheerleaders, served as president of the Booster Club and of the Student Senate, and worked two years on the yearbook and one on the school newspaper. He had a good time, even as the Depression deepened and life became grimmer in Illinois and across America. But in Reagan's autobiography, with all its nostalgic memories of Eureka, there isn't a single story from the classroom. There weren't any in my interviews with him, either. In his early childhood, Reagan had received "A" grades in Tampico and Monmouth. He had a "B" average at Dixon High School. At Eureka, Reagan barely eked out passing grades. Margaret Cleaver, a superior student, thought he was capable of good work but was unwilling to study. Perhaps he never learned to study because he memorized so easily. Neil remembered a professor complaining that his brother never opened a book. "And yet when the test comes, I just have to give him his grade," the professor told Neil. "He has it all cold."[13] Neil believed his brother had a photographic mind. "He would take a book the night before the test and in about a quick hour he would thumb through it and photograph those pages and write a good test," Neil said.[14]

The professor, whom Neil did not name, was Archibald E. Gray, Eureka's only teacher of economics and sociology, the subjects in which

Ronald Reagan ostensibly majored. Gray was popular because he graded leniently and did not work his students hard. He did, however, make them think. Gray's lectures, according to Barrus Dickenson, later a president of Eureka and a weekly newspaper publisher, emphasized social justice. "He taught economics with a special viewpoint," said Dickenson. "The viewpoint was that what was needed was social reform. He talked about the strikes at the coal mines of southern Illinois, the violence there. He made you realize that we had to pay a price for the automobile. He would talk about Henry Ford's assembly line method and what it did to workers to do the same thing, pushing the pieces around, day after day."[15] In his later political career, Reagan took a jaundiced view of professors who indoctrinated their students, but he had no objections at the time to Gray, who doubled as school librarian and recommended a book about Lenin as a "biography of a great man."[16]

Illinois was not in danger of going Leninist in the early 1930s, but it was hard hit by the Great Depression. Wheat and corn prices plummeted, banks closed, and bread lines formed in Chicago. Dixon was dairy-farming country, and milk prices had fallen so low by 1931 that cows were not worth milking. In neighboring Iowa, farmers who were receiving two cents a quart for milk that distributors were selling for eight cents embargoed all deliveries except those going to hospitals.

With Jack Reagan as the principal breadwinner, the Reagans had not been particularly prosperous even in good times. In 1921, with a friend putting up the capital, Jack had opened a shoe store in Dixon that he called The Fashion Boot Shop. It never made much money and closed down for good in 1929. As the Depression deepened, the Reagans moved from a rented home into a less expensive two-room apartment, then sublet a room of the apartment and prepared their meals on a hotplate. A kindly neighbor cooked for them at times, handing the Reagans their meals through the window. Jack took a job at a cheap chain shoe store in Springfield, 150 miles away. Nelle went to work as a seamstress but was always short of money. Ronald, the dependable son, sent $50 home to his mother from his meager savings, most of which he had earned by washing dishes at Lyda's Wood, the women's dormitory at Eureka.

The low point for the Reagan family came on a Christmas Eve when Jack received a special delivery letter telling him he was fired, apparently from the Springfield store. "Well, it's a hell of a Christmas present," Jack said. Ronald Reagan often told this story in his political campaigns, usually to make the point that he understood about hard times. The authenticity of this story is uncontested, but a question lingers about whether Jack received the fateful telegram in 1931 (as Ronald Reagan remembered it) or in 1932 (as Garry Wills reconstructed it).[17] Wills' chronology is more persuasive to me. Whenever it happened, the firing was a devastating blow to Jack Reagan. He never sold shoes again.

Ronald Reagan graduated from Eureka College on June 7, 1932, the same day that 25,000 veterans who called themselves the Bonus Expeditionary Force paraded up Pennsylvania Avenue in Washington, D.C., demanding a bonus payment for their service in World War I. Some of the veterans sported empty sardine cans hooked to belts that had once held shiny mess kits. They carried American flags and signs that read: "The Bonus or the Breadline," "Food and Clothing Now, Not a Tombstone Later," "Wilson's Heroes, Hoover's Bums." The House of Representatives responded to them by approving a bonus bill, but the Senate voted it down. Many of the disillusioned veterans returned home; thousands of others remained in abandoned buildings they had occupied on Pennsylvania Avenue and at a campsite at Anacostia Flats on the outskirts of Washington. On July 28, District of Columbia police attempted to evict them and a riot ensued in which police shot and killed two of the marchers. District authorities appealed for help to President Herbert Hoover, who called out federal troops commanded by General Douglas MacArthur. After the troops routed the unarmed veterans from Pennsylvania Avenue, MacArthur ordered them to Anacostia, where they drove the bonus marchers out with tear gas and then burned down their homemade shacks.

The smashing of the bonus Army was big news in Dixon. The Reagans, Democrats all, shared in the public outrage and blamed Hoover, although MacArthur clearly had exceeded his orders. Ronald Reagan was then in his final summer as a lifeguard at Lowell Park after failing to land a $12.50-a-week job selling sporting goods at Montgomery Ward. Along with millions of other Americans, he had dreams but no prospects. When the summer ended, he would be out of work. But Reagan in this desperate time extended his horizons. The inspiration may have come from his former high school drama teacher, B. J. Frazer, who talked with him one day at Lowell Park. "Aren't you going to have a shot at communications, the field in which you have so much talent?" Frazer asked.[18] This was what Reagan wanted to do, but he didn't know how to go about it. He talked it over with Sid Altschuler, a wealthy Kansas City businessman who had married a Dixon girl and visited each summer for vacation. Reagan had taught Altschuler's two daughters to swim, and the businessman reciprocated by counseling the young lifeguard. However, Altschuler had no connections in the broadcasting industry. He advised Reagan to take the most menial job he could find at any studio, anything to get his foot in the door.

Reagan tried. After discussing his plans with his mother, he hitchhiked to Chicago, then the regional radio center of the Midwest. At night he bunked in the fraternity house of a former Eureka classmate who was attending medical school. By day he made a painful round of the studios, hoping to demonstrate his ability as a sportscaster. No one was interested. He was an inexperienced small-town college graduate competing with hundreds of experienced applicants in the trough of the Depression. Times were so bad in Chicago that half the normal workforce was unemployed. Mayor Anton Cermak had asked for $150 million in federal relief funds. The alternative, he warned, would be riots that would require the government to send in federal troops. Reagan made no headway, but at WMAQ, the NBC station in Chicago, a secretary took a fancy to him and told him he was wasting his time in Chicago. Go find a small station in the "sticks," she told him. Reagan, feeling "pretty down and discouraged," hitchhiked back home.[19]

After a few days, he took the good advice he had been given and bounced back. His father owned a well-worn Oldsmobile. It was rarely driven because Jack had no money to buy gasoline, but he kept it in the hope that someone would once again offer him a selling job on the road. Now, he encouraged his younger son to take the car and make a swing of nearby small-town radio stations. Ronald Reagan's first stop was Davenport, Iowa, 75 miles west across the Mississippi River, the home of WOC, or "World of Chiropractic," a station founded by B. J. Palmer and housed in the same building as his chiropractic school. WOC had been advertising for an announcer for a month before Reagan arrived and had just hired the most promising of the tryouts. There were no other jobs, station manager Peter MacArthur told him. Angered at himself that he hadn't known about the tryouts, Reagan burst out, "How in the hell does a guy ever get to be a sports announcer if he can't get inside a station?"[20]

Something about Reagan impressed MacArthur, who asked him if he could announce a football game. This was the ideal question, for Reagan had the useful experience of announcing scores of imaginary games on his broomstick microphone to his Eureka football teammates. Alone in a studio, with MacArthur listening from the control room, Reagan improvised an account that was based upon a game between Eureka and Western Illinois in which he had played the previous year. As a storyteller, he always tried to improve upon the facts, and his stirring account gave credit to "Dutch Reagan" for making a game-saving block that could be heard in the press box. Eureka didn't have a press box, and in the actual game Reagan missed the block. But Reagan's invented version sounded authoritative to MacArthur, who offered the young lifeguard $5 and round-trip bus fare from Dixon the following Saturday to broadcast a University of Iowa football game.

It was a foot in a door that Reagan would kick wide open.

5

ANNOUNCER

NOVEMBER 1932 was a big month in Ronald Reagan's life—and an even bigger one for the United States of America. For Reagan, it was the month he launched his career as a radio announcer. For the nation, November marked the beginning of a new era as voters turned out President Herbert Hoover and chose Franklin Delano Roosevelt to replace him. Raised as a Democrat, Reagan proudly cast the first ballot of his life for FDR and his "New Deal for the American people."

But Reagan's preoccupation that November was football, not politics. After he impressed Peter MacArthur with his half-remembered and half-improvised account of a Eureka game, the WOC station manager hired him to broadcast four University of Iowa home games for $5 a game—but only on condition that he did well on the first one. In effect, it was a one-game trial, and Reagan needed to memorize the team rosters and quickly master the rudiments of sports broadcasting to take advantage of his opportunity.

On game day, Reagan took the bus from Dixon to Davenport, where MacArthur met him and drove him to the stadium at Iowa City for the game with Minnesota. Reagan was the No. 2 man in the broadcast booth; he was described in the Dixon newspaper as "righthand man to Gene Loffler, WOC announcer." In fact, he was competing with Loffler as well as assisting him in what turned out to be a fairly even match. Loffler was a professional broadcaster with a superficial knowledge of football; Reagan had played football and understood the game but had never been before a real microphone, except at his impromptu tryout. In that first game, Loffler and Reagan broadcast alternate quarters, with Reagan gaining confidence with every play. In the end, he was convinced he had outshone Loffler. While this opinion cannot be verified at this historical distance, Reagan must have done well, for MacArthur asked him back for the three remaining Iowa home games, doubling his pay for each of them to $10.

Reagan spent two anxious months in Dixon after the football season, hoping for a call that would tell him he had a future in radio. MacArthur kept in touch with his young prospect, telephoning him at Christmastime to encourage him. Early in 1933, he called again, this time offering Reagan the staff announcer's job he coveted. It paid $100 a month, good money for a beginner in the depths of the Depression. A machinist in Iowa made 63 cents an hour in 1933, a telephone company technician $16.36 a week, a farm laborer $16.50 a month. When Reagan moved to Davenport, he paid $18 a month in rent for his rooms at the Vale Apartments at the corner of East Fourth and Perry streets, a short walk from the WOC studio, which was on the roof of the Palmer School. He bought a meal ticket at the Palmer School basement cafeteria, entitling him to 18 meals a week for $3.63. He sent money home to Dixon, where his father was still out of work, and $10 a month to Moon so he could finish college at Eureka.[1]

Reagan was twenty-two years old when he broke in as a rookie announcer at WOC. He had a pleasant manner and a remarkable voice, reminiscent to family friends of Nelle Reagan's, which projected warmth, excitement, earnestness. His voice was his great gift. It was a voice, wrote Roger Rosenblatt, that "recedes at the right moments, turning mellow at points of intensity. When it wishes to be most persuasive, it hovers barely above a whisper so as to win you over by intimacy, if not by substance. . . . He likes his voice, treats it like a guest. He makes you part of the hospitality. It was that voice that carried him out of Dixon and away from the Depression."[2]

Still, Reagan struggled in the beginning. He could ad-lib easily but lacked formal training as a broadcaster, and his inexperience showed when he read prepared material. Reading commercials was particularly difficult. "The secret of announcing is to make reading sound like talking," Reagan wrote years later. "I still am not good at a first reading of a script. At that time I was plain awful. I knew it, and so did the listeners. What was worse, so did the sponsors. I couldn't give it that easy conversational persuasive sell."[3]

Reagan overcame this shortcoming. He found that if he memorized the opening passage and repeated it out loud before he delivered it, everything he read would sound spontaneous. Self-discoveries have lasting value, and Reagan would use this technique later in life when rehearsing for major political speeches. Over time, the combination of genuine earnestness and acquired spontaneity made him a persuasive radio salesman, first for products and then for causes 'and candidates. The voice was a gift, to be sure, but the natural-sounding delivery came from practice.

Nonetheless, Reagan almost had his radio career cut short, supposedly out of naiveté about the nature of the broadcasting business. WOC in those days featured an evening program of organ music furnished by a local mortuary, which in exchange received a "free" plug for its services. Reagan said he didn't understand that the plug was really a commercial and that his "dramatic instinct rebelled at mentioning a mortuary in connection with 'Drink To Me Only With Thine Eyes.'" He omitted the plug, the sponsor complained, and Reagan was fired. Good fortune—Reagan called it a "miracle"—intervened. Reagan was assigned to break in his replacement, a schoolteacher who had been interviewed weeks earlier. The teacher was under the impression that the job had been promised to him and that Reagan was filling in until he arrived. When Reagan told him about the circumstances of his firing, the teacher realized that an announcer's life at WOC was precarious and demanded a contract. When he didn't get one, he went back to the security of teaching, and Reagan was rehired for the job.[4]

This is another of those Reagan stories from which something seems missing. It is hard to believe, for instance, that even a novice announcer could be unaware that the plug for the mortuary was actually a commercial. B. J. Palmer, the founder of WOC, was a relentless promoter, and the station, like most businesses during the Depression, was struggling. Sponsors were precious, and announcers were instructed to cater to them.

Reagan didn't say who fired him. It clearly wasn't his mentor, Peter MacArthur, whom Reagan praised as a "saint" and who in turn viewed Reagan as his most promising protégé. Since MacArthur was Reagan's boss, the order to let him go must have come from a higher-up—probably Palmer or his son, Dave, the business manager, either of whom would have been more protective of a regular sponsor than of a new announcer. In any case, the story about the teacher's reaction does not quite ring true. If the teacher asked for a contract, he must have been even more naive than Reagan, for it was known that Palmer did not give contracts, nor were they necessary at a time when jobs were prized and broadcasters lacked union protection. At WOC, in those Depression days, employees could be and were dismissed without notice. When Garry Wills, inquiring into the circumstances of Reagan's firing, asked to see the station's accounting records, he was told they didn't exist. Everyone at WOC was paid in cash.[5]

Whatever the details of the incident, it is typical of Reagan that he remembered the outcome as one of gracious destiny and praised those who helped him learn about radio (especially MacArthur) while erasing from his memory those who did not fully appreciate his abilities (the Palmers). His job security soon became less tenuous. Reagan started at WOC on February 10, 1933, and was fired and rehired in March. In May, WOC was temporarily consolidated with its sister station WHO in Des Moines, which Palmer had upgraded to a 50,000-watt clear channel station that could be heard throughout the region. MacArthur took Reagan with him to WHO, where he was designated the sports broadcaster, and his salary doubled to a munificent $200 a month.

Reagan was elated. He liked the more spacious stage of Des Moines, the capital of Iowa with a population of 142,000 and the largest city in which Reagan had lived except when he was an infant in Chicago. And his move coincided with rare good news from home, where his father, a loyal Democrat, had received as party patronage the steady employment that had long eluded him. Lee County was a white, rural, Republican bastion where Democrats in general and eastern "wet" Catholics in particular were viewed with suspicion. In 1928, Hoover had trounced Jack Reagan's hero and fellow Catholic Al Smith by more than a 2–1 margin in Lee County. Even in 1932, when northwestern Illinois was in distress, Hoover managed to carry Lee County, albeit by only four percentage points. (FDR carried Illinois by a 10 percent margin that year; his national margin over Hoover was nearly 18 percent.)

Political patronage mattered in Illinois, which was third in line for federal relief funds, after New York and Pennsylvania. Jack Reagan's government job was distributing food and scrip that could be exchanged for groceries to the jobless, some of them his friends and neighbors. He was part of the Federal Emergency Relief Administration, later expanded into the Civil Works Administration (CWA), an important "alphabet agency" of the early New Deal and a lifeline for millions of Americans during the Depression.

Ronald Reagan's discussion of the government's rescue of his father is the least satisfactory section of his early autobiography, *Where's the Rest of Me?* At the time of writing, Reagan, having recently delivered his bell-ringing speech for Barry Goldwater in 1964, was trying to reconcile the antigovernment message that formed the core of this speech with his enduring gratitude to FDR for saving his family. His solution was to praise Roosevelt while attacking "Washington" and its faceless bureaucrats for making welfare a way of life. In this early autobiography, and again in his post-presidential memoir, *An American Life*, Reagan lauds the Works Progress Administration (WPA) because it "put people to work building roads, bridges, and other projects." Ronald

Reagan's claim is that his father wound up battling the bureaucrats because, while Jack sought to find work for the unemployed, the "federal welfare workers" wanted to keep them on welfare.

This is a cartoon version of what happened in the early New Deal years, when Jack Reagan distributed welfare not for the WPA (created in 1935) but for the CWA. The latter agency was the brainchild of federal welfare administrator Harry Hopkins, who proposed it as a stopgap measure to help starving Americans weather the difficult years of 1933–1934 while yet another New Deal agency—the Public Works Administration—geared up. Roosevelt, accurately quoted by Reagan as calling relief "a narcotic, a subtle destroyer of the human spirit," never had any intention of making welfare a way of life and disbanded CWA in 1935 after it had come under attack from Republicans and southern Democrats. But it did much good in its short existence. Although CWA fell short of Hopkins' goal of employing 4 million Americans, it provided crucial assistance at a time when social breakdown was a genuine threat.

Jack Reagan seems to have done well, too. In 1934, he obtained federal funds for removing Dixon's streetcar tracks, which were used in the girders of a hangar at the new Dixon Airport, a project planned before the coming of the New Deal that was brought into existence by the CWA. The use of the tracks was crucial, for it kept costs low enough to win federal approval for the airport. As Garry Wills observed, Jack had "finally made his big sale—as a clever bureaucrat."[6]

Ronald Reagan's stories, as we have seen by now, are often instructive in what they omit. Neither in his early biography nor in his later memoir does Reagan mention that his brother, as well as his father, was on the federal payroll distributing relief in Lee County. Neil was hired by Jack, unusual at a time when government policy was to hire only a single unemployed male from each family in order to stretch the limited number of jobs to as many families as possible. Perhaps Ronald was embarrassed by the nepotism involved in Neil's hiring, for he never referred to it in any writing or interview of which I am aware.

While Reagan's stories of this period are incomplete, his sense of familial responsibility was impressive. The money he sent home had enabled Jack to hang on until the New Deal arrived. He also helped Neil graduate from college. In 1935, when Neil left the patronage welfare job in Dixon, he went to Des Moines, where Ronald—now known on the air and to everyone at WHO as "Dutch"—took him into his apartment and secured an audition for him as a broadcaster. The Palmers had always planned to reopen WOC at Davenport after a year. When they did, Neil went to Davenport as an announcer. While he was not his brother's equal as a broadcaster, Neil had commercial skills, and in 1936 he was named program manager for WOC, the first step in what became a successful advertising career. Ronald had managed to get Neil through college and find him work. By any measure, he was his brother's keeper.

Ronald was now embarked safely on the first of his improbable series of careers, but Margaret Cleaver was not making the voyage with him. They had gone steady for most of seven years through high school and college. The only time he had dated anyone else, and then briefly, was in his junior year at college, when Margaret had spent a year at the University of Illinois. She returned to Eureka for her senior year, motivated, it seems, by her affection for Reagan. At the Eureka graduation ceremonies, the graduates—forty-five of them in 1932—stood by custom in a rope of ivy. As their names were called, they stepped forward and the university president cut the ivy strands, symbolically breaking the ties of the students with the past. Students who planned to marry used the ceremony as a means of declaring their intentions. They held the uncut ivy strands around them, as Ronald and Margaret did.

Only they know what happened to their relationship after they left Eureka. Reagan makes a fleeting reference in his autobiography, saying, "Our love and wholesome relationship did not survive growing up."[7] He does not mention that he and Margaret were engaged, or that their parents expected they would soon marry. That they did not set a wedding date after graduation may have reflected the economic realities of the Depression; he had no prospects of work after his summer employment as a lifeguard, and she had been hired to teach in a small high school in Cropsley, Illinois. They continued to write, however, and he hitchhiked out of his way to see her before leaving for his unsuccessful round of interviews in Chicago. In May 1933, when Reagan moved to Des Moines, he called Margaret to tell her about his good fortune. By then, however, they were already drifting apart.

The conventional wisdom, at least in the Reagan family, was that romance was sacrificed to Reagan's determination to make a name in radio. "As soon as he was out of school he was so imbued with the idea of getting a job that he ignored everything," Neil said. "Everything else was put on the shelf temporarily. She went her own direction."[8] A reporter who interviewed friends of Margaret reached a similar conclusion, saying, "She wanted to be a homebody; he was going for the bright lights."[9] Maybe so, but Margaret had no more intention than her fiancé of settling down in Dixon. In 1933, she traveled to Europe with her older sister Helen, who had majored in French. A year later, she wrote Ronald a "dear John" letter from France, returning his engagement ring and saying she had fallen in love with a young man in the U.S. Consular Service whom she planned to wed. He was James Waddell Gordon Jr., of Richmond. They were married by the Reverend Ben Cleaver in the Christian Church in Dixon on June 18, 1935.

The testimony of Reagan's friends at WHO is that he was shattered by the breakup, but his conduct after receiving the letter from Margaret was anything but disconsolate. He began dating almost immediately and in 1936 bought his first new car—a brown Nash convertible. The more difficult news for Reagan came from home, where his father had suffered a serious heart attack that required a long convalescence. Once more, Ronald became the breadwinner of the family. The car is the only extravagance associated with Reagan during his four years in Des Moines. Each week, he sent a third of his paycheck home to his mother.

In his quiet way, Reagan had become popular with the WHO staff. He had the commanding presence that would serve him well in movies and in politics. "As a speaker and as a personality, you were always aware when he came into a room that someone was in the room," recalled Myrtle Williams (then Myrtle Moon), an attractive, dark-haired woman two years older than Reagan who was program director of WHO.[10]

As the sports announcer, Reagan was physically isolated from the news staff of WHO, which was located in the Stoner Building in downtown Des Moines. Reagan was in the back of the ground floor of the three-story building, the front of which housed the Stoner Piano Company. The news staff was on the second floor. This arrangement suited Reagan, who liked people but preferred to work alone. In his cubbyhole of an office, he wrote and delivered a weekly sports commentary in which he at times questioned the commercialism and integrity of professional sports, especially boxing, almost always ending on a moralistic note. Reagan left the building to broadcast a panoply of sports events, but he was best known to WHO sports fans for what he did at the office—reconstruct Chicago Cubs baseball games from a laconic pitch-by-pitch account that he received by telegraph.

This pre-television period was the heyday of baseball "re-creation," as it was called. Broadcasters who mastered this art, and Reagan was very good at it, invented everything from the color of the sky to the actions and expressions of the players and umpires on the field. Their aim was to create a visual scene in which listeners would think the announcer was at the ballpark. "You just couldn't believe that you were not actually there," said Myrtle Williams. "Of course, he knew baseball and that helped."[11]

Reagan's favorite story, from the more than 600 games he re-created, was of a time when the wire went dead and he faked what was happening for twenty minutes. There were some constants to the story, as Reagan recalled it, and some variables. Dizzy Dean was always pitching, and it usually was the ninth inning. The batter varied. Sometimes, as in his autobiography, it was Augie Galan, and at other times it was Billy Jurges. Here is the version, with Jurges the hitter, that Reagan gave to a Baseball Hall of Fame lunch in the White House on March 27, 1981:*

When the slip came through, it said, "The wire's gone dead." Well, I had the ball on the way to the plate. And I figured real quick, I could say we'll tell them what happened and then play transcribed music, but in those days there were at least seven or eight other fellows that were doing the same game. I didn't want to lose the audience. So I thought real quick, "there's one thing that doesn't get in the scorebook," so I had Billy foul one off . . . and I had him foul one back at third base and described the fight between the two kids that were trying to get the ball. Then I had him foul one that just missed being a home run, about a foot and a half. And I did set a world record for successive fouls, or for someone standing there, except that no one keeps records of that kind. I was beginning to sweat when Curley [the monitor in the control booth] sat up straight and started typing . . . and the slip came through the window and I could hardly talk for laughing because it said, "Jurges popped out on the first ball pitched."

Reagan used his imaginative gifts for purposes other than entertainment. On a late-summer Sunday evening a few days after this broadcast, a nursing student named Melba Lohmann returned by bus to Des Moines from her home in Sheffield, Iowa, and was making the short walk to her hospital when a man thrust an object into her back and demanded her purse and suitcase. She offered him the purse, which contained only $3, but the man grabbed the suitcase as well. Then she heard a voice coming from the window of a second-floor apartment above her. "Leave her alone, or I'll shoot you right in the shoulders," said Ronald Reagan. The would-be robber dropped the purse and the suitcase and fled. Reagan then came downstairs in robe and pajamas and walked Lohmann to the hospital, where she told the story to her supervisors.

Reagan saw nothing unusual in this feat. He did not brag about what he had done or stay in touch with Lohmann. But in an interview in the February 1984 issue of the pro-gun magazine *Sports Afield*, President Reagan told the story to make a political point, saying it was fortunate

*I asked Reagan about this discrepancy during a July 31, 1981, interview. He thought a moment, and said, "It was Jurges."

he had a gun in his possession that night. The story was received skeptically by some members of the media who were covering Reagan's re-election campaign, and the campaign staff located Lohmann, now Melba King, and brought her together with the president when he made a swing through Iowa. It was the first time they had seen each other since that night, and she verified that Reagan had indeed scared away the would-be robber. Reagan then told Lohmann that it was a good thing he had fled because the gun was empty and he had no ammunition for it. Garry Wills has questioned whether Reagan even had a gun. Bill Boyarsky, who related the incident in a 1968 book on Reagan, said he had three guns, none loaded.[12] Who knows? But whether Reagan had no guns or one or three, he was well armed with imagination and bravery and a willingness to become involved in a situation where his own life could have been at risk.

Reagan was this way throughout his life. Before a microphone or on stage he lived in a world of make-believe in which it was legitimate to invent or alter a story for dramatic or political purposes. Offstage, he was modest, unassuming, and willing to do the right thing. At Camp Dodge, a National Guard facility where he swam at Des Moines, Reagan spotted a girl going under and, almost by a lifeguard's force of habit, rescued her from drowning. Again, he said nothing about it, believing that it was what anyone would have done.

As Reagan became a celebrity in Des Moines, he was frequently asked to speak to civic or youth groups. In these settings, he often told stories in which he was the hero without ever alluding to his acts of actual heroism. As a speaker, Reagan preferred made-up stories with a moral, reminiscent of the skits in which he appeared as a child in his mother's church. My favorite, perhaps because I heard it so many times in so many different versions, was a fictitious account of how he supposedly called a penalty on himself and cost Dixon High School a football game.* Over the years, this fable showed up in other forms, attributed to other football players. Sometimes Reagan told a version in which a player admitted dropping a touchdown catch in the end zone even

---

*Reagan's account, as reported by the now defunct *Rockford Morning Star*, was this: "I'll never forget one game with Mendota. The Mendota team yelled for a penalty against Dixon at a crucial point. I'd been the culprit and I knew they were right. The official hadn't seen the play, however, so he asked me. I was in an awful spot. But truth-telling had been whaled into me, also a lot of sports ethics which, from the storm that incident raised, evidently weren't exactly practical for fatheads. I told the truth, the penalty was ruled, and Dixon lost the game. I finally wrote a story about it and sold it to a national boys magazine. That sale just about turned the tide for me away from professional sports and coaching on the one hand and acting on the other." There are no contemporary accounts of any incident of this sort, and Dixon High lost to Mendota only once when Reagan was a member of the varsity team. In that game, when Reagan was a senior in 1927, Mendota won 24–0.

though the official hadn't seen it. The story, in any version, was unveri-fiable—and untrue. In Reagan's world, it was legitimate to tell such sto-ries for dramatic effect if they served a moral purpose.

While he told such whoppers easily in speeches, Reagan was other-wise uncomfortable when he found it necessary to lie. Thanks to the generosity of her younger son, Nelle Reagan now was able to afford train trips to Des Moines to visit Ronald. On one of these visits, she complained that Jack was drinking heavily again and urged Ronald to write him. He did, trying to trick his father into abandoning alcohol. "I told him I had the same problem, and I thought it might help him that he could set an example for me," Ronald Reagan told me in 1989.[13] This well-meant falsehood must have seemed transparent to Jack, who con-tinued to drink heavily until the last two weeks of his life. But Ronald Reagan was so bothered by this lie that he remembered it more than a half century later.

This was a rare unpleasant memory for Reagan during his mostly happy years in Des Moines. He blossomed professionally at WHO, first as a sports announcer and then as an announcer on a news program fea-turing Harold Royce Gross, a future Republican member of the House who went by his initials "H. R." and was known for his conservative views. (The two became friends and argued without rancor over meals about FDR, whom Reagan adored and Gross abhorred.) The program was sponsored by Kentucky Club, which made tobacco, and this prompted Reagan to take up pipe smoking.

Reagan also interviewed such celebrities as the famous British actor Leslie Howard—the stage-struck Reagan forgot his name—and the Los Angeles evangelist Aimee Semple McPherson. The latter interview concluded ahead of schedule and Reagan signaled for music to fill in the remaining minutes of the hour. As he told it in his autobiography, "A sleepy engineer in the control room reached out, pulled a record off the stack and nodded to go ahead." Reagan announced there would be "a brief interlude of recorded music" and the station played "Minnie the Moocher's Wedding Day." Years later, the announcer, Harold (Red) Rissler, disputed this account. As Rissler remembered it, Reagan went outside after the interview on a hot night to cool off, a privilege denied engineers. "I thought it would be very good to . . . teach him a lesson," said Rissler, who deliberately played the offending record.[14] His boss didn't think it was funny, and Rissler nearly lost his job.

Hot nights were commonplace in the farm belt during the mid-1930s, when heat and drought were the handmaidens of the Depres-sion. The worst year was 1934, when vast dust storms uprooted millions of acres of land in the central plains, searing crops, killing livestock, and blotting out the midday sun. Des Moines was on the edge of the Dust Bowl, as the catastrophe came to be called, but in the center of the heat wave that created it. Stories about record temperatures, withered crops, and heat deaths dominated the *Des Moines Register and Tribune* in July 1934, when the temperature frequently topped 100 degrees. People slept on roofs and fire escapes or, if they had the price of admission, crowded into the Paramount Theater for the blessing of air conditioning. WHO had an air-conditioning plant, too, but one that was prone to such frequent leakage that people walking by the studio would smell the escaping ammonia fumes and complain. There was no air conditioning in the windowless control room.

On his nights off, Reagan kept cool at Cy's Moonlight Inn on the west edge of town. It was a big barn of a building with a long bar, a dirt floor, dance records, and an air-conditioning system more primitive than WHO's—a huge block of ice in the center of the room over which fans blew to dispel cooled air. Near beer sold for 25 cents a bottle at Cy's and was sometimes spiked with pure alcohol, a practice that began during Prohibition and continued after it was repealed. "Everybody had flat thumbs," recalled Paul McGinn, a hotel manager. "The flat thumbs came from turning the bottle upside down so the alcohol could mix."[15] Reagan liked the club and the girls who came there, but he drank so little that he was often called upon to drive others home, effectively serving as a "designated driver" long before the phrase was coined. He also sometimes visited the nearby Club Belvedere, which had a casino, but he never gambled. What Reagan did instead was keep in excellent physical shape, swimming almost daily at Camp Dodge and riding with Myrtle Williams and her friends at the Valley Riding Club. Later, after passing the eyesight test by means of a ruse, he enlisted as a reserve cavalry officer so that he could ride at Fort Des Moines, a decision Reagan later called "one of the smartest things I ever did."[16] For Reagan, who needed active time alone, horseback riding replaced his boyhood walks along the Rock River.

Reagan had become an asset to the Palmers, who had tried to discard him in Davenport but now raised his pay to keep him. He was soon making $75 a week—more than twice as much as his father had ever made—and saving most of what he did not send home. He dated sporadically until McGinn introduced him to Jeanne Tesdell, a pretty recent Drake graduate. They went steady for a year before breaking up on such good terms that Reagan was invited to—and attended—the party where she celebrated her engagement to a local attorney.

Socially speaking, Reagan already displayed the quiet reserve that would characterize his behavior as a married man in Hollywood and

Sacramento. He liked telling stories or talking politics but kept to himself so much that many of his fellow announcers did not know where he lived. The exception was the easygoing Myrtle Williams, who became a good friend. "He's eaten more eggs at my apartment than anyone," she said, also recalling Reagan's fondness for macaroni-and-cheese dinners.[17] Her memories of their friendship are contented ones: selecting records for Reagan when he was a disc jockey, having lunch together and counting their money beforehand, going to church services at Drake where Williams was a Sunday soloist. When President Roosevelt came to town—on September 4, 1936—Williams and Reagan rushed to the window to see the president go by in his open limousine. She cared little for politics, but Reagan was thrilled by the glimpse of his idol.[18]

Happy as he was in Des Moines, Reagan's dreams of an acting career had never died. In 1936, Gene Autry signed a hillbilly band (the Oklahoma Outlaws) that had appeared on WHO to a contract for one of his western movies. If a nondescript band could make it in Hollywood, why couldn't he? Reagan believed in destiny and luck, and both had favored him in radio. He had never been to the Pacific coast, but he came up with a plan that would allow him to test the waters in Hollywood without cutting his ties to WHO. In those days, the Chicago Cubs held spring training at Catalina Island, off the Southern California coast. (Both the island and the Cubs were owned by Phillip K. Wrigley, the chewing-gum magnate.) Reagan had accumulated a month's vacation, and he offered to use it getting to know the players in spring training (from February 12 through March 15) if the station would pay his expenses. WHO agreed, and Reagan went west with the Cubs. Hollywood, not Catalina, was on his mind.

Reagan had a connection in Hollywood. Her name was Joy Hodges, a Des Moines girl who had worked at WHO. She had become a successful singer and had appeared in some minor roles in RKO films. McGinn had introduced the two of them on a double date when Hodges came to Des Moines on tour, and Reagan had interviewed her on WHO. When he asked her how it felt to be a movie star, she replied, "Well, Mr. Reagan, you may know one day."[19]

A few days after he arrived in Southern California, Reagan sought out Hodges, who was then singing with a band at the Biltmore Bowl. He sent her a note backstage saying he wanted to see her after the performance. She agreed. When they met, Hodges had him take off his horn-rimmed glasses, told him that he was "very handsome" without them, and advised him never to wear them again. The next morning, she called her agent, George Ward, and Reagan went off to see him.

Ward was with the Bill Meiklejohn agency, whose clients included Robert Taylor, Betty Grable, and a little known actress named Jane Wyman. In promoting himself to Ward, Reagan exaggerated his credentials and his salary scale, describing the Eureka Drama Club as a stock company and telling him that he was making $180 a week, twice his salary at the time. None of this mattered to Ward, who recognized that Reagan was a "likeable, clean-cut American," a "type," as he put it, that was valued in Hollywood. Although he didn't mention it to Reagan, Ward knew that Jack Warner was looking for just such an actor to replace Ross Alexander, a promising actor slightly older than Reagan who had committed suicide on January 3, 1937. Reagan's voice reminded Ward of Alexander's. Ward picked up the phone and called Warner Brothers casting director Max Arnow on the spot.*

"I have another Robert Taylor sitting in my office," Ward said with Hollywood hyperbole.[20] Arnow had heard such talk before, but the Meiklejohn agency had sent him useful talent, and he agreed to give Reagan a screen test. At that test, Arnow picked out the suitable part of a clean-cut young man from the Midwest (Johnny Case in *Holiday*, a movie that cast Cary Grant in the lead role when it was made later that year). In Arnow's recollection, Reagan read the part, memorized it, and gave a perfect test on camera. Ward then tried to persuade Reagan to remain in Los Angeles for a few days until Jack Warner had seen the screen test, but Reagan told him he had to return to Des Moines with the Chicago Cubs. He left on Wednesday, March 16, wondering if he had blown his chance by not staying.

As Reagan subsequently realized, however, he had, "through ignorance," done the smart thing. "Hollywood just loves people who don't need Hollywood," he wrote.[21] On March 22, Ward wired him that Warners had offered a seven-year contract with a one-year option for $200 a week and asked what he should do. "Sign before they change their minds," Reagan wired back. He was happy, and so was Hodges, who wired the *Des Moines Register and Tribune* the "scoop" that the city had a star in its midst. Improving on Ward, she said that he was "the greatest bet since Taylor."[22]

All Reagan needed was a screen name. He was then known universally as "Dutch," a nickname he had valued as an undersized boy but now no longer needed. After the screen test, Arnow had discussed a movie name, and Reagan, timidly as he recalled it, suggested that the studio use his real name. In a parody of a movie scene, Arnow repeated

*The Warner brothers were Harry and Albert, who were based in New York, and Jack, who ran the studio in Hollywood and was in charge of film production. Their studio was incorporated as "Warner Bros.," and all of Warners' films carried this label.

the words "Ronald Reagan, Ronald Reagan," and finally declared, "I like it."[23] So, Ronald Reagan it was. Migrating to a place where many people change their names and lose their identities, the young announcer from Iowa had regained the Christian name with which he had been baptized in Tampico twenty-six years earlier.

6

ACTOR

NATIVE SONS AND daughters are a minority in California, a state
conceived in greed and idealism by immigrants who tested its
profound variety of opportunities and climate and supplied its
driving force. The Spaniards swept into California in the sixteenth century to find gold, save souls, and keep out rival powers. They sent
priests, who built missions, and soldiers, who occupied land they rarely
settled. After the fall of the Spanish empire, California became a frontier of Mexico, governed from afar, with lightly populated *rancheros* dependent upon horses and native labor. Then came the Anglo settlers,
eradicating with disease or gunfire the few thousand Native Americans
who had survived the rule of Spain and Mexico. The first wagon train
struck out for California in the spring of 1841 from Independence, Missouri, lured by stories of the fabulous land 2,000 miles to the west.
Other migrants arrived after the gold discovery of 1848. They were
restless folk who came to California in search of gold or land or because
they could not pay their debts at home or were in desperate journey
from a crime. These migrants called the country they had left "the
States" and adopted California as their home. It would later become
home to other waves of immigrants from Mexico, China, Japan, and the
whole wide world.

Ronald Reagan was part of the great migration to California that
began in earnest with the gold rush and has never stopped. Because of
abundant resources and a kindlier climate, remote California was a
more inviting frontier than the inhospitable plains and mountains that
separated it from the nation's populated regions across the continent.
So California developed in a twinkling and burst into the consciousness
of America full-blown. "Elsewhere the tempo of development was slow
at first, and gradually accelerated as energy accumulated," wrote Carey

McWilliams. "But in California the lights went on all at once, in a blaze, and they have never been dimmed."[1]

Most of the migrants, Ronald Reagan among them, couldn't wait to reach this promised land. The morning after the staff of WHO threw a farewell party for him at Cy's Moonlight Inn, Reagan piled his belongings into his Nash convertible and headed west. He pulled up at the Hollywood Plaza Hotel on May 31, 1937, after driving nonstop the last twenty-four hours across what he called "the burning desert" to Los Angeles. He had driven alone, a single current in a torrent of immigration from the nation's great midland and typical in that he came from Illinois by way of Iowa. In the three decades from 1910 to 1940, California's largest source of immigrants was Reagan's home state of Illinois. So many native-born Iowans lived in California when Reagan arrived that one of them, Frank Merriam, was governor of the state. A novel of the period, Darwin Teilhet's *Journey to the West*, called its Southern California section "the Iowa Coast." State societies flourished, with those from Iowa and Illinois among the most prominent, binding together newcomers in nostalgic celebrations at annual picnics. To Reagan, it must have seemed that the world he had known in Dixon and Des Moines had moved with him to Los Angeles.

And, to a large degree, Reagan brought his world with him. He sent for his parents in September, three months after he arrived. His brother soon followed. So did three Teke friends from Des Moines, who decided one merry night at Cy's that they also wanted to partake of the good life in Southern California. Reagan, who recognized the need to stay in touch with his fans, wrote a series on his new career for the *Des Moines Sunday Register*. It began on June 13, 1937, and continued through October 28, providing a useful contemporaneous record of Reagan's early months in Hollywood.

Reading the series today, one is struck by Reagan's fascination with filmmaking and the attention he paid to technique: where to stand, what to wear, how to kiss a girl. While his articles in the Des Moines newspaper are spiced with self-deprecatory stories about how it felt to be "a male *Alice in Wonderland*,"* the focus of the series is on camera location, scene lighting, film editing, and rehearsing. "Picture making continues to amaze me," Reagan wrote with a sense of wonder, after filming a scene a dozen times before the director accepted it.

---

*In one of these stories, written during the filming of his first movie, Reagan tells how he tried to win the attention of June Travis, the female lead, with whom he was infatuated. The director instructed Reagan to whisper something in her ear in the next-to-last scene when he "gets the girl" to make it seem realistic. Reagan asked Travis for a date. She whispered back, and Reagan ruined the scene by saying out loud that he couldn't hear her. The stage hands laughed and shot the scene again. "I whispered my question again, and this time heard her reply," Reagan wrote. "Her answer was 'No.'"

As in radio, Reagan struggled at the beginning. He had a sense of déjà vu from Davenport when he was called upon on his first day at Warners to read his lines in a movie that was being filmed under the title of *Inside Story*. Since he had never seen the script, his reading was flat. This puzzled Nick Grinde, the director, who had directed Reagan's screen test. Reagan, more composed than he had been in his early days at WOC, calmly explained that he never did well at first readings but would be okay after he had memorized the part. Grinde obliged him by shooting scenes in which Reagan did not appear. When Reagan came in the next day, he had perfectly memorized the lines and projected the warmth and earnestness that had impressed Grinde in the screen test.[2]

Reagan's photographic memory and willingness to take direction were suited to the assembly-line production that Jack Warner expected of his B-picture division, then headed by Bryan Foy. The B-division, a consistent moneymaker, turned out rapid-fire, low-budget films without qualms about artistic quality. An actor who quickly memorized scripts was money in the bank, and Reagan's easygoing disposition was an additional asset. In his early years in Hollywood, he did not agitate for star roles, and he was willing, perhaps too willing, to accept a bit role in a big movie after being a hit in a small one. As a result, Reagan lingered in the B-division longer than other actors of equivalent or lesser talent who were more demanding or difficult to deal with on the set.

Reagan's approach to acting was suited to the screen. Years before "method acting" came into vogue, his high school drama teacher, B. J. Frazer, was telling his students to act out the emotions of their characters. "I did not have training as a professional drama coach," said Frazer. "I think my ignorance stood me in good stead. I wanted them to be this character. I used to sit the cast down and ask, 'Why, why, why are the characters doing these things?' When they got out on the stage, they *were* the characters. I understand that this became the standard for Hollywood. Reagan was good. He never forgot his lines or his actions. When he got on the stage, he was the character."[3] This training was reinforced at Eureka by Marie Ellen Johnson, a respected drama teacher who encouraged Reagan to believe he could succeed as an actor.

Reagan also had the asset, which he would later in his career consider a liability, of being typecast. Hollywood valued wholesome, handsome, young male actors whom they could celebrate as epitomizing American values. Reagan filled this bill. In his first film, Reagan was cast as a radio announcer who uncovers small-town corruption. The announcer was cheerful and moralistic, allowing Reagan to play what Garry Wills would later describe as the "heartwarming role" of himself.[4] From beginning to end, it was what he did best.

The film that Reagan described to readers of the *Des Moines Sunday*

Register as *Inside Story* was released in New York on November 12, 1937, under the new title of *Love Is on the Air*, a paraphrase of a popular song. In these days of double features, it took a distant second billing to the feature film *Stage Door*, starring Katharine Hepburn. Even by the B-division standards of Warners, where films usually took six weeks to make, *Love Is on the Air* was a quickie. It was shot in just three weeks at a cost of $119,000. At this pace, it is doubtful if many scenes in the movie were redone a dozen times, as in the example that Reagan breathlessly described in his newspaper series.

Reagan's next role was a bit part in a major film, *Hollywood Hotel*, the last of the great Busby Berkeley musicals of the 1930s. It's worth noting because it marked the beginning of his friendship with the influential gossip columnist Louella Parsons, who was also from Dixon and took a shine to the young actor from her hometown. *Hollywood Hotel* was based on a CBS radio series of the same name that had been conceived by Parsons and featured Dick Powell as the host. In the movie, Reagan appears briefly as an announcer on Parsons' staff—his role was so insignificant that he did not even receive a film credit. But his friendship with Parsons would boost his career and have a significant impact on his personal life.

Reagan made nine films in 1938, ending with *Brother Rat*, a movie adaptation of the George Abbott play in which Eddie Albert had starred on Broadway. Albert also starred in the movie, and the rave reviews he received for his film debut overshadowed the favorable critical comment Reagan received for his portrayal of Virginia Military Institute cadet Dan Crawford, who romances the daughter of the VMI commandant. Jane Wyman plays the daughter in a screen relationship that foreshadowed a real one. *Brother Rat* was entertaining, but most of Reagan's other 1938 movies met his later description of Warners B-division films: "They didn't want them good, they wanted them Thursday."

In 1939, Reagan made eight movies. The standout was *Dark Victory* with Bette Davis, Geraldine Fitzgerald, and Humphrey Bogart. (*Newsweek* praised Reagan, as well as Bogart, for his "excellent" performance.) By the beginning of 1940, Reagan had established himself as a pleasant, second-line lead actor. He wanted more, however, and for the first time battled for a part. By the time Reagan tested for the role of George Gipp in *Knute Rockne—All American* (1940), Warner Brothers had tried out ten other actors. None of them "looked like football players," as Reagan remembers it, adding that few persons of normal build look like football players out of uniform. Reagan felt he was perfect for the role of Gipp, a rakish but talented Notre Dame football player who died young of pneumonia. He also sensed that the role might rescue him from the B-division. Reagan showed Bryan Foy pictures of himself in a Eureka College football uniform. Foy was supportive but said that Reagan had to persuade Hal Wallis, who headed the A-division at Warners and was producing *Rockne*. Reagan then approached Pat O'Brien, the uncontested choice for the Rockne role. The two actors had appeared together in *Submarine D-1* (1937), where Reagan's role was left on the cutting room floor, and again in a 1938 film, *Cowboy from Brooklyn*. O'Brien, a star, liked Reagan and knew of his athletic background.

Years later, O'Brien said:

As far as Jack Warner was concerned, it was just another picture. I was excited about it, being an athletic buff, but there weren't too many contract players at Warners who were athletically inclined. I asked who was going to play the Gipper. "Who's the Gipper?" Warner said. I said, "This is a helluva important role. A lot of the people you have under contract don't know a football from a cantaloupe. This guy does." I said, "I'll tell you what I'll do. I'll make the test with him." Warner said I could do it if I was that excited about it. I made the test with him, and the rest is history. Ronald Reagan breathed life into the Gipper.[5]

Even with a lifeless Gipper the film would have been interesting, because O'Brien was ideal as Rockne, the Norwegian immigrant who became Notre Dame's football star and its most famous coach before losing his life in a plane crash. Gipp is romanticized, but most of the Rockne material is accurate. While Reagan doesn't come on the screen until relatively late in the film, his arrival is worth the wait. The scene is Gipp's first practice at Notre Dame, and Rockne asks him if he can carry the ball. With an insouciance that anticipates candidate Reagan, Gipp looks quizzically at the coach and asks, "How far?"

The Rockne film led to major roles for Reagan in *Santa Fe Trail* (1940) and *The Bad Man* (1941), a melodrama dominated by accomplished scene-stealers Wallace Beery and Lionel Barrymore. In recalling the latter film, Reagan often told of a scene in which he was simultaneously upstaged by Beery and bruised by a wheelchair operated by Barrymore in his role as a crippled rancher. *Santa Fe Trail* makes mincemeat of history. Errol Flynn was cast in the lead role as Confederate cavalryman J. E. B. Stuart, with Reagan playing the second lead as General George Armstrong Custer, supposedly Stuart's friend and a fellow 1854 graduate of West Point. Actually, Custer was fifteen years old when Stuart graduated that year, and the two men never met. Oswald Garrison Villard wrote to *The Saturday Review of Literature* to protest the film's historical inaccuracies. "It was Jefferson Davis, according to this Hollywood version, who was the real champion of the union," declared *The Christian Century*. But Reagan looked good on a horse and performed well enough as Flynn's mythical best friend to give his career another boost.

Three other Reagan films were released in 1941, all to good, if not exceptional, reviews. Reagan was a young pianist in *Million Dollar Baby*, a young newspaperman in *Nine Lives Are Not Enough*, and an American stunt pilot in *International Squadron*. By now, Reagan was knocking on the door of stardom and making $1,000 a week. He was rewarded with roles in two films, one of them forgotten and the other the memorable *Kings Row*.

The forgotten film was *Juke Girl* (1942). Reagan, who would one day characterize the farm workers' march that Cesar Chavez led to Sacramento as an "Easter-egg roll," played a hero fruit picker battling the big packing houses while keeping bad packer Richard Whorf away from Ann Sheridan, then known as the "oomph girl." Manny Farber, reviewing the film for *The New Republic*, thought *Juke Girl* a movie that "wanted to be brave and forthright about the rotten farming conditions in the South, which also wasn't exactly what the producer wanted; so it's coated over with the cheap glazing of any horse opera." But Farber, one of the film's least friendly critics, also thought that Reagan and Sheridan both were "fine to look at—with natural freshness that makes good movies."

Kings Row is based on the Henry Bellamann novel about a turn-of-the-century small town with a darker side than Reagan's memories of Dixon. James Agee, the esteemed film critic who then wrote for *Time*, called director Sam Wood's screen interpretation of the novel "potent, artful cinema." But the film was a challenge for Wood because of a convoluted script that was in part the result of the Hollywood taboo about incest, an important element of the novel's plot. The script changed incest to insanity and tacked on an unconvincing happy ending.

Agee's review focused on Wood's successful effort to "de-oomph" Ann Sheridan. Wood did this so well that Sheridan's excellent acting and larger role overshadowed Reagan's more predictable competence as Drake McHugh, a playboy from the wrong side of the tracks. In the film, McHugh's legs are amputated by sadistic surgeon Charles Coburn as a punishment for his romance with his daughter, played by Nancy Coleman. Reagan awakens from the operation and utters the celebrated line that became the title of his autobiography: "Where's the rest of me?"

Reagan's performance in a film whose cast also included Claude

Rains, Robert Cummings, and Betty Fields, was for the most part well received, although Bosley Crowther of *The New York Times*, who had liked Reagan in lesser roles, was not impressed by either him or Sheridan. Russell Maloney in *The New Yorker* said Reagan "capably breezes through the part," and Philip Hartung in *Commonweal* lauded Reagan for "a splendid performance." In *The New Republic*, Farber said that Reagan and Sheridan "made *Kings Row* feel inside your stomach." This critic was amazed that Sheridan had performed competently but said that Reagan was "good and no surprise."

Reagan, who felt that Wood had drawn the best out of him as well as Sheridan, was so pleased at the favorable reaction and at succeeding in a dramatic part that he subsequently exaggerated his role. He wrote in his autobiography that Sheridan was "not in the shot" when he awakens from the operation and finds that he has lost his legs. In fact, she was in the entire shot, which is told from her point of view. This aside, Reagan had critical ratification for his firm belief that *Kings Row* was his top performance. "It was my best picture," Reagan told me in 1968, adding that the McHugh role illustrated the precepts of acting that he had first learned from B. J. Frazer in Dixon. "I always ask myself how do I, Ronald Reagan, feel about it," he said. "How much is Ronald Reagan with his legs cut off and how much is Drake McHugh? If I divorce myself and say, 'How does Drake McHugh feel?' it's not a good job. But if I scream in horror, 'Where's the rest of me?' and I feel it, that's me, and it's right."[6]

For Reagan, the only downside to this movie that brought him to the brink of stardom was its timing. *Kings Row* was filmed in 1941, the year the Japanese attacked Pearl Harbor and plunged the United States into war. It was released in 1942, when Reagan was in the Army. He had easy work in the war, a subject that will be explored in the next chapter, and a new million-dollar, seven-year contract that agent Lew Wasserman negotiated for him on the strength of *Kings Row*. But Reagan's military service deprived him of the opportunity to take advantage of his breakthrough role, and other rising stars eclipsed him during the war years. This led to a series of postwar conflicts with Warners, which preferred Reagan in light comedies rather than in the dramatic roles he thought his performance in *Kings Row* had earned him.

Reagan was no longer the obliging small-towner of his salad days in Hollywood. His first serious dispute with Warners arose in 1947 over a movie called *Stallion Road* that was supposed to star Humphrey Bogart and his wife Lauren Bacall. Reagan hoped this film would get his career rolling again after the war, but the Bogarts backed out of it and the film was downgraded from a big-budget Technicolor production to an inexpensive black-and-white film. Zachary Scott and Alexis Smith took the place of Bogart and Bacall; Reagan was cast as a hero veterinarian afflicted with anthrax. He performed competently and received reasonably good reviews, but the movie failed commercially. Then came *That Hagen Girl* in the same year, starring Shirley Temple in her first grownup role. Reagan made the film solely because he was contractually obligated to do so; he suspected that American filmgoers weren't ready to accept the childhood sweetheart as an adult, with Reagan as her overage lover. He was right. The film, an artistic and box-office flop, was widely panned.

Retrospectively, Reagan's work on screen during this troubled period of his life looks better at historical distance than it did at the time. He made fifteen films in the postwar period, beginning with *Stallion Road* in 1947 and ending with *The Winning Team* in 1952. Only two of them, *That Hagen Girl* and *Night unto Night* (1949), were clinkers. Four films—*The Voice of the Turtle* (1947), *The Girl from Jones Beach* (1949), *John Loves Mary* (1949), and *The Hasty Heart* (1949)—gave Reagan an opportunity to display his flair for light comedy. The best of these is probably *Voice of the Turtle*, where Reagan has the male lead as an Army sergeant who falls in love with a young actress. In this instance, Jack Warner's judgment was sharper than Reagan's. He had bought the rights to the award-winning play by John Van Druten with Reagan in mind and refused to let his would-be star quit the picture for a bit part in *Treasure of the Sierra Madre* (1948), which became an instant classic. Reagan's dispute with Warner soured him on *The Voice of the Turtle* even though critics praised his acting and applauded new star Eleanor Parker. (Reagan, in an uncharacteristic display of temper, had demanded June Allyson instead of the then-unknown Parker.) "Ronald Reagan turns in a pleasingly sensitive performance as the marooned sergeant," wrote *Newsweek* in a typical review of this film.

Several other Reagan films of this period won critical acclaim. Crowther praised Reagan in *The Girl from Jones Beach*, saying he had "a cheerful way of looking at dames." *Time* thought Reagan was the "only real fun" in this movie, which it disliked. Reagan also won plaudits for his performance in *The Hasty Heart* (1950), where he was a supporting actor in a cast that featured Richard Todd and Patricia Neal. Todd won an Academy Award nomination for his portrayal of a soldier in a Burmese hospital and went on to a big career. Though Crowther found Todd's portrayal of the dying Scottish officer "eloquent" and "irresistible," he also singled out Reagan as "amusingly impatient and blunt" in the role of a wounded American.

After the failure of *That Hagen Girl*, Jack Warner replaced Reagan with Errol Flynn in a western. Reagan felt it was unjust to blame him for the failure of a movie he had never wanted to make and told Bob Thomas of the *Los Angeles Mirror* that he was "going to pick his own pictures" and could do a better job of it than Warner Brothers had done. His comments prompted Jack Warner to write Reagan an angry letter.[7] Lew Wasserman stepped into the breach, negotiating a contract with Warners that required Reagan to do only one picture a year at half his former salary. One week later, Wasserman negotiated a five-year, five-picture deal for Reagan with Universal Studios that also allowed him to do films for other studios. Ironically, Reagan's irritation with Warner Brothers had given him the freelance status he sought at a time when many other postwar feature players were turning to the security of long-term contracts.

But Reagan initially enjoyed his newfound contractual independence, the first fruit of which was *Louisa* (1950), a charming film that suggested that Universal also valued Reagan more for his comedic talents than his dramatic potential. In *Louisa*, Reagan is an amiable architect with a pretty daughter (Piper Laurie) and a mother, Louisa (Spring Byington), who disrupts the family. The movie also features Charles Coburn, the evil surgeon of *Kings Row*, cast as a tycoon who romances the widow Louisa but steps aside in a gentlemanly manner for a local grocer, played by Edmund Glenn. Reagan enjoyed being reunited with Coburn, and the film received positive reviews.

Reagan's new contract gave him the opportunity to make the westerns that Warner Brothers had denied him. Starting with *The Last Outpost* for Paramount in 1951, he made four westerns for three different filmmakers, with the best being *Cattle Queen of Montana* (1954) with Barbara Stanwyck for RKO. The others are run-of-the-plains westerns in which Reagan rides better than he acts. Reagan also made a 1951 comedy, *Bedtime for Bonzo*, which enjoyed a television revival in the late 1960s after it became the staple of opposition political gags. The gags aside, it's an amusing comedy in which the chimpanzee of the title steals most of the scenes and Reagan performs competently. But Reagan's best picture of this period was *The Winning Team* (1952), which he made for Warner Brothers and enjoyed because it brought him into touch with professional athletes. The movie is the story of pitcher Grover Cleveland Alexander, whose drinking bouts masked an epileptic condition he never revealed to his teammates. Even though the word "epilepsy" was taboo on screen, Reagan powerfully suggests that there is more to Alexander's fainting spells than alcoholism.*

*Reagan's stand-in during the baseball scenes of *The Winning Team* was Bob Lemon, an outstanding pitcher for the Cleveland Indians. In one scene, Alexander is practicing for his come-

By the mid-1950s, Reagan's interests had turned to television and politics and he was no longer in demand as a movie actor. He made a single movie in 1955 and none the following year. Reagan's last feature film, *Hellcats of the Navy*, premiered in San Diego on April 11, 1957. The movie, Reagan's fifty-second, was a local hit because of San Diego's large naval population audience but is otherwise remembered mostly because Nancy Davis was the leading lady and because it marked the end of Reagan's movie career. Technically, it wasn't the end, because a fifty-third film, *The Killers* (described in chapter 2) was released in theaters in 1964. But this had started out as a television project; Reagan always considered *Hellcats of the Navy* his "real" final film.

How good was Reagan as a movie actor? There is no single answer to this question. One measure of Reagan's ability as an actor is that he frequently won praise in films panned by the critics. Another is that he did well in movies where he was overshadowed by future stars who were making their debuts, most notably Albert in *Brother Rat*, Parker in *Voice of the Turtle*, and Todd in *The Hasty Heart*. Still another is to observe that Reagan durably held his own in movies for two decades with such acting heavyweights as Humphrey Bogart, Charles Coburn, Claude Rains, James Cagney, Olivia de Havilland, and Bette Davis.

Garry Wills, in a typically thoughtful appraisal, concluded that Reagan's voice and personality were better suited for the romantic and light comedy roles in which Warner Brothers preferred to cast him than the more dramatic or western roles he sought. "He was better than Wayne Morris, who started out billed above him," Wills wrote. "He was in the league of Van Johnson, Peter Lawford, Rod Taylor, Gig Young—not a bad league; they were solid performers. And it is wrong to say he ever failed in this league. . . . Reagan failed in Hollywood because he was not satisfied with his proper rung, with the range he commanded, but attempted heavier roles he could not sustain."[9]

"Failed" seems to me too strong a term for an actor—and a man—who consistently sought more than the accomplishment that was in easy range of his talent. In Hollywood, as in other aspects of his life, Reagan's reach consistently exceeded his grasp. One of his most appealing attributes during his long climb from Dixon to the White House was that he was never content with the roles others assigned to him. He believed in himself. He believed he would become a radio announcer

---

back by throwing baseballs into a catcher's mitt that has been nailed onto a barn. Normally, this would have been easy for Lemon, but he was wild the day of the shooting and couldn't hit the mitt. After several misses, he heard a voice behind him say, "Mind if I try it?" It was Reagan, whose baseball skills were so limited that Lemon doubted if he could hit the barn, much less the mitt. But according to Lemon (in a story recounted by Ron Fimrite), Reagan took the baseball and threw it squarely into the mitt on his first and only try.[8]

when there were no jobs to be had and that he would make it in Hollywood against the odds. Later, he would improbably believe that he could be governor or president. "If there is one thing we are sure of, it is . . . that nothing is impossible, and that man is capable of improving his circumstances beyond what we are told is fact," Reagan would say in announcing his presidential candidacy in 1980. *Nothing is impossible* was his credo.

Reagan's competence on the screen was rarely in dispute as long as he was viewed as "just" an actor. After he became a conservative spokesman and a candidate, some of those who disapproved of his political views also disparaged his acting. Such retrospective criticisms, Reagan told me in 1968, "touch an exposed nerve." Reagan could accept most political attacks with equanimity, but he hadn't expected that his adversaries would also make fun of his films. His defensiveness on this score is understandable. Acting was not a phase of Reagan's life but the essence of it. He spent thirty years of his life in Hollywood, and he did not cease being an actor when he left. When asked, before he ran for office, what kind of governor he would be, Reagan said, "I don't know. I've never played a governor before."[10] Later, near the end of his presidency, he said there had been times in the White House when he "wondered how you could do the job if you hadn't been an actor."[11] He was joking in both instances, to be sure, but he also meant it.

I remember one particular interview in 1968, late at night on a campaign plane when Reagan was returning home to Los Angeles after spending several days on the road campaigning for Republican candidates. Both of us had exhausted political subjects, and Reagan turned to stories about the days he had spent in Hollywood and what had happened there. I listened in fascination when suddenly Reagan, who was tired, interrupted one of his stories to scornfully denounce "this *New York Times* kind of business of referring to me as a B-picture actor." He went on to list a long line of first-rate actors with whom he had appeared, often getting better reviews than they did. No one referred to them as B-picture actors, he said with an intensity that I had never seen before. Then he calmed down, paused, and—almost shyly—added, "I'm proud of having been an actor."[12]

7

FAMILY MAN

Jane Wyman was the pursuer and Ronald Reagan the pursued when their off-screen relationship began during the filming of *Brother Rat*. Reagan and Wyman had arrived separately for a promotional photo shoot; a schedule mix-up caused a delay, and they began talking to each other about their lives while waiting for a photographer to arrive. Wyman, impatient by temperament, was annoyed by the long delay. Reagan, in contrast, was so accepting of it that Wyman wondered if his calm demeanor was an act. "It didn't seem possible that a man could have so even a disposition consistently," she said.[1] His self-assuredness attracted her.

Soon, they were dating. Reagan, six years older, was protective of Wyman and enjoyed her company but was in no hurry to rush into anything. While he seemed self-confident to Wyman, he had been wary of personal commitment ever since his rejection by Margaret Cleaver. In the five years since Cleaver had returned his engagement ring, Reagan had dated frequently but backed away whenever a relationship showed signs of becoming serious. He displayed this wariness with Wyman, whom he described, in terms more appreciative than romantic, as "fun" and a "good scout."[2]

Wyman won him over by becoming a part of the world Reagan had brought with him to Southern California from Dixon and Des Moines. She became friends with Nelle Reagan, who approved of her, and on Sundays often accompanied Nelle to the Beverly Hollywood Christian Church. She took up golf, which Reagan had added to his athletic repertoire. On weekends or when they weren't filming, Wyman went to the beach with Reagan and his Teke friends from Des Moines. They swam and body surfed in the ocean and played volleyball on the beach. At night, they went to the movies. Soon, Wyman was one of the gang, accepted by Reagan's family and friends.[3]

When Reagan and Wyman met, she was married to Myron Futterman, a courtly dress manufacturer from New Orleans nine years her senior whom she had wed while he was on the rebound from a divorce. Because Wyman wanted a baby and Futterman did not, they separated in 1937 after three months of marriage. Wyman filed for divorce two months later and soon reached an amicable settlement. California law required a year for the divorce to become final; the decree was issued late in 1938. Futterman gave Wyman their apartment, its furnishings, and $1,000 in cash.

Born Sarah Jane Fulks in St. Joseph, Missouri, Wyman came from a troubled marriage that was the second for both of her parents.[4] Her father, a police officer, died when she was eleven, and she was raised by a mother who was middle-aged when Sarah Jane was born. Fulks began her Hollywood career as a chorus girl. After several bit parts, she signed a Warner Brothers contract for $60 a week on May 6, 1936, and the studio renamed her Jane Wyman. In 1937, she appeared in seven movies in minor roles. Wyman was typecast as much as Reagan would be but less accurately. She was pretty—except for her snub nose, she might have been a classic beauty—and Warners decided she was a prototypical "dumb blonde" with little to recommend her except sex appeal. In truth, Wyman was bright and talented and her hair a natural brown.

Gossip columnists, particularly Parsons and her rival Hedda Hopper, were then powerful forces in Hollywood. Words of praise from either of them could signal a producer or an agent to the presence of a rising star. To Parsons' credit, she recognized Wyman's talent and tried to help her escape typecasting. The columnist included both Reagan and Wyman on a nine-week "stars of tomorrow" vaudeville tour in 1939. With Wyman taking the initiative, her romance with Reagan blossomed.

"Long before Ronald was aware of Janie's existence, she knew *he was there*," breathlessly reported *Photoplay*. "But Ronnie had had his heart bashed in once and wouldn't look Janie's way for a long time. When he did, it was all over but the wedding."[5] Parsons announced their engagement. Years later, she said, "Life was very much the way Jane wanted it on a certain day our vaudeville tour took us to Philadelphia. . . . Her brown eyes were sparkling and her voice was bubbling with happiness as she told me: 'Have I got a scoop for you! Ronnie and I are engaged!' I had known that Janie worshipped Ronnie, but I hadn't realized he was falling seriously in love with her. I announced the engagement that night from the stage and in the newspapers."[6]

After this column appeared, the Hollywood publicity mills competed to proclaim Reagan and Wyman the ideal couple. One fan magazine offered the couple an expenses-paid trip to Hawaii if they would take a cameraman along to record their marriage ceremony and honeymoon.

Instead, Reagan and Wyman were married in Glendale on January 26, 1940. They attended a reception given by Parsons at her home, honeymooned in Palm Springs, and moved into the Beverly Hills apartment where Wyman had lived before the marriage. On January 4, 1941, Wyman's twenty-fourth birthday, a baby daughter they named Maureen Elizabeth was born to the Reagans.

Founded by immigrants, many of them Jewish, Hollywood was then the mass culture capital of the United States and the valedictorian of Middle American values. In its early days, Hollywood had a carnival atmosphere and was known as "the movie colony," where loose morals prevailed over good manners. Carey McWilliams counted the other side of the coin, crediting Hollywood with liberating Los Angeles "from the sillier rituals of middle-class life."[7] But a series of morals scandals after World War I, coming when filmmaking was emerging as one of the nation's most profitable industries, jolted Hollywood and led to formation of a trade association, a code of conduct, and a censor (the Hays office) empowered to police the themes, messages, and language of every movie. A morals clause became a standard part of an actor's contract, and press agents were hired by the studios to sell and sanitize the private lives of stars. Actors were supposed to be wholesome, and the studios were always on the lookout for "perfect marriages" that could be presented as typical symbols of happy Hollywood home life.

The attractive young Reagan family became a billboard for this idealized Hollywood. The tone of the studio's relentless (and invasive) promotion of the Reagans is captured in a release from the Warner Brothers publicity department on June 2, 1941, headed, "THE HOPEFUL REAGANS. They Are Looking Forward to More of Everything Good—Including Children." Much of it is in banal dialogue between Jane and Ron that would have been more suitable for Jane and Tarzan. The Reagans, with their baby, "show signs of becoming one of the important first families of the film colony, a new dynasty, one might say, which will bear watching. It is a busy little family what with both papa and mama working in Warner Brothers pictures and little Maureen Elizabeth about to cut her first tooth—in advance of all predictions, too." The rest of the release is even gooier. Both parents rave about their baby, and Jane confesses that, unlike Ronald, she was "terribly disappointed" when she learned her baby was a girl. Ronald, ever the average man, is quoted as saying: "The Reagans' home life is probably just like yours, or yours, or yours. We do the same foolish things that other couples do, have the same scraps, about as much fun, typical problems and the most wonderful baby in the world." The only mildly contentious note in the release is a comment from Jane that they are using old furniture and want to buy new when they move into the eight-room house they are building on a hill overlooking Hollywood. Ronald interrupts before Jane can finish. "Depends on conditions and prices and war and things," he says. "We don't intend to get out on a limb."

By August, with her husband filming *Kings Row*, Jane was bragging about the marriage in *Silver Screen* in an article entitled "Making a Double Go of It." Mary Jane Manners quotes "Janie" as saying: "Neither Ronnie nor I were stars. We were both featured players, making $500 a week. I wasn't a glamor queen, and he wasn't a matinee idol. We were just two kids trying to get the breaks in pictures. But look at Ronnie now. He's taken a scooter and gone leaps and bounds ahead of me. But I'm terribly proud of him—all the same." There is more, too much more, about how Ronnie converted her from nightclubbing to swimming, golf, and other sports, and about how they spent their time looking at model houses before finally spotting the one they wanted in a movie. There is another published appeal for new furniture. There is a confession from Wyman that she had "always been the kind of girl that if there was anything I wanted, I'd go and buy it and think about whether I could really afford it afterward but Ronnie won't go in debt." Finally, there is a glimpse of how they get along together. "Ronnie and I are perfect counterparts for each other," she said. "I blow up and Ronnie just laughs at me. We've never had a quarrel because he's just too good-natured. I pop off and am over it in a minute. Then he makes me ashamed of myself because he's so understanding."[8]

Despite this gush, it was a trying time for the Reagans. Jack Reagan died on May 18, 1941, after a series of heart attacks, and Ronald devoted even more time than usual to his mother. This inevitably meant less attention for Wyman, who was struggling with the dual responsibilities of motherhood and movie-making. Although Wyman was the more talented actor, she was insecure about her ability; her observation that her husband had moved "leaps and bounds ahead" of her could hardly have been comforting. Through it all, Wyman stayed busy. Within a few months of Maureen's birth, she was back at work, making four films in 1941 and another three in 1942.

Reagan, who had been a reserve cavalry officer since his days in Des Moines, was scheduled to go on active duty early in 1941. He received a deferment in February after Jack Warner wrote a handwritten letter saying that Reagan's loss would have a negative impact on upcoming Warner Brothers films, the most important of which was *Kings Row*. He received another deferment at the studio's behest in October after his scenes in *Kings Row* were finished because Warner said he was needed for *Juke Girl*. In January 1942, he received a third deferment, also at the behest of Warner, but which Reagan credited to the intervention of his agent Lew Wasserman. This allowed Reagan to finish *Desperate Journey*, in which he costarred with Errol Flynn.*

Such consideration for actors was not unusual. Colonel Lewis B. Hershey, the director of Selective Service, issued a ruling in February 1942 declaring that the film industry was essential "to the national health, safety and interest, and in other instances to war production." Deferments were granted to "actors, directors, writers, producers, camera men, sound engineers and other technicians" whose induction "would cause a serious loss of effectiveness."[10]

It was a questionable ruling. Actors had not been deferred in World War I, and the Screen Actors Guild, in which Reagan and Wyman were active, went on record in World War II as saying that actors should be subject to the "same rules of the draft as the rest of the country." Nevertheless, in early 1942, less than 3 percent of the 30,000 movie industry employees in Hollywood were on active duty.[11] Many of these were reservists who were subject to immediate activation under rules issued by the War Department after Pearl Harbor. Reagan was called up on April 14, 1942, commissioned a second lieutenant, and sent to Fort Mason in San Francisco, after a tearful farewell at a surprise party thrown by Wyman where the guests included Jack Benny, Barbara Stanwyck, and Ann Sheridan. As far as Reagan's fans knew, he might have been headed for action in the South Pacific. Fan magazines showed him in uniform and proclaimed that Reagan was "off to war" and ready for the "grim task before him."

Whatever his profession or connections, it is highly unlikely that Reagan would have seen combat. His eyesight was so poor that when he was retested by the Army before going on active duty it was determined (on March 10, 1942) that he was eligible only for "limited service." At Fort Mason, he served as a liaison officer in charge of loading transports for Australia. After five weeks, Reagan was sent back to Los Angeles and assigned to the Army Air Corps as a member of the First Motion Picture Unit, which was headed by Jack Warner, now a lieutenant colonel. Reagan proclaimed that he was "surprised" by the transfer, which may have been assisted by Wasserman. Surprised or not, Warner and Hal Wallis, who was directing propaganda films for the wartime studio, were glad to have Reagan back. After a few weeks as a public relations officer, Reagan was making movies again.

---

*Reagan performed capably, and the film made money. But it did no credit to the studio. In the words of Tony Thomas, who was usually kind to Reagan's movies, *Desperate Journey* "is the kind of film which presents the German military . . . as such nincompoops that the viewer is left wondering why it took the Allies so long to bring the war to an end."[9]

Reagan did not neglect his fans. When he returned home, he wrote an article for *Photoplay* magazine called "How to Make Yourself Important" that in its folksiness was reminiscent of the series he had written for the Des Moines newspaper after he went to Hollywood. In the *Photoplay* article, Reagan described himself as "a plain guy with a set of homespun features and no frills" whose tastes and preferences were those of the average man. He wrote:

> I like to swim, hike and sleep (eight hours a night). I'm fairly good at every sport except tennis, which I just don't like. My favorite menu is steak smothered with onions and strawberry shortcake. Mr. Norm is my alias. I play bridge adequately, collect guns, always carry a penny as a good-luck charm and knock wood when I make a boast or express a wish. I have a so-so convertible coupe which I drive myself. I'm interested in politics and governmental problems. My favorite books are *Turnabout* by Thorne Smith, *Babbitt, The Adventures of Tom Sawyer* and the works of Pearl Buck, H. G. Wells, Damon Runyon and Erich Remarque. I'm a fan of Bing Crosby. My favorite actress is my wife. I like things colored green and my favorite flower is the Eastern lilac. I love my wife, baby and home. I've just built a new one—home, I mean. Nothing about me to make me stand out on the midway.[12]

Reagan's celebration of his normality was attuned to conventional wartime liberalism in stressing equality over exceptionalism. He credited his film success to average values he said he shared with his fellow Americans. "Average will do it," Reagan wrote, expressing a credo that would survive throughout his various political incarnations. Reagan's identification of himself as an average man gave him standing to speak for "the people." His key advice to the fans he left behind was "(a) love what you are doing with all your heart and soul and (b) believe what you are doing is important—even if you are only grubbing for worms in the back yard."[13]

By the time this article appeared, in August 1942, Reagan had just completed filming *Rear Gunner* for the First Motion Picture Unit, which was then based at Vitagraph Studios in Los Angeles. It moved in October to Hal Roach Studios in Culver City, which became known as "Fort Roach" (or sometimes "Fort Wacky"). *Rear Gunner,* released as a short feature in commercial studios after negotiation between Warner and the War Department, was essentially a recruiting tool. Filmed in Las Vegas and Tucson, it follows the progress of a timid Kansas farm boy as he is drafted, trains in gunnery school, and becomes an expert marksman who wins the Distinguished Service Medal in combat.

Burgess Meredith was cast as the gunner and Reagan as the lieutenant who gives him his chance. Warner later boasted that *Rear Gunner* persuaded thousands of men to enlist.[14]

The First Motion Picture Unit was the result of a collaboration between Warner and General Henry ("Hap") Arnold, who headed the Army Air Corps (later the Army Air Force). Arnold was a visionary who before World War II recognized the potential decisiveness of air power in the coming conflict and predicted that the United States would not "maintain its integrity and continue its existence in its present way of living unless it establishes and maintains the world's strongest air force."[15] He was equally farsighted in recognizing that the best way to advance this concept and recruit needed personnel was through the movies. With this in mind, Arnold cultivated friendships with Jack and Harry Warner and persuaded the War Department to give preferential treatment to the Air Corps in requisitioning personnel for the First Motion Picture Unit. *Rear Gunner* was made at the advocacy of Arnold, who said the Air Corps had sufficient pilots but was in urgent need of gunners.

As recruiting swelled, the First Motion Picture Unit performed another mission envisioned by Arnold: making training films to speed the learning process for Air Force crews and to show simulated bombing targets. Reagan became involved in this process, sometimes as an actor but more often as a narrator. These were ironic roles for Reagan, who had been afraid to fly since being bounced around in a small plane on a turbulent flight to Catalina in 1937, but he performed them well. In *Jap Zero*, which instructed recruits on how to distinguish enemy planes from friendly ones, Reagan plays a pilot in the South Pacific who downs a Zero because he has learned its flying characteristics. In *Beyond the Line of Duty* (1942), a morale-building film (and the only one to feature the voices of both Reagan and President Roosevelt), Reagan's narration breaks in on FDR to remind pilots of techniques learned in flight school.

Reagan also narrated *Westward Bataan*, which lionized General Douglas MacArthur and explained his island-hopping strategy in the South Pacific, and *Target Tokyo*, which celebrated the B-29 bombings of the Japanese homeland. He was an actor in a short subject, *Mr. Gardenia Jones*, and a longer film, *For God and Country*, aimed at promoting unity among Catholics, Protestants, and Jews. Reagan plays a Catholic chaplain who dies a heroic death while trying to save the life of an American Indian. In 1943, Reagan was detached from his unit for a role in *This Is the Army*, a Warner Brothers musical written by Irving Berlin, who appears on screen to sing, "Oh, How I Hate to Get Up in the Morning."

As Reagan recalled it, Berlin approached him during the filming to praise his acting and suggest he go into show business after the war. Reagan thanked him without knowing whether Berlin knew he was a movie actor or if he had forgotten him because he hadn't been on screen for so long.[16] It was an early warning of what Reagan would face as an actor when he tried to connect with the generation of moviegoers who came of age while he was making training films.

While Reagan's wartime service failed to advance his film career, it influenced his political development. Hollywood presented World War II as a clear-cut struggle between freedom and tyranny, and Reagan would display this same uncompromising view in the Cold War when he denounced the Soviet Union and communism in much the same terms he had used to describe Nazi Germany and fascism. His experiences in the film unit also deepened his patriotism and an internationalist outlook that had already been strong when the war began. In the prewar years, Reagan had argued with isolationist friends who opposed military preparedness. As he learned more about the war and the reasons for it, Reagan was reinforced in the view that Hitler should have been stopped earlier and that President Roosevelt had been right to bolster Britain. In a December 29, 1940, "fireside chat," FDR had said of America, "We must be the great arsenal of democracy." Reagan liked the phrase and never forgot it, using it on a dozen occasions when he was president in appeals for rebuilding U.S. military capability and supporting U.S. allies and the Nicaraguan contras.[17]

Reagan emerged from military service believing that he had played an important part in the war effort. Just as he exaggerated or invented incidents to make a point in the football stories of his youth, he would later recount scenes from movies and describe them as real events. He was often criticized for this. What the critics, myself sometimes included, failed to realize was that Reagan often was aware of what he was doing. After his presidency, in the context of defending a U.S. military buildup that had brought the Soviet Union to the bargaining table, Reagan acknowledged that "Maybe I had seen too many war movies, the heroics of which I sometimes confused with real life."[18] On two occasions, which I examined more fully in an earlier Reagan biography, he became so carried away in denouncing the horrors of the Holocaust that he talked about photographing Nazi death camps during World War II.[19]

Such flights of fancy aside, Reagan was quite right in insisting that the First Motion Picture Unit contributed to the war effort. He gave two examples in his autobiography, writing at length about how the careful construction of a filmed model of Tokyo assisted U.S. flight commanders in selecting bombing targets. He wrote more briefly about an arguably more significant Hollywood contribution, the filmed attacks on replicas of German missile-launching sites at Peenemunde that showed they were vulnerable to low-level bombing. This helped U.S. and British bombers (Reagan cites only the U.S. effort) to inflict such destruction upon the launching sites that the massive V-3 missile, which the Germans had hoped to use against London in 1943, did not become available until December 1944, six months after the Allied invasion of Europe.[20]

Reagan's wartime service was comfortable in comparison to that of most of the 12 million Americans who were mobilized and sent far from home. But less than one-fifth of the U.S. male population was in uniform (and a small fraction of that in combat at any given time), and Reagan probably would have been spared military service altogether had he not been a reservist. When I asked him years later if he regretted not having fought in the war, Reagan shook his head and said he would never have been allowed a combat role because of his eyesight.[21] He believed, with good reason, that he had served his country well by staying home and making training films.

Seen in their own terms and not in comparison to the hard and dangerous lives of overseas soldiers, Reagan's wartime years were stressful for him and his young family. The Reagans had moved into a new eight-room house above Sunset Boulevard with a sweeping view of the Pacific Ocean two weeks before he was called to active duty, when Maureen was fifteen months old. His widowed mother lived in a small house below the Sunset Strip that Reagan had bought and deeded to his parents. He gave her $175 a week as long as he could afford it, and then worked out an agreement with Warners to pay Nelle $75 a week to handle his fan mail, with the money to be deducted from his salary after the war. Wyman, who was making films throughout the war, helped support Nelle when Reagan's payments to her stopped in 1943.

For Wyman, her husband was near yet far away. He spent the week billeted at Fort Roach, usually coming home on weekends. She was there as often as possible, but her film schedule was a busy one. Early in 1944, Wyman embarked on a twelve-week national tour to sell war bonds and promote a comedy, *The Doughgirls*, the last film she would make for Warners. By now, precocious Maureen was asking for a baby brother. Her parents wanted more children, too, but Maureen's delivery had been difficult, and Wyman was not eager for a second pregnancy at this time in her career. The Reagans decided to adopt. Michael Edward Reagan, less than a day old, joined the household on March 18, 1945.

Wyman, to use the phrase she had earlier applied to her husband, had now moved "leaps and bounds" ahead of him in acting. Unable to persuade Warners to give her a dramatic role, she asked the studio to loan her to Paramount, where, over the objections of the liquor industry, the gifted Billy Wilder was filming *The Lost Weekend.* Based on a best-selling novel, the film tells a searing story of an alcoholic writer, who is played by Ray Milland. Wyman plays the writer's wife. The film and Milland won Academy Awards in 1945, and Wyman received favorable reviews for a compelling performance. Wilder made effective use of what one biographer called Wyman's "large, sad eyes."[22] Louella Parsons had been right all along about the depth of Wyman's talent, even though Warners had never recognized it. By the time Reagan was released from the Army on July 11, 1945, Wyman was working from dawn to after dusk on her next big film, *The Yearling.* Reagan stayed out of her way and went off to Lake Arrowhead by himself.

Although Reagan was supportive of his wife's emergent career, Wyman's screen success did not translate into happiness at home. Daughter Maureen identified one of the reasons when she wrote that although "there was a lot of Ronald Reagan in almost every role he played," there was "very little Jane Wyman in any of her screen performances, and at the same time there was all of Jane Wyman in each and every role."[23] Maureen recalled that her mother became so deeply involved in her roles that she rarely smiled during six months of filming *The Yearling,* in which she played the gritty, dirt-farmer role of Ma Baxter, for which she was nominated for an Academy Award.

Reagan, while unsure of his own career, still believed the marriage was solid. Wyman became pregnant again. Five months into her pregnancy, Reagan contracted viral pneumonia, the disease that had killed George Gipp. It almost finished off Reagan, too. He believes he would have died at Cedars of Lebanon Hospital except for the efforts of an unnamed nurse who kept coaxing him to take another breath. Reagan said he "kept breathing out of courtesy" and slowly regained his will to live.[24] While Reagan was fighting for his life, Jane gave birth on June 26, 1947, to a baby girl who was four months premature. The baby died the following day. Parsons said afterward that the baby had come early because Jane was "distraught" and "almost out of her mind with worry" over the illness of her husband. Parsons, whose own husband was in Cedars of Lebanon recuperating from an illness, dropped in to see Reagan frequently. "When Jane was stricken, it was Ronald's turn to worry and he was almost desperate," Parsons said. "He was so miserable because he was unable to be with her during her ordeal. He tossed and fretted in his hospital bed, telling me how magnificent Jane had been and how fearful he was of her health. Little did he realize that this illness of hers might bring about their separation within a few months."[25]

After recovering from the trauma of losing her child, Wyman plunged into work on the demanding role of a deaf mute in *Johnny Belinda* (1948). By now, there was gossip of trouble in the marriage, although Reagan seemed oblivious to it. In the February 1948 issue of *Photoplay*, Gladys Hall quoted Wyman as telling a reporter during a 1947 trip to New York: "We're through. We're finished, and it's all my fault." Was it? Hall's article, entitled "Those Fightin' Reagans," asked more questions than it answered.

"Is there some hangover from a past Ronnie does not share?" she wrote. "Some conflict, still unresolved in Jane's memory? Certain it is, however, that Jane last autumn was visibly unhappy; was nervous; was irritable—many times in public—with Ronnie. But Ronnie was cajoling, always very easy with Jane, and very sweet. Always in there, trying."

Hall's sympathy for Reagan was shared by columnists Parsons and Hedda Hopper, both of whom wrote that Reagan was astonished when he read in the newspapers about the comments Jane had made in New York. Parsons was "genuinely shocked" and Hopper "stunned," as if something they had helped create was being destroyed. Parsons tried to save the marriage with a public plea for reconciliation in the April 1948 issue of *Photoplay*: "Last Call for Happiness: This is Ronald Reagan's Heart Speaking, With the Frankness that would be Given Only to an Old Friend." When Ronnie got a chance to say what happened, he replied enigmatically, "Nothing—and everything. I think Jane takes her work too seriously. . . . She is very intense—but she's been a wonderful wife and unsure because of that very thing. The trouble is—she hasn't learned to separate her work from her personal life. Right now Jane needs very much to have a fling and I intend to let her have it."

Reagan also told Parsons that Wyman was "sick and nervous and not herself. Jane says she loves me but is no longer 'in love' with me and points out that this is a fine distinction. That I don't believe. I think she is nervous, despondent and because of this feels our life together has become humdrum." Reagan conceded, however, that he might have spent too much time on union business. "Perhaps I should have let someone else save the world and have saved my own home," he said.

By the time this article appeared, Reagan and Wyman were separated. She received an Academy Award for *Johnny Belinda* and attended the ceremony in the company of the film's leading man, Lew Ayres, whom the *Los Angeles Times* described as "her beau." Ayres, famous for his role as a German soldier in *All Quiet on the Western Front*, had played Wyman's sympathetic doctor in *Johnny Belinda*. Reagan, who attended the awards ceremony alone, had earlier told Hedda Hopper, "If this comes to a divorce, I think I'll name *Johnny Belinda* as the co-respondent."[26]

Some of Reagan's friends considered this ambiguous quip a veiled reference to a rumored romance between Wyman and Ayres; others interpreted it as meaning that Wyman had given up her marriage for her career. The wisecrack, typically Reaganesque, could have had either meaning, or both, and Reagan was too much the gentleman or too hurt to say more. Biographer Anne Edwards, sympathetic to Wyman and fair-minded, believes that her relationship with Ayres was platonic.*

Whatever the nature of the relationship, Reagan was unprepared for separation or divorce. Patricia Neal remembered him at a party soon after the separation was announced, "and it was sad because he did not want a divorce. I remember he went outside. An older woman went with him. He cried."[27] In a later account undoubtedly based on what Reagan had told her, Nancy Reagan said Wyman told him to "get out" when he arrived home one afternoon. "That's pretty hard to take, particularly if you're the kind of person Ronnie is," Nancy Reagan said. "Ronnie is not a sophisticated fellow."[28] Maureen Reagan, who was seven at the time, said in her autobiography that her father was "devastated" by her mother's decision. "It just never occurred to him, no matter what their problems were, that he and Mother would get a divorce, it was so foreign to his way of thinking, to the way he was brought up," she wrote.[29]

Wyman gave her version in court. She announced in February 1948 that she was suing for divorce and filed a complaint in May charging "extreme mental cruelty," then the catchall reason for most California divorces. In the subsequent court proceeding, Wyman said the Screen Actors Guild took up much of her husband's time and that she did not share his interest—even though she was also a member of the union board and remained on it after the divorce. She added that Reagan wanted her around to talk about union issues but that the discussions were "far above me" and that no one was interested in her ideas. "Finally, there was nothing in common between us, nothing to sustain our marriage," she said.

In a divorce decree granted initially on June 28, 1948, and made final on July 18, 1949, Wyman was awarded custody of the two children and $500 a month for their support. Reagan was required to maintain $25,000 life insurance policies on himself and his ex-wife and to allow

---

*Edwards wrote of Wyman, on page 331 of *Early Reagan*: "She claimed she and Ayres did not have an affair while they were making *Johnny Belinda*, that they engaged in talk, not sex, in the time they spent together off the set. Quite probably, this was the truth." But Edwards, in an otherwise well-noted book, does not give a source for Wyman's claim.

Jane horseback riding privileges on an eight-acre ranch they had bought in Northridge. Subsequently, in 1952, Wyman wed film-studio musical director Freddie Karger, but she divorced him two years later. Wyman and Karger married again in 1961, but this marriage also ended in divorce.

Ever after, Wyman refused to comment about her marriage to Reagan. The closest she came was a remark relayed secondhand through a friend, Father Robert Perrella, in a book published when Reagan was governor: "She also admits it was exasperating to awake in the middle of the night, prepare for work, and have someone at the breakfast table, newspaper in hand, expounding on the far right, far left, the conservative right, the conservative left, the middle of the roader. She harbors no ill feeling towards him."[30]

Reagan's feelings were shattered. He moved out with his desk, his books, and a stuffed lamb given him by Maureen and took an apartment in the building where he had lived before his marriage. A close friend of Reagan's in those days told me that after the divorce Reagan was "despondent, in a way I had never seen, because he usually was such a happy, optimistic man." For awhile, Reagan went into a shell—much as he had done when Margaret Cleaver sent him back his ring—but soon he started dating casually, as he had also done after the Cleaver breakup. He stayed busy in the Screen Actors Guild and saw his children regularly, often taking them to the Northridge ranch and later, after he had sold this property, to a 290-acre ranch in Malibu Canyon that (two years after his divorce) he named "Yearling Row," after Wyman's performance in *The Yearling* and his own in *Kings Row*. Maureen said she and her brother Michael saw nearly as much of him after the divorce as before it.

When Reagan discussed the breakup publicly, which was not often, he agreed with the verdict of the columnists and the fan magazines (even while decrying their repeated examinations of his failed marriage) that he had been a "victim" who would never have sought a divorce. Because he did not initiate or want the breakup, Reagan acted as if he had not really been divorced. He never changed this way of looking at what had happened to him. Thirty-two years later, President Reagan told an interviewer: "I was divorced in the sense that the decision was made by somebody else."[31] On the lecture circuit in behalf of the film industry soon after the Wyman divorce, Reagan surprised audiences by invariably including a line or two in his speeches about the high success rate of marriages in Hollywood. The community was divided into two groups by Reagan—the "multiple marriage set," which received all the publicity, and the stable, family people, whom Reagan said were in the vast majority. Even before he met Nancy Davis, he put himself in the latter category.

Reagan had learned in childhood the knack of mentally discarding events in his life that caused him emotional or physical pain. This ability is not unique, but Reagan had an awesome skill at such pretense, which armored his natural optimism. In 1985, after an operation for colon cancer, Reagan insisted in an interview with *Time* magazine that he did not "have cancer" because the cancer had been removed. "So, I am someone who does not have cancer," Reagan said, "but like everyone else, I'm apparently vulnerable to it."[32] It was an unshakable view. In his memoirs published five years later, Reagan said he was still "a little annoyed" at how the operation had been reported. He insisted that what should have been written was, "the president *had* cancer."[33]

Despite Reagan's proficiency at such mental gymnastics, the divorce had dented his self-confidence. He tried not to let it show, however, and his stalled film career soon regained momentum. Reagan owned a Cadillac and a ranch and dated attractive women, often for only a single night. It was outwardly a pleasant life, but not a satisfying one. "I was footloose and fancy free, and I guess down underneath, miserable," Reagan told me years later.[34]

Nancy Davis changed that. Along with the other important women in Reagan's long life—his mother, Margaret Cleaver, and Jane Wyman—she had theatrical interests. And in common with Wyman, she had survived a turbulent childhood and reinvented herself in Hollywood. Born in New York City on July 6, 1921, Nancy Davis was the daughter of stage actress Edith Luckett and Kenneth Robbins, a car salesman who abandoned the family soon after his daughter's birth. When she was two, her mother resumed her stage career and sent her infant daughter to live with an aunt and uncle in Bethesda, Maryland. In 1929, Luckett married Loyal Davis, a successful Chicago neurosurgeon who adored Nancy, adopted her, and gave her his family name. Nancy's life became stable and privileged, and she ever after considered Davis her true father. After graduating from Smith College in 1943, she capitalized on her mother's Hollywood connections and became an actress. On MGM studio records she listed her birth date as July 6, 1923, shaving two years off her age in a familiar Hollywood practice.

The conventional opinion is that Nancy Davis marked time in Hollywood while waiting for the right man to come along. She encouraged this view. Supplying biographical information to MGM in 1949, Nancy Davis said her "greatest ambition" was to have a "successful happy marriage." In 1975, for a compilation on the achievements of Smith College alumni, Nancy Reagan said: "I was never really a career woman but [became one] only because I hadn't found the man I wanted to marry. I couldn't sit around and do nothing, so I became an actress."

Was that all there was to it? Nancy Davis had a background in summer stock, had been in a Broadway musical, and was a reliable performer. When she met Reagan in 1949, she was working for MGM in *East Side, West Side*, which starred Barbara Stanwyck, James Mason, and Ava Gardner. While she did not at all resemble Wyman, both of them had one outstanding physical feature—their eyes, which in Nancy's case are large and luminous. Davis was typecast, too, but as a responsible young mother. In the words of Garry Wills, Nancy was "the steady woman."[35] In 1950, producer Dore Schary chose her as the female lead in *The Next Voice You Hear* to play a pregnant, middle-class mother opposite James Whitmore, who was also in his first lead role. Although Whitmore and Davis received favorable reviews, the film failed commercially. But Davis had proven herself and, like Reagan, continued to hold her own on screen with better-known actors, including Glenn Ford, Frederic March, and Ray Milland, who had starred in Wyman's breakthrough film. Davis appeared with Milland in *Night into Morning* (1951), playing a war widow who talks Milland's character out of committing suicide. In sum, Davis was a solid performer. She appeared in eleven movies, nine of them after she met Reagan. Three of the films were made after they were married. Wills believes she has been underrated because she is best known for the undistinguished *Hellcats of the Navy* (1957), in which Reagan had the lead role.

Nancy Davis differed from both Reagan and Wyman in that she had no illusions of stardom. One reason she so capably played a wife and mother was that she really wanted to become one. The experience of her mother, who had given up the theater to marry Loyal Davis, suggested to her that a marriage was more likely to succeed if the woman set aside her career. While Nancy Reagan may have overstated the case when she said she became an actress because she couldn't "sit around and do nothing," she did want to get married. Some hostile accounts have even suggested that she was desperate for a husband, which seems unlikely for an attractive woman in her twenties who had dated many men, including such enduring stars as Clark Gable. But although she was not desperate, she was certainly determined, and she took the initiative in seeking out Reagan. According to Anne Edwards, Davis told Schary that she wanted to meet Reagan, and Schary's wife, Miriam, arranged a dinner party in September 1949. Nancy sat across from Reagan and listened attentively as he talked politics and denounced communism.[36]

Nancy Reagan does not mention this dinner in her account of how she met Reagan. Her oft-told story (and his) is that the name "Nancy

Davis" showed up on Communist mailing lists and then on a list of left-wing actors published in a Hollywood newspaper. On the set of *East Side, West Side*, Davis mentioned this to director Mervyn LeRoy, who said he would fix matters, first by having Louella Parsons set matters straight in her column (which she did), and then by calling his friend Reagan, who was president of the Screen Actors Guild. "I d never met Ronnie, and certainly Ronnie didn't know me from a hole in the wall, but I told Mervyn it was a fine idea," Nancy Reagan recalled years later, making no secret that her desire to meet Reagan outweighed any fear of being falsely branded a Communist.[37] By the time Reagan called back and reported that it was a case of mistaken identity, LeRoy realized that Davis wanted more than political clearance. LeRoy declined to set up a meeting, but he called Reagan and suggested he take Davis to dinner. Reagan, ever cautious, called Davis (on November 15, 1949) but invented an early morning shooting schedule that would enable him to leave if she proved a dud. She knew this was a common ruse in Hollywood for bailing out of a blind date and responded that she also had an early morning shoot, which was equally untrue. Reagan took her to LaRue's, near the Screen Actors Guild office. She was smitten by the tall, athletic, and courteous actor, who walked with a cane because he had broken a leg in a charity baseball game. Reagan, tired of bachelorhood, enjoyed the company of an attractive woman who was more interested in him than in her own career. They sat at the table long after midnight, talking.

Once again, however, Reagan did not rush the relationship. He saw Nancy often, and she went with him to Screen Actors Guild meetings, where she watched him with rapt attention and said nothing. On February 6, 1950, his thirty-ninth birthday, she accompanied him to the Beverly Hills Hotel, where he was honored by the Friars, a Hollywood group, for service to the film industry. Reagan's friends thought of Nancy as a woman who was "good for Ronnie." They soon became an item in the gossip columns, although both of them would always be more discreet about their personal lives than Reagan and Wyman had been. A Hollywood newspaper account at the time described "the romance of a couple who have no vices" in these terms: "Not for them the hot-house atmosphere of nightclubs, the smoky little rooms and the smell of Scotch. They eat at Dave Chasen's, they spend their evenings in the homes of friends, they drive along the coast and look at the sea and a lot of time they're quiet. They go as 'steady,' according to one reporter, as any couple in Hollywood and Nancy knits Reagan argyle socks, though she doesn't cook for him."

Despite the enthusiasm of the writer and of a Hollywood press corps that regularly asked Reagan if he was going to marry Davis, they were not going steady. "Ronnie was in no hurry to make a commitment," Nancy Reagan wrote in her memoir, *My Turn*. "He had been burned in his first marriage, and the pain went deep. Although we saw each other regularly, he also dated other women."[38] Nancy Davis prodded him, asking him if he wanted her to wait for him. When he said that he did, and no proposal was forthcoming, she told him she had asked her agent to get her a play in New York. Finally, after calling Loyal Davis in Phoenix to ask permission to marry his daughter, Reagan proposed at their favorite booth in Chasen's. They were married on March 4, 1952, without fanfare at the Little Church in the Valley. The only other people in the church were the minister who married them, and their friends Bill Holden, the best man, and Ardis Holden, the matron of honor. Nancy soon became a real-life mother. Patricia Ann Reagan was born by cesarean section seven and a half months after the wedding, on October 22, 1952. On May 28, 1958, the Reagans had a son, whom they named Ronald Prescott Reagan.

Reagan's marriage to Nancy Davis restored his sense of equilibrium shortly before his film career slid into a second and irreversible decline. Nancy seemed on the surface a perfect model of an idealized wife in the days before the rise of the women's movement—she was loyal and supportive, and she believed (or pretended to believe) that her husband would have remained in demand for choice roles except for his "unselfish" devotion to the Screen Actors Guild.[39] But despite her promotion of a 1950s stereotype, Nancy was never the "little woman." While she defended her husband in public, she could be caustic in private when assessing Reagan's union, film, or political associates. Later, in political life, Nancy Reagan would say that her "antenna" about people was better than her husband's, and it was often true. They made a good team. He was better informed and had a sense of destination, if not always a road map for the journey. She was practical, on the lookout for opportunities, and protective of her husband from fellow travelers of all ideological hues who promoted their own agendas. Nancy served ten years with him on the board of the Screen Actors Guild and participated in the selection of the aides and consultants who ran his campaigns for governor and president. From the beginning of the marriage, and especially after he went into politics, those who dealt with Ronald Reagan would learn that it was useful, sometimes necessary, to have the approval of his wife.

Despite the tribulations of his career and tensions within the Screen Actors Guild, Ronald Reagan became happy once again. He liked working with his hands and trimmed trees and built fences on the Malibu ranch, as he would later do at their ranch northwest of Santa Barbara. He also taught Nancy to ride. It was never her favorite activity, but she became a competent rider, believing, as she later wrote, "If you wanted to make your life with a man, you took on whatever his interests were, and they became your interests, too."[40]

Nancy Reagan called herself a "nester," and they bought a house in the Pacific Palisades, the first she ever owned. While she was in the hospital giving birth to their daughter, he planted an olive tree outside their home. The gesture touched Nancy, who after the house was sold would drive by to see how much the tree had grown. Reagan was a devoted husband, with a wit and tenderness reflected in the love letters he sent to his wife, whom he called "Nancy Pants."[41] But he remained forever guarded about his first marriage, bearing scars that recalled the wound. "You can get just so far to Ronnie, and then something happens," Nancy Reagan told me in 1989. "It took him a long time, I think, to feel that he could really trust me."[42]

Reagan would never completely share that trust with the children of either marriage, even though he was by ordinary standards an excellent and loving father. He read to his children and sang songs to them and taught Patti and Ron to swim and ride, as he had similarly taught Maureen and Michael. He was never harsh or abusive, either physically or verbally, and he was patient with his children in tasks and at play. For all that, he was distanced. Ron Reagan said in 1986 that he enjoyed a "friendly and loving" relationship with his dad but added, "You almost get the sense that he gets a little bit antsy if you try and get too close and too personal and too father-and-sonny." The son explained this by saying that his father lacked a role model in his own family and "so what fathering he did, he had to come by on his own."[43]

Reagan's children were unanimous in testifying to their father's difficulty with closeness. Maureen Reagan wrote despairingly in her autobiography of the inability of either of her parents to "get below the surface" and explain to her what had happened to them.[44] Michael Reagan wrote that his father was often "completely oblivious" to others. He recounted an incident at his graduation from an Arizona boarding school where his father did not recognize him in his cap and gown.[45] Patti Davis told me, "I never knew who he was. I could never get through to him."[46] Ron Reagan said, "I know him as well as anybody, outside my mother. But still, you know, there is something that he holds back. You get just so far, and then the curtain drops, and you don't go any farther."[47]

All of Ronald Reagan's children attest to their love for him and prized the rare times they were alone with their father. All felt he cared for them, but they did not think of him as a person in whom they could confide. Maureen Reagan, in some respects the child closest to Ronald Reagan, endured a physically abusive and terrifying first marriage to a police officer without ever telling her father about it even though they were carrying on a lively correspondence about politics. Michael Reagan considered his father "the only adult male I ever trusted" but could not tell him (or his mother) about the oppressive trauma of boyhood molestation by a camp counselor. In 1987, he confided his experience to a sympathetic Nancy Reagan while his father "gazed into the distance."[48] Patti Reagan was unable to tell her father much of anything— or to listen to anything he told her. She thought him mysterious. "It was like he came in smoke, and disappeared in smoke," she said.[49]

Nancy Reagan, more open emotionally than her husband, never fully solved the riddle of what she described to me as "the strange mixture with Ronnie."[50] In her book, *My Turn*, she said: "Although he loves people, he often seems remote, and he doesn't let anybody get too close. There's a wall around him. He lets me come closer than anyone else, but there are times when even I feel that barrier."[51] These words have an ironic ring, for those who lacked access to Reagan often saw Nancy as the barrier. But she knew when she was being an impediment, and there was usually good reason for it. The barrier inside Reagan of which Nancy spoke existed long before she came into his life. She did not build it, and she could not tear it down.

If she did not always get beyond the barrier, Nancy Reagan understood better than anyone else the elements of its construction. She realized that the emotional wall around her husband had been shaped by his reaction to his father's alcoholism, by the hurt and isolation he felt after the collapse of his first marriage, and by the wanderings of the Reagan family through small-town Illinois, where the young Ronald learned the art of living without close friends. Her own childhood dislocation made her especially sensitive to the problems arising from the nomadic nature of her husband's early existence. She recognized a rootlessness in Ronald Reagan that was oddly at variance with his sense of continuity and place. In this respect, Reagan resembled his father, who was a wanderer, more than his mother. Even at rest, Reagan projected what speechwriter Landon Parvin called a "sense of movement."

The movement was geographically confined. Reagan arrived in Hollywood when he was twenty-six years old, and he ever afterward called Southern California his home. When he was governor and lived in Sacramento, he and Nancy, whenever possible, spent weekends, sometimes very long weekends, at their home in Pacific Palisades. During eight years as president, he spent the equivalent of a full year in California, most of it at his ranch near Santa Barbara. When he left the White House, he and Nancy flew to Los Angeles and settled down immediately. In his last campaign, he said of California, "This isn't a place out here; it's a way of life."

Instead of drifting from town to town as his father had, Reagan moved from picture to picture, changing casts and directors along the way. He was pleasant to all but close to none. His pattern in politics was similar. When adviser Martin Anderson, exiled from Reagan's entourage because of a staff purge that the candidate ignored, rejoined the presidential campaign in 1980 after a long absence, he sensed that Reagan was happy to have him back without quite knowing he had been away.[52] Reagan wanted friendly faces around him; too much change on the set disturbed him in movies or in politics. But closeness was a distraction from his goals.

Although he became adept in stagecraft as a movie actor, Ronald Reagan was not a product of Hollywood. By the time he arrived in Southern California, he already lived in a world of illusion. "He who would bring home the wealth of the Indies must carry the wealth of the Indies with him,"[53] it has been said, and Reagan came to California bearing the treasures and burdens of his boyhood experiences. He used his optimistic imagination to transform his difficult childhood into an idyll. He used it to broadcast word pictures of games he never saw. Later, he would invent an America that never was and share with his fellow citizens a bright, shining vision of our country's greatness founded on an imagined version of the past. The vision would have meaning to others because of its power and because of Reagan's belief in it. But it was not a vision that thrived on close encounters.

Reagan was an American, an announcer, an actor, a union leader, and a political activist. Later, he became governor of California and president of the United States. Through it all he was a family man who was devoted to his parents, his two wives, and his four children. He did all he was able to do for his families, but he was by nature and experience a loner who found it hard to reach out to others when he was not on stage. Reagan was also a man with a mission. When his first marriage was failing, he had acknowledged to Louella Parsons that he had devoted too little attention to his home and too much to trying to save the world. But this was a grace note, not an apology. Reagan believed that the world needed saving. He would answer the call.

8

POLITICIAN

W HEN RONALD REAGAN ran for governor of California in 1966, he was dismissed as a greenhorn who gave rousing speeches but was otherwise unprepared for public life. Professionals of both parties pegged Reagan as an out-of-work actor who was trading on his celebrity status to launch a political career. Even after he was elected, legislators regarded Reagan as more of a celebrity than a politician, a perception Reagan encouraged by describing himself as a "citizen-politician" who had answered the call of duty. He often talked as if he were on loan from the entertainment industry and planned to return to his basic calling after serving, like Cincinnatus, when his country needed him.

First impressions die hard, and professional politicians treated Reagan condescendingly even after he had served two terms as governor and was well into the second term of his presidency. This was in part because politicians who rose through the ranks in orthodox fashion were reluctant to admit that a former actor could do so well at their profession and in part because Reagan worked at being underestimated. When House Speaker Thomas P. ("Tip") O'Neill, an accomplished politician, met with President-elect Reagan on November 18, 1980, he tested him by saying that his Sacramento experience was "minor league" and that legislation might not move swiftly for him in Washington. "This is the big leagues," O'Neill told Reagan, who smiled while his aides fumed. Reagan told me later that he thought he would do better if O'Neill underrated him. Six months and two budget defeats later, O'Neill was asked by a constituent in Boston what was happening. "I'm getting the shit whaled out of me," the speaker replied.[1]

O'Neill had not been bested by an amateur. Despite Reagan's disclaimers, Jane Wyman had been right in observing that he was more interested in politics than anything else. He was elected senior class president in high school, participated in the student strike as a freshman at Eureka College, and gave frequent public speeches beginning with his days as a broadcaster in Des Moines. Reagan admired President Roosevelt, whom he credited for saving the country and rescuing his own family, and enjoyed listening to his radio speeches. He was interested in political ideas (but not the mechanics of campaigns) and discussed politics with anyone who could be drawn into conversation on a movie set. In 1942, he wrote that his interests since college had been "dramatics, athletics and politics."

Twice, in 1946 and 1952, Reagan was sounded out as a potential Democratic candidate for Congress. In 1948, he campaigned for President Harry S Truman and future Democratic stars of the Senate, including Hubert H. Humphrey. Friends in the Screen Actors Guild joked that Reagan was the "boy on the burning deck" because he spoke so frequently at union meetings. But he gave good speeches. The Guild elected Reagan president five consecutive times and later brought him back for a sixth term in which he led a successful strike against the movie producers. By any measure, Reagan was a political person.

He was also, for the most part, consistent as he moved during his long lifetime from left to right across the political spectrum. The essence of Reagan's politics in both its Democratic and Republican formulations was a sentimental populism in which he expressed himself as an ordinary man who shared the values of his constituents. Reagan's heroes were, like any good populist, "the people" or the "forgotten Americans." He stood up to the power elites—first in business, then in government and the media. The actor who in *Photoplay* celebrated himself as "Mr. Norm" and proclaimed "average will do it" became the politician who saw himself as the tribune of the American people. A tribune in the Roman sense of the word was a representative of the people, and Reagan envisioned himself in this role long before he became the president of the United States. He was a mirror who reflected the values of everyday Americans and was one with those whom he represented. On the eve of the 1980 presidential election, when a radio reporter asked Reagan what other Americans saw in him, he replied, "Would you laugh if I told you that I think, maybe, they see themselves and that I'm one of them? I've never been able to detach myself or think that I, somehow, am apart from them."[2]

Reagan's belief that his bond with the people was indissoluble gave him an inner security about his politics that was more reassuring than any public opinion survey. It helped him, at various times, to escape the potentially suffocating clutches of the Communist Party, the House

Un-American Activities Committee (HUAC),[3] the John Birch Society, and the Moral Majority. When a suspect group of ideologues embraced Reagan, as he said of the Birchers, they were accepting his philosophy rather than the other way around.

Reagan's temperament and habits were also suited for political life. He declined to call himself a "politician" because of an aversion to the connotations of the word rather than from distaste for politics. Politicians in America are stereotyped as glad-handing opportunists who, in Lincoln's self-deprecatory phrase, are "one long step removed from honest men."[4] But politics often attracts honest men (and women) who, like Reagan, get along well with people but are uncomfortable with personal intimacy. As to his habits, Reagan was disciplined and organized. He read newspapers and periodicals with an eye for information that reinforced core values and beliefs, and his memory, as political ally Paul Laxalt later said, was "frighteningly" retentive.[5] All these were useful traits in politics.

Reagan's first significant political training ground was the Screen Actors Guild, which had won a four-year battle for recognition from recalcitrant movie producers three weeks before he arrived in Hollywood. Except for a few stars, movie actors were peons in an industry operated by primitive entrepreneurs who had traditionally responded to unionization attempts by blacklisting the actors who tried to organize. But in 1933, the producers forced contract players to accept a 50 percent pay cut, enormous even by Depression standards, and created the conditions for the successful organization of the Screen Actors Guild. At the time it was formed, more than half its members made less than $2,000 a year, and many of these "day players," as they were called, worked a day a week for $15. For lesser-known actors, the Guild's success in raising the wages of the day players provided the means of survival in an industry that has never cared well or widely for its own.

Reagan wrote in *Where's the Rest of Me?* that he was recruited into the Guild by actress Helen Broderick, who heard him make an antiunion crack in the Warners commissary and gave him an hour's lecture on the merits of the union. Reagan said he then became a "rabid union man."[6] In Reagan's account, repeated in similar form in his postpresidential memoir, *An American Life*, he was elected to the Guild board in 1938 because union leaders wanted board members representing various levels of experience. Reagan said he was "drafted to represent the industry's young contract players"[7] and accepted with "awe and pleasure."[8] The board included some of the big stars of Hollywood—Robert Montgomery, Edward Arnold, Charles Boyer, James Cagney, Eddie Cantor, Cary Grant, Ralph Morgan, and Dick Powell. At union meetings, they received the young actor as an equal. Reagan was impressed by their commitment because he realized that these actors could have negotiated favorable contracts without the help of a union. He saw their participation as the selfless actions of successful men who remembered what it was like to be young and unknown. "My education was completed when I walked into the board room," Reagan wrote. "I saw it crammed with the famous men of the business. I knew that I was beginning to find the rest of me."[9]

Like so many stories in Reagan's autobiographies, this account must be read with caution. There is no way to verify that Broderick convinced a reluctant Reagan to join the Guild. Reagan came from a pro-union family and had defended labor's right to organize long before he came to Hollywood, but he may have so highly valued artistic individualism that he was skeptical of an actor's need for a union. If he had doubts, he quickly swallowed them. The records of the Screen Actors Guild show that Reagan became a member on June 30, 1937, little more than a month after he arrived in Hollywood, paying a $25 admission fee and $7.50 as his quarterly dues.

These records contradict Reagan's story about the timing of his ascension to the Guild board. They suggest that his entire account of how he became a board member is another Reagan fable with a moralistic message, in this case a story about how he was inspired by the selflessness of successful actors. Reagan became a member of the board not in 1938 but in July 1941, and then as an alternate for Heather Angel. It would have been unlikely that Reagan would have represented new contract actors in 1941; he was then on the verge of stardom. Jane Wyman was the catalyst for bringing her husband into Guild prominence. John ("Jack") Dales, executive secretary of the Guild, asked Wyman to serve as Angel's alternate; instead, Wyman brought Reagan to the union office and suggested he would make a better alternate.* The board accepted Reagan, and his union career was launched. Dales remembered that Reagan made an immediate positive impression. "He was a plain, likable guy who spoke his mind," Dales said. "There was a charm about him."[10]

Reagan left the Guild board when he went into the Army but retained his enthusiasm for the union. In 1945, he resumed his seat on the board, this time as an alternate for Rex Ingram, and after that for Boris Karloff. Reagan did not become a board member in his own right until

---

*Since actors rarely were able to attend board meetings when making films on locations outside Hollywood, as Angel was doing at the time, they routinely sought alternates to replace them. Once alternates were accepted by the board, they often served for months as full participating members, as was true for Reagan.

he was elected third vice president of the Guild in September 1946. He was by then one of the union's best-known spokesmen, and he was about to become even more prominent. On March 10, 1947, the popular Robert Montgomery avoided a potential conflict of interest by resigning as president of the Guild because he was producing and directing a film in which he was also appearing as an actor. Franchot Tone, Dick Powell, and James Cagney resigned as board members at the same time on the identical grounds of having "a financial interest in the production of the pictures in which they will appear." Gene Kelly nominated Reagan to replace Montgomery; Kelly and George Murphy were also nominated. The vote was taken by secret ballot with a majority needed to win. Reagan received a majority and arrived late from a meeting of the leftist American Veterans Committee to learn that he was the Guild's new president.[11]

By 1947, a decade after winning recognition from the studios, the Guild was a prestigious union with a strategic position in an anxious industry threatened by foreign films, the looming menace of television, and jurisdictional disputes among craft unions. Hollywood's anxieties were heightened by the fearful politics of the Cold War, which spurred investigations into alleged Communist influence in the industry by a headline-hunting congressional committee.

The Communists, no less than the committee, were fascinated by Hollywood, then the center of American popular culture. Beginning in the early 1930s, the Communist Party of the United States (CPUSA) gave a high priority to Hollywood because party leaders believed that movies could change the social consciousness of Americans. There was nothing novel about this belief. The American Legion and the Legion of Decency, among others, feared that films had the power to subvert or corrupt moviegoers. Organized crime was also interested in Hollywood, although for more practical reasons. Taking advantage of the shared cupidity of movie producers who were at once naive and unscrupulous, mob-controlled unions entered into "sweetheart" deals with the studios. The residue of this corruption was a factor in a series of jurisdictional strikes that engulfed the film industry from 1945 through 1947 and became crucial to Reagan's political evolution.

The mob had moved into Hollywood in 1936 in the persons of gangsters Willie Bioff and George Browne, who were backed by the Chicago underworld syndicate headed by Frank Nitti, the successor to Al Capone, and assisted by a $100,000 contribution from producer Joseph Schenck. Bioff and Browne took over a moribund industrial union of stagehands, the International Alliance of Theatrical Stage Employees (IATSE), signed up several producers, and assessed each employee 2 percent of his paycheck in union dues. In six years, they raked in $6.5 million, which they divided with the Chicago syndicate. After a series of highly publicized investigations, Bioff and Browne were sentenced to federal prison in 1941 for extorting $550,000 from five major studios. Bioff subsequently was murdered by a bomb set off by the starter in his car.* The International Alliance lived on and prospered under the leadership of a tough-talking Nebraskan named Roy Brewer who had been brought in to clean up the union.

The Communists enjoyed two periods of influence in Hollywood. The first occurred during the Popular Front collaboration of Communists and liberals that began in 1936 and ended with the Nazi-Soviet pact of 1939. The second came after the German invasion of Russia in June 1941 and ended with the collapse of Nazi Germany in April 1945, when, at Stalin's direction, the Communist parties of the world ended their wartime policy of cooperating with the Western democracies. The Conference of Studio Unions (CSU), which contested with the Alliance for labor control of Hollywood, was born in this second period of liberal-Communist cooperation. It was the brainchild of Herbert Sorrell, "whose flattened nose witnessed to an early and not too successful boxing career."[12] This was the description of Sorrell by George Dunne, a liberal Jesuit priest who reported on the labor disputes in Hollywood for *Commonweal*. In Dunne's view, Sorrell was "a rare phenomenon in the moral miasma of Hollywood management-labor relations: a man of honesty and integrity."[13] Others held a less flattering view. Dales considered Sorrell a Communist and untrustworthy, and Reagan, at least retrospectively, concurred. Sorrell was ultimately expelled from the National Executive Board of the Painters Union for having "willfully and knowingly associated with groups subservient to the Communist Party line."†

The CSU, organized in 1941, flourished during the war years. It capitalized on the film community's distrust of the Alliance and a lingering belief that Brewer, while not corrupt, was in bed with the producers. "The Communist Party was very much interested in the success of the Conference of Studio Unions," said Max Silver, a Los Angeles County

*For an account of the mob takeover of IATSE, see "The Life and Times of Willie Bioff" in *The Education of Carey McWilliams*, Simon and Schuster, page 91. McWilliams was an attorney in Los Angeles at the time and represented some of the union members who were fighting criminal control of their local. Of Bioff's murder, McWilliams wrote, "Thus did Willie Bioff depart this life, not with a whimper but with a bang."

†Sorrell was later identified on the basis of handwriting before HUAC in 1947 as a man who had signed a Communist Party document under the name "Herb Stewart." However, Sorrell told the House Education and Labor Subcommittee in 1948, "I am not now nor have I ever been a member of the Communist Party."

Communist leader during this period. "Its interest lay in the main to establish what we called a progressive center in Hollywood instead of the IATSE. . . . The party was interested in establishing a nerve center that would be to some extent influenced by party policy and party people."[14] In 1945, the battle was joined by the 16,000 members of the Alliance and the 10,000 members of the CSU for control of the film industry workforce in Hollywood.

There have been numerous accounts of these conflicts, most of them one-sided. Reagan wrote a highly selective version of the Hollywood labor struggles in *Where's the Rest of Me?* that scoffs at the genuine grievances of the nine craft unions represented by the CSU. Dunne and Garry Wills were similarly dismissive of the Alliance, which Wills referred to as a "thuggish" union. Looking back on this period from his later conservative vantage point, Reagan marveled at his own ignorance. "To say that I was naive is putting it mildly," he told me thirteen years later. "I knew about Browne and Bioff, of course, but I wasn't up on the Communists."[15] Nor was he fully "up," as he should have been, on the economic realities of Hollywood. Studios were cutting back on pictures, and many actors who had done well before the war shared Reagan's concern that they might not appeal to the generation of moviegoers who had come along while they were in military service. The actors wanted to work, and the recurrent strikes were getting in the way. Since both the Alliance and the CSU wanted Guild support, the actors believed they could function as mediators with the help of the American Federation of Labor (AFL), to which all three unions belonged. So the Guild, on Reagan's motion, decided to investigate the causes of the dispute between the Alliance and the CSU.

Despite official neutrality, the Guild leadership began its inquiry with sympathy for the liberal CSU and skepticism about the Alliance, which was still suspect from the days it was under mob control. In October 1945, the Guild honored CSU picket lines during a brief walkout. But when the Conference of Studio Unions struck again in 1946, the actors were reluctant to go out in behalf of the 350 set decorators the union represented. Some Guild leaders, Reagan included, wondered why Sorrell said that his only motive for the strike was to win higher wages for set decorators and other manual workers and insisted he had no jurisdictional goals. Although it was common knowledge that the Alliance and the CSU wanted to put each other out of business, the Guild tried to work out a settlement between Brewer and Sorrell and in July 1946 produced a pact that the actors grandiloquently called "The Treaty of Beverly Hills."

This settlement ended a two-day strike but provided only a brief ceasefire in the Hollywood labor wars. A month later, an AFL arbitration decision confused the jurisdictional issue and threatened the demise of the Alliance at the hands of the mammoth Carpenters Union, headed by the crusty William Hutcheson. Sorrell interpreted the decision as a green light to win control of the set decorators. On September 12, the CSU struck again and picket lines were thrown up around Warner Brothers and MGM. The Guild held an emergency meeting and, with Reagan doing most of the talking, decided to send a delegation to the AFL convention in Chicago. The actors, including Reagan, Wyman, Walter Pidgeon, Dick Powell, Alexis Smith, Gene Kelly, Robert Taylor, and George Murphy, were shunted from meeting to meeting before being allowed to present a resolution calling for binding arbitration of the Hollywood labor dispute. It passed unanimously but was never enforced.

Reagan testified later before the House Labor Committee that he had threatened AFL President William Green with a proposal to fly Hollywood stars to every major American city in denunciation of the labor violence unless Green agreed to the resolution. Green responded to the threat by immediately arranging a meeting between the actors and Hutcheson, who agreed to withdraw his designs on the set decorators but also (according to Reagan) denounced "the Commies" and threatened to "run Sorrell out of Hollywood" and destroy his union.[16]

By now the producers were solidly behind the Alliance, while the Guild wanted the labor dispute to end on almost any terms. Strikers fought pitched battles in front of the Warner Brothers studios with police, who escorted Alliance members across the CSU's picket lines. Each side blamed the other for the violence, but the weaponry was on the side of the Los Angeles and Burbank police and fire departments, which brought in tear gas and fire hoses to quell the strikers. Reagan managed to avoid most of the violence because he was on location in the Sierra Madre, north of Los Angeles, filming *Stallion Road*. Years later, testifying in a lawsuit, Reagan said he was called to the telephone at a gas station near the film location. "I was told that if I made the report [calling for binding arbitration] a squad was ready to take care of me— fix my face so I would never be in pictures again," Reagan said.[17] He took the threat seriously enough to carry a gun and for a time was also under police protection.

Nothing happened to Reagan, however, and it was the CSU that was "fixed" with substantial help from the board of the Screen Actors Guild. The board decided that the Conference of Studio Unions was engaged in a jurisdictional strike, which meant that actors did not have to honor its picket lines. On October 2, 1946, the membership backed up the board by an overwhelming vote; the Guild took the lead in a proclamation of twenty-five unions denouncing Sorrell and the CSU. The actors, and almost everyone else, crossed the picket lines. The strike collapsed. The Conference of Studio Unions disappeared from the face of the earth.

Dunne and Wills demonstrated in detailed accounts of the various Hollywood strikes and negotiations that Reagan's 1965 autobiography is inaccurate on key points of the events that led to the CSU's demise.[18] But even Dunne, a political foe, acknowledged that Reagan was not lying, writing that "he believes his own untruths."[19] And while Dunne may have been right in saying that the CSU might have prevailed if actors had honored the picket lines, it is most unlikely that the Guild would have done so regardless of what Reagan said or did. The actors wanted to work, and the studios preferred Brewer to Sorrell, who, fairly or not, had been tarnished by the repeated insinuations that he was a Communist or at least was following the party line. This was a damning accusation in Hollywood at the time and not a matter on which Reagan was a neutral. Although he made no mention of it in his 1965 autobiography or his 1990 memoirs, Reagan and Wyman, on April 10, 1947, became informants for the FBI to whom they subsequently reported on Communist activity in Hollywood.[20]

Reagan's agreement to serve as one of eighteen FBI informants in the film industry coincided with the investigation by the House Un-American Activities Committee into "Communist infiltration of the motion picture industry." Before the committee was finished, ten screenwriters who refused to cooperate would go to prison and hundreds of others would become unemployable. The reputation of participants on every side of the inquiry would suffer, and Hollywood would be revealed as a repository of cowardice, silliness, and ignorance. But in May 1947, when Committee Chairman J. Parnell Thomas of New Jersey and Representative John McDowell of Pennsylvania convened a closed session of fourteen friendly, anti-Communist witnesses at the Biltmore Hotel in Los Angeles, the power of the committee to divide and harm was underestimated by its opponents, including the Communists.

The film community had historical reasons for believing that investigating committees were harmless hot air. Hollywood had been investigated before, from various sources. In August 1941, isolationist Senator Gerald Nye of North Dakota declared that movies had become "the most gigantic engines of propaganda in existence to rouse . . . war fever in America and plunge the nation into destruction." Senator Nye made his anti-Hollywood speech to a sympathetic audience in St. Louis, which booed as he read the names of movie producers and directors, all of them Jewish. In September, another isolationist, Senator D. Worth Clark of Idaho, led an investigation by a Senate subcommittee and compiled a list of fifty films that Clark said contained war propaganda. Eight were Warner Brothers movies, and two of these starred Reagan—*Murder in the Air* (1940), one of four movies in which Reagan played Secret Service agent Brass Bancroft, and *International Squadron* (1941), in which Reagan was cast as an American who joins the Royal Air Force and learns respect for the British. The isolationists believed, accurately, that Hollywood was supportive of President Roosevelt's effort to aid Britain against Nazi Germany. *Code of the Secret Service* (1939), the second of the Bancroft films, ends with a speech by Bancroft that one writer described as "a call to arms."[21] But the isolationist campaign collapsed after the Japanese attack on Pearl Harbor.

Hollywood had also survived earlier inquiries into supposed Communist influence. Before the investigation led by Thomas, a Republican, two demagogic Democrats had tried without success to stir up Red scares. Representative Martin Dies of Texas, the first chairman of the House Un-American Activities Committee, had tried to embarrass Hollywood in 1938 and wound up embarrassing himself. Jack B. Tenney of Los Angeles, a one-time left-wing legislator who had turned against the Communists and coauthored the bill that removed them from the California ballot, had conducted a state investigation and was laughed out of town in 1943. There were many in Hollywood who believed, until too late, that Thomas and his inquisitors would suffer a similar fate.

Carey McWilliams observed that Hollywood is a community better defined in industrial than in geographic terms, "a world within a world" with a strong sense of group identity.[22] Spokesmen for this community tend to react with one voice when it is threatened from the outside. This defensive impulse after the scandals of the 1920s led to the promotion of "wholesome Hollywood." Two decades later, it led even anti-Communist producers to avoid the Tenney Committee as if it were a plague. But the community's defenses were down in 1947 as stars and studios looked anxiously at a changing economic structure that promised fewer and costlier movies. The external fearfulness that Hollywood would display before the Thomas Committee reflected an internal economic insecurity that prompted even liberal producers to throw radical baggage overboard. When the producers finally capitulated, their fear that continued employment of suspected Communists would hurt box-office receipts was the decisive consideration.

The Thomas investigation coincided with a rising national Red scare. Both the Congress of Industrial Organizations (CIO) and the

United Auto Workers (UAW) were purging their ranks of Communists, and teachers and other public employees were confronted with a spate of loyalty oaths. The same week Reagan testified before the House Un-American Activities Committee, the Soviet Union completed its destruction of democracy in Poland. Through purges or rigged trials, the Communists already had silenced opposition forces in Hungary, Bulgaria, and Rumania. While the Soviets consolidated their domination of Eastern Europe, the Communist parties in Europe and the United States denounced the Marshall Plan for reconstructing Western Europe as "capitalist imperialistic gangsterism." President Truman had acted to prevent Communist takeovers in Greece and Iran, and Communist pressure mounted weekly on the still democratic government of Czechoslovakia.

The changing sentiments of Americans toward the Soviet Union and its defenders during the Cold War were reflected in Hollywood, where the patriotic fervor of World War II had embraced "our gallant Russian allies." Hollywood had been a flagrant instrument of national propaganda during the war. The studios made propaganda films in which Korean Americans and Chinese Americans played malevolent Japanese pilots, the Japanese Americans having been precipitously evacuated from California with little more than the clothes on their backs. The propaganda, encouraged by the Roosevelt administration, included occasional pro-Soviet films, such as *Mission to Moscow* (1943) and *Song of Russia* (1943), and other wartime dramas with a scrap or two of ambiguous dialogue that the Thomas Committee would diligently dredge up as dubious evidence that made-in-Moscow sentiments were being subtly implanted in the minds of American moviegoers. Reviewer James Agee, writing in *The Nation* in 1943, suggested that the "cuddly reverential treatment of President Roosevelt" in *Mission to Moscow* and *This Is the Army*, both produced that year by Warner Brothers, was "subject to charges of indecent exposure and quite possibly of alienation of affections." But Roosevelt was president, after all, and the Soviets were U.S. allies. In retrospect, it is probably a commentary on the anticommunism of many Hollywood producers that there were so few pro-Soviet films. Members of the armed services who saw the well-made Army Signal Corps film *The Battle of Russia* (1943) got a stiffer dose of pro-Russian sentiment than any civilian moviegoer.

Looking back, even in the context of the Cold War, it is difficult to understand the preoccupation of the Thomas Committee with what now seems such a trivial enterprise. The premise of the investigations can be understood only if one recognizes that congressmen, Communists, writers, producers, and Ronald Reagan alike shared the delusion

that millions of Americans could be swayed by the insertion of a fragment of political sentiment into an otherwise benign movie. Not even
the fearful Jack Warner would acknowledge that this had actually happened, but nearly everyone who appeared before the Thomas Committee, including Reagan, agreed that such subversion would be of the
utmost significance. They agreed because the House Un-American Activities Committee, which failed woefully in investigating Communist
penetration into key industrial unions, accepted Hollywood's premise
of its self-importance.

"In those days one of the greatest influences on American life was the
motion picture," said Neil Reagan. "You can't laugh it off."[23] This was
the animating, if unproven, notion underlying the inquiry, and it was accepted as an article of faith by all sides. On the Right, such vigilant anti-
Communists as Lela Rogers, Ginger's mother, said she had turned down
one script for her daughter because it contained the Communist sentiment: "Share and share alike—that's democracy." On the Left, Hollywood Communists expressed great satisfaction with the triumph of
Alvah Bessie, one of the Hollywood Ten, for slipping into *Action in the
North Atlantic* (1943) a scene where a Soviet plane dips its wings to an
American freighter and a U.S. merchant seaman cries out, "It's ours!"

When Reagan left the service in 1945, he doubtless would have
agreed with the sentiments expressed by this seaman (actor Dane
Clark). Reagan was, he once told me, "not smart about the Communists,"[24] and he believed, reasonably, that "Red" was a charge that was
hurled rather indiscriminately at Democrats and liberals. Neil Reagan,
who years earlier had become a conservative Republican, disagreed, and
the brothers would argue whenever Neil mentioned the word "Communist" to Ronald. "He would say right away quick, 'Oh, you're coming out with the Communist story,'" Neil recalled. "And then the
occasion arose as a result of the strike when these people began to hit
him over the head, figuratively speaking. And then, while I'm sure he
would never admit it to me or to anyone else, some of the things I'd
been saying to him began to soak in."[25]

In his autobiography, Reagan described himself as "a near-hopeless
hemophilic liberal"[26] who bled for every cause that came along. This is a
considerable overstatement. Jack Dales referred to Reagan as a "so-
called liberal" who in the late 1940s consistently defended President
Roosevelt but otherwise expressed conservative ideas.[27] Even in his relatively liberal phase, Reagan was no indiscriminate joiner, and most
of his political activity in the postwar years was limited to the Screen
Actors Guild. He took a brief fling with the utopian-minded World
Federalists, but at a time when liberal-sounding Communist-front

organizations were a dime a dozen in Hollywood, Reagan joined only two—the Hollywood branch of the American Veterans Committee (AVC) and the Hollywood Independent Citizens Committee of the Arts, Sciences, and Professions (HICCASP). He left both groups as soon as he realized that Communists were running the show.

Of these organizations, Reagan was most interested in the AVC, which he believed had worthy goals and in which he became an active participant. As noted, he was attending an AVC meeting when he was elected president of the Screen Actors Guild. But he quit soon afterward in disillusionment when a tiny minority with ties to the Communists tried to launch a studio strike in the name of the membership. At HICCASP, Reagan lasted slightly longer and tried to change the direction of the organization. He and Olivia de Havilland (each of whom at first suspected that the other was pro-Communist) joined forces with James Roosevelt in a series of meetings at Roosevelt's home to draft a resolution declaring, "We reaffirm our belief in free enterprise and the democratic system and repudiate communism as desirable for the United States."[28] The Communists and their allies, led by screenwriter John Howard Lawson, refused to let the resolution come to a vote of the members. When the HICCASP executive board, with only de Havilland in support, voted down the resolution, Reagan resigned, as did de Havilland, Roosevelt, and other members of the anti-Communist faction.

Reagan emerged from these experiences as a lifelong anti-Communist but with few personal scars. Unlike radicals or liberals who had looked to the Soviet Union as the hope of mankind and felt disillusioned or betrayed by the purge trials, the Stalin-Hitler pact, or the postwar Soviet takeover of Eastern Europe, Reagan had never paid much attention to what was happening in Russia. Even without his experience in HICCASP, Reagan certainly would have broken with the Communists once he learned that they were determined to undermine the Guild's position on jurisdictional strikes. In his retelling of the stories of this period, Reagan seemed rather to have enjoyed standing up to Lawson and urging him to accept a denunciation of communism. He also proudly claimed credit for exposing Communist influence in the Hollywood strikes, and he would approvingly quote the testimony of Sterling Hayden, who in 1951 related to the House Un-American Activities Committee how the Communists had attempted to mobilize support among actors for the CSU strike. "The move was very successful," Hayden said. "It ran into the board of directors of the Screen Actors Guild, and particularly into Ronald Reagan, who was a one-man battalion against this thing. He was very vocal and clear-thinking on it."[29]

Actually, the Communists in Hollywood had run aground, like Communists elsewhere, on their intransigent Stalinist policies. What is missing from Reagan's one-dimensional account of this period is any recognition of what happened as the wartime alliance came to an end and the Communists, under orders from Stalin, changed from a policy of U.S.-Soviet collaboration to a hard anti-American line. In 1944, U.S. Communist Party leader Earl Browder, at Moscow's orders, renamed the party the Communist Political Association. In 1945, with the Nazis defeated and the Soviets contesting for power in Europe, "Browderism" became a grievous error and the Stalinist William Z. Foster became head of the reconstituted Communist Party. In 1946, Browder was ejected from the party, and his like-minded, generally more moderate followers in Los Angeles and Hollywood were similarly expelled.

The Communist opposition to Reagan's "innocuous" anti-Communist resolution in the Hollywood Citizens Committee of the Arts, Sciences, and Professions, which Reagan found so surprising, was the required expression of the party line. And it wasn't the withdrawal of Reagan and James Roosevelt that killed the organization, as Reagan contended in his autobiography. Instead, the Communists killed it themselves by insisting, as a matter of party discipline, that their supporters oppose liberal but anti-Communist U.S. Senate candidate Will Rogers Jr. in the Democratic primary in favor of a candidate who was willing to accept Communist support.[30] The Communists prevailed on the endorsement, but HICCASP collapsed. What was left of it was absorbed by the Progressive Citizens of America, which became the launching pad for the left-wing presidential candidacy of Henry Wallace in 1948.

Because of their dogmatic behavior, the Communists had lost most of their liberal allies in Hollywood by the time the investigations of the House Un-American Activities Committee began in 1947. Many liberals were especially repelled by the behavior of screenwriter Albert Maltz, one of the best known of the Hollywood Ten and perhaps the most talented. Writing in the *New Masses* of February 12, 1946, Maltz denounced what he called the "vulgarization" of the Communist idea that "art is a weapon." He made the additional mistake, from the Communist point of view, of praising the works of James Farrell, the author of the *Studs Lonigan* trilogy, whom Maltz accurately described as "one of the outstanding writers in America." Maltz was answered in *The Daily Worker* by Communist cultural commissar Mike Gold, who called Farrell "a vicious voluble Trotskyite" and said that "Albert Maltz seems to have let the luxury and phony atmosphere of Hollywood at last to poison him." Maltz recanted in an article in *New Masses*, heaping criticism upon his own "distorted view of the facts, history and contribution of left-wing culture to American life." Maltz's willingness to chastise himself was another of the periodic eye-openers that Communists provided liberals in Hollywood. His two articles, and Gold's, read into the record of the House Un-American Activities Committee, constituted a more impressive indictment of the Communist Party than anything Parnell Thomas was able to devise.

Reagan was by now an intense anti-Communist, but he also regarded Thomas and his committee as "a pretty venal bunch."*31 Reagan's low view of the committee may have been reinforced by his involvement with the FBI, which took a proprietary interest in investigating subversion. To understand Reagan's perspective it must be remembered that FBI director J. Edgar Hoover was not at the time recognized as a sordid figure who spied on civil rights leaders, trampled civil liberties, and used his power to blackmail politicians. In the 1940s, Hoover's skillful propaganda had made him a national icon to conservatives and liberals alike, and the FBI was credited with capturing or killing notorious gangsters and arresting Nazi spies during World War II. (Even the Communists had cheered the FBI for investigating Leon Trotsky's followers, several of whom were successfully prosecuted during the war under a dubious law, the Smith Act, later used to jail most of the CPUSA leadership.) Liberals at the time felt that the FBI was more responsible and restrained than the House Un-American Activities Committee, and Reagan, as an FBI informant, undoubtedly shared this view.

Reagan was wary when the committee's chief investigator, Robert Stripling, came to his hotel room on the night of October 22, 1947, to quiz him about his testimony the following day. They sparred, with Reagan relating his own anti-Communist experiences in HICCASP and declaring the opposition of the Screen Actors Guild to communism. Reagan told Stripling that he couldn't prove that any particular adversary was a Communist and wouldn't make such an identification on the witness stand. When the issue came up the following day, Reagan handled the issue with a politician's touch:

STRIPLING: As a member of the board of directors, as president of the Screen Actors Guild and as an active member, have you at any time observed or noted within the organization a clique of either Commu-

---

*Reagan's feelings about Thomas were justified. An investigation, launched after columnist Drew Pearson reported that Thomas had padded his congressional payroll in return for salary kickbacks, led to an indictment for fraud and one for receiving kickbacks. He pleaded no contest, was fined $10,000, and was sentenced to a Danbury, Connecticut, prison where two members of the Hollywood Ten also were incarcerated. Thomas was paroled on September 9, 1950, after serving nine months.

nists or Fascists who were attempting to exert influence or pressure on the Guild which has consistently opposed the policy of the Guild board and officers of the Guild, as evidenced by the vote on various issues? That small clique referred to has been suspected of more or less following the tactics that we associate with the Communist Party.

REAGAN: Well, sir, my testimony must be very similar to that of Mr. [George] Murphy and Mr. [Robert] Montgomery. There has been a small group within the Screen Actors Guild which has consistently opposed the policy of the Guild board and officers of the Guild, as evidenced by the vote on various issues. That small clique referred to has been suspected of more or less following the tactics that we associate with the Communist Party.

STRIPLING: Would you refer to them as a disruptive influence within the Guild?

REAGAN: I would say that at times they have attempted to be a disruptive influence.

STRIPLING: You have no knowledge yourself as to whether or not any of them are members of the Communist Party?

REAGAN: No, sir; I have no investigative force, or anything, and I do not know.[32]

Reagan's testimony did not delight the red-necked, short-fused Thomas, who a week later smashed a gavel to splinters while putting down a hostile witness. At the time Reagan testified, the committee investigation seemed to be going downhill. In May, at the closed hearings in Los Angeles, the word had been leaked to reporters of a supposedly sensational accusation: Robert Taylor was said to have charged that he had made *Song of Russia* under pressure from the Roosevelt administration. In October, the day before Reagan came before the committee, Taylor labored to correct this impression "lest I look a little silly by saying I was ever forced to do the picture. I was not forced because nobody can force you to do any picture." This testimony by a star who wanted to send the Communists "back to Russia or some other unpleasant place" undercut one of the thin premises of Thomas' investigation and put the chairman in a bad mood. But Thomas was in no position to bully the celebrities he had invited to give luster to his proceedings. As Taylor left the room, according to a contemporary account, "more than half the spectators stamped for the door, clustered happily around him and followed him more than a block down the street to his automobile."[33]

Reagan had never become "another Robert Taylor," as his agent had promised when he signed his first movie contract. But he was a star, too, and younger than Taylor and Montgomery. *The New York Times* reported that when Reagan entered the room, wearing a tan gabardine suit and blue-knitted tie, "there was a long drawn-out 'ooooh' from the jampacked, predominantly feminine audience." Many accounts observed that Reagan looked younger than his thirty-six years. His testimony was careful and controlled. Taylor had named Howard Da Silva and Karen Morley, both well-known Hollywood radicals, as two of the "few who seem to sort of disrupt things once in a while." Reagan did not even do that. Instead, he told a story about how he had been asked to lend his name to a hospital fund recital sponsored by the Joint Anti-Fascist Refugee Committee at which Paul Robeson would sing, and how it turned out not to be a benefit for the hospital.[34]

Reagan's testimony then turned to the strikes in Hollywood. The Screen Actors Guild, Reagan informed the committee, "is better informed on the situation and on the jurisdictional strike than any other group in the motion-picture industry." When Stripling tried to lead Reagan into saying that Communists were responsible for the labor trouble in Hollywood, the actor surrounded the question without ever really answering it. "After all, we must recognize them [the Communists] at present as a political party," Reagan reminded Stripling. "On that basis we have exposed their lies when we came across them, we have opposed their propaganda, and I can certainly testify that in the case of the Screen Actors Guild we have been eminently successful in preventing them from, with the usual tactics, trying to run a majority of an organization with a well-organized minority.

"So that, fundamentally, I would say in opposing those people that the best thing to do is to make democracy work," Reagan continued. "In the Screen Actors Guild we make it work by insuring everyone a vote and by keeping everyone informed. I believe that, as Thomas Jefferson put it, if all the American people know all of the facts they will never make a mistake. Whether that party should be outlawed, I agree with the gentleman that preceded me [George Murphy] that that is a matter for the government to decide. As a citizen I would hesitate, or not like, to see any political party outlawed on the basis of its political ideology."

The Jefferson reference stung Thomas, who replied, "That is just why this committee was created by the House of Representatives, to acquaint the American people with the facts." But Reagan wasn't through. After Thomas had thanked him, Reagan put what might be called the genteel case against the committee in these words: "Sir, if I might in regard to that, say that what I was trying to express, and didn't do very well, was also this other fear. I detest, I abhor their philosophy, but I detest more than that their tactics, which are those of a fifth column, and are dishonest, but at the same time I never as a citizen want to see our country become urged, by either fear or resentment of this group, that we ever compromise with any of our democratic principles through that fear or resentment. I still think that democracy can do it."[35]

Reagan, Murphy, and Montgomery won praise for their testimony from *Life*, *The New York Times*, and other major publications. Even liberal critics agreed that he had done well; Philip Dunne wrote that Reagan had made "a fine statement of civil-libertarian principles on the stand."[36] In his testimony, Reagan had walked a fine line. While agreeing that Communists sought to control the film industry, he had argued that no measures beyond vigorous democratic trade unionism were needed to combat them. He had named no names and recanted no principles. He had defended his union. Years later, he would obscure his own moderate and politically astute conduct by exaggerating the danger the Communists had posed to the film industry, quoting approvingly from the findings of the committee and denying that a blacklist existed. But at the time of his testimony, Reagan was sensible and restrained, paying the minimum homage to the committee and to the fearfulness it had created in the film industry.

Had the movie producers been similarly inclined, the Thomas Committee might have met the fate of its predecessors. When the chairman suspended the hearings after three days of questioning unfriendly witnesses, the widespread view was that the investigation had flopped. Newspaper editors protested Thomas' tactics, and a Gallup Poll showed that the public had a low opinion of the investigation. But the hostile writers also had made a damaging public impression as they followed a prearranged and confusing legal strategy of refusing to answer questions while insisting that they were answering them in their own way.*

Writers were dragged off the stand to the sound of Thomas' gavel-pounding while shouting their attacks on the committee. John Howard Lawson, the premier unfriendly witness, yelled at Thomas: "I am not on trial here, Mr. Chairman. This committee is on trial here before the American people. Let us get that straight." Maltz called Stripling "Mr. Quisling," using the name of the World War II Norwegian traitor. Only Ring Lardner Jr. tried a lighter approach, responding to a ques-

*A Gallup Poll taken November 7–12, 1947, shows that Americans did not have a high opinion of either the writers or the committee. By a margin of 46 to 29 percent, the poll respondents thought that writers who refused to answer questions about their Communist affiliations should be punished. But a question about the way the investigation had been handled produced only a 30 percent approval response, with 36 percent disapproving and 27 percent undecided.

tion about Communist membership, "I could answer it, but if I did I would hate myself in the morning."[37] The performance of the un-friendly witnesses rescued the unfriendly Thomas. The committee voted without dissent to cite the ten uncooperative witnesses for con-tempt. The full House agreed in a vote that was both an assertion of congressional investigative prerogatives and an expression of militant anticommunism. When McDowell called for the contempt citation of Maltz, he read a list of countries that had fallen to the Soviet Union and declared that Maltz was "a colonel in the conspiratorial political army of Soviet Russia."

The contempt citations were a signal to the frightened producers who met at the Waldorf-Astoria Hotel in New York on November 22 and 25, 1947, to decide what to do about the uncooperative writers. Eric Johnston, the head of the Motion Picture Producers Association, warned that boycotts against films written by the Hollywood Ten were already being organized or threatened, including one by the American Legion. Sam Goldwyn argued that this was not sufficient cause to jus-tify a blacklist, but he found no backing among his colleagues. The pro-ducers agreed to blacklist the Hollywood Ten unless and until they had purged themselves of contempt.

This decision, which was made public in a declaration that became known as "the Waldorf Statement," was not immediately communi-cated to the outside world. Instead, a committee of the producers headed by Louis B. Mayer met privately with representatives of the three major guilds—the actors, directors, and writers—on November 27 for the purpose of obtaining their cooperation with the producers' blacklist. Reagan, as president of the Screen Actors Guild, represented the actors. He raised the question of how "innocent people" would be protected under the producers' new policy. Sheridan Gibney for the writers and William Wyler for the directors voiced similar concerns. The producers committee met again with the Guild leaders on Decem-ber 3, the day the Waldorf Statement was finally made public, but failed to win their support. Afterward, the directors opposed the declaration as "fundamentally insincere," while neither the writers nor the actors took a stand. The Screen Actors Guild, with Reagan in support, voted in mid-January to require non-Communist affidavits of its officers, which it later extended to all Guild members. For all practical purposes, this move signaled that the Guild would not oppose the studios for fir-ing actors who refused to say whether or not they were Communists.

Despite his evocation of Thomas Jefferson on the witness stand, Reagan dodged the civil liberties implications of a blacklist. He did this by refusing to acknowledge that a list, as such, existed, and by saying that he would oppose creation of a list of persons unemployable for political reasons. At the same time, he acknowledged the right of studios to be cognizant of actors' outside activities or reputations in employing them. This meant that no Communist or suspected Communist would be employed. Reagan continued, however, to be concerned about "innocent people" who were vulnerable to the unofficial vigilante blacklists that sprang up in Hollywood in the wake of the congressional investigation. The Guild did its best to help repentant actors who were hauled before the House Un-American Activities Committee. This meant, in effect, helping those who were willing to name the names the committee demanded, and letting the unrepentant fend for themselves. When Gale Sondergaard, wife of the Hollywood Ten's Herbert Biberman, took the Fifth Amendment before the committee in 1951, Reagan as president of the Guild told her that the union would oppose any secret blacklist. "On the other hand, if any actor by his actions outside of union activities has so offended public opinion that he has made himself unsaleable at the box office, the Guild cannot and would not force any employers to hire him," Reagan said.[38]

Reagan's views were centrist and unexceptional for the time, similar to those of the Truman administration, which he supported. He was not hysterical about communism, and he denounced "witch-hunters" as well as Communists. The speeches he gave for Truman and other Democratic candidates in 1948 were aimed at what Reagan called "Republican inflation" and did not deal with Communists or foreign policy. Reagan supported the Democratic ticket in 1950, which included Democrat Helen Gahagan Douglas for the U.S. Senate seat in California against Republican Richard Nixon, who won. Nixon was a junior member of the House Un-American Activities Committee when Reagan testified, and Douglas was one of the few House members to vote against the contempt citations of the Hollywood Ten. Reagan later claimed that by the time of the 1950 election, he already thought that Douglas was "awfully naive about the subject of Communists" but wouldn't have "name-called or red-baited" by saying it publicly.[39]

I know of no one, either publicly or privately, whom Reagan called a Communist other than those who proclaimed their own communism. He realized that such accusations often damaged the accuser, and his sense of fairness led him in the direction of scrupulous political dialogue and away from personal vilification. At the same time, he became convinced that domestic Communists were part of an international conspiracy led by the Soviet Union to undermine democratic governments. The following, from an article that Reagan wrote for January 22, 1951, issue of the magazine *Fortnight*, is a fair sample of his thinking:

But suppose we quit using the words Communist and Communism. They are a hoax perpetrated by the Russian government, to aid in securing fifth columnists in other countries and to mask Russian aggression aimed at world conquest. Every time we make the issue one of Communism as a political philosophy, we help in this hoax. Substitute "Pro-Russian" for the word Communist and watch the confusion disappear. Then you can say to any American, "You are free to believe any political theory (including Communism) you want," but the so-called "Communist Party" is nothing less than a "Russian-American Bund" owing allegiance to Russia and supporting Russia in its plan to conquer the world. The very constitution behind which these cynical agents hide becomes a weapon to be used against them. They are traitors practicing treason.

In this article, Reagan asserted, "The real fight with this new totalitarianism belongs to the forces of liberal democracy, just as did the battle with Hitler's totalitarianism." He also denounced professional hate groups that "masked their racial and religious bias" behind anticommunism and those "anti-labor forces [that] used 'red-baiting' to fight unions." But never again would Reagan argue with his brother when Neil told him that the Communists were up to something.

What is most notable about Reagan's immersion in the anticommunism of his time is that he emerged from it in such good mental health. Others on both sides with more complex turns of mind and less balance than Reagan were psychologically trapped by what had happened to them in the great Hollywood Red hunt. Some were forever encumbered by the experience, which became the central reference point of their lives. Reagan was not trapped. He became more wary than he had been before, and his views changed, as they would on other matters, but he was only occasionally obsessive about his new opinions. Looking back on his experiences, he never apologized and hardly ever explained. In a time of hysteria, he could denounce Communists without raising his voice. What had happened to Reagan had changed his mind but not his character. As his on-screen career faded, he had successfully completed his basic training as a politician.

9

COMPANY MAN

Ronald Reagan was at once a family man, a union man, and a company man. The company was Music Corporation of America (MCA), originally a band-booking agency created in 1924 by Jules Stein, a Chicago eye doctor and amateur musician. Expanding his horizons, Stein hired Lew Wasserman, a circumspect public relations man, and sent him to Hollywood. He arrived in 1938, a year after Reagan, whom he befriended and represented as an agent. Wasserman helped MCA become a dominant talent agency, in the process becoming a Hollywood power.

On July 14, 1952, with his movie career on the wane and Nancy Reagan pregnant with their first child, Reagan in his capacity as president of the Screen Actors Guild signed an unprecedented agreement with MCA that gave the agency's Revue Productions a blanket waiver to produce an unlimited number of television shows. The waiver was a sweeping departure from Guild rules, which prohibited actors from retaining agents who produced movies, as MCA planned to do in a large way. In return for a favor that would make it a behemoth of Hollywood, MCA agreed that actors would receive "re-use fees," or residuals, for programs that were shown as repeats.

The waiver was the brainchild of Stein and Wasserman, who broached it to Reagan and Jack Dales, the executive secretary of the Guild. Laurence Beilenson, a former attorney for the Guild who had brought Dales into the union, and was at the time the attorney for Revue Productions, was also involved in the negotiations, which were shrouded in secrecy. Only six board members, two of them Reagan and his wife Nancy, attended the board meeting at which the waiver was approved. Both sides kept the deal confidential; Reagan anticipated opposition within the Guild and MCA knew that other producers opposed paying residuals. Ten years later, testifying before a federal grand jury during a Justice Department investigation of MCA's monopolistic practices, Reagan admitted he had "felt a little self-conscious" about the waiver because of the appearance of a conflict of interest.[1] He had favored it nonetheless, he said, because of a belief that MCA would stem the flight of television production from Hollywood to New York at a time of high unemployment in the acting community. In a similar vein, Dales said subsequently, "We were scared that we were going to lose television" to New York.[2] The Guild also represented actors in New York, but it is understandable that Reagan and Dales gave priority to Hollywood, their home community. This doesn't explain, however, why MCA was given exclusivity. If the motive was preserving jobs, why grant a waiver to a single company? Reagan ducked this question when it was put to him before the grand jury, saying, "We felt we were amply protected, that if any harm started from this, if anything happened to react against the actors' interest—we could always pull the rug out from them [MCA]."[3]

MCA had no worries on this score. All the principals in the deal were friends, especially Reagan and Wasserman. Representing Reagan in 1942 after the success of *Kings Row*, Wasserman had obtained a $1 million contract from Jack Warner, the industry's first. Reagan was also grateful to Wasserman for the assistance he had given him in avoiding military service until he had completed other Warner Brothers films. Their friendship would last throughout their lives, surviving Reagan's political conversion to the Republican Party while Wasserman was becoming a leading donor to Democratic causes and candidates.

The MCA waiver haunted Reagan's reputation in Hollywood. His action in 1952 was compounded in 1954 when the Guild board, on which Reagan continued to serve after stepping down as president, approved a permanent extension of the waiver. Reagan supported the extension even though he was by then host of *General Electric Theater*, one of MCA's most successful shows, and even though the Guild was in the process of applying to television its ban against agents serving as producers. Permanent exclusion from this ban gave MCA a huge advantage over its competitors, which it effectively exploited. Reagan's participation in the 1954 decision was a conflict of interest by any definition. He had become president of the Guild in 1947 after Robert Montgomery resigned to avoid a *potential* conflict when he became a producer as well as an actor. There was nothing potential about Reagan's conflict, since MCA had negotiated his contract with GE.

Some of Reagan's severest critics have described his actions as sinister. Balanced biographers are also skeptical. Wills found Reagan's answers to the federal grand jury in Los Angeles unconvincing.[4] Edwards said they raised questions that remain unanswered.[5] The skepticism about Reagan's conduct was reinforced by his 1962 grand jury testimony when he was being questioned about whether the Guild had granted the 1952 waiver to MCA in exchange for residual fees. Reagan said, "I don't honestly recall" and added that "maybe one of the reasons I don't recall was because . . . in the summer of 1952 I was up in Glacier National Park making a cowboy picture for RKO."[6] The movie was *Cattle Queen of Montana*, which costarred Reagan and Barbara Stanwyck. It was made not in the summer of 1952 but in the summer of 1954. In the summer of 1952, Reagan was in Hollywood.

Reagan's lapse in memory, if that is what it was, oddly foreshadowed a similar lapse on February 11, 1987, when he was being questioned by the Tower Board he had appointed to investigate the secret sale of U.S. weapons to Iran. Reagan's memory of what had happened was then so deficient that the White House counsel concluded he "had no recollection of his own."[7] In neither case, however, did Reagan deny what he had done. He acknowledged to the grand jury that he had favored the MCA waiver, and he told the Tower Board he had authorized the arms sales to Iran.

The problem on both occasions was that Reagan had woven the essential facts into narratives in which he was the hero who had done what was morally right even if it broke the rules. He had been doing that for a long time, as when he misremembered his role in the Eureka strike or recalled long-lost football games as victories. Reagan was a storyteller who made the facts fit the story, rather than building his story on the facts. Those who witnessed Reagan's befuddled performance before the Tower Board had no doubt he could have passed a polygraph test and generally ascribed his confusion to his age, then seventy-six. But he was fifty-one years old, and his mental acuity not in doubt, when he was questioned before the grand jury. Reagan remembered as little about the MCA waiver in 1962 as he did about the arms deal in 1987. Both times, others initiated the proposal and approached Reagan. And both times, despite reservations, Reagan signed off on these dubious deals.

I believe that Reagan, who could rationalize nearly anything, convinced himself that he had done the right thing because Hollywood had benefited from the MCA waiver. If so, the benefit was short-term and marginal. Even Dales acknowledged that Hollywood was destined to become the principal production center for television films within a few years.[8] The waiver may have speeded up this process, but the big beneficiary of the waiver was not Hollywood but MCA.

MCA's expansion after its sweetheart deal with the Guild attracted the attention of the Justice Department, which under Robert F. Kennedy conducted an extensive investigation. The transcript of the grand jury proceedings at which Reagan testified runs to 6,000 pages and shows that federal prosecutors had done their homework. Even so, the investigation turned up no evidence of bribery or other illegality in the granting of the waiver, and a subsequent inquiry by the Internal Revenue Service also found no wrongdoing. Reagan suspected that the investigations by the Kennedy administration were political and conceivably related to his support of Richard Nixon in the 1960 election. There is no evidence of this, either. Whatever the motivation, the results of the MCA probe were a major disappointment for the Justice Department, which was reduced to using the weakest weapon in its legal arsenal, a civil suit against MCA for conspiracy in restraint of trade that named the Guild under Reagan's presidency as a coconspirator. The lawsuit was dropped after MCA sold its talent agency, which had become a minor part of its business. In a meaningless action, the Guild then repealed the waiver. The outcome disgusted Reagan, who complained in his autobiography that actors had been left without representation. But many of the actors kept their MCA agents, who set up shop in other firms or formed their own agencies.

In all likelihood, the Kennedy administration failed to discover criminal conduct because there was none to find. The MCA deals with the Guild are best understood as examples of a cronyism that then pervaded Hollywood, which in many ways operated like a small town. As in any municipal political machine, Hollywood's cronies took care of each other. Reagan was particularly suited to this cronyism, for he was loyal to his agents in a community where many actors made a practice of discarding them, and his agents returned the loyalty. Whenever he had a problem, Reagan was apt to run it by Wasserman or Taft Schreiber at MCA, which was in need of friends as it expanded its business empire. By the time of the federal investigation, a decade after the initial waiver, MCA had gobbled up the backlog of Paramount and Universal films, purchased Decca Records, and then bought the entire Universal studio. Thanks in large part to the boost it had received from Reagan and the Guild board, MCA controlled 60 percent of the entertainment industry.

Good politicians remember their friends, and Stein and Wasserman had long memories. Four of the six actors who voted for the waiver would appear on *General Electric Theater*. Nancy Reagan played the female lead four times; two other board members appeared twice. Ronald Reagan benefited the most, with MCA providing him a lifeline whenever he needed one. In January 1953, MCA found Reagan the western he wanted and money ($75,000) he needed by reactivating his contract with Universal, which cast him in *Law and Order*, a low-budget film in which Reagan played the lead role of a respected lawman who comes out of retirement to save a town. A year later (in February 1954), when the Reagans had a baby in the house and no job in sight, Taft Schreiber booked Reagan into a Las Vegas nightclub act known as the Continentals.

Acting on his friend George Burns' prescription that "truth is the basis of all good comedy," Reagan drew laughs during two weeks at a hotel-casino called the Last Frontier with a routine based on the premise that he needed to introduce other people because he had no talent himself. The act was popular, and Reagan received offers from nightclubs around the country. He turned them down, having quickly discovered that he and a nightclub life were not made for each other. Nancy was anxious to return to their daughter in Pacific Palisades, and neither she nor her husband had any taste for gambling. They spent most of the time he wasn't on stage in their room. "When we were back home, we thought of it as just so many more weeks we'd bought that we could hold out in our waiting game," Reagan wrote in his autobiography.[9]

They didn't have long to wait. Soon after the Reagans returned from Las Vegas, Schreiber called with, as Nancy put it, "more good news."[10] It was the offer to host *General Electric Theater*, at a salary of $125,000 a year, which GE soon raised to $150,000. MCA had solved Reagan's financial problems and launched him on a new career. *General Electric Theater* ran on Sunday nights. Reagan starred in some of the dramas and introduced all of them. His contract also called for him to tour the country for ten weeks a year, meeting GE executives and employees and plugging company products.

Employing Reagan as a "corporate ambassador" was the brainchild of the visionary president of General Electric, Ralph J. Cordiner, who had pioneered in decentralizing his vast company and in promoting the role of GE as "corporate citizen." Reagan did not know Cordiner, but he admired what he had heard about him. He later said:

> He was the man who really was the leader of decentralization of industry and business. They had 139 plants in 38 states, and he was the one that had the courage as the chief executive officer and chairman of the board to say to the managers of those plants, "I want you to run them as if they were your plants." They never had to get a ruling from the board of directors. There'd be a general code of ethics laid down, and this is how the theater came about. Cordiner had the idea that not only would they do this television show but that the spokesman they got to do the theater, which turned out to be me, would [tour] the plants. The employees,

scattered as they were, would realize that the headquarters knew they were there because here's that fellow they saw on Sunday night coming to visit them.[11]

For several years, Reagan had doubled as a spokesman for the movie industry. Reagan's success on what he called "the mashed potato circuit" was one of the reasons Schreiber considered Reagan ideal for the GE job—he could act, introduce, sell products, and make a decent speech. But nothing was said to Reagan about giving speeches when he signed the GE contract, and his speaking was limited to relating brief anecdotes on his first tours for the company. Then, as Reagan told the story, he was asked in a GE plant to speak in behalf of a United Fund drive. He performed so well that a GE public relations man confided to Reagan that he had been rejecting requests for speeches because he didn't want to write them. Reagan said he didn't need a speechwriter. "If you want to accept a speaking date for me, I'll take care of it," he said.[12]

Once GE found that Reagan could speak, the company wouldn't let him stop. By Reagan's account, he gave as many as fourteen speeches a day and spent a total of two years of the eight he was under contract to General Electric on the road, visiting every one of the company's plants and meeting all of its 250,000 employees. Since he was afraid to fly, Reagan's contract specified that his travel would be by train. GE took advantage of this clause the first year, keeping Reagan on the road for eight consecutive weeks. Neither he nor Nancy Reagan found this long absence acceptable, and GE agreed on more frequent but shorter tours, none more than three weeks at a time. Even so, GE was a demanding company that, in the words of former company public relations man Edward Langley, wanted "a Cadillac at Ford prices." It asked and received more than its money's worth from Reagan. "We drove him to the utmost limits," said Langley. "We saturated him in Middle America."[13]

Reagan had "Middle America" inside of him long before he heard of General Electric, but the tours were nonetheless a useful political training ground. Langley recalled that after one tour Reagan said to him: "When I went on those tours and shook hands with all of those people, I began to see that they were very different people than the people Hollywood was talking about. I was seeing the same people that I grew up with in Dixon, Illinois. I realized I was living in a tinsel factory. And this exposure brought me back."[14]

On tour, Reagan learned the economies of campaigning: how to conserve his voice and how to fill his martini glass with water until the last reception of the day. He made mental notes about which jokes succeeded and which statistics served to make his points. Many of the questions asked him by his corporate or service club audiences focused on government excesses. In responding to these questions, Reagan gradually became more critical of government. No one told him to do this, but Reagan paid attention to his audiences. Reagan was already a company man when he began his GE tours, but he was still a nominal Democrat who had been raised to be suspicious of Big Business. Over time, on tour for General Electric, these suspicions diminished and were replaced by distrust for Big Government.

Meanwhile, on Sunday nights, *General Electric Theater* was exceeding even Schreiber's high expectations. It climbed from nineteenth in the ratings in its first year (1954–1955) to third in 1956–1957 and was the leading show in its 9 P.M. time slot following *The Ed Sullivan Show*. *General Electric Theater* presented a wide range of dramatic material, including a memorable western version of Charles Dickens' *Christmas Carol* with Jimmy Stewart. It also made Reagan, an amiable but dignified host, familiar to a new generation of viewers. As Wills observed, "They were the first television generation, being introduced to the man who would use television better than any other politician."[15]

Behind the scenes, the path was not always smooth. For all its advertised progressiveness—the company slogan was "Progress Is Our Most Important Product"—GE guided its television program with a heavy hand. A GE censor vetoed various scripts on the basis of "taste," including several that Reagan thought tasteful. Reagan, however, defended the company in its best-known use of censorship, which was exercised on a script set in a fogbound airplane where the instruments malfunction. General Electric, which manufactures airplane instruments, was "naturally sensitive" about this, said Reagan, and the script was changed.[16]

On the road, Reagan was beginning to stir sensibilities of his own. He had a habit of affixing brand names to products, and GE executives were annoyed by Reagan's use of the term "Frigidaire," manufactured by a competitor, as a generic name for refrigerators. His speech also was beginning to have an edge. In its earliest forms, it blended patriotic themes with a defense of Hollywood, where, said Reagan, the crime rate was low and the divorce rate 10 percent below the national average. But it became more specifically antigovernment over time, with titles such as "Encroaching Control" and "Our Eroding Freedoms." In 1959, Reagan included among his targets the Tennessee Valley Authority, then a revered symbol of New Deal progress to Democrats, and also a $50-million-a-year customer of GE products. Reagan said he did not have this relationship in mind when he made a speech declaring that "the annual interest on the TVA deal is five times as great as the flood damage it prevents." But it wasn't long before Reagan heard that TVA was pressuring GE to drop him or lose its business with the agency. Reagan had never met Cordiner and considered him "a very distant and austere figure up there on the bridge,"*[17] but he called him to see if the GE president was worried by the TVA complaint.

"Mr. Cordiner, I understand you have a problem that has to do with me," Reagan said.

"Well, I'm sorry you found that out," Cordiner replied. "It's my problem. I've told them we don't tell an employee what he can or can't say, and we're not going to start."[18]

Reagan appreciated Cordiner's response. "I suppose I still had some lingering boyhood ideas from the Great Depression about big business being not that way, and I was overwhelmed," Reagan told me.[19] Perhaps, but his response to Cordiner's graciousness was worthy of an experienced politician. He told the GE president that he didn't want to say anything in his speeches that might cost GE workers their jobs. According to Reagan, Cordiner replied, "This is a chance we have to take. It's a matter of principle."

Reagan persisted. "Well, Mr. Cordiner, what if I told you I could make the same speech and be just as effective, and I don't have to use that paragraph at all?"

The GE president replied, in a warm voice: "Well, it would make my job easier."[20] The offending paragraph disappeared, only to make a comeback when Reagan emerged as a spokesman for Goldwater.

By this time, the company man was in demand as a speaker at other companies, and his message of moral uplift, still similar to the speeches he had once given to community groups in Des Moines, was reaching a wider audience. "There appears to be a lessening of certain moral standards and certain principles of honesty and honor in our country, even a lessening of patriotism," he said on a radio show sponsored by the National Association of Manufacturers. On the same program, he agreed with a former commissioner of internal revenue that "the present income tax law is making us a nation of liars and cheats."

Reagan was sensitive to the high tax rates because his income and

---

*As he said these words, Reagan saluted, evoking the image of a ship in which Cordiner was the commanding officer and Reagan his second-in-command. Reagan had never read any of Cordiner's speeches, but his evolving ideas about the harm caused by government interference in the marketplace paralleled the GE executive's. In a lecture to the Columbia Graduate School of Business in 1956, Cordiner said: "The deepest reason why state planning has failed wherever it has been tried is that centralized bureaucratic control fails to provide either the information or the productivity that is provided by the United States' system of incentives and competition in a substantially free market. . . . Where there is little freedom at the marketplace for people to decide what they want and what they will pay for it, one sees the artificial shortages or surpluses that plague every state-planned economy in the world, including the farm economy of the United States." Reagan could have uttered these words.

family responsibilities were increasing. The Reagans, now with a son, had moved into a larger Pacific Palisades home that General Electric turned into a showcase. "We found ourselves with more refrigerators, ovens, and fancy lights than we could use," wrote Nancy Reagan.[21] GE nonetheless kept supplying appliances, including a refrigerated wine cellar, putting such a heavy load on the power supply that a special switch box was needed to handle the intricate wiring. Reagan enjoyed the gadgetry and didn't mind that his family home had become a living advertisement for General Electric. He didn't mind being a corporate spokesman either, and he was good at it. A Hollywood joke of the period, quoted by Sheila Graham, an unfriendly columnist, is that someone watched Reagan give a pitch for General Electric's nuclear submarine and said, "I didn't really want a submarine, but I've got one now."[22]

Reagan remained a union man. In 1959, with a fight brewing between the Screen Actors Guild and movie producers over residual payments to actors, the Guild asked Reagan to return as president, replacing Howard Keel, who had resigned to do a Broadway musical. "We wanted a strong leader," said Dales,[23] who asked Reagan to become president again in behalf of an executive committee that included Walter Pidgeon, George Chandler, and Leon Ames. Reagan was reluctant, in part because Nancy wanted him to turn the Guild down. Instead, Reagan bought time by asking for a few days to think it over. He then called Lew Wasserman, who advised him to accept the Guild's offer. Reagan said in his autobiography that he was surprised by Wasserman's advice, but there doesn't seem to be much mystery about the reasons for it.[24] MCA had a stake in the negotiations, and Reagan was a former client and a friend. True to his pattern of following Wasserman's advice, Reagan told Dales he would take the job.

In subsequent negotiations with the Association of Motion Picture Producers, the Guild asked that actors be compensated for movies from 1948 to 1959 that had been purchased by the studios and reissued for television. The Guild also sought creation of a welfare and pension fund. The producers were open to a pension fund but considered the issue of residuals nonnegotiable. In a meeting at the Hollywood Palladium, with Reagan doing most of the talking for the board, the Guild membership authorized a strike.*

In March, the Guild struck seven major studios. As Nancy had feared,

---

*Once again, Reagan had a conflict of interest that he did not reveal. He had negotiated an agreement in March 1959 for one-fourth ownership in the rerelease rights for *General Electric Theater*. Apparently, Reagan did not tell Dales or the other members of the Guild board about this, for the Guild issued a press release saying that Reagan had no ownership interest in the series.

her husband came under attack from all sides, with a conservative faction led by Hedda Hopper opposed to any fees for residuals and another faction urging that the Guild seek ownership for actors of their pre-1959 films, not merely fees for using them. The studios settled after seven weeks. They accepted a pension plan, which was funded with $2 million in re-use fees paid for from the 1948–1959 films, and they agreed to pay residuals for future films. But the settlement did not end the controversy. Dales thought that Reagan had demonstrated his mettle as a labor leader, but some actors, Glenn Ford and Bob Hope among them, believed that Reagan and the Guild board had given away the older films for a pittance. I find it difficult to believe that Reagan and the board could have done better than they did, especially since many actors were so eager to go back to work that they were willing to settle on lesser terms. Owners of intellectual property in America have always been reluctant to allow creators to share the profits of their creation. Publishers to this day refuse in most cases to pay writers and journalists for re-using their material. No union has been able to make a significant dent in their position.

The strike ended on April 18, 1960, and Reagan resigned from the presidency on June 7. He and his wife also left the Guild board. Reagan believed he had done well for his union, but he was seeking a more overt political role. He was by now a recognized conservative spokesman; a GE executive, he said, told him that he was more in demand as a public speaker than anyone in the country except President Dwight D. Eisenhower. In 1960, the Republican Party asked Reagan to support Richard M. Nixon. Reagan offered to reregister as a Republican but was told he would be more effective if he spoke for Nixon as a Democrat.

Later, Reagan concluded that his support for Nixon made him a liability to General Electric after John F. Kennedy narrowly won the presidential election. Reagan's option came up for renewal in 1962, at a time when *Bonanza* in the NBC time slot opposite *General Electric Theater* on CBS had pulled ahead in the ratings. As Reagan related the story, he received a call from a GE executive who told him the company wanted him to confine his speeches to selling GE products. Reagan got hot about it. He told the executive, whom he had never met, that he was constantly getting requests to speak and would continue to do so on his own time. "There's no way that I could go out now to an audience that is expecting the type of thing I've been doing for the last eight years and suddenly stand up and start selling them electric toasters," Reagan said. "You'd suffer, and so would I. I can't do that."[25] The conversation continued, with the executive reiterating that GE wanted Reagan to speak only on behalf of its products. Finally, Reagan said: "That's it. If it's the speeches, then you only have one choice. Either I don't do the speeches at all for you, or we don't do the program; you get somebody else."[26] Within two days, General Electric had canceled the show. Reagan told me that Cordiner was retired at the time and that GE would not have canceled the show if he had still been in charge, but his memory was again faulty. Cordiner did not step down as chairman of the board and chief executive officer until December 1963, more than a year after *General Electric Theater* went off the air.

General Electric made the decision to drop Reagan in March 1962, a month after he testified before the federal grand jury about his role in the MCA waiver. Garry Wills suggests that the company may have been engaging in damage control because it feared that Reagan would be implicated in the MCA scandal.[27] The indictment against MCA naming the Guild under Reagan's presidency as a coconspirator was filed in July; *General Electric Theater* continued on the air until September.

A less dramatic but more informed explanation than the ones offered by Reagan and Wills comes from Paul Wassmansdorf, a former GE executive who was present at the discussions that led to cancellation of the show. Wassmansdorf said that the decision had nothing to do with MCA, politics, or Reagan's speech but was based solely on the fact that *Bonanza*, after a shaky start in 1959, was routing *General Electric Theater* in the Sunday night television ratings. CBS was worried because millions of viewers were switching over to NBC after watching *The Ed Sullivan Show*. Meanwhile, several of the decentralized divisions at General Electric, all of which were charged a share of the costs for the show, "wanted more value for their advertising dollars and wanted to make their own decisions on how the money was spent."[28]

These concerns led in late 1961 and early 1962 to a series of meetings among executives of GE, CBS, and Batten, Barton, Durstine and Osborne, the advertising agency to which MCA had sold *General Electric Theater*. Wassmansdorf attended these meetings because his boss, Stan Smith, GE vice president of marketing, had been assigned by Cordiner to handle "the Sunday night problem."[29] GE wanted to hang onto the Sunday night slot, if possible, but the consensus that emerged from the meetings was that the format of the program needed to be changed. Reagan was invited to New York to discuss a new format but refused to attend, saying he wanted to stick with the existing format. Smith then asked Reagan if he would consider remaining a spokesman for GE apart from any television show. "He refused," recalled Wassmansdorf. "He wanted the TV exposure, since acting was still his profession." Reagan's unwillingness to consider other options left General Electric with no choice except to fire him.[29]

Reagan's version of what happened and the story related by this GE insider are more compatible than they seem at first glance. Reagan confirmed to me that GE had indeed sought another format and that he had wanted no part of it.[31] When Smith called him with the offer to continue just as a GE spokesman, Reagan may have interpreted this as criticism of his political speeches and reacted accordingly. Wassmansdorf concluded that Reagan was intransigent because he believed he had "an inside track" with Cordiner, who liked Reagan and wanted to keep him.[32] But Cordiner had handed off the solution of the "Sunday night problem" to others, and he backed their decision to let Reagan go.

In the abstract, Reagan admired Cordiner because he delegated authority. He did not like the result when it cost him his job, but Reagan would emulate this behavior as governor and president when he needed to get rid of someone who refused to resign.

10

VISIONARY

THE CONVENTIONAL description of Ronald Reagan's political evolution is that he was a liberal Democrat who awakened to the Communist menace while participating in the postwar labor and political struggles in the film industry and gradually realized that the federal government was encroaching upon individual freedom, at which point he became a conservative Republican. As we have seen, Reagan encouraged this analysis in his 1965 autobiography, even though Jack Dales and others who were familiar with his views doubted that Reagan had ever been much of a liberal. Nonetheless, Reagan's story of his political conversion has largely been accepted as historical truth. There are also those who believe that Reagan became a conservative "extremist," as Democrats tagged him when he ran for governor of California in 1966. Two years earlier, the Democrats had demonized Barry Goldwater in this manner, and they assumed that similar tactics would prevail against a candidate who had come to public attention as Goldwater's disciple. And so it was that Reagan entered the political arena as typecast as he had ever been in Hollywood. He had once been a Liberal. He was now a Conservative.

First impressions die hard. This conventional opinion of Reagan's evolution persists in the face of evidence that he was an orthodox and not a leftist Democrat and solid proof that his conservatism was tempered and pragmatic during his eight years as governor and eight years as president of the United States. That's the last thing most conservatives want to hear. Reagan is an icon of greater value to his adherents as a true believer who once walked in darkness than as a peace-minded president who defied the right wing of his party to win ratification of an arms-reduction treaty with the Soviet Union. But to understand Reagan it is necessary to put aside the myths of both sides and examine the sources of his ideas and vision.

When it comes to ideas, Reagan is the Rodney Dangerfield of American politics—he can't get any respect. While he is routinely described as "the great communicator" and retrospectively valued as a leader, even conservatives rarely consider Reagan an idea man. This underrates him. Reagan was no intellectual, but he knew what he believed and why he believed it, and he wove his ideas, single-handedly and without the help of speechwriters, into one of the most successful thematic speeches in the history of American politics.

When Reagan burst onto the national scene with his speech for Goldwater on October 27, 1964, he was a political unknown. Even conservatives who were dazzled by the speech did not recognize that Reagan had been formulating it for a decade, most of the time as a Democrat, and that the ideas it presented were his own. This was because Reagan was an actor. Although he enjoyed name recognition and popularity beyond the wildest dreams of ordinary politicians, these were discounted in the political community as the product of Reagan's years in movies and television. Despite the similarities of their professions, politicians have a low opinion of actors. When Reagan became a candidate for governor, Democrats dismissed him as a fading star who had been upstaged by a chimpanzee in *Bedtime for Bonzo*. Republicans were kinder to Reagan, and the movie, but largely shared the assumption that an acting background was poor preparation for public life. Reagan recognized that being an actor was an obstacle to being taken seriously. During the "exploratory" phase of his candidacy for governor in 1965, he agreed with his campaign managers that he should travel around California giving short speeches and answering questions. Reagan knew he needed to demonstrate that he could think on his feet without the help of a script.

The cadre of Californians closest to Reagan as governor—William Clark, Edwin Meese, and Michael Deaver—are unanimous in believing that Reagan was underestimated intellectually because he was an actor. (Deaver doubted that an actor could be elected governor and for this reason supported Reagan's opponent, George Christopher, in the 1966 Republican primary.[1]) At the time when Reagan entered partisan politics, "actor" was shorthand for "airhead," and Reagan would be dogged throughout his political career by skepticism about whether he possessed the candlepower to succeed as governor or president. I explored this question in chapter eight of *President Reagan: The Role of a Lifetime*, relying heavily on the insights of Harvard psychologist Howard Gardner and his theory of "multiple intelligences."[2] The short explanation is that Reagan's kind of intelligence differed from the intelligence of most politicians. Reagan had a gift for narrative, and the famous stories he told to make his points with audiences were also his way of explaining to himself how the world worked. Reagan was an inductive thinker; as economist Annelise Anderson observed, he always thought in concrete examples.[3] Her husband, Martin Anderson, also an economist, noted that Reagan's way of approaching issues was coherent without being overtly theoretical. "He never sat down, at least to my knowledge, in the campaign or the [presidential] administration and said, 'Now here is my grand design, what I want to do and all the theory,'" Martin Anderson said. "And yet, if you stepped back and added up all the specific things he said and looked at them, it formed a grand design. In other words, he did it by inference rather than deduction. It's a different way of thinking."[4]

This latter-day understanding of Reagan was unavailable to conservatives in the 1960s. Conservatives at the time tended to be defensive when Reagan's intelligence was questioned. I was told more than once by aides that Reagan was "smart enough" to be governor, hardly a ringing endorsement. The truth was that neither conservatives nor liberals knew much about Reagan's thought processes. William F. Buckley recognized the problem. "People say he is a simpleton, which isn't right, and when they realize he isn't they're apt to go to the other end of the spectrum and compare him to Socrates, which doesn't work either," Buckley told me.[5]

Conservatives may have found it difficult to understand Reagan, but they at least had the compensation of his political success. Liberals were left to explain how an actor they had derided as an ignorant extremist could successfully govern the nation's most populous and macroscopic state. Their insufficient explanation was that Reagan was a master communicator with a winning personality. These were valuable assets, to be sure, but the political landscape is littered with affable political communicators who have no comparable achievements. What made Reagan different was the power of his ideas and his stubborn adherence to them.

As Reagan extended his domination of American politics through the 1980s, liberals could no longer deny that he was an effective politician, but they continued to minimize the importance of his ideas. For conservatives, Reagan had by then become a paragon beyond comparison to ordinary politicians. A typical hagiographic portrait by an eminent conservative member of the Reagan administrations in Sacramento and Washington describes Reagan as having "a star quality" and a "popular message of personal and economic freedom."[6] This is accurate, to be sure, but note how closely this description tracks the liberal view that it is the messenger and not the message that is decisive.

Still, it is understandable that Reagan is more deified than examined on the Right. He is the first (some would say only) nationally popular conservative leader in American history and the man who led his fellow believers out of the political wilderness. This happened at a time when the conservative movement, after capturing the Republican Party in 1964, seemed marginalized by the magnitude of Goldwater's defeat in the presidential election. Conservatives were so grateful that Reagan had emerged in the midst of this political disaster that they did not ask where he came from. For conservatives, he was born full blown as a future president with his stirring speech for Goldwater. The last thing they would have wanted to hear was that Reagan, as a Democrat, had been giving much the same speech for years to service clubs and community groups and working men and women in General Electric plants across America.

Reagan had been doing this since boyhood. There was the strike speech at Eureka College, the talks on moral uplift in Des Moines, and the paeans of praise for Hollywood family life, which were undeterred by the disintegration of Reagan's first marriage. Many of his speeches were absolutist, which is to say that they drew a bright line between right and wrong. While Reagan's effective use of anecdotes and his good humor relieved the sternness of his message, his speeches echoed the sermons he had heard in his mother's Christian Church in Dixon. Reagan advocated a moral code of conduct and assessed the consequences of deviating from it. People must be good sports, and a player who violated the rules should blow the whistle on himself. Nations must also play by civilized rules. America had an obligation to resist evildoers, to use a word that President George W. Bush brought back into vogue after the terrorist attacks of September 11, 2001. It was a word that came easily to the lips of Reagan, who had cheered Franklin D. Roosevelt for supporting Britain against Nazi Germany, which Reagan considered the embodiment of evil. Reagan regarded fascism and communism as equal enemies of freedom. He stood up to the Soviet Union, which he described as the "evil empire."

Reagan's beliefs about America's mission in the world blended his mother's religious teachings (God has a purpose for everything) with an expansive, patriotic view of country widely celebrated by Hollywood during World War II. In political scientist Hugh Heclo's useful phrase, Reagan held a "sacramental vision of America."[7] As evidence, he offered Reagan's commencement address to William Woods College in Fulton, Missouri, in June 1952. The speech, called "America the Beautiful," is an enduring expression of Reagan's belief in American exceptionalism:

I, in my own mind, have thought of America as a place in the divine scheme of things that was set aside as a promised land. It was set here and the price of admission was very simple; the means of selection was very simple as to how this land should be populated. Any place in the world and any person from these places; any person with the courage, with the desire to tear up their roots, to strive for freedom, to attempt and dare to live in a strange and foreign place, to travel half across the world was welcome here. And they have brought with them to the bloodstream that has become America that precious courage, the courage that they and they alone . . . had in the first place, to this land, the unknown, to strive for something better for themselves and for their children and their children's children. I believe that God in shedding his grace on this country has always in this divine scheme of things kept an eye on our land and guided it as a promised land for these people.

Reagan was a Democrat when he gave this speech; later that year, according to Frank Mankiewicz, the Los Angeles County Democratic Central Committee considered endorsing Reagan for an open congressional seat but declined to do so on grounds he was "too liberal."[8] So much for the acumen of the local Democrats, one is tempted to say, but Reagan's vision of America as a free society that drew its strength from the courage and bloodstock of its immigrants was then considered a liberal view. Liberals in those days celebrated the American "melting pot" rather than the diversity of its human ingredients. The genius of America was not that it perpetuated differences but that it obliterated them and created a new being: an American. As President Franklin D. Roosevelt said in a campaign speech, "All of our people all over the country—except the pure-blooded Indians—are immigrants or descendants of immigrants, including even those who came over on the *Mayflower*."[9]

The idea that Americans were made, not born, was the basis of Reagan's steadfast belief in American exceptionalism, a view that changed hardly at all as he marched across the political spectrum. Reagan expressed this belief in an idealistic manner, never allowing it to degenerate into an assertion of American *superiority*. During his 1980 presidential campaign, Reagan made nativist conservatives uneasy by calling for a "North American accord" in which Mexicans, Canadians, and citizens of the United States (and their goods) would move freely across national borders. This idea led Reagan to take the first steps toward what became the North American Free Trade Agreement.[10]

Abroad, President Reagan was also consistent in expressing his appreciation of the contributions that foreigners had made to the creation and renewal of America. In Moscow and other places, he said, "You have to understand that Americans come from every corner of the world. I received a letter from a man [who] said you go to live in France, but you cannot become a Frenchman; you go to Germany, you cannot become a German—or a Turk, or a Greek, whatever. But anyone, from any corner of the world, can come to live in America, and become an American."[11]

Both as Democrat and as Republican, Reagan was a democratic internationalist. The passage quoted above restates and expands the central assertion of "America the Beautiful." It was not enough for America to be the promised land; to fulfill its destiny it must also be an exemplar for other nations equally entitled to the blessings of freedom. President Reagan believed he had a personal mission to make this case. He saw himself as an apostle of freedom when he presented Soviet leader Mikhail Gorbachev with lists of imprisoned dissidents or others held in the Soviet Union against their will. In China, Reagan quoted from the Declaration of Independence and said, "We believe in the dignity of each man, woman, and child. Our entire system is founded on an appreciation of the special genius of each individual, and of his special right to make his own decisions and lead his own life."[12]

Heclo called Reagan's vision sacramental because it interpreted the American experience as "something sacred, a material phenomenon expressing a spiritual reality." He identified three facets of the vision. The first was a belief that "God had chosen America as the agent of His special purposes in history." The second was that America was sanctified not for its own sake but as a "rescuing, redeemer nation." The third is the view that the United States had broken the seemingly inevitable pattern in which nations rise, grow, decline, and fall.[13] Simply put, Reagan believed in the immortality of America. In his campaign speeches, he quoted the revolutionary Tom Paine, "We have it in our power to begin the world over again," a line that came from Reagan's own reading, not the research of an aide. Reagan believed, as he often said, that America's best days are yet to come. He was the oldest president in U.S. history, but he attracted young voters because he had a bright vision of the nation's future. Running for reelection in 1984, President Reagan said America must continue "to help push back our newest frontiers in education, high technology and space." In the same week that his Democratic opponent questioned the costs of the manned space program, Reagan called for its continuance, saying, "The American people would rather reach for the stars than reach for excuses why we shouldn't."[14]

I have written elsewhere that Reagan spoke to America's future with accents of the past. This added to the allure of Reagan's vision, which seemed impervious to the political and cultural developments occurring around him, particularly in the 1960s. "A divinely purposed nation, on a world-redeeming mission, breaking out of time into a millennial realm of endless becoming—this was a sacramental vision as old as any talk about the American republic," Heclo wrote. "Ronald Reagan carried it into a late 20th century supposedly dominated by more modern, skeptical, and materialistic notions."[15]

Reagan's recurrent vision had many permutations. America is "the last best hope of man on earth." America has a "pre-ordained destiny to show all mankind that they, too, can be free without having to leave their native shore." Americans must "live for liberty until liberty is the blessing and birthright of every man, woman, and child on this earth." The first of these quotations, from the peroration of Reagan's nationally televised speech for Barry Goldwater on October 27, 1964, is a famous line of Abraham Lincoln's, although Reagan may have borrowed it from FDR, who also used it without attribution. The second quotation is from a campaign speech Reagan gave to the Veterans of Foreign Wars on August 18, 1980. The third is from a memorial service on May 22, 1987, for sailors on the USS *Stark*, which was attacked by an Iraqi jet fighter as it patrolled the Persian Gulf. These and numerous other Reagan speeches are consistent in describing a divine purpose for America and in emphasizing the duty of Americans to recognize the special nature of their national mission.

Reagan's vision became a pillar of "The Speech," the basic address that evolved during his General Electric days, culminating in the speech for Goldwater. In its later variants, however, Reagan's preoccupation with government growth overshadowed the sacramental vision. As he said in 1959, "Today there is hardly a phase of our daily living that doesn't feel the stultifying hand of government regulation and interference. We are faced with a collection of internal powers and bureaucratic institutions against which the individual citizen is absolutely powerless. This power, under whatever name or ideology, is the very essence of totalitarianism."[16]

Critics saw a contradiction between Reagan's love of country and his growing distrust for its government. They have a point, but the contradiction, like so many of Reagan's expressions, was rooted in the American experience. The United States of America came into existence through a revolution against the British monarchy that was subsequently celebrated as a revolution against central authority in general. In their debates about the nature of the new republic, especially in creating checks on executive power, the Founding Fathers were influenced by the ideas of John Locke. In *A Necessary Evil*, Garry Wills traces the philosophical origins of American antigovernmentalism to Locke's social contract, "which teaches that government is founded on a necessary loss of freedom, not on the *enhancement* of liberty."[17]

In the twentieth century, the Lockean notion that any gain of government came at the expense of freedom provided a philosophical underpinning for opposition to the New Deal, which its foes denounced as tyranny and compared to fascism. Antigovernmentalism subsided during World War II, when the federal government was the great organizing agent of the war against Nazi Germany and imperial Japan. But in the late 1950s, when Reagan was refining "The Speech," and even more so in the 1960s after the unveiling of President Lyndon B. Johnson's Great Society, conservatives resumed a vigorous attack on federal power. This course led them into an inevitable alliance with southerners, some of them conservative and some of them not, whose aim was to maintain a racial status quo that denied or limited black voting rights. Both Goldwater and Reagan opposed the Civil Rights Act of 1964 on what they believed were constitutional grounds. Neither man was a racist, but their alliance with the southerners on this touchstone issue opened a gulf between conservatives and blacks that has never healed.

Outside the South, the conservatives found fertile ground for their message in the Mountain West, the region where Goldwater and especially Reagan were most popular and where antigovernmentalism has its deepest roots. This seems a contradiction, too, since the federal government had made the region habitable for settlers by driving out the native Indians, laying telegraph lines, subsidizing railroads, and building dams to store the region's scarce and precious water. But it is also a region where the government owns more than half the land and has its most conspicuous presence. This was Reagan country, as was Southern California, which in the decades after World War II became a center of explosive entrepreneurial growth. Government had a hand in this expansion, too, through the distribution of aerospace and defense contracts, but small business powered the boom. Orange County, where the John Birch Society flourished, was receptive to the candidacies of Goldwater and Reagan and to their antigovernment message.

To restive conservatives hearing Reagan for the first time in the 1960s, the antigovernment theme was more resonant than the patriotic vision, but the combination was appealing at a time when American values were under attack at home and abroad. As disorders flared in cities and on campuses and the United States became mired in the bog of Vietnam, patriotism and skepticism about the U.S. government coexisted easily. Stuart K. Spencer, Reagan's streetwise political adviser, cared not a whit for sacramental visions, but he realized that his candidate had "the right message at the right time."[18]

The message was authentic, and its construction unique. Unlike anyone else on the national political stage, Reagan composed his central speech on lonely train trips where he had no resort to researchers, speechwriters, fact-checkers, or other useful aides. He built "The Speech" from the bricks of his reading and experience, decorating it with stories clipped out of local newspapers or popular national magazines such as *Reader's Digest*. Most of his speeches were chock full of numbers, for Reagan rarely met a statistic he didn't like, but they were also sprinkled with anecdotes that relieved the strain of so much statistical material. The anecdotes were carefully tested; Reagan listened to his audiences and relentlessly discarded lines that didn't draw a laugh. He also had an ear for the oddball item that made familiar points sound new. Here is Reagan, speaking in 1948 in behalf of President Truman and Hubert Humphrey, then a U.S. Senate candidate:

> The profits of corporations have doubled while workers' wages have increased by only one quarter. In other words, profits have gone up four times as much as wages. And the small increase workers did receive was more than eaten up by rising prices, which have also bored into their savings.
>
> For example, here's an Associated Press dispatch I read the other day about Smith L. Carpenter, a craftsman in Union Springs, New York. Seems that Mr. Carpenter retired some years ago thinking he had enough money saved so that he could live out his last years without having to worry. But he didn't figure on this Republican inflation which ate up all his savings and so he's gone back to work. The reason this is news is Mr. Carpenter is 91 years old.
>
> Now, take as a contrast the Standard Oil Company of New Jersey, which reported a net profit of $210 million after taxes in the first half of 1948. An increase of 70 percent in one year. In other words, high prices have not been caused by higher wages, but by bigger and bigger profits.

By 1964, and the Goldwater speech, big government had replaced big business as the enemy. "Since the beginning of the century our gross national product has increased by 33 times," Reagan said. "In the same period the cost of federal government has increased 234 times and while the work force is only one and one-half times greater, federal employees number 9 times as many." The menace to workers was no longer excessive corporate profits but high taxation and the costly welfare programs financed by these taxes. The following Reagan example was as bizarre and timely as the strange case of Smith L. Carpenter:

> Recently, a judge told me of an incident in his court. A fairly young woman with six children, pregnant with her seventh, came to him for a divorce. Under his questioning it became evident that the husband did not share this desire. Then the whole story came out. Her husband was a laborer earning $250 a month. By divorcing him she could get an $80 raise. She was eligible for $330 a month from the Aid to Dependent Children Program.[19] She had been talked into the divorce by two friends who had already done this very thing.

The Goldwater speech, dubbed "A Time for Choosing" to draw a partisan contrast between the presidential candidates, might as accurately have been called "The Collected Speeches of Ronald Reagan." It was cluttered with even more than the usual quotient of statistics and laden with allusions to Plutarch, Alexander Hamilton, James Madison, Sumner Slichter, Karl Marx, Howard Kershner, Senators Joseph Clark and Harry Byrd, John Ramsey McCulloch, and Howard K. Smith. Other notable borrowings were not identified. The final paragraph of the speech begins with a famous phrase of Franklin D. Roosevelt's, who was persona non grata to Republicans in 1964. (In 1980, when Reagan accepted the Republican presidential nomination and felt free to say what he wanted, he quoted FDR by name.) This peroration also includes the aforementioned borrowing from Abraham Lincoln:

> You and I have a rendezvous with destiny. We can preserve for our children this, the last best hope of man on earth, or we can sentence them to take the first step into a thousand years of darkness. If we fail, at least let our children, and our children's children, say of us we justified our brief moment here. We did all that could be done.

Reagan had used these apocalyptic lines before, but few Americans had ever heard them. Seen coldly on the printed page they echo a strain of pessimism, most mordantly expressed by Whittaker Chambers, that the forces of freedom might lose the global struggle with socialism. To conservatives, this seemed a close question in the 1960s. But Reagan added a note of triumphant optimism, making the climax of his speech sound more encouraging than it read. Believers who heard Reagan felt they were being summoned to a vital battle that would surely end in victory. They responded to Reagan's speech, to which an appeal for donations was appended, with an outpouring of contributions in small denominations that totaled more than $1 million, a record at the time.

For conservatives who had become discouraged as Goldwater's campaign disintegrated under the pressure of a Democratic portrayal of him as a dangerous warmonger, Reagan's speech marked a turning of the tide. The following week, Goldwater lost in a landslide and Republicans suffered such heavy losses that commentators speculated that the party might go the way of the Whigs. Reagan knew better. Instead of a "thousand years of darkness," he was looking forward to the dawn.

With the advantage of hindsight, it is evident that "A Time for Choosing" marked the apogee of the speech that Reagan had created and polished during his train trips for General Electric and his years on the banquet circuit. Amidst the ruins of the Goldwater campaign, "The Speech" was such a beacon for conservatives that Reagan was soon being touted as a probable candidate for governor with the clear intimation that he might someday become president. Reagan, practical as well as idealistic, responded by buffing off the hard edges of his message to make it more acceptable to a larger political audience. Elements of "The Speech" would pop up at odd times throughout the rest of his career, but Reagan softened the apocalyptic tone without ever withdrawing a word of what he had said.

The hardest edge of the message, and therefore the one Reagan dulled the most, was his assertion that the United States was sliding into socialism by degrees, a notion fashionable among conservatives in the 1960s. Reagan often used quotations or paraphrases from Karl Marx or modern socialists to make this point; a favorite line was this supposed prediction of Norman Thomas, who ran for president on the Socialist ticket for six consecutive elections through 1948: "Thomas said that the American people would never knowingly vote for socialism; but under the guise of liberalism, they would adopt every fragment of the socialist platform until one day America would be Socialist without knowing how it came about." This is a suspect quotation, and Reagan gave no reference for it.[*][20] By the 1960s, the deeply pacifist Thomas was more of a social democrat than a socialist, and the United States was not then or ever close to "going socialist."

Instead of warning about a potential socialist America, Reagan took

---

*If Thomas said this, I have been unable to find evidence of it, and Reagan told me in 1968 that he did not know its origin. Thomas often did say, however, that both major political parties had borrowed items from the Socialist Party platform, including Social Security. Reagan was vulnerable to using bogus quotes in his speeches because he clipped so many items out of newspapers in which such quotations abound. For some reason, the problem persisted even after he was no longer dependent on his own research. Reagan used, for instance, several variants of a fake Tocqueville saying: "America is great because America is good. And if America ever ceases to be good, America will cease being great." This bogus quote was also used by Bill Clinton and Ross Perot.[21]

closer aim at the expansive ambitions of the Great Society. Here he was on surer ground. Urban and campus disorders had created a backlash among working-class Democrats, and both George Wallace and Richard Nixon had capitalized on it. By the middle of the 1960s, as observed in the first chapter of this book, beleaguered California Governor Pat Brown had suffered political damage from the disorders in Berkeley and Watts and was struggling to maintain California's welfare state without raising taxes. The Johnson administration, which Brown backed, was also under fire from the Left for the steady expansion of the U.S. military role in Vietnam. This context was made to order for Reagan, whose antigovernment broadsides sounded far less radical in 1966 than they had two years earlier.

The struggle of the 1960s is often described as a cultural clash, which it certainly was, but it was also a debate about the purposes and capacity of government. Despite his rhetoric ("the closest thing to eternal life is a government program"), Reagan did not advocate a *weaker* government. His principal criticism of the Johnson administration in Vietnam was over the conduct of a war in which Americans were being sacrificed by an administration that lacked the will to win. Similarly, Reagan scored points with Californians by criticizing Governor Brown for supposedly timid responses to campus demonstrators and urban rioters. Reagan believed that Brown's concessions, particularly at Berkeley, had encouraged demonstrators rather than deterred them. This was not an antigovernment message but a call for more effective use of government's police power.

In staking out this ground, Reagan was asserting traditional values and traditional uses of governmental authority. Californians were weary of crisis and conflict. They wanted a return to the good life and a leader who promised, as Reagan did, to restore a sense of order and purpose. It was indeed the right message at the right time.

2

GOVERNOR REAGAN

11

CANDIDATE

THE REPUBLICAN PARTY in California to which Reagan offered himself as a candidate was exhausted from a long period of dominance followed by a frantic burst of internecine warfare. Republicans had routinely dominated state politics during the first half of the twentieth century, aided by California's unique cross-filing system that allowed candidates to seek the nominations of all parties on the ballot in the primary election. This system, an innovation of the Progressives led by Hiram Johnson, reduced the power of the political parties in an effort to eliminate corruption.* But it did not have an equal impact on the two major parties. Republicans were the majority party at the time, and cross-filing benefited incumbents, who in most cases were better known and better funded than their challengers. The new system wrecked the minority Democrats, who in many legislative and congressional districts were unable to field credible, well-financed candidates. In these districts, Republican candidates often won both the Republican and Democratic nominations in the primary.

The practical result of cross-filing over time was to create a single incumbent's party in which Republicans and a few powerful newspaper publishers called the shots. Some Democrats were allowed to run unopposed or with token opposition in return for acceptance of their party's overall minority status. Year after year, incumbents were returned to office without serious challenge as the Republican Party became increasingly dominant. By 1954, Republicans held both U.S. Senate seats, the

---

*The Progressives came to power in California in 1910. During the next six years they enacted a series of social and political reforms unmatched in the history of the West. These included workers' compensation, child-labor regulation, civil service, a direct primary, and the initiative, referendum, and recall. Cross-filing was enacted in 1913. It was repealed in 1959. All of the other reform measures have survived in some form.

governorship, and substantial majorities in the House delegation and the State Legislature. Three-term Republican governor Earl Warren had been elevated by President Eisenhower to the Supreme Court in 1953. Another ambitious Californian, Richard Nixon, was Eisenhower's vice president. Pat Brown, then the attorney general of California, was the only Democrat with statewide recognition. He had been elected largely because the Republican incumbent he defeated was widely believed to be corrupt.

In 1958, the Republicans did for the Democrats what they could never have done for themselves. The instigator of what became known as the "Big Switch," or, later, the "Suicide Pact," was U.S. Senator William Knowland, an intractable bull of a man whose lack of diplomacy was exceeded only by his ambition. Knowland wanted to be president. Governors in those days controlled state delegations at national conventions, and Knowland reasoned that Sacramento was his best route to the White House. He was undeterred by the fact that California already had a competent Republican governor in the person of Goodwin Knight, who had moved up from lieutenant governor when Warren was named chief justice, then won election on his own in 1954. Knight had started out as a conservative and, emulating Warren, had moved toward the center after he became governor. Knight had cultivated organized labor and enjoyed good relations with the state's union hierarchy. This put him at odds with Knowland, who favored a right-to-work initiative that employer groups placed on the California ballot in 1958.

Knight wanted a second term as governor, but he lacked Knowland's resources. Using the leverage of conservative contributors and the influence of his newspaper family (publishers of the *Oakland Tribune*), Knowland pressured Knight into changing his plans. Knowland ran for governor, and Knight moved over into the Senate contest. This brought Brown, who had been leery of opposing Knight, into the governor's race as the champion of the union shop. The national AFL-CIO poured money and precinct workers into California to defeat the right-to-work initiative. It lost, and Brown trounced the previously unbeaten Knowland. Knight's compliance with Knowland's demands had made him look weak in the eyes of voters, and he lost as well. The Democrats also gained control of the Legislature, which proceeded to abolish cross-filing.

Brown was reelected in 1962 with a skillful campaign against Nixon, who, after two terms as vice president and a narrow loss in the 1960 presidential election, gave Californians the impression that he considered the governorship a springboard for another presidential race.

Then, to complete the Republican Party's self-destruction, the moderate and conservative wings of the GOP cut each other to pieces in the 1964 presidential primary, where Goldwater was pitted against New York Governor Nelson Rockefeller. Goldwater was depicted as a right-wing bomb-thrower who would undermine Social Security and lead the nation into war. Rockefeller was portrayed as an untrustworthy eastern liberal who had betrayed his party and abandoned his wife. Goldwater won a narrow victory, clinching the Republican presidential nomination. But many of the GOP moderates who had supported Rockefeller deserted Goldwater in the general election.

This self-consuming fratricide left the Republicans without an experienced and broadly acceptable candidate to challenge Governor Brown when he sought a third term in 1966. Warren, Knowland, Knight, and Nixon were out of the picture. The moderate Thomas Kuchel was a leader in the U.S. Senate but persona non grata with conservatives, who blamed him for undermining Goldwater. California's other senator, elected in 1964 over Democrat Pierre Salinger, was Republican George Murphy, Reagan's old friend from the Screen Actors Guild. He had no interest in the governorship.

Murphy's election had been instructive to Reagan on two counts. It demonstrated to him that a former actor with a conservative message could win in California. Murphy's victory also suggested that Californians had rejected Goldwater instead of the Republican Party. Although President Johnson carried the state by some 1 million votes, his percentage of the popular vote in California (58 percent) was lower than it was nationally (61 percent). Goldwater carried only five southern states and, barely, his home state of Arizona, where Johnson received 49 percent of the vote. Democrats picked up 37 seats in the House, for a 295–140 majority, and two in the Senate, for a 68–32 margin. Nationally, Democrats gained 500 state legislative seats. The elections, wrote Theodore H. White, "had left the Republican Party in desperate condition," with Republicans suffering from a lack of common purpose and "a continuing failure to capture the imagination of the American people." In contrast, he wrote, Johnson's Great Society was a "vision which embraces the entire nation."[1]

This vision did not embrace Ronald Reagan. Writing in the December 1, 1964, issue of *National Review*, he declared that the election had demonstrated that 26 million Americans, meaning those who had voted for Goldwater, were committed to freedom. There was also hope of salvation, Reagan believed, for many of those who had cast their ballots for Johnson. "All of the landslide majority did not vote against the conservative philosophy, they voted against a false image our Liberal opponents successfully mounted," Reagan wrote. "Indeed, it was a double false image. Not only did they portray us as advancing a kind of radical departure from the status quo, but they took for themselves a costume of comfortable conservatism." Reagan dismissed this as a "cornpone come-on," about as close as he ever came to a personal swipe at a president. "Time now for the soft sell to prove our radicalism was an optical illusion," Reagan wrote. "We represent the forgotten American—that simple soul who goes to work, bucks for a raise, takes out insurance, pays for his kids' schooling, contributes to his church and charity and knows that there just *'ain't no such thing as a free lunch'*."[2]

Among five contributors who evaluated the election for *National Review*, Reagan alone made no mention of Goldwater, about whom he had mixed feelings.* Although he was careful not to criticize Goldwater publicly, Reagan believed that the "false image" put forward by the Democrats had received a mighty boost from Goldwater's inept campaign. Reagan, though not one to boast, was certain he could have done better. His low opinion of the Goldwater campaign was shared by financial backer Holmes P. Tuttle on the basis of his experience in 1964.

Tuttle, a soft-spoken entrepreneur whose Ford Motor Company dealerships in Los Angeles were the base of a profitable complex of businesses, was Reagan's shrewdest and most influential contributor. Not well known outside his own wealthy circle, he had been a Republican fundraiser since the first Eisenhower campaign. He had supported Goldwater but thought the bitter Republican National Convention of 1964 "a fiasco" in which the nominee had foolishly passed up a chance to unify the party. Tuttle believed Goldwater could have accomplished this by selecting moderate Pennsylvania Governor William Scranton, instead of conservative William Miller, as his running mate.[3] Even so, Tuttle did his best for Goldwater, organizing a $1,000-a-plate dinner in Los Angeles at a time when this was an enormous amount of money to charge for a political event.

Tuttle had known and admired Reagan since the 1940s and invited him to be the speaker. Reagan gave the celebrated speech that became known as "A Time for Choosing," electrifying the Los Angeles audience. Tuttle wanted to put it on national television, but Goldwater's campaign manager, Denison Kitchel, and adviser William Baroody Sr. thought that Reagan's speech was too controversial, particularly in its critical references to Social Security. (This from the manager of a candi-

---

*The other contributors were George Bush, John Cabot Lodge, Russell Kirk, and Gerhart Niemeyer. Bush and Lodge, who had come off losing Senate races in Texas and Connecticut, respectively, in which they had run stronger than Goldwater, called for the Republican Party to be more inclusive.

date who had also criticized Social Security and joked about lobbing a grenade into the men's room of the Kremlin.) Tuttle and a few wealthy friends then aired the speech in California with a trailer on the screen asking for contributions. The Californians raised so much money that they were able to tell the Republican National Committee, which was hard-pressed for funds, that they could pay for the national telecast.

Nonetheless, Kitchel continued to lobby against the Reagan film. He persuaded Goldwater to telephone Reagan at home the Sunday before its scheduled showing and urge him to withdraw the speech. Reagan asked Goldwater if he had seen the taped film, and the Arizona senator replied that he had not. "Well, it's not really that bad, Senator, and I don't think it will do you any harm," Reagan said. "Please read the script or see the film. If you are then of the opinion that it will hurt your campaign, I'll abide by your decision and cancel the release."[4] Though Kitchel remained unconvinced, Goldwater did not call back, and the speech was shown. Tuttle believed that Goldwater's strategists gave in because the campaign was desperate for money. The episode convinced Tuttle, and to some degree Reagan, that they knew more about what appealed to voters than the national leadership of the Goldwater movement.

Reagan had sounded like a prospective candidate in the *National Review* article, written a few days after Goldwater's defeat. I believe he had already decided to seek public office, in no small part because he knew he could better Goldwater's showing. But he had not yet decided to run for governor. Reagan was preoccupied with federal issues and had given little thought to California politics. His daughter Maureen, with whom he conducted a lively political correspondence, tried to shift his focus. In 1962, while working in Washington, Maureen had written her father deploring the advance of liberal policies and urging him to run for governor. She concluded the letter by saying he "could" be governor, to which Reagan, using Maureen's family nickname, replied, "Well, if we're talking about what I could do, Mermie, I *could* be president."[5] After the 1964 election, Maureen visited her father and again urged him to seek the governorship. Gesturing to Nancy with a smile, Reagan said, "Oh, my God, they're closing in all over."[6]

The closing in was led by Tuttle, who two months after Goldwater's defeat convened a meeting of his millionaire friends at his home in Palm Springs. Tuttle and most of his friends were "self-made men," which is to say that they were entrepreneurs who had amassed fortunes without the start-up advantage of inherited wealth. The only Tuttle friend with ties to a major Wall Street corporation was A. C. ("Cy") Rubel, chairman of the board of Union Oil Company. The other oil-

man at the meeting was Henry Salvatori, founder of the Western Geo-
physical Company, who was best known as a fierce anti-Communist
but also hated "big oil," as he called it, for trying to run him out of
business when he was a wildcat oil driller. Also attending the meeting
were Reagan's lawyer, William French Smith, and Taft Schreiber, the
MCA executive who had brought Reagan into television. There was
also Leonard Firestone, president of the tire company that bore his
name; Leland M. Kaiser, a retired investment banker; Edward Mills,
vice president of Holmes Tuttle Enterprises; and two San Franciscans,
Arch Monson Jr., the western manager of Autocall Company, and
Jaquelin Hume, the president of Basic Vegetables Products Incorporated. These men called themselves the "Friends of Ronald Reagan."
What they had in common besides money was a fervent belief in the
efficacy of the marketplace in which they had made their millions and a
conviction that Reagan was uniquely inspirational. Tuttle told Reagan
that he and his friends wanted him to run and would support him. Reagan thanked him but expressed concerns about the costs and difficulties of a statewide campaign. "I told him I knew it would be a sacrifice
but that he was the man we wanted," Tuttle said.[7] Reagan said he
would think it over. Tuttle went home, optimistic that Reagan would
make a commitment if the millionaire backers showed they could put
together a campaign.

The next and crucial step in the process demonstrated Tuttle's commitment to a more broad-gauged campaign than the one that had
brought grief to Goldwater. He sought out Spencer-Roberts, the
Southern California political management firm that had run Rockefeller's near-miss primary campaign against Goldwater in 1964. Stuart
Spencer and Bill Roberts were even more self-made than Tuttle and his
friends. Spencer was an amateur athlete who had been a parks-and-
recreation director in the small Southern California city of Alhambra;
Roberts had been a television salesman—when asked what he did for a
living he would say he was "in television." Moderate Republicans and
supporters of Earl Warren, they had started out working for the Los
Angeles County Republican Central Committee and had gone into
business for themselves as campaign consultants to local candidates.
The candidates won, and Spencer-Roberts branched out. Before managing the Rockefeller campaign, they had won thirty-four of forty congressional races with Republican candidates of various views.

"We checked with people around the country, and they said Spencer-
Roberts was the best," Tuttle told me. "We didn't want anything less
than the best."[8] Among the people he checked with were Goldwater
and his strategists, who still smarted from the hardball-tactics of

Spencer-Roberts in the 1964 California primary but told Tuttle there was no doubt about the firm's competence.

Spencer and Roberts, however, were even less ready than Reagan to make a quick commitment to Tuttle. The partners had the luxury, for the only time in their career, of a choice of gubernatorial candidates. They had been sounded out to manage the campaign of Reagan's prospective Republican opponent, former San Francisco mayor George Christopher. The "Kuchel crowd," as Spencer put it, assumed they would prefer the moderate Christopher to the conservative Reagan, as they had preferred Rockefeller to Goldwater. But Spencer and Roberts had a gambling streak and were intrigued by the notion of winning the governorship with a former actor whose chances were considered remote. They also had reservations about Christopher, who had lost twice in statewide races. Roberts thought that the swarthy, heavy-set former mayor would not look good on television. The partners also doubted that a former San Francisco mayor would appeal to voters in populous Southern California. "We wrestled with it," Spencer recalled years later. "George was the favorite, he was the favorite of the party, the polls, the media, everything. But when push came to shove, we didn't think there was any growth in Christopher."[9]

Roberts and Spencer also had reservations about Reagan. "We had heard that Reagan was a real right-winger and we thought that a right-wing kind of candidacy would not be a successful one," Roberts said. "We'd also heard a lot of other things—that Reagan was a martinet, that he was difficult to work with."[10] But Reagan dispelled these qualms when he met with Roberts and Spencer at Cave de Roy, a Los Angeles key club, to discuss his prospective candidacy. "We found him to be an open and candid person, easy to talk with, and a good listener," said Roberts.[11] He was, as Spencer put it less elegantly, "not a nut," and he had a "moral center . . . always important for a candidate."[12] The partners also respected Tuttle and knew he could raise the money needed to finance an effective campaign. What tipped the scales in Reagan's favor, however, was that both Roberts and Spencer were tantalized with the idea of winning with a long shot. "It was a challenge to us," said Spencer, "because nobody thought it could happen."[13]

Reagan was as impressed by Roberts and Spencer as they by him. It is a sign of Reagan's political pragmatism that he never, then or in any of his presidential races, used ideological tests in choosing campaign strategists, or, when he won, in selecting chiefs of staff. Soon after their first meeting, Reagan called Tuttle and declared he was ready to make the race. Immediately, Reagan began to prod Roberts and Spencer. On their third meeting, this time at Reagan's home, Reagan said, "Well, what about it? Are you going to do it? You've been asking me questions for three meetings now."[14] Roberts quietly answered that the partners were ready to manage the campaign.

It was at first an "exploratory" campaign, for Reagan was at once ambitious and cautious. As Franklyn ("Lyn") Nofziger, a Copley News political reporter whom Spencer recruited as press secretary, subsequently observed, Reagan typically began campaigns with an exploratory effort and a late announcement. "He didn't want to embarrass himself," Nofziger said.[15] In 1966, Reagan agreed with Tuttle and Spencer-Roberts that the Friends of Ronald Reagan would raise money and rouse activists while he tested popular reaction to his prospective candidacy in small towns around the state. "We said, it's like show business," Spencer said. "New York stage plays start out of town. If they have any screwups, they correct them before they come back on Broadway."[16]

Early in June 1965, the Friends of Ronald Reagan sent out its first mailing, written by Roberts and signed by Rubel, to a list of Republican activists. The forty-two names on the letterhead, mostly businessmen, included a smattering of well-known Hollywood figures: James Cagney, Walt Disney, Randolph Scott, Robert Taylor. The letter began with the words, "A time for choosing" and went on:

> For several years, Ronald Reagan has spoken, forcefully and eloquently, to the above subject. Again and again, he has called upon the American people to awaken to a decision they must ultimately make. Simply put, the question was, and still is: Will the people control the government or will the government control the people?
>
> Again the challenge—a time for choosing—but in another way. Today, the question is: Who shall govern this, the largest state in the nation?
>
> Ronald Reagan, out of a deep sense of duty and dedication, is willing to serve his Republican Party as its candidate for governor providing a substantial cross-section of our Party will unite behind his candidacy.

This one letter, which concluded with a parenthetical note that corporate checks were acceptable, raised most of the $135,000 that the Friends of Ronald Reagan spent in the pre-campaign period. Tuttle, who contributed $5,000, observed that the friends could have put up the money themselves, but decided that the solicitation would give a broader group of people a stake in Reagan. The enthusiastic letters that accompanied the donations reinforced the opinion of Roberts and Spencer that they had a live-wire candidate.

Other developments on the Republican side also encouraged the

Reagan team. Kuchel, anathema to conservatives but potentially formidable, briefly considered the race and then decided against it. Lesser-
known moderates who might have been more telegenic than Christopher
either dropped out or decided not to run because they lacked the financial means to run a serious campaign. By the autumn of 1965, it was
clear that Reagan's only major opponent would be Christopher, whom
Spencer-Roberts had accurately assessed as vulnerable despite his continuing lead in the polls. Christopher was confident he could convince a
majority of Republicans that Reagan was unelectable. If Reagan were
the nominee, Christopher envisioned the campaign as a replay of 1964,
with Reagan cast in the Goldwater role of "right-wing extremist."

Ignoring Christopher, Reagan began testing his campaign on the
road, as Spencer-Roberts had suggested, away from the population centers of Los Angeles, San Diego, and San Francisco. I met him in Sacramento, where Reagan spoke to a luncheon group of curious reporters
and lobbyists. The format was a short speech in which Reagan summarized his concerns about government growth and then took questions
from an audience that was knowledgeable about state government. Reagan freely acknowledged that he wasn't. When a reporter asked him if it
wasn't presumptuous to think that someone without a shred of background in public life could be governor, Reagan blandly replied that his
lack of experience would enable him to take a fresh look at state government. I thought this was an astonishing answer, but Reagan was comfortable with it. He was also more comfortable with reporters than most
conservative Republicans. After the lunch, the reporters crowded
around Reagan, shook his hand, and chatted with him about his days in
Hollywood or on *General Electric Theater.* He seemed more a celebrity
than a candidate. Later, when an editor asked my impression of Reagan,
I said I didn't know why anyone would want to run against an opponent
who was so well known and so well liked.[17]

This was not the opinion in Pat Brown's camp, however. Armed with
polls that showed Brown would defeat Reagan but lose to Christopher,
the governor's strategists were cheering for Reagan's nomination. Soon
they would do more than cheer.

At Reagan headquarters on Wilshire Boulevard in Los Angeles,
Spencer-Roberts was receiving mixed reports on the out-of-town tryouts. The summation was that Reagan connected well with audiences
but fumbled too many questions to which he should have known the answers. Occasionally, he scrambled figures, such as when he said that the
state's welfare rate was 15 percent instead of 5 percent. The press coverage of Reagan was relatively tolerant in the early going, but Spencer-
Roberts knew that such mistakes would become an issue once he

became a formal candidate. So his campaign managers embarked on a crash course to educate their fledgling political star.

Their first move, which was not disclosed to the press, was a series of what Spencer called "civics lessons" in which Reagan was the student and Assemblyman Charles J. Conrad the teacher. The crusty Conrad, a legislator since 1947 and an accomplished parliamentarian, was also a bit actor in movies and television, and the kinship of profession made Reagan receptive to him. Realizing that Reagan knew little about state government, Conrad explained to him how legislation was passed and the governor's role in the process. These tutorials were conducted at Reagan's home. Conrad kept the meetings secret; his only reward was that Reagan, who couldn't identify most legislators in his early years as governor, always remembered Conrad and greeted him by name.[18]

Conrad alone was not enough, however. As the campaign progressed, Spencer-Roberts hired a team of behavioral psychologists, Stanley Plog and Kenneth Holden, who taught at Southern California universities and operated the Behavior Science Corporation in Van Nuys. Working from Reagan's speeches and from interviews with him, Plog and Holden isolated seventeen issues, arranging each into a philosophical framework. Eventually, they produced eight black books that contained factual references for Reagan to cite and that ultimately became the partial basis of his first attempts at a legislative program. And they expanded his already wide range of literary allusions to include such names as Tocqueville and Hilaire Belloc, helping Reagan to employ what David S. Broder subsequently called "a sort of wisdom-by-association technique also used by President Kennedy"[19] in his speeches.

Spencer believes that Plog and Holden were of minor importance because neither he nor Roberts, let alone Reagan, understood them. "Bill and I didn't understand it, but we were looking for any angle we could get and so they were brought in," Spencer said. "They'd sit down with Reagan, and Reagan was where we were. He couldn't understand them. And we had a nice, friendly parting. They were honest guys, they were intellectual guys, they were maybe on the cutting edge of some kind of research, but the users didn't know how to use it, so there was no reason to screw around with it."[20]

Even so, Holden, Plog, or an assistant accompanied Reagan on most of his early campaign trips, and it seems likely that Reagan picked up something useful from their research. Reagan was autodidactic; he sopped up material from aides, audiences, conversations, summaries that were handed to him on cards, or articles he read in local newspapers or *Reader's Digest*. One of Reagan's strong points was that he was not a snob—he valued the opinion of his driver as much as the opinion of an expert. This was also a weak point. On matters on which he had no background, which included most state issues, Reagan tended to believe anything he read without considering the source. When he became president, his aides sometimes hid the ultraconservative newspaper *Human Events* from him or cut articles out of it that they thought might send Reagan off the deep end.

Plog and Holden made no attempt to alter Reagan's basic speech and would not have succeeded if they had tried. Reagan's message, minus the more apocalyptic phrases, remained as fundamentally antigovernment as the one that had excited the followers of Barry Goldwater. People were too dependent on government, which had become the master instead of the servant. Government must be reduced in size and taxes lowered. Businessmen should not be strangled by government regulations. Ordinary citizens were competent to take charge of their own government and their own affairs. "I am not a politician," Reagan said in several of his speeches. "I am an ordinary citizen with a deep-seated belief that much of what troubles us has been brought about by politicians; and it's high time that more ordinary citizens brought the fresh air of common-sense thinking to bear on these problems."

This became the theme of Reagan's campaign. Acclaiming common wisdom over expertise, Reagan presented himself as the "citizen-politician" who represented these ordinary citizens against the professional manipulators in Sacramento and Washington. Contrasting the supposed wisdom of the common man to the assumed perfidy of professional politicians was a populist theme at least as old as Andrew Jackson and as contemporary as George Wallace, who in 1966 was completing his second term as the segregationist governor of Alabama. It was a recurrent theme in Hollywood, too, most resonantly in Frank Capra's 1939 film *Mr. Smith Goes to Washington*. In this movie, Jimmy Stewart was cast as Jefferson Smith, a "small-town patriot" appointed to the Senate in his home state by a political machine "whose masterminds think they can control him."[21] Reagan and Stewart were friends, and the film was one of Reagan's favorites. In the movie, Mr. Smith prevails over the devious "special interests" that rule the nation's capital.

Reagan, however, was running for governor, not senator, and he needed to adjust his political targets. This was easier said than done, for Reagan was more anti-Washington than antigovernment. He believed in state's rights, which in the politics of the time was often code for resistance to racial integration. Segregationists had waved the state's rights banner during the battle over the 1964 Civil Rights Act, which Reagan had opposed. Reagan's belief in state's rights was neither racially motivated nor politically useful; he could have won moderate support in

1966 without alienating his conservative base in California by retro-spectively acknowledging the need for a federal guarantee of voting rights. Reagan had no interest in doing so. For all his talk of limited government, Reagan never favored diminishing the authority of California or any other state. He was reasonably consistent on this through-out his career, saying in 1988 that as governor and president he had sought to "re-awaken the federalist impulse and approach the Constitu-tion with a new fidelity—in short, to restore power of the states."[22] Be-cause of these views, Reagan was sometimes called Jeffersonian, although to the best of my knowledge he never described himself in this way. A latter-day admirer wrote a book about Reagan called *The Last Jeffersonian*.[23]

One problem with the Jeffersonian label is determining which Thomas Jefferson the labelers have in mind. Reagan was indeed "Jeffer-sonian" in his belief that a commitment to freedom was what made Americans exceptional; this idea is at the root of Reagan's 1952 speech "America the Beautiful." But if by "Jeffersonian" is meant a preference for limited government, the label is misleading when applied to Rea-gan—as it was in some respects for Jefferson. Neither as governor nor as president would Reagan shrink from using executive power to restore order in cities or on campuses, to fire striking air traffic controllers, or to send American troops wherever he thought they were necessary. Neither did Jefferson, who in his first inaugural speech (in a bow to op-position Federalists), called for "the preservation of the General Gov-ernment in its whole constitutional vigor, as the sheet anchor of our peace at home and safety abroad." This was the Jefferson who doubled the size of the United States with a Louisiana Purchase he suspected was unconstitutional.

Reagan, unlike Jefferson, was no intellectual, nor did he pretend to be. But he was a disciplined professional in all endeavors despite his cel-ebration of political amateurism. Just as he had worked on his technique as a radio announcer and a movie actor, and then as a television host, he practiced his speeches relentlessly. And he mastered, from a standing start, the requirements of a problematic candidacy in a difficult political race. This was partly because he had first-rate advisers, but mostly be-cause Reagan found his true calling in politics. Reagan was a competent actor with limited range. As a politician, however, he was so enormously gifted that he seemed a president-in-waiting almost as soon as he began campaigning. In Bill Boyarsky's analogy, Reagan was the equivalent of a natural hitter in baseball, with skills that are born, not made.[24] Roberts, who had worried about Reagan's right-wing tendencies, recognized this almost at once. So did Nofziger, a rumpled, cigar-chewing reporter who was as conservative as Reagan but not easily impressed by any politician. Nevertheless, when Roberts asked Nofziger for an evaluation of the candidate after one of his first trips with him, Nofziger predicted he would be elected and said he might one day become president. Plog, the academic hired for research purposes, was impressed, too. He recalled a speech at Claremont College, where students greeted Reagan with signs deriding the television show *Death Valley Days*, of which Reagan was then host.* Referring to Boraxo, the program's sponsor, Reagan said, "That may be only soap to you, but it's bread and butter to me."[25]

Reagan formally announced his candidacy for governor on January 4, 1966, in an event that demonstrated the television-age professionalism of his campaign. The speech was taped at the Reagans' home and shown in advance to reporters so they could write about it for their early editions the next day. Reagan appeared at the Statler-Hilton in downtown Los Angeles to answer questions from reporters. After this news conference, the announcement was broadcast on fifteen television stations throughout the state.

The announcement speech reached out to moderates and called for an in-depth study of California's troubled tax system and a possible moratorium on property taxes for the elderly. It extended an olive branch to the Democratic-controlled State Legislature, in which Reagan said service should be fulltime "with compensation as nearly commensurate to the service rendered as we could make it." Reagan was realistic in his assessment of California's problems. "It won't matter much," he said, "if the sky is bigger and bluer out here if you can't see it for the smog, and all our elbow room and open space won't mean much if the unsolved problems are higher than the hills." Then, in a line that might have come from his 1952 speech "America the Beautiful" or his Tom Paine incantation of beginning the world over again, Reagan said, "Our problems are many but our capacity for solving them is limitless."

The announcement speech was a success, and Spencer-Roberts was heartened by campaign polls that showed him rapidly closing the gap on Christopher. In some ways, in this formative period of his candidacy Reagan's managers were too dazzled by their candidate's political gifts. During their discussions with Reagan before they agreed to manage

*Reagan was host on this non-network show for twenty-one episodes in 1965 and 1966. Neil Reagan, an executive at the advertising firm of McCann, Erickson, suggested his brother for the position to Ronald Reagan's agent, Bill Meiklejohn. Ronald Reagan initially was resistant even though he needed the money; he changed his mind because he wanted to keep his lines open in Hollywood if he failed in politics, another example of Reagan's caution. After he announced his candidacy for governor in 1966, the sponsor replaced him on broadcasts of the program in California to prevent his opponents from seeking equal time under prevailing federal regulations.

him, Spencer and Roberts had worried if Reagan could handle the rigors of the campaign. But when he proved a hit with crowds and responded effectively to hecklers and hostile questions, Spencer-Roberts forgot that their natural candidate was far from a finished product and overlooked the pitfalls of working him too hard.

Reagan celebrated his fifty-fifth birthday in February. He was in excellent physical shape and mentally keen but needed daily rest. Since Reagan cheerfully followed whatever schedule was handed to him without complaint, as he had done since his early days as an actor, it was up to his managers to see to it that he was not over-scheduled. In the two months after his announcement, they kept him busy, and no one on his team called a halt when Reagan came down with a severe viral infection late in February. He was still recovering on March 6, 1966, when he appeared, with Christopher, at the convention of the National Negro Republican Assembly in Santa Monica.

Negroes, as most blacks then preferred to be known, were in short supply in the Republican Party, especially after Goldwater's nomination. The Negro vote was not a factor in the Republican primary, but the event gave Christopher an opportunity to make his case that Reagan was too extreme to defeat Pat Brown. He proceeded to do so. In his speech, Christopher twitted Reagan for his opposition to the Civil Rights Act of 1964. This irritated Reagan. Later, near the end of a question-and-answer session, a delegate asked Reagan how he could hope to win the votes of Negro Republicans after opposing this law. Reagan gave a boilerplate answer decrying racial bigotry. Christopher, commenting on Reagan's answer, said he would have voted for the Civil Rights Act and added that Goldwater's opposition to it "did more harm than anything to the Republican Party. . . . This situation still plagues the Republican Party, and unless we cast out this image, we're going to suffer defeat."

The questioning would have ended there except that Reagan rose to his feet to make a point of personal privilege. "I resent the implication that there is any bigotry in my nature," Reagan yelled at the surprised delegates. "Don't anyone ever imply I lack integrity. I will not stand silent and let anyone imply that—in this or any other group." He then stalked out of the meeting. Some reports said Reagan had tears in his eyes. One reporter said Reagan had declared, "I'll get that S.O.B." The plump Nofziger sprinted over to Reagan with surprising speed and caught up with him as he left the hall. Outside, Reagan calmed down but didn't know what to do. Nofziger told him to go home and said he would try to think of something.

After Reagan had departed, Nofziger conferred with Holden and

James Flournoy, one of the few members of the Negro Republican Assembly who was favorable to the Reagan candidacy. Flournoy insisted that Reagan return to the convention. Nofziger conferred by phone with Roberts, who agreed with Flournoy then drove to Reagan's home in Pacific Palisades, getting lost on the way. He arrived to find a subdued candidate who had been discussing the day's events with a worried Nancy Reagan and was eager to make amends. Flournoy had suggested that Reagan attend an evening reception, where he could talk to delegates individually. Reagan did, and his return to the hall blunted the impact of his walkout. Once back, Reagan was his normal, smiling self. He apologized to the delegates for leaving, reiterated his personal abhorrence of discrimination, and declared that his opposition to the Civil Rights Act was based on constitutional grounds.

Reagan's blowup was his first serious setback in the campaign. Stories about the event were unflattering, and *Los Angeles Times* editorial cartoonist Paul Conrad drew a headless Reagan, saying, "I'm looking for the rest of me."* Christopher kept the issue alive for a few days, at one point extending his "sympathy" to Reagan "in this moment of his emotional disturbance." It may have been a low blow, but Spencer-Roberts and Nofziger realized that the incident had indeed raised questions about Reagan's ability to take criticism. Reagan realized it, too, and made it a point to remain unruffled in response to questions from reporters about his mental state. At a news conference in Sacramento four days later, he turned aside one question by quipping, "My wife says I'm very even-tempered."

All in all, Reagan's outburst cost him little. Californians had a reputation for tolerance, but voters had given 2–1 approval to a 1964 ballot initiative sponsored by real estate groups that repealed the Rumford Fair Housing Act, an open-housing measure that Governor Brown had advocated and signed into law. Backers of the initiative had based their campaign on the property rights of homeowners, the functional equivalent of the issue of state's rights as it was raised in opposition to the Civil Rights Act of 1964. And even among white Californians who supported open housing, the mood had changed since the Watts riot of August 1965. That bloody episode had claimed thirty-four lives and left many white Californians more concerned about racial violence in their own state than with the struggles over voting rights in the faraway Deep

---

*Conrad's drawing sent Reagan into orbit. According to Nofziger, Reagan became so angry that he wanted to demand that *Los Angeles Times* publisher Dorothy (Buffy) Chandler fire Conrad. Nofziger talked Reagan out of calling the publisher and suggested that he instead ask Conrad for the autographed original of the cartoon. Reagan followed Nofziger's good advice; the next day he told a *Times* reporter he thought the cartoon was "cute" and said he had asked for the original because "I'd like to have it."[26]

South. On March 15, 1966, nine days after Reagan's walkout in Santa Monica, there was another flare-up in Watts. This incident was quickly controlled by police at the cost of two lives but reminded jittery Southern Californians of the precarious state of race relations in their cities. By a stroke of bad luck, Governor Brown was in an airliner over Denver when the incident erupted. He persuaded the pilot to return to Los Angeles, but newspaper accounts of Brown's action reminded readers that he had been in Greece when the Watts riot broke out.

For many Californians, civil unrest was linked to fear of violent crime, which was on the rise in California. Reagan had brought up the issue when he announced his candidacy. "Our city streets are jungle paths after dark, with more crimes of violence than New York, Massachusetts, and Pennsylvania combined," Reagan said. While he rarely dwelled on the issue in his campaign speeches, concerns about crime—and the prospect of more riots—provided a context of acceptance for Reagan's message.

Still, Roberts told me after the election that Reagan's walkout in Santa Monica might have been damaging if it had occurred later in the year when voters were focused on the election. But it was not big news in March. The *Los Angeles Times* played the story of the walkout on an inside page under a two-column headline. In contrast, the newspaper put out an extra edition on the March 15 eruption in Watts, then ran that story in the home edition under a banner headline on a busy news day—it was the same day that President Johnson signed a $6 billion tax increase to help finance the Vietnam War and that Gemini 8 astronauts were preparing to lift off. Only political aficionados cared about what had happened at the Negro Republican Assembly. Included in the latter category were Pat Brown's strategists, who were encouraged in their belief that Reagan couldn't take the heat.

Reagan's managers learned an important lesson from the Santa Monica incident. The candidate's schedule before Santa Monica had been reminiscent of Reagan's early days on the road for General Electric, when he was on the go from early morning until late at night. After Santa Monica, Spencer-Roberts, prodded by Nancy Reagan, saw to it that Reagan was rested. Although Reagan sublimated his aversion to flying and used a chartered DC-3, known to reporters as "The Turkey," to navigate the expanses of northern California, he campaigned in Southern California mostly by bus. Bill Boyarsky described a typical day:

> A comfortable Greyhound bus was loaded each morning with sweet rolls and coffee for breakfast; soda, beer, sandwiches, and fried chicken for lunch, and whiskey and gin for the long drive back to headquarters. It

was a self-contained home with a lavatory for the long days on the freeways. In the mornings the bus would leave Reagan headquarters and bring the six or seven members of the traveling press, the staff, and the candidate to the first event of the day, which was sometimes a coffee hour with women or a stop at a television station to tape a show for future viewing. After that would be a noon stop for a speech at a luncheon. In the afternoons there would be a rest stop at a motel. After Reagan's [Santa Monica] blowup over civil rights, the afternoon stop was seldom missed. His nap over, the candidate would rise refreshed for a dinner speech, which would end the day. By 10 P.M. he was usually in bed.[27]

Christopher, in contrast to Reagan, was poorly organized. The Spencer-Roberts view that there was no growth in him was demonstrated repeatedly as Christopher showed up late for events and scowled his way through television appearances. His only message was the negative one that Reagan was a sure loser against Brown, an assertion that became more dubious with each passing day. In April, Christopher gave the major television speech of his campaign, which he called "The First Order of Business Is to Win." More than half of the broadcast was devoted to a discussion of Reagan by name. Christopher contended that Reagan's participation in the Eureka College student strike (which most voters had never heard of) and his support of Helen Gahagan Douglas against Richard Nixon in 1950 would be used against him by the Democrats. "Hell, we ought to pay him to give that speech to Democrats after the primary," said one Reagan backer after watching the performance.

Christopher was hindered and Reagan helped by a hitherto-undiscovered scriptural admonition propounded by an astute obstetrician, Republican State Chairman Gaylord Parkinson: "Thou shall not speak ill of any fellow Republican." Parkinson called this the Eleventh Commandment. His motive for promulgating it was not to help Reagan but to unify his divided party by silencing leftover recriminations from the 1964 Goldwater-Rockefeller campaign. Parkinson, an excellent organizer, was valued by party professionals for the "Cal Plan," a strategy of concentrating on vulnerable Democratic legislative districts. Spencer-Roberts had managed several Cal-Plan candidates, respected Parkinson, and latched onto the Eleventh Commandment, which helped Reagan concentrate his campaign against Governor Brown while pretending that Christopher did not exist.

The Eleventh Commandment shackled Christopher, who needed to go after Reagan to make the case that he could not beat Brown. Twice during the primary campaign, Parkinson rebuked Christopher for allegedly violating the Eleventh Commandment, further inhibiting what had already become a defensive campaign.

Pat Brown, preoccupied with Christopher, did not understand the pattern of political change that was occurring in California. Brown was from San Francisco, a city with a distinctive culture that is at once cosmopolitan and provincial. San Francisco had been at the center of the state's political life early in Brown's career, but the city's influence had waned and its population had remained static during a period of mass migration to California. San Francisco's immigrants tended to be foreigners and easterners, not the conservative middle-class whites from the Midwest and the South who then dominated the immigration stream to Southern California. Because San Francisco was his point of political reference, Brown overestimated Christopher, who had been a capable mayor of the city. For the same reason, Brown underestimated the power of the conservative revolt that was brewing in the suburbs of Los Angeles, San Diego, and Orange counties. He also underestimated Reagan, whom he knew only from his movies. Brown, like Christopher, saw Reagan as a Hollywood variant of Goldwater who would be unable to attract moderates. A variety of public opinion surveys bolstered the view. The most respected of them, Mervin Field's California Poll, in February 1966 gave Reagan a narrow 3-point lead over Christopher with 27 percent of the potential Republican voters undecided. In trial match-ups, this same poll showed Christopher beating Brown by 7 points and Brown defeating Reagan by 4. With the polls endorsing his regional misconception about the relative strengths of the Republican candidates, Brown decided to give the Reagan candidacy a boost.

Pat Brown was neither the first nor the last politician who maneuvered to influence the opposition party to nominate a candidate he wanted to face in the general election. But Brown may have been the only such politician ever to do so against the advice of his campaign manager. Don Bradley, the manager, was a traditionalist who believed that no good ever came from meddling in the other party's primary and who also foresaw that Reagan would win the Republican primary no matter what any Democrat said or did. But Brown, encouraged by State Finance Director Hale Champion, overruled Bradley and authorized political in-fighters Dick Kline and Harry Lerner to discredit Christopher. They, in turn, hired Dick Hyer, a former San Francisco newspaperman, who dredged up a 1939 conviction of Christopher for violating a "fair trade" milk-pricing statute that had been resisted by many California dairymen. The prosecutor in the case had termed the violations technical, and the material had been used without success against Christopher in his San Francisco supervisorial and mayoralty campaigns. But the charges were news in Southern California, as Kline knew they would be.

Bradley, loyally abiding by Brown's decision to smear Christopher even though he did not agree with it, leaked the material to Drew Pearson, who wrote a string of columns suggesting that Christopher was corrupt. Christopher, already hamstrung by the Eleventh Commandment, was forced to defend himself at a time when he wanted to go on the attack against Reagan. Christopher, who did not know the source of the Pearson columns, at first suspected Spencer-Roberts. He was furious when he found out that Brown was the actual source. The smear of Christopher did indeed help Reagan, who by May had pulled ahead by 45–32 percent in Mervin Field's poll. But it backfired against Brown, who had a reputation for conducting above-board campaigns. Harry Farrell, the political writer for the *San Jose Mercury-News*, summed up the damage: "Some people thought that Pat Brown was indecisive or bumbling but no one denied his sincerity or dedication. After the Christopher smear he was just another politician."[28]

And a politician with his back to the wall at that. California was often in the forefront of political change, and in 1966 the Democratic Party in the state tore itself to pieces two years before it came apart nationally. On the Left, there was Si Casady, the head of the volunteer California Democratic Council, an implacable foe of the Vietnam War and an intemperate critic of President Johnson. Brown supported the war and the president, and he teamed up with State Controller Alan Cranston to depose Casady, an action that alienated liberal activists.

On the Right, there was Los Angeles Mayor Sam Yorty, a much-traveled demagogue who ran against Brown in the Democratic primary. Yorty received a boost when the California Supreme Court ruled on May 11, 1966, that the initiative repealing the Rumford Act was unconstitutional, a decision that injected open housing into the gubernatorial primary. Yorty assailed Brown for his support of the Rumford Act and accused the court of violating property rights. Reagan said he would support legislation repealing the law. Brown, under pressure, said he opposed discrimination in housing but was willing to accept unspecified modifications in the Rumford Act, a bit of waffling that disappointed liberals without commending him to conservatives.

The timing of the Supreme Court's decision, less than a month before the June 7 primary election, and Yorty's exploitation of it, hurt Brown. In the weeks before the election, the governor became a defensive candidate who was forced to shift his focus away from the Republicans and concentrate on winning the Democratic nomination. Brown, backed by organized labor and regular Democrats who had no use for

Yorty, won but not impressively. He received 52 percent of the Democratic vote in the primary, polling 1,355,262 to 981,088 for Yorty and 234,046 for four other candidates.

Reagan, meanwhile, scored a convincing victory, the first of many times when he proved a ballot-box candidate who fared better on election day than in preelection polls. In the Republican primary, Reagan received 1,417,623 votes to 675,683 for Christopher and 92,751 for three minor candidates. He had exceeded even the expectation of Spencer-Roberts in outpolling Brown. Of more significance, Reagan had instantly unified his party by obtaining 65 percent of the total Republican vote. The magnitude of his victory persuaded moderate GOP politicians who might have sat on their hands after a close election to swing quickly into line. Reagan helped by making a gracious overture to Christopher, and Roberts saw to it that letters were sent out the day after the primary offering positions in the Reagan campaign to prominent Christopher supporters.

But Pat Brown had done more than anyone to unify the Republican Party. Years later, Christopher told me that he disliked Reagan and might have balked at supporting him except for the "Pat Brown–Drew Pearson smear." When Reagan called to ask for his support, Christopher promised that he would do everything he could to help beat Brown in November.[29]

12

WINNER

THE OUTCOME OF the primary election validated Reagan's legiti-
macy as a candidate, and he knew it. When I discussed the campaign with him two years later, he used a sports analogy to
illustrate the importance of his victory. Reagan said that some athletes
perform well in practice. Others, and Reagan claimed to have been one
of them when a college football player at Eureka, practice indifferently
but rise to the occasion in the heat of the game. As Reagan saw it, everything before the primary election had been practice. The primary was
the first game of the season, and Reagan and his team had won. Now he
was no longer "just" an actor.

This was a politician's retrospective assessment. In 1966, Reagan
wouldn't even acknowledge that he was a politician; he admitted only to
the hyphenated "citizen-politician." To say this was a pretense, as many
have done, is beside the point. Of course it was pretense; Reagan was
running for the state's highest office, not auditioning for a movie role.
As a candidate for governor, and ever after, Reagan would prove as professional in politics as Pat Brown. But Reagan didn't see it this way. He
had sold himself on the notion that he was an enlightened amateur who
would run the government differently than a professional politician.
Like all good salesmen, Reagan believed his sales pitch, which in this
case included the dubious claim that governmental experience was a
drawback. "The man who has the job has more experience than anybody," Reagan said time and time again. "That's why I'm running."
Reagan came up with the line to deflect questions about his qualifications, but Roberts realized early in the campaign that his candidate believed it. "Oh, what will that poor soul do if he's ever elected governor?"
Roberts asked Nofziger.[1]

The poor soul who had the job was in trouble. Pat Brown had been one of California's most accomplished governors, but he was on the ropes in 1966. For reasons recounted in the first chapter of this book, most notably disorders on city streets and college campuses, Brown was increasingly seen as ineffective—both Reagan and Sam Yorty had assailed the governor's "failed leadership." While Brown's indecisive manner contributed to the impression that he was a weak executive, much of what was happening was beyond his control. California was on the cutting edge of the national cultural and political upheaval that was tearing apart the Democratic coalition that had seemed so dominant when Lyndon Johnson was elected two years earlier. Working-class Democrats were having second thoughts about the civil rights revolution in the wake of urban riots. In 1966, a significant number of these Democrats voted for Yorty in the primary and became prospective votes for Reagan in the general election. Liberals, particularly young ones, were protesting the widening U.S. military involvement in Vietnam. Though wary of Reagan, liberals had lost enthusiasm for Brown, whom they had supported wholeheartedly four years earlier when his opponent was the detested Richard Nixon.

Brown, meanwhile, had lost his zest for politics. "I think I was tired of the job," he told me subsequently. "I think that manifested itself. Being governor eight years, you lost a little of the zip. You've appointed your friends judges, the people you've grown up with. You've appointed other people to higher office, you've put over a great water plan and a master plan for higher education, and you're building three universities. You're seeking out something to do—what do you do now? Now we get down to the tough parts of politics, like a revenue program, and here's where I ran into the stone wall of Jesse Unruh in the Assembly. That's where Ronald Reagan came along."[2]

This, too, was hindsight. In 1966, Brown believed he could win a third term as governor by changing the subject from his leadership to Reagan's deficiencies. In all of Brown's winning campaigns, beginning with his first local victory in San Francisco, he had made his opponent the issue. Bill Knowland had been the issue when Brown was elected governor in 1958, and Nixon the issue when Brown won reelection in 1962. From Brown's point of view, Reagan was more vulnerable than these "giants," as the governor called them. Brown and his strategists dismissed Reagan as a right-wing clone of Goldwater, minus the latter's experience. They consistently doubted that voters would take an actor seriously, a surprising assumption in view of George Murphy's election to the Senate two years earlier. And they believed that Reagan would surely wilt in the fire of the campaign.

These strategists underestimated Reagan, and they overestimated themselves. Brown's campaign team was divided, like classical Gaul, into three parts. Hale Champion, a former newspaper reporter who held the key post of state finance director, was in charge of Brown. Don Bradley was in charge of the campaign. Frederick Dutton, an old friend whom Brown had appointed to the University of California Board of Regents, was Brown's political adviser. Dutton, who was practicing law in Washington, wasn't eager to spend the election campaign in California, but Brown wanted him around. "You were here for the takeoff, I want you here for the crash landing," Brown told him.[3] Dutton and Bradley did not get along, and they did not hide their disagreements from the press. When a reporter asked Bradley who was directing the campaign, he replied, "It just depends on whose day off it is."[4] The division added to the impression of Brown's indecisiveness.

Despite the inner dissension, the campaign's first efforts to make Reagan the issue were promising. Ridiculing Reagan's "citizen-politician" premise, Brown wondered aloud if people who were ill needed citizen-doctors. Then Brown compared Reagan to a "citizen-pilot" who told passengers it was his first flight "but don't worry—I've always had an active interest in aviation." Such spoofs might have had an impact had Brown stayed with them, for they played on public concern about Reagan's inexperience, an area in which Bill Roberts knew he was vulnerable. But Brown did not discuss this issue in a straightforward way. He could not resist saying that he was solving California's problems when Reagan was making the film *Bedtime for Bonzo*, and he used the word "actor" as if it were a synonym for "know-nothing." This belittling of Reagan's profession impressed neither actors nor voters. Jack Palance walked out of a Democratic telethon in disgust, saying, "Attack him [Reagan] if you wish for lack of experience, but don't go after him just because he is an actor."[5]

Palance's action should have sent a signal to the Brown team, but the governor and his strategists were too impressed with their own supposed cleverness to heed it. Brown rarely gave a speech without a sneering reference to a Reagan movie. His strategists, equally oblivious, commissioned an oddball half-hour "documentary," *Man vs. Actor,* that was offensive even in a state where political smears are commonplace. At the climax of this film, Brown tells an integrated class of young schoolchildren, "I'm running against an actor, and you know who shot Lincoln, don't cha?" The Democrats liked this distasteful line so well that they made it into a one-minute spot that was shown several times during the last week of the campaign.

Along with other chroniclers of the 1966 campaign, I wondered at the time and afterward why Brown, Bradley, Champion, and Dutton, all experienced campaigners, imagined that such foolishness would benefit them. The answer to this mystery was hidden in plain sight. The fatal defect of the Brown campaign leadership was that it contained no one from Southern California, which, depending on how the region is defined, then accounted for 60 to 65 percent of the electorate. Hollywood is one of Southern California's great industries, and movie actors among its most prominent citizens. Brown and Bradley were from San Francisco, which looks down its nose at Southern California. Champion lived in Sacramento, where state government is the leading employer. Dutton, the most thoughtful of this quartet, lived in Washington. He had doubts about the wisdom of the anti-actor strategy, but he did nothing to stop it.

The other way in which the Brown team sought to make Reagan the issue was to demonize him as an extremist. There was what social scientists would call a "cognitive dissonance" to the overall strategy, since it simultaneously depicted Reagan as an amiable lightweight (the anti-actor theme) and a dangerous right-winger who would damage the basic institutions of California government. But while the anti-actor approach never made sense, the anti-extremist component of the strategy had potential. The Democrats, after all, had destroyed Barry Goldwater with this strategy in 1964. And Reagan was saddled with the approval of the John Birch Society, a fringe group whose founder, retired Boston candy maker Robert Welch, had called President Eisenhower "a dedicated, conscious agent of the Communist conspiracy." The western headquarters of the Birch Society was in San Marino, near Pasadena. If Brown could pin the Bircher label on Reagan, he had a chance of rescuing his campaign.

The John Birch Society (JBS), named after an American missionary and U.S. intelligence officer who was killed by the Chinese Communists in 1945, took root in the suburbs of Los Angeles and Orange counties during the hothouse climate of the Cold War. Its membership, as described in a 1961 report by California State Attorney General Stanley Mosk, was composed "primarily of wealthy businessmen, retired military leaders, and little old ladies in tennis shoes" who were bound together by an "obsessive fear" of communism. This was a popular if not entirely accurate description of a secret society whose members included many middle-class family men who were active in community work, school organizations, and church groups. Not all Birchers were as far off the diving board as Welch, who believed the Communists were on the verge of taking over America and the world. Birchers typically were unsophisticated people who had joined the society because they felt the American system was failing and that they had been called to save it. While few in numbers, they became a factor in California politics for the same reasons that members of the Communist Party had been a force in an earlier era: They came to meetings early, stayed late, outworked their adversaries, and believed in their cause. As a result, various Birchers wound up on school boards or other elected bodies much as Communists had attained positions of union leadership or political influence even though their party lacked a mass membership.

The JBS posed a problem for conservative Republicans similar to the problem that Communists once had caused liberals with whom they were in coalition. The energy and discipline of the Birchers were potentially helpful to conservative candidates but only if harnessed without the baggage of Robert Welch. This was tricky business. Running for governor in 1962, Nixon had repudiated the John Birch Society and the two California members of Congress who belonged to it—Edgar Hiestand and John Rousselot. This had been of no visible help to Nixon, whose action was widely (and perhaps unfairly) seen as a decision based solely on political expediency. Hiestand and Rousselot were defeated for reelection, but this had little to do with their Bircher affiliations. They were victims of a Democratic-controlled redistricting that virtually obliterated their districts.

Reagan took a different tack than Nixon had. He had no use for Welch and called his smear of Eisenhower "despicable," but he did not tar every Bircher with the Welch brush. No doubt there was an element of political calculation in Reagan's approach, but I believe he was sincere and accurate in saying, as he did to Bill Roberts, that it was unfair to label all Birchers as "crazies." Reagan, after all, believed with the Birchers that communism was the principal threat to freedom throughout the world. He had no quarrel with the Birch Society's premise, only with its exaggerated view of the success of Communist infiltration of democratic governments.

Roberts and Spencer worried that Reagan's easygoing view of the Birch Society would lead him into trouble. They thrashed the issue out with the candidate in the late summer of 1965, coming up with a formulation that was largely Reagan's: "Any member of the society who supports me will be buying my philosophy. I won't be buying theirs." This was as far as Reagan was willing to go. Spencer and Roberts did not try to push him, for they realized he would not back down on matters of principle. But they did persuade Reagan that it was unwise to be drawn into repeated discussions of the Birch issue. After outlining this basic position on the Birch Society, Reagan mostly stayed away from the issue. Whenever a reporter asked him about the society, Reagan would say he had already given his views and that a printed copy of his statement was available from his press secretary. Since Reagan rarely varied his answer, most reporters eventually stopped asking the question.[6]

Spencer nonetheless remained "scared to death" of the Birch issue. He wanted to keep Birchers out of the Reagan campaign and sought out Rousselot, who had been a friend in the Young Republicans. Spencer-Roberts had managed his campaign in 1960, when the personable Rousselot had defeated a Democratic incumbent. After the election, Spencer flew with Rousselot to Washington to help set up his congressional office. On the late-night flight Rousselot began expounding on the Communist menace and Spencer said, "John, you sound like a Bircher." Rousselot said he was. This shocked the moderate and non-ideological Spencer, who tried to talk his friend into quitting the Birch Society.[7] Rousselot remained a member, however, and he and Spencer rarely saw each other after that until Spencer called on him in 1966. By then, Rousselot was public relations director for the Birch Society and trying to shift the organization's focus from Communist conspiracies to practical issues, such as "support your local police," a slogan Rousselot was credited with coining. In 1966, when Spencer appealed to him to keep Birchers away from the gubernatorial campaign, Rousselot told Spencer to tell Reagan that he would come out for him or against him, whichever would do the most good.

Rousselot was jesting, as he often did, but making a commitment in the process. He had no intention of opposing Reagan, whom he admired. Rousselot was telling Spencer that he understood the political realities and would see to it, as best he could, that the Birch Society did not go overboard for Reagan and damage his political prospects. Rousselot was crucial to any such effort because he was the most prominent and well-liked Bircher in California. Spencer related his conversation to Reagan, who made the mistake of repeating Rousselot's comment, also as a quip, in a speech to a Republican group. The audience included Jane Alexander, a moderate Republican opposed to Reagan. She called friendly reporters, who wrote stories about the exchange between Spencer and Rousselot. The story was discomforting to Spencer, but Reagan took it in stride.[8] In the news conference after his announcement speech on January 4, 1966, Reagan said in response to a question about possible support of John Birch Society members that he was "not going to submit a loyalty oath" to those who wanted to vote for him.

The Democrats continued to pound the "extremist" issue. From a purely political perspective, they had little choice, for the anti-actor strategy was not working, and Brown sank steadily in the polls throughout the spring and early summer. The point man in the attack on Reagan was Robert L. Coate, the state Democratic chairman. On August 4, 1966, he issued a twenty-nine-page document called "Ronald Reagan, Extremist Collaborator—An Exposé." It portrayed Reagan as a "front man" who "collaborated directly with a score of top leaders of the super-secret John Birch Society" and used "his acting skill and TV charm to soft-sell the doctrines of radical rightists who condemn Social Security and other social advances as Communist-inspired." Included in the document, along with various nutty quotations from Robert Welch, were the alleged hate-group links of some two score Reagan supporters. But many of the charges lacked documentation, and most of those who were named, with the exception of Henry Salvatori, had at most a remote connection to the Reagan campaign. The "exposé" quickly ran out of revelations and padded out its twenty-nine pages with paragraphs from the Birch Society Blue Book, six pages of anti-Birch denunciations by various Republicans, and such meaningless tidbits as, "Birch Society and Birch-oriented book stores peddle extremists' materials in the same catalogues that offer Reagan's pamphlets, books, bumper strips, and long-play records."

Many of these allegations resurfaced in a "white paper" issued by State Controller Alan Cranston, who believed his reelection was assured and plunged into the Brown campaign with an undocumented claim that he had new evidence that the Birch Society was riddled with anti-Semitism. Reagan was angered by the suggestion that he was in any way tolerant of anti-Semitism. While married to Jane Wyman, he had quit a Los Angeles country club because it did not admit Jews.[9]

But Reagan had no reason to worry about Cranston. The effort to tar Reagan with the brush of anti-Semitism was so outlandish on its face that no one believed it. Cranston subsequently provided comic relief to the campaign by pursuing Reagan from airport to airport in an effort to give him his "white paper." This publicity stunt backfired. When Cranston finally caught up with his quarry at the Sacramento Airport, Reagan said to him, "All right, you've made your grandstand play. Now why don't you run against your opponent?" Afterward, Reagan dismissed the attempt to link him to the Birch Society as "guilt by disassociation."

Whatever it was called, it was a wasted political maneuver by the Democrats. Reagan emerged from the exchange as the victim of a somewhat desperate political harassment. Cranston's heavy involvement in the extremist issue—one of his staff members devoted months to the "white paper" and his files provided material for the Coate "exposé"—underscored the cynicism that permeated the once idealistic California

Democracy in its final months of power. Cranston was the founder and first president of the liberal California Democratic Council (CDC) and a charter member of a band of California liberals who had opposed guilt by association in the days when Wisconsin Senator Joseph McCarthy was on the rampage. The point was not lost on Cranston's staff, which at one point threatened to quit en masse in protest to their boss' tactics. There were other signs that not all Democrats approved of the strategy of pegging Reagan as an extremist. State Senator George Miller Jr., an influential legislator, bluntly told Brown to "run on your record and forget this Birch thing." But Brown paid no heed to Miller, who had salvaged many of the governor's cherished programs in the State Senate, telling him that he was too unpopular to run on his record. Brown may have been correct, but his tactics worsened his problems.

Political polling in 1966 had not achieved the sophistication of later years, when campaigns conducted daily trackings. However, periodic surveys taken by both sides showed a downward spiral for Brown in August and September, when the anti-extremist theme was most heavily emphasized. Brown was losing significant numbers of the working-class Democrats who had voted for Yorty in the primary; they were unimpressed with the effort to portray Reagan as a closet Bircher. The only voting bloc on which the anti-extremist campaign appeared to have any impact was a relatively small group of Republican liberals centered in San Francisco. One of the latter, John Rothman, chairman of the San Francisco County Teen-Age Republicans, wrote Reagan asking him about Coate's accusations that he had supported hate-mongers and extremists. Reagan replied in an impassioned letter that recounted his longtime opposition to Gerald L. K. Smith and other anti-Semites and denounced Coate's "smear based on demagoguery."[10]

By Labor Day, the traditional formal opening of the fall campaign, Reagan was running loose in the lead. While the Brown campaign sputtered and its strategists and fund-raisers quarreled, the Reagan campaign under the direction of Spencer-Roberts ran smoothly.* Roberts traveled with Reagan while Spencer roved the state and kept tabs on grassroots Republican efforts. Every night they talked by telephone, debriefing each other on the events of the day. Thanks largely to Holmes

---

*The Brown campaign suffered another setback in August at the state Democratic convention, where Harvey Aluminum Company heiress Carmen Warschaw was scheduled to take over as party chairman. A group of liberal Democrats opposed her, exploiting a tactless remark of Warschaw's "that the people with money don't have enough say in the Democratic Party." She lost by four votes to the liberal choice, Assemblyman Charles Warren of Los Angeles. Warschaw blamed Brown for not doing enough to help her and withdrew her support from the governor. This fiasco advertised—and widened—the split among Brown's strategists. Dutton favored Warschaw while Bradley backed Warren.

Tuttle, the Reagan campaign had always been well funded, and corporate contributors who had turned their backs on Goldwater came forward as the likelihood of a Reagan victory increased. The Reagan campaign, at the suggestion of Roberts, had also brought in "new, fresh faces" and put them in positions of authority. Philip M. Battaglia, a thirty-one-year-old attorney, was chairman of the campaign. Thomas C. Reed, a thirty-year-old physicist, was the northern California chairman. Both of them were bright and energetic; neither was scarred by the intra-party battles of past campaigns.

Reagan by now had his campaign lines down pat. He talked consistently, as in the primary, of the "failed leadership" of Brown. All other issues—the university "mess," high taxes, the growing cost of welfare—were tied into this theme. While making his case against Brown and big government, Reagan was careful to say that he would oppose right-to-work legislation or any changes in California's generous program of unemployment insurance. He believed that working-class Democrats would vote for him if assured that he was no threat to their hard-won benefits.

The university "mess" proved an unexpectedly potent issue. Reagan had discovered it on his small-town speaking trips during the exploratory phase of the campaign in 1965, observing to an aide after one speech that "this university thing comes up each time I talk." The surveys commissioned by Spencer-Roberts at the time showed the Berkeley demonstrations to be a minor issue, but Reagan put more stock in his audiences than in any poll. Eventually, the polls caught up with the candidate and found that public concern about demonstrations at the University of California was an animating issue. Long before this happened, Reagan was declaring that student dissidents should "observe the rules or get out."

As a campaigner, Reagan proved effective. Because of his background, Spencer-Roberts had expected him to excel in prepared speeches and especially in television appearances. But to the surprise of his campaign team, Reagan also established a rapport with the reporters assigned to him at a time when it was an article of faith among conservatives that the press was the enemy. Richard Nixon hated the press and had allowed his feelings to spill out in his famous "last press conference" after his defeat in 1962. Goldwater, less of a hater, had nonetheless engaged in a running battle with the press in 1964. Reagan and Nofziger shared the conservative view that reporters, as a group, favored liberal causes and candidates. But Reagan neither advertised this opinion nor patronized the press. (For that matter, I know of no speech in which he called himself a "conservative" in the 1966 election campaign.) Toward reporters he displayed a mixture of reserve and friendliness that was a distinctive feature of his personality.

For their part, reporters had mixed views of Reagan. Many of them found him monumentally ignorant of state issues, but few, if any, disliked him. Nofziger coached Reagan against over-answering and encouraged him to dodge questions designed to pull him into the deep water of the many issues about which he was ignorant. Most of the time this strategy, and Reagan's friendliness, enabled him to survive. Reagan also benefited because reporters, as a rule, had low expectations about his capabilities. As a result, he tended to receive high marks for answers that might have been considered barely adequate for a more experienced candidate.

Expectations aside, Reagan rose to the occasion for big events, as he had often done throughout his life. In the 1966 campaign, the media event that mattered most was a September 11 joint appearance with Brown on *Meet the Press*, the closest the two candidates came to a debate. Sander Vanocur of NBC News, one of four reporters on the show, opened by asking Reagan about his political philosophy, a question he handled deftly. That led to this exchange:

MR. VANOCUR: On this question of party philosophy, California has a rather unique party philosophy going back to Hiram Johnson and Earl Warren and Goodwin Knight. Would you say that your philosophy is in [their] tradition?

MR. REAGAN: Are you talking about the Earl Warren of the Supreme Court or the Earl Warren as Governor of California?

MR. VANOCUR: I am talking about the Earl Warren as Governor of California, sir.

MR. REAGAN: There are some differences, of course. There would be between any two people, but basically, yes, I would go back as far as Hiram Johnson when he destroyed boss rule in California. Here he was striving to return power and authority to the individual, and he set up certain practices for our two political parties that still exist today . . . things that are very difficult for people in the East to understand, when they have been used to more boss rule in the smoke-filled room. Here in California we take the case to the people.

MR. VANOCUR: Sir, are you at all worried that if you stood as an Earl Warren, pre–Supreme Court Republican, this might alienate some of your conservative supporters?

MR. REAGAN: Oh, not at all. I think there are many people who look back with great pride—most Republicans do—on those years under both Earl Warren and Goodwin Knight.[11]

Vanocur told me that when Reagan distinguished between Governor Warren and Chief Justice Warren he suddenly realized he was in the presence of "a real political pro." Reagan continued to display that professionalism later in the show in response to questions from David Broder of *The Washington Post*, Carl Greenberg of the *Los Angeles Times*, and Bill Brown of NBC News, who pressed Reagan about the Berkeley demonstrators. Reagan said they had a right to free speech "but at the university this dissent has been permitted to take place literally where they had violated another freedom, the freedom of someone to listen. You can have free speech, but I don't have to listen. But when you allow this to take place at a point where anyone entering the university campus or anyone going back and forth from their classes must be subjected to the loud speakers and to the stands and to the handouts and to the demonstrations, then you are violating their right of privacy."[12]

Reagan was confident and assured throughout the program. In contrast, Governor Brown seemed tired, and his replies sounded defensive and shrill. Brown described Reagan as an "enemy of the people" and, in response to a question from Greenberg, repeated an earlier accusation that Reagan was "an enemy of the Mexican-American people," based on an insensitive comment that Reagan had made about the Cesar Chavez–led United Farm Workers march from Delano to Sacramento.* The governor also said that Reagan's criticisms of the Berkeley demonstrators had done "a great university incalculable harm by bringing it into a political campaign." Reagan charged, on this program and elsewhere, that Brown himself had politicized the university by using Dutton, whom he had appointed to the university board of regents, as a principal adviser in his reelection campaign.

On balance, Brown was damaged by the continuing protests at the Berkeley campus, less because of what Reagan was saying than because the governor seemed to have no control over the situation. He had even less control over what was happening on the streets. On September 27, police shot and killed a fleeing sixteen-year-old auto theft suspect in the Hunter's Point area of San Francisco. Brown, who was having dinner at a friend's house in San Diego, quickly called out the National Guard and flew to San Francisco the next day. But the incident produced three days of rioting and was a potent reminder of the Watts riot and California's simmering racial tensions.

By October, Reagan had assumed such a commanding lead that

---

*Reagan had referred to the 300-mile march, which ended at the State Capitol on Easter Sunday, as an "Easter-egg roll." The comment horrified Stu Spencer, who respected Chavez. But Brown was in no position to exploit it. After having refused to meet with Chavez and the marchers, he had spent the holiday weekend at the home of Frank Sinatra in Palm Springs.

Roberts and Spencer were convinced he was a sure winner. (Reagan remained cautious and said he would believe it when the votes were counted.) What worried Reagan's managers was the plight of other statewide Republican candidates, called "constitutional officers" in California, who were trailing in the polls. Spencer and Roberts were party men, and they had no difficulty in persuading Reagan that he should invest his popularity in electing other Republicans. So Reagan added a line to his standard speech appealing for election of the entire ticket, saying, "Don't send me up to Sacramento alone."

The final days of the campaign were a celebratory journey throughout the state in which Reagan appeared with the five other statewide GOP candidates, usually accompanied by mariachi bands. He finished each speech with the words, *"Ya basta?,"* the Spanish equivalent of "Had enough?"

California's voters answered the question in the affirmative. Reagan received 3,742,913 votes to 2,749,174 for Brown, a margin of 993,730 votes, and carried traditionally Democratic working-class precincts, especially in Los Angeles, in which Brown had swamped Knowland and Nixon. Reagan did well in suburban and rural areas that also were strongly Democratic in registration. He ran marginally behind traditional Republicans in silk-stocking GOP areas, though he still carried these areas handily, and substantially ahead of most Republicans in Mexican American neighborhoods, which he nonetheless lost. Despite Brown's jibe that Reagan was an enemy of Mexican Americans, he ran more strongly in this community (the estimates are from 38 to 40 percent) than any Republican had ever done. He had also brought in most of the GOP statewide ticket on his coattails. To Reagan's great satisfaction, the Democratic losers included Cranston.* Republican voting trends extended to the Legislature, where the Democratic margin was reduced to four votes in the Assembly and two in the state Senate.

What produced this Reagan landslide? Part of it was the national trend in 1966, when Republicans won ten governorships previously held by Democrats. Part of it was a normal reaction against an incumbent who had worn out his welcome after eight years in office. Part of it was campaign blunders by Brown and his divided staff, and the skillful

---

*Cranston, who believed until election day that he was safe, lost to a moderate young assemblyman named Houston Flournoy, who had entered the campaign after a night of hard drinking when his legislative pals put up his filing fee. Other Republican winners included Nixon ally Robert H. Finch, who was elected lieutenant governor, and the Republican candidates for state treasurer and secretary of state. Finch led all candidates, including Reagan, but polls had shown him trailing before Reagan started campaigning for the GOP ticket. The only Democrat to win statewide was the incumbent attorney general, Thomas Lynch, who waged a notably nonpartisan campaign.

campaign of Spencer-Roberts. And part of it, a large part, was the political skill of Reagan, who proved a superior candidate.

In two interviews conducted many years apart, thoughtful strategists on both sides agreed that a principal key to Reagan's victory was that he was underestimated from beginning to end. "They always had the feeling until late in the campaign that he was just another movie actor and the movie industry is noted for its feather-brained, irresponsible people," Roberts told me in 1968. "They felt he was incapable of putting up a good race and that he'd make a boo-boo some afternoon and they'd catch him and ruin him."[13]

In 1981, a few months after Reagan was elected president, Fred Dutton observed that Brown and his team had underrated Reagan in 1966 and that Democrats had repeated this mistake during the presidential campaign. "Reagan was underestimated, and he still is," Dutton said. "We tried to make him out a sinister figure, as Jimmy Carter did in 1980. It didn't work for us, and it didn't work in subsequent campaigns. Reagan has no harsh edge to him. Part of what happened is that we took him on as an actor, putting down one of the great industries of the state, but the roots of the mistake go deeper. Reagan is terribly pleasant, highly articulate, and has a serious approach about politics. People like him, and we didn't understand that. We missed the human dimension of Ronald Reagan."[14]

13

ADVERSARY

WHEN RONALD REAGAN quipped that he had "never played a governor," it confirmed the prevailing view in Sacramento that he was play-acting at politics and lacked the ability to govern the mega-state of California, which is 800 miles from corner to corner and in 1966 had a population of more than 19 million.[1]

Sacramento, at the confluence of the American and Sacramento rivers, is far from the population centers of Southern California and the San Francisco Bay Area. Situated in the heart of productive farmland, the city became an urban hub during the Gold Rush and was designated the state capital in 1854. Unlike many California cities, Sacramento remains connected to its past. For nearly a century, California's great Central Valley, with Sacramento as its northern anchor, was known as "Superior California," a usage *The Sacramento Bee* still clung to in 1966. To Californians from more temperate coastal climates, Sacramento weather was decidedly inferior—hot and muggy in summer, chilly and foggy in winter. But Sacramento is the political center of California and the only city in the state in which government is the principal industry. It is, on the whole, a competent government. The Progressives who controlled state government early in the twentieth century disdained the spoils system and instituted a professional bureaucracy chosen by civil service. The bureaucracy grew, as bureaucracies do. By the time of Reagan's election, Sacramento was home to a sizable permanent government on the federal model with considerable expertise and a capacity for resisting change.

This bureaucracy had allies in the California Legislature, which narrowly remained in Democratic hands after the Reagan-led Republican sweep of statewide offices in the 1966 election. Democratic control posed no obstacle to Reagan in the forty-member State Senate, which had a bipartisan tradition and a conservative Democratic leadership. It was another story in the eighty-member Assembly, which was led and often ruled by Jesse Marvin Unruh, its flamboyant speaker. Unruh had been such a thorn in Pat Brown's side that a Brown aide told me that the one solace in the governor's crushing defeat was that "the Unruh problem" was now Reagan's.

Unruh would have been a handful for any governor. Nicknamed "Big Daddy" for a supposed resemblance to the rotund and domineering father in the Tennessee Williams play *Cat on a Hot Tin Roof*, Unruh was a contradictory figure with gargantuan appetites for power, food, booze, and sex—especially power. He was alternately principled and devious, sophisticated and crude, thoughtful and impulsive, visionary and myopic. Unruh delighted in the exercise of raw power; his fellow (also powerful) Democrat in the State Senate, George Miller Jr., once called him "Little Nero." In a notable display of pettiness, Unruh refused to replace the broken typewriter of a secretary of a Republican legislator who had voted against him on a minor bill. But Unruh was also the leader of a national movement to improve the seedy image and second-class status of state legislators. Even his numerous enemies acknowledged that he had upgraded the quality of the California Legislature and equipped it with a capable professional staff.

Unruh was as self-taught as Reagan, with even humbler roots. The son of Texas sharecroppers with limited schooling, he had enlisted in the Navy during World War II and improved his language skills by reading self-help texts such as *Thirty Days to a Better Vocabulary*. After World War II, he attended the University of Southern California on the GI Bill of Rights, plunged into campus politics, and wrote for the *Daily Trojan*, then an excellent collegiate newspaper. As a dirt-poor liberal, he was attracted to left-wing causes and had a brief flirtation with the Communists, whom he respected for their organizational skills. "I used to say facetiously that the only reason I didn't join the Communist Party was because I couldn't afford the ten-cents-a-month dues," Unruh told me.[2] But Unruh was too much a political realist to become a Communist. Instead, he and a group of like-minded friends plunged into the chaotic world of Democratic politics just as the Democratic Party was becoming competitive statewide. In 1954, on his second try, Unruh won election to the Assembly.

Unruh, then thirty-three, arrived in Sacramento at a time when a bipartisan group of legislators who called themselves the "Good Government Group" was trying to wipe away the stain of lobbyist domination. Liquor lobbyist Artie Samish, the "secret boss" of California who had pulled legislative strings for nearly two decades, was in federal prison for income tax evasion, and a spirit of reform was in the air.[3] Even so, legislators had little status and less income. This was underscored soon after Unruh's arrival in Sacramento when a newly elected Republican assemblyman resigned to take over Samish's lobbying job with the malt-beverage industry.[4] He more than quadrupled his salary, for legislators made only $3,600 a year, while the lobbyist's job paid $15,000.

Unruh began as a purist who wouldn't let a lobbyist buy him a meal. But he was fascinated by the lobbyists, known in Sacramento as the Third House. Most legislators depended on the lobbyists for basic information about pending bills. While others in the Good Government Group decried the influence of the Third House, Unruh thought about harnessing it for his purposes. Suppose a legislator accepted lobbyist contributions and, instead of pocketing the money, used it to help other legislators? Even as a freshman assemblyman, Unruh was willing to experiment. He felt certain he could win reelection. When lobbyists offered contributions for his 1956 reelection campaign, Unruh suggested they give them to "good guys" in neighboring districts, with the proviso that the lobbyists give credit to Unruh. It was a radical departure from the prevailing practice in California, where legislators looked out for themselves.

Over time, this single creative idea and Unruh's organizational talents made him a dominant force in Sacramento. "Money is the mother's milk of politics," Unruh often said, and he understood how to use the funds he collected from the Third House. Unlike many legislators, Unruh had little interest in enriching himself. Money to him was a means to the end of building a loyal constituency that would help him gain legislative leadership and run for higher office. He did this in stages. In 1957, grateful Assembly members who had been helped by contributions directed by Unruh elected him chairman of the Finance and Insurance Committee, the key committee for business legislation. This post gave Unruh visibility within the business community and brought him to the attention of Howard Ahmanson, an art-loving tycoon who owned the largest savings-and-loan association in Los Angeles County. Unruh met Ahmanson during the performance of a routine political chore. Republican Governor Goodwin Knight asked Ahmanson, his chief bankroller, to revitalize the run-down Los Angeles Museum of Science and Industry. The museum was in Unruh's district, and he became the legislative troubleshooter for the project, in the process convincing Ahmanson that he was an able legislator. Ahmanson became, in his words, "a devoted, unabashed friend of Mr. Unruh."[5]

Unruh was large in size and poor. Ahmanson was diminutive and wealthy. But in ways that mattered more, the two men were quite alike.

Both had good heads for numbers, a swaggering style, and an approach to issues that combined self-interest with appreciation for the common good. Unruh, a bullying chairman who would gavel down hostile witnesses before they had a chance to testify, was progressive on civil rights and other social legislation. Ahmanson, tough and competitive, recognized that business could no longer adopt a "public-be-damned" attitude. In 1963, he told reporter Harry Farrell that "The Right Wing calls me a pink Republican. . . . One of them said I was too rich to be a Democrat and too liberal to be a Republican."[6] Ahmanson's pragmatism made him welcome in Sacramento during Democratic and Republican administrations alike; Unruh became his favorite political beneficiary.

Unruh's rise to power also received a boost from a liberal Democratic resurgence in the 1950s. The California business community realized that Republican control of the Legislature was threatened and feared that liberals with an antibusiness agenda would take over. Unruh, who was in debt, had sponsored legislation protecting the poor from usurious interest rates, but he was not reflexively antibusiness. The fact that many on the Left thought Unruh too willing to compromise with the class enemy made businessmen like him even more.

In 1957 and 1958, Unruh, with Ahmanson's assistance, perfected his system of raising contributions from the Third House. The donors included entrepreneurs Bart Lytton and Louis Warschaw, friends of Ahmanson, plus such big-business powers as Richfield Oil and Prudential Insurance. The money they donated rarely, if ever, passed through Unruh's hands, but lobbyists—and Unruh himself—reminded the candidates where the contributions came from. Robert Finch, the Nixon man on the Los Angeles County Republican Central Committee, appreciated Unruh's skills. "Jesse had a sharper sense of how dollars should be spent than anyone who has come along in a long time," Finch said. "He knew that a relatively small amount of money given to an incumbent or a new candidate at an early time was worth five times that much later on down the road. He could assess with a very sharp eye who had a chance to be elected and who was in trouble."[7]

By 1968, a decade later, Unruh-directed contributions for Assembly candidates would reach a high of $365,000. How much Unruh gave in 1958 is not known because state financial-reporting requirements were then minimal, but the amount was a small fraction of the 1968 figure, even if inflation is taken into account. Whatever the amount, the contributions were sufficient to earn Unruh the lifetime loyalty of up-and-coming Democrats who in 1958 won control of the Legislature. In 1959, when Pat Brown became governor, his colleagues chose Unruh chairman of the Assembly Ways and Means Committee, where he was soon the power behind the throne of Speaker Ralph Brown.

Unruh's increased authority paid dividends for his business backers. One barefaced example of Unruh's value to Ahmanson occurred when State Veterans Director Joseph Farber, a friend of Unruh's, and a Pat Brown appointee, awarded Ahmanson's National American Fire Insurance Company an exclusive five-year contract to write fire policies on all the homes in the state that were financed by Cal-Vet, a popular program for California veterans. The contract drew angry accusations of a political deal from the association of 238 small insurance companies that had previously shared the business, worth $7 million over the next decade. But the contract stuck. Unruh shrugged off the criticism. He appreciated that businessmen with money and influence had come to think of him as reliable. In return, he received tacit business support for such modest excursions into social legislation as the Unruh Civil Rights Act, a well-conceived antidiscrimination law.

By the time the Legislature convened for the 1959 session, Unruh had long since stopped worrying about being bought off by a lobbyist's lunch. His new theory about lobbyists was succinct: "If you can't eat their food, drink their booze, screw their women and then vote against them, you have no business being up here."[8] Sometimes Unruh did vote against them, but on many crucial matters he didn't. With Unruh leading the way, the Assembly leadership in 1959 rammed through a $245 million tax program but deleted a $23 million oil severance tax sought by Governor Brown. On this occasion, Unruh worked in tandem with Senator Miller, his erstwhile Democratic rival, who represented oil-rich Contra Costa County. The oil lobbyists in the initial months of the Brown administration recovered their contributions to Democrats many times over by rejection of this one measure. But when business paybacks did not intrude, Unruh took the lead in pushing through progressive legislation. In the 1959 session, the most productive of the Brown administration, the Legislature increased unemployment compensation, expanded state aid to education programs, passed a Fair Employment Practice Act, and abolished the dead-letter cross-filing law. "Jesse made his reputation on my program, and I made mine on the way he handled it," Governor Brown said in assessing his brief honeymoon with Unruh.[9]

In 1961, Unruh closed in on the speakership. He first arranged a graceful exit for Ralph Brown, a soft-spoken attorney who had authored California's pioneering open-meetings and open-records laws. Unruh authored a bill creating a new appellate court and, with Ralph Brown's help, persuaded the governor to sign it. Governor Brown then appointed his namesake to the new court. With this accomplished, Unruh and a legislative ally, Assemblyman Robert Crown, began counting votes. Unruh already had the support of the Democrats whom he had helped elect with lobbyist contributions; Crown gave him a cushion by drawing a handful of favorable districts for incumbent Republicans with the implicit understanding that they would support Unruh for speaker. The redistricting gave Unruh the best of both worlds; it was partisan enough to guarantee Democratic control of the Assembly but secured the districts of Republicans who would not oppose his rise to power. On September 20, 1961, his thirty-ninth birthday, Unruh was elected speaker.

The new speaker and the governor, egged on by their rivalrous staffs, were soon at odds. Brown looked upon Unruh as an upstart and resented his attempts to substitute his own proposals for the governor's legislative program. Unruh considered the governor a ditherer who was too often influenced by the last person to see him before he made a decision. This view of Brown had taken root with Unruh and the public in 1960 because of the governor's actions in the case of Caryl Chessman, a notorious Los Angeles rapist known as the "Red Light Bandit." Chessman had languished for twelve years on San Quentin's Death Row, where he had become a writer and inspired a campaign to grant him clemency that gained widespread attention, in part because Chessman was not a murderer. On the night before Chessman's scheduled execution in the gas chamber, Brown went home alone after agreeing with his clemency secretary, Cecil Poole, that he would not stop the execution. Brown's wife, Bernice, was away, representing California at the opening of the Winter Olympics in Squaw Valley. Their son, Jerry, who had recently left a Jesuit seminary and was then a twenty-one-year-old student at the University of California at Berkeley, called and asked him to spare Chessman's life. The governor agreed.[10]

This decision was not as impulsive as his son (or Unruh) believed. Pat Brown, alone among the state's prosecutors, had opposed the death penalty when he was district attorney of San Francisco and again when he was attorney general of California. He opposed the death penalty as a candidate for governor, although he promised he would carry out the law. During his eight years as the state's chief executive, Brown spared more condemned men than any other governor of California before or since. He didn't want Chessman executed, especially since he had not killed anyone. But the legal situation, as Brown understood it, was complicated. Chessman had been convicted of multiple felonies; under state law at the time only the California Supreme Court could commute his sentence, which the court had declined to do. Brown could have granted Chessman an indefinite stay of execution, but he didn't want to be seen as thumbing his nose at the law. So in response to his son's telephone call, Brown agreed to ask the Legislature, where bills to abolish the death penalty were usually buried in committee, to consider the issue. He granted Chessman a reprieve pending the outcome of legislative action.

Unruh in 1959 had gone along with Brown's effort to abolish the death penalty and supported an Assembly bill that died in committee. But he was enraged by Brown's decision to spare Chessman.[11] The governor was not on the ballot in 1960, but elections would be held in all eighty Assembly districts, and Unruh knew that marginal Democrats would be put on the spot on the death penalty issue. In deference to Unruh's feelings, Brown did not ask for another Assembly test on the measure but saw to it that the bill proposing to abolish the death penalty was introduced in the State Senate. There, after a prolonged and emotional debate, it was rejected in committee on an 8–7 vote. The Senate was usually more conservative than the Assembly; the only surprise was that the vote was closer than it had ever been on the death penalty issue in California. Since then, no other death penalty repeal bill in California has come this close to passage.

Brown refused to grant another reprieve to Chessman, who after additional legal maneuvering was executed on May 2, 1960. During these last months of Chessman's life, the governor was booed repeatedly at public events for granting the reprieve; after the execution, liberals assailed him for not stopping it. All sides looked upon Brown as a waffler—it was the Chessman affair that prompted Unruh's previously cited description of Brown as a "tower of Jell-O." This was unkind and—in this case—untrue. Brown was certainly indecisive on many issues, but he seems to have acted in the Chessman affair out of moral conviction. He wanted to spare Chessman, but he took seriously his oath to uphold the laws of the state, including the death penalty. Brown may have deceived himself about the possibility that the Legislature would abolish capital punishment, but the closeness of the vote suggests he was not as far off the mark as Unruh believed.

Relations between Unruh and Brown were frigid from the Chessman execution until 1962, when the Democrats faced the common enemy of Richard Nixon. At a time when polls showed Brown and Nixon locked in a tight race for the governorship, Brown swallowed his pride, invited Unruh to the executive mansion in Sacramento, and asked for help. The speaker, the Southern California chairman of the campaign, said he would go all-out for Brown and did. With Unruh's assistance, the Democrats presented a united front that turned back Nixon and maintained control of the Legislature. In return, Unruh wanted a clear path to the Democratic gubernatorial nomination in 1966, and he believed that Brown had promised him at their meeting that he would not seek a third term. Assemblyman Crown, who accompanied Unruh to the mansion, also remembered it this way. Brown did not.* When it later became clear that Brown intended to run again, open political warfare broke out between the governor and the speaker. In the 1966 campaign, Unruh ignored Brown and devoted his resources to preserving the Democratic majority in the Assembly, a feat he barely accomplished. After the election, the Democratic majority was down to four votes.

By the time Reagan arrived on the scene, Unruh was no longer the "Big Daddy" of popular lore. He had suffered a humiliating political defeat in 1963 when he locked up recalcitrant Republicans in the Assembly for several days in an effort to force them to accept a budget bill. The "Lockup," as it became known, backfired. Republicans refused to capitulate and won the propaganda battle in the press; State Republican Chairman Caspar Weinberger hyperbolically accused Unruh of using tactics favored by Hitler and Stalin. Unruh had been drinking and in a rage when he ordered the Lockup; he acknowledged afterward that he had used poor judgment. His response to the criticisms that were heaped upon him was personal and dramatic. Unruh gave up drinking and cigars and went on a four-month diet in which he ate one meal every other day and lost 80 pounds.[13] Although his discipline was impressive, and his figure trim for the first time in his life, Unruh remained insecure. He told a friend that he sometimes dreamed he was a penniless boy back on the farm in Texas. When I interviewed Unruh for my first book in 1968, he insisted on holding the microphone of my primitive tape recorder so he could switch it off if he didn't like the question. While he never stopped the tape, he confided to me in a subsequent interview that it gave him a feeling of control to have that option.

Unruh had no fear of Reagan. He did not share Brown's bias against actors, but he thought that Reagan's lack of governmental experience would be insurmountable. Unruh welcomed the notion of matching wits with a Republican governor. Whenever he had proposed meritorious alternatives to Brown's proposals, Unruh had been labeled an obstructionist. Now, facing a Republican governor, Unruh had the chance

---

*The meeting at which this conversation took place occurred in early October 1962. Unruh and Crown told friends after the meeting that Brown had promised not to run in 1966. Crown told me in 1968 that the governor had made an "absolute commitment" not to seek a third term. Brown denied this but acknowledged to me that he might have encouraged Unruh by saying he would be "helpful" to his ambitions for higher office.[12]

to demonstrate that he was an effective partisan leader. If all went well, he would become the logical Democratic candidate for governor.

Reagan knew that Unruh would be a formidable adversary. What Reagan didn't understand was that he also faced intense skepticism from the Republican minority in the Assembly. The Republican leader in the Assembly was Robert Monagan, a sturdy ex-Marine who was popular with his fellow legislators and the press. Monagan had toyed with running for governor but realized he lacked the financial resources and the name recognition to succeed and backed George Christopher instead. So had all the other Republicans in the Assembly upon whom Monagan depended for advice or counsel. Despite the national resurgence of Republican conservatives in 1966, the leading GOP legislators in the Assembly were moderates or liberals in the Earl Warren mold who believed that government had social responsibilities. This was true even of conservative Republicans. Assemblyman Frank Lanterman, one of the few legislators with a favorable view of Reagan, would soon sponsor a pioneering measure providing community clinics for the mentally ill. Assemblyman John Veneman, a moderate Republican who was close to Unruh, had played a leading role in seeing that California was one of the first states to provide medical care for the poor under the new federal Medicare law. Monagan, in one of his first statements after Reagan became governor, opposed Reagan's promised repeal of the Rumford Fair Housing Act. As a group, these Republicans were able, resolute, and generally progressive. They were not about to roll over for Ronald Reagan, whom few of them had even met.

The fact that Reagan knew so few legislators was an even bigger problem for him than differences in political philosophy. The assemblyman whom Reagan knew best was Charles Conrad, who had tutored him at the behest of Spencer-Roberts, but Conrad was on the outs with the GOP leadership. On the Senate side, Reagan was well acquainted only with George Deukmejian, a freshman from Long Beach who had moved up from the Assembly. Bill Roberts, a friend of Deukmejian's, had brought Reagan to Long Beach to meet him during the campaign. Deukmejian, whose own election was never in doubt, had traveled with Reagan during the campaign and given him political pointers. Reagan appreciated this and would rely on Deukmejian in the months to come. Otherwise, Reagan had few friends in the Legislature and no legislative program beyond a vague promise to "squeeze, cut, and trim" the cost of government.

When Reagan said he had never played a governor, he was making a joke. He had no idea that being governor would be an extraordinarily demanding role.

14

NOVICE

Ronald Reagan became the thirty-third governor of California at fourteen minutes after midnight on January 2, 1967, in an inspirational ceremony conducted on a television platform that shone brightly amidst the semi-darkness of the State Capitol rotunda. Reagan tensed as the University of Southern California chamber singers massed above him in the rotunda balcony sang "America the Beautiful." But he recovered his showman's touch as he stepped forward in a dark business suit to take the oath of office on a 400-year-old Bible brought to California by one of its first immigrants, Father Junipero Serra. After he was sworn in, Reagan turned to Senator George Murphy and said, "Well, George, here we are on the late show again."

This quip was the opening line of a four-minute speech that Reagan wrote, as he later put it, "all by my lonesome." He took note of the unusual timing of the ceremony—"I don't know what the stars prescribed, but we had our reasons for doing it at this hour"—then thanked State Supreme Court Justice Marshall McComb for administering the oath and Senator Murphy for his friendship. To Methodist minister Wilbur Choy, who participated in the ceremony, he said, "Reverend, perhaps you weren't a part of my imagining what this moment would be, but I am deeply grateful for your presence because you remind us, and bring here, the presence of someone else, without whose presence I certainly wouldn't have the nerve to do what I am going to try to do."

"Someone back in our history," Reagan continued, "I think it was Benjamin Franklin, said, 'If ever someone could take public office and bring to public office the teachings and the precepts of the Prince of Peace, he would revolutionize the world and men would be remembering him for a thousand years.' I don't think anyone could ever take office and be so presumptuous to believe he could do that or that he could follow those precepts completely. I can tell you this, I'll try very hard. I think it is needed in today's world."

Because of its timing, this personal and religious speech with which Reagan began his governorship received little news coverage except for the wisecrack about being on the late show with Murphy. No California governor had ever been inaugurated in the dead of night (nor have any since), and most stories of the event that appeared in morning newspapers had, of necessity, been written well in advance and without the benefit of a text of Reagan's speech. There was no round-the-clock television news in those days. Portions of the ceremony were shown on television on January 2, but when morning newspapers picked up the story on January 3 the midnight inaugural was old news. That day's stories focused on upcoming events, including an inaugural concert with Marilyn Horne and "comedian-violinist" Jack Benny and a traditional ceremony on January 5, where Reagan spoke in broad daylight from the west steps of the State Capitol. This more extensive speech was officially designated as Reagan's inaugural message.

The State Capitol press corps, of which I was a member, and legislators of both parties found the two inaugurals confusing. One inauguration had been sufficient for previous governors, a legislator said to me. Why did Reagan need two? I didn't know the answer. Reagan's aides were short on explanations and acted as if a midnight swearing-in was perfectly normal. Encouraged by Reagan's reference to "what the stars prescribed," many of us accepted the widespread rumors that the midnight swearing-in had been astrologically dictated. Two decades later, the ejected White House chief of staff Donald Regan would generate an embarrassing controversy by revealing that Nancy Reagan relied on an astrologist to guide her husband's public schedule. But in 1967 it was no secret that the Reagans often began their day by reading the astrology column written by a Hollywood friend, Carroll Righter. Reagan had taken note of this in his autobiography without creating a stir.[1]

The real reason for the timing of the midnight ceremony was not astrological but political. After the election, Governor Pat Brown focused on finding judgeships and other government jobs for friends, aides, retiring legislators, and party loyalists. Other defeated governors had rewarded their cronies, but Brown's largesse was more stunning than that of any of his predecessors. He appointed or promoted some eighty judges and raised eyebrows even among Democratic jurists when he elevated his brother, who was not highly regarded by his peers, from a lower court to the appellate bench. These actions tarnished Brown's reputation, for most of his preelection judicial appointments had been well qualified, but there was nothing Reagan could do about it. When it seemed in December as if Brown might continue making appointments until the moment Reagan was sworn in, Reagan's chief of staff, Phil Battaglia, came up with the idea of the midnight ceremony to choke off any last-minute appointments. Brown completed most of his appointments gift list soon after Christmas, but he appointed his son, Jerry, to the State Narcotics Board as late as January 1. Long before then, the midnight ceremony was fixed on the schedule, and Battaglia did not want to change it.

Reagan, as was his custom, played no role in this maneuvering. When it came to his public schedule, as governor and president, Reagan was Hollywood's child. He would memorize a script, show up on time, and follow the instructions of the director without fuss. Although he was often criticized for overdependence on his schedulers, Reagan wisely did not worry about such trivia. He did not work hard unless he needed to, but he was disciplined and sensible in the way he used his time.

Instead of fretting over scheduling details, Reagan focused on communicating the ideas that had propelled him into politics, and he lavished attention on the inaugural message he delivered from the State Capitol steps. A key passage of this speech, though secular in content, had religious guidance, albeit from a more obscure source than the inspiration provided by the Prince of Peace. W. S. McBirnie was a right-wing radio evangelist whose weekly program, "Voice of Americanism," was heard on small stations throughout California. In 1965, McBirnie sought out Reagan and pledged his support. Bill Roberts, neither conservative nor religious, realized that McBirnie had a following and invited him to Reagan's home when the gubernatorial campaign was still in the discussion stage. When the talk turned to a label for Reagan's message of more individual freedom and less government, McBirnie suggested that Reagan call his plan "the Creative Society."[2]

By the time of Reagan's inaugural, McBirnie was long gone. In his pragmatic way, and with Roberts' encouragement, Reagan distanced himself from the evangelist during the campaign after Pat Brown tried to link McBirnie to the John Birch Society. But McBirnie's slogan had taken root. This was how Reagan expressed it to a throng of some 10,000 persons gathered at the west front of the State Capitol on an uncommonly warm winter's day in Sacramento: "The path we will chart is not an easy one. It demands much of those chosen to govern, but also from those who did the choosing. And let there be no mistake about this: We have come to a crossroad—a time of decision—and the path we follow turns away from any idea that government and those who serve it are omnipotent. It is a path impossible to follow unless we have faith in the collective wisdom and genius of the people. Along this path government will lead but not rule, listen but not lecture. It is the path of a Creative Society."

As was often the case, Reagan's speech was long on generalities and short on specifics. But the direction was clear. Reagan proposed local property-tax relief and reductions in state spending. In words that fore-shadowed President Bill Clinton by three decades, he also promised to reform a welfare system he said was destructive of "self-reliance, dignity and self respect . . . the very substance of moral fiber." The state would help the aged, the disabled, and "those unfortunates who, through no fault of their own, must depend upon their fellow men. But we are not going to perpetuate poverty by substituting a permanent dole for a pay-check."

Then came the red meat. Reagan received loud applause when he de-clared that students at public universities would be required to observe "reasonable rules and regulations" and that those unwilling to do so "should get their education elsewhere." In words directed to the profes-sors of these students, Reagan said, "It does not constitute political in-terference with intellectual freedom for the taxpaying citizens—who support the college and university systems—to ask that, in addition to teaching, they build character on accepted moral and ethical stan-dards." More loud applause. Reagan had thrown down the gauntlet to Berkeley.

The preparation of this inaugural message was a collaborative effort between Reagan and Lyn Nofziger, who during the campaign had de-veloped into a capable speechwriter. Nofziger preferred short and catchy phrases that could be captured in a headline. Since he followed old-fashioned rules for political speechwriting and gave Reagan the credit for anything he said, the authorship of particular phrases is not always evident. The lines, such as the following, that can clearly be identified as Reagan's were paraphrases of "The Speech" he had been giving since his General Electric days: "For many years now, you and I have been shushed like children and told there are no simple answers to the complex problems which are beyond our comprehension. Well, the truth is, there are simple answers—there just are not easy ones."

This faith in "simple answers" was fundamental to Reagan's political thinking. He clung to it throughout his governorship and well into his presidency. Opponents mocked this assertion—Assemblyman Charles Warren, the Democratic state chairman, called it "baby talk"—but Rea-gan meant it. He was making a valid, if overstated, point that politicians often knew what needed to be done but shrunk from unpopular actions. What was needed in California, Reagan said, was to cut government spending. "We are going to squeeze and cut and trim until we reduce the cost of government," Reagan said in the best-remembered line of his inaugural message. "It won't be easy, nor will it be pleasant, and it will involve every department of government, starting with the governor's office." Reagan's call for spending cuts won praise from Republicans, and from Hugh Burns of Fresno, the conservative Democrat who led his party in the State Senate. Liberals denounced it, but Assembly Speaker Jesse Unruh, the Democrat who mattered most, held his fire. Unruh, not knowing quite what to make of Reagan, decided to play a waiting game. He called the speech "forward looking" and, with only a mild touch of sarcasm, promised the Legislature's "cooperation, understanding, suggestions and prayers."[3]

Reagan was in need of all such help. He gave good speeches, but he had trouble getting his government off the ground or finding others to help him do it. Bill Roberts, brilliant as a political strategist, was uninterested in government and told Reagan as much when he was asked to join the administration. So did his partner, Stu Spencer. Cy Rubel, the titular head of the Friends of Ronald Reagan, was terminally ill.[4] Holmes Tuttle, the most influential of the Friends, took a willing hand in the transition but was as devoid as Reagan of governmental experience. The Reagan governorship, as Nofziger put it, had "materialized out of thin air" without a political machine. "His campaign was run by hired people who then walked away and left it," Nofziger said. "Therefore, when he was elected, the big question was, 'My God, what do we do now?' And really, we were so busy running that though we recognized a month beforehand that we should begin to start doing some things and Phil Battaglia tried in the last two or three weeks of the campaign to line up office space, no one really sat down until after the election and said, 'Where do we get our hired help? What do we do?' We were so innocent that we tried to run government from Los Angeles during the interim and discovered that we couldn't."[5]

This discovery was particularly difficult for Reagan, by choice and inclination a Southern Californian. Although he would become comfortable in the governor's first-floor corner office in the golden-domed State Capitol, he remained a perpetual visitor in Sacramento. Home to Reagan, and even more his wife, was Pacific Palisades, 400 miles away, where the Reagans returned on most weekends and other interludes throughout his governorship. In the seven weeks between the election and the inaugural, Reagan lived at home and worked out of a rented cottage on the grounds of the Ambassador Hotel on Wilshire Boulevard in Los Angeles. This was conveniently close to Tuttle and the other Friends of Ronald Reagan, soon to be known as the Kitchen Cabinet, but an impractical location for dealing with the myriad problems of the transition. Battaglia recognized this. Shortly before the election, he rented office space for the government-in-waiting at 400 Capitol Mall, a short walk from the capitol.

The task of organizing the new administration fell heavily on Battaglia and Thomas Reed, the bright young men of the Reagan team. They had help from Nofziger and guidance, some of it unwanted, from Tuttle and Reagan's other wealthy contributors. Reagan had often talked about the value of business expertise, and he embraced a plan put forward by Battaglia and Tuttle of forming "select" committees of business advisers who would winnow down the long list of applicants to find the best people for the top jobs in state government.

Battaglia was a man in a hurry. He had been admitted to the University of Southern California law school at the age of twenty after only two years of undergraduate work and obtained his law degree at USC while also serving as student body president, editor of the Trojan Bar quarterly, and director of the USC Law Alumni Association. To help pay his way through law school, he worked as a law clerk for the Los Angeles firm of Flint & MacKay. He joined the firm upon graduation and four years later became a partner in the firm. Tuttle, who had scouted around for a Southern California campaign chairman with a top-flight resume and no baggage from past Republican factionalism, brought him aboard. Although Battaglia knew little about politics and even less about policy, he impressed Tuttle and Roberts with his organizational ability. In the general election, he became Reagan's state chairman, to the disappointment of Reed, who wanted the post but was instead designated northern California chairman. Battaglia showed quiet deference to Reagan, who called him "my strong right arm." But Reed would have the greater impact on the governor's appointments.

Reed was an intelligent free spirit with a flair for politics. Although he called himself a conservative Republican, he was libertarian in his social attitudes, skeptical about the Vietnam War, and moderate on environmental issues. Reed, who had become wealthy in land development, had graduated first in his mechanical engineering class at Cornell University in 1955 and received his master's degree in electrical engineering at the University of Southern California. After service in the U.S. Air Force, he helped design nuclear weapons at the University of California's Lawrence Radiation Laboratory. He became involved in the Goldwater presidential campaign, from which he emerged with an obsessive distrust of Lyndon Johnson. Reed believed that Johnson had smeared Goldwater as a warmonger while planning to plunge the United States deeply into the Vietnam War. When he joined the Reagan campaign, Reed was already looking forward to 1968, when he envisioned Reagan as the Republican presidential nominee. Although state service held no attraction for Reed, he realized that Reagan needed good appointees and a fast start as governor to be taken seriously as a presidential candidate. So Reed volunteered to serve as appointments secretary for the first 100 days of the administration.

Reagan did himself a favor by accepting Reed's offer. When Reed was named appointments secretary in mid-December, the transition had bogged down. None of the top twenty state jobs had been filled, and the select committees of businessmen had found few top prospects. Even on the few occasions when they did, the prospects were reluctant to give up lucrative business posts to serve their government. Tuttle talked some of the recalcitrants into serving—"I told 'em, you complain about government all the time, now here's your chance to do something about it"—but he had a problem in matching prospects to available jobs.[6] Reed did most of the matching. He shared Tuttle's and Reagan's preference for successful businessmen but was less inclined to equate business ability with professional competence. Reed believed in political patronage but only for qualified applicants, and he was wary of appointing people who might be tempted by the power and perquisites of office. "We wanted guys who couldn't be bought for lunch," Reed said.[7] The word "guys" is instructive, for there were no women among the highest rung of appointees and only a sprinkling of women in the next level. But racial and ethnic minorities fared better than in any previous Republican administration, including Earl Warren's. Nineteen of the top 100 jobs went to minority applicants. James Johnson, the director of veterans affairs, was the first black to head a California state department.

Reed's greatest triumph came where least expected. Environmentalists shuddered at the election of Reagan, who, while discussing the state's magnificent redwoods during the campaign, had said, "A tree is a tree—how many more do you need to look at?"* But Reed found Reagan an outstanding resources administrator in the person of Norman ("Ike") Livermore, a progressive lumberman who belonged to the Sierra Club. This choice unsettled lumber executives, who were bat-

---

*This remark has been widely misquoted. Speaking to the Western Wood Products Association in San Francisco on March 12, 1966, Reagan said, "I think, too, that we've got to recognize that where the preservation of a natural resource like the redwoods is concerned, that there is a common sense limit. I mean, if you've looked at a hundred thousand acres or so of trees—you know, a tree is a tree, how many more do you need to look at?" A campaign aide to Governor Pat Brown summarized the quotation as, "If you've seen one redwood, you've seen them all." This version was picked up in the press and widely circulated, giving Reagan an opportunity to say he was misquoted even though his actual words were arguably as damaging.

tling a proposed Redwood National Park on the north coast of California, but Reed blandly observed that Livermore had a business background and "sweat equity" because he had chaired the Marin County campaign of a conservative Republican congressman.[8] This irrelevant argument prevailed, and Reagan appointed Livermore, who was committed to preserving California's dwindling wild rivers and other vanishing resources.

Livermore's agency included the State Parks and Recreation Department. As its director, Reed selected William Penn Mott Jr., an empire-building bureaucrat dedicated to creating open space in crowded urban areas. Mott, a conservative conservationist, had won national acclaim in his field by overcoming the resistance of a powerful utility district to expand a unique regional park in Alameda and Contra Costa counties across the bay from San Francisco. Together, Livermore and Mott gave the Reagan administration a conservationist stance that neither friend nor foe had anticipated.

Reed and his deputy, Paul Haerle, a Marin County attorney, recruited bright young attorneys and corporate executives to head key agencies or departments dealing with transportation, savings-and-loan companies, corporations, banks, and licensing standards. Almost all of them were competent, pro-business, and young. The average age of the top 100 appointments was only forty, which seemed old enough to Reed, who was thirty-three. Consumer advocates complained that some of the new appointees had close ties to the industries they were supposed to regulate. Reed acknowledged as much. "There's a very thin line between a guy being a vested interest and a guy being knowledgeable," he told me. "The way to get a guy who isn't a vested interest is to get someone who doesn't know what he's regulating."[9]

All in all, Reed's performance as appointments secretary received high marks, even from Democrats. Reed's self-imposed deadline of 100 days in office had pushed him to make appointments rapidly and allowed him to "play the bad cop" in resisting unqualified applicants put forward by party stalwarts and Reagan's friends.[10] The brevity of Reed's state service also inhibited the development of rivalries with Battaglia and others in the inner circle. Battaglia, not usually a power-sharer, was cooperative, knowing that Reed would soon be gone. On April 1, 1967, as promised, Reed resigned and went off to promote a Reagan presidential candidacy. Haerle took over as appointments secretary.

Long before then, Reagan had in place an inner cabinet of "executive directors" intended to serve as the board of directors of his administration. Originally, this cabinet included six people: Battaglia, Nofziger, Cabinet Secretary William P. Clark, and three administrators who ran

multitudinous departments that were later grouped into four agencies.*
The administrators were Livermore, Gordon Luce for business and
transportation, and Spencer Williams for "human resources," a diverse
grouping of departments that included welfare, state hospitals, and prisons. Later, a fourth agency—agriculture and services—was added. It
was headed by Earl Coke, a former vice president of the Bank of America in charge of agricultural activities and a onetime assistant secretary
of agriculture in the Eisenhower administration. At sixty-six, Coke was
older and had more government experience than anyone else on the
Reagan team. Luce, forty-one, was a savings-and-loan executive who
had become the Reagan point man in San Diego after impressing Tuttle
and Stu Spencer in an early campaign interview that Luce likened to a
"Hollywood casting call."[11] Luce was genial and efficient. Williams,
forty-four, was from San Jose, where he had been Santa Clara County
counsel before becoming the Republican nominee for attorney general.
He was the Republican Party's only statewide loser in the 1966 election.
Reagan felt obligated to find a position for him, and Williams became
the only executive director whose hiring was instigated by the governor.
Williams rounded out an inner cabinet of six business-oriented family
men. All were Republicans and all had college degrees, three of them
from Stanford University.

Overall, this was an impressive team for a novice governor, but Reagan and his principal advisers malfunctioned on the job that mattered
most. In California, the state finance director is second in importance
only to the governor. He has responsibility for preparing a state budget,
which in 1966 was larger than the budgets of all but six nations in the
world, and for defending it before the Legislature. The appointment
was especially critical for Reagan because Governor Brown and his finance director, Hale Champion, had avoided an election-year tax increase in 1966 by changing the state's accounting system so that they
could use anticipated revenues to balance the books. When Champion
was asked after the election what he would have done if Brown had been
reelected, he replied, "Raise taxes."[12] In his inaugural message, Reagan
described Champion's scheme as "a gimmick that solved nothing but
only postponed the day of reckoning." As Reagan accurately noted, the

*This grouping was incorporated into a government reorganization plan later passed by the
Legislature and ballyhooed by Reagan as a "streamlining" of government. But no one waited
for the Legislature—the plan was in operation from the first week of the Reagan governorship, although there were several changes in nomenclature. The reorganization plan originally was called an "interim communications system." After toying with various titles for the
agency heads, including "deputy governors" and "executive secretaries," the administration
settled on "secretaries." For simplicity's sake, I've used the most descriptive nomenclature of
"executive directors" throughout this book.

state was financing a year's spending with fifteen months of income.
The inherited deficit was then estimated at $400 million, and Reagan
was mandated by the state constitution to balance the budget by June
30, the end of the fiscal year. Finding a finance director should have
been Reagan's postelection priority, but he dawdled on the one appointment he could not afford to delay.

Part of the delay arose from Reagan's misconception that the brightest lights in the business community were ready to drop whatever they
were doing to serve their state. Reagan had talked, before and after the
election, of attracting a finance director from "some of the big names in
business—men who make $100,000 a year." No big names volunteered,
and Reagan's first choice for the finance directorship was not a businessman but Legislative Analyst A. Alan Post, whose annual salary was
$31,835. He was the right choice. Gentle and unassuming with an ana-
lytical mind, Post was held in near-universal reverence in Sacramento.
He had transformed the obscure legislative analyst's office into an effective, nonpartisan agency that analyzed the financial impact of legislation
without favoritism. This made him a thorn in the side of governors and
sometimes a problem for Unruh, as well. Post didn't care. He had been
scathingly critical of Pat Brown's unfounded accounting changeover,
pointing out that it would produce a serious revenue shortfall in 1967.
But Post, a moderate in his political views, was uncomfortable when
Reagan said during the campaign that he would appoint him as the next
finance director. "I didn't want to be part of anyone's campaign," Post
told me years later.[13] He also valued the Legislature and did not want to
leave it. When Reagan offered the finance directorship to Post, the legislative analyst thanked him but politely rejected the offer.

Reagan's second choice was another government man, Richard
Krabach, the Ohio state finance director. He, too, declined. Another
possibility, aerospace executive Dudley Browne of Lockheed, was
sounded out but showed no interest. By now, the Kitchen Cabinet was
involved in the search. Tuttle and Henry Salvatori, secure in the conviction that business ability was the true barometer of success in government, put forward the candidacy of one of their own, investment banker
Leland Kaiser. This set off alarm bells in Sacramento, where neither
Battaglia nor Nofziger thought Kaiser was the right man for the job.

Battaglia and Nofziger, supported by Reed, had an alternative. He
was Caspar W. Weinberger, who had come to their attention through
Bill Clark, the rancher-attorney who was Reagan's cabinet secretary.
Weinberger, a San Francisco attorney, had a distinguished resume in
government and private life and was well informed on state financial issues. As a state legislator in the 1950s, working with information sup-

plied in part by Alan Post, Weinberger had investigated corrupt liquor lobbyist Artie Samish and helped reform the state beverage control system. He had chaired the state Republican Party, written a newspaper column, and served as host of a public affairs discussion program on the educational television station KQED. During the Reagan transition, Weinberger chaired a task force that came up with the proposals implemented by Clark in organizing the governor's inner cabinet.

But Weinberger's credentials could not erase his black mark with conservatives: He had backed Nelson Rockefeller against Goldwater in the 1964 presidential primary. This made him a "traitor," to use Reagan's word for Rockefeller supporters who deserted the party after Goldwater's nomination. Weinberger, in fact, had swallowed his doubts about Goldwater and remained loyal to the Republican Party, but he nonetheless remained anathema to the Kitchen Cabinet. Weinberger never fully understood why he was in disfavor; he believed it was because Southern California "ultraconservatives" considered him a "liberal Republican."[14] But their opposition had little to do with Weinberger's supposed liberalism and everything to do with whom he had supported in 1964. Tuttle would have embraced Alan Post, whose opinions were to the left of Weinberger on most issues. But he would not accept a Rockefeller man. Battaglia, Nofziger, and Clark could not overcome the Kitchen Cabinet's resistance, and Reed did not even try. In its most blatant and ill-chosen exercise of power during the transition, the Kitchen Cabinet vetoed Weinberger. All Clark could salvage was the consolation prize of having Reagan appoint Weinberger chairman of the part-time Commission on California State Government and Economy, better known as the Little Hoover Commission. This kept Weinberger waiting in the wings.

With a month to go before the state budget was due at the printer's office, Reagan was now desperate for a state finance director. Post, Krabach, and Browne had turned down the job. The Sacramentans had blocked Kaiser. The Kitchen Cabinet had stopped Weinberger. The impasse opened the door for management consultant Gordon Paul Smith, who was five feet, five inches tall but made up for his lack of height with a rapid-fire verbal delivery, a retentive memory for facts and figures, and a consultant's desire to please. The previous year, he had appeared before the Little Hoover Commission on behalf of the consulting firm Booz, Allen and Hamilton, of which he was vice president, to offer a proposal for a study of state manpower. Smith was determined to win the competitive contract. While other consultants offered restrained presentations about the abilities of their firms, Smith had waxed lyrical over Booz, Allen and Hamilton's extensive capabilities.

This salesmanship irritated Commission Chairman Harold Furst, a banker with a droll sense of humor. With a straight face, he asked Smith whether his study would also provide information on "subversives" in state government. Smith promptly answered that he was confident he could obtain that information. Furst and other commissioners, hard put to keep from laughing in Smith's face, decided then and there against hiring his firm.[15]

This quality of wanting to please his listeners would make Smith the delight of the capitol press corps and the bane of the public relations–conscious Battaglia and Nofziger. Ultimately, it would cost Smith his job. But in that cold late autumn of his election triumph, Reagan was impressed by Smith and desperate for a finance director. On December 16, he appointed Smith, who took a two-thirds cut in salary to become finance director at $31,835 a year.

Smith knew little about the state budget and even less about the legal authority of his new job. He shunned Champion during the transition, even though the outgoing finance director was cooperative with the new administration, and he was unaware of the California constitutional provision that the Department of Finance is the property of the governor-elect. He had no allies on the Reagan team in Sacramento, and his bubbly enthusiasm rubbed some of them the wrong way and suggested to officials in the Finance Department that he didn't understand the magnitude of the fiscal problem facing the state. Edwin Beach, one of two professional deputy directors in the department, tried to be helpful but thought that Smith was "out of his league."[16]

By waiting until Reagan became governor, Smith gave himself too little time in which to prepare a 1,005-page budget. That budget, a then-record $4.6 billion, was unveiled by Reagan on January 31, 1967, without the usual detail found in such documents. For most departments, the budget was the allocation from the previous year adjusted for growth with a notation of "less 10 per cent reduction." It was based on the premise that all state departments and agencies could absorb a 10 percent across-the-board reduction without cuts in services or losses in efficiency. Legislators of both parties derided this plan, which would have penalized departments that operated frugally and rewarded those with padded payrolls. Legislative analyst Post, who had during the Pat Brown years called for significant budget reductions, found himself urging budget increases. Post said that the "flat and undetailed 10 per-cent reductions" provided no guidelines for genuine economies. Smith was the fall guy for this dubious budget, but the idea for the across-the-board cut was Reagan's. He had proposed it at a private meeting organized by Holmes Tuttle during the early days of his exploratory candidacy.[17] It was one of those "simple but not easy" answers Reagan touted in his inaugural message. In this case, it was not an answer at all.

This budget never had a chance of legislative enactment, although Reagan and Smith later insisted that it had encouraged department heads to economize. This claim is doubtful. The criticisms from *Post* and prominent legislators of both parties encouraged bureaucrats to wait out the new governor in hopes the budget would be withdrawn, as it was two months later. Still, Reagan's address to a joint session of the Legislature in which he unveiled the original budget displayed hints of his latent political skills. He complained in this speech that the state treasury had been "looted and drained" and proposed new taxes by April 1 to balance the budget, most of them on liquor, tobacco, and other luxuries. Some Democrats took umbrage at the "looted-and-drained" comment, and Senate Democratic leader Hugh Burns, who was well disposed toward Reagan, said the April 1 deadline was "totally unrealistic," as it proved to be.[18] But almost no Democrat mentioned that Reagan had broken a campaign promise when he proposed to increase taxes. The sleight-of-hand accounting changeover put into place by Brown and Champion had made tax increases necessary and spared Reagan from the charge that he was going back on his word.

Later, with the cover provided by the inherited deficit, Reagan would push his advantage on the tax issue. But in the early months of his governorship, he was still too green to exploit it. Instead, Reagan and his team relied on one-time or cosmetic economies. For these, the governor patted himself on the back in a report giving "an accounting of his stewardship" after 100 days in office:

"We have sold the expensive-to-operate state airplane, the Grizzly, at a savings of more than $200,000 a year.

"We have reduced the number of state employees, largely by not replacing those who quit or retire.

"We have cut out-of-state travel to a minimum.

"We have frozen the purchase of state automobiles.

"We have asked every department to examine its procedures with the hope of reducing expenditures as much as 10 per cent."

Some of these economies were illusory (the automobile freeze contributed to higher maintenance costs), and some, such as the employee reduction, were only temporary. Others, among them a Battaglia brainstorm that state employees work voluntarily on Lincoln's and Washington's birthdays, backfired completely. Less than 2 percent of the state workforce showed up on either holiday, and some high-ranking civil servants who often used days off to get caught up at the office stayed home in protest against the implication that government employees were somehow less productive than other people. Other, more significant, economies also worked in reverse. Departments were unable to hire essential personnel and purchase needed material, a restriction that Lester Halcomb, executive director of the Little Hoover Commission, said was counterproductive. The Department of Public Works had purchased the cabs to forty trucks, but the purchasing freeze prohibited the department from buying the rest of the vehicles. In an examination of the transition, scholar F. Alex Crowley called such practices "ludicrous diseconomies."[19]

The evaluation was accurate, but symbolic victories were needed by Reagan, who had campaigned on a pledge to reduce government growth. "The symbol on our flag is a Golden Bear; it is not a cow to be milked," Reagan declared at the end of his 100-days report. With a political intuitiveness that would have done credit to Jesse Unruh, Reagan was laying the foundation for an immense tax increase. The economies, real and imagined, were preconditions for the acceptance of this tax increase by the Legislature and the people.

Viewed in historical hindsight, Reagan's delay in appointing a finance director, the budget stumbles, and his hyperbole about his cost-cutting achievements were part of a learning experience that might reasonably have been expected. Reagan was, after all, devoid of background in government, and his senior staff was also engaged in on-the-job training. "We were not only amateurs, we were novice amateurs," Nofziger said with his usual bluntness.[20]

That was the way the Reagan governorship began.

15

PRAGMATIST

R ONALD REAGAN WAS determined to succeed as governor. His aspi-
rations were to give California a new sense of direction, which
he did, and to limit the growth of state government, objectives
that anticipated the domestic goals of his presidency. He did not realize
that his second objective bordered on the unattainable. Because he had
lacked any background in government, Reagan did not know that much
of the state budget was predetermined by state laws, federal formulas
regarding matching funds, and voter-approved initiatives he could not
change. Nor did he understand that California's government in 1967
was stretched to meet its existing commitments to education, health,
highways, and law enforcement. To candidate Reagan, it had seemed as
if there was more than enough revenue available to pay for everything.
Governor Reagan would learn differently.

The most systematic record of Reagan's apprenticeship as governor
is contained in the minutes of his meetings with his staff and executive
directors during the first two years of the governorship. This record,
subsequently called "cabinet minutes," was the work of Austrian-born
Helene von Damm, secretary to William P. Clark, Reagan's first cabinet
secretary. Clark instructed the meticulous von Damm to "write it all
down," and she produced minutes that show Reagan and his inner cabinet without promotional gloss.

The minutes of the first eight months are particularly valuable.
Later, after Clark and von Damm moved to other positions, and especially in Reagan's second term, the minutes became terse, unrevealing
summaries.* But the early minutes depict a warts-and-all Reagan who

*Clark made some of the early minutes available for my first book on Reagan in 1968 and pro-
vided all of them for this book. The minutes for the first eight months of the governorship
remain in his custody. Subsequent minutes, after Clark left the post of cabinet secretary, are

acknowledged ignorance without embarrassment and told stories at his own expense. In one meeting, while discussing California's role in a scientific project, Reagan related that he had been offered a ride in a submersible exploring the continental shelf. He declined. The representative of the explorers persisted. "I kept telling him that I had claustrophobia, and he said, 'you don't have to go down deep, we can find a place only 60 feet deep.' He doesn't know that I have claustrophobia when I draw the curtains," Reagan said.[1]

Reagan emerged in these early meetings as a self-assured governor who did not shrink from decision making. He breezily discussed myriad issues, at times punctuating his comments with bursts of antigovernment rhetoric. When informed of a prospective $29 million deficit in Medi-Cal, California's version of the federal-state Medicaid program that provides health care for the poor, Reagan exploded. "Those damn state governments," he said. "They pass legislation without knowing what it costs."[2] But later in the same meeting, Reagan talked approvingly of a government plan in which doctors would take a lesser fee for their Medi-Cal services, comparing this to a personal experience: "You know, years ago before there was help available like this, I was in the hospital with a smashed leg. My bill was $10,000. At the same time there was a truck driver with identical injuries as mine in the hospital, treated by the same physician, but his bill wasn't anything like mine. And I knew then that part of my payment was to take care of services the doctor rendered to the truck driver. Bills varied [according] to persons' ability to pay—that's the way it worked."[3]

Several of the cabinet discussions show similar tension between Reagan's visceral distrust of government and his practicality. As he later demonstrated as president, Reagan was simultaneously conservative and pragmatic. He had a competitive streak that made him determined to succeed, even when success required him to ignore ideology. On most issues, he clung to his opinions without allowing them to undermine his governance.

Reagan turned fifty-six on February 6, 1967, a month into his governorship. His convictions and habits would change little during the next twenty-two years, during which he successively served eight years as governor, six in private life (in which he was campaigning much of the time), and eight as president of the United States. At his first meeting with his executive directors, on January 25, 1967, Governor Reagan plunged earnestly into work. Agreeing with Gordon Luce, his business and transportation director, he decided on the spot to ask President

in the custody of the Ronald Reagan Foundation, which made them available. They are stored in the Ronald Reagan Presidential Library at Simi Valley, California.

Johnson's administration to relax limitations on the billboard industry in a pending federal highway beautification bill that was loaded with money for California. On the next item, Luce gave Reagan a short but lucid report on the financing of the Coronado Bridge, then delayed in court. Reagan asked a series of pertinent questions: Where did people in the [San Diego] area stand? Would the Navy go ahead with its assurance to widen the channel if the bridge was built? Was the contract given to the first bidder? He decided to wait until the court had acted.

As the meeting continued, Reagan authorized looking into a report that California was the only state required to match the federal government dollar for dollar in hospital construction. He questioned Clark and his chief of staff, Phil Battaglia, on requests from the State Water Project for exemptions from the Reagan administration's hiring freeze. "We are not trying to be unreasonable," Battaglia said. Reagan wasn't unreasonable, either, and several of the requests were granted. When Clark pressed Reagan for decisions on issues that had been brought to his attention before the meeting, Reagan said, "I think it should be played by ear." This was his way of saying that he did not want to be rushed.

Nor did Reagan want to be overwhelmed with detail, as Clark realized from the beginning. This meeting marked the debut of the "mini-memo," which was Clark's method of summarizing issues. The memoranda for this particular meeting ran to two or three pages, but Clark subsequently reduced them to a single page. Each memo had four paragraphs, with the first devoted to a statement of the issue, the second to the pertinent facts, the third to discussion, and the fourth to a conclusion and recommendations. Reagan's adversaries ridiculed these memoranda as a shallow approach to decision making, but they performed the necessary function of acquainting a governor who had never spent a day in government with the multitude of issues confronting him. James Alexander, the last cabinet secretary to Governor Brown, thought the memos were useful and praised Clark for initiating them.[4] They worked, for the most part, because Clark was scrupulous in fairly presenting both sides of an issue so as not to "cook" a decision. And on the more crucial issues, as Clark observed, Reagan went beyond the mini-memos and delved into the supporting material that accompanied them. One of Reagan's strengths was his capacity to make a difficult decision without anguishing over the result. He was not, however, by any stretch of the imagination a "policy wonk," the current fashionable term for politicians who enjoy exploring minutiae. Reagan was concerned with outcomes but bored by detailed discussion of issues that did not interest him. As in the presidency, he focused on a few issues that he believed were determinative or had symbolic value.

In 1967, the state's budget crisis was both determinative and symbolic. Reagan needed to eliminate the deficit he had inherited to balance the budget, as required by the state constitution, and to have the resources and the freedom to deal with anything else. And yet, although Reagan had talked recurrently about the budget deficit during the campaign, he seemed surprised by its dimension. "It's just twice as bad as I thought when I was campaigning," he told a career official in the Finance Department who laid out the problems for him.[5] After saying this, however, Reagan did not immediately come to grips with the deficit. Reagan's first budget, submitted in January, would have been wildly unbalanced even if the Legislature had accepted his cookie-cutter solution of a 10 percent across-the-board spending reduction. In this respect, Reagan's first gubernatorial budget anticipated his presidency, in which he never once submitted to Congress a spending plan that would have balanced the budget.

The political situation that Reagan faced in California in 1967 was similar in many respects to the one he would face as president in 1981. The Democrats, under Speaker Jesse Unruh, controlled the State Assembly, just as they would control the House under Speaker Tip O'Neill. Democrats controlled the State Senate in 1967, and Republicans the U.S. Senate in 1981, but Hugh Burns, the State Senate president pro tem, was a conservative who liked Reagan. Both as governor and as president, Reagan usually was able to forge a working majority in the upper house. The situations of the early governorship and early presidency were also similar in that Reagan was more popular than his principal legislative adversaries and, because of his abilities as a communicator, more successful in rousing public support. Neither Unruh nor O'Neill could compete with Reagan on radio or television; they relied on legislative maneuver, in which they were presumed to have an advantage.

Another similarity was that Reagan's fiscal point men were vulnerable, albeit for different reasons. David Stockman, the wunderkind of the Reagan presidency, knew too much, or thought he did. Gordon Paul Smith, Reagan's state finance director in 1967, knew too little. The results were that Stockman overreached and that Smith, in the opinion of the career professionals at the Finance Department, was outwitted by the Legislature. But in both cases the responsibility for the crucial decisions rested with Reagan, not his finance ministers.

On March 2, Smith acknowledged in a speech to a men's club that the Reagan administration could not meet its 10 percent goal on budget reductions; he said the cuts would average about 8.5 percent below what the state would have spent if programs had been allowed normal growth for population increases. Battaglia was infuriated; he held a news conference to say that 10 percent remained the administration's target.[6] But on March 27, Smith, on Reagan's behalf, withdrew the first budget and submitted a second one to the Legislature. The revised budget, supporting Smith and contradicting Battaglia, was $5.06 billion, an increase of $440 million from the first budget and roughly an 8.5 percent cut from the Brown budget adjusted for population growth. The new budget relieved the general anxiety among the state's 169,000 employees but alarmed the Department of Mental Hygiene and the state's higher education system. Budget increases for the University of California and state colleges were dependent upon the imposition of tuition, an issue that will be examined in a subsequent chapter. And Reagan proposed to eliminate 3,700 jobs in the Department of Mental Hygiene, which operated the state's ten mental hospitals.

The Department of Mental Hygiene was a tempting target for budget-cutters because the population of the mental hospitals was declining, thanks to tranquilizing drugs and new medical procedures. The number of patients had dropped from 33,000 in 1963–1964 to a projected total of fewer than 20,000 in 1967–1968. But the numbers were deceptive. The patients leaving the hospitals were the ones who responded best to tranquilizers; those who remained were more apt to need intensive care. And the state's mental hospitals had never been adequately staffed. In a memo to Reagan after Battaglia announced the cuts, Spencer Williams acknowledged that the mental hospitals had yet to reach two-thirds of the recommended 1952 staffing standard for rehabilitation and social services but played down this important point.[7] As a moderate who was trying to burnish his budget-cutting credentials in a conservative administration, Williams instead called attention to the fact that the state had surpassed 90 percent of the 1952 standards in nursing, psychiatric, and psychological services.

By any measure, California's mental hospitals were awful places. A Democratic state senator (whom I accompanied) paid a drop-in visit at one of these antiquated human warehouses in April and found forty patient wards that were watched on some shifts by a single attendant. In one ward, the senator heard pounding from behind a locked door and insisted that it be opened. He found a boy, dressed in his shorts, with only a plastic bucket for furniture. The senator was shaken by his tour of the hospital. "All the governor has to do is make a personal visit to one of these places and he will see we need more staffing—not less," he said.[8]

Reagan dismissed such criticisms as political, even though he was notably less enthusiastic about the cutbacks in the mental hospitals than Smith or Battaglia. They may have anticipated the governor's reluctance, for Reagan was not informed about these particular budget cuts until a week before they were announced. The cabinet minutes of March 7 show Williams downplaying the magnitude of the reductions and claiming that their impact would be offset by a 5 percent pay increase for psychiatric technicians:

WILLIAMS: There will be 1200 layoffs and this [the pay raise] should take the heat off a little. We have to deduct 2600 positions in the Department of Mental Hygiene.

GOVERNOR: Is this justified?

WILLIAMS: While our hospital population is going down, the staff and the budget have not. We fall below the standards recognized nationally. Even with the staff reductions, the patient-staff ratios can be maintained. Unfortunately the bulk of Mental Hygiene is in staff.

CLARK: But the decision has not been made yet?

WILLIAMS: No, we are just telling you of this problem. There is no need to get anybody stirred up yet.[9]

The stirring up occurred a week later, when Battaglia announced the layoffs prematurely in a bungled attempt to prevent the plan from being leaked to the press. The announcement triggered protests from public employee unions and gave Democrats an opening. Senator Stephen Teale, a prominent Democrat and a physician, said the cuts would move the mental hospitals "towards the snake pit conditions of the middle ages."[10] Such criticisms made Reagan uncomfortable, but he did not back down. "We are not going back to the snake pit," Reagan said at an impromptu news conference in the rain before attending a meeting in San Francisco. "We lead the nation in the quality of our mental patient care, and we will keep that lead."[11]

The Reagan administration's ace in the hole in the contest over the budget cuts was Dr. James Lowry, a holdover from the Brown administration and the director of the Department of Mental Hygiene. A year earlier, Lowry had argued for increased staffing at the mental hospitals. But Lowry, as a lobbyist described him, was a military sort of man who supported his higher-ups in the chain of command and "interpreted Reagan's goal of 10 percent as an order to cut 10 percent."[12] This amounted to $19.3 million, which seemed high to Williams, who recommended a lesser reduction of $14.4 million that would have saved about a third of the jobs in the mental hospitals. Battaglia and Smith decided to use Lowry's figure. Judging from the cabinet minutes, Williams did not put up a fight or tell the governor that he thought the layoffs were excessive.

The 10 percent cut was for the entire Department of Mental Hygiene, which had many fixed expenses that were not easily reduced. In the staffing of the mental hospitals, the cuts were well beyond 10 percent. The layoffs of 3,700 employees, most of them psychiatric technicians or their subordinates, amounted to nearly 16 percent of the hospitals' workforce. This was difficult to justify, but Lowry, Battaglia, and Smith contended that the patient-staff ratios at the hospitals would remain nearly the same because of the declining patient population. Within the Reagan inner circle, only Lyn Nofziger was skeptical. He realized it was politically damaging for Reagan to make mental patients and hospital workers bear the brunt of the budget cuts. (He may also have been sympathetic to the patients and workers, for on human issues Nofziger often was less conservative than advertised.) For his part, Reagan identified with the hospital workers who would lose their jobs. He made this clear in a meeting with the cabinet and executive directors on March 14, the day the cuts were announced:

SMITH: If we don't take all of these surpluses, we have two alternatives. In the tax bill we had $55 million that was being restored. . . . If we don't reduce all of the $19 million, it will cause a problem. It will diminish the economy program.

GOVERNOR: You don't realize this is the most dramatic thing you have given me. I'd like to hide. It has nothing to do with the economy but it reminds me of my father who got his slip on Christmas Eve. That was in the Depression days and my imagination is still that of a little kid who gets up and cries. On the other hand, if you fellows tell me that we don't need these employees, I don't see what else we can do. I still like the phasing out better than giving them the slip. And we should help them as much as we can.[13]

When a government action touched a mystic chord of personal memory, Reagan could sound like the New Deal Democrat he once had been. But in this case, he ignored his instincts and therefore missed an opportunity. At the time, the path was open for a lesser reduction in the Department of Mental Hygiene budget than the one Battaglia and Smith had proposed. Reagan might gratefully have embraced a compromise if either his chief of staff or his finance director had been sensitive to his feelings or if Spencer Williams had spoken up in behalf of the lower budget cuts he had proposed. Instead, these advisers armed Reagan with facts and figures to justify the entire reduction. It was the worst thing they could have done. Reagan had a weakness for statistics, which in this case undermined his sensible reaction to an excessive proposal and led him into an abstraction in which the mental patients and the hospital workers became numbers in a mathematical ratio.

From that day forward, Reagan responded to criticisms about the budget cuts by saying that he had maintained the ratio of hospital staff to patients. *The Sacramento Bee*, editorially hostile to Reagan, called the budget cuts "dubious economies"[14] and ran a drumfire of stories in which opponents of the plan predicted neglect and chaos in the hospitals if they went through. Alfred Auerback, vice president of the American Psychiatric Association, disputed the claim that California was first in mental health care among the states, claiming that it really ranked twenty-fifth.[15] But Reagan was heartened by the initial reaction of the *Los Angeles Times*, the newspaper that mattered most to him. Cautioning against a rush to judgment, an editorial in the *Times* concluded, "Under the circumstances we suggest that criticism be held in abeyance at least until the details of the proposed personnel reductions are available."*

Reagan grasped at this straw at a special meeting of the cabinet, where everyone except for a restrained Nofziger was jubilant:

GOVERNOR: Hello everybody. What do you have to offer to make me feel better?

CLARK: We have as the first item reaction to layoffs. I might say that it has not been as violent as we have expected. The *Los Angeles Times* is in the process of writing an editorial in tomorrow's paper.

GOVERNOR: I just read the last line and I can only say, if we would have been as smart in other things.

NOFZIGER: We had the positive approach.

CLARK: . . . We were on the offensive on the first attack. Spence, what is your observation?

WILLIAMS: The press was after me and Lowry all day. We pulled together some of the figures to match them up with the press release.

NOFZIGER: Well, thanks.

WILLIAMS: And we did. This afternoon about four or five TV stations were chasing us around and we had a meeting in the conference room. Lowry did a great job. We did not call it a press conference although major press was there, too. We stressed the fact that we mentioned, about hospital patient and staff ratio and the maintaining of present level care and standards. We said how close the state has already come to the standards set by the Legislature in 1952. . . .

CLARK: As Lyn has advised, we should stay away from saying "standards."

*When the details became available, the *Times* joined in the criticism of the budget cuts. On March 30, another *Times* editorial concluded, "The time to find any faults in the Reagan mental health budget . . . is before it is put into effect and before any needless suffering occurs."

WILLIAMS: Right, they have their own standards.

GOVERNOR: Do you know how hard it is to mispronounce "psychiatric" once
  you know how to pronounce it right? I had to do it in *Kings Row* and
  at first I couldn't do it. It is like deliberately singing a flat note.[16]

In the case of the budget cuts at the Department of Mental Hygiene,
the entire Reagan team was off-key. With patients trickling out of the
mental hospitals onto the streets and community clinics, there was a
strong case to be made for sensible economies, but Reagan did not
make it. Alan Post, the legislative analyst whom Reagan had wanted to
hire as finance director, did. Post suggested to a legislative committee
that the state should close two of the most inefficient mental hospitals
and plow the savings into community treatment centers. A Reagan insider, critical of Battaglia and Smith, said, "We should have sent efficiency experts into each hospital, and each hospital should have been
handled as a separate distinct case."[17] But neither this approach nor
Post's would have produced the quick budget fix that Smith and
Battaglia sought.

Reagan, although failing to override his aides, was never completely
comfortable with what they had done in his name. He avoided mentioning the mental hospitals in speeches touting his economies, and he
was notably defensive when the issue was raised at news conferences.
"We were panicked into a premature announcement of mental health
cuts," Reagan told me a year later, when Smith and Battaglia were no
longer with the administration. "We had no chance to warn legislators
and the roof fell in on the whole thing."[18] But even if he would not
admit anything more than a public relations error, Reagan had learned a
lesson from this episode. Never again in his governorship would he single out a department for such massive layoffs. Nor would he be asked to
do so, for his inner circle, especially Clark and Nofziger, recognized
that their boss wanted no repetition of the mental hospitals fiasco.

The Legislature softened the blow. When the budget passed the
Legislature, the layoffs had been reduced from 3,700 to 2,600, close to
what Williams originally recommended. Reagan accepted the change
without comment, but that was not the end of the story. Soon the trickle
of patients out of the mental hospitals became a torrent and the torrent
became a flood, abetted by court decisions that mentally ill persons who
had committed no crime could not be held against their will. In 1968, a
conservative Republican and a liberal Democrat teamed up in the Assembly to push through progressive legislation that replaced warehous-
ing of the mentally ill with community treatment centers. Reagan
endorsed the bill and signed it into law. In 1969, he reversed course on

his budget-cutting, proposing a record $28 million increase for the Department of Mental Hygiene and also the closing of the notably inefficient Modesto State Hospital, as Alan Post had recommended. As patient-staff ratios improved at the mental hospitals and the first community treatment centers were built, Reagan in 1969 was able to claim, more accurately than two years earlier, that California was "the number one state in the treatment of the mentally ill." The Modesto hospital was the first of several to be shuttered by Reagan and his successors. The mentally ill who had been a state responsibility became instead a burden for local communities, relatives, and themselves. Although Reagan's post-1967 budgets devoted more money than ever before to community treatment, the hope that this was a panacea proved illusory. By the time Reagan became president in 1981, the mentally ill, who had for so long been locked out of sight in hospitals, were living on the streets of America's cities. They are still there.

No amount of budget reductions, even if they had been politically palatable, could have balanced California's budget in 1967. The cornerstone of Governor Reagan's economic program was not the ballyhooed budget reductions but a sweeping tax package four times larger than the previous record California tax increase obtained by Governor Brown in 1959. Reagan's proposal had the distinction of being the largest tax hike ever proposed by any governor in the history of the United States. He sought tax increases on sales, personal income, banks and corporations, insurance companies, liquor, and cigarettes. When Reagan unveiled the plan on March 8, it carried a price tag of $946 million. When it passed the Senate with various attachments, including a tax on services that the press dubbed the "shoeshine tax," the total was $1 billion. And this from a governor two months in office who had campaigned on the virtues of tax reduction! It was a breathtaking display of pragmatism.

Reagan's boldness reflected an intuitive understanding that Pat Brown had done him an unintentional political favor by bequeathing him a deficit that made tax increases necessary. Two days after his inauguration, Reagan said he did not want to wait "until everyone forgets that we did not cause the problem—we only inherited it." His aides interpreted this comment as a mandate to negotiate with the Legislature for tax increases. Before long, Reagan was meeting with Assembly Speaker Jesse Unruh to discuss the tax package.

Reagan and Unruh, already sizing each other up as potential rivals in 1970, were united by self-interest. They would never be friends. To the governor, the speaker was an archetypal wheeler-dealer. To Unruh, Reagan was a cold fish who lectured about larger purposes while pushing a narrow political agenda. It may have bothered Unruh, who was hypersensitive to real or perceived slights, that Reagan was unimpressed by him and uninterested in his views. In truth, legislators as a group did not interest Reagan. He shunned the numerous receptions where liquor flowed and legislators mingled with lobbyists. Whenever possible, Reagan left the capitol by 5:30 P.M. and went home to a quiet dinner with Nancy. In the evening, he read or watched *Mission: Impossible* on television.

No one expected Reagan and Unruh to like each other, but the governor was also a distant figure to Republican legislative leaders. "He wasn't interested in the Legislature at all," said Bob Monagan, the Assembly minority leader and later speaker. "I got along with him fine, but never—not once—during his eight years as governor, did he solicit my views. Pat Brown would call me down and put his feet up and ask me what I thought. We usually disagreed, but we knew where we stood. I had pretty good access to Reagan. If I wanted to see him, I could and he was always polite. But I initiated every meeting I had with him."[19]

As he would later do as president, Reagan compensated for the remoteness of his relationships with individual legislators with a strong legislative office. His first legislative secretary was Jack Lindsey, a savvy businessman whom Bill Roberts had brought into the Reagan campaign. Lindsey shared a hometown (Fresno) with Democratic Senate leader Burns, and the two became friends. Lindsey also forged a friendship with Monagan. George Steffes, who began as Lindsey's deputy and succeeded him, had worked for the Republican State Central Committee and played a role in electing several Republican legislators. Vernon Sturgeon, the liaison to the State Senate, was a former senator and close to Burns. All three aides had the capacity to tell Reagan what he needed to know rather than what he wanted to hear.

Lindsey demonstrated this early in the governorship when Reagan told him and Lyn Nofziger that a horsemen's group, aware that he missed riding in Sacramento, was giving him a horse. Lindsey asked what a horse cost. Guess, said Reagan. Lindsey guessed $500. No, said Reagan, more like $5,000. "Just about the cost of a vicuna coat," said Lindsey, referring to the gift that had led to the resignation of President Eisenhower's chief of staff, Sherman Adams.[20] Reagan flushed. Nofziger chimed in, observing that Reagan had objected to conflicts of interest in the Brown years. "The press would cut us to pieces," he said.[21] Reagan flushed again and then changed the subject. He never brought it up again—but he turned down the gift.

In terms of funding future programs and giving him room to maneuver, the tax bill that Reagan obtained from the Legislature in 1967 was more valuable than any horse. The Legislature was generous because

Unruh, in addition to favoring tax increases on their merits, believed that a huge revenue bill would undermine Reagan. How could the largest tax increase in California's history not harm a conservative governor who had promised tax reductions? Unruh did not yet appreciate how effective Reagan could be in deflecting blame. Neither did a handful of conservative legislators who questioned the amount of the tax increase. Reagan blithely ignored them. "I'm the stingiest fiscal conservative you ever saw," he said.[22]

Political calculations aside, Reagan and Unruh shared a genuine commitment to property tax relief. Reagan was no tax expert, but he was a homeowner, and he realized that retired people who lived on fixed incomes were vulnerable to property tax increases. Unruh had proof of what Reagan knew in his gut. Orthodox Democratic opinion held that sales taxes were the most regressive, which is to say that they proportionally fall heaviest on low-income taxpayers. But a masterful study by an Assembly committee, encouraged by Unruh, showed otherwise. People with low incomes spend most of their money on food, which in California is exempt from the sales tax. Prescription drugs are also exempt. Because of these exemptions the sales tax was less regressive than the property taxes levied by local governments, which took no account of ability to pay. In California at the time, homeowners faced soaring tax bills as houses were reassessed at ever higher values, and local governments raised revenues to build an expanding network of new roads, schools, sewers, and other facilities. This pattern was devastating to seniors living on a pension or Social Security, some of whom were forced to sell their homes because they could not afford to pay the property tax. If they were renters, the tax was passed along to them by landlords in the form of higher rents.

Eventually, the spiral of increased assessments and higher property taxes ignited a revolt that in 1978 led to passage of an extreme tax-limiting initiative (Proposition 13) and copycat measures in other states. Unruh and Reagan were ahead of their time in anticipating this crisis, which would have occurred much sooner if they had not acted. As early as 1965, the Assembly speaker had proposed a tax reform package that gave low-income homeowners a state rebate for a portion of their property taxes. Pat Brown cold-shouldered the idea, not wanting to share credit for the rebate with Unruh. Brown failed to realize that a governor, with greater visibility than any legislator, would gain most of the credit. Reagan realized it right away. In his first meeting with Unruh, he agreed with the speaker that a property tax rebate was a must.

On this first and most significant revenue bill of the Reagan years in

Sacramento, the governor and the speaker saw eye to eye on nearly all the essentials except for income tax withholding, which Unruh favored and Reagan opposed. Unruh believed, accurately, that California lost revenue from "tax cheats" who moved in and out of the state without ever paying income taxes. Reagan foresaw, also accurately, that future legislatures would find it easier to raise income taxes if they were extracted from weekly paychecks rather than collected in a lump sum. "Taxes should hurt," he said. Early in the negotiations, Reagan told Assemblyman John Veneman, the Republican who chaired the Assembly Revenue and Taxation Committee and carried Unruh's version of the tax bill, that his feet were "set in concrete" against withholding.[23]

Reagan's version of the tax bill was introduced by Senator George Deukmejian, a Republican. He was a freshman in the upper house but a veteran of the Assembly, where he was trusted as a straight shooter. Deukmejian, who had campaigned with Reagan and was familiar with his standard pitch for reduced government, was pleasantly surprised by the governor's willingness to raise taxes. "A lot of people, including me, thought he would be ideological," Deukmejian said. "We learned quickly that he was very practical."[24]

Deukmejian, an observant legislator and future governor, believed that Reagan's experience in the Screen Actors Guild had helped prepare him for Sacramento. Legislators who met with the governor in his conference room were accustomed to taking any open chair. At an early meeting, Reagan said to Deukmejian, "We ought to do what we did when we negotiated with the movie producers. They sat on one side of the table, and we sat on the other."[25] So Reagan separated Republicans and Democrats in this way, formalizing negotiations in which he participated effectively and that ended well for him.

As it turned out, however, the crucial division on the tax bill was between Democrats. The Senate gatekeeper on taxes was Finance Committee Chairman George Miller Jr., a feisty rival of Unruh's. Miller called property tax relief a "hoax"; he argued that since business paid more property taxes than homeowners, any increase in the sales tax was a business subsidy. Miller mirrored the myopia of the Senate on this issue, where property tax relief was in disfavor for various reasons. Some senators agreed with Miller that business would benefit too much from such relief. Others considered the property tax a purely local issue in which the state should not involve itself. Still other senators, as David Doerr observed, looked upon local officials who were raising property taxes as potential opponents and didn't want to boost their political careers with a state rebate that would make the taxes less onerous.[26] When Miller's committee marked up Deukmejian's tax bill, it eliminated property tax relief entirely. The Senate then sent the bill to the Assembly, where it languished in Veneman's committee.

Unruh, meanwhile, staked out his ground on income tax withholding, which was included in Veneman's tax bill. Reagan warned that he would veto any measure with this provision, but Unruh insisted on a partisan show of force. After a Republican attempt to delete withholding was defeated on a party-line vote, the Assembly sent the Veneman bill to the Senate. The two sides had reached an impasse that lasted beyond the constitutional deadline of June 30 for passing a budget. The Senate refused to pass the Veneman bill, and Reagan could not get the Deukmejian bill out of the Assembly unless he reached an accommodation with Unruh.

In this situation, with the deficit mounting and both sides digging in, Reagan proved the equal of the master politician Unruh. By standing firm, Reagan made Unruh choose between property tax relief and withholding. Once the choice was cast in these terms, it was no contest. Unruh knew that the Senate Democrats would remain resistant to property tax relief. He also assumed that the state's cash-flow problems would in time persuade Reagan to accept withholding. Reagan realized he risked losing the tax bill altogether but calculated that Unruh would not let the state slip into bankruptcy. The situation reminded the governor of a labor situation in which a settlement was inevitable because neither side could afford to lose. Neither did, but it was Unruh who gave up the most. After several days of negotiation, he agreed to resurrect the Deukmejian bill, which was amended in Veneman's committee. Most of the features of the Veneman bill, minus withholding, were amended into the Deukmejian measure and supported by Democrats and Republicans alike. The Assembly also killed the services, or shoeshine, tax, a dubious provision that would have been difficult to enforce, and under lobbyist prodding removed the tax increase on insurance companies.

The final product gave Unruh the satisfaction of seeing his 1965 tax reform proposal, which Governor Brown had rejected, accepted by Reagan. In return, Reagan gained political credit for property tax relief at the same time he was raising taxes by a billion dollars (more than $5 billion in 2003 dollars) and blocking imposition of withholding. It was a lopsided bargain in Reagan's favor. One of the reasons Unruh agreed to it was that he believed the governor would become unpopular the following April when Californians paid their income taxes. But most of the indignation against the sharply increased personal income tax was directed retroactively at Pat Brown, whom Reagan had succeeded in blaming for the state's financial condition.

At the time of the agreement with Reagan, however, Unruh believed that he had struck a good bargain. The Assembly speaker's part of the deal was to push the tax bill through the Senate, no small task in a state where spending bills require a two-thirds vote. But Unruh delivered, with Reagan's help. First, the amended Deukmejian bill was returned to the Senate. Unruh then allowed Senate bills to accumulate in the Assembly, where they remained on calendar for weeks without any action. Both the governor, working through Vern Sturgeon, and Unruh, operating through ex-assemblymen who had been elevated to the Senate, kept the pressure on the upper house. The senators wanted their bills passed in the Assembly and were amenable, as always, to other political concessions. One of these concessions by the Reagan administration was to trade two judgeships to a key Democratic senator in return for a vote on the tax bill.[27]

Even then, the Unruh and Reagan forces were a vote short when the tax bill came up for final passage on July 28. Proponents of the bill stalled for two hours until they could track down Senator Joseph Kennick, a former assemblyman and Unruh ally, in a Long Beach restaurant. Unruh had steered financial contributions Kennick's way when he first ran for the Assembly. Although Kennick had serious reservations about the tax bill, he agreed to vote for it. At this point, senatorial courtesy prevailed and Senate President Pro Tem Hugh Burns changed his vote from "nay" to "aye" to save Kennick the trouble of flying to Sacramento. It was a victory for Unruh and an even bigger victory for Reagan. "Other Republican governors might not have been able to pull it off," Deukmejian said decades later. "It was sort of like Nixon going to China."[28]

An economist who analyzed the tax bill without knowing its political background might conclude that it had been crafted by a New Deal Democrat. The bill changed California's revenue-raising structure from a regressive one that took little account of ability to pay into a reasonably progressive system. During the Reagan administration, corporation taxes nearly doubled, from 5.5 percent to 9 percent. The tax on banks went from 9.5 to 13 percent. The state's share of the sales tax rose from 3 to 4.75 percent. The maximum on personal income taxes increased from 7 percent to 11 percent, and brackets were narrowed to put more persons in a higher tax bracket.* The bill was especially helpful to low-income seniors who owned their homes; the state gave them a substantial refund of their property taxes. The bill also set aside $190 million of future revenues for broader property tax relief.

*The figures used here are for the tax increases throughout Reagan's eight years as governor and reflect later adjustments. Most of the increases resulted from the 1967 bill.

These mammoth tax increases, substantially more than were needed to close the inherited deficit, earned Reagan a bonus of opposition from the far Right. Although most Republicans voted for the tax bill, the Legislature's most flamboyant right-winger, Senator John G. Schmitz of Santa Ana, opposed it from its introduction. Schmitz, who once quipped that he joined the John Birch Society to get the middle-of-the-road vote in Orange County, voted against the bill and then promoted a book, *Here's the Rest of Him*, written by Kent H. Steffgen with the help of Schmitz's administrative assistant, Warren H. Carroll, which depicted Reagan as a turncoat. "From a governor who campaigned on promises to economize and relieve the tax burden on productive citizens, so that their energies might be released in a 'Creative Society,' this kind of tax increase is utterly indefensible," Steffgen wrote. "It hurts most those he promised to help most."[29]

Reagan took the attack in stride, aware that expressions of displeasure on the Right contributed to his growing reputation as a responsible executive who refused to let ideology interfere with effective governance. "Schmitz strikes me as a guy who jumps off the cliff with flags flying," Reagan told me a year later. "I'm willing to take what I can get."[30] What he got was a government that was fully funded for the first time in four years and a state surplus that allowed him to restore budget cuts and increase educational funding. It was more than even the popular Earl Warren had achieved in his first term and more than most California governors ever attempted. The tax bill also persuaded skeptical legislators that Reagan was an accomplished politician. It marked the end of his novice period as governor.

Looking back on Reagan's accomplishment, some students of government wondered if he had planned all along to raise more revenue than was needed as part of a strategy to avoid tax increases later on. This notion gives Reagan more credit—or blame—than he deserves. Reagan's brilliance as a politician was more intuitive than calculated. He did not know how much money the tax bill would bring into state coffers; indeed, it raised more revenue than Unruh or Alan Post had anticipated because of a surge of inflation in the late 1960s. But Reagan did have a sense, as good politicians do, of the importance of striking while the iron was hot. Like his early idol Franklin Roosevelt, he invested his popularity rather than conserving it for a later day. When I pressed Reagan during a long plane trip in 1968 about the political impact of the tax bill, he was reluctant to talk about it. When I followed up by saying that Unruh thought the tax bill would be an issue when Reagan ran for reelection, he said he had not decided to run again. Then, with a smile, Reagan added almost off-handedly that he had raised taxes in

1967 and that the next election was in 1970. Reagan was not a plotter, but he knew what he had done.

Reagan's other significant display of pragmatism in his first year as governor involved the Rumford Fair Housing Act, and his fingerprints were not on the finished product. The law, intended to prevent bias in housing sales and rentals, was authored by William Byron Rumford, a Berkeley pharmacist and one of the Assembly's four black members. The Legislature had passed the Rumford Act in 1963. As previously recounted, voters in 1964 repealed it by approving a ballot initiative (Proposition 14) promoted by the California Real Estate Association (CREA). In 1966, the California Supreme Court invalidated the initiative, on grounds it violated federally guaranteed rights of equal protection, and reinstated the Rumford Act. Reagan promised in his gubernatorial campaign that he would support repeal of the law. In his first months in office, he gave no hint of having second thoughts. He appointed Burton Smith, a former president of the CREA who had played a leading role in the passage of Proposition 14, as state real estate commissioner. Then he asked Attorney General Thomas Lynch, a Democrat, not to become involved in the appeal to the U.S. Supreme Court of the California Supreme Court's decision striking down Proposition 14.[31] Lynch politely refused, saying he had a duty to represent the California high court's position on appeal. When the Supreme Court declined to overturn its California counterpart, the decision was left to Reagan and the Legislature.

The repeal bill, by Robert Badham, a conservative Orange County Republican, had no chance in the Assembly. Unruh, proud of sponsoring an earlier civil rights bill, was willing to revise but not to repeal the Rumford Act. Bob Monagan, the moderate Republican leader, held similar views. It is a comment on the relatively principled politics of the day that both the Democratic and Republican leaders in the Assembly were willing to oppose a bill they believed was morally flawed even after voters had passed a repeal initiative by a 2–1 margin. There were, however, limits to the risks Unruh was willing to take. The speaker, nursing a four-vote majority in the Assembly, did not want to expose Democrats to an up-or-down floor vote on repeal. He sent the Badham bill to a committee chaired by William T. Bagley, the Assembly's most liberal Republican. Bagley knew what he was supposed to do with the repeal bill. "Unruh wanted it killed, and I wanted to kill it," he said.[32] The Badham bill died in Bagley's committee.

Chances for repeal were better in the Senate, where its leader, President Pro Tem Hugh Burns, opposed the Rumford Act. On March 15, a Senate committee held a stormy hearing in which an NAACP official denounced the repeal attempt as "hate-ridden" and a CREA spokesman defended housing discrimination as a constitutional right. Rumford, by now an ex-legislator, testified. He said seventeen states had stronger laws against housing bias and that not one of them, "not even Alabama," had considered repealing them.

With Senate action pending, Reagan's chief of staff, Phil Battaglia, met secretly with Bagley at the Senator Hotel and said of the repeal bill, "We wouldn't mind if you killed it."[33] Bagley didn't know if the message came from the governor or Battaglia, but he appreciated it. He told Battaglia that he intended to kill or revise the repeal bill if it cleared the Senate.

In these early months of the Reagan administration, Battaglia had the reputation of being more moderate than Reagan, although there was no proof of this. The chief of staff (whose official title was "executive secretary") acted as if he were deputy governor, often using the imperial "we" in discussing Reagan's policies and confiding to a reporter that he could deal with Unruh and other powerful legislators. Battaglia's behavior had begun to worry colleagues on the governor's staff, who suspected him of freelancing. But it is unlikely that Battaglia would have told the garrulous Bagley that it was okay to kill the Rumford Act repeal without some sort of nod from Reagan. Although there is no direct evidence that Reagan knew of Battaglia's maneuvering, the governor increasingly talked about "repeal or revision" of the Rumford Act, the language used in the 1966 platform of the California Republican Party.

If Senator Burns was aware of such nuances, he was undeterred by them. Burns assumed that the governor shared his determination to repeal the Rumford Act, as both he and Reagan had promised to do. The Senate leader's problem was not the repeal bill but its author, John Schmitz, the Legislature's only avowed member of the John Birch Society. Burns epitomized the Senate's Democratic old guard. Crusty in demeanor and conservative by inclination, he was an effective, if cynical, legislator and a friend of Sacramento's most influential lobbyists. In his clubby way, he took care of his Senate pals as well as Unruh did his protégés in the Assembly. Burns told members running for reelection to "point with pride, view with alarm, and wave the American flag," which was how he conducted his own campaigns.[34] But Burns was no extremist. In his view, the Birchers were "crazies" and Schmitz was a zealot. As much as he wanted to repeal the Rumford Act, Burns was unwilling to have a Bircher's name on the bill. So he kept the Schmitz bill bottled up in committee for a month before deciding to appropriate it and bring it to the floor with his name on it. On April 13, the Burns repeal bill passed 23–15 with senators on both sides quoting Abraham Lincoln for their own purposes.[35]

Unruh sent the bill to Bagley's committee, where it was converted into a revision of the Rumford Act that limited the law to subdivision sales plus any sale or rental of multiple units with five or more dwellings. Single-family homeowners would be free to discriminate but could not instruct real estate brokers to do so. Had the bill passed in this form, Bagley estimated, it would have reduced the application of the Rumford Act from about 32 percent to 14 percent of California housing. On August 2, 1967, the Assembly passed the revised bill by a 46–22 vote with the "no" votes cast by liberals who opposed any change in the Rumford Act and conservatives who wanted outright repeal. Unruh called the revision, now known as Burns-Bagley, an answer "to the bigots of both sides."[36] Reagan, in a statement written by Battaglia, endorsed Burns-Bagley. This surprised and irritated Burns, who complained that Reagan had conferred with Unruh and leaders of the real estate industry but not with him. "I think this is somewhat of an affront to the Senate," Burns said.[37]

Time was running out on the legislative session, which was supposed to end Friday, August 4. Instead, clocks were stopped in both the Senate and the Assembly, a device that permitted legislators to work through the weekend. Reagan was not in Sacramento working with them. A routine medical examination had discovered an enlarged prostate, and he had undergone an operation in a Santa Monica hospital, where a small, benign tumor was also removed from his lower lip.[38] While Reagan was recovering from surgery, Battaglia was in charge of negotiations with the Legislature.

Three last-minute attempts were made to change the Rumford Act. On Saturday, August 5, a Senate committee rejected the Assembly version of the bill. Later that night, Burns brought the measure before the full Senate with a motion to reject the amended bill. The motion passed 24–7. Then, as weary legislators worked to midnight on both weekend days, a two-house negotiating committee chaired by Bagley was named to find a compromise. But when two conservative senators appointed by Burns balked at the timetable of the meetings, Bagley decided not to call the committee into session.[39] Even had he convened it, there would have been little chance at resolution because the two Assembly Democratic members—future speakers Bob Moretti and Willie Brown Jr.—wanted no changes in the Rumford Act.

Who saved the Rumford Act? Considerable credit (or blame, depending upon one's point of view) goes to Bagley, who decades later said that his role in the process was the proudest achievement of his legislative career.[40] But credit is also due Unruh and Bob Monagan, who teamed up to kill the Badham bill and then joined in supporting the revision that ran aground in the Senate. Still, the Rumford Act probably would not have survived and certainly would not have survived intact had not Reagan muddied the waters by retreating from his promise for outright repeal and finding revision acceptable. This tactic did not sit well with Republicans in the Senate. Many of them privately blamed Battaglia for leading the governor astray, and only one Republican senator supported revision in the climactic vote the Saturday before adjournment. Politically, the outcome was useful both to Unruh and to Reagan. The speaker and the governor issued separate statements blaming the Senate for failure of revision and saying they had done the best they could.

The following year, when legislative conservatives and the real estate industry were again talking repeal, Reagan cut them off at the pass. Late in March 1968, the governor held a series of meetings with minority groups, all of which opposed outright repeal of the Rumford Act. On April 2, Reagan said in response to a question at a news conference that he would veto a bill that repealed the Rumford Act and left nothing in its place because the law was an important "symbol" to minorities. When a reporter pointed out that supporters of the Rumford Act often had defended it on these grounds, Reagan said, "I frankly admit that I was greatly impressed to find out how much of a symbol this is in many areas, and I think that anything that is done must certainly be done with full communication with these people [minorities]."[41]

Reagan's statement was big news, and Reagan was unhappy with the news coverage. Acting pragmatically was not a problem for Reagan, but he was uncomfortable when anyone observed that he had changed his mind on a matter of principle. In the cabinet meeting of April 4, 1968, Reagan said he was "mad enough to cancel any press conferences" because newspaper stories had described his promise to veto a Rumford Act repeal as an "about-face," which of course it was. Reagan told his cabinet that he had not changed his stand on "constitutional rights," by which he meant the right of individual homeowners to discriminate. After going on in this vein for a few minutes, however, Reagan said, "Real estate people must realize that I hate to see this brought to a referendum again. I have always felt that it should be settled in the Legislature."[42]

Although these remarks were made in private, leaders of the California real estate industry knew where Reagan stood. The governor's call for legislative revision rather than repeal was echoed by Burton Smith, the state real estate commissioner who had in 1964 been a leader in the initiative campaign to repeal the Rumford Act. The backlash from that campaign and the rise of the national civil rights movement had made housing bias a divisive issue within the industry, and the CREA decided to forego another initiative and focus on legislative revision, as Reagan had hoped it would. But the Legislature wanted no repeat battle over the Rumford Act. By 1968, most liberals and all but a handful of conservatives considered Rumford a no-win issue. Senator Schmitz introduced another repeal bill, but it was buried in committee. This time Burns made no attempt to revive it.

Neither did Reagan. He continued to believe that individuals had a right to discriminate in the sale of their homes if they did so without the aid of a realtor, but he made no attempt to pry a bill from the Legislature and wisely let the issue rest.[43] When Congress subsequently passed a federal Fair Housing Act that reduced the Rumford Act's importance, he sidestepped the issue again. Reagan was a conservative, beyond a doubt. He was also a practical and resourceful politician.

16

CONSERVATIVE

THROUGH TAX INCREASES and sundry compromises, Ronald Reagan retained his high standing with mainstream conservatives, some of whom began boosting him as the next president even before he learned the ropes as governor. Conservatives were not blind to Reagan's pragmatism. They liked what he said, even when it required ignoring what he did, because Reagan had a perspective that William F. Buckley described as "essentially undoubting." Although Reagan's policies sometimes changed to meet the realities of governance, his perspective did not. Speaking to a conservative audience after his election as governor, Reagan said he was "just as frightened of government now that I am a part of it" as before he took office. And it wasn't government alone that frightened him. Reagan spoke out against the civil disorders, student rebellions, and cultural licentiousness that many Americans saw as threats to the old order. From the standpoint of the American cultural revolution that became known as "the sixties," Reagan was a counterrevolutionary. Conservatives valued him because he was one of them and took a stand.

In the early months of 1967, California drifted in the turbulent storms of history. The Watts race riot of 1965 was a fading memory; the next such bloody riot, in Detroit, did not erupt until July. Berkeley was quiet. As students returned to what the *San Francisco Chronicle* called the "Great Confrontation Game," the 1965 occupation of Sproul Hall was also a memory. It would take two more years of campus skirmishes and provocations before the game turned deadly. Even in Vietnam, a killing ground since the early days of World War II, there was a brief lull. On New Year's Day, 1967, a column in the *Los Angeles Times* from Saigon said that "enemy forces . . . have no respect for honor or decency" and that the United States should "clobber them" if they broke the holiday truce.[1] The columnist was the writer John Steinbeck. Sixty-seven combat incidents were reported in the next thirty hours. By October, as casualties and war costs mounted, 46 percent of Americans said that U.S. involvement in Vietnam was a mistake, and opponents of the war led a gigantic march on the Pentagon.

Culturally, conservatives remained in control, even on the coasts. At the urging of a Democratic city councilman, the New York Transit Authority removed posters from subways and buses advertising the movie *The Graduate* because they showed Anne Bancroft in bed with Dustin Hoffman. As a condition of appearing on *The Ed Sullivan Show*, the Rolling Stones changed the chorus of a hit song, "Let's Spend the Night Together," to "let's spend some time together."[2] In California, an obscure state legislator named Leo Ryan, later a House member who was murdered in Guyana, failed in an attempt to lift the ban on a school play deemed offensive because of its title, *A Cat Named Jesus.*

These conservative victories were fleeting. *The Graduate* was the top money-maker among 1967 films, and the Rolling Stones never again censored their songs for television. In Sacramento, the Cannes Film Festival winner of 1966, *A Man and a Woman*, played for seven consecutive weeks to packed houses in the winter and early spring of 1967. "Calendar year 1967 saw the emergence of a self-consciously adversarial counter-culture," observed Michael Barone.[3] A gap that was at once a cause and a product of this counterculture erupted between young and old. The badges in this generational war were beards, long hair, and drugs. Ronald and Nancy Reagan worried about the impact of drugs and alienation on their teenage daughter Patti, then attending a boarding school in Arizona. It was a common concern among parents across the land.

One of the least heralded but most important changes occurring in America was the birth of a new feminist movement. The National Organization for Women (NOW) was founded on October 29, 1966, in the John Philip Sousa community room at *The Washington Post*. Its first statement of purpose, over the objection of founder Betty Friedan, omitted mention of abortion on grounds it was too controversial.[4] In February 1967, NOW petitioned the federal Equal Employment Opportunity Commission to end discriminatory help-wanted advertisements in newspapers. On March 16, Aileen Hernandez, vice president of NOW in San Francisco, testified before a California legislative committee during a hearing on a bill by Mervyn Dymally, the only African American in the State Senate, that would have prohibited sexual discrimination in state employment. A senator asked if the California Highway Patrol (CHP) should be required to employ women. "Yes, I don't think it would be difficult to find qualified women for the patrol," Hernandez answered. But the bill was scuttled after a CHP representative told the committee "that the very nature of patrol work disqualifies women as traffic officers."[5] It would be another seven years before the CHP admitted women to its ranks.

Anthony C. Beilenson was in 1967 a young freshman state senator representing an affluent, liberal district in Los Angeles County. He was a transplanted New Yorker who had attended Phillips Andover and graduated from Harvard and Harvard Law School. In 1957, he had joined the Beverly Hills law firm of his cousin, Laurence Beilenson, who had represented the Screen Actors Guild when Reagan was its president. Tony Beilenson, as everyone called him, won election to the Assembly in 1962 as a Democrat less than a month after his thirtieth birthday. In 1964, the Supreme Court's historic "one-man, one-vote" decision changed the character of the rural State Senate from a body in which some members represented more cows than people into a representative body in which Los Angeles County went from one to fourteen senators. Armed with the court decision, Jesse Unruh engineered a skillful reapportionment. It opened up a safe seat for Beilenson, which he won easily.

As a legislator, Beilenson was bright, earnest, competent, intensely liberal, and almost too serious for words. A devoted family man, he eschewed the poker games and hard drinking then common in Sacramento political circles but became deeply involved in the drafting of social legislation. In his first term in the Assembly, he coauthored a bill to liberalize California's abortion law, which allowed abortions only to save the life of the mother. The hearings produced graphic testimony about the deaths and mutilation of women from illegal abortions. Beilenson, who had led a sheltered life, was horrified to learn of the "barbaric" treatment of women who could not afford to travel to countries where abortion was legal. In 1965, the original author of the bill had declined to reintroduce it because of opposition from a Catholic prelate in his district. Beilenson took over the bill and won some additional supporters, but for the second session in a row, it died in committee.

Abortion in the 1960s was discussed in whispers. Until mid-decade, the word itself was taboo in most newspapers, including the *Los Angeles Times*, where abortion was called an "illegal medical procedure." The phrases "pro-choice" and "pro-life" did not yet exist, and battle lines on the issue were drawn almost entirely on religious lines. Conservatives who were not Roman Catholics believed, in a bromide of the day, that government should stay out of "the boardroom and the bedroom." Lib-

eral Democrats who were also Catholics were overwhelmingly an-
tiabortion.* Public attitudes, however, were changing among members
of all faiths. In July 1966, a survey by Mervin Field, the state's most respected pollster, showed that 72 percent of Californians favored liberalized abortion laws, including nearly 59 percent of Catholics. No one on
either side anticipated that the U.S. Supreme Court would eventually
determine the legality of abortion. Before *Roe v. Wade*, decided in January 1973, abortion was a state matter and the rules under which it was
permitted were up to fifty legislatures to decide.

When Senator Beilenson introduced the Therapeutic Abortion Act
in 1967, its chances seemed remote. That it had any chance at all, even
in the new, more urban Senate, was because of a whim of the Senate
leader, Hugh Burns, and his lobbyist pal Daniel Creedon. When
Beilenson called upon Burns to seek support, something about the
earnest young senator impressed the lobbyist, who often sat in with
Burns on such meetings. "Let's give the kid a chance," Creedon said.[6]
Burns agreed and assigned the bill to the Judiciary Committee, on
which Beilenson served. It was the most broad-minded committee in
the Senate.

Beilenson's bill amended California law to allow abortions in cases of
rape or incest, when a doctor deemed that the birth was likely to impair
the physical or mental health of the mother, or when there was "substantial risk" that the child would be born deformed. Events outside
Sacramento gave the measure a push. The Colorado Legislature, with
Republicans in a majority, liberalized abortion. Closer to home, nine
San Francisco Bay Area physicians were criminally charged with performing abortions on mothers with German measles, an illness that can
cause deformity in a child. Women rallied to their defense. Four
women in the suburban counties of San Mateo and Santa Clara south of
San Francisco gathered 8,000 signatures on a petition urging that the
physicians not be punished and calling for a change in the law. They
traveled to Sacramento and dumped the petitions on the desk of a surprised Senator Richard J. Dolwig, who pointed out that the Roman
Catholic Church opposed changes in the law. One of the women,
Teresa Santaferraro, replied that she was a Catholic and had collected
many of the signatures from coreligionists.

These petitions, and Beilenson's persistence, aroused the church,

*The legislative delegation that I covered at the time as a reporter for the *San Jose Mercury-News* demonstrated the typical division on abortion. Senator Clark Bradley, a Republican, a Protestant, and one of the most conservative members of the Legislature, never wavered in his support for the Beilenson bill. Assemblyman John Vasconcellos, a liberal Democrat and a Catholic, opposed the bill and said, "I cherish life whether it's on Death Row or in Vietnam or in the womb."

whose leaders realized that a liberalized abortion law in trend-setting California would spur similar laws in other states. The church launched a vigorous campaign against the bill that generated a record amount of mail. "Most of the incoming mail at the capitol was inspired by Catholic priests who asked, from their pulpits, that their parishioners write to their legislators urging defeat of the bill," reported *San Francisco Examiner* political writer Jack S. McDowell. "In many cases pre-printed envelopes and other aids were provided."[7] This letter-writing campaign had an impact. Senator George Danielson, a Los Angeles Democrat, announced that he was reluctantly voting against the Beilenson bill. "I just can't go against 5,000 votes from my district," Danielson said.

When the bill was heard before the Senate Judiciary Committee, Alden J. Bell, the Catholic bishop of Sacramento, said that it sanctioned legalized murder. "The unborn child, however brief its existence, is clearly identified by science even in embryonic form as belonging to the human family," Bell said. "It needs only to be nourished and cherished to develop its full potential. It has the right to live." Beilenson responded that his bill was "an attempt to restore a degree of freedom of choice and of conscience to many thousands of women." He made his case with parliamentary skill, displaying respect for the church and legislators who disagreed with him, but he was unrelenting on the need for change. "The present law is archaic, barbarous and hypocritical," Beilenson said. "We force women and girls to seek out the services of quacks and criminal abortionists." Beilenson estimated that 100,000 illegal abortions were performed annually in California. This figure seemed high even to some of Beilenson's allies, but a Los Angeles County grand jury had been informed about an epidemic of illegal abortions among the poor. In addition, as Beilenson observed, notorious abortion mills flourished across the border in Mexico, where the practice was illegal but allowed.

Bell, Beilenson, and scores of other witnesses argued the issue before a standing-room-only crowd in the 293-seat hearing room of the Judiciary Committee. The hearing, patiently conducted by its Republican chairman, Donald Grunsky, began at 8 P.M. on April 27 and lasted six hours. At 2 A.M. on April 28, the thirteen-member committee sent the bill to the floor by a bare majority of seven votes, one of which was Grunsky's. Five of the seven affirmative votes were cast by Republicans. Beilenson persuaded only one other Democrat on the committee to vote for the bill.

The Senate committee's action came as a surprise to the governor. Reagan had expressed support for the legislation and communicated this to Beilenson and Craig Biddle, a Republican and former prosecutor who was the floor manager of the bill in the Assembly, but Vern Sturgeon, the governor's Senate liaison, had not anticipated that the bill would reach the floor. Sturgeon and his friend, Senate leader Burns, maneuvered to send it back to committee. The effort failed. But when Beilenson subsequently attempted to bring the bill up for a floor vote, he realized that both the Senate leadership and Sturgeon were working against him. Rather than risk defeat, he put the bill on the inactive file while he attempted to generate more enthusiasm for it in the governor's office.

In his first-floor corner office of the capitol, Reagan was not his usual decisive self. The abortion bill was foreign territory to him, and neither his doctrines nor his staff offered a compass to guide him. Opinions in the governor's office mirrored the division in the Legislature, where most Catholics opposed the bill and most non-Catholics favored it. Usually, Reagan could count on his top aides to reach at least a rough consensus. In this case, Lyn Nofziger and Edwin Meese advised him to support the bill, while Phil Battaglia and Bill Clark urged him to oppose it. The Kitchen Cabinet was also divided along religious lines. Supporters and opponents alike suspected that Nancy Reagan was a closet supporter of the bill, but she withheld comment. Her contribution was to suggest to her husband that he talk to her father Loyal Davis, a retired surgeon who supported liberalization of abortion laws. Reagan did. He also talked to Cardinal Francis McIntyre at a weekend meeting in Los Angeles arranged by his old campaign firm, Spencer-Roberts, which the Catholic Church had hired to lobby against the Beilenson bill. McIntyre, of course, opposed any change in the law.

Faced with an abundance of contradictory and absolutist advice, Reagan behaved as if lost at sea. At a news conference on May 9, he displayed almost total confusion about the bill, freely contradicting himself and claiming he had discovered some "loopholes," which on close examination turned out to be the purpose of the legislation. The clearest sign that the governor was wavering in his support for the bill came when he suggested that California allow Colorado, where a liberalized bill was already in effect, to become the "laboratory" to test changes in abortion law. But Reagan's performance at this news conference angered Republican senators, who had already made themselves political targets by voting for the Beilenson bill and didn't want to go through the process again. "This will keep coming back as an emotional issue year after year," Senate Judiciary Chairman Grunsky told Reagan. "If the Legislature acts now, the issue will be resolved and settled once and for all."[8] Still, Reagan could not decide. He was poring over the written material provided by both sides but could find no clue to a compromise. "I have never done more study on any one thing than on the abortion bill," Reagan told me later.[9]

In the agony of indecision, Reagan lied to reporters, a sure sign he was under stress. On two separate occasions, he denied at news conferences that he had been contacted by Spencer-Roberts or had met with Cardinal McIntyre. (Later, he freely admitted their involvement.) Reagan was playing for time. Before the Senate vote, he issued a statement calling for a compromise of "morality and logic" and describing the provision in the bill allowing abortions for anticipated deformities as "not different from what Hitler tried to do." A disgusted Beilenson commented that the governor "was just talking and talking, hoping no bill gets to him." He was right, but Beilenson was too good a legislator to allow this to happen. Beilenson removed the offending section, and the Senate passed the bill with the minimum twenty-one votes.

The opposition did not quit. The Catholic Church's lobbyist, an urbane former American Legion commander named William Burke, huddled with Stu Spencer and Battaglia, who obtained a legal opinion questioning the impact of the Senate legal changes. Then, at the prodding of Battaglia and the lobbyists, Reagan discovered new "loopholes" in the measure. On June 13, two hours before the Assembly voted on the bill, Reagan discussed them at his weekly press conference, emphasizing the latitude given doctors to authorize abortions to preserve the mental health of the mother. When asked whether he would sign or veto the measure, the governor replied, "I haven't had time to really sit down and marshal my thoughts on that." But Republicans who had taken heat for supporting the bill were tired of Reagan's dithering. After Assemblyman Biddle declared on the floor that the governor would be "breaking a pledge" if he failed to sign the bill, the Assembly passed the measure on a 48–30 vote. As in the Senate, Catholics cast most of the "no" votes. One of the few Catholics who voted for the bill even though he abhorred abortion, was a young up-and-coming Democrat named Bob Moretti who valued Beilenson and realized that many women wanted to reform the abortion law. Moretti wept as he voted "aye."[10]

As soon as the bill passed, Lyn Nofziger demonstrated the leadership that had hitherto been lacking in the governor's office. Nofziger realized that stories in the next wire-service cycle and in the June 14 newspapers would focus on the possibility of a Reagan veto unless he declared his intentions immediately. Striding into the governor's office, Nofziger said he wanted to issue a press release saying that Reagan would sign the bill the following day. Reagan wearily agreed, and Nofziger produced the press release within minutes. The news stories the next day emphasized the potential impact of the legislation and passed over Reagan's indecisive performance before the bill was passed.

There are worse maladies than indecision. In his heart, Reagan agreed with Cardinal McIntyre, not Dr. Davis, and he really wanted to veto the Therapeutic Abortion Act. Instead, he subordinated his personal feelings to the commitment he had made to Republican legislators to sign the bill. He wasn't happy about it. "Those were awful weeks," Reagan told me a year later. He added that he would never have signed the bill if he had been more experienced as governor, the only time as governor or president that Reagan acknowledged a mistake on major legislation. And this was in 1968, when the full consequences of the Beilenson bill were uncertain and when Reagan still believed he had prevented its worst features from becoming law. "You can't allow an abortion on grounds the child won't be born perfect," Reagan said. "Where do you stop? What is the degree of deformity [required] that a person shouldn't be born? Crippled persons have contributed greatly to our society."[11] He never wavered in this view. When legislators in 1970 proposed new liberalizations in the abortion law, Reagan successfully opposed them. In a "Dear Citizen" letter, he said, "Those who summarily advocate a *blanket population control* [Reagan's emphasis] should think carefully. Who might they be doing away with? Another Lincoln, or Beethoven, an Einstein or an Edison? Who shall play God?"

But these musings came after the fact. The Therapeutic Abortion Act of 1967 did what the antiabortionists had feared, as doctors broadly interpreted the provision to allow abortions on mental-health grounds. In 1967, when the measure was enacted, there were only 518 legal abortions in California. In 1980, the year Reagan was elected president, 199,089 abortions were performed in California hospitals and clinics. The total number of abortions performed from 1968 to 1980 was 1,444,778.[12]

As abortions increased exponentially, Reagan claimed that physicians, especially psychiatrists, were taking unfair advantage of the mental-health provision and said he had not known of this "loophole" when he signed the measure.* The best that can be said about this claim was that Reagan had forgotten what he had said at his news conference two hours before the bill was passed. "The prognosis of mental health would be easier to exaggerate than the diagnosis of physical health, and

---

*The cabinet minutes record Reagan as opening the cabinet meeting of March 28, 1968, by declaring, "I discovered I do have a prejudice." At the time the governor was meeting with a series of minority groups, one of which included an "articulate" psychiatrist who rubbed Reagan the wrong way. "I have discovered I am prejudiced . . . against psychiatrists," Reagan said. "I don't care WHAT color they are."

this of course could allow certain leeway for a doctor who wanted to do this [perform an abortion], to make a statement that he believed that this grievous suffering or this mental health deterioration would result," Reagan said at the time. Despite these suspicions, Reagan had no idea of the magnitude of the abortions that the provision would allow. Beilenson himself told me he was surprised that physicians so liberally interpreted the law.[13]

This was not the last word from Reagan on the issue. On July 27, 1979, with *Roe v. Wade* the law of the land, Reagan declared his support for a constitutional amendment that would have returned national abortion law to what it had been in California before the Beilenson bill. In a letter to Representative Henry Hyde, author of the Human Life Amendment, Reagan said, "I personally believe that interrupting a pregnancy is the taking of a human life and can only be justified in self-defense, that is, if the mother's own life is in danger."

Reagan's overall legacy on abortion is mixed. By a pro-life standard, he failed. With a stroke of the pen on June 14, 1967, Reagan signed a bill that permitted more legal abortions in California than occurred in any other state before the advent of *Roe v. Wade*. Later, his support of the Hyde Amendment earned him the support (and baggage) of pro-life forces in his presidential campaigns. I have no doubt that Reagan by then believed that abortion was murder, but the issue was never a high priority for him. Of 1,044 writings in his own hand, most of them radio speeches between the end of his governorship in 1975 and his election as president in 1980, only one was devoted to the abortion issue.[14] As president, Reagan addressed the annual pro-life rallies in Washington by telephone so he would not be seen with leaders of the movement on the evening television news. This practice was ascribed to the public relations savvy of Michael K. Deaver, but it continued after Deaver left the White House. Abortion was a troublesome issue for Reagan. He stayed away from it as much as he could.

On other social issues, Governor Reagan knew his intended destinations but had little help from the Legislature in reaching them. His chief obstacle was the Assembly, where Unruh did not make it easy for any governor. The Democrats had only a four-vote Assembly majority during Reagan's first two years in office, and Unruh realized it was risky for Democrats to challenge the governor directly on such "law-and-order" issues as pornography or campus unrest. But Unruh knew how to bottle up bills as well as pass them, and he sent bills that would have advanced Reagan's social agenda to the graveyard of the Assembly Criminal Procedure Committee.

Civil libertarians revered this committee in the Pat Brown years, when liberals dominated it. To law enforcement, which watched in dismay as bills for stiffer penalties and longer sentences were repeatedly buried or emasculated, it was the "criminal committee." As crime rates rose in the 1960s, there was a clamor to break the bottleneck. Unruh reacted by balancing the committee between five Democrats and five Republicans, all from nominally safe districts. He named a Republican as chairman. During Reagan's first two years as governor, this committee killed Republican proposals that would have outlawed distribution of pornography to minors, increased the penalties for narcotics use and for campus trespass, lengthened mandatory minimum sentences for a number of crimes, and "untied the hands" of law enforcement agencies on arrest procedures to the degree permitted by the courts. At the same time, the committee scuttled Democratic proposals that would have eased penalties for narcotics use, authorized earlier release of prisoners, and imposed wide-ranging gun controls. The stalemate was frustrating to liberals and conservatives alike but acceptable to Unruh, who on these issues was content to maintain the status quo.

Reagan and the conservatives finally broke through with a trio of bills introduced by Senator George Deukmejian, the Republican who had carried the governor's fiscal package. The most important of these bills increased the penalties for persons convicted of inflicting great bodily harm on their victims during a robbery, burglary, or rape from five to fifteen years. These sentences seem tame when compared with modern penalties in California, where a thief with a record of three felonies can be sent to prison for life. At the time, however, they were an achievement. After minor changes, the Deukmejian bills cleared the Assembly Criminal Procedure Committee with Unruh's tacit blessing. Reagan signed them into law with much fanfare.

Many Democrats in the 1960s feared being labeled "soft on crime." Reagan had raised the crime issue in his 1966 campaign, and Richard Nixon and Spiro T. Agnew would exploit it inconclusively in two subsequent elections. But Reagan was less partisan and arguably more effective than Nixon and Agnew in his approach. Instead of portraying Democrats as "soft," Reagan focused on court decisions that he believed had tilted the balance against victims and toward lawbreakers. His target was most often the California Supreme Court, which on criminal-justice issues had blazed a liberal trail before the U.S. Supreme Court under Chief Justice Earl Warren entered the fray. In a speech to the National Sheriffs Association, Reagan attacked court decisions that he said "have narrowed the difference between liberty and license" and "overbalanced the scales of justice so that the rights of society are outweighed by decisions granting new rights to individuals accused of crimes." He then gave an account of a grisly murder of a ten-year-old girl who had been stabbed repeatedly and "mutilated in a savage and depraved manner." The killer was sentenced to death, but his conviction and sentence had been overturned on a 4–3 decision of the California Supreme Court "because there was insufficient evidence that the defendant intended to commit mayhem or torture." Reagan said that such decisions pointed up the need for "common sense and realism in the war on crime." He continued: "Let us have an end to the idea that society is responsible for each and every wrongdoer. We must return to a belief in every individual being responsible for his conduct and his misdeeds with punishment immediate and certain. With all our science and sophistication, our culture and our pride in intellectual accomplishment, the jungle still is waiting to take over. The man with the badge holds it back."[15]

Reagan's certitude was shakier when he was required to make a decision of life or death. He became governor near the end of an undeclared four-year moratorium on the death penalty caused by a series of court stays. The idleness of the apple-green gas chamber at San Quentin had been a blessing not only for the condemned but also for Governor Brown, who always anguished when faced with a clemency decision. Brown had made thirty-five such decisions in his two terms as governor and spared a dozen convicted killers, far more than any other California governor. Reagan had not specifically criticized any of these acts of clemency but had complained about delays in the judicial process and once talked sarcastically about the need for an "urban renewal project" on San Quentin's Death Row, where sixty condemned men had accumulated. But he felt less cocksure when he reviewed the clemency appeal of Aaron Mitchell, a thirty-seven-year-old black man who had killed a Sacramento policeman during a robbery. "Ron talked to his pastor and he said later it was the worst decision he ever had to make," a Reagan associate told me. "It was one thing to be for capital punishment and another to know you had the power to save a man's life."[16]

There were no grounds for sparing Mitchell other than opposition to the death penalty. His victim was killed in the line of duty, and no California governor has ever commuted the death sentence of a cop killer. Governor Brown had heard Mitchell's appeal for clemency in 1966 and swiftly denied it. But Mitchell had since received a stay and was legally entitled to another review of his sentence by the new governor. Reagan, who as a boy had given up raising rabbits with his brother because he could not bear to kill them, did not have the stomach for a clemency hearing. He turned this unpleasant chore over to Edwin Meese III, his thirty-five-year-old legal affairs secretary and a former deputy district attorney from Alameda County who believed strongly that the death penalty was a deterrent.

Meese was scrupulous. He conducted an extensive and detailed hearing during which Mitchell's mother ran sobbing from the room. Afterward, he reviewed the transcript with the governor, but there was never any real doubt about the outcome. On April 11, 1967, the day before Mitchell's scheduled execution, Reagan denied clemency and focused his comments on the victim. "In this particular instance the man, the father of two children, who was killed was a policeman," Reagan told reporters. "I think that if we are going to ask men to engage in an occupation in which they protect us at the risk of their life, we . . . have an obligation to them to let them know that society will do whatever it can to minimize the danger of their occupations. I think any policeman is entitled to that. There are no bands playing or flags flying when he shoots it out with a criminal on our behalf."

On the eve of the execution, demonstrators opposed to the death penalty began an all-night candle vigil in front of the Reagan home in Sacramento. Police kept them separated from another orderly group that was picketing the pickets. Reagan went to bed. At breakfast, he told Nancy Reagan that he did not object to the demonstrators' call for church bells to ring out at 10 A.M., the hour of Mitchell's execution, but thought "it also would be a good idea if church bells would ring out for the murder victim as well."[17] Reagan then went to his office, which was also being picketed. At 10 A.M., Mitchell was granted his last request of a cigarette. Two minutes later, four guards dragged the condemned man into the execution chamber. As they strapped him in, Mitchell screamed, "I'm Jesus Christ."

Two hours after the execution, the Senate Committee on Governmental Efficiency rejected a bill by Senator George Moscone repealing the death penalty. It marked the twenty-first time since 1933 that the California Legislature or one of its committees had rejected such a bill. Reagan was mentioned only once during the testimony, but Moscone pointedly called on the Legislature to prevent the executions of the sixty men remaining on Death Row because "beyond us there is nothing." Moscone later became mayor of San Francisco and was murdered by a disgruntled political foe, who was acquitted. But although Moscone was one of the Senate's most astute members, he was not quite right about Reagan. The governor did not regret his decision in the Mitchell case, but he had learned that there is a vast difference between the abstract rhetoric of retributive deterrence and the executive power to spare or take a life.

The rhetoric would continue, but the power would be carefully used.

The next clemency case to come before Reagan involved Calvin Thomas, twenty-seven, also a black man. He had been convicted of first-degree murder in May 1965 by a Los Angeles County jury for killing the three-year-old son of his girlfriend by hurling a firebomb into her home. Once more, Meese presided over a clemency hearing that Reagan did not attend, but this time he reached a different conclusion than either the jury or the trial judge. Meese told Reagan that an electroencephalogram and a psychiatric examination, conducted after Thomas was convicted, "revealed preexisting brain damage resulting in a chronic mental condition."[18] Claims of brain damage or childhood trauma are often made by defense lawyers desperate to find a judge or a governor willing to look beyond the trial record. They rarely bear fruit. But Reagan gratefully accepted Meese's recommendation and on June 29, 1967, granted clemency to Thomas. No one knew it at the time, but it was the last such decision Reagan would face. In 1972, the California Supreme Court struck down the death penalty. Later that year, the U.S. Supreme Court halted executions while it weighed the constitutionality of the death penalty, a decision it did not reach in the affirmative until after Reagan's governorship.

On issues of penology, Reagan was generally progressive, again despite his rhetoric. Steve Merksamer recalled an early meeting in the governor's office where Reagan was briefed on the state prison system. The briefing concluded with a rundown on the activities of the Catholic and Protestant chaplains in the prisons. What about the Jewish chaplains, Reagan asked. The briefer told him there weren't many Jewish inmates, but that rabbis were brought in for them upon request. That isn't good enough, Reagan said. He directed the appointment of Jewish chaplains, an on-the-spot action that dazzled Merksamer, then a young aide (many years later Governor Deukmejian's chief of staff) and a Jew.[19]

Of more import to more inmates was Reagan's authorization of conjugal visits in California prisons, a policy long advocated within the state Department of Corrections on grounds it would reduce despair and homosexual behavior. Conjugal visits were allowed in such otherwise backward states as Mississippi, but Reagan's predecessors in California had shied away from the issue because of the political risk that they might be portrayed as coddling criminals. That didn't worry Reagan. He agreed with an in-house paper written by Rus Walton, a thoughtful public relations man who hoped to transform the slogan of the "Creative Society" into policies. The paper, after indulging in Reaganesque rhetoric about police officers holding back the "jungle," proposed improving probation services, bail reform, and education on drug abuse. One of Walton's recommendations was that the state should "provide quarters at prisons for conjugal visits between inmates and their wives" because "this should help to alleviate instances of homosexuality in prisons and help to keep the family unit intact while the head of the household is incarcerated." Reagan agreed. Conjugal visits, called "family visits," were tried as a pilot project at the Men's Prison at Tehachapi and then gradually extended throughout the California prison system. Family visits exist to this day in California's prisons, although they were scaled back in the 1990s by Governor Pete Wilson, a Republican usually described as a moderate.

Reagan's record on judicial appointments was also generally constructive, although it was a far cry from the nonpolitical merit system he had advocated during his campaign for governor. California governors have enormous opportunity to leave their mark on the judiciary. They appoint all trial judges without ratification from anyone. They also appoint appellate and Supreme Court judges, which require approval from a judicial commission. The only restraint on governors is the political one of being held to account for unqualified judges. And this is no restraint at all on lame-duck governors, who hold appointive power until they leave office. After his defeat in 1966, Pat Brown made a record eighty appointments to the bench. These included his executive secretary, his clemency secretary, the state banking superintendent, the state resources director, three defeated legislators, and several friends as well as the aforementioned elevation of his brother to an appellate court. This free-wheeling indulgence in doling out judgeships was so shameless that it prompted protests even from Democrats in the Legislature. Critics proposed prohibiting lame-duck appointments, or, at a minimum, making them subject to Senate confirmation, but nothing came of these ideas.

During his campaign for governor, Reagan had repeatedly criticized Brown for appointing "political cronies" and promised to take politics out of judicial appointments. He endorsed a variant of the Missouri Plan in which judges are chosen by a professional commission composed of lawyers and judges. Reagan stood by his "merit plan" proposal, and Senator Grunsky offered a bill to make it law, but only for appellate and Supreme Court judges. When it came to judges in the trial courts, despite Reagan's continued insistence that he sought the most qualified judges his subordinates sought to redress the political balance after eight years of a Democratic governor.

Paul Haerle, the San Francisco attorney who was brought into the administration by Tom Reed and succeeded him as appointments secretary, directed judicial selection. Haerle set up five-person judicial selection boards in all but the smallest of California's fifty-eight counties, each composed of three lay members, one Bar Association representative, and one judge. The names of the board members were kept secret, although their identities often were known within the particular counties. "The three lay members were usually people who had been active in the Reagan campaign," Haerle said. "The Bar Association representative was usually nominated by the bar. The judge I'd usually pick in consultation with a Republican lawyer."[20] Haerle did not operate in a vacuum. William French Smith, the governor's longtime lawyer, took an active interest in Los Angeles County judges, sometimes with input from the Kitchen Cabinet. Nominees in Alameda County (Oakland and Berkeley) were usually vetted with Edwin Meese. Gordon Luce, although not a lawyer, often was consulted on prospective San Diego County nominees.

This process produced an abundance of prospective Republican judges, whose names were submitted for ranking to the State Bar. The bar ranked nominees on a four-point scale, from "exceptionally well qualified" to "not qualified." None of the latter were appointed. Most prospective nominees were in the middle range, either "well-qualified" or "qualified." Haerle, Smith, and others in the inner circle agreed that Reagan needed to appoint good judges, even to the point of taking a highly qualified Democrat over an unqualified Republican. But politics was always part of the process. In Monterey County, Reagan appointed his local campaign manager over two qualified candidates who were recommended by the Reagan selection committee. He also appointed his trusted aide Bill Clark to three successively higher courts, each time provoking controversy. The Clark appointments will be examined in a subsequent chapter; suffice here to say that Clark was an exception in that he was one of the few state judges ever named by Reagan whose qualifications were questioned.

Considering Reagan's avowed commitment to a merit system, which he continued to advocate well into his governorship, Haerle was remarkably candid about the Reagan team's approach to judicial selection. "Political registration has got to be of importance," Haerle told me in 1968. "It's terribly demoralizing to the [Republican] party if a Democrat is appointed, particularly on the first round."[21] But Haerle was leery of party hacks or anyone too eager to become a judge. "The guys who want these judicial jobs are often the least desirable," he said. "The quality ones who are forty-five and fifty, you have to go out and ask them to serve. If they're making a lot of money, they may want to wait until they're sixty, but that's not when you want them."[22]

Reagan signed off on the judicial selection boards and welcomed the ratings of the State Bar as a useful tool for weeding out loyalists who were unqualified to be judges. But he characteristically insisted that "the boys," as he referred to his team, work it out among themselves when there was a controversy over two or more qualified candidates. Even when a selection was uncontroversial, Reagan hesitated to call the successful applicant and congratulate him. Haerle urged him to make such calls, believing it was good politics, but Reagan usually had Haerle make them instead.[23] Haerle surmised that Reagan's behavior reflected a general distaste for lawyers. More probably, Reagan was demonstrating his normal reluctance to become involved in the rewards-and-punishment aspects of politics. He cared about ideas and communicating with people. The nuts and bolts of politics did not interest him.

The Reagan team played politics nonetheless, quickly mastering the art of using judgeships as commodities that could be traded for votes. Battaglia was aggressive in this regard. He swapped four judges with Unruh in return for legislative concessions to the administration and doled out two judges to Democratic Senator Alfred Alquist to obtain his vote on the $1 billion tax bill. Senator Alfred Song's law partner wound up with a lower court judgeship after Song switched his vote in favor of the merit plan for appellate and Supreme Court judges.

The merit plan, however, did not make it through the Legislature. Grunsky had sufficient muscle to pry the bill out of his committee, and Song's vote enabled it to clear the Senate, but it died in an Assembly committee. Various learned-sounding arguments were made against the Grunsky bill, but the merit plan was killed because of politics. Under the prevailing system, which still exists, lawyer-legislators have an inside track to judicial appointment, and they did not want to give up this opportunity for a merit plan. Unruh, no lawyer, let the attorneys in the Democratic caucus do the dirty work, but he was pleased with the outcome. He believed in political appointments, had benefited from trading votes for judgeships, and looked forward to one day being governor himself.

Later, after Republicans won control of the Assembly in 1968, the dealing in judgeships continued. In 1969, Republicans sought to induce a Democratic legislator from a marginal Assembly district in Los Angeles County to take a judgeship in the hope they could elect a Republican to succeed him. Lewis Uhler of Public Affairs Associates, a Republican organization, approached the law partner of Democratic Assemblyman Harvey Johnson and asked if Johnson was interested in a judgeship. Subsequently, Republican Assemblyman William Campbell, who represented a neighboring district, told Johnson, "You know, that judgeship is yours if you want it."[24]

Johnson, notably honest, was one of the few Democrats who had supported the merit plan for judicial selection. He turned down the judgeship and exposed the maneuver as a Republican attempt to create a special election and ensure control of the Assembly. "Perhaps our citizen politician should climb down off his high horse of hypocrisy and rename [the merit plan] his barter plan for political advancement," Johnson said.[25] When Reagan was questioned about the offer at a subsequent press conference, he denied knowledge of it. I was skeptical at the time of his denial but believe now that he made it in good faith. The offer originated with Assembly Republicans anxious to preserve a slim majority.[26] Had it been accepted, the governor's staff would have been required to produce a judgeship, but that would have been easy to do because there were several judicial vacancies in Los Angeles County. There would have been no need to tell Reagan about the maneuverings while the deal was in an exploratory stage. In fact, there was an advantage in not telling him because it enabled him to deny, truthfully, that he was not part of the deal. That is what he did.

Despite the wheeling and dealing, Reagan's overall record in appointing judges was a good one. Reagan named more than 600 judges in eight years as governor, and even critics of the administration agreed that most were of high quality. Reagan was no judicial activist. What he wanted, as he had told the National Sheriffs Association, was "common sense and reason" on the bench, and that is pretty much what he got. But his judicial selection process, while producing qualified judges, was as partisan as his predecessor's. Eighty percent of Reagan's appointees were Republicans, almost exactly the percentage of Democrats who had been appointed to the bench by Pat Brown.

Governor Reagan's most significant judicial appointment was his selection on April 6, 1970, of Donald R. Wright of Pasadena as chief justice of the California Supreme Court, following the retirement of Roger Traynor. Wright, a third-generation Californian descended from a family that had crossed the plains in a covered wagon, had graduated with honors from Stanford and Harvard Law School. Governor Earl Warren had appointed him to the bench in 1953. In 1967, when Wright was presiding judge of a trial court in Glendale, William French Smith asked him to help the Reagan team with judicial appointments. Several of Wright's recommendations were appointed judges. The following year, Reagan promoted Wright to the appellate court.

In announcing what he called "one of the most important decisions I shall ever make as governor," Reagan said that he had picked Wright as chief justice after an "exhaustive search which encompassed the entire judiciary and legal profession of the state." Indeed, the governor had been part of the search. Although Reagan had rubber-stamped the choices of his appointments team for lower courts, he took an active role in the selection of a chief justice. His goal, as he said in the announcement, was a justice who would return the California high court "to a policy of judicial restraint." Wright seemed ideal for this purpose. William French Smith had discussed his credentials with several judges and lawyers, all of whom agreed he was balanced and capable. In politics, he was a moderate Republican. In his record fifteen years as a trial judge, he had rarely been reversed. In the words of legal scholar Preble Stolz, "Wright was a judge's judge—professional, quiet and undramatic in demeanor—who seemed to exude dignity, open-mindedness, fairness, and compassion." Previous chief justices had been respected, but Wright was "loved as well as admired" by his colleagues, whom he led through "gentle persuasion."[27] There was nothing in Wright's background to suggest he was a judicial activist.

Politicians far less conservative than Reagan believed that the court needed a calming influence. Beginning in the mid-1950s, the California Supreme Court became nationally known for liberal judicial activism. Its decisions restricting police searches (notably *People v. Cahan* in 1955) anticipated the Warren court and provoked harsh denunciations of the court from law enforcement officials.[28] The Wright court, from April 1970 until February 1977, was on most issues balanced and centrist. But on the basis of a single dramatic decision, Wright forever alienated conservatives and forfeited the confidence of the governor who had appointed him.

The California Supreme Court is legally required to review all trials that result in death sentences. Early in 1972, the court for the second time heard such an appeal from Robert Page Anderson, who in 1965 had been convicted of shooting to death a San Diego pawnshop clerk during a robbery. On appeal, the California Supreme Court under Chief Justice Traynor had affirmed the conviction but set aside the death penalty on grounds that opponents of capital punishment had been improperly excluded from the jury. The court ordered a new penalty trial at which Anderson was again sentenced to death.

In their second appeal to the California high court, Anderson's lawyers challenged the constitutionality of capital punishment. They focused on the peculiar wording of the California Constitution, which prohibits "cruel *or* unusual punishment" instead of "cruel *and* unusual punishment," the phrase used in the Eighth Amendment to the U.S. Constitution. Wright found the conjunctive difference significant. Whatever its merits, the death penalty is certainly "cruel" in the common meaning of the word—indeed, few who support capital punishment would want it to be otherwise. Writing for a 6–1 majority of the court in *People v. Anderson*, Wright on February 18, 1972, declared capital punishment unconstitutional in California. Anderson's sentence was reduced to life imprisonment. So were the death sentences of 101 other inmates, among them, Sirhan Sirhan and Charles Manson, who were awaiting execution on San Quentin's Death Row.[29]

Reagan was shocked. He issued a statement declaring that Wright's decision made "a mockery of the constitutional process involved in establishing the laws of California" and called the court's distinction between "or" and "and" a "one-word technicality." Reagan also told reporters that Wright had not been against the death penalty when he appointed him. Privately, Reagan was harsher, accusing Wright of misleading him. According to Edwin Meese, who was present during the conversation, Wright told Reagan in a Sacramento meeting before his appointment that he favored the death penalty.[30] Wright denied that he had discussed the issue with Reagan. But whatever he said, or didn't, was irrelevant. Wright had a judicial duty to address the constitutional issues raised in *People v. Anderson* and to decide the case on its merits. That is what he believed he had done.

Wright, however, invited criticism with a ruling that was more expansive than necessary. Assemblyman John Burton of San Francisco, a leading liberal and foe of capital punishment, put his finger on the difficulty when he called Wright "Reagan's Earl Warren."[31] This was meant as a compliment, but in *People v. Anderson* Wright demonstrated Warren's penchant for making gratuitous comments that provided political ammunition to critics of the court. Wright could have struck down the death penalty law on the sole basis of the state constitutional wording "cruel or unusual." But he added that the death penalty was also cruel because long imprisonment before execution was psychological torture. As critics of the ruling noted, most of the delays between convictions and executions were the result of appeals made by the condemned. Wright's ruling also found that the death penalty was "unusual" as well as cruel because of "the evolving standards of decency that mark the process of a maturing society." So much for judicial restraint. The ensuing controversy, in the words of legal scholar Stolz, "left an indelible stain on numerous political leaders and gravely damaged the public credibility of the court."[32]

Police officers were especially offended by Wright's ruling. Outspoken Los Angeles Police Chief Ed Davis said the decision would "result in the slaughter of many California citizens by an army of murderers who have been waiting for years in Death Row for such an unrealistic judicial judgment."[33] The *Los Angeles Times* ran a front-page picture of Mary Sirhan, mother of Sirhan Sirhan, who was awaiting execution for the murder of Robert Kennedy. The caption said, "Elated by the Ruling." The *San Francisco Examiner* said editorially that capital punishment was "an issue of such overriding importance that it should never be abolished except by a vote of the people or their chosen legislative representatives."[34] In Sacramento, Senator Deukmejian introduced a state constitutional amendment to restore the death penalty.

Although Deukmejian's amendment was promptly approved by the Legislature and by voters, it took two U.S. Supreme Court decisions, two legislative measures, and a ballot initiative to restore the death penalty in California. Even then, it was not applied. Wright's successor, Rose Bird, reversed so many death sentences that she sparked a successful conservative campaign to remove her and two other liberal justices from the court. The gas chamber in San Quentin remained idle until April 21, 1992, when Robert Alton Harris was executed for the murder of two San Diego teenagers in 1978. It was the first execution since Aaron Mitchell had gone to his death in the early months of Reagan's governorship twenty-five years earlier. Although Reagan had not intended it, he had with Wright's appointment set in motion a long California moratorium on the death penalty.

17

LEADER

RONALD REAGAN, the actor who had never played a governor, discovered during his first months in office that he enjoyed the demanding role. He arrived in Sacramento not knowing what governors did except make speeches, and he struggled in the beginning to learn what was expected of him. He learned. Reagan was no method actor, but he needed to think of himself as a governor before he could behave like a governor, and he also needed to acquire the techniques of governance.

Technique was important to Reagan. He had been on the brink of losing his first adult job as a radio announcer because he could not read commercials when he hit upon the technique of memorizing the first paragraph so his reading would sound conversational. He had misread the lines of his first part in Hollywood, too, but reassured the worried director that he would memorize them. He did. His initial speeches as a traveling corporate salesman for General Electric were platitudinous, but Reagan practiced on his audiences and found the words to express his sacramental vision. He became an inspiring political speaker. As governor, he knew so little about state issues when he began that his most frequent answer at early news conferences was, "I don't know."[1] But he gained knowledge and confidence with practice, and the news conferences, sometimes televised, became an effective instrument of communication. Reagan was a performer who required regular rehearsals to keep his edge. As governor, he learned the technique—and the political utility—of saying less than he wanted to say about a given issue. The controversy over the Therapeutic Abortion Act was a learning experience that taught Reagan to withhold commitment until a bill had reached his desk.

Reagan needed help, and would always need help, with the fine print.

He was an idea man, not an analyst. He needed a system that utilized the expertise of others, for Reagan did not know—could not possibly have known, with his background—how government worked. Expertise, fortunately, was close at hand. Beginning with the governorship of Hiram Johnson (1911–1917), California had developed a professional bureaucracy that kept the machinery of government humming as the state built and operated roads, dams, universities, hospitals, and prisons and developed a complex network of social services. In Reagan's early months, the skill of the bureaucracy was particularly evident in the Department of Finance, where two professional holdovers, Roy Bell and Ed Beach, compensated for the deficiencies of Reagan's appointed finance director, Gordon Paul Smith.

Reagan's theory of administration was sound. He believed in hiring people of proven ability who tapped into the available expertise while nudging the bureaucracy in the direction he wanted it to go. This is what Reagan and his team mostly did, although the bureaucracy, in Sacramento as in Washington, was skilled at passive resistance to an executive who tried to move too swiftly. (Such resistance is irksome to governors and presidents but can be useful, as Reagan discovered when the bureaucracy joined forces with the Legislature to slow down the excessive reduction of the workforce at the state mental hospitals.) Without announcing it, Reagan learned to value the California state bureaucracy. While he continued to denounce government in his stump speeches, his targets were not in Sacramento but in Washington, where he took aim at the Johnson administration and the unnamed bureaucrats who held sway in the "puzzle palaces of the Potomac."

Reagan's reliance on bureaucratic expertise ratified his life's experience at the expense of his ideology. Movie-making is a collaborative enterprise in which expertise is critical. Reagan relied as an actor on the expertise of men and women who created the films, wrote the scripts, devised the sets, and operated the cameras, sound, and lighting systems. Directors appreciated Reagan because he was punctual, memorized his lines, and did what he was told. He behaved similarly in the governor's office, where he was the putative director. In fact, he provided little direction beyond what aides could glean from his speeches. Reagan had core beliefs and values, a welcome fearlessness, and a capacity for decision making. But he rarely reached out and even more rarely initiated a course of action. "He was a reactor, not an actor," said George Steffes, then a young legislative aide and a careful student of Reagan's modes of behavior.[2]

Reagan required a daily schedule that told him what to do, where to go, and whom to see. He adhered closely to this schedule, for he did not like to be kept waiting or to keep others waiting. Most of his meetings started and ended on time. Busy officials and reporters on deadline welcomed Reagan's discipline and punctuality, which at times unnerved legislators accustomed to small talk and a looser routine. The minutes of Governor Reagan's twice-weekly cabinet meetings show that he moved crisply through most discussion items. While he punctuated his comments with pithy one-liners that encouraged a relaxed atmosphere, he did not linger at cabinet meetings.

Reagan mastered his role as governor because he was competitive, organized, and on most issues a quick study. He was also a good listener, when he wanted to listen, and he intuitively absorbed information. Blessed with a low ego, Reagan was unafraid to show ignorance, an unusual quality in politicians. Asked at a news conference about the contents of his legislative program, Reagan turned to his aides and said plaintively, "Can anyone tell me what's in my legislative program?" Reporters laughed. What Reagan lacked in knowledge, he made up for with a candor that appealed to many members of the media.

Still, he often seemed to be doing it with mirrors. Legislators, reporters, and (behind his back) even members of his staff lampooned Reagan as a nine-to-five acting governor who made spot decisions based on Bill Clark's mini-memos and over-delegated to his subordinates. There was a kernel of truth to this stereotype, but it reflected the usual underestimation of Reagan. While his understanding of complex issues was sometimes superficial, Reagan's political and managerial instincts were, up to a point, secure. He understood that a governor should not waste his time in micromanagement. "Show me an executive who works long overtime hours, and I'll show you a bad executive," Reagan said.[3]

But while Reagan never burned the midnight oil for the sake of staying busy, he would stick around when there was work to do. "He took the business of reviewing legislation very seriously," said Steffes, who remembers poring over scores of bills with Reagan and experts brought in from various departments of government.[4] Reagan also stayed late if the Legislature was working and aides wanted him around for last-minute negotiations. "At some of the budget sessions, he would be in his office after midnight in case he was needed," Steffes said. "But you had to ask him to be there."[5]

In discussing political leadership, James MacGregor Burns wrote, "The most important instrument a leader has to work with is himself—his own personality and its impact on other people."[6] Burns was writing about Franklin Delano Roosevelt, whose words of hope had thrilled Reagan as a young man, but his perception applies with equal force to

Reagan. In his first months as governor, Reagan concentrated on reviving the faith of Californians in their government—a goal that anticipated the larger task of renewing the damaged confidence of Americans at the outset of his presidency in 1981. Reagan, like FDR, focused on economic issues because he knew they were the key to advancing broader goals. Reagan would never have said, "It's the economy, stupid," the slogan of Bill Clinton's political team in 1992, for he did not inflate himself by insulting others, but he grasped the essence of the fiscal situation when he took office. He also realized, as FDR did, that dealing effectively with the economic realities that confronted him was more important than fulfilling a campaign promise. This is why Reagan agreed, without embarrassment, to a massive state tax increase that contradicted the thrust of his campaign message. This is also why he was willing as president to increase budget deficits that he had promised, as Roosevelt did in his 1932 campaign, to eliminate or reduce. Reagan was less experimental than FDR but equally determined to succeed.

Perhaps Reagan knew so little about his legislative program because there was not much in it at first except budget cuts and tax increases. Jesse Unruh, wise in the ways of Sacramento, realized this. "I think all in all he did very well," Unruh said of Reagan on the final day of the 1967 legislative session. "But the reason he did so well is he did as little as he had to. His whole strategy was not to get involved in major problems facing the state other than the budget and taxes."[7] As Unruh knew, however, the budget and taxes were the major problems facing California at the time, or at least the problems that a governor could successfully address. Reagan had addressed them. "He no longer can be termed an amateur politician," Unruh said. "He has learned every trick of the trade."[8]

One of the tricks Reagan learned was to circumvent troublesome lobbyists whose support was vital on crucial legislation by talking to the top executives of the company or industry that employed them.[9] This may have been a holdover from his days as president of the Screen Actors Guild, when Reagan dealt directly with producers. Reagan drew upon his Hollywood experience whenever possible. In a letter to William Meiklejohn on July 31, 1967, Reagan joked with his former agent that he was sorry he couldn't pay him a commission for "this new part" of governor. "Of course I could complain that the contract makes little provision for time off and no provision for overtime, and while I'm trying to play the 'Good guy,' the script is written so that most of the time I feel out-numbered," wrote Reagan.[10]

In large measure, it was this sense of humor and the ability to see himself as others saw him that rescued Reagan in Sacramento. Offstage, he had a decent respect for the opinions of others and a gentle perceptiveness that made him responsive to criticism. Steffes was displeased when Reagan became involved in a series of public recriminations with Pat Brown, the governor he had defeated. When Steffes said to Reagan that such criticism should be "beneath" the governor of California, Reagan looked up at him quietly and said, "You're right, and I won't do it anymore."[11] On another occasion, at a lobbyist's reception where Reagan had uncharacteristically imbibed a pair of vodka martinis, he was drawn into verbal sparring with Bill Bagley, the bright and volatile assemblyman who made no secret of his opinion that the governor was a know-nothing. Reagan had little use for Bagley, whom he regarded as a Democrat in Republican clothing. On the ride home after the reception, he thought about what had happened and said to an aide, "You know, all Bill really wants is attention, and we're going to give it to him. Find some bills we can work together on and have him be the author."[12]

In such ways, drawing upon his personality, Reagan learned bit by bit to be an effective governor. What he had to overcome, even more than his lack of background on state issues, was a misconception about politics embedded in his antipolitical rhetoric. Reagan entered public life believing that the legislators were connivers intent only on feathering their nests and perpetuating themselves in office. There was a grain of truth to this notion, but it was, like many of Reagan's political perceptions, a caricature. Over time, Reagan learned that legislators really were not much different from other people and that the approaches that had worked for him in Dixon, Des Moines, and Hollywood could also help him succeed in Sacramento.

They would also help him succeed in Washington. Nationally, conservatives still smarted from the debacle of the 1964 presidential election. Reagan seemed to them a dream come true and a logical challenger to President Johnson, whom they assumed would run for reelection in 1968. Johnson was still formidable, but his popularity had begun to fade. The Republican front-runner, as Reagan learned the ropes as governor, was the former auto magnate George Romney, elected in 1966 to a third term as governor of Michigan. Richard Nixon was considered a long shot who had been once too often around the track. Political strategists in the Reagan camp shared the conventional assumption that Nixon was a proven loser. When Tom Reed left Sacramento to promote a subterranean Reagan presidential candidacy, he thought that Romney or Governor Nelson Rockefeller of New York were the Republicans to beat.

Reagan was not yet ready to become a national candidate, and he was mindful that Californians would react negatively if they believed that he was interested in the governorship solely as a stepping stone to the White House. Reagan's only early foray to Washington was an obligatory performance on March 2, 1967, at a $500-a-plate victory dinner honoring new Republican governors and senators while paying off some of the party's debts in the process. To the delight of Reed and Lyn Nofziger, Reagan stole the show. The featured speaker of the evening was Romney, whose appearance, as described by Warren Weaver of *The New York Times*, "consisted almost entirely of jokes that failed to produce much laughter."[13] Reagan did better. He began his brief remarks by saying, "It's a pleasure to be in the only capital city that's in worse shape than our own." Reagan then issued what Weaver called "a rousing summons to Republican conservatives" to base their 1968 campaign on the lessons of 1966. These lessons, he said, were that people had voted against piling up debts with no plans to pay them and against "sharing the fruits of our toil with those who can't and won't work." But while reaching out to his base, Reagan sounded a grace note by suggesting that President Johnson consider Pat Brown for a seat on the Supreme Court. In his only foreign policy comment, Reagan said of the Vietnam War, "Any cause worth fighting for is a cause worth winning."[14]

The Republican audience, as well as *The New York Times* and *The Sacramento Bee*, agreed that Reagan was a hit. Reagan, however, did not want to fuel speculation about a presidential candidacy. When he returned to Los Angeles the next day, he emphasized to reporters that he had no ambition to run for president in 1968. That didn't close the door, for Reagan had agreed to head California's mammoth delegation to the Republican National Convention as a "favorite son," a common practice in those days. Reagan said his purpose was to "keep harmony and avoid any bitter campaigning in California which might split the Republican Party."[15]

Back in Sacramento, the governor's legislative aides ignored national politics and focused on improving relations with legislators who considered Reagan standoffish. The aides arranged for lobbyists to throw an elaborate dinner for Reagan and other leading politicians at The Firehouse, one of Sacramento's better restaurants. The host for the evening was a popular Democratic assemblyman named John T. Knox, who was mildly surprised when Reagan held his own in a pre-dinner discussion about wine, a subject on which Knox was conversant. Reagan had begun drinking wine in 1947 while recovering from the pneumonia that had nearly killed him. At a doctor's suggestion, he had a glass of red wine with dinners during his recuperation. Although Reagan never became much of a drinker, he learned enough about wine to maintain an adequate wine cellar in his Pacific Palisades home that, courtesy of General Electric, was thermostatically controlled to maintain an ideal temperature. Since consuming liquor was a vice to this alcoholic's son, Reagan justified his limited drinking on nutritional grounds. ("You're not allowed to advertise that any alcohol has food value, but wine has," Reagan told me two decades before the *New England Journal of Medicine* found medicinal value to moderate wine-drinking.[16])

There was ample drinking and eating at The Firehouse on the rainy evening of March 15, 1967. Waiters in maroon jackets served seven courses, with tornados Rossini as the entrée, each accompanied by a vintage wine. There was champagne for toasts, and brandy and cigars after dinner. Reagan, typically, tasted each course and sipped from each wine but neither cleaned his plates nor drained his wine glasses. He skipped the cigars and the brandy entirely. During dinner each guest told a story, several of them politically barbed and most of them off-color. The format was made to order for Reagan, who specialized in self-deprecating humor and was a veteran of Hollywood "roasts," where the aim is to insult the honored guest.

Reagan and State Senator George Miller Jr., an accomplished raconteur with a storehouse of off-color stories, dominated the evening. "Reagan went through a series of ethnic jokes, dialect jokes, and political jokes, all of them hilarious," said one participant.[17] One of the few printable jokes was at the expense of Controller Houston Flournoy, a moderate Republican who did not hold his liquor well. Flournoy had defeated Democrat Alan Cranston in part because Cranston, as recounted earlier, had spent too much of the 1966 campaign chasing Reagan around various airports to hand him a "white paper" accusing him of being a right-wing extremist. Noting that he hadn't seen Flournoy at any airports, Reagan said, "You've been in office for three months, and you still haven't started acting like a controller." Flournoy unsteadily told the governor what to do with himself, using a familiar four-letter word.[18] Then he laughed. Reagan laughed, too. According to some accounts, Flournoy soon nodded off.

There would be other such dinners during the Reagan governorship but not many of them. Reagan was convivial, but he had neither a genuine interest in socializing with other politicians nor a need to demonstrate that he was one of the boys. Some legislators thought their celebrity governor looked down on them; the prosaic truth was that Reagan was tired at the end of the day and preferred to spend evenings at home. As an actor, he had been accustomed to working intensely for weeks on a film, followed by several weeks off. As governor, he worked harder on a daily basis than he had since coming to California at the age of twenty-six. Whenever possible, Reagan left his corner office in the capitol before 6 P.M. for the seven-minute drive in his chauffeured state car to his home, where he watched the news, showered, and ate a simple dinner in his pajamas with Nancy. After dinner, he watched television, wrote letters, or read from a mélange of newspaper and magazine articles, science fiction, and memos about the next day's work schedule. In Sacramento, as later in Washington, Reagan's aides emphasized his memo reading and downplayed the rest of it. But Reagan rarely missed an episode of *Mission: Impossible, Mannix,* or *Bonanza,* the show that had sent *General Electric Theater* into oblivion. On Sundays, he sometimes watched professional football with his son Ron, who was nine when Reagan became governor and known to his parents as "Skipper."

This routine was manageable for Reagan but difficult for Nancy Reagan, who was unprepared for the demands of being a governor's wife faraway from home and friends. Nancy Reagan did not care much for Sacramento, nor Sacramento for her. The city was then an almost pastoral community equidistant from the bright lights of San Francisco to the west and the outdoor life of the high Sierra to the east. Although it was a pleasant place in which to live, Sacramento lacked the excitement and amenities of Los Angeles. Nancy Reagan's friends were in Hollywood, Malibu, Pacific Palisades, and Santa Monica. She shopped in Beverly Hills. She missed the Pacific Ocean and the mild Southern California weather. In Sacramento, the Reagans were supposed to live in the governor's mansion, a forbidding and dilapidated heap of Victorian gingerbread on a busy and noisy one-way street that carried traffic from San Francisco to Reno. No children had lived there for more than twenty years.[19]

Trading Pacific Palisades for Sacramento was bad enough. Living in a relic that was more suitable as a museum (which it is today) than a residence was unthinkable. Nancy Reagan rebelled. She realized that the mansion, which had ropes in the bedrooms instead of fire escapes, was a "firetrap." A rusted screen that wouldn't budge covered the window of her son's second-story bedroom. In case of fire, her son was supposed to smash the screen by running at it with a bureau drawer and then climb onto the roof.[20] Nancy Reagan had no difficulty in persuading her husband to move out of the mansion.* The Reagans, at their own expense, leased a two-story, twelve-room Tudor house in an exclusive section of

---

*The governor didn't think much of the mansion either. The cabinet minutes of May 23, 1967, when the Reagans were no longer living there, quote him as saying he was "amazed" to find out that Democratic leaders in the State Senate were intent upon preserving the mansion. After commenting on the costs of preserving it and the difficulty of parking, Reagan critically described the architecture. "The only thing that is interesting is the downstairs and the high ceiling and marble fire place," he said.

eastern Sacramento. When the owner, a city councilman, later decided to sell the house, members of the Kitchen Cabinet bought it for $150,000, leasing it back to the Reagans and making a good investment in the process. The Reagans lived in this house throughout the governorship.[21]

Sacramento, however, was never really home to the Reagans. On weekends, many of which began on Thursday when the Legislature was not in session, they retreated to Pacific Palisades. There, at home, Nancy Reagan could escape the demands of being a politician's wife, which in Sacramento included participation in a social organization composed of spouses of public officials and lobbyists. Nancy Reagan could not bear making small talk with the wives of legislators who, as she saw it, were disparaging her husband on the Assembly or Senate floor. Staff members, except for her loyal press assistant Nancy Clark Reynolds and a young aide named Michael Deaver, feared her and gave her a wide berth.* Newspaper reporters assigned to write about her, stereotypically women in those days, found her snobbish. Nancy Reagan was so annoyed by *The Sacramento Bee*, with its incessant editorial criticisms of her husband, that she barred the newspaper from her home. "I don't let him see it," she told me, adding that she had told a reporter from the paper, "I think you're very shortsighted; you're so heavy-handed in your approach. Nobody's as bad as you describe the governor."[23]

Ronald Reagan also held a negative opinion of *The Sacramento Bee*, but it was the newspaper of record in the capital and required reading. Sounding like a child who had outwitted his parents, the governor told me cheerfully that he had canceled the home subscription to please Nancy but read *The Bee* at the office.[24] Reagan was an inveterate newspaper reader who subscribed to seven newspapers at home.[25] Following the practice of his General Electric days, he clipped items of interest and used them in his speeches.

Nancy Reagan would over time become as sophisticated as her husband, in some ways more so, in dealing with the media. She was a better judge of people than he was and would learn to cultivate political alliances across party lines. But when Nancy Reagan arrived in Sacra-

---

*The opinion of Paul Haerle was typical. "Nancy treated staff like servants," he said. He recalled a 1968 incident where Reagan was hosting the Republican Governors Association in Palm Springs. "I was the appointments secretary, in charge of appointing judges," Haerle said. "My assignment from Nancy was to go to all the frigging lobbyists around town and try to arrange gift packages to give to the Republican governors as they checked into their hotel. I did it. But it was kind of demeaning to be calling the lobbyists, [saying] 'Can you give us some wine, can you give us some canned salmon?' She kept asking if I had talked to so-and-so. It was not a pleasant experience."[22]

mento, she was even more of a novice than her husband. Nothing in her experience had prepared her for the goldfish bowl of politics. In Chicago, under the doting eye of Loyal Davis, she had lived the sheltered life of a debutante and social registerite. What limited experience she had with the media was with a Hollywood press corps more cuddly and reverential toward its subjects than the political press was toward governors and legislators. Ronald Reagan had also faced a difficult adjustment when he entered partisan politics, but he at least had been exposed to critical coverage during Hollywood's union struggles and Red-hunting controversies.

Nancy Reagan was an easy target for the press, which treated her less generously than her husband. He could mangle statistics, distort facts, and forget his legislative program and emerge as a big, likable lug of a citizen-politician who was striving to do his best for the citizens of California. She could turn on the charm and say all the right things and be depicted as brittle, suspicious, and shallow. Reporters mocked "the Gaze," which was Nancy's transfixed way of looking at her husband in public. And then, just as the national press was becoming aware that Reagan had something other than tinsel between his ears, Nancy was savagely portrayed in *The Saturday Evening Post* by Joan Didion, who described Nancy's famous smile as a study in frozen insincerity. In an article that also carried the byline of Didion's husband, John Gregory Dunne, Didion portrayed the Reagan home and garden in Sacramento as a movie set in which everyone, including the state guard, the cook, and the gardeners, smiled relentlessly. "Nancy Reagan says almost everything with spirit," Didion wrote, "perhaps because she was an actress for a couple of years and has the beginning actress' habit of investing even the most casual lines with a good deal more dramatic emphasis than is ordinarily called for on a Tuesday morning on 45th Street in Sacramento."[26]

Nancy Reagan was crushed by this piece, which Katharine Graham later said set the tone for other articles. Nancy Skelton, an observant reporter, interviewed Nancy Reagan for *The Sacramento Bee* soon after the Didion article was published and found her "moved almost to the point of tears of anger that she had taken Didion into her house and down to the capitol and had spent a lot of time with her."[27] Skelton quoted Nancy Reagan as saying of Didion: "I thought we were getting along fine together. Maybe it would have been better if I snarled a bit."[28]

One reason for Nancy Reagan's bad press may have been that the most detailed stories about her were written by women. In those days, Nancy Reagan related poorly to women, allegedly because she saw them as competitors for her husband's attention. This changed in

Washington when Nancy Reagan became friends with Graham, the publisher of *The Washington Post*, and Meg Greenfield, the paper's influential editorial page editor. But she had no such friendships in Sacramento. Another reason for Nancy Reagan's problems was that she was, to use a psychological term, a "grievance collector." In her autobiography, she remembered every unflattering description: "Queen Nancy. The Iron Butterfly. The Belle of Rodeo Drive. Fancy Nancy. The Cutout Doll. On the *Tonight* show Johnny Carson joked that my favorite junk food was caviar."[29]

More favorable descriptions were forgotten. Nancy Reagan's autobiography does not mention a flattering article by Lynn Lilliston in the *Los Angeles Times* a few months after the Didion piece that was headlined: "Nancy Reagan: A Model First Lady."[30] (The article was written because the newspaper had chosen Nancy Reagan as a "*Times* Woman of the Year.") Nor did she recall an even more glowing pre-Didion piece in *Look* by Eleanor Harris, a friend of the family. The Harris article cited Nancy Reagan's frequent description of her husband as "my hero" and said she was also "his heroine." It quoted him as saying, "How do you describe coming into a warm room from out of the cold? Never waking up bored? The only thing wrong is, she's made a coward out of me. Whenever she's out of sight, I'm a worrier about her." Tears came to his eyes as he spoke, Harris reported. She concluded, "I *don't* believe that these two are a couple of actors acting. I *do* believe that they are genuinely devoted to each other."[31] No one who knew the Reagans doubted it.

Nancy Reagan's principal difficulty, with reporters and staff and allies of her husband alike, was the opposite of the pretense described by Didion. She alienated even those who were disposed to like her with statements that were bluntly honest and undiplomatic. I had a small taste of this when, prideful and naive, I showed the Reagans the cover of my first book, which depicted Reagan and Unruh overlaid on a map of California. Nancy Reagan said tightly that she had not expected Unruh to be on the cover. He smiled and said, "At least I got top billing." As Eleanor Harris observed, Nancy Reagan did not even know how to accept compliments for her husband. Strangers would come up to her at receptions and say they had talked to him and "found him so wonderfully bright and honest." She would bridle, saying that her husband had always been bright and honest, "sending the enthusiast away somewhat dispirited."[32]

Ronald Reagan accepted her as she was. In later presidential campaigns and in the White House, she would prod him to make needed staff changes and to come to grips with the consequences of wrong decisions, notably after the Iran-contra affair. But in Sacramento, at this stage of their political development, he was the protector who took his wife's calls even during cabinet meetings, caring little that it gave some the impression that she was "Governor Nancy." Once, an aide overheard a phone exchange in which Nancy Reagan called to complain about black militant Eldridge Cleaver, who had just delivered a number of foul-mouthed opinions of Reagan. "But, honey, I can't have him arrested just because he says those things," Reagan told her.[33] When I asked Reagan about this, he was philosophical. "She bleeds pretty good," he said with a chuckle. "Sometimes I come home and find she's pretty sore about something I laugh off. It's much harder on them [women] than it is on us—there's no way for them to fight back."[34]

Reagan was a gentleman before he was a leader. By treating his wife with respect, he set an example of stability and helped her adjust to the frequent cruelties of political life. She learned from him, but she helped him, in no small measure because she was often more sensitive to the needs of others than he was. Escaping from the routine of home and social life, she threw herself into the useful Foster Grandparents Program, begun by Sargent Shriver, which brought older people into regular contact with children who had been institutionalized as "mentally retarded." This was well publicized, but Nancy Reagan also reached out in situations that were never reported by the press.

Early in 1973, the Reagans held a reception at their Sacramento home for the legislative freshman class, which included Assemblyman Lou Papan, a Democrat. "It was a large class and they put us in the basement, which didn't set well with many of the wives," recalled Papan years later. He was annoyed by the perfunctory behavior of the governor, "who was a bit removed," but charmed by Nancy Reagan, who warmly greeted Papan and his wife Irene. The Papans had a son who was seriously ill. Nancy told Irene Papan that she was a doctor's daughter and did her best to comfort the distressed mother. The Papans lost their son, but memories of Nancy Reagan's empathy lingered. "I think Nancy smoothed over her husband's rough edges," Papan said.[35]

It was an assessment rarely heard in Sacramento.

18

SURVIVOR

S AN DIEGO, where Father Junipero Serra in 1769 proclaimed the first permanent Christian settlement in California, is serene in August, when residents and visitors flock to its broad beaches, spacious Balboa Park, the famous San Diego Zoo, or the Del Mar racetrack. Among its favorite hideaways is the sleepy little peninsula of Coronado, home to the Hotel Del Coronado, a "great, lumbering, white Victorian wonder."[1] Today "The Del," as locals call it, is a ten-minute drive from downtown San Diego across a picturesque bridge. But in August 1967, when Ronald Reagan and his wife escaped to this elegant haven, it was accessible only by ferry.

Reagan, recovering from the surgery that had caused him to miss the final hours of the legislative session, was in good spirits. In his first year as governor, despite his inexperience and a Democratic-controlled Legislature, he had rescued the state from fiscal chaos with a balanced budget and a progressive tax bill. After early stumbles, he had emerged from the legislative session to the praise of opposition editorialists and even the Democratic leader, Jesse Unruh. Only the extreme Right blamed Reagan for resorting to liberal fiscal remedies, and this marginal opposition made him seem more reasonable.

Reagan was fortunate in other ways. The state's economy was on the upswing. California had been spared the violent civil disorders that rocked eastern cities that spring and summer. From a political standpoint, Reagan's situation looked too good to be true. It was. On the pleasant Friday afternoon of August 25, as the fog retreated over the horizon and temperatures lingered in the mid-seventies, eleven of the governor's most trusted aides and supporters barged into the Reagan suite at The Del to accuse his chief of staff, Phil Battaglia, of inappropriate conduct and demand that he be fired.

Battaglia, a natty dresser with dark good looks and a receding hair-line, had been brought into Reagan's 1966 campaign by Holmes Tuttle as Southern California chairman and promoted to the state chairman-ship after the primary. Though something of a mystery man to other members of the Reagan team, he had an excellent resume. Battaglia had been a big man on campus at the University of Southern California, where he had served as student body president and editor of the *Trojan Bar Quarterly*, and compiled a solid academic record. When Tuttle tapped him for political service, he was an up-and-coming partner in a major Los Angeles law firm. In addition to these achievements, Battaglia met the Spencer-Roberts test of lacking a political history; Reagan's campaign management team wanted bright young men who were unscarred by internecine party warfare. After the election, Battaglia, almost by default, became Reagan's executive secretary, as the chief of staff was then called. He had the vital blessings of Tuttle and Nancy Reagan, toward whom he was deferential. As previously noted, the governor often called him "my strong right arm."

Battaglia presented two faces to the world in Sacramento. He treated powerful politicians, especially Unruh, with courtesy and respect. With those who had less influence, both on the governor's staff and outside it, he was often curt and dismissive. Battaglia made an alliance with Nof-ziger, who agreed that one of them would be present in all meetings with Reagan. Other top members of the Reagan team disliked the way Battaglia operated. Gordon Luce, the executive secretary for trans-portation and commerce, considered him overly protective of Reagan. Ike Livermore, the resources executive secretary, thought that Battaglia didn't do his homework. Livermore was appalled when Battaglia, on a short ride to the airport before he flew to Washington, asked for a quick fill on the controversy over creation of a Redwoods National Park. Liv-ermore didn't know where to start, and he balked at trying to summa-rize in a short compass a complex issue about which he had strong feelings. He told Battaglia he couldn't do what he was asking and sug-gested they talk in depth about the issue when the chief of staff re-turned.[2] They never did. Bill Clark, the cabinet secretary, got along well with Battaglia but was mystified by his many absences. "I tried to run everything by him, whenever I could find him," Clark said.[3] That be-came increasingly difficult. During the crucial months of May and June, for instance, the cabinet minutes show that Battaglia attended only six of twenty-four cabinet meetings.

Despite his inattention to the cabinet, Battaglia cultivated the media. Trying to control "background" communications, he laid down a rule that only he and Nofziger could talk with reporters. Battaglia naturally

favored the *Los Angeles Times*, his hometown paper, and the Los Angeles af-
filiates of the three television networks represented in the capitol, but he
also provided information to reporters for the wire services and for the
San Diego, Sacramento, and San Francisco newspapers. The *San Jose
Mercury-News*, for which I worked, was not on Battaglia's big-battalion
list, but he usually took my calls when he was in town. I found him but-
toned-down and careful, except for an expansive moment when he confided to me that he could "handle" Unruh. It was an odd statement; the
formidable Assembly speaker could not easily be handled by anyone.

Battaglia had a mixed reputation with the press corps. Reporters
value anyone who provides them with information, and Battaglia, by
dint of controlling access, did better on this score than most other Reagan aides. But reporters tend to be suspicious of those with high opinions of themselves. Battaglia behaved as if he ran the place, and some
reporters sarcastically called him "deputy governor" before Nofziger
began using this phrase. My opinion at the time was that Battaglia patronized Reagan. He acted as if he were smarter than his boss, foreshadowing the conduct of Reagan's campaign strategist John Sears in 1980
and of Donald Regan, who became White House chief of staff in 1985.
But Battaglia had far less experience that either Sears or Regan, and his
political instincts were shakier. It was Battaglia, for instance, who proposed that state employees work voluntarily on Lincoln's and Washington's birthdays, a silly gimmick during the novice period of Reagan's
governorship that proved a flop.

Such nonproductive experiments aside, it was widely believed that
Battaglia was more liberal than Reagan. The evidence for that view is
scant and contradictory. Battaglia wanted Reagan to veto the Beilenson
bill that liberalized abortions. The cabinet minutes show that Battaglia
was more rigid and adamant than the governor on cutting the workforce at the mental hospitals. Only on the Rumford Fair Housing Act
can it be argued that Battaglia was more moderate than Reagan. Even
on this issue it is a close call, for Battaglia was not far apart from Reagan
in his views, although he may have recognized the need for compromise
before the governor did. Thomas C. Reed, Reagan's first appointments
secretary and a rival, thought that Battaglia was nonideological and interested only in acquiring power, a view that eventually became a collective opinion in the governor's office.

The "inappropriate conduct" of which Battaglia was accused by the
Reaganites who interrupted the governor's vacation at the Hotel Del
Coronado was homosexuality. These rumors had circulated for months
within the governor's staff, although Reagan was unaware of them.
They were first directed not at Battaglia but at a young scheduling aide,

who for reasons never fully clear had displeased senior Reagan aides. They took their complaints to Battaglia, who dismissed them. "We were a little surprised at that," Clark recalled.[4] Soon, it was noticed that Battaglia disappeared on trips, sometimes with his scheduler, for no apparent governmental purpose. Then a report came in from Edgar Gillenwaters, the governor's representative in Washington, D.C., that raised questions about Battaglia's conduct while he was in the nation's capital. Gillenwaters was not a rumormonger, and his report sounded alarm bells in Sacramento.* Clark and Nofziger were concerned but reluctant to share this information. Neither knew quite what to do.

Public attitudes toward homosexuality have changed enormously since 1967, nowhere more than in California. Despite lingering prejudice and periodic hate crimes directed against gays and lesbians, most Californians now regard sexuality as a matter of biology instead of choice. It is not news today in California if a public official puts a homosexual in a position of trust. Today, two openly gay men and three proclaimed lesbians are valued members of the Legislature, and another lesbian is a state constitutional officer. Their sexuality has never been an issue.

For all anyone knows, there were as many homosexuals working in California state government in 1967 as there are now. But they were of necessity circumspect about their sexual orientation, for they invited dismissal if they announced it to the outside world. Leland Nichols, a former television reporter who had worked for Pat Brown and was in 1967 on Jesse Unruh's staff, described the period as one of "fairly high paranoia" for gay men in politics or government.[6] Nichols, who many years later revealed that he was gay, said he knew in the mid-1960s of legislators, members of the governor's staff, and other state officials who were homosexual.[†] They kept this secret to themselves.

The members of the Reagan team who set out to bring down Battaglia were not motivated by homophobia. Nofziger referred disparagingly to the "daisy chain" in the governor's office, but his concern about "the homosexual ring" was political. He realized that the Reagans came from Hollywood, "where dwell and work a significant number of

---

*Gillenwaters was a former aide to a House member, Bob Wilson of San Diego. Reagan and his team trusted him, valued his experience, and relied on his advice. In what appears to be a veiled reference to Battaglia, Gillenwaters said in a 1983 interview that Reagan aides claimed credit for "good news" about their boss while allowing the governor to be blamed for "bad news."[5] Gillenwaters thought it should be the other way around.

†Nichols, who in the early years of the Reagan governorship worked for a public television station, was a family friend who lived a block away in Sacramento. We often discussed Unruh and Brown. Four 1991 interviews of Nichols for the State Government Oral History program offer vivid insights into the lives of gay men employed in state government during this period, all of them "in the closet" at the time.[7]

homosexuals," Nofziger wrote in his memoirs. "As a result both were tolerant of this sort of aberrant sexual behavior."[8] The sentiment about Reagan's tolerance is accurate—Reagan would a decade later play a pivotal and courageous role in defeating a ballot initiative that discriminated against homosexual teachers. Reagan did not think homosexuality was aberrational; indeed, there is no record that he thought about it at all—not once in 1,044 speeches written in his own hand did he mention it. When Reagan was president, Nancy Reagan's openly gay interior decorator and his partner were overnight guests at the White House without comment.

Tom Reed, who had returned to his development company in San Rafael and was running what he called "a crypto-campaign" for the Reagan presidency, cared even less about homosexuality, if that is possible, than Reagan. Reed was and is a libertarian on social issues. He believed that the government had no business inquiring into sexuality and favored liberalized abortion laws. But he also thought that Battaglia was a menace. "I was involved with the Reagan campaign in the first place because I wanted to get rid of Lyndon Johnson, who was a fraud and killing people in Vietnam," Reed told me years later. "We needed to defeat LBJ, and Reagan seemed to me the best chance of accomplishing that. I thought Battaglia was making it impossible for Reagan to govern as he should."[9]

Unlike Reed and Nofziger, Bill Clark had no interest in a Reagan presidential campaign in 1968. His concern was that the governor's effectiveness was being steadily undermined by Battaglia's inattentiveness and frequent absences. "The sexual issue was the trip wire," Clark said. "It wasn't the reason that we needed to make a change."[10]

The details of how this change was accomplished vary depending upon who does the telling. My reconstruction of the final weeks of the anti-Battaglia conspiracy relies heavily on the records of Reed, who kept a contemporaneous diary. It shows that on August 11, 1967, a Friday, Reed responded to Clark's request and met him in the Admiral's Lounge of American Airlines at the San Francisco airport. Clark told him about the Gillenwaters report and the suspicions about Battaglia and his scheduler. This was the first Reed had heard of the allegations, but the report came "as a flashbulb."[11] Reed had no doubt they were true. He remembered that during the transition, he and Clark would come to work in the morning and find that decisions had already been made, as if at an earlier meeting. Reed's diary for August 11 shows that Clark was uncertain about how to proceed. "He hoped it would go away, and it hadn't," the entry said.[12]

Reed offered to help, as Clark had anticipated he would. The conspirators needed a coconspirator outside the governor's office who had the resources to underwrite an investigation. The "coup plotters," as Reed called them, enlisted the aid of Art Van Court, Reagan's security aide and a former Los Angeles police detective with contacts in the law enforcement community. Van Court recruited Curtis Patrick, an earnest young aide in the governor's office who was in charge of setting up telephones for Reagan and his aides on their travels. The coup plotters hired a private detective to tail Battaglia and his scheduler.

With this sort of assistance, the coup plotters should have found something if there was anything to find. But the results of their botched and frantic investigation ranged from unproductive to comic. Nofziger candidly described what happened in his memoirs: "We made the Keystone Cops look good. When Van Court went to investigate [the scheduler's] apartment, he couldn't get in. We tried and failed to bug Battaglia's office. We sent a man to tail Battaglia and [Jack] Kemp [an intern in the governor's office] and he lost them even though they didn't know they were being followed. We searched out their room arrangements in a hotel in San Francisco and discovered they took separate non-adjoining rooms and slept in them all night."[13] Scandal-mongering syndicated columnist Drew Pearson later wrote that the investigators took pictures and taped sounds of "orgies." This was untrue. This was indeed the intention of the coup plotters, but they found nothing to photograph or tape.

By late August, the circle of coup plotters included Reed, Clark, Nofziger, Luce, Gillenwaters, Van Court, Patrick, Haerle, and Meese. Reed and Haerle are friends, and the latter had succeeded Reed as appointments secretary. Meese, the legal affairs secretary and a rising power within the administration, was on military reserve training when he received a phone call informing him about the intended coup. In the absence of evidence, the conspirators decided to write down what they knew—or suspected—in a report, which Reed called an "indictment," and sign their names to it. The report, although explicit in its description of alleged sexual acts, contained nothing that would have been admissible in a court of law. The absence of legal evidence bothered the lawyers among the coup plotters, but they plowed ahead nonetheless. As Clark later said wryly, "People have been hanged on the basis of circumstantial evidence."[14]

In terms of his political career, the conspirators had judged Battaglia guilty of a hanging offense, assuming Reagan went along with their findings. No one was certain that he would. As governor, Reagan treated aides courteously but paid little attention to their comings and goings. Reagan was the star of the show in Sacramento, and staff members the supporting cast. The star's role was to make decisions, which Reagan did willingly, and to communicate with the public, at which he excelled. As long as the production went smoothly, Reagan was oblivious to any tensions among the supporting players.

The first draft of the "indictment" against Battaglia was written by Nofziger and reworked by Reed. It was shown to Haerle and Meese, both lawyers, whom Reed said removed inflammatory adjectives and sharpened the document. On Thursday, August 24, Reed called Holmes Tuttle and then William French Smith in Los Angeles to tell them a "Walter Jenkins situation" existed in the governor's office.* That night, Reed's secretary in his San Rafael office typed a final version of the indictment. She made four carbon copies. Reed carried the original and the carbons with him when he flew to San Diego the next morning.[15]

The other coup plotters had slipped out of Sacramento and also flown to San Diego. They gathered on Friday morning, August 25, at the home of a savings-and-loan executive, a friend of Gordon Luce's. Tuttle and Smith joined them, bringing the number of conspirators to eleven. Reed gave one of the carbons to Tuttle and passed the others around. They talked for awhile, then drove in different cars to the Coronado ferry and rendezvoused in the parking lot of the Hotel Del Coronado. Van Court was not with them. He was on duty as Reagan's security guard and, by prearrangement, told the governor that "the boys" needed to see him. Reagan had no idea why they were there.

It was now late afternoon, and Reagan greeted them in his bathrobe with his usual unfailing good humor. "Golly, are you quitting all at once?" he said. But he stopped joking when he read the report Reed had handed him; some of the coup plotters recalled that Reagan's face turned white. The plotters were tense. Haerle noticed that Nofziger's hands were shaking, which he remembered because Nofziger was usually steady and composed. Reed and Nofziger spoke briefly, followed by Tuttle. The others said nothing. All of them could see that the governor was stunned by the report.

During his presidency, Reagan often remained silent when contending officials aired their policy differences in his presence. On several occasions, they left the Oval Office or the national security chambers not

---

*Walter Jenkins, a close associate of President Johnson's, was arrested on October 7, 1964, in the men's room of the YMCA in Washington, D.C., a gathering place for homosexuals then under police surveillance. Subsequent investigation revealed a similar episode in 1959. With the election less than a month away, the arrest was of intense concern to the president's political operatives, but polls soon showed that the Jenkins affair had no impact on Johnson's lead over Barry Goldwater. Theodore White credits Goldwater for referring to the episode "only rarely—and with conspicuous lack of relish."[16] Clark Clifford gives an illuminating and sympathetic account of the affair in his memoirs.[17]

knowing what, if anything, Reagan had decided. So it is perhaps not surprising that the coup plotters have different recollections of what Reagan said and did on that Friday afternoon in his hotel suite. One participant told me, for my first book on Reagan in 1969, that the governor said, "My God, has government failed?" No one else mentioned that particular phrase, and it seems an unlikely reaction, since nothing that Reagan was being told involved the failure (or success) of government. Still, it was a typically Reaganesque comment. Reed recalled that Reagan initially made excuses for Battaglia, suggesting he had been ill or under strain.[18] This account has the ring of truth, for Reagan liked Battaglia and his first reaction, as governor and as president, was to defend any subordinate accused of misconduct.

Several of the coup plotters recalled that Reagan conveyed through body language that he accepted the basic findings of the report. "I had no doubt as we left that this was going to be resolved in our favor," Haerle said. "This was 1967. Practicing homosexuals on our staff, oh my God."[19] One clue to Reagan's acceptance was that he agreed that it was necessary to make an immediate change in "security arrangements"—a euphemism of the coup plotters for changing the locks on the doors in the governor's staff offices. The one thing Reagan said that all who were there remember is, "I want to sleep on this." The coup plotters accurately assumed from this response that Reagan wanted to think about the manner of Battaglia's departure and the way it would be handled in the press. In reality, Reagan's choices were limited. Had he rejected the report, he risked losing the services of his senior staff, his principal fund-raiser (Tuttle), and his longtime lawyer (Smith).

The coup plotters were relieved—and ecstatic. They retired to the lounge at the San Diego airport. Reed later remembered proclaiming that it was "the end of an era,"[20] but many of the others did not remember anything from the postmortem at the airport bar because they drank so much. Nofziger and Haerle said honestly that they became intoxicated, and they were not alone.[21]

Reagan did not fire Battaglia. He could never fire anyone, as the world learned in 1987 when he couldn't bring himself to tell White House Chief of Staff Donald Regan that he was being replaced even after he had chosen his replacement. Regan learned about it on CNN and walked out. There was no cable news network to send the message to Battaglia in 1967. That task fell to Tuttle, who on Saturday, August 26, met Battaglia in Los Angeles, where the chief of staff had flown for the weekend on unrelated business. As best as I could determine from a cryptic conversation with Tuttle a year after the meeting occurred, Battaglia was surprised.[22] The view jibes with the recollection of

Battaglia's scheduler, the other target of the coup plotters, who was in Washington, D.C., that weekend. He later told me that at the time he was unaware that he and Battaglia were under suspicion and does not believe that Battaglia knew it either.

Most of what the scheduler learned about the investigation he subsequently read in the newspapers or in my first book. But, surprised or not, Battaglia did not admit he had done anything wrong. Instead of offering to resign, he bargained for a judgeship. Tuttle said no. It was obvious to him that Reagan would be damaged if news leaked out that the governor had given his accused chief of staff a judgeship to secure his resignation. Tuttle told Battaglia he would be allowed to quit and that none of the allegations against him would be released to the press. While they were talking, the locks in the governor's office were being changed at Van Court's order. After sleeping on it, as he had promised, Reagan held separate telephone conversations with Reed and Nofziger telling them he wanted Bill Clark to succeed Battaglia. They agreed. Reagan's call was a relief to Nofziger, who had worried that the governor might think he deserved Battaglia's job. Nofziger was a political creature with minimal interest in government administration. The last thing he wanted was to be chief of staff.

On Monday, August 28, at a news conference with Clark in a first-floor room in the State Capitol, Battaglia announced that he was leaving to return to his law practice and said Clark was his "personal choice" to replace him. Appropriating a favorite Reagan phrase, Battaglia said, "This citizen-politician has determined it is time to go back to citizen life." Reporters, surprised by the announcement, pressed Battaglia on whether he was leaving to promote a Reagan-for-President campaign. Battaglia deflected the questions. Anticipating skepticism, Nofziger had included a sentence in the official resignation announcement quoting Reagan as saying that he had known all along that Battaglia would soon return to private life.* He also planted the story with Carl Greenberg, the influential political editor of the *Los Angeles Times*. On August 29, Greenberg's story quoted unnamed "intimate friends" as saying that Battaglia had from the beginning planned to serve no more than a year.

---

*The press release announcing Battaglia's resignation was issued by Paul Beck, Reagan's press secretary. (Nofziger was now director of communications.) Reagan reviewed the release before it was issued, apparently to make sure that it sufficiently praised Battaglia. "I am sorry to see Phil Battaglia leave," the release quoted Reagan as saying. "His loss will be felt keenly by this administration and even more so by me. He has been a good personal friend, a trusted advisor and the hardest worker on my staff. His brilliance and his leadership are responsible for much of what this administration has been able to accomplish. However, I knew from the beginning that his service would be limited and that he would have to return to his profession. I wish him Godspeed."

Greenberg, however, was too good a reporter to take anything he was told at face value. By the fifth paragraph of his story, Greenberg was disputing the premise of his lead paragraph. He wrote that associates in state government "hinted they were surprised by the abruptness of Battaglia's decision."[23]

They were not the only ones surprised. Battaglia's scheduler, the other target of the coup plotters, checked in from Washington on Monday on a routine call. A receptionist or a secretary, he's not sure which, asked if he'd heard the news about the changes. He hadn't. When the scheduler returned to Sacramento later in the week, Haerle politely told him his services were no longer needed and allowed him to resign.

With Battaglia gone and Clark in place, the coup plotters congratulated themselves on their success in misleading the press. They were premature. In truth, reporters misled themselves, first with the speculation that Battaglia was leaving to run the presidential campaign and then by persuading themselves that he had been the loser in an ideological struggle won by "right-wingers."

Perhaps the story would then have vanished into the mists of history had Battaglia kept a low profile. Instead, he soon returned to Sacramento on behalf of legal clients, which put him back into the news. Bill Clark, convinced that Battaglia was trading on his former relationship with Reagan, issued a memo instructing department heads to report immediately any communication they received from him. I wrote a front-page story for the *San Jose Mercury** detailing specific contacts between Battaglia and administration officials.[24] Battaglia's behavior infuriated Nancy Reagan. "Why doesn't someone do something about Phil?" she said in Nofziger's presence. Nofziger, afterward describing himself as a "damn fool" for doing so, undertook to do something.[25] Among other things, he briefed a half dozen reporters about the reasons for Battaglia's overthrow, swearing them to secrecy in the process. President Johnson's aides had done much the same after the Jenkins incident and suppressed the story for several days. By then, Jenkins was gone. With Battaglia back on the Sacramento scene, Nofziger's predicament was more difficult. His major mistake, as he later wrote, was that he did not anticipate that anyone would write about "a homosexual scandal."[26]

Someone did. In September, the "Periscope" column of *Newsweek* reported that a "top GOP presidential prospect has a potentially sordid scandal on his hands. Private investigators he hired found evidence that two of his aides had committed homosexual acts. The men are no

---

*At the time there were three newspapers, all under the same ownership: the *San Jose Mercury* in the morning, the *San Jose News* in the afternoon, and the *San Jose Mercury-News* on Sunday. Now there is one newspaper, daily and Sunday, in the morning, the *San Jose Mercury News*.

longer working for the GOP leader but the whole story may surface any day." The blind item was the work of Karl Fleming, the respected Los Angeles bureau chief for *Newsweek*. It signified to Nofziger that the story was now making the rounds and beyond his control.

He tried, nonetheless, to keep a lid on it. The National Governors Conference that year was a monumental nine-day junket in the Virgin Islands held in mid-October aboard the chartered USS *Independence* at the instigation of New York Governor Nelson Rockefeller. Aboard the cruise vessel, which reporters called the "ship of fools," Nofziger was persistently questioned about the rumors circulating in the wake of the "Periscope" item. He denied them. According to Nofziger, David S. Broder of *The Washington Post* took him aside and said to him, "Lyn, you told me all about it." Nofziger was dumbfounded because he did not remember that he had done this. "I knew he wasn't lying," Nofziger said of Broder. "I don't think he has a lie in him."[27] By now, Nofziger was alarmed. How many others had he told? He decided he had been talking too much in "naive belief that no one would write the story."

I didn't attend the National Governors Conference but learned about the reason for Battaglia's demise from other sources. When Nofziger returned to Sacramento, I confronted him. He said he would discuss the story if I agreed not to write it. I declined to make this commitment, so we did not discuss it again until after the story became public. (It made no difference, as it turned out, for the *San Jose Mercury* decided not to run my story, which identified the conspirators and their targets.) But it was clear to me, as it must have been to other reporters, that disclosure was now only a matter of time.

The story broke in an October 31, 1967, column by Drew Pearson. The column, with a Los Angeles dateline, began: "The most interesting speculation among political leaders in this key state of California is whether the magic charm of Governor Ronald Reagan can survive the discovery that a homosexual ring has been operating in his office." The column compared Reagan's action with President Johnson's in the Jenkins case. "Johnson acted immediately," Pearson wrote. "Reagan, on the other hand, waited for about six months."

The column was typical of Pearson, who was bold in tackling taboo subjects but reckless with facts. Reagan hadn't known anything until the coup plotters had burst into his suite to inform him two months earlier. And the cases were dissimilar in that there was a police record, in fact two police records, in the Jenkins case. The coup plotters on the Reagan staff had searched for similar evidence to no avail. Pearson's column also said that, "Van Court came up with a tape recording of a sex orgy which had taken place at a cabin near Lake Tahoe leased by two members of Reagan's staff." This was a tidbit of truth buried beneath a mound of inaccuracy. Battaglia and Kemp had purchased a cabin together at Lake Tahoe, in which Kemp later sold his half-interest back to Battaglia, but there was no tape or record or any other evidence of a "sex orgy."

Pearson's column galvanized Reagan, who had been more sanguine than his wife or Nofziger about keeping the story out of print. Reagan, not without reason, believed that Pearson was bent on discrediting him, and he recast the story in his mind as a morality drama in which he was the hero and the columnist the villain. "There are innocent wives and children involved," he said to an aide, in reference to Battaglia's two young adopted children.[28] Publication of the Pearson column coincided with Reagan's weekly news conference. When Reagan was asked about the column, he said:

> No, there is no truth to that report and I know where the report comes from. . . . Most Californians won't see it, because I think that the best clue to the veracity of the report—is the fact that as far as we know most of the major papers are refusing to run the Drew Pearson column in which it appears. Drew Pearson has been sort of riding my back for a number of years, long before I ever got into this business, back when I was just making speeches along the banquet trail. . . . I myself wonder how respectable newspapers can continue to carry this column of a man who has done what he's done, and this is about the lowest, this is just stooping to destroy human beings, innocent people, and there is just no sense in getting into that kind of contest with him.

Reporters pressed the issue, asking Reagan about news leaks aboard the USS *Independence*. Reagan denied any leaks, then turned to Nofziger and asked: "Want to confirm it, Lyn?"

"Confirmed," Nofziger replied without hesitation.

Reporters in the room who knew better shifted uncomfortably but said nothing. The next day, Jack McDowell reported in the *San Francisco Examiner*: "The resignation of certain officials serving in Governor Reagan's administration were demanded and were received. Their departure came after a private investigation was made into some of their activities, personal and political. The investigation was ordered without Reagan's knowledge."[29] McDowell, who in an earlier story had described the Battaglia ouster as the culmination of an ideological struggle, went on to observe that no criminal charges had been filed and added that identification of the officials "is not privileged by the knowledge that a private investigation, made in secret and without official status, was made." Nofziger nonetheless named the officials in his memoirs.

Newspaper readers must have been confused. As Reagan had predicted, most California newspapers suppressed the Pearson column but were now carrying a running story on what was referred to as "the homosexual scandal." Pearson added fuel to the flames, saying the facts were "incontrovertible" and blasting Reagan. "He has been posing as Mr. Clean and yet tolerated homosexuals for approximately six months and did not act regarding them until he was pressured,"[30] Pearson said. Reagan called Pearson "a liar" and said that he had better "not spit on the sidewalk" if he came to California, a statement he afterward regretted.

At his November 14 news conference, the governor blew up when reporters persisted in questioning him about the Pearson column and the leaks of the story. This was the exchange:

REAGAN: Look, let me ask you something. I just can't believe you fellows want to continue to pursue this thing. Now I told you a few days ago that I had made my last statement on the subject. I have never had and do not have any evidence that would warrant an accusation. No accusation or any charge has been made. Now, if there is a credibility gap, and I'm responsible, it is because I refuse to participate in trying to destroy human beings with no factual evidence. And I'm not going to do that, and if that means there is a credibility gap, so be it. There is a credibility gap.

PRESS: Mr. Nofziger has been accused by six newsmen of not owning up to telling them confidentially that people left the administration because of immoral behavior.

REAGAN: Yes, I don't know that this is true, and I told you this subject, as far as I'm concerned, is closed. Now do we want to have a press conference or do we want to just stand here with me refusing to talk?

By now, Reagan was lying, almost defiantly, about what he had done. He saw no reason to name anyone, and he was sorry that he had embarrassed Nofziger at the October 31 news conference. "The thing that I have always regretted was that I should never have put Lyn on that spot," Reagan told me a year later. "You know I should never have turned to him. I should have waited until I could have talked to him and said, 'Lyn, why did they ask that question?'"[31] Nancy Reagan was less forgiving. She refused to talk to Nofziger for five months. Feeling that his role as communications director was impaired, Nofziger told the governor that Nancy Reagan was undermining him and offered to resign. Reagan, as always, defended his wife but told Nofziger that he would no longer have difficulty with her and rejected the resignation. Nofziger stayed until he left to join a Senate campaign in 1968. After serving as a congressional liaison in the Nixon administration, he returned to play a significant role in Reagan's later presidential campaigns. In the Reagan presidency he was a political advisor. He remains a Reagan loyalist to this day.

Battaglia, only thirty-two when he was forced out, was understandably bitter. His accusers had plotted behind his back without ever giving him a chance to face them. No one had proven that he had done anything wrong, even accepting the premise of the time that homosexual conduct was inappropriate. Stu Spencer, informed of the coup after it occurred, said that Battaglia came to him indignantly and over sandwiches in Spencer's office talked about filing a lawsuit. Spencer told Battaglia he had no case and would harm himself if he went after the new Reagan team.[32]

Battaglia returned to his law practice, prospered, and contributed to the communities in which he lived. He founded the Watts Youth Center and became a leader of the Pacific Conservatory of the Performing Arts, which supports theater groups along California's central coast. He served a term as mayor of Rolling Hills but never sought partisan political office.

The scheduler, younger than Battaglia, eventually landed a good job. Looking back on what happened years later, he remembered feeling simultaneously "horrified" at the method of his dismissal and "relieved" that he no longer had to work in the competitive, hothouse environment of the governor's office.

Not everyone caught up in the scandal was as fortunate. A political consultant who is now deceased and whose name is not mentioned in this book lost his job and became despondent. Reed valued him and became so worried about his emotional stability that he put him on his payroll.

Jack Kemp, the young intern in the office who had bought the cabin with Battaglia, was hurt politically by rumors emanating from the scandal but showed fortitude in overcoming them. Kemp was a professional football player, at that time the quarterback for the Buffalo Bills. He was essentially a "gofer" in the governor's office, thrilled to be around Reagan and happy to work for his chief of staff. The conspirators who had ousted Battaglia faulted him only for his naiveté. Kemp, who was in football training camp when the coup occurred, played three more years with the Bills, served nine terms in the House of Representatives, ran for president, became secretary of housing and urban development in the cabinet of the first President Bush, and in 1996 was Republican presidential nominee Bob Dole's vice-presidential running mate.

"During these years the scandal was resurrected from time to time, but Kemp rode it out with courage and an absolute refusal to let it ruin him, his family, or his career," Nofziger wrote.[33] This is true. Over the years, I became inured to receiving telephone calls from opposition political consultants inquiring about Kemp's role in "the homosexual scandal." I told them that Kemp was simply in the wrong place at the wrong time.

The scandal also dogged Reagan, probably more than he realized. When he ran for president in 1976, information was received at *The Washington Post* from sources who claimed that Reagan had been part of the "homosexual ring" and directed the cover-up. I was assigned to check out these allegations, which meant retracing the ground I had covered in 1967 for the *San Jose Mercury*. The allegations were unfounded. When Reagan ran again in 1980, the process repeated itself. By now I felt like the television weatherman portrayed by Bill Murray in the movie *Groundhog Day*, who relives the same day over and over again. But several weeks later, Reagan's principal accuser wrote me a letter acknowledging that the charges were false. "Save the letter," executive editor Ben Bradlee told me. I did. The accusations against Reagan were never raised again.

Reagan's response to the homosexual scandal in the main reflected well on him while also revealing a weakness of his governance. He was steadfast at his October 31 news conference when he lied to protect the men who had been fired and their families. Although he had a political motive for lying, he would have been better served politically by naming Battaglia and taking credit for ousting him. Instead, he prolonged a mystery that kept the story alive for several additional weeks. Reagan knew this. He also knew that following this course would make it easier for him to rebut Pearson's more extravagant assertions. But Reagan had his back up and did not want to make any concessions to a columnist whom he regarded as a smear artist. (He remembered, too, that Pearson had teamed up with Democratic operatives to smear George Christopher in the 1966 primary campaign, an action that helped Reagan but which he nonetheless thought dirty pool.) Reagan had compassion for Battaglia, whom he liked and believed had served him well. In addition, as Nofziger realized, Reagan did not consider homosexuality—in this case, alleged and unproven homosexuality—a big deal.

Although Reagan's conduct was decent and principled, the incident demonstrated his incredible distance from the operation of his governorship. It makes sense for a governor, and even more for a president, to focus on long-range objectives and delegate implementation to others. Reagan did this well enough, but he paid so little attention to what was going on in his office that he was unaware of pitched battles occurring down the hall. This happened again in the White House, sometimes with disturbing results. I was reminded of the famous George Price cartoon where a man has a gun battle with the police in his home while a woman continues to play cards with her friends. "Don't ask *me* what it's all about," she explains to her friends. "He leads his life, and I lead mine."[34] That was true of Reagan and his staff. How could Battaglia miss so many meetings and Reagan not notice it or mention it to anyone? As president, he would complain about the source of "leaks" to people who were doing the leaking and have no inkling of what had happened. During his years as both governor and president, many things were done in Reagan's name of which he was only dimly aware, as investigators learned in 1986 and 1987 while looking into the diversion of funds from the secret Iran arms sales to the Nicaraguan contras.

It is often said that Reagan over-delegated, but this was not the root deficiency of his governance. Reagan's deeper problem was twofold. The first part of it was that he was a kind and genial man who accepted people at face value and tended to believe that anyone who professed support of his agenda was suitable to work for him. (Naive acceptance was not unique to Reagan. Hubert Humphrey, another happy warrior whom I covered for many years, also believed that everyone who worked for him was solid gold.) The second and even more serious problem was that Reagan rarely followed up by asking his subordinates what they were doing with the enormous grants of authority he had ceded to them. Reagan needed at all times a strong chief of staff who looked out for his interests, and his alone.

For Reagan's staff, the last four months of 1967 were the most difficult period of the governorship. During the two months between the coup and the publication of the Pearson column, aides lived in daily fear that the story would become public. They could not talk about it with outsiders and were reluctant to discuss it even among themselves, since they had different levels of involvement. Reagan was withdrawn and lacking in his customary optimism. As one of the coup participants told me at the time: "It was a heart transplant where one wasn't replaced and where the operation was performed with a dull knife. The trauma was so severe that the patient—the governor's office—went into a state of shock for four months. And the governor cut himself off from a lot of things that he shouldn't. The governorship went into receivership."[35]

If so, it was fortunate that the receiver was William P. Clark Jr., who was thirty-five when he became Reagan's chief of staff. Like Battaglia, he was a lawyer and a Roman Catholic. But while Battaglia was a city boy, Clark came from a ranching family and was president of the family business, the Clark Land and Cattle Company. After attending a Catholic preparatory school and Stanford University for two years, he had joined the Army as a counterintelligence officer. In Munich, he met Joan Brauner, a German who was working for another U.S. officer as a military secretary. They were soon married. After his Army service, he attended night classes at Loyola University in Los Angeles. The Clarks had a young family and a meager income, and he dropped out of Loyola without graduating and passed the bar examination, then practiced law in the coastal town of Oxnard. In politics, he was a conservative Democrat who found Barry Goldwater's campaign against big government appealing. Clark became a Republican in 1964 and chairman of Ronald Reagan's campaign in Ventura County in 1966. His hobbies, he said when he became chief of staff, were "horses and kids."[36] The Clarks had five children, all of them, at that time, between the ages of five and eleven.

Clark, lanky and soft-spoken, was suited for the job that had been thrust upon him. In many respects, he was a chief of staff in waiting, for he had often chaired cabinet meetings during Battaglia's frequent absences. Battaglia had set up what Haerle called "a curtain" around Reagan; Clark exposed the governor to a range of people and a variety of viewpoints and encouraged him to call new appointees and visit the state agencies and departments scattered around Sacramento. Clark's only drawback in his relationship with the governor, he quipped, was that he had never seen any of his movies.[37] But Reagan liked strong, silent types, and he needed a supportive chief of staff, not a film critic. Despite (or perhaps because of) the reserved nature of both men, they forged a closer bond than Reagan did with any other aide during his governorship. Under Clark, Reagan adopted a "chairman of the board" style that became his preferred method of governance in Sacramento and during the first term of his presidency. Reagan responded to the tonic of greater exposure to members of his government; he was too much the natural optimist to stay discouraged for long. Reagan was a survivor. The change of leadership in his office, especially the ascension of Clark, had helped pulled Reagan through.

Other changes were in store. As recounted earlier, the Kitchen Cabinet had resisted the unanimous recommendation of Reed, Clark, Battaglia, and Nofziger to make the capable Caspar W. Weinberger state finance director. Clark had stashed Weinberger away as chairman of the Little Hoover Commission, a watchdog group, and Weinberger did good work and stayed in touch.

Smith was in constant hot water with the Legislature, where Democrats and Republicans agreed that he was not up to the job. He was a persistent target of Unruh's and an annoyance to Assembly Republican leader Bob Monagan, who made no attempt to defend him. Democrats and moderate Republicans were particularly incensed over Smith's contention that the state budget could not be balanced unless $160 million was taken from Medi-Cal, the California version of the federal Medicaid program providing medical care for the poor. Reagan approved the reductions, which were blocked in the courts. But at a press conference on January 4, 1968, Smith had the candor and poor judgment to acknowledge that the Democrats had been right in saying that the Medi-Cal cuts had been unnecessary. He conceded too much. By then, the state's fiscal crisis had been resolved in the old-fashioned way, by raising taxes. Neither Smith nor Reagan had known that the tax bill would pass when the Medi-Cal cuts were proposed. But Smith's artless performance at the press conference gave Democrats an opportunity to accuse Reagan of trying to balance the budget on the backs of the poor, a charge that would follow him into the White House. Unruh predicted that Smith would be fired. On January 17, at another press conference, Smith accused Unruh of taking a "cheap shot" at him and said he had offered to bet the Assembly speaker $1,000 that he wouldn't be forced out. Fortunately for Smith, Unruh didn't take the bet. On February 1, 1968, Smith resigned "for personal reasons" and was praised by Reagan for his service.[38] Weinberger was named to replace him.

Smith departed with a touch of class. The cabinet minutes show that he briefed Reagan on the upcoming budget the day he left office. Then, in the presence of his civil service deputy, Ed Beach, he praised the professional bureaucrats in the Department of Finance as the best in the nation. Reagan agreed. The governor and his finance director had undergone on-the-job training together, and Reagan thanked Smith for his part in ending "fiscal irresponsibility" in California.[39] Reagan was free of the scandal that had almost wrecked his governorship. His next act would be running for president of the United States.

19

NONCANDIDATE

T HE NATIONAL POLITICAL landscape changed during the four months that Reagan and his team were recovering from the impact of the homosexual scandal. George Romney, the earnest but inarticulate front-runner, was struggling, but President Johnson was struggling even more. In the late summer of 1967, Romney clung to a slight lead over the president in public opinion surveys as Americans became increasingly disillusioned with Johnson because of domestic civil disorders and increased casualties in Vietnam.

On August 31, 1967, three days after the staff shakeup in Reagan's office, Romney taped a television interview in Detroit with a regional broadcaster named Lou Gordon, a former reporter for the Drew Pearson column. Romney, originally supportive of Johnson's policies, had visited Vietnam and gradually reconsidered his position on the war, as many Americans were doing. (U.S. casualties in Vietnam in 1967 were 9,500 killed and 20,000 wounded, compared to 6,500 killed and 11,000 wounded in the previous four years of U.S. involvement in the war.) At the taping, Gordon asked Romney if his criticism of the administration was inconsistent with his past support for the war. Romney replied: "Well, you know when I came back from Vietnam, I just had the greatest brainwashing that anybody can get when you go over to Vietnam. Not only by the generals, but also by the diplomatic corps over there, and they do a very thorough job." Romney went on to say that he had since reviewed the history of Vietnam and concluded, "I no longer believe that it is necessary for us to get involved in South Vietnam to stop Communist aggression."

The taping was on a Thursday, with broadcast scheduled for the following Sunday. Gordon read the transcript and decided that "brainwashing" was news. He telephoned a correspondent for *The New York*

Times, which reported Romney's comments on September 5.[1] During the next weeks, Romney was bombarded with questions about why he had been brainwashed. (Senator Eugene McCarthy of Minnesota said tartly that he thought a "light rinse" would have sufficed.) Many of the news reports overlooked Romney's larger point, which was a sensible rejection of Johnson's continued support for the South Vietnamese government.

Given his deficiencies on the stump, Romney probably would not have secured the Republican nomination in 1968 no matter what he said. But "brainwashing" finished him. He dropped steadily in the polls during the fall and winter. On February 28, 1968, facing defeat at the hands of Richard Nixon in the New Hampshire primary, he withdrew from the race. Nixon, who had yet to make a statement on Vietnam, was a triple winner. Romney was out, but his withdrawal came too late for Governor Nelson Rockefeller of New York, a more potent rival, to enter the New Hampshire primary. Meanwhile, on the Democratic side in New Hampshire, Gene McCarthy's strong showing stunned President Johnson and set in motion a chain of events that prompted Johnson, on March 31, to announce that he would not seek reelection.

In the Reagan camp, Nixon's rise seemed a mixed blessing. Reed and Nofziger, along with many other conservatives, were not wild about Nixon but preferred him to Romney or Rockefeller. They doubted, however, that Nixon could win. Nixon had carried California in 1960 when John F. Kennedy won the presidency in a virtual dead heat. But Nixon's disastrous 1962 race for governor against the Democratic incumbent, Pat Brown, had labeled him a loser. After his defeat, Nixon held his famous "last press conference," mostly a tirade against the newspaper coverage of his campaign. ABC responded with a half-hour program called "The Political Obituary of Richard Nixon" that rubbed salt into Nixon's wounds by including commentary from Alger Hiss. The conventional wisdom was that Nixon was down for the count.

Jules Witcover, in his 1970 book, *The Resurrection of Richard Nixon,* and Theodore White, in *The Making of the President: 1968,* published in 1969, meticulously chronicled the remarkable Nixon campaign that carried him from political oblivion to the White House. White's retrospective judgment on Reagan was that the timing and emotional impact of the homosexual scandal prevented Reagan from becoming a credible presidential candidate in 1968.[2] That may be true, but well before the scandal Reagan was ambivalent about running for president. He approached the campaign with a combination of caution and ambition that in hindsight can be seen as typical. Even in 1976 and 1980, when Reagan was less ambivalent about running, he formed exploratory committees and announced his candidacy at the last moment—far too late, in Nofziger's view. "Clearly, anyone who runs for president three times is ambitious, but he didn't want to embarrass himself, he didn't want to look like a damn fool," said Nofziger. "He was a very careful guy."[3]

Reed and Nofziger were less cautious, and they believed that Reagan was destined to become president. On November 17, 1966, nine days after Reagan was elected governor, Reed had met with the Reagans at their home in Pacific Palisades to discuss the pursuit of the presidency. Nofziger and Battaglia were there, representing the Reagan staff. So were Stu Spencer and Bill Roberts and another member of their firm. Reed was authorized to contact Peter O'Donnell, the Texas Republican chairman, and F. Clifton White, an astute New Yorker who had masterminded Barry Goldwater's nomination in 1964. That night, Reed had dinner with William Rusher, the publisher of *National Review* and a Reagan enthusiast, who also urged him to recruit White.[4]

O'Donnell wasn't interested, but White was intrigued. The following Sunday, Reed and White had lunch at the Appawamis Club in Rye, New York. They agreed that Reagan would be the best challenger to Johnson in 1968 but that no overt moves toward a presidential candidacy should be made until Reagan established a track record as governor. To Reed, that meant Labor Day of 1967, which would turn out to be a few days after the staff shakeup in the governor's office. After his discussion with White, Reed flew back to California and gave the Reagans a report at breakfast the next day. On November 20, Reed and Reagan met at the St. Francis Hotel in San Francisco to discuss the presidential race. Reed's diary entry for that day shows that Reagan signed off on the plan to hire White as a consultant.* Later, when rumors of a Reagan presidential campaign began to make the rounds, Reagan disclaimed knowledge of Reed's activities. This, Reed told me, was "bunk."[6]

But the situation that confronted Reagan in early 1968 was different from the one that Reed and White had anticipated late in 1966. Had Romney remained the Republican front-runner, Reagan would have been an attractive alternative to conservatives in the South and West. Romney's collapse and Nixon's resurgence changed the equation. The Nixon team, aware of Reagan's appeal in the South, gave high priority to nailing down early commitments from Dixie's most prominent con-

---

*The plan, according to Reed's notes, included a role for Spencer-Roberts, mostly in arranging strategic speaking engagements outside California. But Stu Spencer believed that it was premature to talk about running Reagan for president before he had even served a day as governor. He later discounted the seriousness of the Reed-White effort and told me he wanted no part of it.[5]

servatives. What became known as Nixon's "southern strategy" relied, among others, on Strom Thurmond in South Carolina, John Grenier in Mississippi, and John Tower and GOP chairman O'Donnell, whom Reed had courted, in Texas.

Reagan's reluctance to become an avowed candidate aided Nixon's effort to line up southern conservatives who had supported Goldwater in 1964. The underlying Reagan problem in 1968, as Nofziger understood better than anyone else, was Reagan's cautious nature, compounded by inner doubts about whether he was ready to be president. The redoubtable David S. Broder of *The Washington Post* discussed this ambivalence in a January 14, 1968, article, in which he said of Reagan, "He is described by his associates as fatalistic almost to the point of naiveté in his belief that events will order themselves. 'Ron honestly believes that God will arrange things for the best,' says one Republican colleague. 'But some of the people who made him governor are willing to give God a hand in making him President, and they're not too happy with the slowdown.'"[7]

Others on Reagan's staff, however, encouraged Reagan's hesitancy. Bill Clark, the new chief of staff, believed that Reagan had plenty to do in Sacramento and was not anxious for him to become a quixotic presidential candidate. Neither was Rus Walton, a brainy idea man, who had been brought into the governor's office to put rhetorical flesh on the bones of the Creative Society that Reagan had promised as a gubernatorial candidate. This divided staff counsel, and Nixon's surge, hampered Nofziger, who was busily promoting a Reagan presidential candidacy without much help from his boss or his chief of staff. Instead of becoming a candidate, Reagan became an avowed noncandidate. His weekly news conferences became ritual dances in which reporters tried to push Reagan into saying he was running for president. He never did, but he also refused to emulate William Tecumseh Sherman, the Civil War general who had declined the 1884 Republican presidential nomination by saying, "I will not accept the nomination and will not serve if elected." Asked to make a Sherman-like statement disavowing his candidacy, Reagan said, "Nobody else made the statement except Sherman, and it wasn't a particularly good idea for him."[8]

For all his indecision and liabilities, Reagan was a far more appealing personality than Nixon. He was the party's premium fund-raiser and most charismatic speaker. His ability to attract large, responsive crowds and fill Republican coffers made him welcome everywhere and gave White and Reed the opportunity of selecting speaking engagements deemed the most beneficial to Reagan's shadow candidacy. Reagan was also more forthright than Nixon. He believed in himself and his ideas and did not shrink from expressing them. On May 15, 1967, he had debated Robert F. Kennedy on a CBS program called "Town Meeting of the World" that linked Reagan in Sacramento and Kennedy in New York with eighteen students in London. Reagan, who had carefully prepared for the encounter, bested Kennedy in a program that was mostly devoted to the Vietnam War.*

Reagan believed that President Johnson had legitimate reasons for committing U.S. military forces to Vietnam, but he also was convinced that the United States should try to win the war, or failing that, withdraw. Reagan said as much repeatedly. Nixon followed a shrewder strategy of playing the middle and saying as little as possible about Vietnam. It made him seem more moderate and would help him win the election, but the war continued throughout the Nixon presidency.

Even if Reagan had been a less reluctant candidate, the time was out of joint for him in 1968. His conservative image was a liability in the Northeast and the Midwest, where Republican leaders rebuilding from the 1964 debacle wanted a mainstream candidate. In the South and Mountain West, Republican leaders worried that an impulse toward moderation would push the party leftward and result in the nomination of Romney or Rockefeller. To these practical conservatives, a Nixon in the hand was worth a Reagan in the bush.

White recognized that the confluence of events favored Nixon. I think Reagan realized it, too, for he and Reed discussed the situation with Barry Goldwater when the Reagans vacationed in Arizona during Easter week in 1968. Goldwater, then preparing for his return to the U.S. Senate, remarked to Reagan and Reed that Republicans would "know who the nominee would be" by mid-June.[10] Reagan returned home realizing that Goldwater was committed to Nixon but believing that the convention might deadlock. At this point, Reagan's fatalism prevailed. He told Holmes Tuttle it was important for him to "enunciate my principles" and pull the Republican Party in a conservative direction. This was not the statement of a man who was lusting to be president, but Reagan nonetheless stepped up the pace of his noncandidacy after the meeting with Goldwater. In April, Reagan campaigned in Idaho and Colorado, where he warned about untrammeled welfare growth. In Boise, Reagan denounced the "credibility gap" and "morality gap" of the Johnson administration, contending that "together these

---

*The press verdict that Reagan won the debate was virtually unanimous. David Halberstam wrote that Reagan had "destroyed" his opponent. Kennedy after the debate asked, "Who the fuck got me into this?" Weeks later Kennedy upbraided Frank Mankiewicz by saying, "You're the guy who got me into this Reagan thing."[9] The sponsors of Reagan's campaign in the 1968 Oregon primary sought to use a portion of the CBS program in a political commercial. The Kennedy camp refused to give permission.

two gaps form a leadership gap on a scale we have never known and should no longer tolerate."

But Reagan was opening his own credibility gap. Earlier that week, at a news conference in Sacramento, he had made a standard declaration that he was not "an announced candidate" for president. On this occasion, when reporters pressed him on his "availability," Reagan said, "I think any citizen of the United States is available for that office if his fellow citizens decided he was the individual they wanted." Reagan reiterated this message in Boise at a private meeting with Oregon supporters who had traveled to Idaho to meet with him. Once again, however, his prospective candidacy was hampered by ambivalence. Reagan gave the Oregonians the impression that he would eventually become a candidate but disappointed them by saying he would not make appearances in their state before the Oregon primary on May 28.

From Boise, Reagan flew to Boulder, where on the same day that Hubert Humphrey formally announced his presidential candidacy the California governor told a cheering student audience at the University of Colorado that the principles of individual freedom required abolishing the peacetime draft. "We've gone down a bad and dangerous road with peacetime conscription, and I would turn to a professional Army and eliminate the draft," Reagan said. He stayed on the auditorium stage for an hour, masterfully responding to questions. When students applauded his assertion that a university administration has responsibility for maintaining order on campus, Reagan paused and asked, a bit plaintively, "Have you ever thought about transferring to Berkeley?"[11]

Nixon, meanwhile, was amassing delegates in presidential primaries where he was uncontested except by write-in campaigns. After winning New Hampshire on March 12 and Wisconsin in April, both with more than 79 percent of the vote, he added Indiana, Nebraska, and West Virginia on the first two Tuesdays of May. Reagan needed a victory, or at least a strong showing, in the free-for-all Oregon primary, which in other years had been the graveyard for the presidential dreams of Harold Stassen and Henry Cabot Lodge. Reagan was on the ballot in Oregon. He had refused to file a noncandidate affidavit that would have removed his name on the creative grounds that this would be tantamount to "committing perjury," since his name was on the ballot as a favorite-son candidate in California the following week. His Oregon backers interpreted this as a sign that Reagan was in the race, and they gave his candidacy the hard sell even though their sales product stayed out of the state. The lead salesman was Bob Hazen, a Portland savings-and-loan executive who had spearheaded Nelson Rockefeller's successful 1964 Oregon campaign. Hazen was motivated by practical politics;

he believed Nixon would lose in November but that Reagan could win.

But the Reagan campaign in Oregon was a dud. Reagan received only 23 percent of the vote compared to 73 percent for Nixon. Reagan's performance in California on June 5, the following Tuesday, was also unimpressive. He was unopposed as the favorite-son candidate for president, but 52 percent of Republican voters did not cast ballots for the Reagan slate. Only political professionals paid attention to the Republican results, however. The California story was in the Democratic primary, where Robert F. Kennedy won a hard-fought victory over Gene McCarthy. That night, Kennedy entered the kitchen of the Ambassador Hotel on Wilshire Boulevard in Los Angeles, where his supporters had gathered. He was shot by Sirhan Sirhan and died two days later. Kennedy, wrote Theodore White, "had aroused the best and the beast in man. And the beast waited for him in the kitchen."[12]

The assassination of Kennedy was the last of three murderous events that in the first half of 1968 transformed America. The first of these was the Tet offensive, which began in Vietnam on January 31, 1968, and lasted for twenty-six days. U.S. commanders were caught by surprise, and Americans watched in amazement on television as Communist troops stormed the South Vietnamese presidential palace and the U.S. embassy. The bloody fighting that followed was a disaster for both sides. Militarily, Tet was a Communist defeat. The North Vietnamese and Viet Cong lost 10,000 troops compared to 500 for the United States and were forced out of the cities or strategic positions they had captured. Politically, however, Tet was a decisive setback for the Johnson administration. More than any other event, Tet spurred McCarthy's antiwar campaign in New Hampshire and led to Johnson's withdrawal.

The second event that changed America occurred on April 4, when Martin Luther King Jr. was shot on the second-floor balcony of the Lorraine Hotel in Memphis as he chatted with friends in the courtyard below. He died an hour later. Riots erupted in Washington, D.C., then in Boston, Chicago, Detroit, Pittsburgh, and San Francisco. Within a week, disorders broke out in a hundred cities. By the time federal and National Guard troops had quelled the riots, thirty-nine people had been killed and thousands arrested.

These nationally traumatic events had a profound impact on Reagan. Tet persuaded him (as it did Jesse Unruh) that the American people would not indefinitely support a war of attrition in Vietnam. King's assassination, even though the subsequent civil disorders in California were mild in comparison to what had happened in most other states, reminded Reagan that discontent and anger among black Americans held the potential to produce a repetition of the Watts riot.

At the suggestion of Rus Walton, Reagan held a series of private meetings with African American and other minority leaders throughout California. They had the dual purpose of educating Reagan about the problems of minorities and making the public relations point that the governor was reaching out to them. Reagan listened attentively when African Americans criticized his administration to his face and on one occasion dissuaded an angry black militant from walking out of a meeting. Two of these meetings were held after the assassination of Robert Kennedy, and one of the participants in his comments to the governor linked Kennedy's killing to the murder of Martin Luther King. The two Americans who had given the most hope to blacks had been gunned down, he said. Blacks felt that any champion of their cause was in mortal danger.[13]

In subsequent campaign speeches, Reagan often cited these meetings as evidence of a creative approach to racial problems. "I listened as one man told me, 'We would pull ourselves up by our own bootstraps, but we have no boots,'" Reagan said in a July 14 televised report on equal opportunity. This speech took cognizance of the "legitimate grievances" of blacks and other minorities and promised them "an equal place on the starting line" and a "restoration and perpetuation" of the American dream that "every man has the right to live, to be himself and to become whatever thing his manhood and his vision can combine to make him—that he will be free to be whatever God intended he should be."

It wasn't all talk. Reagan made more minority appointments than any previous California governor. He also from the early days of his governorship encouraged the efforts of Los Angeles industrialist H. C. ("Chad") McClellan to find jobs for blacks in Watts and South Los Angeles, which had never recovered from the devastation of the 1965 riot. McClellan obtained $90,000 from a private foundation after the riot, established an employment center, and embarked on a drive to recruit unemployed blacks. He claimed to have found jobs for nearly 18,000 of them.[14] Although critics claimed that these figures were exaggerated, McClellan's effort was genuine. Reagan was impressed with McClellan's program and lauded it in speeches and at cabinet meetings.

But Reagan's outreach toward minorities during his governorship, more purposeful and sustained than any similar effort during his presidency, was undermined by his response to the racial politics of 1968. The backlash candidate that year and for some time to come was George Corley Wallace, the segregationist former governor of Alabama. He was the champion of whites in the South and the North who hated and feared the civil rights advances and racial disorders that marked the Great Society. Four years later, in 1972, Wallace would help Republicans by competing in Democratic primaries and splitting the party. But in 1968, when Wallace was a third-party candidate, his threat was to Republicans. As Michael Barone has observed, southern Democrats had been on the defensive ever since President Kennedy supported civil rights legislation in 1963.[15] Polls taken in 1967 and 1968 showed that any Republican nominee would defeat President Johnson (and later Hubert Humphrey) in most southern states in a two-way race. With Wallace in the mix as a third-party candidate, however, Republicans trailed Democrats in some states and Wallace in others. By May 1968, when Reagan was meeting with minority groups, polls showed Wallace receiving 14 percent of the vote nationally and a higher percentage in the South. He stayed at this level throughout the campaign, winning 13.5 percent of the national vote in November and carrying five southern states.

Wallace posed a special problem for Reagan. Without Wallace, Reagan was the strongest potential nominee of any party in the South. With Wallace, he was a question mark, for their appeal to white conservatives overlapped. Had Reagan become the GOP nominee, this would have been a strategic concern. Reagan would have been stronger in the South than Nixon, but he was not as well positioned to hold the center. In July 1968, as Reagan prepared for a belated appeal to southern delegates to the Republican National Convention, White and Reed had the more limited goal of trying to avoid alienating southerners with an attack on Wallace. This tactic produced a dismal news conference on July 16, at which Reagan repeatedly declined to draw any difference with Wallace on racial issues. The highlight was this exchange:

PRESS: What views of George Wallace do you disagree with?

REAGAN: Well, now, lately on the basis of his speeches that would be kind of hard to pin down because he's been speaking a lot of things that I think the people of America are in agreement with. But I would have to say on the basis of his past record . . . that I can't believe that he has the philosophy that I believe in . . . because on his past record and as a governor he showed no opposition particularly to great programs of federal aid and spending programs and so forth. Right at the moment he's dwelling mainly on law and order, patriotism, and so forth, and these are attractive subjects, and I'm sure that there are very few people in disagreement and I think this perhaps is responsible for some of the gains he's made.

Unruh charged after the news conference that the governor had "endorsed" Wallace's segregationist views. This was an overstatement, but it reminded minority voters, if any reminder was needed, that their governor was the same Ronald Reagan who had opposed the Civil Rights Act of 1964 and had made his national debut as a spokesman for Goldwater. The irony was not lost on Reagan, who resented Goldwater for not returning the favor. On June 19, Goldwater had written Reagan a letter recalling their Easter conversation and in effect told him to get lost. "The middle of June has come and I would hasten a very strong guess that Nixon can well win on the first ballot," Goldwater wrote. "This, of course, would be guaranteed if a large state such as yours or Texas moved in his direction. I told you at the time [Easter week] that California, which means you, could become the leading power in the Republican Party if Nixon were assured of victory because of a decision on your part to release your delegates together with a statement that your vote would go to Dick. I fully respect and understand why you have refrained from doing this, but the outward reasons for this plan and for this action no longer exist, so a new area of decision now faces you."[16]

Reagan knew that Goldwater was telling him to get out of the race, which may have made him more inclined to stay in it. While still ambivalent about the presidency, Reagan resisted being pushed around, and he didn't think Goldwater's track record as a presidential candidate entitled him to lecture anyone. Still an undeclared candidate, Reagan left Sacramento in a chartered jetliner on July 19 in a far-fetched attempt to win over the South without Goldwater, Thurmond, Tower, or the state party chairmen whose support Nixon had locked up months earlier. With Reagan on this pilgrimage were the usual suspects—Clif White, Tom Reed, Holmes Tuttle, and William French Smith, plus all the reporters whom Nofziger could induce to come along.* "It's more of a Southern solicitation than a Southern strategy," quipped Reed as the plane took off from Los Angeles.[17]

The first stop was Amarillo, Texas, where Reagan addressed a fund-raising barbecue and met with pro-Reagan delegates from five states. He told them he would not become a formal candidate until his name

*The Kitchen Cabinet raised or contributed most of the money needed for the Reagan presidential campaign. Tuttle, as usual, took the lead, although Henry Salvatori was also an important contributor and fund-raiser. Reed's records show that the 1967 budget was $100,000, which included Clif White's salary as a consultant. This would be equivalent to $530,000 in 2003 dollars. The budget for 1968 was $440,000, which proved to be more than Reagan needed and more than his financial backers raised. The actual 1968 spending was $366,000, just under $2 million in 2003 dollars, of which $163,000 was spent at the Republican National Convention at Miami Beach.

was placed in nomination. When asked what he would do if he were nominated, Reagan replied, "I won't be a reluctant candidate. I'll run like hell." After Reagan left the room, White left no doubt that Reagan would be a candidate. He called him the man of "courage, common sense and charisma" that the nation needed as president.

From Amarillo the Southern Solicitation proceeded to Little Rock, Arkansas, where Reagan predicted multiple ballots at the forthcoming convention. When I interviewed him on the flight from Little Rock to Charlottesville, Virginia, Reagan told me that by multiple he meant "more than two" and then made a distinction that he would fail to share with any of his southern audiences. "We won't get the racist vote," Reagan said. "We don't want it. Neither party wants it."[18] Wallace, he went on, was a passing phenomenon whose candidacy threatened the orderly growth of a two-party system in the South. "We've got a chance to elect some Republicans and may lose some very wonderful opportunities because of the Wallace candidacy," Reagan said.[19] He was sending me a message. I had written a story for the *San Jose Mercury* drawing attention to his refusal to take issue with Wallace.[20] Reagan did not complain about the story, or even mention it, but this was his way of telling me he was pulling his punches against Wallace solely for tactical reasons.

From Charlottesville, Reagan flew to Baltimore and then to Cincinnati for the National Governors Conference. He took a side trip to Frankfort, Kentucky, where he dined with Governor Louie B. Nunn and all but one of the state's twenty-four Republican delegates. The Kentucky delegation, however, remained solidly pro-Nixon.

Back at the Governors Conference, there was a curious sidelight. Reagan and Nelson Rockefeller, at opposite ends of the Republican spectrum, praised each other while governors of smaller states watched in amusement. Rockefeller was banking on the Southern Solicitation to stop Nixon, a hope Reagan kept alive by joining with southern governors in voting against a Romney-sponsored "declaration of conscience" that included a pledge to eradicate discrimination in housing. This maneuver exposed the precarious balance Reagan was trying to maintain in reaching out to minorities in California while courting Wallace sympathizers in Dixie. After conferring with his staff, Reagan changed his "no" vote on the Romney resolution to an abstention.

Reagan then flew to Birmingham, Alabama, where he met with delegates from several southern states behind a security cordon so tight that the elevator operator for a time refused to let Nofziger off at the governor's floor. That night he gave a speech in which he urged southerners not to "throw their vote away in a futile protest" for a third party. The *Birmingham News*, in an editorial entitled "Why Reagan's Here," had no doubts he was a candidate. "So far he's fiddled around the edges of open declaration . . . but he is a candidate, period." The editorial said that Reagan's appearance "can't harm the candidacies of Republican campaigners for Congress and the Senate." The stop-off, however, was of little benefit to Reagan. He had raised bundles of money for the Republican Party on his trip, and won many a conservative cheer, but he had barely dented Nixon's delegate count.

In the interval between the Southern Solicitation and the Republican National Convention in Miami Beach, senior members of the governor's staff in Sacramento approached Reagan with a gentler version of the point made bluntly by Goldwater in his June 19 letter. Bill Clark and Rus Walton were concerned that Reagan had widened his credibility gap by declaring that he was not a candidate as he campaigned for delegates across the South. In a six-page memo to Clark on July 31 that referred to Reagan as "the Boss," Walton factually assessed the strength of the Nixon candidacy and the desperation of the Rockefeller forces, whose "only chance now (and it is extremely remote, at that) is to drive a wedge between the Nixon and Reagan forces—split the conservative forces, weld a new amalgam." Rockefeller, in Walton's eyes, was a "wrecker" with nothing to lose; "this is his last desperate try." But anything that hurt Nixon could also damage Reagan and his position in the party. "So far the Boss has handled himself beautifully in most respects," Walton's memo continued. "It is what happens from here on out that counts. We must not let others push him into untenable positions." Walton proposed a "hard" delegate count on Monday, August 5, the opening day of the convention. If the count showed Nixon the winner, Reagan would allow his name to be placed in nomination, then rise to a point of personal privilege and "with the eyes of the nation upon him . . . decline the nomination and urge his people to vote for Nixon." It was good advice, but Reagan didn't take it.

At the convention, Rockefeller and Reagan were dependent on each other. Nixon needed 667 delegates to be nominated. The hope, or fantasy, of both governors was that Nixon would fall below 600 delegates on the first ballot. Then, support would fall away in the center to Rockefeller and on the right to Reagan, and it would become apparent that Nixon could not be nominated. The skillful White had sequestered a formidable amount of second-ballot strength for Reagan, who was the preferred candidate of rank-and-file southern delegates. If only he could get to a second ballot.

Politics is a litany of "ifs." If Rockefeller could chip away at Nixon in the Northeast on the first ballot. If White could break the unit rule in Florida and Mississippi so that delegates in these states could vote their preferences. If Louisiana State Chairman Charlton Lyons, who liked Reagan so much that there were tears in his eyes when White appealed to him, would let his delegation go.[21] These were the "ifs" of Miami Beach.

The California delegation at the Deauville Hotel on Collins Avenue, however, was pondering a different possibility. Should Reagan, who had repeatedly insisted that he was not a candidate, abandon his favorite-son status? He wasn't inclined to do it when he arrived in Miami Beach, but a prominent member of the California delegation thought otherwise. Former U.S. Senator Bill Knowland, notorious for his poor judgment, approached Nofziger on nomination day, August 7, with a proposal that Reagan become a full-fledged candidate. Nofziger, who later faulted himself for not consulting first with White and Reed, took Knowland to Reagan's suite, where the senator told him that his favorite-son candidacy would become credible if he declared.[22] Reagan, weary of walking the tightrope of noncandidacy, gave in. "I felt I was running the risk of becoming like a Stassen joke," Reagan told me retrospectively. "I was keeping my fingers crossed because I was afraid of a battle inside our delegation if I did. When I got the word that it was unanimous for me, it did make it easier. I was getting edgy in having to address all these delegations and tell them that I would be a candidate when my name was placed in nomination and they could so consider me at that time."[23]

The announcement simplified life for Reagan but enabled Nixon operatives to claim that the California governor had broken his promise. The Nixon team, never loath to attack, organized a campaign of telegraphs and letters calling upon Reagan to pull out. Some of the telegrams said, "Keep your word, Ron." Reagan's announcement astonished his wife, whom he usually consulted before making political decisions. Not this time. "I was the most surprised person in the world when it happened," said Nancy Reagan, who heard the news over the radio as she was preparing to grant a press interview.[24]

Reagan was not a candidate for long. On the first ballot that evening, Nixon received 697 votes to 277 for Rockefeller and 182 for Reagan. White later told Reagan that he had fallen only eight votes short, by which he meant the number of votes needed to break the unit rule in Florida, Mississippi, and South Carolina. "We were a lot closer than many people think," Reagan said.[25] Reed was similarly convinced. "The first ballot was Nixon, the third ballot was Reagan, the fifth ballot was Rocky and those were the ones they had to win it on," said Reed, recounting both a convention that occurred and one that might have been.[26] But a Reagan nomination, after his hesitant start, had always been a long shot.

All that was left for Reagan was to salvage a tiny shred of the bold strategy Walton had urged on him at the convention. Shortly after 2 A.M. on August 8, Reagan strode to the podium and urged that the convention "declare itself unanimously and unitedly behind the candidate Richard Nixon as the next President of the United States."

Afterward, Reagan was faulted for not declaring his candidacy sooner and for declaring it at all. California Lieutenant Governor Robert Finch, a Nixon confidant who had dutifully cast his vote for Reagan, believed that Reagan should have remained a favorite son. "He was getting bum dope from White, Reed, and Knowland," Finch said. "The governor would have gotten the same number of votes as a favorite son that he received as an avowed candidate. As long as Nixon had Tower, Thurmond, and Goldwater, there was no way that Reagan could take any massive amount of southern delegates."[27]

Reagan's friend William F. Buckley, who also had supported Nixon, was more charitable. Buckley saw Reagan as a contingency candidate whose presence had provided an alternative for conservatives if Nixon collapsed in the primaries. "Accordingly, friends of Ronald Reagan asked him to stand by, and contrived the favorite-son façade to spare him the embarrassment of an unbecomingly precipitate ambitiousness," Buckley wrote in his syndicated column. "What then happened is what often happens in politics. Contingent operations become vested interests. The royalist passions of the entourage take over, and before long the principal is carried along into the vortex without the rationale he had been promised to hang on to."[28]

Buckley thought it "spooky" that conservatives, such as Tower and Thurmond, had stuck with Nixon when it was Reagan who embodied conservative ideals. "It must have been especially hard for Reagan," wrote Buckley. He continued:

> He is a man expansively generous, considerate; and it must be both (a) that he never considered, at least not after Nixon's primary victories, the possibility that he would beat Nixon and (b) that he nevertheless shrank from overruling his idealistic, devoted and optimistic coterie, who asked him to suspend thought and dream; dreaming being the substance of the whole elating caper. It is seldom recognized in politics, in particular where presidential candidates are involved, that gentle and obliging and self-effacing men are capable of asserting themselves into presidential politics. Ronald Reagan was one such.[29]

The validity of this generous judgment was accentuated by Reagan's wise reaction to his defeat. He confided immediately to Nofziger that he "wasn't ready to be president" and he made a similar statement soon afterward to Michael Deaver. Reagan told me that fall, while campaigning without rancor for Nixon and the Republican ticket, that he felt a "sense of relief" when Nixon was nominated.[30]

In 1968, Reagan agreed in his heart with Clark and Walton more than with Reed and Nofziger about the wisdom of running for president. He was his mother's fatalistic son. His day would come, if that was God's plan. He was tired but not unhappy after the Miami Beach convention. Borrowing a yacht from one of his millionaire friends, Reagan and his wife cruised the Florida Keys for a long weekend. "I averaged sleeping 14 hours at night and then I would take a nap in the afternoon," said Reagan. "We both felt the same way."[31]

In retrospect, Reagan's abortive 1968 campaign prepared him for sterner tests. He learned in the process of running half-heartedly for president about delegates and party politics and the media swirl at conventions. (He also learned, said Tom Reed, in a reference to a Machiavellian GOP state chairman from Mississippi, that "when Clarke Reed says yes, he means no.")[32]

It is an axiom of life and politics, accepted by Reagan, that defeats teach more than victories. Reagan was a good politician, and he had paid attention, as good politicians do. John F. Kennedy's unsuccessful bid for the vice presidency at the 1956 Democratic convention helped propel his successful candidacy for president in 1960. Goldwater's stirring speech for Nixon at the 1960 convention gave the Arizonan a running start for 1964. Many of those whom Reagan roused in 1968 remembered him eight years later and followed his banner to Kansas City and beyond. Reagan came out of Miami Beach a loser. But defeat had laid the groundwork for victory.

20

REGENT

Ronald Reagan discovered the "mess at Berkeley" in his campaign for governor and did his best, by his lights, to clean it up. In the early years of his governorship, Berkeley was Reagan's most effective populist issue, resonating more with voters than his denunciations of other messes, real or imagined, in welfare, Washington, or Vietnam. Berkeley was Reagan's symbol of what had gone wrong in America. The University of California at Berkeley was on the barricades of the cultural revolution that divided our country in the 1960s and in some respects divides it even now. The revolution was in its nascent stages when Reagan ran for governor, but Reagan took his stand as a counterrevolutionary, denouncing what he called "the spirit of permissiveness" and defending traditional values. He acted from conviction rather than calculation, raising "Berkeley" as a political issue when it was a minor blip in the polls. It proved good politics nonetheless.

Initially, Reagan's political advisers doubted the wisdom of making Berkeley a major campaign theme. Californians are proud of their education system, and Berkeley was the state's premier public university, famed for the depth and breadth of its educational achievements. In the eyes of Clark Kerr, its president, Berkeley was not a university but a "multiversity." Berkeley boasted a dozen Nobel laureates and ninety-seven members of the National Academy of Sciences, the most in the nation. Although most famous for its physics department and the work of the Lawrence Radiation Laboratory, UC Berkeley also had first-rate departments in subjects ranging from biochemistry to English. In 1966, when Reagan first made an issue of Berkeley, the American Council of Education found that the university's graduate departments made it "the best balanced, distinguished university in the country."

But UC Berkeley was inaccessible to most Californians. Although gifted students flocked to the university from all over the world, only an elite sliver of California high school graduates qualified for admission by dint of grades, test scores, or special status.* Parents of the 88 percent who didn't qualify—particularly parents struggling to pay for college educations—agreed with Reagan that Berkeley's privileged students should study more and demonstrate less. They responded approvingly to candidate Reagan's allegation that UC Berkeley was dominated by a "minority of malcontents, beatniks, and filthy-speech advocates" who engaged in sex-and-dope orgies "so vile that I cannot describe them to you." They cheered when Reagan declared that students should "observe the rules or get out."

Populism is polarizing, and Reagan's militance affronted an academic community that never cared for him in the first place. He was, after all, an actor and a conservative Republican, a combination that led liberal academics to assume that he was also a know-nothing. Reagan was reassuring to a majority of Californians. He frightened Berkeley, where he was viewed as a menace who sought to bring a great university to heel.

Anti-Reagan academics would have been surprised to learn that H. R. Haldeman, a member of the Board of Regents, the university's governing body, shared their concerns. Haldeman, an alumnus of the University of Southern California, represented university alumni associations on the board. A conservative Republican, he would later achieve notoriety as President Richard Nixon's chief of staff and serve a prison sentence for his role in the Watergate cover-up. But as a regent, Haldeman was effective and responsible. He was a friend of two liberal Democratic regents, Fred Dutton and William Coblentz. They disagreed on many issues but also worked together. Haldeman wanted to curb campus demonstrations and change the leadership of the university, but he worried that Reagan's incitement against Berkeley would be counterproductive.

Early in 1966, as Reagan began to exploit the Berkeley issue, Haldeman sent a private message to Reagan contributor Henry Salvatori, an old friend. Haldeman told Salvatori that he understood the political reasons for raising the issue but questioned Reagan's tactics. "I became concerned about the conduct of the campaign in terms of using the university as a campaign issue and doing it with the wrong facts," Halde-

*The University of California was open to the top 12.5 percent of California high school graduates, plus a limited number of out-of-state students who were in the top 6 percent of their high school class. Even this elite upper rung did not necessarily have a choice of campuses; Berkeley was the choosiest. Black leaders complained that the university's admissions policy severely restricted the percentage of minority students, then only 2 percent (among California residents) of the student body. Affirmative action policies later increased the percentage of minority students.

man said.[1] Salvatori, without mentioning Haldeman, once told me that "Nixon people" had urged him to ask Reagan to soft-pedal his attacks on Berkeley and that he had passed on the message.[2] Whether this message had an impact is not clear, but Reagan's provocative allusions to "orgies" at Berkeley became less frequent in the later stages of his campaign.

Reagan never retreated on his central position that student demonstrators who refused to comply with university rules should be expelled. But he did not immediately address this issue. When Reagan became governor in 1967, the campuses were relatively quiet and the battle lines between his administration and the university were drawn on fiscal grounds. State government had lavished money on higher education as California's population exploded in the decades after World War II. UC Berkeley, the crown jewel of the public higher education system, fared best. During Pat Brown's eight years as governor, the university averaged 95 percent of its budget requests from the Legislature, an achievement unmatched even by the powerful highway lobby. Such largesse could not continue indefinitely, and the fiscal crisis of 1967 would have required cutbacks in the university budget even had Brown been reelected. But Brown was considered a friend of the university, and Reagan an enemy. When Reagan called for reductions in higher education spending and the first-ever tuition charge for resident students, the university took this as a declaration of war.

The opening battle in this war determined the fate of Clark Kerr, a distinguished educator and former labor mediator. In 1952, he became the first chancellor at Berkeley. In 1958, Kerr succeeded Robert Gordon Sproul, who had been president of the entire university system since 1930. Sproul, a capable administrator and awesome politician, was a big, back-slapping Rotarian booster of a man who lobbied the Legislature as easily as he gave a welcoming speech to the freshman class. He formed alliances with the scientific-defense community to fund the cyclotron. He teamed up with agribusiness to obtain legislative grants for university agricultural research. His "secret weapon" was the Order of the Golden Bear, a university alumni club once described as "a pack of onetime Berkeley campus big shots who come out of hibernation whenever Golden Bear Sproul cries for help."[3] The big shots were manufacturers, brokers, lawyers, and scientists who lobbied legislators at Sproul's command.

Sproul's skill at manipulating the alumni and soft-soaping the Legislature cushioned UC in the late 1940s and early 1950s when ardent Communist hunters saw Reds behind every professor's desk and tried to foist a special teachers' loyalty oath upon the university. Even during this difficult period, the university received financially tender treatment from state government. Later, as the demands of the baby boom pushed up education costs, Pat Brown trimmed the budgets of the less prestigious state colleges and left the university pretty much alone.

Kerr, a thinker, a planner, and a pacifist, was not Sproul's equal as a politician. He did, however, have a vision for the university, devising a master plan for higher education and expanding the university from six to nine campuses, each with a special mandate. But as Kerr proclaimed the glories of the multiversity, students on these vast and impersonal campuses became increasingly alienated. Berkeley was heaven for talented researchers, but it was also an educational factory where ordinary students struggled to find their way. A UC official once acknowledged "that the quiet, nonaggressive, A-average high school student who goes to the University of California will get a worse education than he would at a mediocre college where the faculty have time and interest to work with students."[4]

Alienation and idealism coexisted at Berkeley. Busloads of students journeyed to the South during the "freedom summer" of 1964 to work for civil rights. Many who returned from this experience became mainstays of the Free Speech Movement and participated in demonstrations against the multiversity and the Vietnam War. Campus radicals flourished in this milieu. Some of these militants, the physics student Mario Savio in particular, were talented organizers. "The principles of revolution can be applied to a campus as well as to a country," said one UC Berkeley official.[5] Considering that Berkeley was a leader in many experimental endeavors, it is not surprising that it also became a laboratory for student rebellion.

Kerr, however, was surprised. While he often said that "the university is not engaged in making ideas safe for students; it is engaged in making students safe for ideas," neither students nor ideas seemed safe at Berkeley in the troubled 1960s. The regents had doubted Kerr's leadership since the December 1964 occupation of Sproul Hall (described in the first chapter of this book) that ended with the forcible expulsion and arrest of 773 students. The Free Speech Movement of 1964 was followed by the "filthy speech movement" of 1965, various antiwar demonstrations, and a short-lived student strike labeled the "Yellow Submarine Movement." Kerr was powerless to control these disorders. Later, as the Vietnam War intensified, other university leaders across the land would prove equally incapable of restraining demonstrations. But at the time, Kerr's ineffectiveness puzzled even his supporters. Liberal regents wondered why a skilled labor mediator could not reach an accommodation with student activists. Conservative regents complained that Kerr was too indulgent. Haldeman thought he was a poor administrator. "There's an old saying in business that if you promote your top salesman to sales manager you have two losses: you get a lousy sales manager and you lose a great salesman," Haldeman said in evaluating Kerr's performance.[6]

Kerr reacted emotionally to the regents' dissatisfaction with him. On March 9, 1965, three months after the Sproul Hall takeover, he resigned as president, an action leaked in advance to the press. At Governor Brown's urging, the regents rejected the resignation, and Kerr stayed. But the regents resented Kerr for putting them on the spot. As campus demonstrations continued, several of the regents who had gone along with Brown began second-guessing themselves and decided they should have accepted Kerr's resignation when they had the chance.

The Board of Regents of the University of California consists of sixteen members appointed by the governor for sixteen-year terms, plus eight ex-officio members. The latter include the governor, the Assembly speaker, five other public officials, and the university president. The sixteen-year terms are in theory supposed to prevent any single governor from dominating the board and to insulate regents from undue political influence. In practice, the board is pulled into politics whenever the ex-officio members are at odds. Brown had rarely attended regents' meetings, but Reagan was faithful in attendance during the first two years of his governorship. Since the regents had the final say on tuition, an issue on which Reagan and Assembly Speaker Jesse Unruh disagreed, the meetings of the board inevitably became a political battleground.

Even without such direct rivalry, political considerations often influence the Board of Regents. The post of regent is prestigious. Governors use these coveted appointments to reward contributors, political aides, or media moguls, most of them men and women of means with strong opinions. The board meetings were usually genteel; regents made it a practice to hear each other out, which often made them seem indecisive. After Reagan's election, however, the regents recognized that they were likely to face another vote on Kerr. Anti-Kerr members of the board hoped they would have a chance to oust the university president.

Kerr, rather than Reagan, gave them this opportunity. In mid-January, he sent a confidential telegram to all chancellors of the university campuses ordering them to stop accepting new registrants until the budget situation was clarified. Such a message was bound to find its way into the press (as Kerr surely knew), and it did. Meanwhile, the university's public relations apparatus made daily attacks on the Reagan budget, predicting the departure of famous professors and talented students if it passed. UC Vice President Charles Hitch said that university campuses at Irvine, San Diego, and Santa Cruz might have to be closed if Reagan's budget was approved by the Legislature.

This campaign damaged Kerr's standing with Reagan and the regents. "They're not even going to give me a chance," Reagan told an intimate. "They're trying to discredit me."[7] The regents, while sharing Kerr's reservations about the budget and tuition, were also alarmed. Regent Dorothy Chandler, wife of the *Los Angeles Times* publisher and later publisher herself, believed that Kerr's tactics had prejudiced the new administration against him. She had already said as much to Kerr, who related in his memoirs that Chandler had told him the previous November that she would support Reagan in his desire for a new university president because he "had been elected overwhelmingly in an expression of public opinion, and that the board was bound by this vote."[8]

The Board of Regents convened for a two-day meeting on Thursday, January 19, 1967, at its administrative offices across the street from the Berkeley campus. Reagan, governor for less than three weeks, listened as Theodore Meyer, the chairman of the board, presided and the board disposed of routine business.

The first day of the meetings was the Thursday calm before the Friday storm. Before the regents reconvened on January 20, Kerr asked to meet with Meyer and Chandler, the vice chairman of the board, in what he later described as an attempt to clarify his situation. Kerr told them he could not effectively represent the university in budget negotiations as a lame-duck president. Meyer and Chandler, both of whom doubted that Kerr could effectively deal with Reagan even if he had unanimous backing from the regents, urged him to resign. Kerr said that was an issue for the full board to decide.

This was, at best, a miscalculation. Meyer, who wanted Kerr out, blandly agreed that he was entitled to a vote of confidence. When the regents convened, Meyer told the board about the meeting with Kerr. Reagan was surprised. "Who said what to whom I'll never know," Governor Reagan told me. "But Chairman Meyer told us that Kerr had said he wanted a settlement of the Affaire Clark Kerr. That was a bombshell and most of all to me."[9]

The settlement took two hours of closed-door wrangling, with Kerr excluded from the room. Unruh, by some accounts, played the role of agitator. At one point he accused the regents of "vacillating" and threatened to make a motion to fire Kerr, then vote against it.* The motion

---

*Unruh subsequently acknowledged to me that he threatened to make such a motion but said he was expressing exasperation with the indecision of the regents, not trying to provoke them into firing Kerr.

Baby picture of Ronald Wilson Reagan, born February 6, 1911
(Courtesy Ronald Reagan Library)

Main Street in Tampico, Illinois, circa 1912 *(Courtesy Ronald Reagan Library)*

Reagan in Dixon, Illinois, 1923 *(Courtesy Ronald Reagan Library)*

DOROTHY RANDALL
"*An A-1 student, the teacher's joy.*"
Gym 2, 3; Cinean Lit. 1, 2; Joyce
Kilmer 3, 4; Play 3; Annual Staff.

DONALD REAGAN
"Dutch"
"*Life is just one grand sweet song, so start the music.*"
Pres. N. S. Student Body 4; Pres.
2; Play 3, 4; Dram. Club 3, 4, Pres.
4; Fresh.-Soph. Drama Club 1, 2,
Pres. 2; Football 3, 4; Annual Staff;
Hi-Y 3, 4, Vice-Pres. 4; Art. 1, 2;
Lit. Contest 2; Track 2, 3.

Dutch Reagan's photo in high-school yearbook, with first name misspelled "Donald." And the Reagan creed: "Life is just one grand sweet song, so start the music" *(Courtesy Ronald Reagan Library)*

LEFT: Reagan at Lowell Park, where in seven years as a lifeguard he saved 77 people from drowning *(Courtesy Ronald Reagan Library)*

RIGHT: Dutch Reagan, radio announcer at WHO in Des Moines on program sponsored by Kentucky Club tobacco *(Courtesy Ronald Reagan Library)*

Reagan cast as announcer in first film, *Love Is On the Air*, in 1937
(Courtesy Ronald Reagan Library)

LEFT: Reagan with mother Nelle, a determinative influence
(Courtesy Ronald Reagan Library)

RIGHT: Wedding picture of Ronald and Nancy Reagan, March 4, 1952
(Courtesy Ronald Reagan Library)

Reading *The Night Before Christmas* to Patti in 1957 and again in 1964
to Patti and Ron *(Courtesy Reagan Family Collection/Ronald Reagan Library)*

Barry Goldwater in Senate office a few years before his 1964 campaign for the presidency *(Globe Photos)*

National Guardsmen protect Governor Pat Brown as he tours Watts after the August 1965 riot *(AP/Wide World Photos)*

Reagan's 1966 campaign for governor *(Courtesy Ronald Reagan Library)*

The Reagans campaigning, September 8, 1966 *(© 1966, Los Angeles Times)*

The Reagans in victory on November 8, 1966

(Courtesy Ronald Reagan Library)

Reagan sworn in as governor just after midnight on January 2, 1967, by State Supreme Court Justice Marshall McComb. The Reverend Wilbur Choy is in center *(Courtesy Ronald Reagan Library)*

Reagan shakes hands with his nemesis, Assembly Speaker Jesse Unruh, after being sworn in as governor. Lieutenant Governor Robert Finch is in background *(Corbis)*

Reagan meets with S. I. Hayakawa on January 17, 1969. The sign in foreground was over Reagan's office door when he was governor *(Sacramento Bee)*

Sather Gate, entrance to the University of California, under guard in 1968 *(Globe Photos)*

Reagan addresses students after a Board of Regents meeting at University of California-Santa Cruz, October 18, 1968
(AP/Wide World Photos)

Phil Battaglia *(Sacramento Bee)*

ABOVE: Reagan, on October 31, 1967, after denying that a "homosexual ring" existed in the governor's office. From left: security aide Art Van Court, press secretary Paul Beck, Reagan, and communications director Lyn Nofziger *(AP/Wide World Photos)*

The Reagans on the beach at the Del Coronado in 1965 and where Reagan received the news in 1967 that his staff wanted Battaglia out *(Courtesy Ronald Reagan Library)*

The Reagans moved out of this mansion, which Nancy called a "firetrap" and into this traditional Sacramento house where they lived during the governorship *(Courtesy Ronald Reagan Library)*

Legal Affairs Secretary Edwin Meese III talks with reporters in Sacramento in 1967 *(AP/Wide World Photos)*

Ike Livermore, Reagan's state resources director, points to a picture showing him leading a packing expedition into the high Sierra, May 3, 1967 *(AP/Wide World Photos)*

ABOVE: Richard Wilson, Reagan, and Ida Soares in Covelo, 1974. Reagan blocked the high dam that would have flooded the town and Round Valley *(Courtesy of Richard Wilson)*

Bill Clark, then Reagan's chief of staff, with the governor at the Clark ranch in 1967 *(Les Walsh/Courtesy of William P. Clark)*

LEFT: Assembly Speaker Bob Moretti, Reagan's co-architect on welfare reform, shown in 1973, after leading campaign that defeated Reagan's tax-limitation initiative *(AP/Wide World Photos)*

BELOW: Paul Haerle, left, chats with his mentor Tom Reed on April 11, 1967, the day he succeeded Reed as Governor Reagan's appointments secretary *(AP/Wide World Photos)*

Reagan with his legislative liaison, George Steffes *(Courtesy George Steffes)*

Nancy Reagan and son Ron at the 1968 Republican Convention in Miami
Beach *(Courtesy Ronald Reagan Library)*

The Reagan family in 1976: Patti, Nancy, Ronald, Michael, Maureen, and Ron
(Courtesy Ronald Reagan Library)

ABOVE: The 1980 television debate in Nashua, New Hampshire, between Reagan and George Bush that put Reagan on the road to the presidential nomination. In background, from left, are John Anderson, Howard Baker, Robert Dole, and Philip Crane. The moderator is Jon Breen *(Corbis)*

Reagan surprises President Jimmy Carter by shaking hands with him at the beginning of their debate in Cleveland, October 28, 1980 *(Corbis)*

Near the moment of victory, Ford, Reagan, and Bush in Peoria on the last day of the campaign, November 3, 1980 *(AP/Wide World Photos)*

Mike Deaver, Reagan, and Stuart Spencer *(Courtesy Stuart Spencer)*

Ronald Reagan becomes the 40th president of the United States on January 20, 1981. Chief Justice Warren Burger administers the oath *(Courtesy Ronald Reagan Library)*

was made instead by Allan Grant, newly installed by Reagan as president of the State Agriculture Board. Other regents said that dismissing Kerr would seem a partisan act if initiated by a Reagan appointee. Grant withdrew the motion. It was resubmitted by Laurence J. Kennedy Jr. of Redding, an attorney and appointee of Governor Brown. The vote to dismiss Kerr was 14–8. Reagan and Lieutenant Governor Robert Finch voted for the Kennedy motion, and Unruh voted against it. For reasons never explained, Superintendent of Public Instruction Max Rafferty absented himself from the discussion on Kerr and did not say how he would have voted. The other regent who did not vote was Kerr, who was excluded during the balloting. Kerr returned to the room after the vote and calmly presented several routine issues to the regents without reference to his ouster.

Despite conducting himself professionally, Kerr was angry. He charged that Reagan had played "a substantial role" in his dismissal and disputed Meyer's account that he had sought a vote of confidence. Asking for a clarification of his status, Kerr said, "was about as far from asking for a vote of confidence as it could possibly be."[10] This was a semantic quibble. By insisting that the full board decide his fate, Kerr was seeking the equivalent of a vote of confidence, whatever he preferred to call it.

Reagan denied that he had maneuvered to oust Kerr, and the political logic of the "Affaire Clark Kerr" is on his side. Although Reagan believed that Kerr had "outlived his usefulness," the governor was not then seeking a showdown. "We had tuition and the budget on our hands, and I would have preferred to wait until June or so," Reagan told me. "But you can't turn around and give a man a vote of confidence in January and then fire him five months later."[11] Although these comments leave little doubt that Reagan eventually would have moved against Kerr, the governor had nothing to gain by taking the action in January.* His tuition proposal, which was critical to his budget, was at the mercy of the regents.

But Reagan, while not the schemer that Kerr made him out to be, had more to do with his dismissal than he realized. What the anti-Kerr regents needed was not Reagan's participation in their maneuvering but his vote. Thirteen votes, a majority of the board including ex-officio members, were needed to oust a president. In an interview many years later, Haldeman made it clear that he and other regents who had lost confidence in Kerr believed they needed the votes of Reagan and Finch

---

*Lyn Nofziger said that Kerr dropped in on him many years later in Washington. "He freely admitted that Reagan had not done him in, and I just as freely admitted that it had just been a matter of time," Nofziger wrote.[12]

to dismiss him. Governor Brown and Lieutenant Governor Glenn Anderson would have supported Kerr. With Brown and Anderson replaced by Reagan and Finch, and another vote against Kerr provided by Grant, the political arithmetic had changed. Haldeman and the other anti-Kerr regents had wanted to fire Kerr for a long time. When they had the votes to do so, they did.[13]

Kerr's ouster ignited a political firestorm. Democratic legislators in Washington and Sacramento denounced Reagan and the regents. Flags flew at half-mast on UC campuses, where students and faculty held rallies to protest the dismissal. The lead editorial in *The New York Times* was headed "Twilight of a Great University" and predicted an exodus of professors due to Kerr's firing and the Reagan budget. But Kerr's ouster delighted the militant Left. The UC Student Strike Committee huddled with Mario Savio, who was no longer a student, and issued a statement saying: "Good riddance to bad rubbish. The new Reagan administration has begun auspiciously. The multiversity is dead. Long live the university."[14]

Reagan acknowledged at a press conference that the timing of Kerr's ouster was "bad." Even so, it probably saved the university from something worse—a commission to "investigate the charges of communism and blatant sexual misbehavior on the Berkeley campus." Reagan had used these words in promising during his campaign to appoint such a commission, which he suggested should be headed by John McCone, a former director of the Central Intelligence Agency. In the climate that existed after the Kerr firing, such a commission would have poured kerosene on the flickering flames of rebellion at Berkeley, and Reagan dropped the idea.[15]

Kerr's ouster complicated Reagan's budget negotiations with the university. These negotiations were now directed by UC Vice President Hitch, who was less of a target than Kerr but just as committed to resisting tuition and obtaining budget concessions. Hitch had the advantage of commanding support among the regents, who also wanted more money for the university than Reagan was offering. The regents had asked for $278 million in their budget request (more than $1 billion in 2003 dollars). The first budget submitted by Reagan's state finance director, Gordon Paul Smith, had offered $196.8 million plus $20 million to be raised by tuition and $19 million from the regents' own funds, mostly federal grants paid to the university for research contracts. The total of $236 million was $5 million less than the previous year's budget and 15 percent below the regents' request. The university, which for years had demanded and received the cream of the state budget, was now being served skim milk.

Tuition was a particular sticking point. Out-of-state students paid hefty tuitions, but "free tuition" for California students was a university tradition, even though something of a misnomer. As education costs climbed, free tuition had been maintained through steep student fee increases, which by 1967 averaged $250 a year (or $1,250 in 2003 dollars). As early as 1964, Governor Brown's state finance director, Hale Champion, had given a prescient but little-noticed speech in which he said that California was close to "breaching the tuition-free system" with fees "which produce the very kind of unfortunate economic screening that the free-tuition system was supposed to avoid." Champion suggested that the university should hold the line on fees, charge tuition, and plow back some of the tuition money into grants for low-income students.[16]

This idea was the wave of the future, as Reagan soon realized, but no one was pushing it in the wake of the Kerr dismissal. Instead, "no tuition" became the battle cry on university and state college campuses throughout the state. Students at the University of California at Santa Barbara took the lead. They raised $4,000 and rented a fleet of buses for the 400-mile trip to Sacramento, where, on February 9, they marched on the State Capitol beneath a blue-and-white banner proclaiming, "Keep Politics Out of Education." In a deliberate attempt to counteract the "beatnik" image of Berkeley, male students were clean-shaven and wore suits and ties; female students wore dresses.[17] Reagan calmly addressed the 2,500 marchers from the west steps of the capitol, urging them to consider the state's "dire" fiscal plight and "weigh carefully both sides of the question." The students, unimpressed but polite, respectfully applauded. Later, student leaders from the nine university campuses met with Reagan to urge restoration of the budget cuts and withdrawal of the tuition plan. Again, it was a polite encounter, but Reagan gave no ground.

The rally signaled the end of the short-lived honeymoon between Reagan and Unruh. The Assembly speaker had refrained from criticizing the governor during the debate over Kerr, but after Reagan had addressed the students and departed, Unruh gave a fiery speech on the capitol steps in which he told the cheering students, "Tuition is a tax and it's a tax of the worst kind—a tax on education. I do not know of a single Democratic vote in the Assembly for tuition."

Two days later, on a chilly and foggy Saturday, 7,500 students and professors, a majority of them from Berkeley, staged another rally at the capitol, this one organized by the American Federation of Teachers. These marchers, many of them bearded, were rambunctious and disrespectful, matching Reagan's stereotype of demonstrators. They carried signs saying "Tax the Rich" and posters with caricatures of Reagan as a gangster or military officer. Reagan was supposed to be out of town, giving a Lincoln Day speech in Eugene, Oregon. Against the advice of his staff, however, he insisted on delaying his departure. "I wouldn't miss this for anything," he told his aides.[18]

Reagan was at his best in confrontations. Some of the marchers had just finished chanting, "Hey, Hey, Ronald Reagan Ran Away," when Reagan, wearing a trench coat over his suit, appeared on the west steps of the capitol. The surprised marchers greeted him with a chorus of boos. "Ladies and gentlemen, if there are any," Reagan began, and was drowned out with another round of boos. He persisted. "The people do have some right to have a voice in the principles and basic philosophy that will go along with the education they provide," Reagan declared. "As governor, I am going to represent the people of the state." He was drowned out again by boos and angry chants of "We are people." The chants were ringing in Reagan's ears as he turned to catch his Oregon-bound plane. He stopped long enough in the capitol rotunda to say of the marchers, "If they represent the majority of the student body of California, then God help the university and the college system."

When the confrontation was replayed that night on television, it was a public relations triumph for Reagan, whose articulate determination to represent "the people of the state" contrasted favorably with the behavior of the wild-eyed, unruly demonstrators. Reporters kidded Nofziger that he had assembled the rowdy crowd from Central Casting. A disgusted Unruh criticized the demonstrators for booing the governor. Unruh realized that what he called this "rude display" undermined Democratic efforts to resist tuition. Such scenes played out frequently during the next two years, and Reagan was the winner every time. As Unruh put it, "the left wing is really giving Reagan a lot of help."[19]

While the militants were marching, the university was negotiating. Reagan, in the revised budget that Smith presented on March 28, restored to the university and state colleges the money that was to have been raised from collection of tuition. University officials pressed for more. "The estimates as to how many students would have to be turned down at various possible budget levels was almost a comedy of scare tactics, misinterpretation of statistics, and false estimates by university officials," wrote F. Alex Crowley, whose study of the early Reagan administration was otherwise unsympathetic to the governor's education policies.[20] When the dust had settled, both the university and the state colleges received less than their "minimum" requests, although considerably more than Reagan had promised initially.*

*After many maneuvers, the regents settled on a "minimum" budget of $255 million from state funds. UC wound up with $250 million, including $229.1 million from the state and

Reagan, meanwhile, had made a strategic withdrawal on tuition. He had pushed for tuition in February, but the regents closed ranks and voted it down, with the governor casting the lone dissenting vote. Reagan backed off, de-linking tuition from the budget in the revised March 28 budget. This action somewhat appeased the regents, who after voting down tuition in February appointed a commission to report on the possible financial implications of a tuition requirement. The commission proceeded in a leisurely manner; no one wanted to revisit the issue until the budget was passed.

The showdown on tuition came at a regents meeting at the faculty center of the University of California at Los Angeles (UCLA) on August 31, 1967. By then, Reagan's tuition proposal had been transformed. The figure for in-state tuition had been reduced from $400 per year to $250. With the help of Reagan idea man Rus Walton, tuition had been recast as an "equal-opportunity plan." Half of tuition proceeds were earmarked for scholarships and grants, a fourth for new faculty positions, and a fourth for university construction. This was the proposal that Reagan put before the regents.

The report that the regents commissioned after voting down tuition in February found that the University of California, with its $250 average fee scale, ranked fifty-seventh among the nation's major public universities in the charges levied upon students. Adding a $250 tuition would have made UC the fifth most expensive public university in America for resident students. Another report submitted to the board showed that additional funds for scholarships and grants were needed even without tuition. Reagan argued that his equal-opportunity tuition plan would address this need. He warned that state government was too overextended to increase its scholarship program and that spiraling costs of government borne by middle-income taxpayers made tuition imperative. "There is no leeway left for squeezing the people for any state program," he said.

Jesse Unruh took up the challenge, speaking directly to the students and professors who jammed the faculty center. The Assembly speaker did not mention the governor by name, but his comments were directed at Reagan's tuition plan. Tuition, said Unruh, would squeeze the middle-income taxpayers whom Reagan claimed he wanted to protect. Families in the $8,000-to-$20,000 bracket, already hard hit by the $1 billion state tax increase, would pay most of the charges. "Tuition, or a

---

$20.9 million from the regents' funds. The state colleges requested $213 million from the state and received $189 million. Reagan used his line-item veto power to remove $10 million that the Legislature added to the budget for the two systems. These figures do not include construction funds, which were budgeted separately.

service charge, or whatever you call it, amounts to an incredible imposition on the middle-income people of this state," Unruh said. He looked at Reagan as he finished, and the students applauded. Chairman Meyer admonished the audience to be quiet. Reagan accused Unruh of "playing to the gallery" when he was supposed to be addressing the regents.

The regents did not want to be lectured on tuition either by Reagan or by Unruh. As the morning wore on and the regents spoke, it became evident that many of them were uncomfortable with the choices: rejecting the governor for a second time or abandoning the university's historic commitment to "free tuition." Reagan would not yield. He assured the regents that he was flexible about the amount of the charge and the purposes of its use but said there was no turning back from tuition and that it must not be called by any other name. Still, the regents hesitated. Regent Edwin Pauley, an oilman and conservative Democrat, pleaded with Reagan against pressing for a vote. Pauley said he did not want to oppose the governor but could not support tuition in principle. Reagan was undeterred. "I, for one, have no intention of discussing anything except tuition," he said. "Tuition, yes or no."

Unruh also clamored for a vote. But the regents might well have postponed a decision except for Dorothy Chandler, who wanted the issue resolved so that the regents could move on to the question of naming a university president, a post that had been vacant since Kerr's dismissal. "The university is without a captain of the ship," she said. "We must settle the tuition question and go on to the next issue." With this, the regents decided to act. They rejected Reagan's tuition plan on a 14–7 vote. Four of the seven votes in favor of tuition came from ex-officio members: Reagan, Finch, Grant, and Superintendent of Public Instruction Max Rafferty. Immediately after the vote was announced, Reagan proposed a luncheon recess. Tight-lipped in defeat, he said to Nofziger, "You never leave the stadium at the half."

Halftime was behind closed doors in the cafeteria of the faculty center, where groups of regents and staff members clustered at dining tables of their choice. Many of the regents were dismayed by what they had done. They liked Reagan personally, respected him as governor, and realized they were dependent upon him for next year's budget. In the warm quiet of the cafeteria, the regents searched for a compromise. They explained their objections to the word "tuition." Host Chancellor Franklin Murphy pointed out that many educators feared that tuition would be increased once it was removed from the restrictions of student service imposed by the definition of "fees." Pauley agreed and said again that he did not want to vote against the governor. Reagan listened quietly. "What's the alternative?" he said at one point. The other regents, with a draft prepared mostly by Murphy, showed him. It was a new game when Reagan returned to the field after lunch.[21]

Unruh played no direct role in the halftime negotiations. He huddled with a group of "Pat Brown regents"—Dutton, Coblentz, and William Roth—all of whom realized that their morning victory might not survive the afternoon. In the morning, Reagan had said that it would be "hypocrisy" to call tuition by any other name. After lunch, he submitted a new proposal, based on the Murphy draft, which did not mention the hated word. The new plan proposed a "charge . . . to be paid by all students, other than nonresidents, to finance a program of student aid, faculty enrichment and/or other uses to be determined by the regents." Reagan, now smiling, said the charge should be $250, but he graciously agreed to an amendment by Pauley lowering the amount to $200. When Dutton offered a series of technical amendments that could have tied the board up for hours, Reagan agreed to delete any figure from the resolution. The amount would be determined by the regents later. Reagan had won, and he knew it. The resolution was adopted by voice vote with Unruh and a handful of others loudly voting no.

Now it was Unruh's turn to be angry. The Assembly speaker declared that the regents' reversal of its position showed a need for a "complete overhaul" of the board. "This board is no longer competent or able to give leadership to the university," he said. His words brought a retort from Catherine Campbell Hearst of Hillsborough, one of three appointed regents who had voted with Reagan in the morning. "Speaker Unruh comes so seldom to the regents' meetings that he is always able to give cool, clear advice," she said with an icy smile. Unruh had attended only one of the first forty-four meetings of the regents after he had been appointed speaker. His interest in the regents dated from Reagan's election and the subsequent controversies over Kerr, the budget, and tuition.

Thus ended a decisive meeting of the regents. They had preserved the euphemism of "free tuition" while agreeing to charge students for the privilege of attending the university. "If it walks like a duck and quacks like a duck, it must be a duck," Reagan said to Nofziger in the flush of victory. But when the board delayed for months in specifying the amount of the charge, Reagan became as disgusted with the regents as Unruh had been. "That was like throwing a fish to a seal," Reagan told me more than a year later.[22] Still, Reagan had moved the regents in the direction he wanted to go, and tuition was eventually instituted.

The tuition controversy marked another milestone in Reagan's steady evolution as a politician. He had begun by laying down a marker:

a flat tuition charge of $400 that would be used to make up a portion of the deep budget cuts he was asking of the university. Then tuition and the budget cuts were de-linked, and the charge reduced. Then it was "tuition, yes, or no." Finally, Reagan dropped the word "tuition" and allowed the regents to determine what the charge would be. After all these compromises, he proclaimed total victory, a tactic he would often employ as governor and president.

Reagan's maneuvering to obtain tuition was the model for a political style that would guide his governorship and foreshadow his presidency on issues ranging from taxes to arms control. It was a style that owed much to his days in the Screen Actors Guild, where he had mastered the art of negotiation.[23] The genius of Reagan as a politician was that his reach almost always exceeded his grasp, and that he didn't seem to mind. He typically sought more, often much more, than was obtainable, then settled for the best deal he could get.

Three crucial actions, occurring in a period of thirty-four summer days in 1967, set the pattern for Reagan's governorship. On July 28, the Legislature's approval of Reagan's $1 billion tax bill gave him fiscal running room. On August 28, the appointment of Bill Clark as chief of staff established a comfort level within the governor's office that would continue through the much longer reign of his successor, Edwin Meese. On August 31, Reagan won his compromise victory on tuition, a remarkable accomplishment for a governor who had no vote except his own on the same issue seven months earlier.

The university benefited, however, from its rearguard action against tuition and the budget cuts. While the university's scare tactics did not deter Reagan, they drove 1968 admissions below even the regents' most conservative estimates, which reduced expenses. By the time admissions rose again in 1969, Reagan had restored most of the higher education budget cuts. The revenues from his tax bill assured adequate funding for the university and the state colleges throughout his governorship.

The most immediate impact of Reagan's confrontation with the university was to complicate the search for a successor to Clark Kerr. The regents sought to lure a big-name educator but found no one willing to assume the dual risk of controlling Berkeley and dealing with Governor Reagan. Nine months after Kerr's ouster, the regents settled for a proven commodity in plain sight, Acting President Charles Hitch. He proved an able administrator and a realistic leader. Much later, Hitch told the *Los Angeles Times* that his greatest achievement as UC president was to survive.

Hitch was in place and the budget salvaged, but the campus militants remained. When students had occupied Sproul Hall back in 1964, campus protests were a Berkeley peculiarity. But as casualties mounted in Vietnam and racial disorders ripped apart the Great Society, Berkeley became the leading edge of a larger story. In April 1968, students occupied the president's office at Columbia University until a previously indulgent administration had police remove them. The same year, there was a heralded and widely copied "teach-in" at the University of Michigan. Student riots erupted in France, Northern Ireland, Italy, West Germany, and Britain—"seemingly," wrote Michael Barone, "a worldwide uprising by the young."[24] The American component of this uprising continued in 1969 with student disorders at Harvard, the City College of New York, and San Francisco State College.

Reagan was peripheral to these events but preoccupied with them. He believed it was his duty to set an example on California campuses so that students, most of whom had never participated in any demonstration, could attend class safely and focus on their studies. Peaceful protests did not bother him, but he drew the line at disorderly, disruptive behavior. Reagan enjoyed the give-and-take with antagonistic students whom he encountered at meetings of the regents, which were rotated among the university's nine campuses. Lyn Nofziger told of one such encounter at the Santa Barbara campus. When Reagan returned to the regents meeting after a lunch break, the sidewalk was lined on both sides with students who stood in silent protest. As Reagan reached the meeting room, he turned, put his fingers to his lips and said, "Shhhh." The students burst into laughter.[25]

At another regents meeting, this one on the Santa Cruz campus, hostile students noisily greeted Reagan. As the governor's limousine threaded its way at a snail's pace through the students, a bearded demonstrator approached, yelling, "We are the future!" Police were nervous; Reagan was amused. Borrowing a scrap of paper from an aide, Reagan scrawled a message and held it up to the window in the face of the demonstrator. It said, "I'll sell my bonds."[26]

This action was spontaneous, but many of Reagan's barbed one-liners were scripted, and usually by him. "Their signs said, 'make love, not war,' but it didn't look like they could do either," was a surefire applause line. So was a more dubious jape that became a staple of Reagan's 1967 political speeches outside the state: "We have some hippies in California. For those of you who don't know what a hippie is, he's a fellow who dresses like Tarzan, has hair like Jane, and smells like Cheetah."[27]

Some members of Reagan's staff, notably Rus Walton, thought that the governor overdid the hippie-baiting. Reagan's one-liners wowed conservative audiences, but they offended academics and students and made it seem as if his motive for challenging the radicals was purely political. In fact, Reagan was compartmentalized. He had one standard for political speeches, when he threw red meat to his audiences, and another for everything else. His principal limitation in dealing with campus disorder was not his mockery of the militants but his suspicion that all of them were linked together in a "conspiracy." Reagan wanted the conspirators expelled. His saving grace was that he distinguished between advocacy and action. "You outlaw them when the actions they take interfere with the lives of others," Reagan told me.[28]

Reagan's academic critics accused him of anti-intellectualism. He gave them ammunition by saying, or so it was reported, that the University of California "subsidized intellectual curiosity."* But while Reagan, in the long tradition of populism, certainly exploited the anti-intellectual biases of his constituencies, he was in awe of people with advanced degrees. One of the reasons that Reagan was offended by the demonstrations was that he took higher education seriously. Although he had been an indifferent student at Eureka College, more concerned with dramatics and athletics than with his studies, he was the first of his family to graduate from college. His pride in this achievement was tempered by a realization that Eureka was not especially prestigious. In compensation, Reagan romanticized his college days.

Reagan's sentimentality about Eureka led him to interrupt his hard-fought 1980 presidential campaign for a trip to his alma mater on October 17, 1980. There, he made a speech extolling the college's virtues and expressing his appreciation for the start it had given him in life. While Reagan's affection for Eureka was genuine, he was in fact an autodidact who had learned most of what he knew outside of college. Humble in background and democratic in impulse, he never judged people on the basis of educational attainment. It mattered not at all to Reagan that Bill Clark had failed to graduate from law school, that Ed Meese had obtained high marks at Yale, or that James Baker, his first and best White House chief of staff, was an honors graduate from Princeton.

But Reagan always appreciated it when a prestigious university honored him. His appointments secretary, Paul Haerle, a Yale graduate, arranged for Reagan to become a Chubb Fellow at Yale, where in November 1967 he spoke and mingled with the students. Reagan was then being scrutinized as a presidential candidate, and *Time* and *Newsweek* gave him high marks for his performance. Reagan had a good time. When he returned, he told his cabinet, "Okay fellows, keep these meet-

---

*This remark was widely quoted, but I have been unable to find the source of it. William F. Buckley, taking the quotation at face value, suggested that "frivolity" would have been a better word.

ings on a high plane. I am now a Yale man. I want you to know, though, that the Yale hippies are just as dirty and unshaven as the ones we have in California."[29]

While Reagan was at Yale, violence erupted at San Francisco State College. State colleges, many of them excellent institutions, were the middle tier of California's higher education system. They lacked the research mission of the university, which gave college professors more time for their students. When Reagan took office, there were eighteen state colleges. They had a total enrollment of 225,000 compared to 88,000 at the nine university campuses.*

Glenn Dumke, chancellor of the state college system, was appalled by Reagan's higher education budget but diplomatic in his comments, even though he imposed a freeze on new registrants at the same time as Kerr did. When Reagan subsequently revised the budget, Dumke quickly lifted the freeze. Reagan, grateful for small favors at this point, announced that he favored retention of Dumke as chancellor.

Dumke and the state college trustees had their own agenda, on which the top priority was redesignation of the colleges as "state universities." In Dumke's view, the larger state colleges were already de facto universities; he pointed out that they would become eligible for additional grants if so designated. But the University of California, with more clout in the Legislature than the state colleges, opposed creation of another university system, and a bill to do this failed to make it out of committee in 1967. Dumke needed Reagan's backing on this issue to have any chance of success. He also needed public support, which was being steadily undermined by campus disturbances.

The center of these disturbances was San Francisco State College. Two years before the disorder began at the University of California, liberal and radical students at San Francisco State launched tutorial programs financed by student fees and sent student teachers into the poor, black neighborhoods of Hunter's Point and the Fillmore. By 1965, the students were financing fifteen separate "action programs" and had created an experimental college in which 1,500 students were enrolled in subjects ranging from black culture to guerrilla warfare. These pro-

---

*On the bottom tier were the community (formerly junior) colleges, an institution pioneered in California. They gave two-year degrees in technical or vocational subjects and prepared liberal arts students for four-year institutions. California had ninety-three such colleges in 1970, with 800,000 students, nearly ten times the enrollment of the University of California. Most students worked part-time. Community colleges provided bedrock education for children of working-class families. With isolated exceptions, they were immune to the demonstrations that afflicted university and state college campuses during the Reagan years. Reagan's first finance director, Gordon Paul Smith, said on October 16, 1967, that it "might be a good idea" to charge tuition for community college students, but Reagan immediately disavowed the idea.

grams gave birth to the Black Students Union (BSU), which became the focal point of campus controversy.

The experimental college program and the BSU attracted liberals and militant students from all over the country to San Francisco State, which in the fall of 1968 had 18,000 students. The college was not a happy place. Students complained that the militants who ran the student government were short-changing traditional activities such as athletics and the creative arts. Conservatives charged additionally that student-body and federal work-study funds were being diverted into anti-white plays and instruction in "draft dodging." In 1967, a coalition of moderate and conservative student leaders won election and, after a physical clash with BSU leaders, reduced funds for the "action programs." The issue was shunted to the chancellor's office, where an assistant vice-chancellor sided with the radicals while acknowledging that "it is also evident that communication problems exist between students of opposing political persuasions."

On November 6, 1967, members of the BSU tried to solve the communications problem by breaking into the offices of the student newspaper and beating up the editor, who was hospitalized after being punched and kicked in the head and back. A month later, while Reagan was at Yale, a small force of black and white students invaded the college administration building, looted the college bookstore, and attacked bystanders. It was the most serious outbreak of campus violence in California since Reagan's election. From Yale, Reagan talked to his staff, and Press Secretary Paul Beck issued a statement calling upon state college trustees to establish guidelines that included campus cooperation with police "in maintaining liaison and coordination for the prevention of criminal activity and law violations."

Jesse Unruh went further. "I think the situation has become totally intolerable," he said at a Sacramento press conference. "It not only threatens the lives and properties of our state colleges and our state college and university students but it also threatens the existence of our very important public higher education." The students were defenseless, Unruh said, "in the face of an unruly mob," and he added, "I am inclined to believe that President [John] Summerskill ought to be fired."

Unruh's reaction underscored the predicament of the Democrats, who had made common cause with the higher education establishment in opposing tuition and budget cuts but wanted to demonstrate that they were as intolerant of campus disorders as Reagan. This played into Reagan's hands. The governor moved a step at a time against the radicals, always through channels, while Unruh demanded stricter action than Reagan was willing to endorse. What the campus militants accomplished at San Francisco State in 1967 was a foretaste of 1968, when radical demonstrations and their suppression by Chicago police tore apart the Democratic Party at its national convention. Democrats who tolerated mob violence looked weak. Democrats such as Unruh, who called for a crackdown, made Reagan seem reasonable. In fact, he often was.

At San Francisco State, the governor and the state college trustees moved to restore order. College president Summerskill resigned in February 1968 after complaining that "political interference and financial starvation" were ruining higher education. He was supposed to stay until the end of the semester, but Dumke encouraged him to depart abruptly on May 24 for a job in Ethiopia after a three-day sit-in at the administration building brought the college to a standstill. A mild-mannered college administrator named Robert Smith, well-liked by the faculty, replaced Summerskill. On November 14, after renewed violence, Smith closed the college. Unruh demanded that San Francisco State be kept open. Reagan called the closure "an act of capitulation—surrender, if you will—to a small unrepresentative faction of faculty and student militants." But he did not order the campus reopened until two days later, and even then he insisted that the trustees initiate the action. The decision led to more violence. Smith resigned on November 26, 1968, at a Los Angeles meeting of the state trustees that Reagan attended.

Reagan had learned in advance that Smith would quit. The governor discussed the question of a replacement with his educational adviser, Alex Sheriffs. "I said we would be far better off if we found someone on the campus among the ranks because of the efforts of the radicals to make it appear that their autonomy was being invaded," Reagan told me later.[30] He asked Sheriffs about a professor named S. I. Hayakawa, who had been quoted at a faculty convocation as saying that the college should be kept open. Sheriffs said Hayakawa had a reputation for being a man of his word. Two other faculty members were also nominated as Smith's replacement at the Los Angeles meeting, but it was clear to the trustees that Reagan leaned to Hayakawa.

The trustees then drafted a resolution declaring that San Francisco State College must be kept open. They agreed that Hayakawa was the most likely candidate to accomplish this objective and instructed Dumke to offer him the job. Dumke left the room and returned minutes later, a faint smile on his face. "He couldn't help but tease us a little bit," said Reagan. "Chancellor Dumke said, 'Yes, he'll take the job, but there are some strings.' Everybody groaned and then Dumke recited the strings and the strings were the very things we had framed in resolution about keeping the college open and disciplining the students and faculty members who wouldn't play ball. I said, 'We'll not only go along with the strings but we'll even forgive him for Pearl Harbor'."[31]

Samuel I. Hayakawa was a renowned semanticist who had written books and articles explaining the techniques of Nazi and fascist propaganda. He had been a columnist for the liberal *Chicago Defender* and had helped organize the Anti-Digit Dialing League, an unsuccessful campaign to force the Pacific Telephone Company to retain telephone prefixes. For a semanticist, he made some odd and clumsy public statements. When nine people were hurt in campus violence, Hayakawa said, "It's the most exciting thing since my tenth birthday, when I rode a roller coaster for the first time." Hayakawa, the child of Japanese-born Canadians, was married to a Caucasian. One of their three children had Down syndrome, and Hayakawa became active in efforts to help the mentally retarded. He was also a jazz critic, a fencer, and an excellent fisherman who sported a tam-o'-shanter he originally wore as foul-weather gear when fishing. He continued to wear it at San Francisco State, where he stood his ground against the campus militants. "You are," he said, describing himself, "a hero to some and a son of a bitch to others."

From Reagan's standpoint, Hayakawa was ideal. But as the strike at San Francisco State persisted through the winter and into early spring, legislators began to doubt his effectiveness. Later, Hayakawa would become a conservative folk hero and a U.S. senator. But at the time, conservatives had their doubts. When Michael O'Connor of the *Sacramento Union* interviewed the State Senate's most liberal and conservative members, it was the liberal, Al Rodda, who defended the San Francisco State president, and the conservative, John Schmitz, who criticized him. Rodda said, "Dr. Hayakawa is handling the problem in the classic liberal tradition that if there is to be freedom, there must be order." Schmitz quipped, "I think he talks tough but doesn't act tough. He agrees with the students but is trying to accomplish their goals through different means."[32] Both senators had a point. Hayakawa had attempted to create a separate black studies department in a form proposed by the college's sociology department. His answer from the militants was renewed violence.

Hayakawa's flamboyance and the militants' intransigence deflected attention from Reagan, who early in the San Francisco State strike had dropped his opposition to a black studies department. Liberals seemed not to notice, and when they did, they distorted his position. On January 17, 1969, Chet Huntley said on *NBC News* that Reagan had no objection to a black studies department as long as the chairman of the department was white. It was an absurd error, for the choice of a black person to head the department was part of a proposal that Reagan had repeatedly endorsed. Reagan angrily denied the false report, and Huntley sent a letter of apology, saying that the item had come in by telephone and was handed to him while he was on the air. "Please know and understand that this was just plain error and in no way contained any malice or premeditation," Huntley said.[33] This was doubtless true, for Huntley was an honest journalist, but the item demonstrated how readily even the most respected figures in television news were willing to believe the worst about Reagan.

Huntley's item was part of a report on Reagan's first meeting with Hayakawa, a dual press conference in Sacramento. It was clear by then to Reagan that the embattled San Francisco State president, for all his brave words, needed help to keep order on the campus. Reagan was willing to provide it. On January 5, eleven days before his meeting with Hayakawa, Reagan had said he would keep San Francisco State College open by force if necessary. "Those who want to get an education, those who want to teach, should be protected in that at the point of bayonet if necessary," Reagan said at an airport interview in Sacramento.

But with San Francisco State still shut down by strikers, armed confrontation came instead at UC Berkeley, where a group calling itself the Third World Liberation Front launched a strike on January 22, 1969. By February 4, according to University Chancellor Roger Heyns, there had been seven attempts at arson or fire-bombing, which had damaged fourteen buildings, and "innumerable bomb threats" against students and faculty members. On February 5, students entering UC Berkeley through Sather Gate were mauled by strikers. Police responded and were greeted by a hail of rocks and cans. Three officers and six students who had tried to cross the picket lines required hospital treatment.

This was too much for Reagan. Throughout the morning of February 5, Reagan waited impatiently in his office while his staff assembled reports of the incident from the chancellor's office. Then he told reporters that he was proclaiming "a state of emergency" and calling out the California Highway Patrol to protect the university from "criminal anarchists" and "off-campus revolutionaries." "Students have been assaulted and severely beaten as they attempted to attend classes," Reagan said. "Streets and sidewalks providing access to the campus have been physically blocked. Classes have been disrupted. Arsons and fire-bombings have occurred and the university property has been destroyed." Reagan was comfortable with what he had done. On the way back to his office, he told his press secretary, Paul Beck, "I'll sleep well tonight."[34]

Democrats, most notably Unruh, agreed that Reagan was right to proclaim a state of emergency. But it did not bring peace to Berkeley, where sporadic riots and fire-bombings continued both on and off campus. In May, a group of radicals and street people occupied university-owned land they had designated as "People's Park" and stoned police who tried to eject them. Berkeley police sought help from the California Highway Patrol and from Alameda County sheriff's deputies. On May 15, a bloody riot ensued in which marchers threw rocks and bottles at the officers, who responded with tear gas. Some of the tear gas canisters were hurled back into police ranks. Heavily outnumbered, the deputies fired shotguns loaded with buckshot into the crowd. James Rector, twenty-five, of San Jose, standing on the roof of a bookstore, was hit in the abdomen by a shotgun blast and died later in a local hospital. By day's end, sixty people, including a half dozen law enforcement officers and two reporters, had been treated in hospitals and forty-seven persons arrested. Leaders of the three law enforcement agencies that had tried to quell the disorder declared they could no longer guarantee the safety of the city and asked Reagan to send in the National Guard. Reagan complied, and the Guard enforced an unofficial martial law in Berkeley for seventeen days.

In conversations and cabinet meetings, Reagan blamed Rector's death on the demonstrators. He said police were attacked by a "well-prepared and well-armed mass of people who had stockpiled all kinds of weapons and missiles" including bricks, rocks, chunks of cement, and iron pipes. Reagan believed—and no investigation ever contradicted him—that the law enforcement agencies had shown restraint. This was certainly true of the Berkeley police, who had refrained from firing their revolvers even when officers were repeatedly struck by rocks. On July 13, after a review of the incident, Reagan claimed that the arrival of the sheriff's deputies and their shotguns had prevented isolated police officers from being stoned to death and that deployment of the National Guard also had saved lives. "No one can take pleasure from seeing bayonets in an American community or on a college campus," Reagan said. "But the arrival of the Guard with bayonets brought almost total de-escalation of hand-to-hand fighting and violence." Reagan acknowledged that the Guard's use of tear gas had brought distress to innocent people but said the Guardsmen had no choice. "There also can be no question that the alternative to the gas—hand-to-hand combat between the mob and the Guardsmen—could have produced real tragedy," Reagan said.[35]

The deployment of the Guard broke the back of the rebellion at Berkeley and enabled students to attend classes. In time, order was restored at San Francisco State College and also at San Jose State College, which had been paralyzed by a largely nonviolent strike. UC Berkeley was again a scene of demonstrations after the U.S. invasion of Cambodia on June 30, 1970, but university authorities maintained control. Republicans (and many Democrats, including Unruh) credited Reagan for his resolution in the face of the 1969 UC Berkeley uprising. They believed he had sent the radicals a message.

If so, the message failed to reach Isla Vista, a coastal town adjacent to the University of California at Santa Barbara (UCSB). No one in the university system or the Reagan administration anticipated violence at UCSB, which in 1967 had had been the font of the peaceful march to Sacramento against student tuition. Even this orderly protest had been surprising, for UCSB had the reputation of being a fun-loving school at which laid-back students were more interested in surfing and parties than in studies or politics. But the student body population of UCSB had nearly doubled in ten years to 13,000. The counterculture flourished on campus and in neighboring Isla Vista, where students were crowded together in high-rent, ramshackle apartments—"isolated, inbred, and powerless."[36] It was a powder keg ripe for explosion.

On February 24, 1970, police officers patrolling near a popular student hangout lit the fuse when they attempted to arrest two activists for disturbing the peace. A crowd formed and hurled rocks at the officers, who fled on foot. Then the crowd, now a mob, overturned the abandoned police car and burned it. They marched a block to the Isla Vista branch of the Bank of America and set fire to the draperies. The bank, said radicals, symbolized the "capitalist establishment." The UCSB student government had earlier withdrawn its accounts from the bank for "support of the Vietnam War and the growers of the San Joaquin Valley" in their struggle against farm labor organizer Cesar Chavez.

On Wednesday, February 25, civil rights attorney William Kunstler gave a fiery speech in the UCSB football stadium. He denounced police violence and said, "I think the shadow of the swastika is on every courthouse, on universities, on government buildings, maybe even on the apartment door next to you." As students returned to their apartments late in the afternoon, police officers clubbed one of them who was carrying a bottle of wine. Word of the attack spread, and hundreds of students stoned police officers and stores in Isla Vista's tiny downtown. The outnumbered police withdrew. That night, the demonstrators burned the Bank of America to the ground.

Reagan flew to Santa Barbara the following day, February 26. He called the demonstrators "cowardly little bums" and declared a state of emergency. But that night, students again drove the police from Isla Vista. Not until Friday night, February 27, did 500 members of the National Guard and a drenching rainstorm that reduced the ranks of the demonstrators bring Isla Vista under control.

The Isla Vista violence was more destructive than anything that had happened at UC Berkeley or San Francisco State. Most of it, however, was directed at the police and corporations rather than at the university. "Burn, baby, burn," students shouted as they heaped cardboard on the fire at the Bank of America. "Death to corporations."[37] During the next three months, militants periodically attacked stores and battled police in Isla Vista as moderate students tried to control the situation. On April 18, the UCSB student body president broadcast a request for students to fight fires in Isla Vista. Three students left their apartment, extinguished a blaze at a Taco Bell, and moved down the street to put out another fire at a new, temporary headquarters of the Bank of America. Riot police entered the town. Student Kevin Patrick Moran, twenty-two, who had helped douse the fire, was standing in the doorway of the bank when he was struck by a stray bullet and killed.

No one ever determined who killed Moran, although the fatal shot was apparently a ricochet from a police bullet. Reagan, distraught and angry, telephoned Moran's father to offer his condolences. "It isn't very important where the bullet came from," he told reporters afterward. "The bullet was brought about and the bullet was sent on its way several years ago when a certain element in this society decided they could take the law into their own hands."[38]

Resentment simmered on all sides during the remainder of the semester. Thirty police officers and Santa Barbara County sheriff's deputies had been injured at Isla Vista, mostly from rocks and projectiles thrown during the February melees, and some of them had responded with rough treatment of student and faculty demonstrators. On June 10, during and after a mass demonstration at Perfect Park, next to the Bank of America, officers made 667 arrests. The conduct of the officers was criticized; some militants accused them of smashing down doors of apartments in Isla Vista and dragging out students and beating them. Police and sheriff's deputies acknowledged using pepper spray but said they were reacting to more rock-throwing.[39]

A judge dismissed charges against the arrested demonstrators, bringing an end to five months of disorder, but disturbances continued elsewhere in California. "Showing a frightful lack of originality," as Neal Peirce put it, "violence-prone agitators attacked the 990 California branches of the Bank of America some thirty-nine times" with explosive devices or firebombs during the fifteen months after the burning of the Isla Vista bank.[40]

Isla Vista had a constructive aftermath, if not quite a happy ending.

Hundreds of fearful or disillusioned students did not return to UCSB in the fall. Those who came back rejected the radicals and turned to traditional liberal causes such as environmentalism and legal aid for the poor. In an echo of their peaceful protest against tuition, UCSB students hired a lobbyist to present their views on housing and other needs in Sacramento. A new Service Center to advance these goals was financed, in part, by a $25,000 donation from Louis Lundborg in what might be described as an act of enlightened self-interest. Lundborg was chairman of the board of the Bank of America.

.   .   .

When Ronald Reagan became governor of California, an aide installed a bronze and walnut plaque above the doorway to his office on the first floor of the State Capitol. No one remembers where it came from, but it remained there throughout Reagan's eight years as governor, recording his most memorable words about student demonstrators: "Observe the Rules or Get Out—Dec. 3, 1966."[41]

Reagan never deviated from this policy. While he always preferred to have "the rules" enforced by the university and state college systems, Reagan demonstrated at Berkeley in 1969 and Santa Barbara in 1970 that he was prepared to send in the National Guard when administrators could not control their campuses. This consistency stiffened the spine of university chancellors and college presidents inclined to temporize, for the alternative to losing control of the campus to militant agitators was to lose control to the state. Even as the Vietnam War continued and the counterculture flourished, campus disorders in California dwindled to insignificance during Reagan's second term as governor.

Despite the overall success of Reagan's policies in dealing with campus disorders, his rhetoric was at times excessive. He was at his most inflammatory not in the heat of crisis but when defending his policies before friendly audiences. On April 7, 1970, addressing the California Council of Growers at Yosemite, Reagan was asked about the on-campus tactics of the New Left. "If it takes a bloodbath, let's get it over with," Reagan responded. "No more appeasement." This was an irresponsible statement, but the governor's press secretary, Paul Beck, told me that Reagan did not realize that he had used the word "bloodbath." Beck had to play Reagan's remarks back to him on a tape recorder before Reagan would believe him.[42]

On fiscal policies, Reagan made concessions but won most of his battles with the university and state college systems. On February 20,

1970, the university regents finally imposed tuition for resident students, largely along the lines of the compromise that Reagan and the regents had hammered out in the UCLA cafeteria on August 31, 1967. In the interim, Reagan had relented on many of his higher education budget cuts, although not enough to satisfy his academic and legislative critics. The critics pointed out that the university averaged only 90 percent of its budget requests under Reagan compared to 95 percent under Pat Brown. But this reflected Reagan's effort to control state spending rather than a punitive attitude toward the university. Spending for higher education during the Reagan years rose 136 percent, compared to a 100 percent increase in overall state spending. State scholarship spending during these eight years soared from $6 million to $43 million. This helped all higher education but especially private colleges and universities. With Reagan's support, the state colleges meanwhile became "state universities," achieving Chancellor Dumke's long-sought goal. This morale-boosting designation was accompanied by a salary boost for state college professors that narrowed the gap with their higher-paid university counterparts.

As on many issues, Reagan's critics could not decide whether he deserved credit for doing less harm than they expected or blame for doing any damage at all. In a skeptical evaluation near the end of Reagan's second term, *Los Angeles Times* education writer William Trombley said the university had suffered in terms of student-faculty ratio and research spending because of Reagan's initial budget cuts. Trombley wrote that the University of California, "once clearly the best public university in the land," was "now just one of the best."[43] But in the same issue of the newspaper, UC President Charles Hitch was quoted as saying, "Eight years ago this was the best public university in the country. We still are."[44]

Many agreed with Hitch. When Reagan left office, the respected Dean McHenry, chancellor emeritus at the University of California at Santa Cruz, summed up what he said was a widespread feeling about Reagan in the academic community: "His bark proved worse than his bite."[45] It is an assessment that has withstood the test of time.

21

CONSERVATIONIST

I F A MODERN Rip Van Winkle fell fast asleep at the end of Reagan's governorship and awakened after his presidency, he would not have been surprised to learn that Reagan had been underestimated by his adversaries at home and abroad. That was par for the course in California. Nor would Rip, remembering how the realism of Reagan's mammoth 1967 tax bill had trumped the antitax rhetoric of his 1966 campaign, have been startled to find that President Reagan had reduced federal taxes with fanfare and later raised them quietly under the rubric of "tax reform." The demise of the Soviet Union might have taken some explanation. But since Rip knew that Reagan believed in negotiating from strength, he would have understood that he had conducted a military buildup to bring the Soviets to the bargaining table, where he signed a key nuclear arms–control treaty with the leader of a system he had described as an "evil empire."

But our imaginary Rip, I believe, would have been amazed by President Reagan's environmental record and, if he were an environmentalist, dismayed by it.* In this arena, Rip's knowledge of the Reagan governorship would be worthless. Governor Reagan's actions foreshadowed his presidency on many issues, but his environmental policies in Sacramento were contradicted by what he did in Washington. President Reagan turned over the Environmental Protection Agency (EPA), one of Richard Nixon's better deeds, to incompetent political hacks. He appointed the retrograde James Watt as secretary of the interior. "We will mine more, drill more, cut more timber to use our resources rather

*For simplicity's sake, I have used "environmentalist" and "conservationist" interchangeably, as Reagan did. Some draw a distinction between the two words, applying "conservationist" to those who maintain land for use by people such as hunters or fishermen, and "environmentalist" to those who seek to preserve the land for future generations.[1]

than simply keep them locked up," Watt pledged.[2] He would have done this, too, except for Congress and his own ineptitude.

The president who appointed Watt had been the governor who named Norman ("Ike") Livermore Jr. as executive director for resources (or resources secretary), roughly equivalent to California's secretary of the interior. Livermore was Watt's antithesis. He wanted to preserve more, cut less, and build fewer roads into the wilderness. And while Livermore—like Watt, or Reagan himself—lacked government experience, he proved an able politician.

Livermore, born less than two months after Ronald Reagan, on March 27, 1911, had been an adventurer since boyhood. At the age of eighteen, he rode hundreds of miles from his boarding school in Ojai to Monterey, living on pan-fried bread called "bannocks" in imitation of the pioneers. The trip left him emaciated but ready for more adventures.

While recuperating from his long ride, Livermore read the journals of John Muir, the iconographic naturalist responsible for Yosemite and Sequoia national parks. Later, Livermore trekked the 250-mile John Muir Trail. He organized mule pack trains that explored the high Sierra, in the process developing a life-long affection for mules. In 1936, he became a member of the Sierra Club, founded by Muir, and later initiated the club's first wilderness conference.

Livermore, gangly and Lincolnesque in appearance, was a practical man with quixotic dreams. As a youth he envisioned a life in the mountains financed by mule-packing. Marriage and the precarious economics of pack trains changed his plans. Livermore earned a master's degree in business from Stanford and went to work for the Pacific Lumber Company, which he served as treasurer for fifteen years. All the while, he stayed active in the Save-the-Redwoods League. Bill Boyarsky related that Livermore enjoyed visiting Jedediah Smith Redwood State Park, where on the right side of the road are "primeval, almost religiously inspiring coast redwoods and on the left is a sawmill. They're both necessary."[3] Livermore's friend, the Sierra Club president and noted environmentalist David Brower, valued his counsel even though they argued as often as they agreed. Livermore understood Brower, who rarely saw a tree he didn't want to save, but he also understood the timber industry, which translates trees into board feet of lumber. Brower called Livermore "the man in the middle."* Livermore called himself "a living contradiction."[4]

---

*The phrase became the title of a fascinating 1983 Livermore oral history. Brower, who once said the "sun never sets on a Livermore argument," wrote an admiring introduction that celebrated his disagreements with Livermore. One disagreement was over breeding the endangered California condor in captivity, which Livermore advocated and Brower opposed. The breeding program, introduced many years later, has been a qualified success.

In terms of lasting achievement, the Livermore appointment was far and away Appointment Secretary Tom Reed's most valuable contribution to the Reagan cabinet. Reed slipped Livermore by the Kitchen Cabinet, to which the north coast of California was as remote as the moon, by exaggerating his partisan credentials. Livermore was a Republican, to be sure, and had served as finance director in a successful Republican congressional campaign, but that was not why Reed chose him. What commended Livermore to Reed was that he was a conservationist with a business background, a surefire selling point with Reagan. On environmental issues, Livermore stood in the Republican tradition of Theodore Roosevelt, Hiram Johnson, and Earl Warren, all more conservationist than conservative. This approach was typical of Marin County, where Reed and Livermore lived.

Reagan liked Livermore at first meeting. Rugged outdoorsmen appealed to him, especially if they rode horses. Only Bill Clark and Livermore shared this bond with Reagan within the governor's inner circle. Livermore and Clark hit it off, too. Both had an adventuresome spirit. Clark liked to fly and later barely survived a crash in his small plane. Livermore, who had once taken a trek to the highlands of Kashmir, kept wandering off into the mountains.

Within the Reagan cabinet, Livermore was outspoken, too much so for some of his colleagues. Clark, more of a conciliator, was a much-needed ally during the crucial first two years of the administration. But Reagan also appreciated Livermore. This most Southern Californian of governors liked having a cabinet member from the north who could serve as an honest broker on environmental issues. Livermore realized he had a special value to Reagan and took advantage of it, much as George Shultz later would do as President Reagan's secretary of state. Both men used hints of resignation to influence policy, although neither ever quit.[5] Livermore became the only cabinet member to serve the entire eight years of Reagan's governorship.

Reagan's knowledge of environmental issues, except for air pollution, was minimal. Even the geography of the north coast, where trees outnumber people, eluded him. During the 1966 campaign, a reporter asked Reagan a question about the Eel River. Reagan asked where it was. The reporter told the embarrassed candidate that he was standing alongside it. But as governor, Reagan learned the importance of the Eel, which became a battleground between those who wanted to dam its middle fork and those who sought to preserve it as a wild river.

Few such rivers remained in California. The Eel was one of the last rivers in the state with a summer run of the threatened steelhead trout, which spend their lives in the ocean before returning to their river of origin to spawn. On some rivers, dams and other structures that di-

verted water for irrigation prevented steelhead from swimming up-
stream to spawn; on others, erosion from heavily logged hillsides
clogged the spawning grounds with silt and debris. The steelhead could
not be saved unless wild rivers were preserved. And the rivers could not
be protected without sparing some of the hillside trees.

The trees that mattered most were the mighty redwoods, which
Congress hoped to rescue from the chain saws by preserving them in a
Redwood National Park. On this issue, conservationists had reason to
be fearful of Reagan. They remembered his campaign declaration to a
conference of wood producers: "A tree is a tree—how many more do
you need to look at?"[6]

Conservationists would have been even more frightened had they realized how perfectly this vacuous comment expressed Reagan's opinion.
The conventional view of Reagan's statement—often misstated as "If
you've seen one redwood, you've seen them all"—was that he had used
artless language while pandering to an industry for campaign support.
But the wood producers were already in Reagan's corner, and his well-
financed campaign was not in need of their contributions. Reagan had
said what he believed.

Why he believed what he said, however, remains a mystery. Reagan,
who was often attuned to nature, was strangely insensitive to the mag-
nificence of the redwoods, long recognized as natural wonders of the
world. These splendid trees, rising to heights of more than 300 feet,
flourish in a narrow coastal zone influenced by the Pacific Ocean fog.
They were an early cause for conservationists, who formed the Save-
the-Redwoods League in 1913, embarked on a fund-raising campaign,
and persuaded the Legislature to create three redwood state parks en-
compassing 27,500 acres. The league donated half the land, and the
state purchased the remainder from the lumber companies. This was an
impressive achievement, but the parks were tiny in relation to the remaining redwood habitat of 1.5 million acres, reduced by logging to
one-tenth its original size. Lumber companies, including Pacific Lumber, had their eyes on the surviving old-growth redwoods, which are
more resistant than younger trees to rot and decay. A single redwood
2,000 years old yields 480,000 board feet of lumber.

The lumber companies had long opposed a national redwoods park.
By the time Reagan took office, however, the industry had retreated
under conservationist fire to the more defensible position of accepting a
small national park in return for unrestricted logging outside of it.
"Small" was the operative word. Timber executives claimed that a large
park would eliminate thousands of jobs. Using jobs as their battle cry,
they mobilized business and labor support in the two counties (Del

Norte and Humboldt) where land would be set aside for the Redwood National Park.

Reagan, meanwhile, was expressing his feelings about a park—and the redwoods—in cabinet meetings. This is a sample of what he said:

"People seem to think that all redwoods that are not protected through a national park will disappear."[7]

"You know, those people from the Save-the-Redwood League scare me sometimes. I know they are basically good people. But, for instance, there was that old man who said suppose there are a few more hundred people that have to be supported by welfare—the government is spending so much already. How do they say things like that? They show no regard for human beings—these people aren't welfare cases."[8]

"I'll be damned if I take away all this privately owned land for no reason. I owe that much to those people in these counties [where the redwood park would be created]. I wonder, has anybody ever asked the Sierra Club if they think that these trees will grow forever?"[9]

Reagan was reluctant even to acknowledge the grandeur of the trees. Of one of the oldest and loveliest grove of redwoods, he said, (on March 15, 1967), "I saw them; there is nothing beautiful about them, just that they are a little higher than the others."

Livermore ignored such absurdities. He recognized that Reagan had a stubborn streak—Livermore had one, too—and that his statements in part reflected his unwillingness to be pushed around by environmental groups. Livermore worked with the governor instead of against him. He never criticized Reagan to outsiders, and he wrote letters to newspapers extolling his environmental record.* Inside the cabinet, however, he waged a valiant struggle to educate Reagan on the need to get beyond the minimalist positions of the lumber companies.

The cabinet minutes are testimony to the effectiveness of Livermore's step-by-step tutelage of the governor—and to Reagan's flair for effective political compromise. Livermore did not waste time telling Reagan that redwoods are magnificent. With Clark's help, he steered the cabinet into discussions about ways to save a maximum number of redwoods with a minimum impact on logging jobs. This approach played to Reagan's strengths. He was better at weighing policy options than at assessing the aesthetics of the redwoods. As Livermore realized, Reagan's acquiescence was crucial to the creation of a Redwood National Park. Although the final decision was up to Congress, the viabil-

---

*Defending Reagan's environmental record in a letter to the editor in the *San Francisco Chronicle* on February 10, 1969, Livermore wrote: "I cannot recall a single instance where a decision was made by the Governor that was inimical to the philosophy of concern for the quality of our natural environment."

ity of a national park required the inclusion of the contiguous state parks.

The idea that softened Reagan's resistance to a meaningful national park was a proposal, brokered by Livermore, that traded federal land managed by the U.S. Forest Service for privately held land containing many of the prize old-growth redwoods. This "exchange provision," as it was known, appealed to Reagan because it reduced job losses in the north coast communities. The idea had been floated in Congress to reduce the cost of the park; Wayne Aspinall, the imperious chairman of the House Interior Committee, contended that the government could not afford to buy prime redwood acreage outright.

Even the exchange provision did not persuade Aspinall. The bill he allowed to emerge from the House provided for a paltry national park of 24,500 acres. The Senate bill—largely the work of Senator Thomas Kuchel, a California Republican who was barely on speaking terms with Reagan—provided for a 64,000-acre park. The two versions went to a Senate-House conference, where conservationists prevailed. The compromise was a 58,000-acre park that included the 23,500 acres of state parks and some 5,000 acres of valuable beach property owned by the lumber companies. The exchange provision was crucial to the compromise—the lumber companies received 13,000 acres of Forest Service land that Reagan said would stabilize employment in the counties where the park was located. Livermore and the Sierra Club called this exchange a "tremendous victory."[10] But the greater victory was Livermore's success in making Reagan part of the solution.

Despite the hosannas from conservationists, the national park established in 1968 was a work in progress. Many of the park's tallest trees were in a twelve-mile strip along Redwood Creek, which became a turbulent river during winter storms. Runoff from the creek and hillsides denuded by heavy logging outside the park threatened the redwoods within it. Armed with a National Park Service study that declared redwoods an "endangered species," Representative Phillip Burton, a leading liberal Democrat from San Francisco, persuaded Congress to pass legislation expanding the Redwood National Park by 76,000 acres. President Jimmy Carter signed the bill into law on March 21, 1978, by which time Reagan was a former governor who was eyeing Carter's job.

The expanded Redwood National Park is so much bigger and better than the original that the struggles in creating the first park have largely been forgotten. Ike Livermore is not even mentioned in the most comprehensive account of the park's expansion.* But several of the taller, old-

*This account can be found on pages 333–350 of *A Rage for Justice: The Passion and Politics of Phillip Burton*, by John Jacobs, University of California Press, 1995.[11]

growth redwoods that are now stellar attractions in the national park would probably have become decks or picnic tables long before 1978 had they not been saved in the Reagan years. Livermore deserves credit for his straight talk to the governor who appointed him. Reagan deserves credit for listening. The second park stands on the shoulders of the first.

Reagan, usually responsive to natural beauty, needed less convincing on other environmental issues. As a boy, he enjoyed solitary walks in Dixon along the Rock River, where he observed the water birds and other wildlife. As a man, he sought out scenic landscapes on horseback rides. His letters to Nancy Reagan in 1954 during the filming of *Cattle Queen of Montana* in Glacier National Park rhapsodize about the scenery. Nancy Reagan believed that her husband perceived nature "more intensely" than most people. "At the Santa Barbara ranch, we'd ride uphill, and he'd admire the way the trees looked in silhouette against the sky," she recalled.[12]

This appreciation of nature, and especially of wildlife, is reflected in the cabinet minutes. Early in 1968, sheep owners in northern California were literally up in arms over supposed depredations to their flocks by golden eagles. Environmentalists claimed that eagles rarely killed sheep, except for stray or sickly lambs, but ranchers in remote Glenn County believed otherwise and shot eagles they said were preying on their flocks. Reagan read about the shootings and raised the issue at a cabinet meeting. Livermore, focused on the redwoods, thought it politically unwise to take sides in an emotional controversy in which state jurisdiction was questionable. That produced this exchange:

LIVERMORE: Sheep men feel strongly about this. Our recommendation: that you do not get involved.
GOVERNOR: Is the problem THAT widespread? How many sheep do the eagles kill? I hate to see them shot.
LIVERMORE: Eagles are scarce, and we will be in hot water if we support them being shot.
GOVERNOR: I'd rather pay for lambs than shoot them. Besides, I don't like lamb chops.[13]

Reagan usually accepted the recommendations of his executive directors in their areas of expertise, and he followed Livermore's advice and stayed out of the controversy. But Reagan continued to express his opinions on issues affecting California's land, skies, and water, not always predictably. When it came to the environment, he was a study in contradictions, much like the West he loved.

Reagan held a romantic view of the West, formed from Zane Grey novels long before he went to Hollywood. He kept a gun collection. He became an accomplished rider in Des Moines, thanks to his service in the cavalry reserve. In Hollywood he longed to be cast in westerns, an ambition that went unfulfilled for his first fourteen years as a movie actor. By the time he appeared in his first western, *The Last Outpost,* Reagan was already on his second ranch.[14]

His first ranch, purchased in the late 1940s, was an 8-acre horse farm in then-pastoral Northridge, long since overrun by the relentless sprawl of Los Angeles. Reagan sold this property shortly before he married Nancy. In 1951, he bought two parcels of land totaling 290 acres in the rugged Santa Monica Mountains north of Los Angeles. He paid $85,000 for the property, which had a Malibu address and abutted 2,500 acres owned by 20th Century-Fox that had been used for location shots in several westerns.

Reagan decided to sell most of this land after he became a candidate for governor in 1966. "I could not have run for office unless I sold the ranch," he told me in 1968, although the sale was not consummated until a month after the election.[15] He sold the larger of the two parcels, 236 acres, to 20th Century-Fox, which retained an option to buy the remaining 54 acres. Reagan made $1,931,000 from the sale. In 1974, shortly before Reagan left the governorship, the California Parks and Recreation Department purchased all of 20th Century-Fox's land in the area for $4.8 million, paying less than a fourth as much per acre as the film company had paid for the Reagan property. Reagan's holdings while he was governor were in a trust administered by Jules Stein, his old benefactor from the Music Corporation of America. Stein and Taft Schreiber, another MCA ally, negotiated the sale. Some of Reagan's critics smelled a sweetheart deal. Reporters (including me) and political opponents intensively investigated the transactions. No one found any evidence of wrongdoing.[16]

Reagan, however, made more from his land dealings than from any of his movies. He retained ownership of the smaller, 54-acre parcel of his Malibu ranch, on which 20th Century-Fox never exercised its option. In 1968, Reagan used this parcel as a down payment on a 778-acre ranch in Riverside County, southeast of Los Angeles. He paid $347,000 for this property, known as Rancho California, which he said he intended to develop as a working ranch. This never happened, as Reagan could not obtain water or power service for the remote property. In 1973, Reagan said that he was "getting a little impatient about having a ranch" in Riverside County that couldn't be used. "The thought has entered my mind that I might have to look for one that is already established instead of starting one from scratch," he said.[17]

The Riverside County Board of Supervisors allowed Reagan to sub-divide the land, but he had a difficult time finding a buyer. He finally sold the hilly, undeveloped land in December 1976 for $856,000 to James E. Wilson, a real estate broker and land developer, in a transaction that was kept secret. The *Riverside Press-Enterprise* unearthed the details nearly three years later. By that time, Wilson had subdivided the parcel into thirty-five lots, most of them 20-acre parcels, and sold seventeen of them for a total price of $1,065,800.

Near the end of his governorship, Reagan bought his final and favorite ranch, Rancho del Cielo, northwest of Santa Barbara. That is a story for a later chapter. What is important to note here is that Reagan thought of himself as a rancher throughout his governorship. He sympathized with ranchers and farmers in resistance to rezonings that boosted the assessed value and taxes on their properties and forced them to sell pastoral land that was converted into subdivisions.

This sympathy was, on balance, favorable to the conservationist cause. So was Reagan's skepticism about the relentless push of the federal government for high dams on nearly every western river. And in a state that invented the freeway culture, Reagan usefully departed from conventional wisdom and questioned the value of such high-speed roads when they transected scenic forests in the high Sierra. Stopping such road building was a Livermore priority, but Reagan had arrived at a similar position before they met. On September 14, 1966, when he was running for governor, Reagan said in a letter: "I have long been critical of the Highway Commission for its tendency to go by the rule of the shortest distance between two points, regardless of what scenic wonder must be destroyed, to hold to that rule."[18]

Unlike his statements about redwoods, Reagan's conservationist impulses went almost unnoticed. It did not occur to the road builders and the state's powerful water establishment—an interlocking directorate of big farmers, water boards, state agencies, and supportive legislators—that Reagan's desire to rein in government might apply to them. Builders were kings in California. Governor Pat Brown had celebrated the ethos of development. Brown was fond of freeways and proud of his central role in winning voter approval of the California Water Plan, which, through a giant aqueduct, provided water for thirsty Southern California at huge environmental cost to the San Francisco Bay estuary and wetlands known as the Delta. The issue was regional rather than partisan. Reagan was a Southern Californian and presumed to be a friend of all such development.

The first sign that Reagan would not be a pushover for the water establishment came soon after he took office in 1967. Rice growers hoped to dam the middle fork of the Feather River, a favorite stream for trout fishermen hardy enough to hike a steep canyon to reach it. To the growers, the river could be better used for irrigation and hydroelectric power. Plans for the dam were well advanced when Reagan took office; Governor Brown and two state water boards had approved it. But Reagan went along with Livermore's recommendation to fight the project in court, and the governor signed a legislative resolution asking the Federal Power Commission not to license it. This action saved the middle fork of the Feather, which later received permanent protection from federal legislation.

Reagan also sided with an environmentalist effort to save San Francisco Bay, which was threatened by industrial and residential development. The target of the developers was a commission that controlled bay-fill applications. It had rejected so many applications that leaders of the Leslie Salt Company, the largest landowner on the 435-square-mile bay, accused the commission of "Fabian socialism." At the urging of Livermore and State Finance Director Caspar Weinberger, who had been pro-environment as a state legislator, Reagan extended the life of the commission. In his 1969 State of the State Address, Reagan termed the bay "a priceless resource."

Lake Tahoe, which Mark Twain called "the fairest picture the whole earth affords," is also priceless. This high Sierra lake is one of the clearest in the world because the waters that flow into it from sixty-three streams are low in sediment. As in most western streams and lakes, the native cutthroat trout were fished out long ago, but Tahoe has abundant populations of the landlocked Kokanee salmon as well as Mackinaw, rainbow, and brown trout. In the 1960s, the purity of the lake was imperiled by waste waters from resort development, especially from hotel casinos on the Nevada side. Restraining this development required a regional solution, but the California-Nevada border bisects Lake Tahoe. Political control of the lake was balkanized between two states, five counties, and various special districts.

Reagan had a near-Jeffersonian preference for local control. Fortunately for Lake Tahoe, however, this preference did not withstand a personal inspection of the lake, which persuaded him that Tahoe's problems required an interstate solution. It helped that Nevada's governor was Paul Laxalt, an ally and fellow conservative Republican who had reached a similar conclusion. The two governors signed an interstate compact that was ratified by the legislatures of both states and gave control of the lake to the Tahoe Regional Planning Agency (TRPA).

That was not the end of the story. TRPA developed a land-use plan and reviewed proposed developments at the lake, slowing but not stopping the expansion of resorts and subdivisions. But the members of the governing board were all from the Tahoe area, and they faced political pressure to approve development. In 1973, the Reagan administration, at Livermore's behest, revived the California Tahoe Regional Planning Agency, which included public members from outside the region and imposed more stringent building and pollution standards.

The results have been mixed. By the beginning of the twenty-first century, the area around the lake had a permanent population of 50,000 and a summer population of 200,000. The bowl-shaped Tahoe basin has a natural inversion that traps air pollutants; on some summer days its smog levels exceed those of downtown Los Angeles. But the combined efforts of TRPA and the California planning agency, augmented by aggressive land-purchasing policies of the U.S. Forest Service, have made a difference. Two-thirds of the land around the lake is now in public ownership. The lake itself, or most of it, remains an azure blue. Kokanee and trout are flourishing, and the population of crayfish, which clean up the lake, has increased. Three decades after creation of the regional agency, it cannot be said with certainty that Lake Tahoe has been saved. But by acting together, Reagan and Laxalt gave it a chance.

Results were also mixed in California's unending battle to curb air pollution, in which Reagan was a reluctant but moderately successful warrior. In 1967, Reagan also supported and signed bipartisan legislation that merged two agencies and created the California Air Resources Board. For the next seven years, the board struggled to establish stiff standards for car and truck emissions over the resistance of the Detroit automobile industry and its congressional supporters, who wanted to preempt state standards with weaker federal ones.

Reagan, always willing to stand up to the federal government, backed the board. For California, choking in smog, and with 12 million registered vehicles on the road in 1970, the issue transcended partisanship or ideology. Finally, in 1974, with Reagan's support, the Legislature passed a bill authored by Assemblyman Frank Lanterman, a conservative Republican, that a spokesman for the California Air Resources Board called the "ultimate weapon." It gave the board the power to prohibit the sale or registration of vehicles in California that failed to meet state auto emissions standards. Unwilling to abandon the nation's largest market, Detroit capitulated and began making cars to meet the California standards. Because of this bill and restrictions on industrial and residential pollutants, air quality has gradually improved in many parts of the state. But with so many cars on the road and so many people in Southern California, the battle against air pollution is far from won.

.   .   .

The environmental movement, despite isolated successes in saving endangered species, threatened lakes, and redwood trees, was still struggling to become a mass movement during Reagan's early years as governor. Gallup began polling on environmental issues in 1965, when only 28 percent of the public considered air pollution a serious problem and only 35 percent were similarly concerned about water pollution. By 1969, these percentages had risen to 69 and 74 percent, respectively.[19] This public concern was reflected in the California Legislature, which that year passed a tough water quality act with stiff $6,000-a-day fines for polluters. Reagan signed it into law.

Late in 1969, President Nixon consolidated several public agencies into what (in 1970) became the new Environmental Protection Agency. The public approved, but the environment remained mostly a back-burner issue except when a catastrophe occurred. That happened on January 28, 1969, at a blowout on Union Oil Platform A less than 6 miles off the Santa Barbara coast that caused what was then the worst oil spill in U.S. history. Before the well was capped eleven days later, more than 200,000 gallons of oil had escaped into the Pacific Ocean, coating beaches and killing wildlife.

Contrary to predictions at the time, the long-term biological effects of the spill were negligible. The political impact, however, was enormous. The spill led to suspension of drilling in the federal waters off the central California coast and environmentally radicalized Santa Barbara. Even today, political candidates in the area emphasize their opposition to federal offshore oil drilling.

Drilling in state-regulated waters closer to land continued at a reduced pace. Because state regulations on offshore drilling are stricter than the federal government's, Reagan was able to finesse the issue. But the blowout at Platform A was a wake-up call. Another call occurred at 2 A.M. on January 19, 1971, when two Standard Oil tankers collided beneath the Golden Gate Bridge in dense fog. They spilled 840,000 gallons of oil that fouled shores and killed many birds. These spills made Reagan aware that environmental issues had a politically explosive potential.

The Santa Barbara oil spill was a particular boon to environmentalists. Sierra Club membership surged. In Sacramento, a new environmental coalition challenged the prevailing orthodoxy that gave priority to agriculture in the Central Valley and urban development in Southern California. This orthodoxy had ancient roots. In America, development had been synonymous with progress since the first European settlers arrived in the New World. As President Johnson's secretary of the interior Stewart Udall observed, "Every act that overcame the wilderness was considered good. Subjugation meant growth, and growth was next to Godliness in the American scheme of things. Since Plymouth Rock, growth and expansion have been synonymous with survival and success."

This assumption was bipartisan. Republicans were more likely to favor private initiative (logging redwoods), and the Democrats government action (building high dams), but the difference was in shadings. In a 1948 radio broadcast in which he was introduced by Reagan, Democratic Senate candidate Hubert Humphrey said that the Tennessee Valley Authority had turned "a poor house into a treasure house" and advocated establishing other authorities modeled after the TVA. "We must develop every river valley for all of our people," said Humphrey, expressing a sentiment that James Watt would surely have shared. Reagan shared it, too. In his lyrical 1952 speech, "America the Beautiful," Reagan described our country as a "promised land" for freedom-seeking people. He saw the United States as a land of limitless opportunity, with resources to match.

Reagan became more skeptical of federal solutions, including TVA, after he became a Republican, but his view of the land was little changed. Reagan thought like a rancher. The vastness of the West misled him into underestimating its ecological fragility. On a flight from Los Angeles to Denver in 1969, Reagan turned to me and, with a gesture toward an expanse of mountain wilderness below, remarked on the abundance of unspoiled land still available to Americans. He seemed comforted by this thought.

Others were not. Much of the available land in the West was arid desert in which water was a commodity more precious than oil or gold. As Walter Prescott Webb put it, "The heart of the west is a desert, unqualified and absolute." Water was the key to developing this desert, which originally included much of Los Angeles and most of the irrigation-dependent Central Valley.

The California Water Plan, approved by the voters in 1960, was supposed to hold back the desert forever. It authorized $1.75 billion in bonds to construct a 730-foot high dam at Oroville to store more than a trillion gallons of water for hydroelectric production, irrigation, and drinking water. The water was transported via the 444-mile-long California Aqueduct, a remarkable engineering feat, to Southern California. Pat Brown, in a crowning achievement of his governorship, had overcome regional objections to the water plan and sold it to the Legislature and the voters. Reagan, who disapproved of much else that Brown had done, took no issue with the California Water Plan and unwisely exempted water resources from his promised review of Brown's policies.

Reagan appointed William R. Gianelli, a conservative Democrat and able civil engineer, as state water resources director. Gianelli had helped formulate the legislation that created the California Water Plan and had played a primary role in selling it to the Legislature. The next step in the plan was to build high dams on the state's few remaining wild rivers in northern California.

A handful of conservationists stood in the way. The skeptics included a new conservationist organization, California Tomorrow, founded by philanthropist Alfred Heller and Samuel Wood, a Sacramento planner. They published a quarterly magazine, *Cry California*, that questioned the need for additional dams and challenged the assumptions of the water plan. The summer 1968 issue of *Cry California* featured an article by Frank Stead, who had served as chief of the California Department of Public Health's division of environmental sanitation during the Brown administration. Stead argued that the water plan was "only half a system" and that it did not make effective provision for ridding the land of waste water. "We are losing the water battle," he wrote.

> We are spending $2 billion to transport water from our own matchless Sierra to the Southern California coastal areas where daily we pour into the ocean one billion gallons of water of better chemical quality than the water now imported from the Colorado River for use in the same area. And in the process, we are writing off as expendable the matchless water wonderland of the Delta, while the very areas in whose behalf we are per-petuating this colossal ecological blunder lie alongside an inexhaustible supply of water. Finally we are making the fatal mistake that has destroyed every civilization in history which has attempted to build an irrigated agri-culture on an imported water supply without providing for the exportation of minerals equal to those in the incoming water to maintain a balance.[20]

The water establishment of California dismissed such jeremiads as the ravings of a lunatic fringe. By the time Stead's article appeared, the U.S. Army Corps of Engineers, backed by Gianelli and the State De-partment of Water Resources, was planning its next high dam. This was a 730-foot structure at Dos Rios on the middle fork of the Eel, the river Ronald Reagan had been unable to identify during the 1966 campaign when he was standing on its banks. The reservoir behind this dam would have flooded picturesque Round Valley, home to the town of Covelo, a few hundred farms, and an Indian tribe called the Yuki that may have been 9,000 years old.* The lovely valley had a sad history; a

*I have used the term "Indian" rather than "Native American" in my discussion of the Dos Rios controversy because the Yuki referred to themselves as Indians.

hundred years earlier it had been the place where U.S. Army soldiers had herded survivors of seven Indian tribes, including the Yuki.

As envisioned, the Dos Rios dam would have cost $400 million in 1968 dollars, created an artificial lake of 40,000 surface acres, and impounded more water than the Oroville and Shasta reservoirs combined. It would also have destroyed the Eel River fishery, including its summer steelhead run. And it would have been the beginning of the end for the remaining wild rivers on California's north coast. The Grindstone tunnel, which would have started Dos Rios water on its long journey southward, was designed to accommodate the flows of all these rivers.

A majority of those who lived in Round Valley didn't want it flooded despite promises of generous compensation from the federal government. Richard Wilson, a politically savvy cattle rancher with a Dartmouth education, organized a group to oppose the dam, which he afterward expanded into the Save the Eel River Association. He had the backing of the Yuki, who said the proposed dam would drown more than 400 tribal archeological sites, and of California Tomorrow.*

At its outset, Wilson's campaign seemed quixotic. The Army was used to crushing Indian opposition, and conservationists and small farmers had rarely stopped a major proposal of the Corps of Engineers. The entire water establishment, a grouping that included the Corps, the State Department of Water Resources, big agriculture, and such powerful regional agencies as the Metropolitan Water District in Los Angeles County, favored the super-dam at Dos Rios. The water bureaucracy foresaw no serious objection to the dam from the Legislature or the governor, since the federal government would put up the construction money and the state would gain the benefit of additional water storage. This was the classic argument that had littered the West with high dams. In the case of Dos Rios, however, the cost-benefit analysis conducted by the Corps of Engineers showed that the dam would provide minimal flood control, supposedly the reason for the Corps' involvement.

Still, neither Gianelli nor Colonel Frank Boerger, the San Francisco district engineer for the Corps, thought that the dam could be stopped. They had expected Ike Livermore and Walter Shannon, the conserva-

---

*He also had my backing. William Bronson, editor of *Cry California*, asked me to write an article about the proposed flooding of Round Valley. I wasn't interested. I believed that dams were inevitable and assumed that Wilson was just a wealthy rancher standing in the way of progress. Bronson urged me to visit Round Valley and see for myself. I did. The valley was lovely, and Wilson and the Yuki made a strong case for preserving it. Subsequently, I talked to a Corps of Engineers official who acknowledged that the dam would have marginal benefits. I found this a decisive admission. My article, "High Dam in the Valley of the Tall Grass," from which a few passages in this chapter are taken, appeared in the summer 1968 issue of *Cry California*. Bill Clark gave a copy of the article to Reagan, who told me he agreed with it. It was the only time Reagan ever complimented me on anything I wrote.

tionist-minded director of the State Fish and Game Commission, to haggle about costs and wildlife protection and were prepared to make marginal concessions.* But they were surprised and angry when Livermore refused to sign a contract that would have sped the project on its way. Still, Gianelli was confident. No governor of California had ever rejected money for a dam that the federal government wanted to build.

Livermore was buying time. He was preoccupied with the battle over the redwoods and did not want to open a second front in the war to save the California north coast. It took awhile for Wilson to get Livermore's attention. When he did, the resources director was impressed with Wilson's clear-eyed argument that the dam would needlessly sacrifice the Eel River's entire middle fork. In time, Livermore spoke with the fervency of a convert. Addressing the Commonwealth Club, he said: "How could any fair-minded person possibly argue for the destruction of the historic and picturesque town of Covelo and its Indian community by obliterating a beautiful valley of 14,000 acres . . . under the guise of protection against occasional flooding of downstream areas on the Eel River of 20,000 acres?" This, said Livermore, exchanged "permanent destruction" for "occasional protection."[21]

Once the redwoods compromise had been reached, Livermore gave priority to the Dos Rios dam at cabinet meetings, making arguments he knew would interest the governor: the opposition of the Indians, the objections from local interests, and the costs. Reagan was unimpressed that the federal government would bear the cost of the dam. ("It's all our money," he told me.) Livermore had support from Bill Clark, who asked Caspar Weinberger about the cost-effectiveness of Dos Rios. Weinberger, adding another voice to the opposition, told him that the economics were questionable.

Gianelli fought back. He had a cabinet ally in Earl Coke, the agricultural director, who told Reagan that the reservoir created by Dos Rios would provide insurance in drought years for farmers in the Central Valley. Reagan typically did not want to offend any of his cabinet members, and he respected both Coke and Gianelli. Neither Clark nor Livermore knew what the governor would do.

Then, on December 10, 1968, Livermore received a telephone call from Reagan. "Ike," he said, "I hate to see a beautiful valley destroyed. Just between us, I feel we should pause in destroying a beautiful valley."[22]

As the conversation continued, Reagan explained that he had consid-

---

*Shannon, a holdover from the Brown administration and an unrecognized conservationist hero of the era, was often a thorn in the side of lumber companies, developers, and government agencies because of his persistent insistence on mitigation for wildlife losses.

ered Dos Rios a federal project and had not at first realized that it would also require his approval. He then repeated that he did not want to be part of destroying a "beautiful valley" and thought that the state should "hang loose" on the project.[23]

This conversation marked the beginning of the end for the Dos Rios dam. Over the next several months, both sides continued to argue, but Livermore was confident that Reagan would not allow Round Valley to be flooded. To clinch the case, Livermore brought a small delegation from Covelo to the governor's office on April 24, 1969. It included Norman Whipple, a Yuki whose ancestors had been driven into Round Valley by the Army.

According to Ted Simon, whose book *The River Stops Here* gives a definitive account of the Dos Rios struggle, Whipple talked of past injustices to Indians in simple, homespun language. Treaties had been repeatedly broken, including the treaty that had given Round Valley to the Indians. Would there never be an end to it? Simon related that Reagan was on the verge of tears. "Agreements are made to be kept, and we should live with them," the governor said.[24] Later, when he rejected Dos Rios, Reagan would say, in an eloquent pun, "We've broken too many damn treaties."[25] It was his finest environmental moment.

Gianelli and the water establishment continued to wage a rearguard battle in behalf of a Dos Rios dam. Gianelli envisioned an even higher 785-foot dam on the Klamath, the brightest jewel of the north coast wild rivers. Round Valley had been saved for the time being, but Richard Wilson and his allies knew that the dam builders would make their case again to Reagan or his successor unless the rivers were legally protected. It was at this point that another friend of wild rivers entered the picture. His name was Peter Behr, a member of the Marin County clique of conservation-minded Republicans.

Behr, urbane and elegant, was born in 1915, four years after Reagan and Livermore. He typified the elite strand of California immigrants who had attended a prestigious prep school, graduated from an Ivy League university (Yale, and then Yale Law School), served in World War II (Behr rose to the rank of lieutenant commander in the Navy), and then married and settled down in a pastoral suburb of San Francisco. Behr chose Mill Valley, where "quality of life" was in vogue before most Americans had heard this phrase. He served on the Mill Valley Planning Commission and was elected to the City Council and then to the Marin County Board of Supervisors. Soft-spoken but persuasive, Behr led the board in a successful crusade to preserve the panoramic west Marin coast, where Congress established the Point Reyes National Seashore in 1962.

The Point Reyes campaign established Behr, a successful lawyer with a taste for public life, as one of Marin's premier conservationists. He was elected to the State Senate on a rising tide of environmentalism in 1970. This was the year that Senator Gaylord Nelson of Wisconsin proclaimed the first Earth Day, which he called "a turning point in American history." *Time* magazine said that the environment was the "issue of the year," and Reagan emphasized environmental issues in his State of the State Address. In Sacramento, the Sierra Club, the Planning and Conservation League, and other conservationist groups formed the California Coastal Alliance, which raised coastal protection as an issue in the 1970 legislative elections. In 1971, the Alliance drafted a comprehensive plan for coastline protection.

Covelo rancher Richard Wilson had become president of the Planning and Conservation League during the Dos Rios struggle and was seeking ways to preserve his victory. The first line of defense was the Legislature, and the first bill that Behr offered as a freshman senator after consulting with Wilson proposed to create a "wild and scenic river system" on the undeveloped portions of three north coast rivers: the Eel, the Klamath, and the Trinity. The bill's "fatal flaw," as *California Journal* observed, was that Randolph Collier, the white-maned dean of the Senate, was not a party to the measure, and the rivers were in his district.[26] Collier, a pro-development Democrat who was known as the "father of the freeways," was a frequent ally of the water establishment. Behr's bill reached the Senate floor but lost by two votes.

At this point, the Legislature had done little to justify the brave optimism of Earth Day. The conservationist plight was summed up in the headline on the cover story of the November 1971 issue of *California Journal*: "Environmentalists Suffer Second Year of Defeat." It wasn't quite that bad. The story didn't mention Dos Rios or observe that environmentalists, thanks to Livermore, had Reagan's support on most of their priority issues. The problem was the State Senate, which ignored Reagan and the liberal Democratic leadership in the Assembly and killed a coastline preservation bill as well as Behr's measure to protect wild and scenic rivers.

Although not much remarked on at the time, 1972 was a breakthrough year for the environmental movement. Nationally, it was the year when Congress passed the Clean Water Act and the Environmental Protection Agency banned the pesticide DDT. In California, the California Coastal Alliance, after a State Senate committee again blocked a coastline-protection measure, redrafted the bill as a ballot initiative and took its case to the people. The initiative, Proposition 20 on the November 1972 ballot, created a commission with broad powers to grant access to beaches and block projects inimical to the coastline. Reagan opposed it, arguing that the state should enforce existing coastal protection standards instead of creating a new layer of government. Voters, however, approved the initiative by a 55–45 percent margin.

In 1972, Behr reintroduced an even stronger bill to protect California's north coast rivers. On this issue, Reagan was in tune with the voters. Even the recalcitrant Senator Collier was hearing from constituents at home who didn't want to give up their rivers to help farmers in the San Joaquin Valley or urban water users in Los Angeles. Recognizing that he would find it difficult to kill Behr's bill again, Collier introduced a milder rival measure that would have banned dams on the Klamath and Trinity rivers but permitted "planning" for dams on the Eel River. Conservationists saw this as a backdoor attempt to resurrect the Dos Rios dam and endorsed the Behr bill. The Legislature, responding to prevailing conservationist sentiment, passed both bills. This left the decision to the governor, who, by signing both bills, would have left it to the courts to resolved the differences.

Reagan, however, was committed to preserving California's wild rivers and didn't want to leave the decision to a judge. It didn't hurt the conservationist cause that *The Sacramento Bee*, which Reagan detested, urged him to veto both bills on the dubious claim that Central Valley agriculture would need the rivers of the north coast. Nor did it hurt that Behr was a Republican and Collier a Democrat.

But Reagan made his decision on the merits. Without comment, he vetoed Collier's bill. On December 20, 1972, he signed the Behr measure and resolved one of California's great environmental controversies in favor of the conservationists. No one would have realized this from Reagan's bland words when he signed the Behr bill, for he made it sound as if everyone had reasoned together and reached a consensus. "I am delighted that we have been able to resolve several years of controversy over the preservation of our north coast rivers," Reagan said. Behr praised the governor for displaying "the same courage and concern" that caused him to stop the high dam at Dos Rios.[27]

Many laws promise more than they deliver, but Behr's measure establishing a California Wild and Scenic Rivers System did better than advertised. The bill barred dams on five wild rivers, including the Klamath and the Trinity, and a portion of another. Behr had been forced to compromise on the Eel River to get his bill through the Senate; the final version of the legislation imposed a twelve-year moratorium on construction or planning. Long before the moratorium expired, however, the federal Wild Rivers Act gave permanent protection to the Eel River. Taken together, Reagan's decisions on Dos Rios and on Behr's bill saved wild rivers that would have been destroyed. It is a tribute to Reagan—and to Livermore, Behr, Wilson, and a disciplined environmental coalition—that these rivers still flow free to the sea.

Thousands of acres of parklands more accessible to urban populations than the north coast redwoods or wild rivers were also set aside for public use during the Reagan years. The point man in this effort was William Mott, the state parks director. He reported to Livermore, whom he much admired, and had been an ally in the fight against the Dos Rios dam by arguing that the dam's recreational values would be negligible.

Mott, who was trained as a landscape architect and had worked in the National Park Service, had built a national reputation during his fifteen years as parks director in Oakland and five years as general manager of the East Bay Regional Parks District in the rolling hills east of Oakland. He advocated a "balanced" park system, by which he meant parks with something for every conceivable user: backpackers, skiers, ballplayers, swimmers, off-road-vehicle users, and ordinary families who wanted to cook on an outdoor grill. When Tom Reed, in his whirlwind 100 days as Governor Reagan's first appointments secretary, was searching for a state parks director, he found that Mott was nearly everyone's first choice and offered him the job. Livermore weighed in, too, but Mott said he wanted to talk to the governor before deciding. Reed arranged a meeting in which Mott told Reagan that he wanted to manage state parks professionally without political interference. Reagan looked him straight in the eye and agreed. "You run the department; I'll handle the politics," Reagan said.[28] Mott accepted on the spot.

It wasn't that simple, of course. Decisions about the purchase and development of parks are political, and it was fortunate that Mott was an adept politician with commitment and vision. He pioneered in hiring women as state park rangers in defiance of a tradition that such jobs were suitable only for men. (Reagan's support on this issue, Mott said, enabled him to overcome resistance from the Civil Service Commission.[29]) Mott also armed park rangers after seeing to it that they received extensive training in which it was emphasized that use of firearms was a last resort. No state ranger fired a shot in anger during the Reagan years.

Various legislators disagreed with Mott over his definition of "balance." Liberals such as Senator Anthony Beilenson didn't want off-road vehicles in state parks; conservatives such as Senator Collier thought highways should go through parks rather than around them. A highway that ran down the middle of one state redwood park was on the drawing boards when Mott was appointed, and he was unable to stop it. But

Mott persuaded Collier to redraw the route at another state redwood park so that the highway skirted it. Collier, chairman of the Senate committees dealing with finance and highways, respected Mott because he did his homework and had a grasp of the issues. To Mott's delight, Collier agreed to change the gas-tax formula and give the State Parks and Recreation Department a portion of gas-tax revenues during summer months when recreational use was high.[30]

California land values, pushed by population increase and inflation, escalated during Mott's tenure. Mott wanted to buy parkland before the price went higher. This put him in conflict with legislative analyst Alan Post, who believed the state should develop previously purchased parkland before adding parks to the system. Mott had the better argument; California land prices soared to such high levels later in the twentieth century that parkland acquisition slowed to a crawl. In his expansionist views Mott was backed by Reagan, who realized from personal experience that land was the best of all California investments. During the Reagan years, California added 145,000 acres of land and two underwater Pacific Ocean preserves to the state park system. This was an achievement that matched in two Reagan terms what Earl Warren had done in three. No other modern California governor has come close.

Reagan's reputation as a conservationist governor, however, rests more on projects he halted than on the parkland acquired on his watch. In 1969, it was the Dos Rios dam. In 1972, the project was a federal highway between the John Muir and Minarets wilderness areas in the eastern Sierra, which, like Dos Rios, was advocated by persistent government bureaucracies and by powerful agricultural interests in the Central Valley and would have caused significant environmental damage in exchange for meager economic benefits. In both cases, Reagan intervened after planning for the projects had acquired seemingly irresistible momentum.

The trans-Sierra highway had been a dream of farmers in the Central Valley for half a century. They saw it as a way to send products east over the Sierra. But the communities on the eastern slope of the mountains were so thinly populated that projections showed the highway would be lightly used. Conservationists were aghast, for the proposed road would have sliced through one of the most picturesque sections of the John Muir Trail.

Livermore was determined to stop the highway, and Reagan agreed with him. By 1972, Reagan had become more sophisticated about environmental issues and no longer needed his resources director to lead him by the hand. When the trans-Sierra highway first came to Reagan's attention, he expressed skepticism. The immediate issue was a proposal by the U.S. Forest Service to spend $2.3 million to build 2.7 miles of paved road to replace a dirt road (since partially paved) to the Devil's Postpile National Monument. This was, as Reagan recognized, a foot in the door for the trans-Sierra highway. Livermore and Edwin Meese, now the governor's chief of staff, reinforced Reagan's skepticism and waged a delaying action, arguing that the environmental impact statement for the road was inadequate.

Reagan was no deskbound general in this campaign. As he had done at Lake Tahoe, he resolved to make his own field inspection of the Minarets area. This wasn't strictly necessary, since Reagan had for several months sent letters to U.S. Forest Service officials and President Nixon's secretary of transportation, John Volpe, questioning the highway. Some of Reagan's aides suspected that his real motivation was to get out of Sacramento and ride the trail.*

Whatever the motivation, the Minarets trip was one of the more successful media events of the Reagan governorship. "I still have this image of Reagan waving a white hat, on a tall horse, suddenly trotting through a pack station—then bounding over boulders into the high Sierra as staffers and reporters struggled to mount and hang on to some strange beast," George Skelton of the *Los Angeles Times* wrote a quarter century later.[31] Skelton was no greenhorn. An outdoorsman and avid fisherman, he had taken pack trips before, including one with Governor Brown. Although Skelton had often written critically about Reagan, he was impressed with him that day. "It was like the cavalry coming to the rescue," Skelton told me thirty years later.[32] That was how Reagan thought of it, too.[33]

On the warm day of June 27, 1972, Reagan and his party, with 100 packhorses in tow, started out from Red's Meadow, near Devil's Postpile National Monument. They overnighted at a high Sierra lake. Skelton noticed that highway surveyors were at work when they reached the John Muir Trail. Reagan rode 6 miles along steep trails to a meadow beneath the 13,000-foot Minaret Summit. There, he dismounted and made a dramatic speech.

Reagan began by recounting the history of the effort to build a trans-Sierra highway. "Because such a crossing would do irreparable harm to the wilderness beauty and wildlife of the area—and because we simply don't need another highway—we have vigorously opposed such a crossing," Reagan said. He noted that wildlife in the surrounding wilderness—Reagan listed wolverines, deer, bears, mountain lions, and big horn sheep—"are becoming endangered and cannot tolerate any fur-

*Livermore organized the expedition, although he did not join it because of a conflict with the International Environmental Conference in Stockholm, to which he was a delegate.

ther human disturbance. Any additional motorized access through this part of the southern Sierra will have a major adverse impact on the fragile wilderness values we hold so dear."

The governor then announced that he had received a telegram from the White House "detailing the president's complete support for our position." He concluded by proposing "a permanent solution to this problem—to close this corridor forever by merging the existing Minarets and John Muir wildernesses into one." This, he said, would block the trans-Sierra highway forever "and preserve the vast, primitive beauty of this wilderness for generations of Californians yet to come."

Reagan did not stop there. On August 8, he wrote all members of the California congressional delegation calling upon them to join a "cause to which my administration is deeply committed—permanently closing the Minarets Corridor in the high Sierra and effectively blocking a long-proposed trans-Sierra highway."[34] As Skelton observed a quarter century later, "Congress later agreed and today, the John Muir Trail remains unbroken for 250 miles between Yosemite and south of Mt. Whitney."[35]

·   ·   ·

How did a governor who saved Round Valley from extinction and preserved the sanctity of the Minaret wilderness become a president who favored oil drilling, timber cutting, and mining exploration in some of the nation's most scenic lands? The first and most obvious answer is that Reagan largely followed the antithetical advice of his custodians of natural resources, Ike Livermore in Sacramento and James Watt in Washington. Watt called himself "a symbol of free enterprise" and proposed an offshore oil-drilling program of such magnitude that even the oil industry balked at it.[36] He sought to open wilderness areas, which he disdained, to development. Livermore adored the wilderness. "They'd say, 'Stick to the facts,'" he said, speaking of the proponents of the Dos Rios high dam. "I'd say, 'Look, emotion is a fact. The solitude of the wilderness, the beauty of a flower—those are facts.'"[37]

How, then, did Reagan wind up with such dissimilar custodians? The simple answer is that they were selected by different people—Tom Reed picked Livermore and Paul Laxalt recommended Watt. Laxalt, then the senior senator from Nevada and a vital ally in Reagan's presidential campaigns, rarely asked favors of Reagan but wanted a say in selection of the secretary of the interior. Reagan said he would nominate whomever he proposed. Laxalt, however, did not start out with Watt. As I have recounted in an earlier book, Laxalt's first choice was Clifford Hansen, a former two-term Republican senator from Wyoming. Hansen was no Livermore, but he was a reasonable man who in 1968 had supported the more generous Senate version of the legislation creating Redwood National Park. But Hansen didn't want to disclose his financial records and withdrew his name, which opened the door to Watt. So there was a certain accidental quality to Watt's appointment.[38]

In some ways, Livermore was as much of an aberration as Watt. Even though Livermore had Reed's backing, the Kitchen Cabinet, influential in the early days of the governorship, might have vetoed him if it had known how much of a lightning rod he would become. Later, when these wealthy constituents did know, Livermore had solidified himself with Reagan and was also supported by the governor's chiefs of staff, first Bill Clark and then Ed Meese. But Livermore was seen as a potential troublemaker by pro-development forces that backed Reagan's presidential candidacy. Had Reagan taken Livermore with him to Washington as secretary of the interior, he might have become the most environmentally successful Republican president since Theodore Roosevelt. But Livermore was not asked to participate in the Reagan presidency. He had become anathema to those who, as Watt put it, wanted to "mine more, drill more, [and] cut more timber."

Reagan never acknowledged a contradiction in his selections of Livermore and Watt, probably because environmental issues ranked low on his political agenda. On issues that mattered most to him, Reagan was forceful and not a creature of his staff. He came into office, as governor and as president, with firm ideas about taxes and government growth. He believed strongly in restoring the nation's defenses in order to negotiate with the Soviet Union from a position of strength. No one could have talked him out of these positions. Indeed, Al Haig, his first secretary of state, failed in his effort to prevent Reagan from writing an appeal for negotiations to Soviet leader Leonid Brezhnev during Reagan's first months in office.[39] But Reagan had focused on taxation, government growth, and the Soviet Union for decades, in and out of office. The environment was never a similar fixation.

The contrasting environmental records of Governor Reagan and President Reagan are not symmetrical, however. Watt's rhetoric was so extreme that he galvanized environmentalists and their congressional supporters. Environmental groups used mailers with Watt's name and picture as potent recruiting posters. The Wilderness Society tripled its fund-raising, and Sierra Club membership grew 25 percent in a single year. "If there hadn't been a James Watt we would have had to invent one," said Doug Scott, the club's director of federal affairs.[40] Congress blocked most of Watt's initiatives. And fortunately for the conservation- ist cause, Watt self-destructed before he could do serious damage.*

In contrast, Reagan and Livermore together saved imperiled envi- ronmental treasures in California. Had Pat Brown been reelected in 1966, there would now be a high dam on the middle fork of the Eel River at Dos Rios, for Brown favored such developments. If Dos Rios and the accompanying Grindstone tunnel had been built, the Eel would have been destroyed and the remaining wild rivers on the north coast would have become a lost cause. Once the means existed to transport this water south, these rivers almost certainly would have been tapped during the drought years later in the century.

Similarly, the sanctity of the John Muir Trail, once bridged by a trans-Sierra highway, would have been violated. The Yosemite and Se- quoia wildernesses could not have been joined. Commercial develop- ment would have spread in the southern Sierra.

Stopping the Dos Rios dam and the trans-Sierra highway would have been monumental achievements for any governor, let alone one who entered office with a reputation as a foe of the environment. That repu- tation was based almost entirely on Reagan's misguided statements about the redwoods. But Reagan's actions on behalf of the environment during his governorship transcended these words. Governor Reagan saved the wild rivers of the north coast, and he saved the John Muir Trail. It is a valuable legacy.

---

*At a breakfast speech to the U.S. Chamber of Commerce on September 21, 1983, Watt extolled a commission that was reviewing the Interior Department's coal-leasing program: "We have every kind of mix you can have. I have a black, I have a woman, two Jews, and a cripple. And we have talent." Soon afterward, Senator Laxalt privately urged Watt to resign. Watt stepped down on October 9, acknowledging in a letter to Reagan that he would be bet- ter served by "a different type of leadership" at Interior. He was replaced by Bill Clark, who served until 1985, when he was succeeded by Donald Hodel. Neither of these appointments was controversial.

22

INCUMBENT

ONALD REAGAN, a strong swimmer since boyhood, battled a
Democratic current in the lower and more populist house of the
legislative branch for all but two of his sixteen years as governor
and president. Republicans never held a majority in the House while
Reagan was in the White House. They controlled the Assembly during
only two of Reagan's eight years as governor.

This brief Republican legislative interregnum in Sacramento was the
result of the 1968 elections, which completed the work of the Reagan
landslide of 1966. Considering the magnitude of Reagan's victory, Republicans should have captured the Legislature in 1966 but were out-
maneuvered by Assembly Speaker Jesse Unruh, who concentrated the
party's resources in a handful of districts where Democratic candidates
were endangered.

It was different in 1968. Unruh was with Robert Kennedy in the
kitchen of the Ambassador Hotel when he was gunned down on June 5,
1968, the night he won the California primary. Unruh was traumatized.
Later, as head of the California delegation at the discordant Democratic
National Convention in Chicago, he was part of the futile attempt to
block Hubert Humphrey's coronation as the party's presidential nominee. Unruh left Chicago disillusioned. In a speech in Santa Cruz on October 7, less than a month before the election, he came close to
breaking with the national ticket. He claimed that the Johnson administration's domestic polices were "on the whole" as much a failure as its
foreign policies. "The end result is that this nation's people are almost
totally frustrated," Unruh said. "The promises made in the name of the
Great Society have turned into a virtual nightmare of racial tensions,
dispirited youth, rising crime and a mushrooming federal bureaucracy."

These words could have come from Reagan or any other Republican—and soon did. Assembly Minority Leader Bob Monagan, campaigning for Republican control of the Legislature, began using them as the opening lines of his speeches. After his partisan audiences applauded, Monagan would say he was quoting Unruh, which produced more applause. Republican exploitation of Unruh's assault on the Great Society prompted his opponents within the Democratic Party to accuse him of disloyalty, which reduced his effectiveness in the 1968 campaign.

Reagan, meanwhile, campaigned effectively for the Republican ticket in California and banked future political points by speaking for GOP candidates around the country. I accompanied Reagan on two of these trips, interviewing him for my first book, a dual biography of Reagan and Unruh. Tom Reed and Bill Clark made the arrangements. They explained that Reagan would have more time for extensive interviews on campaign trips than in Sacramento. This was true, but there was more to it than that. Reagan, then fifty-seven, had never been comfortable with air travel since his first turbulent plane ride from Los Angeles to Catalina in a storm more than thirty years earlier. I made the mistake, on a flight from New York to Jacksonville, of asking about the clause in Reagan's contract with General Electric, which stipulated that his trips to GE plants would be by train.

"Does flying still concern you?" I asked.

Reagan explained to me that he had decided when he agreed to run for governor that he would have to fly. Then he looked out the plane window at the coastline below and said, "But it's still an awful long way down." We both laughed, but the conversation had reminded Reagan that he was several thousand feet above the earth in a small plane. He was so uneasy for the rest of the flight that I switched off my tape recorder.

Later in the trip, with the plane on the ground in Jacksonville, an inspection turned up a mechanical problem. Reagan, standing on the tarmac while the pilot received a report from the mechanic, was nervous. Paul Beck, Reagan's press secretary, suggested to the governor that he return to the plane while the mechanic worked on the problem. Reagan did. Then Beck turned to me and asked me to go back to the plane and talk with him. I said I was out of questions. "Think of some," Beck said.[1]

Reagan understood that I was being sent to calm him down. He asked me how I felt about flying. I told him about a scary personal experience on a small plane in bad weather and said I understood how he felt. He nodded. We chatted for nearly two hours while the mechanic made a simple repair (or so we were told) involving replacement of a 75-cent spark plug. Reagan was calm and reflective, and we never discussed fear of flying again. But I was impressed that he would travel all over the country in a small plane to speak for obscure candidates when he was so afraid to fly. Reagan strategist Stu Spencer had a similar view. Years later, he told me that Reagan's acceptance of the necessity of flying had made him aware that Reagan was more ambitious than he seemed.

That ambition was often hidden. In part, that was because Reagan was modest. But it was also hidden because Reagan did not see himself as someone who compromised and cut corners, as ordinary politicians do. Reagan believed he was a "citizen-politician." Citizen-politicians do not make deals. Because Reagan had convinced himself that he was never motivated by political considerations, he found it difficult to acknowledge, even in private conversations, that he had a political strategy in mind when he agreed to a massive tax increase early in his governorship. That would be giving away the game. There were many in Sacramento, and later in Washington, who could not believe that a grown-up could engage in such pretense. They missed the point. Reagan genuinely believed that he was "not a politician," so much so that he bridled if I referred to him as such in an interview or article. It was the secret of his political success.

Reagan demonstrated his political acumen in 1968 by waging an all-out campaign against Proposition 9, a California ballot initiative that was the first ripple in the populist antitax tidal wave that would crest a decade later with passage of Proposition 13. Proposition 9 was the brainchild of Phil Watson, the Los Angeles County assessor. It would have restricted property tax and property assessments to 1 percent of value and phased out property tax support for education, welfare, and other "people-related services." The measure, observed State Finance Director Caspar Weinberger, would have been "a complete disaster for the state."[2] He estimated it would have required a $4.5 billion state tax increase by the fifth year of operation, when property tax support for the people-related services would have been completely phased out. The initiative would have nullified the Reagan tax bill and required significant cutbacks in government services—as Proposition 13 did when it became law four years after the end of Reagan's governorship. Early polls gave Proposition 9 a reasonable chance of passage. Reagan and Weinberger wanted to defeat it decisively, so that no one would try to put it on the ballot again in 1970. Reagan's campaign was persuasive, and 68 percent of the electorate voted against Proposition 9.

Overall, the 1968 election went well for the Republicans. Nixon carried California and was elected president. The Republicans ended Democratic control of the California Legislature for the first time in a decade. Democrats held a 42–38 margin in the Assembly and a 21–19 margin in the State Senate before the election. Afterward, Republicans controlled the Assembly, 41–39, and the Senate was tied 20–20. Mona-gan replaced Unruh as Assembly speaker.

The only dark cloud for Republicans in California was the victory in the U.S. Senate race of Democrat Alan Cranston, the former state con-troller whom Reagan had helped defeat in 1966. Cranston beat Repub-lican Max Rafferty, a right-wing superintendent of public instruction who had narrowly upset moderate incumbent Senator Thomas Kuchel in the Republican primary. (Kuchel suffered both from the hostility of conservatives and a lazy campaign.[3]) Reagan stayed neutral in the pri-mary and afterward made a desultory and unsuccessful effort to per-suade Kuchel to endorse Rafferty. The truth was that Reagan didn't like any of the choices: Cranston was anathema, Kuchel was too liberal, and Rafferty was an unpredictable character whose campaign was run by ul-traconservatives who had denounced Reagan for betraying the conser-vative cause when he raised taxes.

But Rafferty was the Republican nominee, and Reagan endorsed him. Instead of taking a leaf from Reagan's playbook and reaching out to Kuchel's supporters, Rafferty conducted a disorganized, extremist campaign that repelled moderate Republicans and independents. Cranston organized a "Gopocrats" committee to woo these voters. The campaign was not edifying. Rafferty suggested that Cranston counte-nanced treason, and Cranston, drawing on an investigative article in the *Long Beach Press-Telegram*, accused Rafferty of being a draft dodger in World War II.

Reagan was barely going through the motions in support of Rafferty until Tom Reed, then Republican national committeeman from Cali-fornia, and Stu Spencer, who was directing the party's state legislative campaigns, informed him that Rafferty was dragging down the party's legislative ticket. This caught the attention of the governor, who wanted Unruh off the University of California Board of Regents, a post he held by virtue of his Assembly speakership.

With Rafferty trailing by 20 percentage points in the polls, Reed, Spencer, and Republican State Chairman Jim Halley discussed replac-ing him as the Republican nominee with Lieutenant Governor Robert Finch. But this was not possible under California law, even if Rafferty had gone along. On September 28, Reagan was drawn into discussion of a more practical solution to the Rafferty problem. The governor agreed with Reed, Halley, and Spencer that they should move into Rafferty's campaign and attempt to salvage it.

Changes occurred immediately. Holmes Tuttle took over finance management from an ultraconservative Rafferty contributor, and Reed and Nofziger ran the campaign. Rafferty stopped talking about Cranston's alleged (and nonexistent) pro-communism and began talking, Reagan-style, about the necessity of maintaining order on university and college campuses. Rafferty, who was facing a million-vote defeat at the beginning of October, steadily closed the gap, but he still lost by 351,000 votes.* But the Reagan team accomplished its purpose: With Rafferty less of a drag on the ticket, Republicans saved four Assembly seats that were in jeopardy and picked up three others from the Democrats.

The elections were followed by changes in the Sacramento cast. Nofziger, who had left the governor's office to help Rafferty, departed for Washington to work for President Nixon in his congressional relations office. Finch, an old Nixon associate, left California to join the cabinet as secretary of health, education, and welfare. Although lieutenant governors are elected independently in California, governors appoint replacements if they leave before completing their terms. Reagan replaced Finch with Ed Reinecke, an obscure conservative member of Congress from Tujunga in Los Angeles County.

The most significant change in Sacramento was the departure of Bill Clark as Reagan's chief of staff. As cabinet secretary, Clark had played a crucial role during Reagan's novice period as governor, filling in during the frequent absences of Phil Battaglia. As chief of staff, Clark had been effective and kept the staff focused on the governor's legislative agenda during Reagan's flirtation with the presidential nomination in the summer of 1968. Clark was devoted to Reagan but wanted to spend more time with his family on their ranch near Paso Robles—and also wanted an appointment to the bench. On November 25, 1968, Reagan announced that he had "reluctantly agreed" to appoint Clark to a Superior Court vacancy in San Luis Obispo County within driving distance of his ranch. "I will miss him," said Reagan, and he did.

The new chief of staff (the formal job title was then "executive secretary") was Edwin Meese III, the legal affairs secretary, who had been among the coup plotters who ousted Battaglia. Clark and Meese had decided privately that Meese would succeed him when he stepped down, an arrangement that dismayed other coup plotters when they learned about it after the fact.† But Meese, a graduate of Yale and UC Berkeley

*Nixon carried California over Humphrey by 223,000 votes. He had 48 percent of the vote, Humphrey 44.7 percent, and George Wallace, the nominee of the American Independent Party, 6.7 percent. Nofziger believed that Rafferty could have won if the Reagan team had taken over his campaign sooner. Recalling the words of the famous sportswriter Ring Lardner about baseball players who could have made it to the major leagues but never did, Nofziger wrote in his memoirs: "Well, Max Rafferty could have been elected U.S. senator but somehow never was."[4]

†The coup plotters, said Reed, had agreed among themselves that they would consult with one another when any major staff change was contemplated.[5] Nofziger was also surprised by Clark's abrupt departure. It is likely, however, that Meese would have been the choice in any case.

law school, was the logical successor. He understood Reagan's modes of behavior and had experience in Sacramento dating back to the days when he had lobbied there for a law enforcement group.

Meese's promotion, however, established a contradictory pattern that persisted into Reagan's presidency. While Reagan delegated immense authority to his chiefs of staff and relied on them for advice, he was only peripherally involved in their selection. Clark picked Meese. After the 1980 campaign, Stu Spencer teamed up with Mike Deaver and Nancy Reagan to select James A. Baker III as Reagan's chief of staff in the White House. At the beginning of Reagan's second term as president, Baker and Treasury Secretary Donald Regan (with Deaver's connivance) agreed to swap jobs, informing Reagan almost as an afterthought. Reagan did not question these arrangements or suggest alternatives. He was the star. Others determined the identity of the director.

Meese was, on balance, an effective chief of staff. Loyal and hard working, he followed Clark's practice of round-tabling decisions before springing them on the governor. He also shared Clark's understanding that Reagan wanted tangible accomplishments, even if they fell short of his conservative goals. This insight would make Meese a significant player in negotiations over welfare and tax legislation in Reagan's second term.

To understand Meese's value to Reagan in Sacramento, it is necessary to see him in the context of the governorship rather than from the perspective of the Reagan presidency. In the latter situation, he was passed over for White House chief of staff and marginalized by Baker and Deaver, who were Meese's superiors in the craft of maneuver. Meese then became the darling of conservatives who believed that the pragmatists were leading Reagan astray. But in Sacramento, where he had Reagan's confidence and no rivals for power, Meese was more often than not the leading pragmatist.

As chief of staff to Governor Reagan, Meese was more outgoing than Clark but less daring in policy initiation. He was at once highly structured and poorly organized. "He had these boxes and boxes of stuff in the office, at home, in which he never knew where anything was," said George Steffes, Reagan's legislative liaison.[6] But in a curious way, Meese complemented Reagan, who cleaned off his desk at the end of every working day, even if it meant discarding into the wastebasket papers he ought to have preserved. Meese filed everything, even if he could not always remember where he had filed it.

Meese more than compensated for any managerial deficiencies with a unique ability to explain intricate issues to Reagan and translate even the most inarticulate of Reagan's ideas into coherent policy. In his discussions with Reagan, Meese avoided legal language and made ample use of stories and anecdotes, which he knew was the way Reagan made sense of the world. (And, like Reagan, Meese could also memorize an apocryphal or invented story and persuade himself that it was true.) Meese was sometimes sycophantic but always trustworthy. He knew what Governor Reagan wanted to accomplish, spoke for him with authority, and never pursued an independent agenda.[7] I once referred to Meese as "Reagan's geographer." He drew maps of Reagan's world and charted courses that led the governor to his destinations.

But most of Reagan's legislative goals were incapable of achievement in 1969, no matter who was guiding him. Republicans had nominal control of the Legislature, but not much more. California is one of a handful of states that requires a two-thirds majority to pass legislation that has a fiscal impact. This meant that Speaker Monagan, with a 41–39 majority in the Assembly, needed the votes of every Republican plus thirteen Democrats to pass a fiscal bill.

The State Senate was even more problematic. The tie that had existed after the 1968 elections was broken when influential Democrat George Miller Jr., revered by his colleagues, died of a heart attack on New Year's Day, 1969. In March, a Republican won a special election to fill the vacancy, giving the GOP a 21–19 majority. But the Senate was politically a mess, with divisions that cut across party lines.

The Senate had done well by Reagan during the first two years of his governorship, principally because the governor's liaison to the upper house was Vern Sturgeon, a former senator and friend of Hugh Burns', the Democratic president pro tem, or Senate leader. The "one-man, one-vote" reapportionment ordered by the courts was in the process of changing the Senate from a rural club of old white men in which partisanship counted for little and friendships mattered a lot into a more partisan, urban, and representative body. Sturgeon had lost his Senate seat in the reapportionment. But Burns, whose cronies included some of Sacramento's most powerful lobbyists, was not easily dislodged. Even after Republicans gained a majority in 1969, he did not step down.

Reagan put no pressure on Burns to do so. The governor's willingness to accept the Senate status quo with its Democratic leadership was frustrating to idealistic members of his staff. One Reagan aide who considered Burns corrupt confided his frustration to me under protection of anonymity. "We're eating our own blood in the Senate," he said. "Instead of pushing our capable, young senators, we're doing business with the very people we came up here to get rid of, and I damn well don't like it. The governor was elected on an integrity platform."

But Reagan arguably was acting in his best interests by refusing to become the point man of Senate reform. Burns had been more a help than a hindrance, and Reagan was understandably cautious about meddling in the organization of the Senate. While Reagan in principle would have preferred a Republican leadership, his political instincts (and Sturgeon) told him that no legislative body welcomes the intrusion of a governor. So Reagan left it to Republicans in the Senate to redress their own grievances.

They did, but slowly. During the early months of the 1969 session, the Senate remained in the grip of Burns and his lobby-ridden cabal. Then, Republican Senator Howard Way, a farmer from Exeter in the San Joaquin Valley, violated an unwritten Senate rule by publicly accusing Burns of a conflict of interest because he had shared in the profits of an insurance company that benefited from legislation he had sponsored.[8] Way's call for an investigation by the Senate turned into a full-fledged challenge to Burns' leadership. Reform-minded Democrats chimed in, urging Burns to quit. He didn't. When Burns was asked if his opponents had the votes to depose him, he chuckled and answered, "No Way."

Burns underestimated Way's challenge. The Senate had been tolerant of Burns' conflicts of interest, in large measure because many senators had conflicts of their own. But younger senators complained that Burns hogged major legislation by referring most bills to a handful of committees dominated by lobbyists. Some senators resented this on principled grounds; others wanted a piece of the action. Way quietly put together a bipartisan coalition that included the most liberal Democrats and the most conservative Republicans and was dominated by senators known for their integrity. Without any help from the Republican governor who had campaigned for a Republican Legislature, Way nurtured his many-sided alliance and counted his votes. On May 13, 1969, Burns, wearied of the battle, impulsively called a closed caucus of the entire Senate to decide the issue. Way won with the minimal majority of twenty-one votes. His supporters included thirteen Republicans and eight Democrats.*

Way wanted to liberate the Senate from the domination of the lobbyists but was undone by his virtues. His biggest mistake was generosity. Burns, then sixty-six, had served in the Legislature since 1936, and Way did not want to humiliate him. After he won, Way gave Burns a conso-

---

*Way informed the governor's office after his victory that Sturgeon was unacceptable to him as Reagan's liaison to the State Senate. Sturgeon stepped aside, and Reagan appointed him to a vacancy on the state Public Utilities Commission. George Steffes, who had been liaison to the Assembly, took over as liaison to both houses.

lation prize of chairmanship of the Senate Agriculture Committee. To do this, he removed Fred Marler, the Republican chairman, who had voted for Way against Burns. Marler never forgave Way, and Burns did not reciprocate Way's kindness. Way's unsteady coalition could not withstand such blunders. On February 10, 1970, the Senate old guard struck back in a counter-coup led by Burns and Republican Jack Schrade, one of the Third House's favorite senators. Twelve Democrats and nine Republicans voted out the surprised Way on a secret ballot and replaced him with Schrade, who promised to be a "senator's senator."[9] That night, the lobbyists celebrated with the victors.

The Senate was in too much turmoil in 1969 and much of 1970 to grapple with the major items on Reagan's legislative agenda. This turned out to be of less consequence than it seemed at the time because Reagan could not even get his program out of the Republican-controlled Assembly. Reagan's top priority in 1969 was property tax relief for homeowners, who were suffering from spiraling increases in local property taxes and assessments. This relief was a key feature of omnibus tax legislation introduced on the governor's behalf by Craig Biddle, the Assembly majority leader. The measure included unpopular remnants that had been discarded from Reagan's 1967 tax proposal, among them the tax on services that was widely known as the "shoeshine tax." It also included an oddball provision for "voluntary withholding" of state income taxes, which was as far as Reagan was willing to go on the issue. This idea was a non-starter. It would have been costly for businesses, which would have been required to do separate bookkeeping for employees who withheld and those who didn't. And it would not have solved the state's cash flow problem, since no one knew how many people would opt for voluntary withholding.

In contrast, property tax relief had broad support. It was seen as necessary by Reagan, as well as by Unruh and Monagan, not to mention elderly Californians who were in some cases literally being taxed out of their homes by increases in local assessments. But the political attractiveness of such relief worked against its enactment, for much the same reason as the popularity of adding prescription-drug coverage to Medicare would delay its enactment by Congress early in the twenty-first century. In the late 1960s and early 1970s, nearly every politician of note in California wanted to take credit for property tax relief. They consequently proposed a variety of plans rather than uniting behind one of them. All of the proposals carried a hefty price tag since providing property tax relief within the confines of a balanced budget meant raising other taxes or reducing services.

Despite these difficulties, and even with an election in the offing, it is conceivable that Reagan and Unruh, now the minority leader, might have reached a compromise if Republicans had been united. They were not. Although Assembly Speaker Monagan faced no challenge to his leadership as Way did in the Senate, Assembly Republicans were all over the map on property tax relief and other issues. George Steffes, the Reagan legislative liaison, was invited by Monagan to attend the GOP caucuses in the Assembly. He was amazed at what he found. "Everyone had his own tax bill, everyone wanted to be governor," Steffes said. "They all talked at once and never agreed on anything."[10]

The problem was that the Republicans had been so long in the minority that they were more adept at opposition than they were at governance. Democrats had controlled the Assembly since 1958, which meant that most Republican members had never been part of a majority. GOP old-timers remembered what it was like, but they had been in the majority during the cross-filing era when the Legislature was less partisan. Monagan could not line up the GOP caucus behind a single plan for property tax relief, let alone control the Assembly. Five separate major tax bills, four of which provided for noteworthy property tax relief, were introduced in the Assembly in 1969. None made it to the Senate.

Reagan, still seen as standoffish by many legislators, was in a typical reactive mode. He never called in warring members of his party in an attempt to forge a consensus on a tax package, and Steffes is probably right in saying that Reagan would have been unsuccessful if he had tried. In the only two years of Reagan's governorship that Republicans had control of the Legislature, the Senate was too unstable and the Assembly too divided for major legislative accomplishment.

In these difficult political circumstances, Reagan and the Legislature acted on issues that cut across party lines or took refuge in small accomplishments. The first category included legislation imposing stronger pollution controls on automobiles than either the auto industry or the federal government desired. The second included a mild bill aimed at restricting legislative conflicts of interest, essentially a response to the alarms sounded by Senator Way and others about excessive lobbyist influence. And with state revenues rapidly accumulating because of the 1967 tax bill, the Legislature passed a measure by Senator George Deukmejian providing a one-time state income tax reduction of $87 million through a 10 percent tax credit. In this case, the Republican majority stood firm and turned back a Democratic attempt to use the money for schools. Reagan wanted the money returned as an across-the-board reduction but compromised with the Legislature on a cap that limited refunds to $200 for a joint return and $100 for a single taxpayer.

Most of what Reagan achieved during the last two years of his first term, however, was done through executive rather than legislative action. These were the years when he cracked down on campus disorders, stopped the Dos Rios dam, and waged a backdoor battle against the Nixon administration's most liberal initiatives, notably the Family Assistance Plan of 1969, which would have expanded federal-state welfare programs for the poor. It was also the only period in Reagan's political career when he enjoyed a respite from the national spotlight. Prior to Nixon's nomination in 1968, Reagan could not get through a press conference without being asked if he was seeking the presidency. This speculation would resurface in 1973, as Nixon's fortunes fell steadily during the Watergate investigations. But Reagan was largely off the national screen in 1969 and 1970.

He never fretted about this turn of events. Reagan was his mother's son—whatever happened was part of God's plan. Although Reagan remained a draw at party fund-raisers, he gave fewer national speeches than early in his governorship and spent more weekends with his family, most of them in Pacific Palisades but some of them in Sacramento.

All the while, he remained the lifeguard who from habit kept his eye on the water. On one Sunday (June 15, 1969), the Reagans held a family picnic for his staff in the backyard of their home in east Sacramento. Reagan was chatting with an aide when he abruptly broke off the discussion and dived fully clothed into a crowded swimming pool to rescue Alicia Berry, the seven-year-old daughter of a file clerk who worked in the governor's office. The child, one of about thirty youngsters playing in or around the pool, was on a raft in four feet of water when it tipped over. Her mother said her daughter did not know how to swim and "swallowed quite a bit water" before Reagan reached her. Another staff member told me the next day what Reagan had done, and I asked him about it. He downplayed the incident, saying, "The water wasn't over my head; it was over hers." But Reagan had a lifeguard's insight into how people drown. "You learn as a lifeguard that you never wait for excitement because there never is any," he said. "Usually it happens so quickly that no one knows what is going on."[11]

.   .   .

Reagan began the election year of 1970 with a new state finance director, Caspar Weinberger having departed to become director of the Federal Trade Commission at the request of President Nixon. Weinberger was succeeded by Verne Orr, a Holmes Tuttle protégé who had performed capably in the low-visibility post of state director of motor vehicles.

Weinberger, in nearly two years of service, had stabilized an office that was in shambles when he took over and effectively managed the budget process. But he also had alienated legislators, who found him too high-handed and unwilling to compromise. This foreshadowed complaints that members of Congress would make when Weinberger was President Reagan's secretary of defense in the 1980s and resistant to even minor reductions in military spending. In both cases, Weinberger stood his ground.

He did not, however, stand up to Reagan. Weinberger had entered the governor's administration under the cloud (with the Kitchen Cabinet, at least) of being a liberal who had supported Nelson Rockefeller. He lived down this reputation by becoming a Reagan cheerleader. Weinberger could be counted upon to give good advice, especially on environmental issues, when Reagan was genuinely undecided. But he disappointed other staff members and Republican legislators, including Assembly Speaker Monagan, by refusing to talk candidly with the governor about state income tax withholding.

Orr, soft-spoken and unknown to the public, lacked Weinberger's extensive background in government but brought other assets to the job. He was gregarious by nature and often had a drink at the end of the day with key Republican legislators, notably Assemblyman Bill Bagley, the chairman of the Assembly Finance Committee. Bagley, a bright and liberal Republican who held himself in high regard, enjoyed baiting Reagan and did not get along well with Weinberger. He liked Orr, who with the help of Monagan enlisted Bagley to carry the administration's fiscal program in 1970.

During the first three years of his governorship, Reagan had been at odds with Assembly leaders, Republicans and Democrats alike, on the withholding issue. Reagan was opposed to withholding because he was convinced that the Legislature would find it easier to increase state income taxes if they were extracted from weekly paychecks in small amounts rather than paid in a lump sum. By 1970, however, the need for withholding had become overwhelming. Each year the state borrowed heavily to cover revenue shortfalls before the lump-sum tax payments were collected. Orr thought this a senseless business practice and decided to make the case for withholding to the governor.[12]

A decision was needed before the state budget was presented in February. So in the first week of January 1970, which was also his first week on the job, Orr asked Meese if he could make a presentation to Reagan and the full cabinet. Meese set up the meeting. Cabinet meetings were then being rotated among different agencies; this one was held at the Department of Agriculture. Orr had prepared elaborate charts on butcher paper to demonstrate the state revenue problems created by the absence of withholding. State Controller Houston Flournoy supported Orr. Reagan, tight-lipped, was impressed with Orr's presentation but wanted to know why no one had told him of the severity of the revenue shortfall. After an uncomfortable silence, the governor answered his own question. "You mean it's like the emperor's clothes," he said.[13]

Afterward, legislative liaison George Steffes met with Reagan in his office to discuss pending bills. Reagan, still simmering from the cabinet meeting, asked Steffes why no one had explained to him before how much the state was suffering from the absence of withholding. "Because Cap told you what you wanted to hear," Steffes replied.[14] Reagan threw his glasses down on the table in anger. It was never easy for Reagan to abandon a cherished position, but in this case he did. "The facts and Verne Orr changed Reagan's mind," Steffes said.[15]*

Reagan unveiled the budget, with income tax withholding included, at a press conference on February 4. When a reporter noted that Reagan had often said his feet were in concrete in opposition to withholding, he replied with a wry smile, "The sound you hear is the concrete cracking around my feet."

By now, the governor and Republican legislative leaders were also on the same page on property tax relief and other issues on which they had competed in 1969. The most noteworthy feature of Reagan's 1970 fiscal program, soon introduced in two bills by Assemblyman Bagley, would have given homeowners a property tax exemption of $1,000 plus 20 percent of the assessed value of their homes. Bagley estimated it would have decreased property taxes by an average of 27 percent.

Democrats, who had been battering Reagan on withholding for three years, couldn't take yes for an answer when he agreed to it. For one thing, they didn't want to ease Reagan's budget problems in an election year. For another, public employee unions and the California Teachers Association, mainstays of Democratic support, objected to other features of Reagan's fiscal program. They particularly disliked a provision that would have imposed spending controls on local governments to ensure that property taxes were lowered.

Tax legislation is always problematic in an election year, but Reagan's 1970 plan would have become law except for California's burdensome requirement of a two-thirds majority for any bill with a fiscal impact.

---

*Meese told me that Reagan never changed his mind on withholding but agreed to it because he realized that a majority of Californians wanted it.[16] The problem with this argument is that Reagan held out against withholding long after the people favored it. In 1967, public opinion, as recorded in the Field Poll, showed a nearly even division on the issue. By January 1968, the poll found that 55 percent of respondents favored withholding compared to 37 percent who were opposed.

Since a sprinkling of Democrats in both houses favored Reagan's plan, the Bagley bills easily would have carried the day in most states, where only a simple majority is needed. Even with the two-thirds requirement, Reagan made the outcome close.

Reagan's principal assets, as governor and as president, were his communicative skills and his willingness to invest his popularity in causes to which he was committed. After Assembly Democrats held up the Bagley bills in May, the governor announced he would enter the districts of members who refused to vote for the measures and campaign against them. This threat, coupled with Republican solidarity, produced enough Democratic defections to send the bills to the Senate. There, the legislation stalled until July 28, when Republican leader Schrade called up the principal Bagley bill for a vote.

Schrade faced a difficult task. With the two-thirds requirement, he needed 27 of the 40 senators. One seat was vacant because a Republican senator had been elected to Congress, leaving Republicans with a slim 20–19 majority. If every Republican voted for the bill, Schrade needed 7 Democrats. He managed to get them, with help from the governor's office, but he failed to deliver one Republican. The holdout was Senator Clark Bradley of San Jose, a fiscal conservative who was opposed to withholding. There were senators who could be induced to vote for legislation with promises of judgeships or other favors, but Bradley was not among them. Honest and stubborn, he refused to budge. The vote in favor of the bill was 26–13, one less than the majority required.

With the session drawing to an end, Schrade waited until Republican Dennis Carpenter, a Reagan supporter, was elected on August 18 to fill the Senate vacancy. Carpenter would have provided the twenty-seventh vote except that Senator Tom Carrell of Los Angeles, a Democrat who had voted for the bills in July, was recuperating from a heart attack. Bagley and Schrade suggested flying Carrell to Sacramento in a hospital plane. Carrell was willing, but Reagan called Carrell's wife and then his doctor and decided against it. The governor made a humane decision rather than a political one, and it cost him his tax plan. On August 20, the Senate voted again on the first and most important of the Bagley bills. Once more, it failed by a single vote.[17]

Reagan was philosophical in defeat. He assumed he would win another term as governor and have another chance to reduce property taxes. That is the way it happened, but few politicians would have been similarly sanguine. Reagan, however, almost never second-guessed himself. One of his most appealing attributes was his willingness to ignore defeats and focus on the battle ahead. This cheery persistence would carry him to the White House, but his strategists didn't know that in the summer of 1970. Tom Reed, who was running the reelection campaign, wasn't even certain that the governor could defeat Unruh.

On the face of it, Reagan's reelection seemed no contest. When the respected Field Poll surveyed the principal candidates in a November 1969 trial heat, Reagan was favored by 53 percent of voters compared to 34 percent for Unruh. A private poll taken for Reagan showed a similar result. It was not surprising that Unruh was such an underdog, for he entered the campaign with obvious handicaps. Unruh had never run statewide, and his political career had stamped him as a wheeler-dealer. He had lost 100 pounds (and dropped the last "e" from his name to become "Jess" Unruh), but the stories about his dieting achievements invariably pointed out that he used to be known as "Big Daddy" and described how he once kept the Assembly under lock and key in an effort to get his own way. Unruh also had accumulated enemies within his own party, some of whom still blamed him for undermining Pat Brown. Despite his fund-raising prowess, he had less money than Reagan and was no match for him on television. Outside his own circle, Unruh was given little chance. But as Reed and Stu Spencer realized, this had been true of Reagan in 1966.

Unruh declared his candidacy on December 4, 1969, hoping through an early announcement to discourage any serious competition in the Democratic primary. San Francisco Mayor Joseph Alioto, who seemed formidable at the time, stayed out of the race, but Los Angeles Mayor Sam Yorty once again sought the Democratic nomination.[18] Unruh wisely ignored Yorty and defeated him by a 2–1 margin in the June 2, 1970, primary election. But Yorty's presence in the race required the Unruh campaign to spend money that would be needed in the fall.

Reagan waited until March 10 to declare that he was seeking reelection, acknowledging to Californians in a 15-minute film that the announcement "will come as no great surprise to any of you." The only surprise was that Reagan had decided to run as a team with Lieutenant Governor Reinecke, who also appeared in the film. This was a boon to Reinecke, who was barely known to voters. The filmed announcement reprised Reagan's 1970 State of the State Address in which he pointed with pride to passage of "the toughest air and water quality control laws in history," viewed with alarm the "physical and mental destruction of our young people" with drugs, and promised, without specifics, to work for welfare reform in his second term. After making his announcement in Sacramento, Reagan flew to Ontario to campaign in the Southern California counties of San Bernardino and Riverside, which he had won handily in 1966. Martin Smith of *The Sacramento Bee* observed that Reagan looked "a little older in appearance and more relaxed in campaign style than he was four years ago as a novice citizen-politician."[19]

Reagan was indeed relaxed. The same could not be said of his political strategists, who, unknown to the press, were fighting among themselves for control of the campaign. At the center of the storm was Bill Roberts, the senior member of the Spencer-Roberts consulting firm that had performed so brilliantly in 1966 and had a contract to run the 1970 campaign. But Roberts and his partner Stu Spencer had become disenchanted with Reagan's staff in Sacramento, whom they accused of bad-mouthing them and referring potential clients to other firms.[20]

Tom Reed, the Republican national committeeman who had been the initiating force in Reagan's abortive 1968 presidential campaign, was not involved in this controversy but had differences with Roberts. In the spring of 1970, Roberts was often missing in action from strategy sessions at Reagan campaign headquarters at 1250 Western Avenue in Los Angeles. Reed saw the election as an opportunity for the Republican Party in California. Democrats had controlled the governorship and the Legislature in 1961 and used their advantage to draw favorable congressional and legislative districts on the basis of the 1960 census. If the Republicans could hold the Legislature while Reagan was reelected, they would be able to redraw these districts after the 1970 census. Reed scheduled a series of meetings with candidates and their managers so the Republicans could plan unified campaigns. Roberts didn't attend. He was nowhere to be found.[21]

Spencer was cognizant of his partner's problems. Spencer-Roberts was spread thin with candidates in several western states, including Hawaii, which Roberts visited at every opportunity. But there was more to it than that. Spencer realized, as Reed didn't because Roberts never told him, that his partner had diabetes and other medical problems and had become severely depressed.* "Bill was a basket case around the office," Spencer said, which was one of the reasons for Roberts' increasing absences.[22]

The blowup that forced a change in campaign management came on June 18, when Reed confronted Roberts unexpectedly at the airport as he returned from a three-day visit to Honolulu. Reed insisted that he go directly from the airport to a campaign meeting. Roberts said he had a dinner engagement and refused. There was a shouting match. Roberts appealed to Spencer for help. Spencer called Reed, who told him that Roberts could no longer manage the campaign.[23]

---

*Roberts and Spencer dissolved their partnership in 1973. Spencer paid for the right to continue using "Spencer-Roberts" as the name of the firm. The two men remained good friends until Roberts' death on June 30, 1988.

The situation, as Spencer realized, was "out of control" and required prompt intervention from Holmes Tuttle, leader of the Kitchen Cabinet. Tuttle, in addition to being Reagan's premium fund-raiser, was the ultimate arbiter in these kinds of crises. He had the trust of all parties, including the governor. Spencer acknowledged that there were problems with Roberts but told him it would look bad if the firm was removed from the campaign. Tuttle agreed, conferred briefly with Reagan, and brokered a face-saving arrangement. Reed would manage the Reagan campaign with strategic advice from Spencer. Roberts would join the campaign of Reagan's old pal, Senator George Murphy, who faced a stiff challenge for reelection from John Tunney, a House member from Riverside and son of the famous heavyweight boxing champion. The deal was a good one for Reagan, who had been largely unaware of the friction within his campaign team until Tuttle called him. Spencer and Reed got along well. "I enjoyed working with him because he would make things happen," Spencer said. "Tom enjoyed me because I kept him from making mistakes."[24]

While the Reagan campaign sorted itself out, the mood of America was changing. On April 22, 1970, the first Earth Day attracted public attention and support, ratifying the wisdom of Reagan's emphasis on environmental issues in his State of the State Address and campaign announcement. Then, on April 30, President Nixon announced that U.S. troops had entered Cambodia to attack bases that North Vietnamese troops were using as a sanctuary for attacks in South Vietnam. As invasions go (Nixon called it an "incursion"), the operation was small, but the impact on the American home front was immense. Two hundred State Department employees and four members of Henry Kissinger's staff resigned in protest. Demonstrations erupted on hundreds of campuses, and 100,000 demonstrators, many of them students, marched on Washington.

On May 4, inexperienced National Guardsmen called in by Ohio Governor James Rhodes opened fire on peaceful young demonstrators at Kent State University, killing four of them.[25] Kent State changed attitudes. Polls taken for the Reagan campaign by Richard Wirthlin's firm of Decision Making Information (DMI) showed that Americans were shocked by the shootings. "Kent State really flipped the switch," said Reed. "The parents of America said, 'Hey, that's our own kids getting killed.'"[26] Before Kent State, even Reagan was viewed as "sort of squishy soft on campus radicals."[27] Afterward, voters became more tolerant of peaceful student protests—or at least more critical of politicians who attempted to exploit them.

Reagan was potentially vulnerable to this change in public opinion.

Kent State occurred less than a month after Reagan, in the wake of the Isla Vista violence, had denounced campus radicals by saying, "If it takes a bloodbath, let's get it over with. No more appeasement." Sensing an opportunity, Unruh claimed that Reagan had "forfeited any right to hold public office."[28] Spencer and Reed laughed off Unruh's hyperbole, but they didn't want to hear any more provocative statements from their candidate. Reagan went along. He was a disciplined campaigner who recognized the change in public mood.

The mood was changing in other ways, too. As the economy faltered and inflation increased, Democrats in many states began returning home to their party. Democratic registration was up in California. The California electorate was 55 percent Democratic and 40 percent Republican, with the other 5 percent divided among minor parties and voters who declined to state a partisan affiliation.

The first priority of Reagan and his strategists was to bring Republicans together. Reagan was a party unifier by inclination; he realized that the deep wounds caused by the 1964 Goldwater-Rockefeller presidential primary had been reopened by the Rafferty-Kuchel contest in the 1968 Senate primary. The ultraconservative Rafferty was on the ballot in 1970, too, seeking reelection as state superintendent of public instruction against Wilson Riles, a moderate Democrat. Knowing that an endorsement of Rafferty would offend Republican moderates, Reagan stayed out of the race on the grounds that the superintendent's post was nonpartisan. This neutrality opened the door to a determined effort by Reed, with back-channel help from Holmes Tuttle, to get former Senator Kuchel on board the Reagan reelection train. For disenchanted Republican moderates, Kuchel was the key.

Kuchel and Reagan did not like each other. In 1962, Reagan had served as campaign chairman for Loyd Wright, a right-winger who challenged Kuchel ineffectually in the Republican primary. In 1968, Reagan sat on the sidelines while Rafferty waged a nasty campaign and defeated Kuchel. But Kuchel was a party man, and Reagan knew the importance of party unity. On August 26, the Reagans invited the Kuchels for dinner at a Malibu beach house they had rented for the campaign. Reagan turned on the charm, paid tribute to Kuchel's public service, and asked for his support. Reed followed up the next day with a two-hour meeting with Kuchel in his Beverly Hills law office.[29] Kuchel came around, endorsing Reagan on September 2 in a statement that was well covered in the press. The endorsement stamped Reagan as the candidate of the entire Republican Party, not just its conservative wing.

Unruh had more difficulty in overcoming lingering resentments within his party. Most Democrats supported him, but some elements of organized labor, cheered on behind the scenes by Spencer, refused to forgive Unruh for what they regarded as his sabotage of Pat Brown's programs in the Legislature. These labor leaders, including the influential Joseph T. DeSilva, head of the 25,000-member Retail Clerks 770 in Los Angeles, organized a labor committee for Reagan. The Reagan fund-raising operation also stroked former business contributors to Brown, convincing some of them to donate to the Reagan campaign. Reagan didn't need the money, but Reed saw to it that stories about defections were given to the papers, fostering the impression that a bipartisan consensus was building for the governor.

There was little Unruh could do about this. He lacked the resources of the governor, and from beginning to end, as John Van de Kamp put it, "campaigned on the cheap."[30] Van de Kamp, a Los Angeles lawyer who later became state attorney general, advised Unruh early in the campaign, then left for Washington. Unruh put Phil Schott, his administrative assistant in Sacramento, in charge of the campaign. Schott was capable and focused, but he was only thirty years old and inexperienced in statewide politics.

On overall strategy, Unruh served as his own campaign manager. His theme, which he enunciated in his declaration of candidacy, was that California under Reagan was run by a "handful of half-hidden millionaires," by which he meant the governor's wealthy contributors in the Kitchen Cabinet. What this populist message lacked in accuracy, it made up in purpose. Unruh knew he was not a physically attractive candidate, especially in comparison to Reagan. His hope of winning rested in making the contest a test between Democrats as the "party of the people" and Republicans as the "party of the rich" who were using Reagan as their tool. This was a tough sell, but Unruh thought it was the best strategy for winning back the blue-collar Democrats who had deserted Brown in 1966.

Exhibit A in Unruh's argument that Reagan's policies favored the wealthy was the 1970 property tax relief bill, which provided larger breaks to higher-income Californians than to those in lower tax brackets. But the tax bill had died in the Senate, and most voters had only a vague idea of what it would have done. Unruh decided to dramatize the issue.

California political campaigns traditionally begin on Labor Day, which on September 7, 1970, dawned bright and sunny in Los Angeles. Unruh's campaign, as *Los Angeles Times* reporter Richard Bergholz put it, got off to a "slam-bang start." Up early, Unruh stood outside the Bel-Air mansion of Henry Salvatori, a prominent member of the Kitchen Cabinet. Two busloads of reporters filled the narrow street, listening to

Unruh explain that Salvatori would have received $4,113 in property tax relief from the governor's tax bill. Salvatori's house was assessed at $700,000, Unruh said. He claimed that every renter in the state with an annual income of $8,000 or less would have paid $25 to the "Henry Salvatori tax relief fund."

Unruh, who believed the Salvatoris were away for the day, intended to use their home as a television backdrop for his message. But Unruh's advance team had goofed. The Salvatoris were home. Tipped off by a neighbor, an angry Grace Salvatori awaited Unruh's arrival behind a closed iron gate. Soon she was joined by her husband, in tennis garb, who refused Unruh's proffered hand through the gate and said, "Is this the way you have to get your publicity? You have to get it at a private home? It's the most ridiculous campaign trick."

The Salvatoris then came outside the gate while Unruh, with charts and easel, delivered his pitch in the driveway. When Unruh brought up the $4,113 "tax break," Salvatori interrupted, "Oh, you ass you, stop being so silly." When Unruh mentioned the "Henry Salvatori tax relief fund," the industrialist looked squarely at him and said scornfully, "You're a liar, Mr. Unruh." Grace Salvatori joined the fray, outshouting the men. "We worked for the money to pay for it," she said of the house. "We pay taxes, and we support every university in this state, practically." In response to Unruh's charge that he benefited from tax loopholes, Henry Salvatori told reporters: "I have no tax loopholes. I earned my money. If he's trying to imply that I supported Reagan to get a $4,000 tax relief, he's stupid."[31]

Unruh eventually retreated. That night his staff members were excited because, as one young aide said, "We had made the national news." He had indeed. His home invasion was the lead story in the *Los Angeles Times* and most other California newspapers. It made *The Washington Post* and played on national television, and Unruh never quite recovered from the impact. In a single stroke, he had revived the image of "Big Daddy," the domineering political bully who had no respect for the rights of others. "It put us in a deep hole," said Schott.[32]*

California's traditional populists, beginning with Hiram Johnson, had demonized business "special interests" by depicting them as monster, depersonalized corporations. Unruh had unwittingly done the opposite and personalized the forces he was supposed to be depersonal-

---

*Two Unruh aides told me that Unruh had been told the Salvatoris were away. Schott, interviewed thirty-three years later, did not remember this but faulted the advance team for failing to examine the layout of the street on which the Salvatoris lived. "We didn't know until we reached the home that this was a street with no outlet," Schott said. "We thought of turning back but couldn't—we were trapped."[33]

izing. Californians value their holidays and their privacy and identified with the nice-looking elderly couple whose castle Unruh had invaded on a holiday. Rarely has any campaign been launched with such a self-inflicted wound.

More were to come. Unruh's companion strategy was to force Reagan, who had been ignoring him, into a debate. He believed he could show up the governor in a face-to-face confrontation despite Reagan's demonstrated skills on television. Spencer and Reed recognized that this was a possibility, and they were not about to give Unruh this chance.

The day after the Salvatori affair, Unruh went off in pursuit of Reagan, armed with the governor's schedule. First, he searched for him at the San Jose Airport but missed him. The next day, Unruh changed his own schedule so he could picket the Reagan residence in Sacramento. Unlike the Salvatoris, Reagan was away, campaigning in Southern California, where he told reporters that he had an opponent who "paid house calls." Unruh was rapidly becoming a laughingstock. Late in the week, he blundered again, saying that an appointee of Reagan's was being rewarded for work his father had done in the 1968 Reagan presidential campaign. This time Unruh had to apologize. The Reagan appointee's father had been dead for ten years.

Reagan used Unruh's tactics as an alibi for avoiding a debate he had already rejected. "One thing my opponent has done is make it clear I was right in refusing to debate him," Reagan told reporters in Santa Rosa on September 9. "His idea of debate obviously is cheap demagoguery." Reagan also refused to disclose his assets, as Unruh had done, saying this would be "an invasion of privacy" and adding, "I have no conflict of interest whatsoever."

In his 1966 campaign for governor, and in all his campaigns for president, Reagan was slow off the mark. In 1970, he benefited from letting his opponent make the first moves. One of the unintended consequences of Unruh's shaky beginning was that it instilled a high level of confidence in the governor. In the early weeks of his campaign, Reagan was a safe, front-running candidate defending his record before safe, friendly crowds with safe, defensible statements. Always most comfortable in his self-defined role of citizen-politician, Reagan campaigned as if he were going to Sacramento to clean up a mess someone else had left behind. "Welfare," said Reagan repeatedly, "is the greatest domestic problem facing the nation today and the reason for the high cost of government."

Reagan's managers—and Nancy Reagan—remembered the lessons of the first campaign and saw to it that the governor had plenty of rest.

Because he was both rested and confident, reporters who covered Reagan in 1966 found him more polished the second time around. When pickets showed up in Modesto bearing a sign, "Get Lost Ronnie," Reagan gave a good account of himself. "In 1966 the novice Reagan would have given them a dirty look, waved shyly to his supporters and then hustled into his car to get away from it all," wrote Bill Boyarsky in the *Los Angeles Times*. "Not the 1970 model Ronald Reagan. He walked directly to the fence, shook a few friendly hands and when the unfriendly people began to heckle them, he heckled them back."[34] Along with this new polish came occasional hints that the citizen-politician had learned some truths about politics. When a South Gate worker yelled at him, "When are you going to clean up politics?" Reagan answered, "Politics is far more honest than you may think."

Reagan's strategists were less confident than their candidate. The sour economy and the decline of student unrest as a salient issue worried Reed as the campaign moved into its final stages. He was running the campaign not from the light and airy public headquarters on Western Avenue but from a windowless 1,500-square-foot office five blocks away at 5119 Sunset Boulevard. Reed called it the Bomb Shelter. There he and his operatives conducted a closely monitored campaign that coordinated Richard Wirthlin's polling, Reagan's schedule, and a $2.3 million (more than $10 million in 2003 dollars) advertising budget that relied on commercials written by Rus Walton. The Reagan ads—progenitors of the stirring "Morning Again in America" commercials that President Reagan's reelection team would use in 1984—celebrated California, hyped Reagan's record as governor, and ignored Unruh. By mid-October, Wirthlin's polls showed Reagan leading Unruh by 51–39 percent.

Unruh never gave up. Recovering from his blundering beginning, he stuck to his message, trying to provoke the governor into a personal exchange. During a Watts speech, Unruh said that Reagan's millionaire backers "don't need a governor because they can buy the governor's house and probably even the governor." Unruh's television commercials, what few he had of them, were well made and expressed the same theme less stridently. His young campaign management team improved with each passing week except for the advance operation, which remained a source of embarrassment. "We were thinking of having Jesse kidnapped to create some sympathy," quipped an Unruh aide during the final week of the campaign. "But we canceled the plan because we were afraid the advance men would go to the wrong house and kidnap the wrong man."[35]

Nonetheless, Unruh gained ground as the economy worsened and Democrats began returning to the fold. On October 23, with the election eleven days away, Reagan's lead over Unruh had shrunk in the DMI trackings to 46–41 percent, a 7-point drop in a week. It was nail-biting time in the Bomb Shelter. Reed, Spencer, Wirthlin, and Walton conferred. They could see from their polls that student unrest was no longer a big issue and, at Spencer's suggestion, pulled television commercials that celebrated Reagan's restoration of "law and order" on California campuses.[36] The television time had already been purchased; the Reagan team substituted spots that stressed Reagan's support of tax relief, smog control, and other environmental issues.

This shift in strategy was accompanied by an attack on Unruh, aided by a story in the *San Francisco Examiner* that revisited his financial dealings with lobbyists. Reagan, going after his opponent by name for the first time, brought up an old charge that Unruh had misrepresented his interest in a Long Beach apartment building. This was a preplanned tactic designed to look spontaneous, but Reagan had been stung by Unruh's repeated attacks on his friends in the Kitchen Cabinet and went beyond his script. In a speech he called Unruh "a demagogue," "a hypocrite," "dishonest," and "a man who has no regard for the truth." Unruh, who had never stopped attacking Reagan, added a new fillip. Posing for a picture with a young woman on either side, Unruh recalled the homosexual scandal and said with a smile: "We used to have a saying in Sacramento in those days. Prove you're straight and take a girl to lunch."[37]

Pollster Wirthlin's daily trackings during the final week of the campaign showed that Unruh's momentum had stalled and that Reagan was leading again by 6 to 7 percentage points. There was a sigh of relief in the Bomb Shelter. But Reed couldn't wait for election day, and millions of Americans probably shared his feelings. Even by the smear-and-fear standards of Nixon-era politics, it was a raw campaign year across the nation. Vice President Spiro Agnew campaigned for the defeat of Democratic "radiclibs," his shorthand for radical liberals, in a shrill attempt to change the composition of the Senate. And in the concluding weeks of the campaign, President Nixon launched a cross-country trip in which he denounced the peace activists who heckled him as unpatriotic and obscene.

On October 29, the Thursday before the election, Nixon arrived in San Jose for a rally with Republican candidates in California. Covering the California campaign for Ridder Publications, I traveled with the Reagan entourage to San Jose to watch the rally and to join the White House press corps for the preelection weekend. Demonstrators were massing outside the civic auditorium when we arrived. Reagan and Murphy gave short, stock speeches. By the time Nixon spoke, the chants of the demonstrators could be heard within the auditorium; some were beating on the building. Nixon defended U.S. troops. "They are fighting in Vietnam so that those young men that are outside shouting their obscene slogans won't have to fight in Vietnam or anyplace any time in the future," he said.

When the rally ended, a security man escorted me to the White House press bus in the parking lot. We passed directly by the president. The demonstrators were shouting, "One, two, three, four—we don't want your fucking war." A smiling Nixon stood atop his car, giving the V-for-victory sign and goading the hecklers. I couldn't make out his words, but the next day it was reported that he said, "That's what they hate to see."[38]

Nixon, a champion hater, used the right word. William Safire, who was there, called the San Jose event "an orgy of generalized hate."[39] It was directed at anyone whom the demonstrators associated with the White House. Rocks hit the press bus in which I was riding as it left the parking lot, shattering a few windows. The shower of rocks, eggs, and bottles missed the presidential limousine, but Nixon told his press secretary, Ronald Ziegler, that he felt an egg brush by his face. Ziegler replied that a Secret Service agent said it was a rock.[40]

Nixon tried to exploit the stoning of the presidential motorcade for political advantage. At a Republican rally in Phoenix two days later, he said that Americans had "appeased aggression here at home" and created further violence. "The time has come for the great silent majority of Americans of all ages and of every political persuasion, to stand up and be counted against appeasement of the rock throwers and the obscenity shouters," he said.

Senator Murphy did not know what to make of the incident but expressed hope that it would boost his lagging campaign. Asked if it would help his election chances, Murphy replied, "I don't see how it can hurt."[41]

Reagan, composed throughout, proved more politically sure-handed than Nixon or Murphy. "Violence never helps anyone," he said before issuing his own condemnation of the rock throwers.[42]*

.   .   .

Voters rewarded Reagan with a second term as governor. He received 3,439,664 votes (52.9 percent) to Unruh's 2,938,607 votes (45.1

*Reagan also called plainclothes National Guard military policemen to active duty to protect any candidates who faced threats of violence from radical groups in the waning days of the campaign. Unruh called this "political grandstanding" and said he had not been threatened.

percent), with candidates for two minor parties receiving the other 2 percent. Reagan's margin of victory was half of what it had been over Pat Brown. Unruh did better than Brown in traditionally Democratic areas, especially in Los Angeles County. Reagan nonetheless narrowly carried the county and ran ahead of the Republican ticket in almost every Democratic working-class area. Although Unruh had done better than any other Democrat would ever do against him, Reagan still won at least 20 percent of the Democratic vote.[43]

Nationally, except for Reagan's reelection and Governor Nelson Rockefeller's unprecedented fourth-term victory in New York, Republicans had little to cheer. Republicans lost eleven governorships. Nixon's hard-edged campaign to win the Senate by questioning Democratic patriotism fell short, with Republicans posting a net gain of only two Senate seats. Republicans lost nine seats in the House.

The Republican Party also suffered setbacks in California. The most notable was John Tunney's victory in the U.S. Senate race over George Murphy. The most surprising was the defeat of Max Rafferty by Wilson Riles, an African American, in the race for state superintendent of public instruction.* And the most important was Republican loss of the Legislature. Democrats picked up three seats in the State Assembly and two in the State Senate, winning control of both houses. This result would have consequences for the next two decades, more than offsetting Republican victories for state constitutional offices. Republicans won four of five of these contests, including the lieutenant governorship. The only Democratic winner was newcomer Edmund G. ("Jerry") Brown, son of the former governor, who was elected secretary of state.

Could Unruh, given more money and a better beginning to his campaign, have defeated Reagan in 1970? It was a tantalizing question for postelection analysis. One factor that cannot be quantified is the intangible of ticket splitting, commonplace in California during the middle decades of the twentieth century. In 1964, Californians had voted for a Democratic president and a Republican senator. In 1968, they had voted for a Republican president and a Democratic senator. In 1970, they elected Reagan and Tunney. Half a million Californians, about one in twelve voters, split tickets in this way. Most of the ticket splitters were registered Democrats. To Democrats willing to split their tickets, Reagan was a more comfortable choice than Murphy, who ran a poor campaign and never recovered from revelations that he had accepted

*Riles overcame a 25-point deficit in the final month of the campaign, which pollster Mervin Field called "one of the most dramatic shifts in public opinion ever measured" by his poll. When Riles paid a courtesy visit to the governor's office after the election, he said Reagan told him, "You'd be surprised at how some of us around here voted."[44]

salary-like payments from Technicolor while in office.[45] Tunney received slightly more votes than Reagan; he won with 53.8 percent of the vote to 44.4 percent for Murphy.

It is hard to see how Unruh, after the disaster of his campaign opening, could have overcome the twin handicaps of lack of money and the California proclivity for ticket splitting. The Reagan campaign spent $3,350,549 in the primary and general election and Unruh $1,207,684. A *California Journal* computation found that Reagan spent $1.05 a vote and Unruh 42 cents. But Unruh's disadvantage was even greater than these figures indicate. He spent $300,000 to win the contested Democratic primary, while Reagan was unopposed for the Republican nomination.*

Reagan did not waste time in postelection analysis. He had conducted himself well in the campaign and had done what his strategists had asked of him. In the closing days of the campaign, Reagan had trotted out a line from the 1966 campaign, telling his supporters that "President Dewey" had warned him not to be overconfident. But I think Reagan felt assured of victory from beginning to end.

He did not, however, anticipate what he would face after the election. Reagan had slowly become accustomed to working with a Republican legislature, which he expected would be ready to pass property tax relief legislation in 1971. He had also promised action to limit California's welfare costs. Reagan meant to keep his campaign promises, but the Republicans had lost the Legislature. If Reagan were to succeed in his second term, he would have to find ways of working with a Democratic legislature that no longer counted Unruh as a member and had new leaders in each house.

---

*An analysis by Tom Reed based on postelection polls taken by Richard Wirthlin shows how difficult it would have been for Unruh to win and also demonstrates the wisdom of Spencer's suggestion to replace the "law-and-order" commercials with "soft" ads stressing the environment and tax relief. The poll shows that voters considered pollution the most important issue, followed by taxes and unemployment. Campus protest ranked eighth. Two-thirds of those who voted for Reagan liked his record or trusted him personally. A fifth of Reagan voters said they voted for him because they disliked Unruh. Half of the Unruh voters were motivated by dislike of Reagan. No Unruh voter said he voted for the Democratic candidate because of his record.[46]

23

REFORMER

OVERNOR RONALD REAGAN began his first term as a novice who
promised to "squeeze, cut, and trim" the costs of government
without having the foggiest notion of how to do it and with a
chief of staff and state finance director who knew as little as he did. As
we have seen, Reagan nonetheless muddled through with middling success. By the beginning of his second term in 1971, he was an experienced politician with an able finance director in the person of Verne
Orr and a competent chief of staff, Edwin Meese, who understood the
governor's needs. Orr and Meese knew, as did Reagan, that the last two
years of the first term had been longer on promise than accomplishment. They meant to change that in 1971.

Reagan's State of the State Address, delivered to a joint session of the
Legislature on January 12, 1971, reflected his maturation. He gave a
sober assessment of the state's fiscal problems, which were aggravated
by a national economic recession, and urged legislators to help him
solve them. Not once did he call himself a "citizen-politician." He held
out an olive branch to the University of California and pledged to work
with Wilson Riles, the new superintendent of public instruction, to improve the quality of education. He promised property tax relief, and, in
an ironic note, chided the Legislature for not accepting income tax
withholding, which Reagan had resisted for three of his first four years
as governor. After observing that the state would deal with its cash flow
problems by internal borrowing, Reagan said: "California will face re-
curring problems which would not exist if withholding had been enacted last year."

Reagan was now committed to withholding, which had been part of
the tax package that had died by one vote in the Senate the previous
summer. But his emphasis in the speech was on welfare reform, which

was crucial to a balanced budget. At the time, there were many local government officials calling for welfare reform strictly on fiscal grounds. Reagan made a broader appeal, questioning the underlying premise of welfare as President Bill Clinton would do a generation later. In Reagan's case, this meant recycling one of his favorite quotations from his first political icon, Franklin Delano Roosevelt, who in 1935 had called government relief "a narcotic, a subtle destroyer of the human spirit." In Reagan's view, welfare was as harmful to those who received it as it was to the taxpayer. "Our goal must be to reform and restructure the entire welfare system," Reagan said.

Reagan had promised welfare reform in his reelection campaign, and Meese had gone to work on it even earlier. On August 4, 1970, a confidential memo drafted by Meese was sent under Reagan's name to members of the governor's cabinet and senior staff. Announcing a study of the state's public assistance and education programs, the memo said: "This study will place heavy emphasis on the tax-payer as opposed to the tax-taker; on the truly needy as opposed to the lazy unemployable; on the student as opposed to educational frills; on basic needs as opposed to unmanageable enrichment programs; on measurable results as opposed to blind faith that an educator can do no wrong."[1] The memo sought recommendations for administrative action and legislation and for pinpointing problems with federal and local governments. "I am determined to reduce these programs to essential services at a cost the taxpayers can afford to pay," the memo concluded. "This is our NUMBER ONE priority. We must bring all our resources to bear on this endeavor. Therefore, I am asking you to make available your best employees including directors for this all-out war on the tax-taker. If we fail, no one ever again will be able to try. We must succeed."[2]

This call to action vaguely echoed the peroration of Reagan's "Time for Choosing" speech for Barry Goldwater in 1964. ("If we fail, at least let our children, and our children's children, say of us we justified our brief moment here.") Unlike that jeremiad, however, when Reagan warned of a gloomy descent into a "thousand years of darkness," he was now sermonizing in a major key. Reagan was determined to reform welfare, not just deplore it. The August memo was the first step in what became a focused effort. The second step was appointment of a task force of state officials and private citizens headed by Ned Hutchinson, who had succeeded Paul Haerle as the governor's appointments secretary. It reviewed welfare issues, concentrating on the costly and much-maligned program known as Aid to Families with Dependent Children (AFDC). Unless AFDC was curbed, the task force and Verne Orr agreed, a huge tax increase would be necessary in fiscal 1972.

AFDC had begun as a minor section of the Social Security Act of 1935. It was designed to strengthen "mothers' pensions," which were state programs to support children whose fathers were disabled or had abandoned their families. The federal government shared the costs, but Congress left the determination of benefits to the states. Benefits were highest in states with a tradition of social legislation, such as California and New York, but they had not kept pace with inflation. Although it was a mantra of liberal Democrats that Reagan lacked compassion for the needy, California had not raised AFDC grants a penny during Pat Brown's eight years as governor, during six of which the Democrats also controlled the Legislature. The grants hadn't been raised in Reagan's first four years, either. As a result, AFDC recipients had suffered a huge decline in real income since their last increase in 1957, which had been approved by a Republican-dominated Legislature and signed into law by a Republican governor.[3] The State Department of Welfare determined in 1971 that the minimum monthly income required for a subsistence existence by a family of three in San Francisco was $271. The maximum such an AFDC family could receive was $172.

These were not the figures that Reagan emphasized, although he did take them into account in designing his welfare plan. What alarmed the governor and his aides was a surge in AFDC caseload. In 1963, there were 375,000 AFDC recipients in California. When Reagan took office in 1967, the number had doubled to 769,000. By December 1969, the AFDC rolls listed 1,150,687. A year later, a month after Reagan's re-election, there were 1,566,000 people on the AFDC rolls—nearly one out of every thirteen Californians. Caseload was increasing by 40,000 a month, and Orr warned that a continued increase of this magnitude would bust the budget in 1972. Reagan conceded after the election that the deepening recession had contributed to the problem. "But the big villain . . . that has kept virtually all of our savings from being returned to the people in reduced cost of government is the thirty-five-year heritage of welfare programs that are out of control," Reagan said in a December 16, 1970, interview with *California Journal*. "And we find ourselves in a position of cutting back on the type of things people should ask of government—parks and everything else—actually cutting those to feed this welfare monster."

The appetite of this "monster" grew during the first two months of 1971 as the task force completed its recommendations. Robert B. Carleson, the state welfare director, and Meese felt a sense of urgency. Reagan joined them and Earl Brian, director of the State Health and Welfare Agency, in formulating the legislation that evolved into the California Welfare Reform Act. This was a departure from the first term, when Reagan had been content to set the tone and leave the details of legislation to aides.

Reagan planned to unveil his proposals before a joint session of the Legislature. But James Mills, the president pro tem of the Senate, and Assembly Speaker Robert (Bob) Moretti, the new Democratic leaders of the Legislature, took the unprecedented step of denying the request. Their weak rationale for this rejection was that the governor was making only general proposals that had not yet been incorporated into a bill. The real reason was that Mills and Moretti realized that welfare was a potent issue and they didn't want to give Reagan a platform. But their clumsy strategy gave the governor an excuse to go over the heads of the Legislature.

Reagan made the most of this opportunity. He sent his welfare-reform proposals in writing to the Legislature and presented them in person on March 3 at Town Hall, a luncheon group in Los Angeles. The event was billed as "the speech the Legislature didn't want to hear" and attracted more television coverage than Reagan would have received had he been permitted to speak to the Legislature. Reagan began with a typical quip. He said he had been asked if his honeymoon with the Democratic-controlled Legislature was over. "I'm not sure it ever started," he said. "On the wedding night someone said something about stepping into the next room to slip into something comfortable—and they never came back."[4]

The governor's welfare plan, most of it culled from recommendations of the Hutchinson task force, called for seventy legislative and administrative changes and was described by Reagan as the "lengthiest, most detailed and specific legislative proposal ever originated by a California governor." In presenting it, Reagan reiterated his usual condemnation of the welfare system but for the first time also acknowledged that welfare recipients were underpaid. He said:

> The crisis in Welfare and Medi-Cal [the California version of Medicaid] presents a challenge to all Californians. We simply cannot sit idly by and do nothing to prevent an uncontrolled upward spiraling of the welfare caseload, as most other states and the federal government appear resigned to do. The whole system itself is about to collapse, nationwide, from the burden it is placing on the taxpayer each year. . . .
>
> Additionally, the system does not adequately provide for the truly needy. Virtually everywhere in California the truly needy are barely subsisting, many below the poverty line, while thousands of the less needy with other sources of income and various exemptions and disregards are getting a disproportionate share of the available money.

The four goals of the Reagan program were to "increase assistance to the truly needy who have nowhere else to turn to meet their basic needs," to require those who were able to work to seek a job or job training, to place Medi-Cal benefits on the same footing as health benefits for those not on the program, and to "strengthen family responsibility as the basic element in our society." The public response was favorable. Thousands of letters calling for enactment of the Reagan plan poured into legislative offices and newspapers, the latter reinforced by editorials calling for reform. Democratic legislative leaders were unmoved. Ignoring the fact that the AFDC rolls had been rising even before the economic downturn, they blamed soaring welfare caseloads on the recession. Democrats conceded that the rising caseload posed a fiscal problem for the state, but their preferred solution was a federal takeover of the system. Ironically, this was also the solution favored by the Republican president whom Democrats blamed for the recession. President Nixon, on August 8, 1969, had unveiled the Family Assistance Plan (FAP), which would have federalized the system and provided a guaranteed income for welfare recipients.

Nixon's proposal, as Steven Hayward has pointed out, had a respectable conservative pedigree going back to 1948, when Senator Robert Taft of Ohio had discussed a similar idea.[5] Milton Friedman, the icon of conservative economists who was often quoted by Reagan, also favored the idea, which he called a "negative income tax." At the time Nixon proposed FAP, there appeared to be a national welfare crisis, fueled by changes in the family structure and by congressional and judicial mandates that made access to AFDC easier. Among the latter was a 1968 U.S. Supreme Court decision that struck down residency requirements in forty states principally on grounds that they violated an American's right to travel.

Many states responded to the welfare crisis less thoughtfully than either Nixon or Reagan. In Nevada, a Democratic governor permitted house-to-house searches for nonsupporting fathers; in Kansas, benefits were cut 20 percent across the board; in New Jersey, grants were eliminated for families with unemployed fathers. Other states postponed changes, waiting to see how Congress would react to FAP, which would have raised federal costs but reduced the burden on the states.

Reagan, almost alone among prominent Republican state officeholders, opposed the Family Assistance Plan. He testified against it before a U.S. Senate committee that was holding hearings in the summer of 1970. That December, in a television debate, he challenged the idea of a guaranteed income. "I believe that the government is supposed to promote the general welfare," Reagan said. "I don't believe it is supposed to provide it."[6]

Although his position was clear, Reagan in early 1971 muted his criticism of the Family Assistance Plan because he wanted help from the Nixon administration on a related welfare issue. For two years, the federal Department of Health, Education and Welfare (HEW) had been pressuring the state of California to increase its maximum AFDC payments to reflect cost-of-living changes. Reagan thought the department was picking on California because of his opposition to the Family Assistance Plan. The villains, in Reagan's eyes, were HEW Secretary Elliot Richardson and his undersecretary, John G. Veneman, a former Republican assemblyman from California whom Robert Finch had brought to Washington.

While state welfare officials were negotiating with Veneman, the courts dealt the Reagan administration a blow. On September 10, 1970, a federal judge ruled in a lawsuit filed by the San Francisco Neighborhood Legal Assistance Foundation that the state must increase its payment schedule or lose the more than $400 million a year it received in federal funds for the AFDC program. HEW announced that these funds would be cut off on April 1, 1971, unless California complied.

With the deadline near, Reagan called Vice President Spiro Agnew, who promised to help. What he did, if anything, is not known, but HEW relented on its deadline. This bought Reagan time, but he knew that the state faced additional lawsuits unless the payments were increased. In March, he met with President Nixon in San Clemente and reached a broad agreement with the president. What Nixon wanted, and got, was Reagan's agreement to bring California into compliance with federal regulations and to soften his public denunciations of the Family Assistance Plan. What Reagan wanted, and also got, was an assurance that HEW would cooperate with a pilot program in California requiring able-bodied AFDC recipients to work for their welfare checks. On July 1, California increased its maximum payments, and a federal court ruled that retroactive payments were not required.

After the concordat with Nixon, Reagan turned his attention to the Legislature, where it was stalemate as usual. Reagan's welfare plan was buried in committee. His proposed budget, which he sought to balance by eliminating the traditional open-ended welfare appropriation, was buried with it. Democrats accused Reagan of conducting government by press release, while Republicans denounced Democrats as obstructionists who had no plan of their own. By June, the legislative session appeared headed for a train wreck. Reagan could not significantly change the welfare system without cooperation from the Democratic-controlled Legislature, which didn't have the votes to pass a bill over Reagan's veto. The Democrats couldn't shape the budget, either, for Reagan stood ready to use his line-item veto power, as he had demonstrated in every budget of his first term.

The impasse was broken by an unanticipated demonstration of leadership from Bob Moretti, the Democrat who had succeeded Bob Monagan as Assembly speaker. Moretti, brash and energetic, was a young man in a hurry, almost as if he realized that he was short of time. His father was born in Italy, and his mother was of Armenian descent. They lived in a poor section of Detroit but moved to Los Angeles while Bob Moretti was a teenager. He attended a Catholic high school and then was an honors student at Notre Dame, from which he graduated with a degree in accounting. John F. Kennedy inspired him to go into politics. Moretti and a brother attended the 1960 Democratic National Convention where Kennedy was nominated for president. "Bobby came back with hats and pennants and banners and all this excitement about Kennedy," recalled his sister, Marie Moretti. "He was hooked."[7]

For Catholic kids like Moretti, Kennedy had broken down barriers that would never be reconstructed again. Moretti, a tough-talker who sounded as if he came right off the streets, met the world with a smile on his face and a purpose in his heart. While generally liberal in politics, he had a low opinion of ideologues of any sort. Details bored him almost as much as they did Reagan. And like Reagan, he dreamed of becoming president. At the age of twenty-eight, Moretti was elected to the Assembly, where he operated on a private code of personal trust, never giving or asking for commitments in writing. Soon after he was elected, Jesse Unruh's chief of staff asked him to sign a pledge of support. Moretti refused. "If my word isn't good enough for you, to hell with you," he said.[8]

During the two years of Republican control of the Assembly in 1969 and 1970, as Unruh became preoccupied with running for governor, Moretti emerged as Reagan's most effective opponent in the Assembly. Long before the Democrats reorganized the Assembly in 1971, he had lined up the support necessary to win the speakership. But apart from the distinction of being, at thirty-four, the youngest speaker in history, Moretti had little to show for his victory. During the early months of 1971, he found himself on the short end of a running rhetorical battle with Reagan. Neither the speaker nor the governor appeared to have a clue about what to do next.

What Reagan and Moretti had in common, in addition to competitive determination, was a desire for results. Though they didn't go around quoting Voltaire, they recognized the validity of his dictum that "the best is the enemy of the good."[9] Moretti represented a middle-class district in the San Fernando Valley where his constituents had become impatient with the posturing of the Legislature and the governor. Welfare costs were out of hand, and voters wanted action.

At this point in their careers, Moretti and Reagan were blessed with aides who were willing to tell them what they needed to know. Bill Hauck, the speaker's thoughtful chief of staff, suggested to Moretti that he take the initiative. "This blasting back and forth has become debilitating to both of you," Hauck said to Moretti one day in June when the prospects for legislative action looked particularly hopeless.[10] On June 28, 1971, Hauck wrote and Moretti signed a letter to Reagan that proposed "that we set aside our personal and philosophical disagreements and work to assure the people that our state will prosper.* As we have both said publicly on a number of occasions this year, if we do not act positively on at least a few of our major state issues the people of California will properly hold us all accountable." Moretti proposed, "in the spirit of reasonable compromise and agreement," an immediate meeting with Reagan. Hauck wanted the meeting on the same day because he knew that there were those in the governor's office who would oppose it.

Downstairs in the corner office of the governor, Reagan legislative liaison George Steffes had been waiting to hear from Moretti. He and Hauck were friends, and they had explored ideas for ending the deadlock. Steffes had the tougher task in selling a summit meeting because several of Reagan's advisers, including Welfare Director Carleson, were reluctant to compromise. But Steffes knew that the governor wanted action, and he believed that Moretti was also serious, in part because the speaker wanted to establish a record on which he could run for governor.[12] Soon after Steffes received the letter, he called Hauck and asked him when Moretti would release it to the press. "We're not," Hauck told him. "He wants to get something started and the condition for starting it is that the two of them meet alone with no one there."[13] Steffes said he would get back to him.

Moretti wasn't sure that Reagan would respond. He had a low opinion of Reagan and believed that the governor felt the same way about him. "I shared an image of him as a pitch man who was a good communicator, who was more interested in selling himself and his administration than he was in accomplishment," Moretti said. "We knew how powerful he was when he was on the media, that he did have a good way of persuading people. We thought that he either exaggerated or stressed

---

*Meese kept a copy of the letter. The words "work to assure the people that our state will prosper" are underlined in pen, apparently by Meese.[11]

unimportant points to get something across. But he was the governor, and it was get together or do nothing."[14]

In the governor's office, there was never a debate about whether Reagan should respond positively to Moretti's overture. The only question was if he should do it alone. Some aides thought the speaker might be setting a trap. Steffes pressed for the meeting on Moretti's terms. Meese weighed the arguments. Reagan listened and decided on a private meeting. It would have been surprising if he had reached any other conclusion, for Reagan was confident of his negotiating skills and impatient to crack what until then had been a united front of Democratic resistance to his welfare proposals. He told Steffes to accept the offer. Late that afternoon, Steffes called Hauck and asked if Moretti could come down within the hour.[15]

Moretti never forgot his first private meeting with Reagan, whom he had seen previously only on ceremonial or social occasions. "I remember he was sitting at his desk and there was a chair right off to the right where I sat and he said, 'Yeah, what do you want to talk to me about?' And I said, 'Look, governor, I don't like you particularly and I know you don't like me but we don't have to be in love to work together. If you're serious about doing some things, then let's sit down and start doing it."[16]

Reagan had a more stylized recollection of the meeting, which he incorporated into an anecdote he later used on the campaign trail. The point of the anecdote was that Reagan took his case to the people when the Legislature blocked his programs. As a result, he often said, legislators who refused to "see the light" instead were made to "feel the heat." In Reagan's telling of the story, a Democratic leader (he rarely mentioned Moretti by name) came to him on the welfare bill and said, "Stop those cards and letters from coming."

It is quite possible that Moretti said this or something like it, for that was the way he talked. But if he did, it was not because he felt vulnerable to any pressure that Reagan could generate. Moretti was fearless. He went to Reagan because he could see no other way to break the impasse with the governor. What surprised him was that Reagan was as genuinely interested in a productive outcome as he was. Reagan was not similarly surprised. He had one mode of behavior for campaigning and another for negotiating. When he gave a stump speech, Reagan used his adversaries as straight men to set up his punch lines. When he negotiated, he took them seriously and tried to get the best deal he could. The secrecy of Moretti's overture convinced Reagan that it was genuine. Within a few minutes, he reached an agreement with Moretti to hold a series of meetings in an effort to reach a welfare accord.

In *Reagan*, more than a decade later, I wrote that this first meeting with Moretti was the turning point in Reagan's transformation from communicator to governor. That is an overstatement. Even when he was a novice governor, Reagan had shown political skill in dealing with opposition legislators, particularly on the 1967 tax bill and in his maneuvering with the University of California Board of Regents on tuition. But in these situations, Reagan was never alone. What was significant about his private meeting with Moretti was that Reagan emerged from it with a new measure of self-confidence. To a degree he had never experienced in his first term, Reagan now felt that he was in command. He was the governor. The speaker had come to him. Never again would Reagan doubt that he was the equal of any other politician.

Although this meeting was an epiphany for both Reagan and Moretti, it was only the first step on an arduous path of negotiation that lasted nearly two weeks and involved many participants. During the negotiations, Reagan and Moretti swore at each other and questioned the other's motivations but also gradually developed a mutual respect. Reagan came to regard Moretti as tough and principled, likening him to the negotiators he'd faced in his Screen Actors Guild days.* Once, when an aide expressed doubt that Moretti would do something he promised to do, Reagan said, "He gave me his word."[18]

Moretti also changed his opinion of Reagan. "Both he and I developed a grudging respect for each other," Moretti said. "We came from different kinds of worlds. I don't think that socially we'd ever have mixed, but when the governor gave a commitment he kept it, and when I gave a commitment, I kept it. So that working on the development of legislation with him was relatively easy because we always knew where the other guy stood."[19]

This rapport between Reagan and Moretti opened the door for the constructive efforts of Senator Anthony Beilenson, the author of the pioneer abortion-rights legislation passed during Reagan's first year in office. In the interim, Beilenson had been involved in every battle to reform the Senate, where he had an unassailable record of integrity. Beilenson had stood with Howard Way in the fight to depose Hugh Burns and reduce the influence of the Third House. He had been among the minority of Democrats who stuck with Way when the lobbyists staged their counter-coup and installed the compliant Jack Schrade as president pro tem. Now, in 1971, Beilenson stood on solid ground, for he had been a friend and colleague of James Mills's, the new Senate president pro tem, when they were Unruh allies in the Assembly.

---

*This was a recurrent analogy. Ed Meese recalled that President Reagan, in a discussion of his negotiations with Soviet leader Mikhail Gorbachev, said, "It was easier than dealing with Jack Warner."[17]

In the early months of 1971, while Reagan and Moretti were still denouncing one another in press releases, Beilenson did the heavy lifting
on welfare reform. As chairman of the Senate Health and Welfare
Committee, he conducted a series of hearings on the governor's plan,
conferring often with his friend Clair Burgener, the Republican point
man for welfare in the Senate. Beilenson was a consistent liberal who
thought that welfare payments were inadequate. He recognized
nonetheless that Republican concern about welfare fraud was genuine
even though he believed Reagan exaggerated the problem. The bill that
emerged from Beilenson's committee became the blueprint for the final
compromise on welfare reform. That was because Beilenson had made
himself knowledgeable on the complex details of welfare legislation and
because Moretti had told him he would back him up on anything he
did.[20] Beilenson put into the bill a provision for job training for welfare
recipients similar to a measure Reagan had vetoed the year before. He
added other provisions for day-care centers and cost-of-living increases
for welfare recipients. "The governor wanted a bill he could call welfare
reform and we gave him one," said Beilenson.[21] In Beilenson's view,
Reagan cared little about the bill's actual contents, but the same could
have been said about Moretti.

Still, it was the governor and the speaker who hammered out the
compromise on welfare reform. It took five days of intense negotiation
at meetings presided over by Reagan and Moretti, followed by six days
of additional negotiations where details were resolved by Reagan's staff
and legislators. Some days, the negotiations would start at nine in the
morning and last into the night. The key negotiators, in addition to
Reagan and Moretti, were Meese, Carleson, Steffes, and Brian for the
governor, and Beilenson and Assemblymen John Burton and Leo Mc-
Carthy for the speaker. The Reagan team was suspicious of Burton, a
blunt-spoken liberal. Recognizing this, Moretti arranged for Burton to
feign angry outbursts and to pronounce provisions Carleson wanted as
unacceptable. The Democrats could not stand Carleson, whom Moretti
said "would drive the Pope to drink in a couple of weeks."[22] Carleson,
later the U.S. commissioner of welfare during the Reagan presidency,
knew more about welfare regulations than anyone else on the Reagan
team but posed a problem in the negotiations because the Democrats
did not trust him. "He would give a 40-page answer to a question that
demanded a yes or no, and a yes or no when something demanded 40
pages," Steffes said. "He drove Tony Beilenson, who was a good guy,
crazy. Tony walked out on the negotiations at one point; I had to get
him back. He played a big role in the final settlement."[23]

The other person who played a big role was Meese, who won the respect of the Democratic negotiators as the administration official who spoke most reliably for the governor. "He's a very intelligent guy with a stick-to-itiveness that can sometimes drive you up the wall," Moretti said of Meese. "But were I in the governor's seat, I would like to have someone like that on my side."[24]

Meese had more than "stick-to-itiveness." While affable in manner, he had a realistic sense of how the game of politics was played in Sacramento and was willing to do what it took to win. Not everyone in the Senate was as high-minded as Beilenson. As Meese's painstaking notes of the meetings show, other senators expected something in return for their votes. On one Meese note about a myriad of details on the welfare bill are jotted the words, "RR: quid pro quo for welf reform out of Senate committee."[25] Following are the names of three Democratic senators who were notorious for trading their votes for appointments. One of Meese's notes records the name of a lawyer whom one of these senators wanted appointed to the bench. After the name of another Democratic senator who was less particular in his judicial preferences, Meese wrote "anyone." It was through such careful attention to backroom politics that the Reagan program finally prevailed in a Senate more accustomed to payoffs than idealism.

The California Welfare Reform Act (CWRA) of 1971 was a seminal achievement of the Reagan governorship. As the product of a compromise, it necessarily contained something for everyone; what made the law distinctive was that it incorporated many of the best features of both Republican and Democratic welfare proposals. The biggest beneficiaries were honest welfare recipients. Eighty percent had their grants increased. The San Francisco family of three that had been getting a maximum of $172 a month at the beginning of the year received $235 after the cost-of-living increase and passage of the welfare bill.

While increasing aid to most recipients, the new law also tightened eligibility in several ways. It reduced the number of hours an unemployed father could work and have his family qualify for assistance. Household furnishings were counted as assets for the first time. A complex and confusing "needs standard" was simplified into a uniform statewide measurement in which family size was the only variable. A one-year residency requirement, long advocated by Reagan, was written into the law despite warnings that it would probably be held unconstitutional in light of the U.S. Supreme Court's 1968 decision outlawing such requirements in other states. Antifraud measures included a state cross-check between county welfare records and employer earnings records. Counties were given financial incentives to recover support payments from absentee fathers. A demonstration project called the

Community Work Experience Program was introduced in some counties. It required fathers and AFDC mothers without young children to work at public service jobs.

Welfare rolls started to decline immediately after passage of the California Welfare Reform Act. Within three years, the AFDC caseload dropped from a high of 1,608,000 to 1,330,000. Conservatives beyond California's borders were impressed. Before passage of the welfare law, Reagan had been their champion because of his inspirational expression of conservative values; afterward, he was increasingly celebrated as a governor who had made a difference. The CWRA became the cornerstone of the Reagan record. When he sought the presidency in 1980, Reagan said, "When I took office, California was the welfare capital of the nation. Sixteen percent of all those receiving welfare in the country were in California. The caseload was increasing 40,000 a month. We turned that 40,000 a month increase into an 8,000 a month decrease. We returned to the taxpayers $2 billion and we increased grants to the truly needy by forty-three percent."

These claims were reasonably accurate, but Reagan usually went on to give a glowing account of the success of the Community Work Experience Program. In fact, this pet Reagan program barely got off the ground, in large measure because HEW dragged its bureaucratic feet in giving the state the waivers it needed for a significant experiment. When the program was tried, most of those who were enrolled in it lacked the work experience to make them useful employees. The program was discontinued by Governor Jerry Brown on July 1, 1975. Although only 9,600 persons had been assigned to jobs during the four years that the program was in effect, it played a pioneering role nonetheless. A generation later, Wisconsin tried a work experience plan with enhanced job training that proved moderately successful. This, in turn, became a model for similar programs after federal overhaul of the welfare system in 1996.

Passage of the California Welfare Reform Act enabled Reagan and Democratic legislative leaders to claim they had delivered on their promises to reform the welfare system. The political benefits, however, were not symmetrical. Reagan received a disproportionate share of the credit, in part because he was more skilled than his rivals at claiming it and in part because a governor has higher visibility than any legislator. When it became clear that the public saw welfare reform as largely a Reagan achievement, the Democrats tried to downplay its impact by saying that California's declining caseload was the result of an improving economy. This was certainly part of the story, but Robert Carleson was accurate in his observation that California's welfare rolls had increased during prosperous years in the past. He was also right in noting that, after passage of the CWRA, the welfare rolls declined more rapidly in California than they did nationally.

Other factors had an impact on welfare caseload. The courts, as Democrats had predicted, struck down the residency requirement. But Carleson, as director of welfare, introduced a requirement for monthly reporting of income, which may have restricted caseload as much as any provision of the law. Beilenson, writing in the *Pacific Law Journal* of July 1972, said that "expanding use of family planning among AFDC dependents" also may have reduced the welfare rolls. Some analysts suspected that this contention was a euphemism for increased use of the abortion option provided by Beilenson's controversial 1967 bill.*

In a report for the Urban Institute, public policy analyst Frank Levy carved out a middle ground. Levy, no fan of Reagan, believed that the dynamic increase of welfare caseload in the 1960s was bound to level off because most of the eligible recipients were on the rolls by 1971. But Levy also estimated that the Reagan reforms, including Carleson's regulations, reduced the welfare rolls by 6 percent (about 21,000 people) more than they would otherwise have declined. "Governor Reagan is a man who works very hard, but he is also blessed with abundant good luck," Levy wrote in 1977. He continued:

> In the case of the CWRA, he had the luck to institute a fairly moderate policy just at the time when demographic factors would cause the "welfare explosion" to end both in California and the rest of the country. . . . At the same time, CWRA is a one-in-a-thousand policy success. The combination of CWRA and associated regulations mandated a large number of changes in a $1 billion program involving thirty-five counties and numerous personnel. . . . The result was a welfare program which, as the governor intended, was reoriented toward fiscal considerations and away from clients—particularly clients with earned income. On balance, however, more recipients appear to have been helped than hurt by this change.[27]

Passage of the California Welfare Reform Act had other consequences. The Family Assistance Plan had been on life support ever since Reagan first opposed it. The CWRA drove the final nail into the

---

*Assemblyman Bagley often said that the reduction of the AFDC rolls in the years 1968–1974 roughly equaled the increase of interrupted pregnancies that occurred as a result of the Beilenson bill. He implied that the decrease in welfare caseload was because of greater resort to abortion by welfare mothers. This is misleading. In California, the birthrate declined from 1963 through 1967. It turned upward in 1968, the year the Beilenson bill went into effect, as women in the postwar "baby boom" came of age.[26]

coffin. With welfare rolls declining, President Nixon abandoned the idea of federalizing the welfare system. Reagan and Moretti, meanwhile, earned editorial praise for their statesmanship. As Steffes suspected, Moretti was indeed building a record on which to run for governor—and Reagan was building one on which to run for president, as unlikely as this seemed in 1971.

Reagan's first foray into the taxation thicket that year was inadvertent and discomforting. On April 5, news reports based on anonymous sources disclosed that Reagan had paid no state income taxes in 1970. Reagan's press office acknowledged the accuracy of the stories and put out a statement saying that the governor had paid no income taxes because he had suffered "business reverses" the year before. Reagan was angry about the stories, which he said invaded his privacy, and both the Democrats and the media had a field day. In an editorial posing as a news story, *The Sacramento Bee* breathlessly compared Reagan's perfectly legal tax return to the secret Nixon slush fund of the 1952 campaign and other questionable Republican practices.[28]

Moretti, who was in Washington at the time, said that Reagan "lives well, he makes a large salary, [then $44,000] and he pays no state taxes. I'm just beginning to understand why the governor opposed state withholding of income taxes for so long."[29] It was a low blow and misplaced, all the more so because Democrats had blocked enactment of withholding after Reagan agreed to it. But the disclosure embarrassed Reagan. "Obviously, I would have preferred to make money and to owe a tax than to lose money and not pay a tax," Reagan told reporters.[30] Years later, William French Smith told me that Reagan had called after the story broke and said he wanted to pay taxes every time he filed a return. When Smith persisted in saying that Reagan shouldn't pay taxes unless he owed them, the governor became angry. "You don't get it," Smith remembered him as saying. "I want to pay taxes whether I owe them or not."[31]

Reagan had always expected, even with a Democratic Legislature, that he would be able to obtain property tax relief legislation in 1971. After he and Moretti reached their welfare accord on August 6, the governor looked forward to a new round of negotiations with the speaker. In the heady glow that prevailed after the welfare agreement, Reagan and Moretti probably would have reached agreement on a tax package had it not been for a stunning decision of the California Supreme Court. On August 30, in a case known as *Serrano v. Priest*, the court found that California's system of financing education from kindergarten through high school by local property taxes was unconstitutional because it treated children inequitably. The state's wealthiest district spent

$952,000 annually on each child, while the poorest district spent only $103.*[32] *Serrano* stopped property tax relief in its tracks. As *California Journal* observed, the ruling abruptly created "strong pressure against a major restructuring of the state's taxes until the school finance system can be reformed to meet the court's test for nondiscrimination."[33]

Trying to find a formula that could pass political muster and meet the court's demanding test for equity was too much for the Legislature, which adjourned a 333-day session on December 2 without reforming school financing or acting on a property tax bill. The state faced a fiscal crisis and the prospect of issuing IOUs to pay its bills.[34] Reagan called the Legislature back into special session and demanded action. On December 7, after much maneuvering, both houses passed a "mini-tax" bill by Assemblyman William Bagley that provided only minor property tax relief but averted a fiscal crisis. The measure raised $508 million, chiefly by increasing bank and corporation taxes from 7 to 7.6 percent and adding a new state income tax bracket. And it finally ended the long-running dispute over state income tax withholding, which was adopted beginning in 1972.

Reagan claimed victory, at which he was adept. But he was frustrated that he had been unable to parlay the welfare compromise into an agreement on property tax relief. Reagan did not fault Moretti, who was just as frustrated as he was. The governor's State of the State Address, delivered on January 6, 1972, was conciliatory. He said property tax relief and school financing were "the most urgent unfinished tasks before us" and appealed to the Legislature for help: "We have tried for three years to adopt a comprehensive property tax reform program. Again I ask you to work with the executive branch and with [Superintendent of Public Instruction] Wilson Riles to eliminate the chronic crisis in public school financing by shifting the burden from the homeowner to a broader based tax. Time is growing short. If we fail this year, the people may act themselves through the initiative process."

The Legislature was also in a conciliatory mood. When Reagan presented his budget later that month, *California Journal* observed that the Democratic response "was markedly restrained and altogether much more moderate in tone than had come to be customary."[35] This was in part because the budget was more generous, especially to higher educa-

---

*In the subsequent debate over a solution to *Serrano*, the distinction was sometimes lost between poor districts and poor children. School districts with low-income families in industrial cities (Emeryville, near Oakland, for instance, or the City of Commerce in Los Angeles County) were wealthy because of tax income from industries. The typical "low-wealth" district was a middle-class, suburban district that lacked industry and had little commercial development. In these districts, schools depended almost entirely on the property taxes paid by homeowners.

tion, than the Democrats had expected it to be. But it was also because legislative leaders, Moretti in particular, realized that Reagan was right in warning that advocates of property tax relief would take their case to the voters if the Legislature again failed to act.

Reagan and Moretti did not have long to wait. Los Angeles County Assessor Phil Watson, whose first ballot initiative (Proposition 9) had been rejected by voters in 1968 after a strong Reagan campaign against it, qualified a second initiative for the November 1972 ballot. This measure, designated as Proposition 14 and popularly known as "Watson II," was widely perceived as more of a threat than the first initiative had been because property taxes had soared in the interim since Proposition 9 was rejected. Watson II would have overhauled the state's tax structure, limited property taxes, and prohibited them from being used to pay for welfare costs. It would have raised sales taxes by two cents, increased corporation taxes, and imposed a new oil severance tax. The sales-tax increase alone posed a threat to a weak economy that was struggling to emerge from recession.

Most evaluations of Reagan's second-term accomplishments focus on the welfare bill and other constructive legislation that emerged from Reagan-Moretti negotiations. But what a governor opposes can be as important as what he initiates, as Reagan demonstrated in the environmental arena by blocking the Dos Rios dam and the trans-Sierra highway. On fiscal issues, Reagan helped thwart various crackpot plans of the sort that regularly find their way onto the California ballot through the initiative process. Watson II was one such scheme. Despite a superficial appeal to highly taxed homeowners, it would have gutted school budgets and forced the state to assume all welfare costs. One legislator said Watson II was like "curing a nosebleed by cutting your throat."[36] Reagan, even though he favored spending limits on government, was not enticed by a radical plan that its sponsor described as conservative. He denounced Watson II and tried to use it as a lever to pry a property tax relief bill out of the Legislature.

That wasn't as easy as it should have been. Moretti had one plan for property tax relief, and Reagan had another. Moretti said that Reagan's plan was too generous to business, and Reagan said that Moretti's plan had no mechanism for keeping property taxes down once they were lowered. But the debate was civil, and Moretti and Reagan again entered into negotiations with the aim of replicating their welfare accord. The problem this time was that the Senate was not part of the negotiations—as it had been on the welfare bill through the presence of Senator Beilenson.

After the Reagan-Moretti compromise (which essentially split the difference between the governor and speaker) passed the Assembly, it was buried in the Senate Finance Committee, where real estate and agricultural interests had strong leverage. These interest groups were supporting Proposition 14, the Watson initiative, which they believed had a better chance of passage if the Legislature killed property tax relief. Moretti then took Senate Bill 90, an education measure that had already been passed by the Senate, and amended the entire Reagan-Moretti compromise into it.[37] The Assembly passed this bill and sent it back to the Senate for a floor vote, bypassing the Senate Finance Committee. There, Moretti was blocked by California's restrictive rule requiring a two-thirds vote for measures with a fiscal impact and by disagreements with Senate leader James Mills, who had quarreled with Moretti over reapportionment and other political issues. Mills' lack of enthusiasm for the compromise was decisive, and the Senate recessed for the 1972 election without action on property tax relief.

The Senate's lack of action should have opened the door for passage of Watson II but didn't. Reagan campaigned forcefully against Proposition 14, promising that he would put his own property tax relief measure on the ballot at the next election if the Legislature refused to act. Norman Topping, chancellor of the University of Southern California and chairman of a statewide coalition opposed to the Watson measure, made a similar promise. Moretti also campaigned against the initiative, using information supplied by legislative analyst Alan Post. He pointed out that the bill would hurt renters, who would receive no relief while paying higher state taxes to benefit homeowners. Most of the state's major newspapers joined in the campaign against Proposition 14. It was rejected, 66–34 percent, only slightly less than the margin by which Watson's first initiative had been defeated four years earlier.

Reagan now made a final push for property tax relief. Senate Bill 90 was sent to an Assembly-Senate conference committee, where both the governor and Moretti made concessions. A proposed income-tax increase was removed from the bill, and renters were guaranteed relief in the form of tax credits. The latter provision brought support from mayors and city governments. San Francisco Mayor Joseph Alioto, who had been neutral, endorsed the bill on November 28.

However, when supporters of the bill brought it to the Senate floor on November 29, they were still two votes short. Some of the Senate holdouts wanted more concessions. Reagan refused. "Once again," he told reporters, "this little band of recalcitrant senators has shown that their only motivations in asking for impossible changes at this eleventh hour amounts to nothing more than an attempt to justify their votes to kill the bill."[38] Reagan warned again that he would carry out his promise to take the measure to the people if the Senate failed to act.

Four senators were under particular pressure. The first to cave was Milton Marks of San Francisco, the most liberal Republican in the Legislature, who later became a Democrat. Marks said he was persuaded by the school lobbyists, but he may also have been influenced by Mayor Alioto's endorsement.[39] However, Moretti and Reagan were still a vote short. Their prime target was David Roberti, a freshman senator from Los Angeles who had been Moretti's seatmate in the Assembly. Roberti, a liberal Democrat who would one day be the Senate leader, disliked the package because it raised the sales tax by a penny.

"There was a lot of pressure," Roberti recalled three decades later. "The school lobbyist was camped outside my office. I had respect for Moretti. He came into my office, got down on one knee and said, 'Paisano, I need your vote.' What could you do? I voted for the bill, which in retrospect was a very good bill. And Reagan called me after I voted and said thank you. That was nice of him because he didn't need to do it."[40]

On December 1, the last day of the session, Roberti provided the twenty-seventh vote for a bill that saved the schools and generated $780 million in property tax relief. Two other Democratic senators who had been waiting to see how the wind blew joined him.[41] Reagan and Moretti had done it again.

Ever afterward, Moretti considered Senate Bill 90 the most significant achievement of his legislative career. It raised the homeowner's property tax exemption from $750 to $1,750, provided a then-record $332 million increase in school funding, and laid the groundwork for a useful state response to school needs after a second *Serrano* decision years later.[42] Reagan was also proud of Senate Bill 90; it would become part of the record on which he sought the presidency.

Reagan and Moretti had more escapes than Houdini during the protracted negotiations, off-stage maneuvering, and public politicking that produced the California Welfare Reform Act and the package of school financing and tax relief contained in Senate Bill 90. Neither of them could have done what they did without the other. Together, they were unstoppable. In the process of these negotiations, Moretti changed his mind about Reagan. He decided he was a good governor ("better than Pat Brown, miles, and planets, and universes better than Jerry Brown") who made the most of his opportunities.[43]

"He had certain assets," Moretti said. "One, he had a philosophy that he was willing to pursue, that he was willing to enunciate, that he was willing to attempt to push. And, secondly, he's a strong personality. . . . Leaders are people who are willing to take positions and stand up and fight for those positions. [Reagan] had an enduring desire to accomplish something, to leave something behind that really improved things."[44]

Because of Moretti's cooperation, Reagan was able to write a record of accomplishment in California on which he could run for president.

Moretti ran for governor in 1974 but failed to win the Democratic nomination. He died of a heart attack on May 12, 1984, while playing tennis with a legislator. He was forty-seven years old.

24

SALESMAN

RONALD REAGAN reached the zenith of his governorship in 1972. He had kept his promise to deliver property tax relief and, working with the Legislature, responded to the school financing issue thrust upon him by the courts. The California Welfare Reform Act was producing results. Reagan had protected the wild rivers of California's north coast and blocked forever the highway that would have bisected the John Muir Trail. The campuses were quiet. Reagan dominated the political scene. And then, when everything was going his way, Reagan proposed a radical and complicated tax-limitation initiative that led to the most damaging political defeat of his career.

The story of Reagan's overreach in 1973 is a cautionary tale about the dangers of indulging ideology at the expense of common sense. It is also a story of misjudgment by aides who ignored historical lessons and political realities and thereby failed Reagan in the penultimate year of his governorship.

It is not unusual for popular California governors to falter in their second terms. Reagan's predecessor, Pat Brown, had done so, as would his successor, Jerry Brown.* It has been true of governors in other states and of presidents as well. Indeed, Reagan's own second presidential term would be salvaged from the misadventure of the Iran-contra affair largely because of his success in dealing with the Soviet Union. What was unique about Governor Reagan's situation in 1973 was that his troubles were self-caused. Never before had a governor of California sponsored a ballot initiative and called a special statewide election to

---

*Before Pat Brown, only two California governors had been elected to two or more four-year terms, and one of these did not complete his second term. Hiram Johnson was elected governor in 1910. He was reelected in 1914 but departed for the U.S. Senate in 1916, where he served for twenty-nine years. Earl Warren was elected governor three times, the last in 1952, and was appointed Chief Justice of the United States in 1953.

decide it. And never again, after the fiasco known as Proposition 1, would a California governor be similarly tempted.

Proposition 1 was the brainchild of Lewis K. Uhler, a former member of the John Birch Society and a classmate of Edwin Meese's at Boalt Hall, the University of California law school. Meese brought Uhler into the Reagan administration in 1970 as director of the state Office of Economic Opportunity, where he took aim at several agencies that were fighting rearguard battles in the "war on poverty." Uhler's principal target was California Rural Legal Assistance (CRLA), which had successfully sued the Reagan administration to increase Medi-Cal benefits and had tried to block the importation of farm labor from Mexico. He prepared a 258-page report that accused the organization of incompetence and incitement of prison riots. Acting on the basis of this report, Reagan vetoed a $2 million federal grant for CRLA. It was restored by the Nixon administration after a three-judge panel found Uhler's charges to be "totally irresponsible and without foundation."

Uhler, a resourceful ideologue with a robust agenda, was undeterred by such setbacks. Although he claimed to be a Reagan loyalist, he did not appreciate the governor's pragmatic agreements with Assembly Speaker Bob Moretti that produced welfare reform in 1971 and property tax relief and school financing accord in 1972. As Uhler saw it, this was doing business with the enemy. In an April 1972 memo cited by Bill Boyarsky, Uhler declared: "I am absolutely convinced that legislators, if left to their own devices, will, in short order, put an end to the Republic in the name of improving it unless we, the people, take aggressive action, change the environment in which they operate, change the rules of the game."[1]

In September 1972, Meese selected Uhler to head the Tax Reduction Task Force, one of three groups charged with drawing up an agenda for the last two years of Reagan's governorship. This appointment gave Uhler an opportunity to advance the cause of tax limitation and his belief that a republic is strengthened when the power of its Legislature is diminished. The task force had distinguished advisers, including Milton Friedman, a Nobel Prize–winning economist; Martin Anderson, an economist who would later become chief domestic adviser in the Reagan presidency; and Anthony Kennedy, a Sacramento law professor whom President Reagan would one day name to the U.S. Supreme Court. But Uhler was the driving force. Because of his extreme views and Bircher associations, he would subsequently be airbrushed out of the memoirs and histories written by Reagan and his cheerleaders.* But

---

*Uhler isn't mentioned in Reagan's memoirs, *An American Life* (Simon and Schuster, 1990), or in the most comprehensive conservative accounts of the Reagan era, *Revolution*, by Martin Anderson (Harcourt, 1988), and *The Age of Reagan*, by Steven Hayward (Forum, 2002). Meese mentioned Uhler once in his memoir, *With Reagan: The Inside Story* (Regnery, 1992).[2]

Uhler was the unquestioned leader of the Tax Reduction Task Force and the architect of its principal proposal: a state constitutional amendment to restrict government spending through strict tax-rate limitations and limits on legislative authority.

This idea had resonance in a state where distrust of majority rule and of the Legislature is embedded in the political culture. A state constitutional provision dating from the 1930s protected the propertied minority of California from the presumed tyranny of the propertyless majority by requiring a two-thirds majority in the Legislature for bills with a fiscal impact, except for education appropriations, and a two-thirds majority of voters for approval of local school bond issues. Coming from another direction, the Progressives in the early twentieth century also distrusted the Legislature. Instead of fearing that the Legislature would be too responsive to the passions of the majority, the Progressives were concerned that it would not be responsive at all. The Progressive remedy was "direct democracy," including the initiative and the referendum. When the Legislature failed to act, the people could.

Proposition 1 married these two misgivings about republican government. It would have written into the state constitution a complex tax-reduction requirement that could be changed only through a referendum approved by two-thirds of the Legislature and then a majority of voters or by the voters themselves through the initiative process. Reagan was intrigued by the idea, all the more so because the state was awash in revenue after years of fiscal crisis. The Reagan-Moretti compromise on the 1972 tax bill had combined with an improving economy and a boost in tax collections from withholding to raise more revenue than anyone had predicted. When State Finance Director Verne Orr presented the state's $9.3 billion budget in January 1973, he found there was an $851 million budget surplus with a $1.1 billion surplus projected for the following year.

Reagan worried that the Legislature would spend this money, which he wanted to give back to the people. "It would indeed be foolish to initiate vast new programs or levels of expenditures higher than absolutely necessary simply because for a short period in the span of government we have an operating surplus," he said.[3] Reagan proposed to return the money by delaying imposition of the one-cent sales tax increase and giving taxpayers a one-time income tax credit. Moretti favored delaying the sales tax increase but contended that the income tax credit favored the wealthy.

The situation was made to order for the kind of accord that Moretti and Reagan had negotiated on welfare, property tax relief, and school financing in the two previous years. On its face, a compromise should have been more easily attainable in 1973 than in prior years because the state had ample revenue to accomplish the objectives of both the governor and the speaker. But the constitutional amendment devised by Uhler stood in the way.

Reagan announced the proposal, which he called a "once-in-a-lifetime opportunity," on February 8 in a televised report to the people and a speech to the California Newspaper Publishers Association. "This idea of allowing the people to decide whether government should take more of their earnings in taxes may be a novel one to some, but unless they have an opportunity to provide a break to spending, in a few short years they will be paying more than half their income in taxes," Reagan said. Moretti said Reagan had declared "economic war on the interests of most of the people in California."

Such hyperbole had in the past been a prelude to negotiation. In 1971, and again in 1972, the governor and the speaker had staked out extreme rhetorical positions before negotiating compromises on welfare reform, school financing, and property tax relief. In 1972, Reagan had used the threat of an initiative on property tax relief to obtain the final votes for his fiscal package. But in 1973, at the beginning of negotiations with the Legislature, Reagan allowed himself to be stampeded into a petition-circulating campaign to bring the tax-limitation initiative to a vote at a special election in November. Since it was the only ballot measure, it was designated Proposition 1. Once the initiative qualified for the ballot, the conditions for compromise no longer existed. Moretti and other Democratic leaders were willing to make concessions to Reagan on the disposition of the budget surplus, and they did. But they were unwilling to surrender legislative power by agreeing to the arbitrary limits of Proposition 1.

By any standard, the initiative was bewilderingly complex. It would have given Californians an immediate 20 percent credit on their state income tax, which was possible because of the budget surplus. This was the only provision of the measure that voters could easily comprehend. Proposition 1 otherwise proposed that state tax revenues be reduced from the 1973 percentage of state personal income, estimated at 8.3 percent, by one-tenth of a percentage point a year until they reached 7 percent. The proponents claimed this would take fifteen years; opponents said the 7 percent ceiling would be reached several years sooner. If the state collected more than the allotted percentage of taxes in any year, the Legislature would have to refund the surplus to the taxpayers. The Legislature was required to establish an emergency fund of not more than 0.2 percent of personal income, but only the governor would be able to declare an emergency. Tax-rate limits were established for cities, counties, and special districts. And these were only the highlights of a plan that ran to 5,700 words of technical legal language.

Uhler and Meese, who had been assisted in the draftsmanship of Proposition 1 by Anthony Kennedy, were proud of their handiwork. It is hard to see why. Californians had a long history of rejecting complicated tax initiatives. As pollster Mervin Field observed, voters suspected that such measures would wind up raising their taxes, even if that was not the declared intent of their sponsors.[4] The Watson tax-limitation initiatives, which Reagan had campaigned against in 1968 and 1972, had been criticized for their complexity but were much simpler than Proposition 1. Voters had overwhelmingly rejected them.

Why, then, did Reagan, normally cautious about changing the constitution, agree to sponsor Proposition 1? And why did he accept a hasty timetable for an initiative that under the usual procedures would have been placed on the ballot at the next scheduled election, the June 1974 primary? To put an initiative on the ballot took the signatures of 8 percent of the voters registered at the time of the previous gubernatorial election, roughly half a million signatures in this case. This goal would have been relatively easy to reach with a year's head start. Qualifying the initiative for the November 1973 ballot, however, required an intense effort. According to conservative analyst Charles Hobbs, "The task force had recommended a grassroots campaign in which Reagan would support, but not head, the thrust for change. Unfortunately, the early need for the use of Reagan's personal strength to stimulate the signature petition drive foreclosed the use of a grassroots strategy. For better or for worse, to the public Proposition 1 belonged to Ronald Reagan."[5]

It is doubtful, however, that Reagan had decided on the timetable. Reagan was interested in ideas and policy, not political strategy. With the significant exception of his decision to debate President Jimmy Carter in 1980, he rarely made decisions on strategy or schedule during his two campaigns for governor or in his three for the presidency. Meese loyally insisted that Reagan made all such decisions, but other strategists and aides demurred.

The more interesting—and unanswered—question is whether Reagan was given any options in 1973 by his team of advisers. The tax-limitation initiative was favored not only by Meese and Uhler but by Michael Deaver, Reagan's deputy chief of staff, who ran the campaign for Proposition 1. Their primitive political calculus was that the measure would receive more attention at a special election when it did not have to compete with other ballot issues for attention. In reality, this was an advantage for the initiative's opponents, who were short of money and largely dependent upon media coverage to get their message across.

Getting the media's attention would have been more difficult in an election where they had to compete with other issues. The Reagan brain trust also believed that the electorate would be more Republican and therefore more likely to favor tax limitation at a special election in 1973 than at a general election in 1974. The benefit of having a more elite electorate, however, was offset by the liability of a shorter and more pressure-packed campaign. Reagan was a good salesman, but Proposition 1 was a hard sale, and he did not have the time to make it.

The details of how these decisions were made are not known. There is no written record of an inner debate over Proposition 1, if any such debate occurred. Under Meese, the cabinet minutes, which in the early governorship had so vividly recorded Reagan's comments, had been reduced to brief summaries. They shed no light on the discussions that led to the proposition. Meese asserted that Reagan was the prime mover but gave no details.[6] He disliked news accounts that focused on the administration's decision-making processes.

The only prominent opponent to Proposition 1 within the administration was State Finance Director Verne Orr, who three years earlier had persuaded Reagan to abandon his opposition to state income tax withholding. Orr would have been comfortable with a more modest initiative to hold taxes at their 1973 level, but he had "heartburn" at Uhler's plan to roll them back to an arbitrary 7 percent figure.[7] Alone among Reagan's advisers, Orr recognized that such a proposal was a leap into the unknown that would stoke public fears about loss of services. "I thought it would be better to stop taxes at the level they were at the time and made my opinion known," Orr recalled thirty years later. "Lew Uhler sold the governor on his idea."[8] Orr thought Uhler was intelligent but a "loudmouth." But on Proposition 1, the soft-spoken and practical finance director was no match for the fervent Uhler, who believed that tax limitation was an idea whose time had come.

Reagan, of course, bears the ultimate responsibility for Proposition 1. He, not Meese or Uhler, was the governor, and the idea of tax limitation appealed to him. Still, it is hard to imagine Reagan taking the plunge on such a complicated proposal, especially on a hasty timetable, if he had been adequately advised of the political risks. As Mervin Field observed, there was no public clamor for state tax limitation as there had been for welfare reform. (Hobbs made a similar point.) Reagan had strong convictions, but he was not a gambler, and he rarely invested his popularity in lost causes. He was also a practical politician. During his reelection campaign in 1970 he had soft-pedaled the campus unrest issue, on which he felt strongly, when the mood of the country changed after the shootings at Kent State.

But Reagan had been advised in that campaign by Tom Reed and Stu Spencer. The governor lacked such savvy political advisers in 1973. Uhler was a zealot. Meese, probably because he favored tax limitation, had a blind spot about the political salability of such a complex measure. Deaver, who took a leave of absence from the governor's office and set up shop six blocks away, was running a statewide political campaign for the first (and only) time. He was, he said, "naive about the power of the teachers," who opposed Proposition 1.[9] This is a stunning admission. The California Teachers Association, one of California's most influential interest groups, had opposed the Watson initiatives and perceived any tax-limitation measure as a threat to education financing. There was never any doubt that the teachers, who were no fans of Reagan in the first place, would go all-out to defeat Proposition 1.

The strategists and aides who might have warned Reagan of the risks he faced were no longer around. Spencer, who with Bill Roberts had been the guiding light of the 1966 campaign, was estranged from the administration and so angry at Meese that he gave quiet help to Moretti in opposing Proposition 1.* Reed, after developing a ski resort in Colorado, was a consultant in the Pentagon en route to becoming secretary of the Air Force. Rus Walton, who had questioned the premises of Reagan's 1968 presidential campaign, and George Steffes, who had encouraged Reagan to negotiate with Moretti on welfare reform in 1971, had left the administration. Holmes Tuttle, who often gave good political advice, was in poor health. Only Orr foresaw the pitfalls, and he was valued for his fiscal insights rather than for political counsel. His warnings were ignored.

Reagan, as Steffes frequently observed, usually made good decisions if he knew the facts but rarely reached out on his own to get them. The first to realize this was Bill Clark, who as cabinet secretary had devised the "mini-memos" that summarized the options available to the governor. When Clark became chief of staff, he saw to it that Reagan knew the pros and cons of all controversial proposals. James Baker did the same during most of his four-year tenure as White House chief of staff. Many of Reagan's setbacks, from Proposition 1 to the Iran arms sales when he was president, occurred in situations where he was not informed of the potential downsides of a particular course of action.

In the case of Proposition 1, it may be that Reagan was not ade-

---

*Spencer believed that Meese had bad-mouthed Spencer-Roberts to potential clients. "He was costing us business," Spencer said. Meese said this accusation is "absolutely untrue." True or not, Spencer was convinced of it and on several occasions shared his political insights about Proposition 1 with Moretti or his top aide, Bill Hauck. "I did what I could to defeat it," Spencer said.[10]

quately apprised of the downsides because his advisers did not recognize them. Meese and Deaver initially were confident. In addition to the demonstrated prowess of Reagan's salesmanship, they enjoyed a commanding financial advantage. Before the campaign was over, proponents of Proposition 1 would spend $1.5 million, not counting $385,000 that it cost to obtain the signatures to qualify the initiative. Opponents spent only $375,000, insufficient to mount a substantial television advertising campaign. Proposition 1 also had editorial endorsements from 85 percent of California's newspapers. This was thought to be a huge advantage; as Mervin Field observed, voters often rely on newspaper editorials in making decisions on ballot measures. But some of the endorsements were hedged. The editorial endorsing Proposition 1 in the influential *Los Angeles Times* pointed out several of the defects in the measure and was undercut by a biting editorial cartoon by Paul Conrad the day before the election that drew the governor as "Reagan Hood," who robs the poor to help the wealthy.

Assembly Speaker Bob Moretti, who was gearing up to run for governor in 1974, became the point man in the campaign against Proposition 1. He opposed it on principle, and he also saw his leadership against the measure as an opportunity to let voters "see me in some other light than Assembly speaker."[11] Moretti loaned the campaign staff some of his aides and $65,000 from his lobbyist-funded Assembly treasure chest, which paid for television commercials in which the speaker denounced the initiative.

For information and arguments, Moretti and other Democrats relied on legislative analyst Alan Post, a trenchant critic of Proposition 1. Post said that the wordy initiative, because of poor drafting, would unintentionally shift tax burdens from the state to local taxpayers. Although Proposition 1 contained provisions to shield local governments from new tax burdens, Post said these provisions did not protect senior citizens, who received property tax relief payments from the state as individuals. Renters who received credits from the state also were not protected. As a result, said Post, it was the programs of property tax relief and renter credits that would "feel the pressure for cutbacks when the budget squeeze is on."[12]

Reagan did his salesman's best with Proposition 1. Many of the editorial endorsements for the measure were obtained through his personal appeals. He also tried to gain the support of Superintendent of Public Instruction Wilson Riles to offset the opposition of the California Teachers Association. Riles respected Reagan but wouldn't go along. "I didn't want to oppose him, I didn't need a fight, but all our studies showed it [Proposition 1] would be detrimental," Riles said. "When it became clear it would hurt education, I knew I would have to oppose it. I did, and told him so, at his house."[13]

Once he realized that passage of Proposition 1 was not the cakewalk he had been led to believe, Reagan campaigned even harder. He went up and down the state with a statistics-laden, antigovernment message that echoed "The Speech" he had molded in the General Electric days and given to conservative forums in the early 1960s. Reagan quoted Cicero, a staple of these stump speeches, as saying, "When a government becomes powerful, it is destructive, extravagant and violent." As Reagan saw it, government was again on the march against the citizenry. He said government spending had averaged 15 percent of the people's total personal income until 1930, rising to 32 percent by 1950 and to 44 percent by 1973. "The fact is, our tax burden has grown steadily through good times and bad for more than 40 years," Reagan said. "Somehow, the law of gravity does not seem to work with government spending."[14]

Alan Post scoffed at Reagan's statistics. In a presentation condensed by *California Journal*, he wrote: "[The proponents of Proposition 1] have erroneously classified the following receipts as taxes in order to obtain this 44 percent figure: admissions to the University basketball and football games, University bookstore receipts, board and room charges of students, private donations to the University, bridge tolls, employee retirement contributions, local airport receipts, local hospital charges, U.S. Postal receipts, and receipts from the sale of agricultural products by the federal government."[15] After removing these and other items, Post calculated the correct percentage of income that was taken as taxes at 32 percent.

Not all of Proposition 1's critics were as analytical as Post. Some Democrats waged a scare campaign that made contradictory claims about the perils of Proposition 1. While Moretti was saying the measure would cut taxes and "strike hardest at low-income and middle-income people," others claimed Proposition 1 would encourage spending. One creative and widely circulated analysis by a UCLA professor maintained that spending for higher education and road building were tapering off and would soon fall below the mandated limits of Proposition 1.[16] Then, he said, legislators would treat the tax ceiling as a floor and increase spending.

This was a preposterous argument in a dynamic state where university and college systems were expanding and the need for new roads was continual. Nevertheless, it had an impact upon voters confused by the intricacies of Proposition 1. Mervin Field's polls showed that opponents of the measure were evenly divided on the question of whether Proposition 1 would limit or increase spending. Supporters of the measure thought it would hold down taxes but were almost evenly split on the question of whether it would reduce services.

Unfortunately for the proponents of Proposition 1, the confusion extended to Governor Reagan—or so it seemed. On October 26, eleven days before the election, Reagan appeared on television station KTVU in Oakland to discuss the measure. The host of the show, George Reading, asked Reagan, "Do you think the average voter really understands the language of the proposition?"

"No," Reagan replied good-naturedly. "He shouldn't try. I don't, either."

This was a facetious response, as Reagan vainly tried to explain in the days ahead. It was also the opportunity that Harry Lerner had been waiting for. Lerner was a political street fighter who was running the heavily outspent advertising campaign against the initiative for Whittaker and Baxter, the pioneer California political merchandising firm. Lerner was one of the strategists who had devised the Democratic smear of George Christopher in the 1966 Republican primary, a maneuver that had helped Reagan in his successful race against Governor Pat Brown. In this case, no smear was necessary. All Lerner needed were Reagan's own words, which became part of newspaper advertisements that proclaimed, "When a proposition's chief sponsor doesn't understand it, it's time for the rest of us to vote no on Proposition 1."

Reagan's quip and Lerner's exploitation of it cemented Reagan's dual role as the principal asset and main liability of the campaign. By this time, for better and for worse, Reagan was Proposition 1. He had participated in the petition drive to put the measure on the ballot by collecting signatures in his Pacific Palisades neighborhood and made so many speeches in its behalf that Proposition 1 had become as much a referendum on Reagan as on tax limitation. In a preelection poll, Mervin Field found that "Governor Reagan's personality seems to have had a polarizing effect. That is, there were just as many people saying they are voting for the measure because Governor Reagan was advocating it as there were people saying they were voting against it because of his advocacy."*[17]

In the end, as voters became increasingly suspicious about the potential impact of Proposition 1, Reagan's identification with the measure

---

*Mervin Field, California's most trusted pollster, decided he wanted to go into survey research after meeting George Gallup in 1937 when Field was a student at Princeton High School in New Jersey. Field began polling California in 1946. Scrupulously nonpartisan, he declined to do polls for candidates and sold his surveys to newspapers. In 1973, he polled on Proposition 1 for the *Los Angeles Times*. Field's surveys were officially called the "California Poll" but were popularly known as the "Field Poll." In 1992, Mark DiCamillo became director of the poll and formally renamed the survey the Field Poll.

may have boosted the vote for the measure among Republicans. By co-incidence, Field had begun polling on October 27, the day after Reagan's wisecrack about not understanding the measure. He found voters confused, with two-thirds of those interviewed saying they wanted to know more about Proposition 1 before making a decision. By November 1, five days before the election, 47 percent of voters had made up their mind. Field's poll had picked up a trend. Proposition 1 was down by 4 percentage points on the first day of his survey and by 11 points on the last day.

There was no suspense on election night. Proposition 1 lost by a margin of 54–46 percent, carrying only eleven of the state's fifty-eight counties and only two populous counties—Orange and San Diego. Turnout was low, and only slightly higher in Republican areas than in Democratic ones. The *Los Angeles Times* announced the verdict: "Gov. Reagan lost his first major election in California Tuesday, and he wasn't even a candidate."[18]

Many election postmortems suggested that the outcome hinged on last-minute decisions of undecided voters to reject a wordy initiative that they did not understand. Field's polls, the only objective measurements of this unusual election, support this view. As *California Journal* put it, "For many individual citizens, confusion undoubtedly played a part in their deliberations. And the conventional wisdom obtained: When in doubt, oppose."[19]

For Reagan, Proposition 1 was a resounding—and unnecessary—defeat. It did far better than Watson's tax-limitation initiatives had in 1968 and 1972 and would have won with less than a 4 percent swing in the vote. This suggests that Reagan might well have sold a simpler plan, such as Orr's idea to hold spending at current levels. He might even have sold a rollback that was more comprehensible and straightforward. Reagan realized after the election that some of those who voted against the measure believed it would raise taxes instead of lower them. He blamed this misunderstanding on a demagogic campaign by Proposition 1's opponents, which gives them too much credit. The fault lies with the drafters of the confusing measure, and with Reagan for accepting it.

Reagan was normally the apostle of simplicity. Like many populists, he chided government for talking down to people. In a passage of his basic stump speech that he had incorporated into his first inaugural message, Reagan said as previously noted, "You and I have been shushed like children and told there are no simple answers to the complex problems which are beyond our comprehension. Well, the truth is, there are simple answers—there just are not easy ones." Proposition 1 was neither simple nor easy. It was deliberately drafted to be beyond the grasp of ordinary people, who responded by rejecting it.

Too late, campaign manager Michael Deaver understood the gravity of this mistake. Deaver had swallowed his doubts about the complexity of the measure, largely because he believed that Ronald Reagan could convince the voters of the merits of any idea he favored. But there are limits to salesmanship, as Deaver realized in retrospect. Looking back on the election with the perspective of history, he said, "I really do think we underestimated the people."[20] Not even Reagan could persuade the voters to buy the deficient product known as Proposition 1.

25

ACHIEVER

Ronald Reagan was defiant, if not introspective, in defeat. He wrote a cover story for *National Review* celebrating the virtues of tax limitation and blaming Proposition 1's defeat on distortions by its opponents. "Naturally, I am disappointed," he wrote. "It was and is a daring idea and I do not regret the exercise. It served a positive purpose. As a result of the battle waged in California, people all over America have been alerted to the staggering burden which taxes impose on our economy and on every family in this country."[1]

At least Americans had again been alerted to Reagan's presence on the political scene. Michael Deaver, who had managed the campaign, found the governor sanguine when he called upon him to apologize for the loss of Proposition 1. Deaver felt he had let Reagan down and told him so.[2]* Reagan tried to bolster Deaver's spirits, telling him that everything would turn out for the best. Once again, Nelle Reagan spoke through her son, saying that all that happens is part of God's plan.

Whether by divine plan or good fortune, Reagan weathered the defeat. He had lost his aura of political invincibility but looked good in comparison to President Nixon, whose fortunes sank with each twist and turn of the Watergate scandal. In the issue of *National Review* for which Reagan wrote "Reflections on the Failure of Proposition #1," George Will wrote a column that concluded: "Mr. Nixon's support is thin and the water below is cold and deep. It is going to be an interesting winter."[4]

As the ice cracked and Nixon sank, conservatives paid increasing

---

*Deaver was a target of conservatives in the wake of Proposition 1's defeat and ever after. State Senator H. L. Richardson, an ultraconservative, said the measure was defeated because "the governor assigned some of his top pygmies to it. Their only good characteristics were mixing a drink, and he gave them responsibility for running a campaign."[3]

attention to Reagan. He was their champion, he was far away from Washington, and his campaign for tax limitation had caught their eye. Proposition 1 was indeed a "daring idea," even if its boldness had been muddied by turgid language. But conservatives didn't bother with the fine print. The tax issue was the wave of the future, and Reagan was riding it. It was a powerful wave. Three years later, in California, a folksy populist named Howard Jarvis fell only 10,000 votes short of qualifying a property tax–limitation measure for the ballot. Two years after that, in 1978, Jarvis teamed up with Paul Gann, another antitax promoter, and qualified the initiative as Proposition 13. Jarvis and Gann had learned from Proposition 1 to keep their initiative simple. With homeowners panicked by inflation and soaring property tax assessments, Proposition 13 passed overwhelmingly. It was so extreme that Proposition 1 resembled a Mother's Day resolution in comparison, but it touched off a nationwide tax rebellion that lasted for two decades.*

In *Paradise Lost: California's Experience, America's Future* (1998), the writer Peter Schrag contended that Proposition 13 "set the stage for the Reagan era and became both fact and symbol of a radical shift in governmental priorities, public attitudes, and social relationships that is as nearly fundamental in American politics as the changes brought by the New Deal."[5] If this premise is accurate, Reagan helped set the stage for his own presidency when he put forward Proposition 1. By the time Reagan became president in 1981, the antitax craze had spread to more than forty states. The clamor for lower taxes of all kinds made it easier for President Reagan to persuade Congress on the virtues of a massive income tax cut. Jarvis was the architect of tax limitation, but Reagan was its prophet.

He was, however, a prophet honored in defeat only by his fellow conservatives. Reagan's political position in California was fragile during the last two years of his governorship. Republicans were demoralized by the Watergate scandal. Democrats controlled the Legislature. They had lost their fear of Reagan, even before Proposition 1, largely because he seemed to have no political future. Reagan encouraged the view that his second gubernatorial term was a last hurrah by turning down Holmes Tuttle when his top money man urged him to seek a third term as governor. Reagan pointed out to Tuttle that he had promised to serve only two terms and had pushed a constitutional amendment requiring such a limitation. When the amendment died in the Legislature, Rea-

---

*Proposition 13 rolled back property values to their 1975 assessed value. They could not be raised by more than 2 percent a year until the property was sold. Property tax rates were limited to 1 percent of value. State taxes and local special taxes, that is, taxes for a specific purpose such as libraries or parks, could be raised only by a two-thirds vote of the people.

gan again promised not to seek a third term. For good measure, he also
ruled out running against Democratic Senator Alan Cranston in 1974.[6]
Reagan had no interest in the Senate. "There's nothing I can do in the
Senate for what I believe in that I won't be able to do anyway," he told
Tuttle.[7]

Reagan was stymied in the Legislature but did what he could outside
it to advance his conservative agenda. He touched off a firestorm in the
legal community by appointing his former chief of staff, William P.
Clark Jr., to the California Supreme Court. Clark had moved rapidly up
the judicial ladder since Reagan had appointed him to a Superior Court
vacancy in 1969. In 1970, Clark ran for the judgeship to which he had
been appointed and won with more than 70 percent of the vote. In
1971, Reagan elevated him to the State Court of Appeals. On January 9,
1973, a week after the death of Supreme Court Justice Raymond E. Pe-
ters, Reagan named Clark to fill the vacancy.

The appointment was fiercely criticized, ostensibly on grounds that
Clark was unqualified. Clark had attended Stanford University and
then Loyola Law School. His Loyola grades were mediocre; Clark said
this was because he was working as an insurance adjuster to support his
family while he attended law school. It took him two tries to pass the
California bar examination. But he had been a successful small-town attorney who as a trial judge was viewed as hard working, fair-minded,
and conservative. He had a similar reputation on the appellate court.

Reagan described Clark as an "outstanding jurist" and believed that
the clamor over his qualifications was a smokescreen for ideological opposition. He trusted Clark and couldn't have cared less whether he had
graduated from law school. History was on Reagan's side in this regard.
Fifteen of the forty-three persons who had until 1973 served as justices
of the California Supreme Court during the twentieth century (and ten
of the forty-four justices of the U.S. Supreme Court) had not graduated
from law school. Marvin Anderson, dean of University of California's
Hastings College of Law, said the state high court would have been deprived of many valuable members "if we were to apply the standard that
one must have a brilliant academic record from a prestigious law school
as the sole criteria."[8]

But in a battle that was a distant early warning of the fight that would
be waged against Senate confirmation of President Reagan's appointment of Robert Bork to the Supreme Court in 1987, liberal groups
challenged the Clark appointment. The California Trial Lawyers Association described the appointment as "indefensible." Democratic
lawyers in the Legislature, the National Lawyers Guild, and the National Organization for Women lined up against Clark, while Republi-

cans gave him across-the-board support. Reagan inadvertently fueled the opposition by overstating Clark's qualifications.*

In California, appointees to the Supreme Court require the confirmation of a three-member Judicial Appointments Commission. Its members at the time were Supreme Court Chief Justice Donald Wright, State Attorney General Evelle Younger, and Parker Wood of Los Angeles, who served on the commission by virtue of his rank as the senior appellate justice in the state. There was bad blood between the governor and Wright, who had disappointed Reagan by striking down California's death penalty law. With Wright considered a likely "no" vote and opposition to the appointment mounting, Clark offered to withdraw his name. Reagan wouldn't hear of it. He sent Clark an octagonal crystal inscribed, "ILLEGITMUS NON CARBORRUNDUM— To Bill from Ron." (The inscription was popularly translated: "Don't let the bastards grind you down.")

The controversy dragged on for nearly two months before the commission took a vote on March 3, 1973. Wright, who had approved Clark's elevation to the appellate court, voted against his appointment to the Supreme Court. He said Clark had demonstrated "promise of growth" but was "not qualified by education, training, and experience" for the Supreme Court.[9] Younger, a Republican who would later run for governor, voted for Clark. So did Justice Wood, the only member of the panel who had served with Clark on a court. Wood and Clark did not always see eye to eye on cases, but the senior justice liked Clark and respected his legal abilities. Because of this, Clark's appointment to the Supreme Court prevailed on a 2–1 vote.

But Reagan was running out of victories.

A new federal law gave states an option of turning over their welfare programs for the aged, blind, and disabled to the federal government. In the summer of 1973, Reagan exercised his option to do so. Since federal payments were less than California's, he agreed that the recipients should receive a modest augmentation from the state. This did not satisfy Democrats in the Legislature, who insisted that recipients receive the full amount of their state grants and introduced legislation to accomplish this.

Reagan persuaded Republican state senators to block the Democratic bill and, on the advice of Earl Brian, his health and welfare secretary,

---

*After he announced the appointment on January 9, Reagan was asked at a press conference if Clark's four years on the bench gave him "sufficient" experience for the Supreme Court. "I think he has actually had a legal career that has been pretty outstanding for about 15 years," Reagan said. "He served on the bench with 150 decisions, none of which was ever overturned." Clark had actually written 125 opinions, five of which were unanimously reversed by the California Supreme Court.

implemented a plan with lesser payments. Welfare groups sued, claiming that Reagan had exceeded his powers in acting without legislative approval. On November 19, 1973, a state appellate court agreed with the plaintiffs. The Reagan administration capitulated and accepted a $122 million Democratic bill with higher aid payments than he wanted. Mike Deaver acknowledged that Reagan had received "bad staff advice." Privately, Deaver and Republican legislators blamed Brian, who they said was preoccupied with running for the U.S. Senate and hadn't done his homework.[10]

Reagan was not involved in the negotiations on the welfare bill, which was signed into law by Lieutenant Governor Ed Reinecke. The governor was on a twelve-day tour of the Far East for President Nixon, an assignment he welcomed. A year earlier, Reagan had dutifully carried the news to the government on Taiwan that Nixon was recognizing the People's Republic of China. Reagan kept his reservations about this decision to himself but freely expressed a growing interest in foreign affairs as his governorship drew to a close.

On January 9, 1974, Reagan gave his last State of the State Address. It contained no new proposals, and his delivery was flat. On January 29, Reagan's perfect record of having 797 vetoes sustained was broken when the Legislature overrode a bill that would have given the governor final authority in closing any of the state's mental hospitals. It was the first time a California governor's veto had been overridden in twenty-eight years. On February 5, a front-page analysis of Reagan's troubles appeared in the *Los Angeles Times*. Written by the knowledgeable George Skelton, who had covered the administration since its early days, the story concluded with the harsh judgment of an anonymous Republican strategist who was described as close to Reagan. "There's no way a governor is going to lose an override by one vote," the strategist was quoted as saying. "There are too many ways to keep legislators happy, too many tradeoffs that can be made. But that takes work, doesn't it? There is a definite sickness in the administration."[11]

Reagan wasn't sick, but he was drifting. I traveled with him to the South in the fall of 1973 and interviewed him twice in 1974, once for *The Washington Post* and once for an analysis of his governorship in *California Journal*.[12] Each time Reagan came across as conflicted. Should he run for President? Should he return to what he called "the mashed potato circuit" and make millions of dollars as an inspirational speaker? Should he retire, with Nancy, to his ranch? At different times he expressed all of these attitudes. Sometimes it seemed to me he wanted to do all three things—and at the same time. Within the Reagan entourage, all aspects of these options were represented. Some were ready for the next political battle. Some needed to make money, more desperately than Reagan ever did. And some, tired from sixteen-hour days while their leader went home early, just wanted out of government. They had been in Sacramento a long time.

Richard Nixon's fall added to Reagan's uncertainty. As the Watergate cover-up closed in upon the president, no Republican officeholder in the country defended Nixon more staunchly than Reagan. (Against the advice of Deaver, Reagan also defended Nixon's money-grubbing Vice President Spiro Agnew, perhaps remembering the help Agnew had given the Reagan administration during its battle with the federal welfare bureaucracy.) Reagan was slow to recognize the implications of the Watergate scandal for the Republican Party and even slower to distance himself from those who were under investigation. On May 1, 1973, he said that the Watergate conspirators were "not criminals at heart."[13] He did not seem to entertain any thoughts that the spreading investigation would bring down the administration, or even cripple it, and he rarely watched the televised hearings of the Senate Judiciary Committee. Touring the South in November 1973, Reagan said Nixon was governing well despite Watergate. When it became apparent that Watergate would not go away, Reagan upped the ante in his defense of Nixon. In private he talked of "a lynch mob" forming to get the president. In public he counterattacked. Speaking to Republicans at a Lincoln Day dinner in Oklahoma City on February 12, 1974, Reagan urged his listeners to shed any guilt feelings and go on the offensive. "We in our party have too often been the victims of big city political machines voting tombstones, warehouses and empty lots against us in every election," he declared in a heavily applauded non sequitur.

Throughout the spring and summer of Nixon's discontent, Reagan remained a Nixon loyalist. On June 11, 1974, Reagan was asked about a report by the columnists Rowland Evans and Robert Novak that "the Reagan inner circle flinches over Reagan's refusal to find any fault with the embattled President." Reagan said the columnists were "stretching it a little bit" and repeated a frequent statement that Nixon and his advisers should be presumed innocent. Not until August 6, when Nixon's resignation speech was being prepared and the pro-Nixon Republicans on the House Judiciary Committee had deserted the president, did Reagan acknowledge, "Now, for the first time, it has been revealed that neither the Congress nor the American people had been told the entire truth about Watergate." Even then, he did not demand resignation but said it was "absolutely imperative" that Nixon go before Congress and make a full disclosure—as if that were any longer an alternative. On August 27, eighteen days after Nixon had resigned and two weeks before

President Gerald Ford pardoned him, Reagan said that for the former president, "the punishment of resignation certainly is more than adequate for the crime."[14]

Perhaps alone among prominent Republicans who stuck with the president, Reagan never suffered a moment from his loyalty. Soon after he made his statement about the Watergate conspirators not being "criminals at heart," I asked pollster Robert Teeter if statements like this would damage Reagan in the public opinion polls. "No, not at all," Teeter replied. "It will just show to everybody that he doesn't know what's going on and isn't involved."[15] Teeter was right. Reagan's popularity increased during this period, even though his administration was in a slump. Partly, that was because Reagan's loyalty to a sinking president reinforced the idea that the California governor was a man of his convictions. But more than anything, Reagan profited from Watergate because it encouraged voters to examine the character of their leaders.

·   ·   ·

In an assessment of Reagan's governorship three months before he left office, Tom Goff of the *Los Angeles Times* said Reagan had left footprints on the government of California that "can be swept away as easily as if he had walked on sand." He credited Reagan with providing "a necessary and desirable breathing spell" after the era of growth and expansion that began during World War II but questioned the permanency of anything he had accomplished. "History probably will conclude that Reagan was a check-point, rather than a turning-point in the basically liberal political direction of California," Goff wrote.[16]

History has concluded otherwise. Apart from his specific accomplishments, Reagan set a tone of skepticism about liberal, expansionist government that persists to this day in California. Before Reagan, the prevailing view in Sacramento was that government should be a protective benefactor of the people. This belief, rooted in the Progressive era, flourished under Republican governors Earl Warren and Goodwin Knight and blossomed during the Democratic years of Pat Brown's governorship and Jesse Unruh's speakership. Under Reagan, this faith in government was banished, never to return. Jerry Brown, who succeeded Reagan, preached a minimalist doctrine and squeezed higher education, the mental hospitals, and many social programs. The Republicans who succeeded Brown accepted Reaganesque doctrines of limited government and paid homage to Reagan for instilling them. By then, Reagan had carried his act to the national political stage, from which he tugged the nation in a conservative direction. The "Reagan

Revolution"—an overstatement that I prefer to call the "Reagan Redirection"—that came to power in Washington was rooted in the Reagan governorship.

In California, Reagan casts a long political shadow. He had more influence on public attitudes toward government and on government's sense of its mission than he did on the fortunes of the Republican Party, where his national impact was greater than it was in California. Even when Reagan was governor, the Legislature remained in Democratic hands, as it has, except for a single session, ever since. In time, the destiny of demographics overwhelmed California Republicans, who worshiped Reagan without emulating him and failed miserably to cultivate a growing Latino electorate. California, once secure for Republicans, became a Democratic redoubt in national and state elections alike. But when Democrats regained the governorship in 1998, it was under a banner of cautious centralism. None of the Republican imitators who currently fly the conservative flag is Ronald Reagan, and Gray Davis is no Pat Brown.

In the immediate aftermath of the Reagan governorship, before his longer legacy was evident, evaluations of Reagan's performance focused on the budget, education, the environment, and welfare reform. Reagan overstated his accomplishments on these matters, in large part to establish his credentials as a presidential candidate. Reagan's adversaries disparaged his record, also because he was running for president. It is, by any reasonable judgment, a mixed record, although on balance more positive than negative. Overall, there is much to be said for an observation made twenty years ago by my friend Judson Clark, who had served as a legislative aide to Assembly speakers of both parties: "Reagan was not so much an underachiever as he was an over committer. He did some important things, but not as much as he said he would do and not as much as he said he did."[17]

Governor Reagan did not operate in a vacuum. Faced during most of his tenure in Sacramento with an opposition Legislature, he needed to compromise and did. Many of these compromises turned out well, for Reagan had the dual advantages of strong convictions and a practical temperament that enabled him to seize a useful half-measure and celebrate it as total victory. Reagan was ideological and practical in nearly equal measure, and this balanced combination of attributes was crucial to his political accomplishments. This was not well understood, either in Sacramento or in Washington. Reagan's supporters said he succeeded because of his conservative convictions. His critics maintained that he succeeded in spite of them. Both sides were right.

Reagan's compromises were especially productive in the educational arena. He had an excellent record of funding elementary and secondary education, but this was as much the doing of Democratic legislative leaders, especially Bob Moretti, as it was the governor's. Education spending increased 89 percent during Reagan's eight years in office compared to 71 percent during Pat Brown's eight years. These figures are even more impressive than this comparison indicates: Elementary and secondary enrollment increased 37.6 percent during the Brown years and only 2.6 percent during Reagan's terms. Spending on higher education during the Reagan years increased by 136 percent. Reagan backed a program for early childhood education and supported a master plan for special education advocated by Wilson Riles, the progressive state superintendent of public instruction. "We did not go backward under Reagan's regime," said Riles. "We went forward."[18]

Going forward, however, proved considerably more difficult than Reagan had anticipated when, announcing his candidacy for governor, he had promised to make California "first in more than size and crime and taxes." During the Reagan years, California's rate of population growth slowed after three decades of dynamic increase, but crime and taxes did not. Although Reagan signed more than forty bills providing stiffer sentences for criminals or other intended improvements in the criminal justice system, California was not safer when Reagan left office in 1974. In eight years, the homicide rate had doubled and the rate of armed robberies had increased even more. There isn't much a governor can do about the crime rate, but taxes increased under Reagan as they had never increased in California before. On the presidential campaign trail, Reagan boasted of returning $5.7 billion in taxes, including $4 billion in property tax relief, to Californians. He never said that these taxes came from increases he sponsored that were at the time the largest in the history of any state. Under Reagan, the state budget increased from $4.6 billion annually to $10.2 billion. The operations portion of the budget, over which the governor has the most control, went from $2.2 billion to $3.5 billion. State taxes per $100 of personal income increased from $6.64 to $7.62.

This is the way Reagan's critics preferred to state his fiscal record. But if the $4 billion in direct property-tax relief is subtracted from the Reagan budgets, they increased only slightly more than inflation. And there is no doubt that Reagan and his three finance directors did much to control the growth of state government. During Pat Brown's eight years in office, the state workforce increased nearly 50 percent. The growth rate was less than half of that during Reagan's eight years, rising from 158,400 to 192,400 positions. If higher education, where a governor's control was indirect, is excluded, the growth was 6.5 percent (from

108,090 to 115,090) at a time when government workforces in other populous states were growing at far more rapid rates.

Reagan did more than can be measured by statistics. From a standing start as a governmental novice, he mastered the intricacies of governing the nation's most populous and macroscopic state. He roused the public and demonstrated, as no one had done before him, that it is possible to succeed as governor of a major state without abandoning conservative convictions. "Reagan will be a hard act to follow," proclaimed a headline in the *San Francisco Sunday Examiner & Chronicle* shortly before he left office. The analysis below the headline, written by the liberal Sydney Kossen, gave Reagan credit for keeping his promises to trim state spending and for saving Round Valley by blocking construction of the Dos Rios dam.[19]

Even Reagan's most persistent editorial nemesis, *The Sacramento Bee*, found good points in his governorship: "Reagan can cite an administration free of major scandal. The state payroll has barely grown numerically since 1966. Not known as a conservationist, he did sign some of the strictest air quality laws in the nation. He also signed legislation easing the state's 100-year-old abortion law in the face of strong opposition. The man who finally got to play a governor has proved himself a capable administrator who did as well as most in trying to do what he set out to do."[20]

A majority of Californians agreed. Pollster Mervin Field's survey in August 1974, just after President Nixon resigned in disgrace, found that three Californians thought that Reagan had done a good or excellent job for every two who thought he did a poor one.[21] Reagan's overall ratings during his eight years were much higher than Pat Brown's. And this last survey of Reagan's approval rating came at a time when overall approval for the Republican Party, and Republican registration in California, were plummeting.

Bathed in praise during the final weeks of his governorship, Reagan could scarcely believe what he was reading. Guided by an inner sense of destiny, he was never one to take much stock in polls. In the final months of 1974, Reagan kept his own counsel and disappointed firebrand former aides such as Lyn Nofziger by refusing, at first, to criticize the Republican president in the White House. But Reagan was keeping his options open and looking ahead.

The option that most intrigued him was the presidency.

III

THE PURSUIT OF
THE PRESIDENCY

26

CHALLENGER

R EPUBLICAN MISFORTUNES paved the path of opportunity for
Ronald Reagan throughout his political career. Richard Nixon's
unsuccessful run for governor of California in 1962 left that office in the hands of a Democrat and gave Reagan an opening four years
later. Barry Goldwater's landslide defeat in 1964 took Republican officeholders across the nation down with him and left the GOP especially bereft of conservative luminaries. Reagan, whose "Time for
Choosing" speech had been the bright spot of the Goldwater campaign,
emerged from that debacle as the conservative political star at a time
when the Republican Party, and the country, were moving to the right.

In 1974, Reagan's eighth and final year as governor, two political
calamities opened a path to the presidency. The first, on August 9, was
the resignation of President Nixon after a taped conversation known as
"the smoking gun" persuaded even diehard congressional defenders of
Nixon's complicity in the Watergate cover-up. The second, on September 8, was President Gerald Ford's unconditional pardon of Nixon, who
had been named an unindicted coconspirator in the Watergate prosecu-
tions. Ford believed that America needed "recovery, not revenge." He
insisted that he was pardoning Nixon to prevent a period of "prolonged
vituperation and recrimination [that] would be disastrous for the nation"[1] and testified before the House Judiciary Committee that "there
was no deal, period." No evidence has ever contradicted this claim, but
the pardon was politically catastrophic for Ford and his party in the climate of cynicism induced by Watergate and the seemingly unending
war in Vietnam. Ford dropped almost overnight from 66 percent to 50
percent in the Gallup Poll and never rose significantly above this figure
during the remainder of his presidency.

The public registered its verdict forcefully in the November midterm elections, another Republican debacle that brought Reagan to the fore. The Democrats gained forty-six seats, including several that were historically safe Republican, and boosted their margin in the House to 290–145, sufficient to override a presidential veto. Republicans also lost four U.S. Senate seats and four governorships, including California, where the winner was Jerry Brown, the son of the man whom Reagan had defeated eight years earlier.*

Republican prospects for recovery seemed even bleaker than after Goldwater's defeat. In January 1975, pollster Robert Teeter gave a stark assessment to Republican state chairmen meeting in Chicago. He told them that most Americans thought of the Republican Party as untrustworthy, incompetent, and closely allied with big business. Only 18 percent of the American people identified themselves as Republicans. Worse yet, Teeter found "unbelievable increases in cynicism toward politics and American institutions in general and toward the Republican Party in particular."[2] The Watergate scandal and the pardon of Nixon had cost the Republicans an asset they had retained even after Goldwater's loss, when the GOP was still seen by voters as a party of higher integrity than the Democrats. Now, the Democrats were regarded as more honest. It was in this context of widespread distrust of the Republican Party that Reagan became an undeclared, uncertain, and frequently underestimated candidate for president.

Reagan's natural optimism served him well in this dark moment. Never one to take comfort in his fears, he tried to buoy the spirits of his fellow Republicans. The day after Nixon's resignation, Reagan addressed the National Young Republicans in the casino country of South Lake Tahoe. At a time when most Republicans were more disheartened than a busted gambler, Reagan urged his listeners to forget their fallen leader and put their trust in conservative ideology. "You can have faith in the Republican philosophy of fiscal common sense, limited government and individual freedom," Reagan said. "Let me offer the experience of the past seven and one-half years in California to support that assurance." He then recounted his achievements in welfare reform but warned that such struggles are "a never-ending battle." Even while California was cutting welfare costs, food stamps—"intended for a worthy

---

*Reagan had expected his handpicked lieutenant governor, Ed Reinecke, to succeed him. But Reinecke was defeated in the June 1974 primary by Houston Flournoy, the state controller, who narrowly lost to Brown. Reinecke resigned as lieutenant governor on October 3, 1974, after being convicted of perjury for lying to a Senate committee that was investigating alleged improprieties by the Nixon administration in settling antitrust suits against the International Telephone and Telegraph Corporation. An appellate court reversed the conviction on grounds that a quorum was not present at the Senate committee session at which Reinecke testified.

purpose"—had become an "administrative nightmare, a staggering financial burden at the federal level and the newest nesting place for welfare abuse and fraud."

Reagan's speech presented his policies in California as a model for the federal government, and many in the cheering crowd no doubt considered Reagan a personal model for the presidency. The address could have been the opening address of his 1976 presidential campaign; indeed, many of its passages would be replicated in speeches he gave after he became a candidate. But although running for president was much on his mind, Reagan was at this point a long way from making a firm decision.

In May 1974, when it still seemed that Nixon might weather the storm, Reagan had discussed his prospects with old and new advisers at a long meeting at his Pacific Palisades home. This meeting had aspects of his early discussions about the governorship with Holmes Tuttle and his wealthy friends. Tuttle was at the May meeting along with Justin Dart, a latecomer to the Kitchen Cabinet, and David Packard, a Republican financial power. The old Reagan hands in attendance included Lyn Nofziger, Ed Meese, Mike Deaver, and Peter Hannaford, a public relations specialist who would become Deaver's partner after the governorship. Some newer members of the Reagan team were there, too: Jim Lake, who represented the governor in Washington, and staff aides Jim Jenkins and Robert Walker from Sacramento.[3]

In 1967, when Reagan was beginning his governorship, Walker had helped a cerebral Washington lawyer named John P. Sears run the early Nixon-for-President campaign. Sears and Mississippi State Republican Chairman Clarke Reed were the only outsiders at the Pacific Palisades meeting. Reagan did not know Sears but listened attentively when he predicted that Nixon would not survive and that Ford would be unable to lead the country after he was gone. Sears was suggesting that Reagan could run for president in 1976 no matter what happened. If Nixon lasted, there would be an open run for the nomination. If Ford inherited the presidency, then Reagan could contest the nomination in the Republican primaries.

This was a heretical notion, and the Reagan team was not ready for it. Reagan, Nofziger, and Meese were too much the loyalists to concede that Nixon was done for politically, and Sears did not have much support for his proposition. But everyone was impressed with the bold analysis of this thirty-four-year-old lawyer, who had skillfully directed Nixon's delegate search in 1968 and had been a rising figure in the Nixon administration until forced out by John Mitchell in 1969. Sears was then committed to Vice President Spiro Agnew, whom he believed would be the Republican nominee in 1976. When Agnew resigned as an alternative to being prosecuted, Sears was left without a candidate. Ford was surrounded by old congressional pals and aides inherited from the Nixon administration. The best Sears could hope for from the Ford crowd was a subordinate job, which did not interest him. Sears wanted to run a presidential campaign. Walker, with help from Jim Lake, convinced Sears that he was the right man for Reagan and that Reagan would be right for him.

People in the Reagan camp who later became sworn enemies of Sears still value the contribution he made in this uncertain time. The Californians around Reagan were resourceful, but the Watergate scandal had deprived them of the chart by which they set their compass. All the grand plans for a 1976 Reagan presidential campaign were now worthless, and Reagan was running in place, waiting for something to happen. It was at this moment that Sears arrived.* While many of his ideas were initially rejected, he planted the seeds for the Reagan challenge to President Ford. Nofziger believes that Reagan would have wound up running in 1976 no matter who was president,[5] and he may well be right. But it was Sears who persuaded Reagan that he could challenge a president of his own party and get away with it. This idea blossomed slowly but steadily in the late spring and summer of 1974 as Nixon's troubles deepened.

The decisive action after Nixon's resignation that cinched the Reagan challenge was Ford's selection of Nelson Rockefeller as vice president. Conservatives who might otherwise have been tempted to give Ford a chance were infuriated at the prospect that Rockefeller might inherit the presidency. More than any other single act of Ford's, or indeed all of them combined, it was the selection of Rockefeller that fueled national interest among conservatives in a Reagan candidacy. Eventually, Ford would yield to conservative pressure and prod Rockefeller to take himself off the 1976 ticket. But by the time this happened—November 3, 1975—Reagan was long committed to the challenge.

In 1974, the prevailing view among the Reagan entourage was that the Rockefeller nomination was designed to stop Reagan. As far back as

---

*Jules Witcover, who was close to Sears, described him as having "a deceptively shy outer crust that camouflaged a biting humor and political toughness and skepticism. Also, his appreciation of and affinity with members of the Washington press corps set him apart from most of the political operatives around both Nixon and Reagan. Where many of the paranoid Nixon types looked upon reporters as the enemy, to be warded off at every turn, Sears saw them as an essential and unavoidable element in the drama of electing a president."[4] Reagan did not have Nixon's preoccupation with "enemies" but believed the Washington press corps was predominantly liberal and distrustful of westerners and conservatives. Sears' rapport with Washington reporters was a recommendation in his favor with Reagan.

December 1973, Rockefeller's decision to resign as governor of New York had been interpreted in Sacramento as an attempt to gain a head start over Reagan in the race for the 1976 presidential nomination. Larry Stammer, the Sacramento correspondent for the *San Jose Mercury-News*, reported that Rockefeller's decision "has renewed interest within the Reagan administration about the California governor's future."[6]

After Nixon resigned, that interest was focused on the vice presidency. On the weekend after Ford became president, Reagan said, "I have always felt that for too long a time we have turned to the legislative branch of our government for our candidates for president and have ignored the fact that those with the most executive experience are governors." By itself, this statement made a case both for Rockefeller and Reagan. But when Reagan was asked whether Ford might select a liberal or a moderate as vice president, he replied, "I happen to believe that what is termed by many as the conservative philosophy is the basic Republican philosophy. It is a libertarian philosophy, a belief in individual freedom and the reduction of government. And so, obviously, I would feel that we were more committed to the mandate of 1972, the philosophical mandate, that people handed down in such overwhelming numbers, if the president should choose someone representative of the Republican Party."[7]

Reagan insisted that he was not campaigning for vice president. But Gordon Luce, who had left Reagan's cabinet to become California Republican chairman and remained close to the governor, sent a different signal. Luce telegrammed the forty-nine other Republican state chairmen urging them to back Ford's selection of Reagan as vice president.[8] How many did so is unknown, but the telegrams went unacknowledged by the White House. Ford's selection of Rockefeller a week later was regarded in Sacramento as a slap in the face. To Republican conservatives who recalled the primary battle of '64, the selection of their old enemy was an unbelievable insult. What concerned Reagan, however, was not that Ford had departed from "the conservative philosophy." He was, instead, disappointed that he had been passed over himself—and would have been even more so had he known at the time, as Ford later revealed, that he was not even on the five-man list from which Rockefeller was chosen.[9]

As the months went by, Reagan and the conservative movement accumulated more grievances against President Ford. The day before Rockefeller was named vice president, Ford had flown to Chicago to address the convention of the Veterans of Foreign Wars. There, he surprised his audience by proposing limited amnesty for Vietnam War draft evaders and deserters, an idea Reagan sharply opposed. While Reagan said he approved of "compassion based on the individual situation for each individual," he also observed that many of those who had refused to fight in Vietnam had no regrets about their conduct. "They didn't feel they did anything wrong in choosing the laws they would break, and they simply want the country to recognize them as somehow being in the moral right," Reagan said.[10]

When I interviewed Reagan in October 1974, he said nothing positive about Ford and claimed it was too early to judge his administration. But he defended Nixon despite the "mistakes" of Watergate and said "that history [is] probably going to be far more kind to that administration with regard to accomplishments."[11] Reagan added that in matters of "world leadership" Nixon was "far more effective than anything we've had for a great many years." Reagan clearly doubted if Ford would be Nixon's equal in foreign policy, an opinion not limited to conservatives. In a November 11 radio commentary that did not mention Ford by name, Reagan criticized the United States for abstaining at a meeting of the Organization of American States in the vote on a resolution to lift the trade embargo on Cuba. Reagan insisted that the conditions for any American dealings with Castro should be removal of Soviet bases, a pledge that Cuba would no longer train Communist guerrillas for military action in other countries, and the settling of claims of American citizens whose property was seized after the Castro takeover.

Ford had even less respect for Reagan than Reagan had for Ford. The president dismissed warnings from advisers that Reagan would present a difficult challenge. "I hadn't taken those warnings seriously because I didn't take Reagan seriously," Ford wrote in his memoirs, in which he observed that Reagan was "one of the few political leaders I have ever met whose public speeches revealed more than his private conversations." Ford criticized Reagan for "his penchant for offering simplistic solutions to hideously complex problems," a belief that he was "always right in every argument," and his supposed nine-to-five work habits.[12]

Despite his low regard for Reagan, Ford was worried enough about his drawing power among conservatives who were angry over the Rockefeller selection that he sought to neutralize Reagan by offering him a cabinet post. Ford called Reagan and they discussed a number of possibilities, including an ambassadorship to the Court of St. James. Ford finally asked Reagan if he would accept an appointment as secretary of transportation. Reagan declined. I had heard about the possible ambassadorship (although not the cabinet offer) when I interviewed Reagan in October and asked him about it. "Hell, I can't afford to be an ambassador," said Reagan, who went on to rule out running for the U.S. Senate in 1976.[13] "Now don't automatically assume the other," he went on, although I had not asked him if he would run for president. After drawing attention to his own high standing with Republican voters in the polls, Reagan issued a disclaimer about his ambitions: "Now, I hope and pray that this administration is successful. And that would take care of '76. Because it's never—in my book—it's never been important who's in the White House; it's what's done. And that's what I mean about the mandate. Whatever may happen, I would like to feel that I can continue to be a voice in the Republican Party insuring that the party pursues the philosophy that I believe should be the Republican philosophy."[14]

In this circuitous fashion, Reagan preserved his options in late 1974 and early 1975. His curious notion that he would serve as a sort of watchdog who would carefully eye the Ford administration for signs of ideological defection disappointed conservatives, especially Nofziger, who had already judged Ford and found him wanting. The pragmatic Sears, who knew that potential Reagan supporters would commit to Ford if Reagan dallied too long before getting into the race, was also disappointed. But Reagan, in a mood reminiscent of his reluctance in 1968, could not be pushed to make a decision. "I'm not going to make a fool of myself," he told Tuttle, adding that he really did want to see how Ford performed before he decided what he would do.

Reagan's wait-and-see attitude was accepted philosophically by Meese, then leaving the administration for a position with the San Diego–based Rohr Corporation. He knew from experience that Reagan stubbornly resisted when pushed too hard to make a decision he was not ready to make. Reagan's caution was a boon to Deaver, who, months before the end of the governorship, had secured a lucrative agreement to manage Reagan's affairs after he left office. Deaver's plan, which Nancy Reagan also signed off on, was to open an advertising agency with Hannaford in Sacramento and Los Angeles that would book Reagan's speeches and research and sell his radio commentaries and a syndicated column. In this way, Reagan became Deaver and Hannaford's meal ticket. Within three months of leaving office, Reagan was making eight to ten speeches a month at an average fee of $5,000 a speech. His column was appearing in 174 newspapers, and his commentaries aired on more than 200 radio stations. His income, $49,100 a year during the governorship, was a closely guarded secret but was estimated at more than $800,000 in 1975. Reagan told friends he was happy to be earning money again. He was in no hurry to give up the column and the radio commentaries, as he would have to do if he became an avowed candidate for president.

Reagan could have made more money and gained even higher visibility if he had taken an offer that Deaver disclosed in an interview for this book. The offer came from CBS, where the iconic Walter Cronkite anchored the evening newscasts and made the network the undisputed leader in television news. The proposal from CBS was that Reagan would do commentary two nights a week. Eric Sevareid, a respected liberal journalist, would do commentary on two other nights. Deaver was excited about the idea, which he thought put in the shade Hannaford's plan for a syndicated radio commentary. He took the CBS offer to Reagan, who said, "I am going to do the radio broadcast."

"Why?" Deaver asked.

"People will tire of me on television," Reagan replied. "They won't tire of me on the radio."[15]

Reagan's bearings shifted rightward as his focus moved from the governorship to the banquet circuit. In Sacramento, the give-and-take of governance had kept Reagan's ideological and pragmatic tendencies in balance. He read the mini-memos, met regularly with the press, and dealt with strong-minded legislators. Clark, and after him Meese, had seen to it that Reagan heard from all sides before making an important decision, with perhaps the notable exception of the ill-fated Proposition 1. But Reagan was isolated on the lecture circuit, though he saw, and spoke to, many more thousands of people than he had met in the governor's office. These audiences wanted ideological comfort, and Reagan gave them what they wanted, including a story of a Chicago "welfare queen" who had "eighty names, thirty addresses, twelve Social Security cards" and was "collecting veterans benefits on four nonexisting deceased husbands." The woman, subsequently convicted of using two aliases to collect public aid checks totaling $8,000, became an enduring symbol of welfare fraud.

As a governor, Reagan had displayed an executive's temperament: He had the ability to go to the heart of an issue and balance conflicting claims in ways that gave solace to the losers. As a speaker before conservative audiences, he retreated to the simplicities of "A Time for Choosing," rousing listeners rather than educating them. Away from Sacramento, he had no Meese, no Clark, and no mini-memos to give him all sides of an issue. His favorite reading on the road was *Reader's Digest*, which was full of those amazing stories and statistics Reagan loved, and *Human Events*, which provided ideological certainty.

Briefly, Reagan toyed with a third-party candidacy. He was impressed with the thoughtful exposition of this idea by *National Review* publisher William A. Rusher, who sought to realize an old dream of forming a third party from disgruntled Republican and Democratic conservatives. "There could be one of those moments in time, I don't know," Reagan told reporters in Sacramento on October 15, 1974, after he had returned from a speaking tour. "I see the statements of disaffection of people in both parties—the loss of confidence. And you wonder which is the easiest. Do you restore the confidence or do you change the name or something? I don't know. I really don't." But the men who bankrolled Reagan's campaigns knew. "You're a Republican, and you're going to stay one," Reagan was told by Tuttle, a party man who had been raising money for Republican candidates since Eisenhower. On this issue, the Reagan contributors were on the same wavelength as Sears and Nofziger. Reagan, no windmill-tilter, was quickly convinced. When he appeared before the State Capitol press corps on November 7, a day after Democrats won the California governorship and lopsided margins in the state's congressional and legislative delegations, Reagan punctured the trial balloon he had set aloft. "I am not starting a third party," he said. "I do not believe the Republican Party is dead. I believe the Republican Party represents basically the thinking of the people of this country, if we can get that message across to the people. I'm going to try to do that."

The party was not dead, but many conservatives agreed that it was comatose. Third-party advocates observed the same phenomenon that Teeter had found in his polls. Few Americans respected the Republican Party or identified with it. Conservatives worried that the Democrats would nominate a liberal in 1976 while the Republicans would be stuck with Ford. M. Stanton Evans, the veteran chairman of the American Conservative Union, told a national conservative political action conference meeting in Washington in February 1975 that conservatives should work "to keep the Republican Party as conservative as possible in states, localities and Congress" but also declared to loud applause: "At the presidential level, we need a new political party in 1976."

Reagan didn't buy it. Speaking to the conference on February 15 after Evans' speech, he asked rhetorically: "Is it a third party we need or is it a new and revitalized second party, raising a banner of no pale pastels but bold colors which make it unmistakably clear where we stand on all the issues troubling the people?"

Reagan's great value to the Republican Party in its time of post-Watergate despair was his persistent optimism. He typically warmed up audiences with a display of gallows humor, saying to them, "There are those who will suggest that any mode of optimism expressed at this meeting would be as inappropriate as the captain of the *Titanic* saying, 'Never mind all that ice. Throw a party on Saturday night.'" Then, he would tell stories intended to encourage his partisan audiences, such as his favorite anecdote about the boy who was looking for a pony amid the horse manure, followed by an old joke about a farmer who gets tired of hearing a minister thank the Lord for his bountiful crops and finally says to him, "Reverend, I wish you could have seen this place when the Lord was doing it by himself." These stories were a prelude to the Reagan message, which was that Republicans should take the nation's political fate into their own hands and recreate America in a conservative image.

Reagan did not advocate ideological warfare within the Republican Party. Rather, he proceeded on the assumption that the GOP activists who came to hear him shared a common faith. He knew that his audiences agreed with him about the evils of government spending, and he knew, too, that many of his listeners were vaguely uncomfortable with the cheerful, inarticulate presidency of Gerald Ford, whom Reagan almost never mentioned. Instead, he suggested that the "mandate" of 1972 was in danger of being betrayed. "The '72 election gave us a new majority, a long-overdue realignment based not on party labels—but on basic philosophy," Reagan said. "The tragedy of Watergate and the traumatic experience of these past years since then has obscured the meaning of that '72 election. But the mandate registered by the people still remains. The people have not changed in philosophy."

Despite the clarity of his politics, Reagan was as reluctant as ever to make a personal decision before it was absolutely necessary. As always, he drifted in the direction of where he wanted to go. What Reagan wanted to do in 1975 was run for president, preferably against a Democrat rather than a Republican incumbent. Ford was in the way. Reagan keenly remembered the GOP split of 1964 and his own insistence on party unity as a precondition of victory in 1966. He knew that he risked being cast as the spoiler who would hand over the White House to a Democrat. Still, Reagan wanted to run. He wanted it so much that Ford's lapses became magnified into crises of presidential leadership. Ford vetoed Democratic spending bills as readily as Reagan had done in California, but Reagan nonetheless saw the $52 billion federal deficit as a Ford failing. The appointment of Rockefeller rankled, and there were those in the Reagan entourage who took seriously the rumors that Ford might decide at the last moment not to run and attempt to hand Rockefeller the prize of the Republican nomination. Ford was not a leader, Reagan told his intimates. In private conversations, Reagan referred to him as a "caretaker" who had been in Congress too long. Slowly—too slowly for Sears and Nofziger—Reagan was selling himself on running for president.

Ford helped make the sale. A traditionalist who accepted the conventional wisdom of Washington, Ford did not believe that the Republican Party would tear itself to pieces again by ousting an incumbent president. Nor, despite Rockefeller, did he believe that many Republicans would accept the far-fetched notion that he was a liberal president. Preoccupied with the problems of the presidency and pulled in different directions by a staff divided between Nixon holdovers and old congressional aides, Ford did not pay consistent attention to the Reagan challenge or treat it seriously enough once he became aware of what was happening. When he acted at all, he did the wrong things. Reagan was particularly insulted when Ford had his chief of staff, Donald Rumsfeld, offer him another cabinet job, this time secretary of commerce. "They're working their way down the scale," a Reagan intimate said when he heard of this offer. He might have heard the line from Reagan, for this was Reagan's view.

Rumsfeld at least acted in private. Worse than this weak offer was the muddle-headed approach of Ford's former congressional cronies, notably Melvin R. Laird, who told reporters that Reagan would not enter the race once he had weighed the options. Ford and his friends, no less than Reagan, were demonstrating that they could talk themselves into believing whatever they wanted to believe. When these stories drifted back to Pacific Palisades, it seemed to Reagan as if he were being described as afraid to take on the president. But there was no way to scare Reagan out of the race.

If Ford had respected Reagan more or understood him better, he would have realized that he had other options. He might have brought Reagan back to the White House for high-visibility meetings, heard him out, and given the appearance of taking his guidance. Some Reagan intimates who knew that the governor was susceptible to flattery, especially from the president of the United States, were worried that Ford might try this approach. Sears knew better. He realized that Ford, after a quarter century in Congress, had a parochial view of national politics and did not grasp the magnitude of the Reagan challenge. He also realized that Ford was hampered by his selection of Secretary of the Army Howard ("Bo") Callaway, a wealthy Georgia conservative, to head his election committee. Callaway had neither standing with the Reaganites nor any experience directing a national campaign. Sears remembered how Callaway had bungled the job as Nixon's southern coordinator in 1968 by inviting George Wallace into the Republican Party and allowing the Nixon campaign to be tagged as racist. Ford either did not know about this incident or did not remember it. To a president of the United States who had spent his entire political life before Agnew's demise in the House of Representatives, Callaway had one sterling quality that commended him as a political manager: He also had been a member of the House.

In California, some Republicans grumbled at Reagan's unwillingness to give Ford the benefit of any doubt. A Reagan intimate with Nixon and Watergate on his mind anonymously expressed his disgust to me late in 1974, saying, "Now is the time for loyalty to a Republican, not when the president is an unindicted coconspirator." Within the Reagan ranks, the most prominent defector was Henry Salvatori, a Kitchen Cabinet member who had been second only to Tuttle in his enthusiasm for Reagan and one of the original trio of fund-raisers (with Tuttle and Cy Rubel) for Reagan in the 1966 campaign. Salvatori, the most conservative member of the Kitchen Cabinet, told Tuttle in 1975 that a Reagan campaign would be divisive and could cost the GOP the White House. Less surprisingly, Reagan also failed to win over the more moderate David Packard, who had been invited to the May 1974 strategy session at which Sears was introduced to the governor. Packard would have been willing to help Reagan in an open race; instead, he became Ford's national finance chairman.

Two savvy political advisers who had helped Reagan in his campaigns for governor were also on Ford's team or waiting to join it. Tom Reed was an assistant secretary in the Pentagon who in November 1975 was appointed secretary of the Air Force. He kept in touch with Richard Cheney, who had succeeded Rumsfeld as White House chief of staff, and suggested he talk to Tuttle in an effort to discourage Reagan from running.[16] But nothing came of this. Stuart Spencer, the premier Republican strategist in California, was estranged from the Reagan staff and waiting for a call from Ford. Paul Haerle, who had succeeded Reed as Reagan's appointments secretary and Luce as the state Republican chairman, openly supported Ford. All of these defections, especially Spencer, were damaging, but the one person who might have dissuaded Reagan from challenging Ford, other than Nancy Reagan, stuck with him. Tuttle had by the spring of 1975 decided that Reagan would be a stronger Republican nominee than Ford and agreed with Sears and Nofziger that an "exploratory committee" should be formed. Once Tuttle was aboard, the Reagan challenge was assured.

Sears persuaded congenial Senator Paul Laxalt of Nevada to head the exploratory committee. Laxalt would later become Reagan's staunchest ally on Capitol Hill, but he was not at that time a close friend. When Laxalt was running for the Senate in Nevada in 1974, he told me that Reagan talked to him in private as if he were giving a speech. "Same stories, same one-liners," Laxalt said. But he liked Reagan nonetheless, shared his views, and admired him as a governor and national conservative leader. Because of this, Laxalt had resisted Minority Leader Hugh Scott's efforts to line up Republican senators on behalf of Ford's candidacy. The Nevadan was shrewd enough to see that Reagan would wind up running for president, and he wanted to be part of the effort. At the time Sears called upon him, Laxalt was one of the few prominent Republican office-holders willing to identify himself with a Reagan campaign. But he would have been an excellent choice even if Reagan and Sears had the entire Senate to choose from.

Laxalt, the son of a Basque sheepherder and member of a large and successful Nevada family, realized that the Republican Party had a problem no matter what it did. Ford was not a strong candidate against a capable Democrat. Reagan might be, but only if he could win the nomination without tearing the party apart. Laxalt knew what it was like to run on a ticket headed by a divisive candidate. In 1964, he had narrowly lost his first Senate race because he had refused to distance himself from Barry Goldwater. It was the only election Laxalt would ever lose. He emerged from the campaign with a reputation for loyalty and sticking to his convictions. For Reagan to win, Laxalt realized, he also must be seen as loyal to principle. This involved, at the outset, a stealth campaign in which an organization could be quietly assembled while Reagan presented himself as a superior alternative to Ford without openly attacking the president. As Sears had recognized, Laxalt's personable style made him perfect for this task.

Citizens for Reagan, as the exploratory committee was called, came into being on July 15, 1975, a week after Ford formally announced that he would seek election in his own right. The Reagan committee's avowed mission, reminiscent of 1966, was to determine the extent of public support for a Reagan candidacy. Everyone who counted—Sears, Tuttle, Nofziger, Laxalt, and such rising political aides as Jim Lake—knew that the exploration was a formality. But it enabled Reagan to keep his radio show and his column, which were important to him and to Deaver and Hannaford. The message of the committee was that Ford was good but that Reagan was better. "We're not saying President Ford is not doing a good job," said Laxalt blandly in making the announcement. "We feel he is. But Governor Reagan could do a better job, because he is totally independent of the federal government scene."

While the committee organized and raised money, the once and future candidate continued to work the banquet circuit with the 1975 version of his 1964 antigovernment speech. The difference, and it was a big one, was that Reagan was no longer a novice who had never held office but a successful California governor who could plausibly contend that he had translated his conservative theories into practice. California reporters accompanying Reagan on his tours marveled at the former governor's stirring stories of how he had returned the state to fiscal solvency and achieved welfare reform and property tax relief by arousing the public to support him against a Democratic Legislature. These accounts ignored the seminal role played by Assembly Speaker Bob Moretti, and much else, and never mentioned that Reagan had agreed to tax increases well beyond the amount needed to close the deficit he had inherited. They were a comic-book version of the history of the Reagan governorship, but there was enough truth in them for Reagan to get away with it. And the speeches succeeded in their main purpose: persuading Republican audiences who had not kept track of what was happening in California that Reagan had the practical experience needed for the presidency.

Reagan's speech, however, did not please the "movement conservatives" of the American Conservative Union, several of whom had grumbled about the performance of their hero at the February political action conference in Washington. They wanted Reagan to challenge Ford directly on détente and the unbalanced federal budget. Above all, they wanted Reagan's speeches to reflect something beyond a general preference for the marketplace and a celebration of his governorship. Nofziger, whose conservative credentials were unassailable, disputed this view. He realized that Reagan's audiences were as happy with his California stories and his bromides as they would be with new ideas and saw no reason to fiddle with the speech. But Nofziger's view did not prevail. The movement conservatives had unlikely allies among reporters who had covered Reagan for a long time and clamored for "something new" to write about. Nofziger resisted them, too, saying that Reagan wasn't trying to make news. Later, Nofziger would quarrel with Sears about the relative blandness of Reagan's approach, but in the summer of 1975 he was content to let Reagan recycle "A Time for Choosing." Sears and his aides David Keene and Jim Lake were too busy organizing to pay attention to Reagan's speeches. As they saw it, if there was one thing Reagan knew how to do, it was speak. Sears and Lake were creating an organization for Reagan in the first primary state of New Hampshire, and Keene was trying to shore up Reagan's southern base. So they gave Nofziger no help in his losing battle to save Reagan from a new speech he did not need.

The speech that arguably prevented Reagan from winning the 1976 Republican presidential nomination was drafted by Jeffrey Bell, a personable conservative on the exploratory committee staff in Washington. Bell had heard Reagan's speech in February before the conservative conference and found it devoid of ideas. "Reagan had absolutely nothing to say," Bell told Jules Witcover later, "so I hit on decentralization as his vision of the future. It was anti-Washington; he could talk about it without attacking Ford. People should have more control, and Washington less. You could get out of the old right-wing rut of calling for repeal of everything and saying that spending for things like education was bad."[17]

Bell's proposal dovetailed neatly with Reagan's frequent claim as governor that states and local governments could run programs such as welfare better than the federal government could. After Stan Evans polished the draft, Bell shipped it to Hannaford in Los Angeles. Hannaford liked the speech, called Sears to praise it, and asked Bell to send him backup material. Before he sent it, Bell discussed the speech with Sears, Keene, and Nofziger. He never discussed it with Reagan, but that didn't matter. When Reagan saw what Bell had written, he remarked to an aide that it was in line with what he would hope to accomplish if he became president.

The formal title of the luncheon speech Reagan gave to the Executive Club of Chicago at McCormick Place on September 26, 1975, was "Let The People Rule." It is remembered in political histories, however, as the "Ninety Billion Speech," as it is called in these pages. The central premise of the speech was that the ills of the nation "all stem from a single source: the belief that government, particularly the federal government, has the answer to our ills and that the proper method of dealing with social problems is to transfer power from the private to the public sector, and within the public sector from state and local governments to the ultimate power center in Washington." With a simplicity and directness that equaled Reagan's, Bell spelled out the consequences of this transfer. "This collectivist, centralizing approach, whatever name or party label it wears, has created our economic problems," he wrote. "By taxing and consuming an ever-greater share of the national wealth, it has imposed an intolerable burden of taxation on American citizens. By spending above and beyond even this level of taxation, it has created the horrendous inflation of the past decade. And by saddling our economy with an ever-greater burden of controls and regulations, it has generated economic problems—from the raising of consumer prices to the destruction of jobs, to choking off vital supplies of energy."

After declaring that "the crushing weight of central government has distorted our federal system and altered the relationship between the levels of government," the speech then broached the solution that was to sink Reagan politically:

> What I propose is nothing less than a systematic transfer of authority and resources to the states—a program of creative federalism for America's third century.

Federal authority has clearly failed to do the job. Indeed, it has created more problems in welfare, education, housing, food stamps, Medicaid, community and regional development, and revenue sharing, to name a few. The sums involved and the potential savings to the taxpayer are large. Transfer of authority in whole or part in all of these areas would reduce the outlay of the federal government by more than $90 billion, using the spending levels of fiscal 1975. With such a savings it would be possible to balance the federal budget, make an initial $5 billion payment on the national debt and cut the federal personal income burden of every American by an average of 23 percent.

Rarely has so much been promised so sweepingly by a presidential candidate-in-waiting. Reagan exempted national defense and space programs, Social Security, Medicare, TVA, "and some aspects of agriculture, energy transportation and the environment" from his transfer proposal. Even so, what he proposed was a mammoth undertaking. Worse yet, from a political standpoint, the backup material that Hannaford had requested from Bell specified reductions in education and manpower training, community and regional development, commerce and transportation, income security, law enforcement, revenue sharing, Medicaid, and health programs.

Reagan's top campaign aides flew in from Los Angeles and Washington to hear him deliver the speech. "We thought the speech was an important issue thrust for him," said Hannaford. "The press treated the whole thing with a yawn."[18] Although the press had been calling for specifics from Reagan, only one Washington-based reporter covered the speech, and he kissed off the proposal in three paragraphs at the end of the story, preferring to write about the unannounced but long-decided question of whether Reagan would run for president. Joel Weisman, a Chicago-based correspondent for *The Washington Post*, filed a story devoted almost entirely to the speech, but it was buried inside the paper. The complaint of Reagan's advisers at the time, as Robert Shogan of the *Los Angeles Times* later observed, was that the speech didn't receive sufficient attention. But Stuart Spencer would change that.

Ford's campaign committee had been an embarrassment since its creation. Packard had failed to deliver as finance chairman. Neither the president nor Callaway had a clue about how to handle Reagan. Callaway had repeatedly and clumsily given the impression that he was trying to force Rockefeller off the ticket, at one point describing the vice president as "the number one problem." It would have been a better description of Reagan. Finally, in October, at Richard Cheney's urging, Ford brought Spencer from California to Washington as his political strategist while leaving Callaway technically in charge of the campaign. Spencer arrived bearing a grudge and an irrepressibly candid spokesman named Peter Kaye. The grudge was against Deaver, whom Spencer believed had joined Ed Meese in bad-mouthing him to potential clients and damaging his consulting business.

Spencer's complaint against the staff masked a deeper resentment that was shared over the years in Sacramento and Washington by many who performed valuable services for Reagan. The truth was that Reagan often took his best aides for granted, especially in the political arena. He did not fully appreciate what Spencer and Roberts had accomplished in 1966 or what Reed and Spencer had accomplished in 1970. As Martin Anderson understatedly observed, Reagan was not "overly thoughtful to those who worked for him," and he "rarely acknowledged what they had done for him."[19] Spencer was secure enough about his abilities not to require praise, but Reagan's lack of appreciation rankled nonetheless.

Spencer, however, was a savvy and combative professional with the ability to put aside his feelings and coolly assess the assets and liabilities of his candidates and their opponents. In 1976, Spencer was contemptuous of Reagan's work habits, saying openly that the former governor was "lazy." But he was equally appalled by the underestimation of Reagan in the Ford camp. "Hell, they were asking me if he was going to run at a time Sears had organized New Hampshire and Reagan had set an announcement date," Spencer told me.[20] He knew, and said, that Ford could not match Reagan as a candidate, particularly on television. Ford was an unelected president. The only way he could win the nomination, as Spencer saw it, was by discrediting Reagan. Spencer and Kaye immediately applied themselves to this task, using the Ninety Billion Speech as their primary weapon. First, they gave the speech to research director Fred Slight for analysis. Then, Kaye began calling reporters, most of whom were unaware of the speech, to provide them with copies and discuss its financial implications. Kaye had credibility with the press because he was as forthright about Ford's deficiencies as he was about Reagan's, a characteristic rare among spokesmen.*

On November 19, 1975, the day before Reagan formally announced

*Eventually, Kaye's frankness, unappreciated at headquarters except by Spencer, cost him his job, but he was useful while he lasted to a president still held in suspicion by the press for his pardon of Nixon. Rogers C. B. Morton, who succeeded Callaway, fired Kaye because he thought he was too candid. Ironically, Morton's own candor subsequently provided one of the Ford campaign's most embarrassing moments. At the Ford committee headquarters in Washington on May 4, when Reagan won 130 of 139 delegates in Alabama, Georgia, and Indiana, Morton allowed himself to be photographed before a collection of half-empty liquor bottles, saying, "I'm not going to rearrange the furniture on the deck of the *Titanic*."

his candidacy, Slight gave Kaye an analysis of the Ninety Billion plan. Listed among its potential effects were high unemployment because of federal cutbacks, probable bankruptcy for some states and municipalities, and a slump in the recession-ridden housing and construction industries. "Finally, such grand rhetoric is completely out of touch with reality," Slight's report concluded. "The question of raising the public's expectations and over-promising on the federal government's ability to deliver smacks of the same faults which Reagan has blamed on other presidents, especially LBJ."

Oblivious to what was about to happen, the Reagans and a few top aides celebrated in a Washington hotel on the eve of the announcement. Hannaford had brought along a bottle of champagne. Before he opened it, he remarked that Reagan had never told them that he was going to run.[21] Everyone laughed. The next day, Reagan opened his campaign at the National Press Club, where he talked vaguely about growing Soviet military superiority abroad and declining economic conditions at home. As always, he blamed government, which he said absorbed more than 44 percent of the national income and "has become more intrusive, more coercive, more meddlesome and less effective." His only slap at Ford was both indirect and unmistakable: "In my opinion, the root of these problems lies right here—in Washington, D.C. Our nation's capital has become the seat of a 'buddy' system that functions for its own benefit—increasingly insensitive to the needs of the American worker who supports it with his taxes."

In the press conference that followed this statement, Reagan demonstrated a lack of specific knowledge about defense issues and the New York City fiscal crisis but, on the whole, fielded questions adequately. Immediately after the speech, he left on a two-day tour of early primary states. At his first stop, a Ramada Inn near the Miami airport, a young man pointed a plastic toy pistol at Reagan. Secret Service men wrestled him to the ground, and Reagan ignored the incident. At a press conference in Charlotte, North Carolina, Reagan gave a cinematic version of how the armed services had been integrated. "When the first bombs were dropped on Pearl Harbor, there was great segregation in the military forces. In World War II, this was corrected. . . . One great story that I think of at the time, that reveals a change was occurring, was when the Japanese dropped the bomb on Pearl Harbor there was a Negro sailor whose total duties involved kitchen-type duties. . . . He cradled a machine gun in his arms, which is not an easy thing to do, and stood on the end of a pier blazing away at Japanese airplanes that were coming down and strafing him and that [segregation] was all changed." When a reporter observed that segregation in the armed services actually ended when President Truman signed an executive order in 1948, three years after the end of the war, Reagan stood his ground. "I remember the scene," Reagan told me on the campaign plane later. "It was very powerful."[22]*

There was as yet no hint of the trouble that was to come with Ninety Billion. When a question about the proposal came up at a rally in Bedford, New Hampshire, Reagan successfully deflected it. Nofziger, the one member of the Reagan team who sensed the potential danger of the issue, took a deep breath. Maybe Ninety Billion would not be such a problem after all.

The following Sunday, on ABC's *Issues and Answers*, the hope of Reagan and Sears that Ninety Billion might go away was revealed as wishful thinking. Reagan sprang the trap on himself after he was pressed by Frank Reynolds, who observed that the federal government paid 62 percent of New Hampshire's welfare costs and that the state would have to either reduce welfare or raise taxes under Reagan's transfer plan. Reagan said that states and local governments could be in a position to pay for these plans if the federal government "stopped pre-empting so much of the tax dollar." This answer was of little help, for New Hampshire is a tourist-oriented state that prides itself on the absence of sales and income taxes. When another ABC correspondent followed up by asking Reagan whether "in all candor" he wouldn't have to tell New Hampshire voters that either an income tax or a sales tax would be necessary, Reagan responded with a rhetorical question: "But isn't this a proper decision for the people of the state to make?"

By now, Reagan's managers knew they had two problems. The first was the Ninety Billion plan, with its damaging specificity. The second was Reagan, who was winging his answers and not paying attention to the backup material that had been given to him. Like other candidates before and after him, Reagan had failed to recognize that the media gives special scrutiny to fledgling presidential candidates. The scrutiny was severe in Reagan's case because he was not well known in the East and because the transfer proposal and Reagan's off-the-cuff statements reminded reporters of Barry Goldwater.

*The 1970 film *Tora, Tora, Tora* contains a scene similar to the one Reagan described except for the cradling of the gun. In the movie, the black messman takes over a machine-gun turret in which the crew has been killed and begins firing at the Japanese planes, one of which begins to trail smoke. There is a factual basis for the scene. After the USS *West Virginia* was struck by a torpedo in the Pearl Harbor attack, Doris (Dorie) Miller, a black messman attendant second class, ran to a machine gun and started firing—one account credits him for five of the twenty-nine Japanese planes that were downed that day. For his heroism, Miller was awarded the Navy Cross and seven other decorations, but he remained a messman. Miller survived the Pearl Harbor attack but was lost at sea in 1943 when the USS *Lipscomb Bay* sank in the central Pacific.[23]

Sears was supposed to help Reagan with the eastern press, and this now became the focus of his activity. He brought in an old Nixon hand, Stanford economics professor Martin Anderson, who battened on a passage in the Ninety Billion Speech in which Reagan had talked about transferring tax resources to the states along with federal programs. Anderson was creative. He dug up an obscure and unsuccessful proposal by former New Hampshire Senator Norris Cotton, who wanted to give states a percentage of federal liquor taxes. He found precedents for the transfer plan in statements by Dwight Eisenhower, John Kennedy, and Hubert Humphrey. When Anderson had finished, the Ninety Billion tiger had been transformed into a tame tabby-cat of a plan for reexamining federal, state, and local government relationships.

But Spencer and Kaye had done their work well. Reagan's recitation of the useful generalities constructed for him by Anderson was undermined by the specifics of his original proposal, which kept being thrown back in his face by the opposition and the press. One survey taken for Reagan by his pollster Richard Wirthlin showed that a majority of voters in New Hampshire actually favored the concept enunciated by Reagan. But the poll did not measure—could not measure—the incalculable impact of the Ninety Billion Speech on the campaign and on Reagan's confidence. He was thrown on the defensive at the very time he had built momentum and was pulling away from Ford. Sears and Lake had built a competent organization in New Hampshire headed by former Governor Hugh Gregg. They expected to win and almost certainly would have, had Reagan thrown Jeff Bell's brainchild into the wastebasket and stuck with his bland and basic speech.

Reagan's own supporters in New Hampshire also damaged his cause. He had the enthusiastic support of William Loeb, the opinionated publisher of the *Manchester Union Leader*, but this was a mixed blessing. "When you get Loeb's support, you also get his enemies and there are lots of them around," Lake observed.[24] The *Union Leader* routinely described President Ford as "Jerry the Jerk." True to his reputation, Loeb extended his attacks to the families of those whom he opposed, calling Betty Ford "stupid" and "immoral" after she defended her daughter's right to have an affair in an interview with Morley Safer on *60 Minutes*.

New Hampshire Governor Meldrim Thomson was also a millstone on the Reagan campaign despite the efforts of Sears and Lake to keep him away from the candidate. Thomson, whose positions on many issues made Reagan look like a liberal, was restricted to a single day of travel with Reagan in favorable Manchester. "He killed us on that one day, though," said Lake in retrospect, remembering how Thomson predicted a 55 percent victory for Reagan on this occasion.[25]

Gregg made no such predictions, wisely declaring that Reagan would do well to win 40 to 45 percent of the vote. But Gregg, whose political perceptions had been formed in the organizational trench warfare of New Hampshire, committed a more serious mistake. He believed that the key to victory was election-day mobilization, which was easier to accomplish if the candidate spent the last two days before the primary out of state. Gregg failed to recognize that Reagan was his own best campaign asset and could make a difference between victory and defeat in a close race. Sears and Lake went along with Gregg. They said afterward that they yielded to him because Wirthlin's polls showed that Reagan would win.

Wirthlin's four surveys, which Sears but not Lake had seen, gave a more ambiguous picture. The first survey, on February 6, 1976, gave Reagan a decisive lead. By February 15, however, Ford had surged ahead on the strength of a two-day visit to New Hampshire that attracted large crowds and favorable coverage from every news outlet except the *Union Leader.* The president planned another trip to New Hampshire before the February 24 primary. Because Wirthlin's polls showed that Reagan's personal campaigning was highly effective, the pollster wanted Reagan to stay in the state to offset the second Ford visit. Wirthlin had not been told of Gregg's intention to export the candidate out of state two days before the election, and he did not realize that Sears had kept the conclusions of the February 15 survey to himself. "John believed that knowledge is power," said Deaver much later, looking back on what he came to regard as an early warning of the uncommunicative conduct that would cause Sears' downfall four years later.

Wirthlin took his final poll on February 18, six days before the primary. The results were ominous. Reagan was four points ahead in the raw tally, but the undecided vote was high. Ford had swung undecided voters in his direction on his first trip to New Hampshire, and Wirthlin assumed he would do the same on his second visit. If the undecideds went 2–1 for the president, the assumption of Wirthlin's analysis accompanying his final poll, Ford would have a tiny lead of 50.7 to 49.3 percent. Wirthlin did not pull his punches in the final survey report he sent to Sears. "On February 18 it appears that Ronald Reagan enjoys a whisper of a lead over Gerald Ford," Wirthlin wrote in his summary:

Given a confidence interval of plus-or-minus 5.2 percent [the margin of error], it would, nevertheless, be folly to project a winner. Further, at least three important events will intervene between now and next Tuesday. First, Gerald Ford will revisit the state. While research conducted in the past indicates that second visits do not have the potency of the first visit, this event should not be underrated since the foregoing data show that Ford shifted the electorate dramatically through his personal appearance. *Second, Governor Reagan will be in the state between now and the election* [my italics]. That visit, the issues it raises, and the play received in the press can also impact the rather large bloc of undecideds.[26]*

The Sunday before the election, Wirthlin met Deaver at Los Angeles International Airport, believing that they were flying to New Hampshire to meet Reagan. Instead, Deaver informed the pollster that they were booked on a Chicago-bound flight with an eventual destination of Peoria. "Why are we going to Illinois?" Wirthlin wanted to know. "To meet the governor," replied Deaver. Wirthlin told me he had a sinking feeling when he heard this because he recognized that Reagan's presence in New Hampshire until the primary was vital. He did not know that Reagan had not been shown the poll in which he had "a whisper of a lead." Reagan, with his usual reliance on his campaign staff, had not protested when Sears, without mentioning Wirthlin's latest poll, had told him of Gregg's desires to mobilize the campaign workers. Instead, he had obediently flown off to campaign in Illinois, where the primary was not until March 16. After a day of useless campaigning in the Peoria area, Reagan flew back to New Hampshire on the Monday evening before the primary, still not knowing that his pollster had told his campaign manager that he should never have left the state.

On this return flight, Reagan heard the bad news. It came from Wirthlin, whom Sears finally had instructed to brief the candidate about what he could expect on Tuesday. Wirthlin uneasily went through the poll with Reagan, trying to put the best face on it but telling him that the race was so close that the break of the undecided voters would determine the outcome. For the first time, as the plane began to descend in the gathering darkness above Manchester, Reagan recognized that he might lose the primary, and with it the presidential nomination. As always, his customary optimism had been telling him that he would win. But Reagan knew that Wirthlin was an optimist, too, and he recognized as well as his pollster that it was not good enough to be tied with the president going into election day.

Later, Reagan would second-guess the wasted time in Peoria and,

*The third factor cited by Wirthlin as important was voter turnout. The pollster wrote that "the conventional wisdom" in New Hampshire predicted a 100,000-vote turnout, which would have been beneficial to Reagan. But Wirthlin warned that his survey pointed to a turnout of about 115,000 votes, which favored Ford. "Without question, a large turnout will erode Ronald Reagan's vote margin," Wirthlin reported in his survey. This was because Reagan's supporters, who were ideologically committed, were most likely to vote.

later still, question why Sears had kept the vital polling information from him. But he did not do that at the time. As the plane began its final approach for a landing in Manchester, Reagan turned to Wirthlin and smiled. "I hope someone down there lights a candle for me," he said.[27]

27

CONTENDER

Reagan awoke on the crisp, clear New Hampshire morning of February 24, 1976, with a winning feeling. His doubts of the night before had faded, and Reagan was once again confident that he would win the primary. His strategist, John Sears, wasn't so sure. Neither was Ford's strategist, Stuart Spencer, who told the president at the White House that the outcome would be close. Richard Nixon had added a complication by choosing the weekend before the primary to return to public life with a visit to the People's Republic of China. The Chinese government's enthusiastic welcome of Nixon had dominated the weekend news coverage and was still a television story on Tuesday morning, when there were no results from New Hampshire to report. Spencer worried that the timing of the former president's trip might remind voters of the pardon and tip the scales against Ford.[1]

Reagan's optimism appeared justified in the early returns. He jumped out to a 4-point lead and held it throughout the evening. By now, Reagan felt so assured of victory that he discarded his election-night superstition for the only time in his career and permitted himself to be photographed with a newspaper headline showing him leading Ford. The lead lasted until 1 A.M. the next morning, when Ford surged ahead. Reagan lost by only 1,317 votes out of more than 108,000 ballots cast. The "whisper of a lead" that Wirthlin had mentioned in his final survey belonged to the president—and by almost precisely the margin the pollster had predicted if the undecideds broke for Ford.[2]

Spencer had been saying for months that Ford needed to win New Hampshire to have any chance of being the Republican presidential nominee. Sears also realized that the primary was critical, but Reagan had it in his head that he would be considered a winner even if he narrowly lost. Meeting with reporters in the early morning hours of Febru-

ary 25, Reagan observed that the press had considered Eugene Mc-
Carthy a winner after he was defeated by President Johnson in the 1968
New Hampshire primary, and had made a similar judgment about
George McGovern after he lost badly to Senator Edmund Muskie in
1972.

The comparison with these Democratic primaries was misplaced.
Neither McCarthy nor McGovern had predicted victory, and neither
had expected to win. Reagan was favored in New Hampshire. Reporters
might have discounted Governor Thomson's public forecast of a Reagan victory had not Sears or Lake privately told several of them that
Reagan would win the primary. This contradicted the usual political
tactic of lowering media expectations by underestimation, but Reagan
was not involved in a usual race. Sears and his team had tried to establish the inevitability of Reagan by diminishing Ford's credentials. They
had portrayed Ford as an accidental president who had no following except for those who reflexively favored a White House incumbent. Reporters who accepted this premise, as many did, logically decided that
Reagan would defeat Ford in a state as conservative as New Hampshire.
Sears did not discourage forecasts along these lines because that would
have undermined his argument of Reagan's inevitability. And so the
press, often criticized in the past for deciding that a candidate who lost
but "did well" in New Hampshire was really the winner, in 1976 used a
simple and appropriate standard: The winner was the candidate who received the most votes.

Sears and Wirthlin did not go to bed the night of the New Hampshire primary. They stayed up, concocting in the dark hours of Reagan's
defeat the strategy that would lead to his brightest victories. Both men
recognized that Reagan needed to go after Ford on foreign policy,
where the president was most vulnerable among conservative voters.
This meant openly attacking Secretary of State Henry Kissinger, who
had been persona non grata with conservatives ever since he pioneered
Nixon's rapprochement with China.

Reagan had discussed foreign policy during the New Hampshire
campaign but in a relatively genteel fashion and without mentioning
Ford or Kissinger by name. Two weeks before the election, when Reagan was still trying to deflect attention away from the Ninety Billion
Speech, he gave a forty-minute address on foreign policy at Philips Exeter Academy. The principal thrust of this speech, which was crafted by
Peter Hannaford, was that the United States should not sacrifice development of the cruise missile for the illusory comfort of a strategic arms
agreement with the Soviets. Tucked into the middle of the address were
these two paragraphs:

Our foreign policy in recent years seems to be a matter of placating potential adversaries. Does our government fear that the American people lack willpower? If it does, that may explain its reluctance to assert our interests in international relations.

How else can we explain the government's bowing to the propaganda campaign of the military dictator of Panama and signing a memorandum with his representative signifying our intention to give up control and ownership of the Panama Canal and the Canal Zone?

On its face, the question of whether the United States should turn over the jurisdiction of the 51-mile Panama Canal to Panama did not seem a promising issue on which to turn the tide against a sitting president of the United States. Three presidents, beginning with Lyndon Johnson, had tried to renegotiate a treaty with Panama, and only a small percentage of voters were even aware of the issue. But Wirthlin, in his surveys, had picked up something else. The something was the backlash that had developed in the aftermath of the Vietnam War, which had ended on Ford's watch with the fall of Saigon on April 30, 1975. In the wake of the ignominious evacuation of U.S. military and diplomatic personnel, many Americans felt humiliated by the outcome in Vietnam. Conservatives increasingly said that the United States was allowing itself to be pushed around in the world without doing anything about it.

In this context, Reagan's denunciation of the Panamanian leader, Omar Torrijos, as a "tinhorn dictator" struck a responsive chord. Most Americans took U.S. control of the Panama Canal for granted. They saw it as an example of American altruism and stability, not colonialism. Wirthlin's polls found that even voters who believed that the United States had no business in Vietnam tended to regard the canal as a legitimate object of American interest. While Reagan slept away his disappointment in the predawn hours of February 25, Wirthlin and Sears decided to make the Panama Canal an issue. Their candidate was more than willing.

The impact of the New Hampshire defeat on Reagan's campaign imparted urgency to the attack. When the pollsters checked their surveys after New Hampshire, they found that Ford's previously narrow lead in Florida had become a runaway. The president had gained 16 points in his own polls and 14 points in Reagan's on the strength of his eyelash victory. This was staggering news for the Reagan forces, and this time Sears told the candidate what was happening. Reagan already was hearing speculation that he would drop out of a race he thought had barely begun. Former Illinois Governor Richard Ogilvie, heading the Ford forces in Illinois, predicted that Reagan's loyalists would desert him if he lost Florida. "One thing about Republicans—they don't like to work for losers," Ogilvie said.

Reagan, who quickly talked himself into believing that he had really won New Hampshire, was at first surprised and then annoyed by such comments. He told aides and reporters he was going all the way to the Republican National Convention at Kansas City no matter what happened—and he meant it. But Florida was not promising. Crossover voting is not permitted in Florida primaries, where the Republican electorate includes many retired midwesterners and easterners. Thirty-eight percent of the eligible GOP voters in 1976 were over sixty-five years old. These older voters tended to vote the way they voted back in Michigan, Ohio, and Illinois and in general were resistant to change and supportive of incumbents. Some of these retirees were susceptible to suggestions from the Ford side that Reagan was "another Goldwater" who would do away with Social Security. Even if Reagan had won in New Hampshire, Florida might have been a struggle. After losing in New Hampshire, his task seemed almost impossible.

But Ford, whose reliance on old buddies from the House of Representatives had led to the unfortunate selection of Bo Callaway as his campaign manager, made a similar mistake in Florida. His campaign manager in the state was Representative Louis Frey Jr., whose horizons were those of a congressional district candidate. Statewide, Frey was quickly out-organized by Reagan forces led by David Keene and L. E. ("Tommy") Thomas, a Panama City automobile dealer. Unfortunately for Reagan, the ebullient Thomas undermined his own efforts with an extravagant prediction that Reagan would carry the state by a 2–1 margin. Although no one else believed this, the forecast saddled Reagan with an unreachable level of expectation. Still, Thomas and Keene were so effective organizationally that Spencer, back in Washington, became worried that the Ford team would not be able to deliver on election day. His solution was to bring in Bill Roberts from California to set things right.

Roberts and Spencer were no longer partners, and Roberts had suffered from illness and misfortune since his palmy days as Reagan's campaign manager in 1966. Nonetheless, he was an accomplished professional with unsurpassed insights into Reagan's vulnerabilities. Within days of Roberts' arrival in Florida in early February, moribund headquarters all over the state had sprung to life in a busy recruitment of volunteers. A glossy, eight-page mailer was distributed to Republican voters, featuring a full-length color picture of "the President" sitting in front of an American flag and saying, "I'm proud to be an American . . .

just like you." Ford was presented as the safe and sure candidate who would "preserve the integrity and solvency of the Social Security system." The none-too-veiled implication was that Reagan wouldn't. Roberts also regaled Florida reporters with stories about how Reagan had required naps when he ran for governor. They made an impression. When Reagan flew home for a weekend of rest in mid-campaign, this normal event was depicted in some Florida newspapers as evidence that he lacked the stamina for the presidency.

Hampered by Roberts' virtuoso performance and increasing media skepticism about his prospects, Reagan struggled to establish his foreign policy themes. Five days before the primary, at a televised news conference and rally at Rollins College near Orlando, Reagan said that Ford had shown "neither the vision nor the leadership necessary to halt and reverse the diplomatic and military decline of the United States." After asserting that the Soviet Union had achieved military supremacy over the United States, Reagan said, "Mr. Ford and Dr. Kissinger ask us to trust their leadership. Well, I find that more and more difficult to do. Henry Kissinger's recent stewardship of U.S. foreign policy has coincided precisely with the loss of U.S. military supremacy." Ford's answer was to use the power of the presidency to demonstrate his commitment to military spending. The day before Reagan accused Ford of presiding over the military decline of the United States, the big news in Orlando was that Martin Marietta, one of the area's largest employers, had been awarded a $33.6 million Air Force contract for an advanced strategic air system.

Reagan made up ground with his attacks on Ford's foreign and defense policies, but not enough. On March 9, Ford won the Florida primary by a 53–47 margin on the strength of the retirement vote, which went heavily for the president. The White House promptly embarked on a campaign to force Reagan out of the race by encouraging Republican office-holders to say he should quit in the interest of "party unity." Reagan was discouraged, Sears was drinking heavily, the campaign was running out of money, and aides were quarreling among themselves. Reagan had lost four primaries, including uncontested ones in Massachusetts and Vermont a week after New Hampshire. Illinois, on March 16, took him further down the downhill slope. On the eve of the primary, Reagan said he would be "happy" with 40 percent of the vote, slightly below what Wirthlin's polls predicted. He received almost exactly 40 percent and wasn't happy at all. But Reagan again repeated, grimly this time, what he had said before Florida. Brushing aside questions about his mounting campaign deficit, Reagan declared he was going all the way to Kansas City.

The North Carolina primary on March 23 was next. Many reporters suspected it would be Reagan's endgame. Sears thought so, too. Without telling his candidate, Sears met secretly in his Washington office on March 20 with Rogers Morton, who had been authorized by Ford to discuss conditions under which Reagan might withdraw from the race. Sears knew that the campaign would soon be out of money because contributions had dried up after Reagan's series of defeats and because the Federal Elections Commission (FEC), which dispensed federal subsidies to presidential candidates, was due to go out of business the day before the North Carolina primary.*

Reagan realized that his campaign was in precarious financial shape, but he knew nothing of the Sears-Morton meeting. Later, he told me that he would never have withdrawn, no matter what Sears agreed to do. He expressed a similar feeling in even stronger terms to Lyn Nofziger and Mike Deaver. Both Californians had more respect for Reagan than Sears did, and they were struck with Reagan's determination. Until this time, Reagan had followed the lead of his political advisers in his various campaigns. Now he was drifting toward the leadership of his campaign at a time when his chief strategist was willing to surrender. Sears believed he was being realistic, not disloyal. He had not factored Reagan's determination into the equation.

Luck, in which Reagan believed, then came to his aid in the form of problems for Bo Callaway, the beleaguered Ford campaign manager. Callaway was accused of improperly influencing a U.S. Forest Service decision that benefited a Colorado ski resort in which he had an interest. In the long run, nothing came of the charges, but White House Chief of Staff Dick Cheney eased Callaway out of the campaign. Cheney offered the job to Spencer, who knew that he was a strategist, not a manager, and turned it down. Rogers Morton replaced Callaway. Ultimately, Callaway's departure was beneficial to the Ford campaign. At that point, however, it was a distraction that for the first time put the White House rather than the Reagan campaign on the defensive.

On the heels of the Callaway affair, Ford demonstrated his limitations as a front-running candidate. Appearing in Charlotte on March

---

*On January 30, 1976, the Supreme Court upheld the constitutionality of much of the Federal Election Campaign Act, passed in 1974 in response to Watergate. This law provided federal financing for presidential candidates. But the court also found that the constitutional doctrine of the separation of powers was violated by the way in which commission members were chosen, since four of the six commissioners were named by Congress to a body that exercised executive powers. Congress was unable to agree on how the commission should be reconstituted, and the FEC temporarily went out of business on March 22, at a time when the bankrupt Reagan campaign owed $1 million. By the time the new commission was back in business on May 21, Reagan had lost a vital opportunity to compete in the Wisconsin primary.

20, the same day Sears was meeting with Morton, Ford gave one of the most vacuous speeches in the annals of presidential campaigning. Speaking to the Future Homemakers of America, Ford said: "I regret that some people in this country have disparaged and demeaned the role of the homemaker. I say—and I say it with emphasis and conviction—that homemaking is good for America. I say that homemaking is not out of date and I reject strongly such accusations." Ford did not identify the evil forces that were trying to destroy homemaking. But he made himself the butt of ridicule among reporters who had been told beforehand by White House Press Secretary Ron Nessen that the speech would be Ford's major pronouncement of the day.

Reagan had more interesting themes, and he was presenting them more forcefully than he had in the Florida and Illinois primaries. Responding to a suggestion from Senator Paul Laxalt, Reagan discarded his five-by-seven cards and spoke without notes as he made his case against the foreign policy of the Ford administration. His fiery extemporaneous presentation roused audiences as Reagan deplored the purported decline of U.S. military power and denounced the "giveaway" of the Panama Canal. "We bought it, we paid for it, it's ours, and we're going to keep it," Reagan said.

North Carolina voters were receptive to the Panama Canal issue, in part because it was also a favorite topic of Senator Jesse Helms, who was Reagan's most outspoken advocate in the state. Helms had been critical of Sears in the early stretches of the campaign, blaming him for what he considered the softness of Reagan's criticisms of administration foreign policy. Reagan's sharpening of the attack, particularly against Kissinger, pleased Helms, and he said so to Reagan. Encouraged both by the audience response and the approval of his North Carolina backers, Reagan stepped up the pace of his attack. In Lenoir, he declared:

> Our party, the Republican Party, has been traditionally the party of fiscal responsibility. For forty years we have opposed the profligate tax and tax, spend and spend, elect and elect policies of our opponents. How will we campaign in November if the Democrats can point to our candidate having presided over the greatest budget deficit in our nation's history?
>
> The Republicans in Congress opposed the Democratic efforts to cut defense spending. . . . How will we respond in the campaign when the Democrats point out that under our candidate we have become second to the Soviet Union in military strength in a world where it is perhaps fatal to be second best?
>
> Mr. Ford and Dr. Kissinger have objected to my criticizing their foreign policy. The Democrats are going to criticize it. How will we defend

defending Castro while he exports revolution and makes Cuba a Soviet satellite?

How can we defend the giveaway of the Panama Canal . . . ?

How can we criticize the disastrous energy legislation passed by the Democratic Congress but signed by our candidate into law?

How will we defend a candidate who fired Dr. Schlesinger and said he will retain Dr. Kissinger if he is elected president?*

Reagan insisted on confining his criticisms to policy matters. When Thomas Ellis, Helms' chief aide and Reagan's North Carolina campaign manager, suggested to Reagan that he make Callaway an issue, the candidate refused, saying the charges had not been proved. Reagan was even firmer in rejecting a leaflet prepared by Ellis that openly appealed to racial prejudice. The leaflet reproduced a story quoting Ford as saying he would consider Senator Edward W. Brooke of Massachusetts, an African American, as a running mate and another story quoting Brooke as favoring busing to achieve racial integration. Ford had mentioned Brooke on a laundry list of possible nominees, but everyone in politics, including Reagan, knew the Massachusetts senator was not a serious vice-presidential possibility. Reagan was furious when he heard about the leaflet and directed that it not be distributed. "That wasn't discussed with us," Deaver told me at a rally where the leaflets were supposed to be handed out. "The governor has never campaigned on race or used it as an issue, never will, and feels strongly about that," Deaver said. When it was pointed out to Deaver that boxes of the leaflets were present at the rally for distribution, he walked over to the campaign worker who had charge of them and ordered that they be put aboard the Reagan campaign plane so they could not be distributed after the candidate had left.[3] The leaflets were destroyed.

Ellis, however, was responsible for the most productive tactic of the North Carolina campaign, which was to show a half-hour Reagan television speech on stations throughout the state. Sears doubted whether many people would watch a half-hour speech by anyone, but Ellis pressured Nofziger into coming up with a poor-quality, vintage Reagan speech that the candidate had made during the Florida primary. Nofziger cut out the Florida references and added an appeal for funds. The half-hour shows appeared on fifteen stations and introduced North

---

*Ford fired Secretary of Defense James Schlesinger on November 2, 1975, and replaced him with Donald Rumsfeld in a so-called "Sunday massacre" that shook up the Ford cabinet and caused an adverse reaction to his administration in the press and the polls. As with the dismissal of Callaway, however, the change eventually proved beneficial to Ford because Cheney, who worked well with Spencer, succeeded Rumsfeld as White House chief of staff.

Carolinians to the old-fashioned Reagan doing what he did best, which was giving his latest version of "A Time for Choosing."

Without fully recognizing it, Reagan had now reached a moment in his own political career as critical as the time he gave his famous speech for Goldwater in 1964. Without that speech, and the enthusiastic response it produced among millions of Republicans, Reagan would not have been able to run for governor of California in 1966. Without his performance in North Carolina, in person and on television, Reagan would have faded from contention before Kansas City and it is unlikely that he would have won the presidential nomination four years later. While neither Reagan nor those who worked for him fully comprehended the significance of the North Carolina primary at the time, Reagan sensed that something was happening among his audiences. Paul Laxalt, who had flown down from Washington to cheer him up, and who dates their friendship from this primary, noticed it, too. "He was the old Ron Reagan," said Laxalt, remembering the way Reagan had roused audiences in his gubernatorial campaigns.[4]

Laxalt was a factor in the Reagan resurgence. Talking with Reagan as an equal, the Nevada senator realized that both he and Reagan had underestimated the patronage power of the presidency. In Florida and Illinois, Reagan had sounded resentful of Ford's dispensing of grants and favors, which is standard operating procedure for any incumbent president. In North Carolina, Reagan began to turn Ford's largesse against him through the potent weapon of ridicule. "I understand Mr. Ford has arrived in the state," Reagan said the Saturday before the primary. "If he comes here with the same list of goodies as he did in Florida, the band won't know whether to play 'Hail to the Chief' or 'Santa Claus Is Coming to Town.'"

Despite his turnaround, Reagan did not know how to deal with a recurrent question from reporters: "When are you going to drop out?" The Ford campaign was orchestrating appeals from public officials urging Reagan to quit. At a Greensboro television station, Reagan reacted to one such statement issued by a group of mayors by saying, "For heaven's sakes, fellows, let's not be naive. That pressure is engineered from the same place that they engineered the pressure for me not to run in the first place—the White House. . . . I'm not going to pay any attention to them now [that] they suggest that I should quit. Tell him [Ford] to quit." Reagan's irritation reflected a recognition that marginal voters might be tempted to vote for Ford if they regarded the president as the certain winner. "You have to think that the undecided voters are not necessarily those who are the most committed, and you wonder what the effect will be on them," Reagan told me in an interview two days before the primary.

My most vivid memories of the 1976 campaign are of two attempts by Reagan to deal with the question about when he would quit. One was on election day, when Reagan held airport press conferences in four North Carolina cities. "Win, lose or draw, I am continuing in this campaign," he said defiantly. Then, when reporters continued to badger him about what he would do if he lost, Reagan refused to answer again, saying he would respond only to other questions. There was a long moment of silence before someone ended the impasse with a question on another subject. The scene was reminiscent of that other defiant time eight years earlier when Reagan had refused at a press conference to take any more questions on the homosexual scandal. Both times, Reagan had persisted in his tactic, and both times he had prevailed.

My other memory is more personal. It occurred in the same airplane interview in which I asked Reagan whether he was being damaged by the constant questioning about when he would withdraw. Reagan acknowledged this was a possibility, and we talked about other issues. Later in the interview, I felt obligated, as the reporter for *The Washington Post* who was assigned to the North Carolina campaign, to get Reagan on the record on the question that was most on the minds of my editors.

"When are you going to quit?" I asked him.

"You, too, Lou?" he said, his lips tightening. Then Reagan looked directly at me and said firmly, as if he were on camera: "I'm *not* going to quit."

In retrospect, I believe it was this determination—an echo of the stubbornness Reagan had shown on several occasions in Sacramento and a foreshadowing of the determination he would display in New Hampshire four years later—that was the most important reason that Reagan eventually became president of the United States. This was not apparent at the time. "Reagan Virtually Concedes Defeat in North Carolina," said the headline of *The New York Times* story the day before the primary.[5] The headline was based on Reagan's observation that "a close race here would be satisfactory to me," a statement that Reagan did not realize would be interpreted as a concession.

The truth is that Reagan did not expect to win the North Carolina primary and was being honest with the reporter who asked for his assessment. By the time the North Carolina vote came in, Reagan was in La Crosse, Wisconsin, speaking to a sportsmen's group. The news that he was winning North Carolina was relayed to him by Nofziger, who was as surprised by the results as anyone else. Nofziger urged Reagan to meet with reporters and crow about his upset victory. Reagan wouldn't do it. The final results were not in, and Reagan remembered New

Hampshire. He had prematurely claimed victory there and learned a lesson he would always remember. Reagan left Wisconsin without making a victory statement, but the results spoke for themselves. In the final tally, Reagan won 52 percent of the vote to 46 percent for Ford. He won the delegate count 28–26.

North Carolina was the turning point in Reagan's pursuit of the presidency. It kept him in the race to Kansas City, from which he emerged as the presumptive front-runner in 1980. After the North Carolina primary, Reagan was at all times a legitimate, full-fledged presidential candidate, even though his campaign was so starved for funds that he had to abandon efforts to contest Wisconsin, where he won 45 percent of the vote anyway. There would be no more organized pressure from the White House urging him to withdraw from the race.

But to capitalize on his victory, Reagan needed to raise money and fast. The quickest way to do this was on national television, where Reagan had been an effective fund-raiser since his debut speech for Goldwater. When Sears proposed making a nationally televised appeal for funds, Reagan looked at him and said he had favored doing this all along. This was true, but Reagan had made no effort to impose his view. "No one paid any attention when I told them what we could do with television," Reagan told me subsequently. Had he been insistent earlier, it is conceivable the speech would have been scheduled sooner and Reagan would have raised enough money to win delegates in Wisconsin, which he could ill afford to concede to Ford.

The speech that Reagan gave on the NBC network on March 31 was a message for true believers patterned after his speeches in North Carolina. After establishing his credentials by giving a glowing account of his governorship, Reagan questioned Ford's leadership on economic issues and attacked Kissinger, whom Reagan depicted as ready to negotiate away American freedoms. Militarily, Reagan asserted again, the United States was now "Number Two in a world where it is dangerous, if not fatal, to be second best." In response to Reagan's attack on his foreign policy, Ford had dropped use of the word "détente" and replaced it with the phrase "peace through strength." Reagan mocked this euphemism as "a slogan with a nice ring to it" that did not reflect military realities.

The content of Reagan's speech delighted conservatives. Sears was pleased because it raised $1.5 million and enabled Reagan to stay in the race. Heading for the Texas primary on May 1, Sears used the prophetic words "new beginning," which would become the Reagan campaign slogan of 1980, to describe the candidate's opportunity. But the beginning came too late in 1976. By the time of the Texas primary, Sears had already been forced to concede in Pennsylvania and New York, where the delegates were controlled by Nelson Rockefeller and his allies. Sears' own preferred field of battle was the Northeast, but he was in no position to contest the Republican power structure there in 1976. Among Republicans in this region, memories of 1964 were still painful, and there were many who compared Reagan to Goldwater. The attacks on Kissinger and Ford's foreign policy that rallied conservatives to Reagan's banner in North Carolina and would help him in the South and West reinforced suspicion of him in the Northeast.

Reagan continued the attacks on friendly ground in Texas, where he hammered away on détente and the Panama Canal. Since Texas was a crossover state, Reagan also openly appealed to the former followers of the crippled George Wallace, whom Jimmy Carter had decisively beaten in the Florida primary. Wallace voters detested the federal government, and Reagan and Carter appealed to them in messages that could have been written by the same speechwriter. "Anything you don't like about Washington, I suggest you blame it on Jerry Ford," said Carter, who was then wrapping up the Democratic nomination. From Reagan came the same song: "I consider it an asset that I am not a member of the Washington establishment."

.It was certainly an asset in Texas. Reagan swept all 96 delegates in the Texas primary May 1 and three days later won 130 of 139 delegates at stake in the Alabama, Georgia, and Indiana primaries. He won in Nebraska on May 11 (while Ford was winning West Virginia) and added more delegates at Republican state conventions throughout the West. Then Reagan rolled to a big victory in California, where his margin was swelled by a ferocious Spencer attack.* But Ford won in his home state of Michigan on May 18 and captured a majority of the vote and most of the delegates in Ohio and New Jersey on June 8, the same day as the California primary.

This was the last round of primaries. In the subsequent six weeks, the

---

*Answering questions before the Sacramento Press Club, Reagan said he would provide a token contingent of U.S. troops as part of a United Nations command if Rhodesia requested it to fight guerrillas. Spencer and Kaye ran a television commercial with a punchline that said, "When you vote Tuesday, remember: Governor Ronald Reagan couldn't start a war. President Ronald Reagan could." Spencer claimed that this commercial made Reagan concentrate on California at a time when he needed to campaign elsewhere. But Reagan kept to his schedule (which was insufficient in Ohio, anyway), and surveys showed that voters did not believe the commercial. Nofziger reran it as a Reagan spot, confident that it would be regarded as a smear. Reagan carried California by a 2–1 margin. Long afterward, a Ford aide told me that during the filming of the commercial, his aides had spoofed the president in an ad made for internal consumption. The anti-Reagan commercial had shown a hand reaching for a red phone in the White House situation room. In the parody, Ford reaches for the phone and knocks it off the desk.

Ford and Reagan forces battled for delegates in convention states, with Reagan sweeping some he might have lost (notably, Missouri) and losing one he needed to win (North Dakota). During this period, Ford's steadily improving campaign came up with a new find in James A. Baker III, a wealthy Houston lawyer and undersecretary of commerce who took over the Ford delegate hunt. Baker possessed the Spencer-Kaye virtues of candor, and he also realized the need to establish credibility with the press and any genuinely uncommitted delegates. Baker recognized that some of Ford's support was soft. A false delegate claim that was exposed by the press might persuade some of the waverers to conclude that the president was going to lose the nomination and precipitate a bolt toward Reagan. So Baker was cautious in his public pronouncements, claiming only those delegates who were legally bound to Ford or who had proclaimed their support for him.

Sears could not afford such pristine tactics. Reagan needed delegates, and Sears claimed, among other things, that they were available among technically uncommitted delegates in Pennsylvania. In fact, the delegation had been screened for loyalty to Ford, and interviews by reporters of members of the delegation did not disclose any hidden Reagan strength. By mid-July, it was clear that Reagan, despite his impressive comeback, had fallen short of the 1,130 delegate votes needed for nomination. *The Washington Post* count gave Ford 1,093 delegates and Reagan 1,030, with 136 uncommitted. This meant that Ford needed only 37 delegates, slightly more than one-fourth of the uncommitted, to be nominated. The private counts on both sides indicated that Ford would do better than that. One prominent member of the Reagan entourage and two lesser aides talked to me about their plans in the fall, undecided whether they should work for Ford or leave the world of politics. It was a sign that they knew Reagan did not have enough delegates to win.

On the flight to Los Angeles after Reagan spoke to a final GOP state convention in Utah, I interviewed the candidate and realized that he also was aware he might lose. "I think my candidacy has been worthwhile," Reagan said. The story based on the not-for-attribution interviews of the aides and the on-the-record interview of Reagan ran Monday, July 19, across eight columns at the top of page 1 in *The Washington Post*. "Reagan's Camp: Air of Resignation," said the banner headline. Underneath was an even more damaging subhead that reflected the story: "He Speaks Not So Much of Victory As of a 'Worthwhile' Bid." Sears and Deaver were furious at this account and refused to talk to me for more than a year. Reagan denied in television interviews the next day that he was resigned to defeat. Nofziger called in reporters and played a recording of the interview in an effort to demonstrate that Reagan had been quoted out of context. But Nofziger knew, too, that some of his fellow Reaganites were already looking for their next jobs.[6]

My story came at a time when Sears was preparing a surprise that would delay recognition of Ford's impending victory. Sears had learned that CBS News planned to broadcast a projection showing that Ford had clinched the nomination. Before this could happen, Reagan introduced a new factor into the equation. On July 26, he announced that he would choose Senator Richard S. Schweiker of Pennsylvania as his running mate if he was nominated for president. The selection stunned Reagan's conservative supporters in the South, especially in the key delegation of Mississippi. It ultimately gave Clarke Reed, the power-conscious Mississippi Republican chairman, the excuse he had been seeking to support Ford. It also failed to gain Reagan any identifiable support in the Northeast, where Schweiker's 100 percent labor-union voting record might have been expected to make a Reagan ticket more palatable. But it did accomplish its purpose of preventing the networks from declaring that Ford had wrapped up the nomination. Before any news organization was willing to go this far, it was necessary to poll the delegates again, especially in Pennsylvania. The Pennsylvania delegates enjoyed their moment in the sun, and several of them delighted in announcing their undecided status to media representatives, even though they planned to, and did, vote for Ford at the convention. But the Schweiker selection had bought time, allowing Sears to maneuver at Kansas City.

Schweiker's selection was a compelling example of Reagan's proclivity for delegation. Unlike some of his actions, however, the delegation in this case was specific and initiated by Reagan, who thought that the last-minute selection of a vice president in the hurly-burly of a national convention was undignified and unnecessary. He had talked to Laxalt about it, who agreed. Two months before the convention he also had discussed the idea with Sears, who saw the advantage of an early selection in terms of constructing a ticket for the general election.

Sears and Laxalt agreed to find Reagan a vice president. During the first week in July, Sears sounded out William D. Ruckelshaus, the Nixon deputy attorney general who had resigned rather than carry out the president's instructions to fire Special Prosecutor Archibald Cox. Ruckelshaus, a Catholic, believed that he was being offered a place on the ticket to give it balance in the fall. But nothing came of the overture. Ruckelshaus would have been an attractive vice-presidential nominee in the fall campaign, but he did not offer any hope of switching Ford delegates to Reagan.[7] And there were not many others who held this promise either. Sears and Laxalt ran through a short list of possibilities. Most were out of the question. Well-known liberals like Senator Jacob Javits of New York would not have met the test of philosophical compatibility. Others, such as Representative Jack Kemp of New York, who would have met the test, were not well known. Schweiker soon emerged as the only likely possibility. Laxalt was enthusiastic about him, which made the selection easier to sell to Reagan.

Reagan told me after the election that he knew "very little" about Schweiker when Sears came to his house on July 23 to make the case for the Pennsylvania senator. Even this may have been an overstatement. Sears told Reagan about Schweiker's liberal record on labor issues but emphasized the senator's opposition to gun control and abortion. Reagan did not know that Sears and Laxalt already had interviewed Schweiker and accepted him. But Reagan's question was direct and political. "Do you think he'd do it?" Reagan asked. Sears assured him that he would. The next day, Laxalt and Sears arrived with Schweiker. Schweiker and Reagan hit it off. Reagan recalled that Schweiker agreed with most of his positions and said he would support even those he didn't as long as he was first allowed to give his opinion. "I have a strong feeling that I'm looking at myself some years ago," Reagan told Schweiker, referring to his own conversion to conservatism. "I'm not a knee-jerk liberal," Schweiker said. "And I'm not a knee-jerk conservative," Reagan replied.[8] In later years, Reagan readily acknowledged that his acceptance of Schweiker as his running mate was an act of political expedience but also insisted that Schweiker's commitment to conservative principles during their long discussion on July 24 was genuine. He may have been right. During the next four years in the Senate, for whatever reasons, Schweiker's voting record did take a conservative turn.

The selection of Schweiker demonstrated the political creativity of John Sears more than anything else Sears did. Many members of the Reagan team who later decided that Sears was on balance a baneful influence on the candidate defend the Schweiker strategy to this day. At different times I asked Reagan, Laxalt, Meese, Nofziger, Hannaford, and Deaver their views of the Schweiker gambit. All of them said that it kept the Republican convention from being a cut-and-dried coronation of Ford. "Sears can be faulted for lots of things, but not for Schweiker," said Deaver, in a typical view. "It kept the whole thing alive."[9]

The way Sears made use of the Schweiker selection at the national convention wound up helping the Republican Party, although Sears didn't get much credit for it. Sears forced a vote on a rule, known as 16-C, that would have required Ford to name his running mate in advance. If this happened, Sears reasoned, anyone whom Ford selected would irritate some faction or region and give the Reagan team a chance to go after the disaffected delegates. This was a long-shot strategy, but one that probably prevented the convention from becoming a donnybrook of the kind that had torn apart the GOP in 1964.

The strategy angered conservatives, who argued that Reagan's followers could be rallied only by an appeal to the causes that made them follow Reagan in the first place. But it delighted Spencer, who knew that Reagan would have won the nomination if the delegates could cast a secret ballot. "I knew that in their heart of hearts a majority of delegates loved Ronald Reagan but were with us because of the incumbency or we'd bought them or got a commitment," Spencer said many years later. "There were delegates of ours who were voting [for Ford] on the floor crying. I was scared to death that Sears could get a policy issue on the floor of the convention that could bust it wide open. And to this day, I don't know why he couldn't have found one. When he decided to go with the rules, I was the happiest politician in America, because we could beat back a rules thing. That had no emotional impact."[10]

Still, a fight on issues that pushed Ford into a corner would have left the convention in shambles, produced a politically ruined nominee, and damaged Reagan's chances in 1980. Sears knew this and walked a fine line in Kansas City, where the challenges to Ford's policies were made within the Platform Committee rather than on the convention floor. The most substantial of these challenges, proposed by Senator Helms and others, was a "Morality in Foreign Policy" plank that praised the Soviet exiled writer Aleksandr Solzhenitsyn for his "human courage and morality" and denounced the 1975 Helsinki Agreement as "taking from those who do not have freedom the hope of one day getting it." Ford had signed the agreement. He had also declined to meet with Solzhenitsyn. The plank, as Ford saw it, "added up to nothing less than a slick denunciation of administration foreign policy."[11] But at the urging of Spencer, Cheney, and Ron Nessen—and over the objections of Henry Kissinger—Ford swallowed it. On every issue that the press might have interpreted as a conservative victory, Ford's people simply capitulated. James Baker suggested afterward that the Reagan team could have come up with a proposal to fire Kissinger, which the president would have been required to resist. But this was not an option that Reagan seriously considered. "I wouldn't have done something like that," Reagan told me when I asked him about Baker's idea.[12] Neither Reagan nor Sears wanted to leave Kansas City labeled as party wreckers.

With the contest limited to process instead of principles, Rule 16-C was defeated and Ford was nominated. Reagan was counted out at 12:30 A.M. on August 19, when West Virginia's delegates voted unanimously for Ford. Despite all the powers of the presidency and all his early victories and all the delegates locked up by Rockefeller and his allies in the Northeast, Ford won by only 1,187 delegates to 1,070 for Reagan. He was the nominee, to be sure, but Reagan had won the hearts and minds of his fellow Republicans in a way that stamped him as more than a gallant loser.

Ford knew that many of his own delegates were sympathetic to Reagan, and he waved him up to the platform in a show of unity. Reagan walked to the podium to the cheers of the emotionally drained delegates and gave a dramatic, six-minute speech that was more a call to battle than a concession. Speaking without notes or cue cards, Reagan told the delegates that they faced the dual challenge of preserving individual freedom and keeping the world safe from nuclear destruction. "We live in a world in which the great powers have poised and aimed at each other horrible missiles of destruction that can, in a matter of minutes, arrive in each other's country and destroy virtually the civilized world we live in," he said. This was not a curtain call, but a salvo against the doctrine of "mutual assured destruction" that would prompt Reagan, as president, to propose a missile-defense system.[13]

Reagan was weary after this speech and a subsequent meeting with Ford.* But he was up after a few hours' sleep to prepare a speech of consolation for those who had stood by his side. "Don't get cynical," Reagan told his followers in the crowded ballroom of the Alameda Plaza Hotel late that morning. "Don't get cynical because, look at yourselves and what you were willing to do and recognize that there are millions and millions of Americans out there that want what you want, that want it to be that way, that want it to be a shining city on the hill." It was one of Reagan's most familiar lines, but Nancy Reagan wept when she heard it. Reagan's supporters, many of them youthful, wept, too. They had stood with their candidate from New Hampshire to Kansas City, and now he was here before them, thanking them for carrying his bags, wav-

---

*In a meeting arranged by Sears and Cheney, Ford called on Reagan at his hotel room. It was an awkward moment. Reagan was an obvious choice for vice president but told Sears he didn't want to be asked to join the ticket. Sears made this a condition of the meeting, telling Cheney that Reagan would be embarrassed at having to turn Ford down. But there were some members of the Reagan entourage who expected Ford to ask anyway, and Justin Dart had urged Reagan to accept the nomination if he did. Reagan told Dart he would consider it, although he told others subsequently that he had not expected Ford to ask. Ford said in his memoirs that he did not know whether he would have asked even if he had not felt bound by the condition imposed by Sears. Would Reagan have accepted if he had? He never said. I suspect that Reagan would have found it difficult to turn down Ford if the president, as Dart suggested he might, had said that it was Reagan's "patriotic duty" to accept. Instead, Ford told Reagan his list of vice-presidential prospects included William Simon, John Connally, Bob Dole, Howard Baker, Elliott Richardson, and William Ruckelshaus.[14]

ing his banners, and putting up his campaign signs in scores of towns and airports. Reagan knew the importance of the team. Reaching back to his movie days for a metaphor, he recalled how seventy-five persons had been required to film a single scene of a farmer running from his field to tell of an airplane crash.

To his weeping supporters in the ballroom, Reagan said farewell but not goodbye. He looked ahead to other battles, quoting a line from an English ballad he had memorized in childhood. "Lay me down and bleed a while," Reagan said. "Though I am wounded, I am not slain. I shall rise and fight again."*

Reagan healed quickly. Within a few weeks he was sending out what Wirthlin called "distinct signals" that he was going to remain a presence on the national scene.[15] The first and clearest of these signals came even before the Ford-Carter campaign began in earnest, at a luncheon meeting at Reagan's Pacific Palisades home early in September 1976. Over seafood salad served on avocado wedges and a raspberry dessert, Reagan shared his views with Sears, Wirthlin, Lake, Deaver, Hannaford, Meese, and Republican field organizer Charles Black. One participant expected the meal to be a farewell and found Reagan talking instead about the issues he would raise in 1977. Another guest remembers that Reagan spoke of the "victory" of the conservative platform that the Ford forces had conceded at Kansas City and said he would support the GOP ticket in the fall without accommodating Ford on issues on which they disagreed.

Reagan campaigned in twenty states, doing more for Ford than the president acknowledged, but he refused to schedule vital, extra appearances in Mississippi and Texas that the Ford committee wanted. Introducing Ford at a fund-raising dinner in Beverly Hills on October 7, Reagan spent his time contrasting the Republican and Democratic platforms. He barely mentioned Ford, and his body language suggested he was uncomfortable sharing a platform with the president. When Ford returned to California later in the campaign and asked Reagan to join him, Reagan declined on grounds of scheduling conflicts.

With or without Reagan, however, Ford, who was 33 points behind in one poll in midsummer, rapidly made up ground on Carter, who had peaked earlier in the year and lost several late Democratic primaries to Jerry Brown and Frank Church after he had nailed down the nomination.[16] Ultimately, Ford lost by less than 3 percentage points. There are those, Cheney and Spencer included, who thought Ford might have

---

*The ballad by Dryden, a famous seventeenth-century poet, was called *Johnnie Armstrong's Last Goodnight*. It reads: "Fight on, my merry men all / I'm a little wounded, but I am not slain; / I will lay me down for to bleed a while, / Then I'll rise and fight with you again."

won except for an astonishing error in his second debate with Carter, in which Ford said that there was "no Soviet domination of Eastern Europe, and there never will be in a Ford administration." (Ford meant, apparently, to say that the spirit of the Polish people had not been conquered, as indeed it had not.) For three days, Ford stubbornly refused to concede that he had misspoken. When he finally did, the damage was done. It was a mistake that cost Ford more than any damage inflicted on him by Reagan.

Ford was convinced, however, that Reagan had played a spoiler's role. When I interviewed Ford in Palm Springs the following year, he blamed Reagan for his defeat, focusing on the fact of Reagan's challenge rather than his role in the general election campaign.[17] Ford repeated this claim in his memoirs, saying: "I think he really believed his candidacy wouldn't be divisive, but I knew he was wrong. How can you challenge an incumbent president of your own party and *not* be divisive?"[18]

On the other side, Reagan and several of his strategists, including Sears and Lake, believed in retrospect that Carter would have lost if Reagan had been the nominee. "So much of Ford's troubles related to Nixon and Watergate and the pardon," Lake said. "He had pardoned Nixon. People were voting against that, and against Washington."[19]

One never knows what might have been, but a persuasive case can be made that both Ford and Reagan were wrong in their postelection speculation. Reagan's challenge was certainly divisive in some respects; it drove Ford to the right on foreign policy and exposed some of the clumsier aspects of his candidacy. (Michael Barone speculated that Ford had the Helsinki accords in mind when he made his blunder about the Soviets not dominating Poland.[20]) But it is also true that Ford, who had no prior experience as a national candidate, was sharpened by the Reagan challenge and that his campaign was forged in the crucible of the contested primaries. Except for Reagan, it is unlikely that Spencer and Baker would have been involved in any important way in the campaign. Ford's campaign cadre—the capable quartet of Spencer, Baker, Cheney, and Robert Teeter—was formed because of the Reagan threat. These four, plus the advertising duo of Doug Bailey and John Deardourff, brought Ford from a threatened summer defeat of landslide proportions to near-victory in the fall. Absent the Reagan challenge, the campaign would have been run by the Callaways, the Freys, the Mortons, the Lairds, and the host of present and former House members upon whose political judgment Ford relied. It is difficult to imagine that Ford could have posed a threat to Carter with such a parochial team.

But the notion that Reagan would have defeated Carter in 1976 is even harder to accept. Conceivably, Reagan might have won if Ford had decided not to run and he had been handed the nomination through the acclamation of the Republican primaries. Perhaps Reagan might also have won if Ford had proved a paper tiger who dropped out after being defeated in the New Hampshire and Florida primaries. In the actual situation that confronted him, Reagan lost these primaries and mounted a comeback with an ideological campaign that advanced his cause in the restricted world of Sun Belt primaries while casting him as a narrow conservative among the electorate as a whole.

Reagan's vulnerability was defined by pollster Louis Harris in a survey published May 6 that showed Reagan losing ground among independents and Democrats as he was making the case against the Panama Canal treaty and Kissinger, the issues that brought him back in the GOP primaries. The Harris poll found Carter defeating Ford by 4 points and beating Reagan by 19. "It is apparent that Reagan has lost ground among the more affluent, better educated, more independent and less ideological groups in the electorate," Harris reported. "Thus, his strategy in appealing to conservative areas and groups has cut him off from the mainstream of the voting public, which he will need so badly in November if he should be nominated." While less dramatic, Wirthlin's polls showed a similar trend.

Even if Reagan had been able to scramble back to the center after securing the nomination, he would have faced the unprecedented political obstacle of campaigning while the president of his own party, whom he had defeated for nomination, occupied the White House. Ford is a generous man, and loyal to his party, but this would have asked too much of even his generosity and loyalty. "It would have been 1964 all over again," said Deaver. "The Republicans would have torn themselves to ribbons."[21] Nor would Reagan's litany about the ills inflicted on the economy by the free-spending federal government have been potent weapons against Carter in 1976. The Georgian was, after all, an outsider, too, and he was at this point promising a balanced budget. Carter gave Democrats who wanted to vote against Washington an opportunity to do so without abandoning their party. "The people wanted an outsider, but they weren't ready for Reagan," Hannaford said.[22]

Stuart Spencer, the only high-level political operative to work for Reagan (in his gubernatorial campaigns and in the presidential elections of 1980 and 1984) and against him (in 1976), believed that Reagan was a naturally gifted politician and the clear choice of the rank and file of his party. He also thought that Reagan was the luckiest candidate he ever knew.

"After Watergate, Reagan was the heir apparent," Spencer said. "He thought so. A lot of people thought so. Ford was an interim piece of business, an appointment. Reagan believed in destiny, he'd put his time in the vineyards, he was going to go after it. But he was very fortunate that he lost in '76. He would have not won because his base was in the South, and southerners had finally found a candidate in Jimmy Carter they could support, and they were going to support him. Sure, they turned on him four years later because he was so bad, but they wouldn't have then. And in 1976, Reagan still had hangover problems in the big states. He could not have won it."[23]

The weight of historical and demographic evidence supports Spencer's view. In 1976, Carter was a fresh face on the national scene and especially attractive in the states of the old Confederacy, which he swept except for Virginia, where the northern part of the state is tied to Washington. For southerners who believed (as Catholics had in 1960) that they might never have another chance to elect one of their own as president, Carter was a redemptive candidate. He was the last Democratic presidential nominee to run about even among white voters in the region.[24]

As the overall election results in 1976 show, the Watergate tide was still running against the Republican Party. The memories of Nixon's presidency and pardon were raw, and Democrats held a 25-point edge in party identification. All but two of the forty-some Democratic "Watergate babies" who had won election to the House of Representatives in 1974 were reelected. The Democrats maintained their overwhelming majority in the House and a solid one in the Senate, where Republicans made a one-seat gain. "The net result," wrote Barone, "was a government that looked overwhelmingly Democratic" but had many fissures beneath the surface.[25]

Many Republicans, taking it all in, were pessimistic about the future. Reagan, as usual, was not. He was standing on the sidelines in 1977, but he was eager to get back into the game. Once more, he had a winning feeling.

28

HEIR APPARENT

T HE FIRST YEAR of the Carter administration was a productive and pleasant time for Ronald Reagan. No longer bound by the demands of campaigning or governance that had preoccupied him since 1965, he was able to pick and choose from hundreds of speaking requests and to resume his column and radio show. Peter Hannaford drafted the columns, but Reagan wrote the radio scripts himself.[1] Many of Reagan's commentaries early in 1977 were more detached and theoretical than they had been in the run-up to his 1976 presidential campaign. While continuing to deplore the Soviet military buildup, Reagan also discussed abuses of the civil service system, income-tax indexing, and bureaucratic "fumbling" in the Food and Drug Administration. He rarely mentioned President Jimmy Carter. Reagan believed that Carter deserved a chance to show what he could do and had the political sense to know it would be counterproductive to criticize him prematurely.

Reagan's columns and radio shows kept him in the public eye, but he was not ready for any political heavy lifting. He knew, and Nancy did, too, that he needed time to himself. Much of this time was spent at his fourth and favorite ranch, the find of wealthy investment counselor William Wilson, a member of the Kitchen Cabinet. Wilson and his wife, Betty, had a ranch at the base of Refugio Canyon northwest of Santa Barbara, where they had hosted birthday parties for Nancy Reagan. Reagan liked the area and asked Wilson if he could find a ranch for him. Wilson knew of another place nearby. The Reagans purchased it through their trust for $527,000 on November 13, 1974, in the last weeks of his governorship.[2] The property had been known as Tip Top Ranch. Reagan renamed it "Rancho del Cielo," Spanish for "ranch in the sky" but with a connotation of "heavenly ranch," which was the way Reagan thought about it. If the ranch wasn't heaven, he said at a birthday tribute to Nancy Reagan many years later, it "probably has the same ZIP code."

Rancho del Cielo satisfied what Nancy Reagan called her husband's "preference for heights." Nestled on a 2,250-foot-high mountaintop 29 miles northwest of Santa Barbara, it is often bathed in bright sunlight when fog shrouds the Pacific Ocean below. The 688 acres of Rancho del Cielo are covered with coastal oaks, madrone, dense brush, pasture, and riding trails. Access, except by helicopter, is over a tortuous one-lane road that winds upward for 7 miles through a brush-covered canyon from Refugio State Beach and the Pacific Coast Highway. In 1955, the devastating Refugio Fire swept through the area, burning 80,000 acres of brush and timber. By the time the Reagans bought the ranch, the brush had grown back on the steep hillsides. But the ranch house was in a clearing next to a small lake that served as the water supply. Reagan named it Lake Lucky and assured his wife that it would protect them if there was ever another fire.

Reagan took care of his horses, and liked to work with his hands. He did not leave Rancho del Cielo as he found it. Working alongside Willard ("Barney") Barnett, a retired California Highway Patrol officer who had been Reagan's driver as governor, and a young aide, Dennis LeBlanc, he rebuilt the 1870s-vintage adobe house that was the center-piece of Rancho del Cielo. They knocked out walls, redesigned the kitchen, tore out a screened-in porch, and replaced it with a sturdy family room. They ripped off the corrugated roof, replaced it with old fence boards, and covered the boards with fake tile. They built a fence around the home of old telephone poles and constructed a rock patio. To build the patio, Reagan and Barnett dragged flat rocks into place, put cement in the crevices, and sprayed the cement with water.

Surveying this handiwork in 1976, when Reagan was on the verge of losing the Republican presidential nomination to Gerald Ford, I was reminded of the haunting scene in *Death of a Salesman* when Biff Loman talks about how his dead father had enjoyed building a bathroom and a new porch and putting up the garage. "You know, Charley, there's more of him in that front stoop than in all the sales he ever made," Biff says. As I listened to Reagan describe his work on the ranch house with genuine enthusiasm rather than the stage polish of his political talks, I thought there might be more of him in Rancho del Cielo than in most of his speeches. On this warm Sunday in July, he seemed to care more about the way he had carved the tile to fit around a meandering stone fireplace than he ever did about the Panama Canal.

The fictional Loman, old and weary from the road, had lost his prowess and his job. This is where the analogy ran into trouble. Reagan still enjoyed selling the conservative elixir, and he was very good at it. He gave seventy-five speeches in 1977, warming up for the next presidential campaign, which his supporters considered inevitable. But even some of these supporters were beginning to notice the wrinkles. Reagan was sixty-six years old in 1977; newspaper profiles and columns pointed out that he would be seventy within a month of assuming the presidency if he won in 1980. "William Henry Harrison, old Tippecanoe, was the only president to be inaugurated at that age, and he died of pneumonia six weeks later," wrote Marquis Childs in a comment typical of those then being written about Reagan.[3] Unlike many other liberals, however, the sagacious Childs did not discount Reagan's chances, observing that he was "more serious than ever" about becoming president.

Reagan deployed his sense of humor against the age issue. He said he had watched a rerun of *Knute Rockne—All American* and that it was like "seeing a younger son I never knew I had." He compared himself to Giuseppe Verdi, who composed *Falstaff* when he was eighty, or to Antonius Stradivarius, who made his best violins after he turned sixty and was still making them in the year of his death at ninety-one. Reagan watched his weight, drank infrequently, and did not smoke. He rode or swam at every opportunity, laughed away the rumors that he dyed his hair, and talked about himself as if he were middle-aged. At a birthday party at the Alexandria, Virginia, home of his former press aide, Nancy Reynolds, on the night he turned sixty-six, Reagan said, "Middle-age is when you're faced with two temptations and you choose the one that will get you home at 9:30."

There is a famous Sherlock Holmes story in which the fictional detective figures out the identity of an intruder because a dog does not bark in the night, and Holmes realizes that the dog knew the criminal. In the four years between his two presidential campaigns, Reagan's age was the great mystery issue, the dog that didn't bark in the night. Nearly everyone expected Reagan's age to be important. Reagan pollster Richard Wirthlin approached the issue in a dozen different ways, trying to find out if people thought Reagan was too old, too tired, too out of touch, or simply not up to the demands of the presidency. He found that people over sixty-five, more aware than younger people of their infirmities, were concerned about Reagan's age, but that this concern didn't carry over into the voting booth. Still, Wirthlin wondered if age was a hidden issue, like racial prejudice or gender preference, that didn't necessarily show up in the polls.

Reagan field-workers were as worried as Wirthlin. "All of us would like to see him ten years younger," said Reagan's Oklahoma coordinator, Clarence Warner, to Richard Bergholz of the *Los Angeles Times* in

April 1977. Warner went on to say, however, that if Reagan "looks as well in 1980 as he does now, I don't think his chronological age will be so important."[4] This proved to be the key. Robert Teeter, who had polled for Gerald Ford in 1976 and would poll for George Bush in 1980, found that Reagan's vigorous appearance trumped the age issue. "If there is some way to quantify it, the concern over the age issue is an inverse relationship to his exposure to the voters," Teeter said.[5]

On balance, the potential of the age issue had the positive impact for Reagan of making him realize that his key aides and supporters would be shopping around for alternative candidates if he showed any reluctance about running. As a result, Reagan dropped his characteristic coyness and talked no more of becoming a candidate only if lightning struck or his fellow Republicans begged him to run. He first signaled his intentions at the September 1976 meeting at his Pacific Palisades home and then dispelled any lingering doubts after the November election by forming a political action committee, Citizens for the Republic (CFTR), which was financed by $1 million in leftover campaign funds. Reagan had this money because his late surge in the primaries had brought him more contributions than he could spend. It was legally his own. "He could have taken that money and bought a palomino ranch if he had wanted to," said a supporter who attended the September meeting. "When he decided to form a political action committee instead, I realized that the country hadn't heard the last of Ronald Reagan."

CFTR was headed by Lyn Nofziger and became a billboard for Reagan and Nofziger to send the kind of messages that made the hearts of true believers go pit-a-pat. Throughout 1977, CFTR newsletters stoked the conservative fires with periodic attacks on the "giveaway" of the Panama Canal, the decline in U.S. military strength compared to the Soviet Union, the supposed danger posed by Communist Cuba, and government "destruction" of the work ethic. It was an insufficient platform for winning a national election, but it kept the conservative activists waiting in the wings.

Nofziger was fifty-three years old in 1977, and he had been consumed since 1966 with the dream of a Reagan presidency. Sensitive and abrasive, Nofziger was a valuable Reagan link to western and southern conservatives, whose certitude about the Panama Canal issue was exceeded only by their suspicion of the pragmatic course on which John Sears seemed to be leading their hero. Nofziger was trusted by these conservatives for his ideology—"I'm much more conservative than Reagan," he told me in 1968—and for his opposition to Sears. Beginning December 3, 1976, in Phoenix and continuing over the next six months in western, midwestern, and southern states, Nofziger and

CFTR promoted a series of regional meetings to discuss the future of Republican conservatism. Ostensibly, these were gatherings of the political faithful who were not pledged to any candidate. In fact, they were Reagan rallies that kept alive a grassroots organization at a time when John Connally was winning the battle of the boardrooms.

Nofziger had personal reasons to oppose Sears. In 1976, working with the cooperation of Nancy Reagan and Mike Deaver, Sears had replaced Nofziger with Jim Lake as Reagan's press secretary. Nofziger was left to direct a California primary campaign in which Reagan's victory was a foregone conclusion. Perhaps because he was himself an organizational infighter, Nofziger recognized before any of the other Californians that Sears meant to pick them off one by one and take control of the Reagan organization.* Aside from his personal feelings, Nofziger disagreed with Sears' political strategy. He thought Sears in 1976 had relied too much on winning over the Washington media and too little on the conservative grassroots organization that was waiting to raise money and walk precincts for Reagan. The difference was as much regional as ideological. Nofziger was a western conservative who believed that the best prospects for his party and his candidate lay south of the Mason-Dixon line and west of the 100th meridian. His vision was of a Goldwater approach writ large, a so-called Sun Belt strategy plus the conservative mountain and plains states of the West. Because Nofziger had been out of favor with Nancy Reagan since the "homosexual scandal" of 1967, he could not match Sears in influence. But Nofziger had a powerful ally in Paul Laxalt, the Nevada senator whom Sears had recruited in 1976 as Reagan's national chairman. Ever since the North Carolina primary, Laxalt had been fielding conservative complaints that Sears did not appreciate the ideological and regional roots of Reagan's appeal.

As a U.S. senator and former governor, Laxalt was the only member of the entourage to approach Reagan as an equal. Other members of the team, including Sears and Deaver, addressed Reagan as "Governor." Laxalt called him "Ron." The Nevada senator's position, courtly manners, and good looks made him a favorite of Nancy Reagan's. His openness commended him to the press. Ronald Reagan valued his counsel, in part because they were both genial conservatives who shared a gift for attracting Democratic and independent voters, as Laxalt had done in campaigns for governor and senator in his home state. Laxalt had been the only senator to support Reagan in his challenge against Ford

---

*Stuart Spencer said that at a governor's conference he had drinks with Sears and warned him that he needed to keep at least one of the Californians in the campaign. "One day Ronald Reagan is going to wake up in the morning, and if he doesn't see a familiar face there, he's going to start asking you some questions you can't answer," Spencer said he told Sears.[6]

in 1976, and he wanted to be more than a figurehead chairman of the campaign in 1980. He believed that it was both possible and necessary to weld the conflicting factions of the Reagan constituency into a cohesive force. Laxalt recognized that Sears was a good idea man but a poor manager and recalled that Sears in 1976 had refused to accept an office manager in Washington out of fear that he would lose organizational control. Essentially, Laxalt was, like Nofziger, a Sun Belt strategist. Unlike Nofziger, however, he recognized that Sears was useful in the Northeast, particularly if Ford ran again. The Nevadan's solution, forcefully expressed to Reagan in 1977, was that Sears should be a leading member of the team rather than captain of it, and that his energies should be focused on the constituencies he knew best—the Northeast delegates and the skeptical Washington press.

Sears, brilliant and moody, had his own struggles. He had shown discipline and courage in overcoming a drinking problem, and he felt up to the challenge of directing the campaign of a candidate with whom he had almost defeated a sitting president. As Sears saw it, Nofziger and his uncompromising western allies were afflicted with the virus of Goldwaterism, a disease known to be fatal to Republican candidates in November. Sears, a pragmatist of the Nixon school, preferred the craft of maneuver to ideological warfare. His frame of reference was thoroughly eastern. A New Yorker by birth, a Notre Dame graduate by choice, a lawyer by training, and a politician by inclination, Sears was fascinated by the challenge of making Reagan the political toast of New York and Pennsylvania. He knew that if Reagan could accomplish this and then establish a solid base in the Midwest, his nomination would be assured. But Sears, no less than Nofziger, was haunted by memories of past slights. Some who knew Sears said that he had never forgotten the aftermath of 1968, when his reward for rounding up vital delegates for Nixon was banishment from the White House by John Mitchell. In the transition period between Reagan's 1976 and 1980 presidential campaigns, Sears gave the impression that he was a man who was never going to allow himself to be elbowed aside again.

Reagan, dividing his time between Rancho del Cielo, his Pacific Palisades home, and his speaking trips, knew everything and nothing. He was bored by the details of Northeast politics that Sears relayed to him but fascinated with the notion that the region was ripe for the taking. Reagan knew of Laxalt's misgivings and Nofziger's distrust of Sears, but he, as well as Nancy Reagan, realized that Sears brought a dimension to the campaign that otherwise would have been lacking. Ironically, in view of what happened later, Reagan was encouraged in his view by Deaver, then a strong Sears booster.

"We had kind of a western inferiority complex," Deaver told me after Reagan was president and he was White House deputy chief of staff. "We didn't realize that what we had to do was do the things that got us where we were."[7] Reagan, who was present during this conversation, nodded in agreement, adding that he had valued Sears because of his access to the Washington press corps. And it wasn't just the press. Until 1980, Reagan had always been spooked at what he regarded as a stereotypical reaction to him in the Northeast. I remember one occasion in Massachusetts in the fall of 1968 when Reagan expressed pleasurable surprise at applause he would have regarded as normal anywhere else. Over the years, he had developed the theory that his gubernatorial record in California was unknown to eastern voters, who, he once said, thought of him as "some sort of conservative cowboy from the West." Reagan did not realize that his view of the "liberal" East was dated and stereotyped in many respects. But he knew that the region remained a mystery to him and that he was dependent on those who understood its ways. Reagan did indeed have a western inferiority complex, and Sears at the time seemed the best antidote to it.

Because of his past successes as a negotiator, Reagan had a strong belief in his ability to reconcile differences of approach. Removed, as always, from the daily struggles of his staff, he did not at this time believe that any of the conflicts were irreconcilable. In an effort to keep every member of his team on board, Reagan adopted a variant of the strategy and structure that Laxalt had suggested. He set up a team leadership that he compared to his California cabinet. Sears, who kept the title of campaign director, was supposed to plot political strategy while Ed Meese kept Reagan briefed on issues and served as chief of staff. The other members of the collective leadership were Deaver, Hannaford, Lake, and Charles Black. Pollster Wirthlin, although not a member of this formal leadership, also played a key role. Laxalt remained an influential, long-distance consultant and the national chairman.

This new structure was not pleasing to Sears, but he was soon again exercising operational control. He had most of his old team back, except for David Keene, who had opted for a major role with George Bush rather than a minor one with Reagan. Sears concentrated on New York, where he sent in an energetic young organizer named Roger Stone, and where he also courted Representative Jack Kemp, a favorite with conservatives. In Pennsylvania, Sears enlisted the brainy Drew Lewis, who in 1976 had held the line for Ford against Sears and Schweiker. In the Midwest, Sears resurrected Keith Bulen of Indiana, an old-timer who had promoted Richard Lugar from obscurity to national fame as "Nixon's favorite mayor" and then to the U.S. Senate.

Bulen had lost a step or two by 1980, but he was still a top political organizer. The most vital, and the most unsung, cog in this rapidly turning wheel was Black, who served as political director of the National
Conservative Political Action Committee and the Republican National
Committee before coming to work for Reagan. Black knew who the
doers and the talkers were among conservatives and Republican field
organizers. As Sears' chief field operator, he gave Reagan a long organizational head start.

With the campaign organization taking shape, Reagan stayed above
the clouds at Rancho del Cielo. He agreed with Sears that he should not
expose himself as a candidate before it was absolutely necessary. Deaver
and Hannaford supported this strategy. They were still marketing the
columns and radio shows that would have to be abandoned once Reagan became a declared candidate. These regular commentaries made
money for the candidate and for Deaver and Hannaford and kept Reagan in the public view.

Reagan had by now achieved a level of national acceptability that can
be claimed by very few politicians at any given time. After his governorship and two campaigns for the presidency, Reagan was, as Bob Teeter
put it, in "the major leagues of presidential candidates," that small
group of people of whom the public has such high awareness that they
accept them as presidential even though they may not vote for them.
"Seniority is how you get into that league," said Teeter, "and the fact
that Reagan had been around since 1964 had made him one of those figures."[8] A Gallup Poll found in August 1977 that Reagan was known by
nine in ten Americans and was their first choice as the next Republican
presidential nominee. The Republican division of the major league of
presidential candidates then included only Reagan and Ford. Nelson
Rockefeller, who had been a major leaguer for a long time, had dropped
out of politics after Ford discarded him from the ticket. He died of a
heart attack on January 26, 1979.

Ford was a worrisome figure to the Reagan team during this period.
Reagan did not believe Ford would run again, but the public opinion
polls gave him scant comfort. Ford led Reagan by 2 percentage points
as the preferred presidential candidate of respondents in a Gallup Poll
of April 1978, and by 14 points in a trial heat in July. These were polls of
all adults, not just Republicans, among whom Wirthlin's polls showed
Reagan with a slight advantage. Still, it would obviously be better for
Reagan if Ford decided not to run.

The hope of the Reagan entourage was that Ford was enjoying his
retirement so much that he would not abandon it for the rigors of a primary campaign. Ford could literally walk out of his Palm Springs office

and be on the golf course for a round of his favorite sport. In the winter, there was skiing at his Colorado vacation retreat at Vail. Betty Ford's illness was also thought to be a deterrent to another Ford campaign.* Still, Ford campaigned for twenty-two Republican candidates in thirty states in the midterm elections of 1978, and he teased reporters into writing speculative stories about a prospective second presidential race. It was with great relief that the Reaganites read a story by David S. Broder in *The Washington Post* on September 29, 1978, concluding that Ford, despite appearances to the contrary, was unlikely to be a presidential candidate again. "Most of those in his inner circle believe that when the time comes, Ford will say 'no' to another presidential campaign," Broder wrote. "And almost to a man, they hope that is his answer."[9] It was.

Two events in the spring and summer of 1978 foreshadowed important aspects of Reagan's candidacy. In May, Jack Kemp asked Reagan to endorse Jeffrey Bell in the Republican primary in New Jersey. Bell, author of the Ninety Billion Speech that had caused Reagan so much trouble in 1976, was opposing a venerable liberal senator, Clifford Case. Reagan consulted with Laxalt, who warned him that it would be unwise to get mixed up in a GOP primary. Reagan declined to endorse Bell or to contribute to his campaign from his political action committee, Citizens for the Republic. (Nofziger donated $50 on his own.) As it turned out, Reagan's prudence cost him little among conservatives, for Bell defeated Case anyway. Reagan then supported Bell in his losing race against Democrat Bill Bradley in the fall.

Reagan's refusal to get involved in the New Jersey primary was an important signal to those looking for such signs. It meant that Reagan intended to present himself as a unity Republican candidate for president in 1980, as he had done when running for governor of California in 1966. Laxalt's advice in this matter demonstrated that Sears did not have a corner on all the pragmatism in the Reagan market. Similar political realism was exhibited in 1978 by Deaver and Wirthlin, who were concerned that Reagan had become too much of a Johnny-one-note in his opposition to treaties that would give control of the Panama Canal to Panama.

Reagan listened to their concern. Without ever actually abandoning the position that had sparked his 1976 comeback, Reagan began talking about making the canal an internationally operated waterway. This pro-

---

*On April 19, 1978, Betty Ford was admitted to the Long Beach Naval Hospital for treatment of drug and alcohol abuse originally arising from addiction to a medication she had been taking to relieve severe arthritis. She was cured and released and became an effective spokeswoman against drug and alcohol abuse.

posal did not attract much attention from the media, but it demonstrated Reagan's political flexibility. In the Senate, Laxalt dutifully led
the opposition to two treaties negotiated by the Carter administration
turning over the canal to Panama. Once they were approved on April
20, 1978, Reagan rarely mentioned the Panama Canal again. Several
Democratic senators found that their votes for the treaties were politically costly, but Reagan had moved on.* Increasingly, his columns and
radio broadcasts focused upon President Carter's purported lack of
leadership, inconsistencies in his administration's energy policy, and the
plight of the economy.

The second event that influenced the direction of the Reagan candidacy was voter approval, in June 1978, of Proposition 13 in California.
With its draconian limits on local and state taxation, this initiative went
so far beyond the spending limits of the rejected Proposition 1 of 1973
that many opponents of Proposition 13 cited the Reagan plan as a
model by comparison. Reagan cautiously supported Proposition 13.
When the initiative passed, he expressed satisfaction and gave retroactive credit to Proposition 1, which he described as a measure ahead of
its time.

In California, the baleful impact on government services that opponents of Proposition 13 had predicted was cushioned and delayed because the Legislature had squirreled away a huge surplus that it doled
out to local governments after the initiative passed. Nationally, however, Proposition 13 had immediate consequences, fueling similar
measures in other states and giving impetus to the Kemp-Roth tax proposal calling for a 30 percent reduction in federal income taxes over
three years. It was named for its authors, Representative Jack Kemp of
Buffalo, the former Buffalo Bills quarterback who had worked for Reagan as an intern in 1967, and Senator William Roth of Delaware.
Kemp-Roth had more popular appeal than most Democrats realized.
Inflation and a steady lowering of the tax brackets had transformed an
income-tax structure that as late as World War II had mostly taxed the
rich into a system that affected nearly everyone. Middle-class Americans felt heavily taxed, all the more so after Social Security taxes were
raised in December 1977 to pay for benefit increases that President
Nixon had produced just in time for the 1972 election.

Kemp-Roth became a rallying cry for Republicans in the midterm
1978 elections, in which they picked up fifteen seats in the House and
three in the Senate. The Republicans had expected to do even better,
but their gains were muted because President Carter was then enjoying

---

*Michael Barone noted that nine of the senators who voted for the treaties, many of them
heavy favorites to win reelection, were defeated in November 1978 or November 1980.[10]

a temporary spurt in popularity as the result of the September peace agreement at Camp David between President Anwar Sadat of Egypt and Prime Minister Menachem Begin of Israel. But Kemp had succeeded in getting nearly every prominent Republican to endorse his tax plan. Backing Kemp-Roth had been an easy decision for Reagan, who had started earning big money for the first time in Hollywood after World War II, when marginal tax rates were at an all-time high. As a Democrat, he had favored reducing federal income taxes (and individual income averaging, not then allowed) and had called for a "human depreciation allowance" akin to the write-offs allowed the oil industry for depreciation. Reagan was reflexively a tax-cutter, and his feelings had not changed despite the pragmatism he had shown in endorsing the largest state tax increase in history as governor of California.

Reagan also identified with Kemp's political motives for accepting what came to be known as "supply-side economics." The supply-siders argued that lower taxes would spur productivity and produce more than enough tax revenues to make up for the lower rates. Kemp, who represented a Democratic, blue-collar district, was attracted by this nostrum because it gave Republicans something other than a recession to offer as an antidote to inflation. Reagan, anxious to reach out to blue-collar voters, saw Kemp-Roth as a means of going after Democrats who were disillusioned with Carter.

Sears accepted Kemp-Roth because Kemp's support helped with his strategy of amassing strength in the Northeast. By the fall of 1979, with Roger Stone's help, Sears had come up with a list of New York party regulars willing to stand up and be counted for Reagan. As a further advertisement of Reagan's interest in the Northeast, his formal announcement of candidacy was scheduled for New York City on November 13. By this time, every other Republican candidate had long since entered the race. There was John Connally, who confided to me during a visit to Los Angeles that he was confident he could beat Reagan if he could only get him one-on-one. But that was also the hope of nearly everyone in a GOP field that also included George Bush, Senators Howard H. Baker Jr. and Robert Dole, and Representatives John B. Anderson and Philip Crane. Connally was far ahead in fund-raising. Sears believed that Baker, who wanted Sears to run his campaign, had the possibility of catching on with the public. No one on the Reagan team worried about Bush, who had been busy for a year working the political vineyards of New Hampshire and Iowa.

The Reagan campaign's most serious problems were internal. The collective leadership had not worked, and Reagan was troubled by constant friction among his principal lieutenants. The first to leave was

Nofziger, who had been given a fund-raising responsibility for which he was temperamentally unsuited. At Sears' behest, Deaver persuaded Reagan to let Nofziger go. Nofziger was hurt and angered by this decision; when Deaver brought the news to him, Nofziger told him that he would be next on Sears' hit list. Nofziger's dismissal fanned the conservative fires that ultimately engulfed the power-conscious Sears. On October 26, 1979, Nofziger told reporters in Los Angeles that "some of the people around the governor are insensitive to his long-term supporters and to the needs of the media." The following day, in *Human Events*, M. Stanton Evans attacked Sears as "a graduate of the Richard Nixon school of politics . . . a devout pragmatist who has little affinity for issues in general, and even less affinity for conservatives." Evans warned that the departure of Nofziger "removes an important potential counterweight to Sears' influence within the Reagan inner circle."[11]

Laxalt agreed and privately told Reagan that conservatives were dismayed at the loss of Nofziger.[12] The Nevada senator also suspected he might be next, for he had heard of a Sears plan to replace him as national chairman and "broaden" the campaign with a dual chairmanship of Kemp and Iowa Governor Robert Ray. Reagan promised Laxalt that he would remain as chairman and kept his word, leaving Kemp with an undefined and largely meaningless title of "campaign spokesman." But the infighting was getting to Reagan, who confessed to a friend that he was spending too much time on internal problems and "couldn't seem to keep everyone on track." By now, Deaver was trying, with little success, to take up the slack in fund-raising and was having his own problems with Sears. On November 2, in Boston for a fund-raiser with Frank Sinatra and Dean Martin, Reagan discussed the friction with Press Secretary Jim Lake, who liked Deaver but distrusted the other Californians. "Governor, there are two people who are absolutely critical to your campaign," Lake said. "One is John Sears and the other is Mike Deaver, and you need them both."[13] At the time, Reagan thought so, too. But the infighting continued, and Reagan, at his wife's suggestion, summoned Deaver, Sears, Lake, and Black to a meeting at his Pacific Palisades home November 26 in an effort to resolve the differences.

What followed was not reconciliation but a showdown. With Deaver and Nancy alongside him, Reagan found himself faced with a united front of Sears, Lake, and Black demanding that he make a decision between keeping Deaver or the three of them. "I can't understand this," Reagan said to Lake. "Three weeks ago you told me that both John and Mike were indispensable to my campaign, and now you're telling me that I have to choose between them." Lake uncomfortably replied that

Reagan could no longer keep both men and that Sears was the more valuable to his campaign.*

As the meeting wound on, Sears accused Deaver of ineffective fundraising, and Deaver insisted that the complaints about him were merely excuses that Sears was using to take total control of the campaign. Reagan wanted a compromise, but Sears and his allies remained adamant, unwilling to accept any arrangement that would keep Deaver in the campaign. Seeing what was happening, Nancy Reagan said to her husband: "Yes, honey, you're going to have to make a choice." Before Reagan could respond, Deaver spoke up and said, "No, governor, you don't have to make that choice. I'll resign." And with that he walked to the front door. Reagan followed him, agitated, and insisted that he didn't want Deaver to leave.

Reagan returned to the living room in a fury. "The biggest man here just left the room," he said. "He was willing to accommodate and compromise and you bastards wouldn't." Reagan never talked warmly to Sears again. The confrontation left him depressed and angry at himself about what he had allowed to happen. His mood was not improved when old friends and allies, who had rarely criticized him to his face, bluntly told him that he had made a mistake. Nancy Reynolds, close to the Reagans and to Deaver, protested the decision in a telephone conversation. It was the only time that Reagan was ever testy with her.[15] Meese forcefully told Reagan that he had made a mistake and didn't understand what was happening in his own campaign. Reagan told me much later that he hadn't needed anyone to tell him that he had done wrong. "But Mike precipitated it," he added. "I really didn't expect him to go."[16]

There are private incidents in every campaign that are special, forever remembered by the participants when memories of celebrated public occasions have dimmed. The November 26, 1979, meeting in Reagan's home was one of those events. For Sears, it marked the beginning of the end. In insisting on Deaver's resignation, Sears had made an adversary of the one California insider who had defended him to the candidate and Nancy Reagan and who had accepted the premise that Sears needed operational control. Others in the inner circle thought that Deaver had been too trusting of Sears, particularly after Nofziger's dismissal. Sears was aware that Deaver had on many occasions spoken well of him, but he was unable to restrain his impulse to achieve full control. A friend of Sears' compared him to a figure in a Greek tragedy

---

*Lake had long seen himself as the man in the middle who had tried with little success to explain Deaver's value to Sears and Sears' importance to Deaver. "I was just worn out being the broker," Lake said to me in 1981. "I couldn't do it anymore."[14]

whose strength is also his fatal flaw. Sears wanted to run the campaign his way or not at all. He could not risk insiders who were closer to Reagan than he was. By eliminating Deaver, he insured his own downfall.

For Reagan, November 26, 1979, marked the day that he became a participant in the operation of his campaign. From the moment Deaver walked out on him, Reagan began to question the wisdom of turning over his political future to a man who patronized him and didn't laugh at his old movie jokes. "I look him in the eye, and he looks me in the tie," Reagan said, reverting to a standard used in his boyhood for evaluating the trustworthiness of a man. Now, at last, the passive candidate was angry enough to say what he really thought and felt about his campaign manager. Once he started doing that, although it took a defeat in Iowa and Nancy Reagan to force him to act, the ultimate decision became inevitable.

It was only after Deaver was gone that the Reagans realized how much they had depended on their longtime aide. Deaver was the faithful adjutant who had maintained the atmosphere of harmony that was vital to the candidate, particularly on the road. Deaver had intervened when contributors, or other aides or reporters, needed to speak with Reagan outside normal channels. Deaver, not Sears, was Reagan's indispensable man. Reagan still needed Sears at this point of the campaign. But after November 26, he would be guided more by his political instincts and less by the judgment of outside professionals whom he did not know. He would listen to those he trusted and felt knew him best—Nancy Reagan, Ed Meese, Paul Laxalt, old members of the Kitchen Cabinet such as Holmes Tuttle and William French Smith, and old campaign managers like Stu Spencer. After Sears had gone, Reagan would welcome Deaver back like a lost son and keep him at his side throughout the rest of the campaign and into the White House.

Campaigns are won in the hearts of candidates before they are won at the ballot box. They are won by candidates who trust their instincts and feel secure in their actions. On November 26, 1979, Reagan began to realize that he did not understand what was happening in his campaign. The struggle to gain that understanding, to speak in his own voice, and to campaign in a way that he felt comfortable with would free Reagan from the restraints of his collective leadership and the disharmony it had produced. Because of what happened in his living room after Deaver walked out on him, Reagan would become his own candidate for president of the United States. It would make a difference.

29

DEBATER

TWO WEEKS BEFORE this pivotal meeting, Sears brought Ronald Reagan to New York to show the flag of his northeastern strategy. Reagan was introduced at one gathering by Barry Gray, a New York radio personality, who proclaimed, "The nation cries out for desperate leadership." By the time Reagan announced his candidacy in the ballroom of the New York Hilton the night of November 13, 1979, there were those in the press corps and in the political community who suspected that is what they would be getting from Reagan.

In his bid for the Republican presidential nomination, Reagan held a huge lead in every poll over the nine other candidates in the race. But many thought he was a suspect favorite who was too old, too unintelligent, or too out of touch to be nominated. "I think a man approaching seventy is going to have a hard time giving a new speech when he's given the same speech two hundred nights a year for twenty years," the political consultant John Deardourff told reporters.[1] It was a prevalent opinion. On the night of his announcement, Reagan fueled the suspicions about him by stumbling through a formula speech that had reporters groping for a lead. He misread some passages, although this was evident only to reporters in the ballroom, for Reagan had smoothly pretaped the speech earlier for a national television audience.

The only new element in the speech was a vague call for "a North American accord," which as best as anyone could understand it was a kind of encounter group among the leaders of Canada, Mexico, and the United States. This idea, which was contributed by Sears, quickly disappeared from public discourse after serving its purpose of demonstrating that Reagan could say something original. The only other whiff of originality in the speech was a mild declaration that Americans had not "been given all the information we need to make a judgment" about the magnitude of excess oil company profits. This comment displeased Jack Kemp, who opposed a windfall profits tax and wanted Reagan to say more about the Kemp-Roth tax cut. Other conservatives were bothered by a lack of specifics on defense and foreign policy. Summing up a consensus shared by the press and conservatives, Laxalt told me that he thought the speech was "mostly mush."*

Reagan's speech looks better in retrospect. The North American accord became the basis for the "framework agreement" in the Reagan presidency that in turn became the basis for the North American Free Trade Agreement in later presidencies. While the speech was uninspiring to those familiar with the collected works of Ronald Reagan, its target was neither movement conservatives nor the national press. Reagan's audience was the millions of Americans watching television, who had learned from experience not to trust the promises of their presidents. These Americans had been disappointed by Johnson, disillusioned by Nixon, and had found little to cheer about in the subsequent performances of Ford and Carter. Carter's approval rating, in a Gallup Poll of November 2–5, had slumped to 32 percent.

Reagan spoke to these disappointed Americans. If he did not have all the answers, he at least was able to establish bonds of association and trust with his audience. Reagan had been doing this for so long that many of us had forgotten how important it was. He did it again the night of his announcement, in words that never made it into most of the news stories, and he did it well. While other candidates were saying what they could do to save America, Reagan was telling the story of his life. "I'm sure that each of us has seen our country from a number of different viewpoints depending on where we've lived and what we've done," he said:

> For me it has been as a boy growing up in several small towns in Illinois. As a young man in Iowa trying to get a start in the years of the great Depression and later in California for most of my adult life, I've seen America from the stadium press box as a sportscaster, as an actor, officer of my labor union, soldier, office-holder, and as both Democrat and Republican. I've lived in an America where those who often had too little to eat outnumbered those who had enough. There have been four wars in my

*The New York Times led its story with the North American accord, and the Los Angeles Times with Reagan's line, "I cannot and will not stand by and see this great country destroy itself." In The Washington Post, I wrote that Reagan had launched his campaign "with a call for the restoration of American influence abroad and American confidence at home." A similar disparity was reflected in the network television coverage. Laxalt observed that the lack of a clear theme or catch phrase in the speech cost Reagan the opportunity of presenting a focused message at the outset of his formal campaign.

lifetime and I've seen our country face financial ruin in the Depression. I have also seen the great strength of this nation as it pulled itself up from that ruin to become the dominant force in the world.

Later in his speech, Reagan told how his father had been fired on Christmas Eve in the depth of the Depression. With moist eyes, he said, "I cannot and will not stand by while inflation and joblessness destroy the dignity of our people." His message was that he was one with his audience. It reinforced an earlier comment to a reporter, "I am what I always have been and I intend to remain that way."[2]

The press missed the significance of Reagan's message while focusing on the tentative beginning of his campaign. The morning of the announcement speech, on NBC's *Today*, Reagan said that if he was elected president he would be younger than most world leaders.

"Giscard d'Estaing of France is younger than you," said interviewer Tom Brokaw.

"Who?" asked Reagan.

"Giscard d'Estaing of France," repeated Brokaw.

"Yes, possibly," said Reagan, who was fifteen years older than the then French president. "Not an awfully lot more."

Reporters laughed at this exchange, and many believed that Reagan could not identify the president of France. In the process of dampening this concern, Press Secretary Jim Lake raised another. He said Reagan had not heard the question from Brokaw, who was directly across from him a few feet away. "We could run a correction in *The Washington Post*," I said to Lake. "We could say that the good news is that Ronald Reagan knows who the president of France is and that the bad news is that he can't hear." Lake, who had done well in fending off the age issue, laughed and shook his head. "We'd rather have you say he's too ignorant than too old," he replied.*

Jack Kemp didn't help. The day after the announcement, he introduced Reagan at a Washington news conference as the "oldest and wisest candidate" while other members of the entourage winced. The

---

*Lake's equanimity did not survive a story I wrote in January, which noted that a question had to be repeated five times at an Iowa rally before Reagan could understand it. The story quoted a former aide who had seen Reagan for the first time in four years and said, "The only difference I have noticed is that his hearing has slipped." Lake told other reporters this story was a "cheap shot," even though Reagan's hearing loss was obvious to anyone who had seen him in earlier campaigns. Subsequently, on a plane trip from Los Angeles to New Hampshire, Reagan told me he had suffered from a minor hearing impairment in his right ear since the late 1930s because of an incident during the filming of one of the movies in which he played Secret Service agent Brass Bancroft. According to Reagan, another actor was supposed to fire a blank .38 cartridge from a distance. Instead, he fired it next to Reagan's ear. I had never heard the story before, and never heard it again, either.

phrase caught on with the campaign press corps, who started referring to Reagan in pool reports as "The Oldest and Wisest," soon shortened to "The O&W."

It was the question of Reagan's wisdom rather than his age that worried Sears and motivated his front-running strategy. Reagan's knowledge gap showed up immediately. After his Washington press conference, Reagan flew back to New York City and confronted reporters again at the Waldorf-Astoria the following morning. He bobbled an easy question about federal aid to New York City, which he didn't know came with strings attached. In Grand Rapids, Michigan, the next day, Reagan proved even less knowledgeable about pending legislation to bail out the troubled Chrysler Corporation, which was of key importance to the state and community in which he was campaigning. Reagan knew he disagreed with Carter on the plan but didn't know why. Later, Ed Meese came back on the plane to explain to reporters what Reagan "really meant" to say. Sears was infuriated with Meese for what he saw as inadequate preparation of the candidate, but Reagan's performance also ratified Sears' low opinion of his candidate's intelligence.

My evaluation of Reagan's first trip, written for *The Washington Post* of November 19, was that the candidate had erased questions about his vitality "while raising new doubts about his capacity to serve as President."[3] I had seen Reagan on the ropes before but couldn't understand why he was so ill-prepared after starting so late. What wasn't apparent then was the draining effect of the staff struggles, which would culminate a week later with the walkout of Deaver. Reagan was distracted. "What I should have pointed out is that the system is in place and it's working," Reagan told me in discussing his muff on New York City aid during an interview en route to the West Coast.[4] He was blunter about his stumbles to his aides, acknowledging to one of them that he had "blown it" in Grand Rapids. This realism would come in handy for Reagan after the Iowa caucuses.

Reagan's schedule was deliberately brisk that first week because Sears wanted to show that he was up to the rigors of a campaign. But Sears slowed him down after that, keeping the candidate on a carefully paced course. Sears' strategy, accepted by the candidate despite his misgivings about the campaign manager, was to cast Reagan as the presumed nominee. Reagan traveled everywhere by air, avoiding the grubby, ground-level combat in which he might be tripped up by the press or local issues and ducking proposed debates with other Republicans.

The high costs of Reagan's constant coast-to-coast travel tested the new campaign spending limitation laws, but Sears was convinced that

Reagan could wrap up the nomination early in the Northeast and then sit out most of the primaries. The campaign manager devoted organizational resources to this target region, concentrating on New York, Connecticut, and New Hampshire, the first primary state. Even there, Reagan's presence was not regarded as essential; New Hampshire Chairman Gerald Carmen pleaded in vain for more appearances. But Reagan was everywhere, and nowhere. In the final seven weeks of 1979 and the first three of 1980, he was an airborne celebrity candidate, soaring above the earthbound struggles of mortal contenders for the Republican nomination. By the second week of December, the pace was so leisurely that a baggage call in South Carolina was listed on the campaign schedule as an "event."

For a time, this front-running strategy, which really was more like front-walking, seemed to be working. A week before Reagan's announcement, *The New York Times*-CBS poll found him far ahead among Republican voters, with 37 percent to John Connally's 15 percent. The following week, *The Washington Post* poll showed Reagan gaining among moderate Republican voters. In California, a poll taken by Mervin Field gave Reagan 61 percent to 12 percent for runner-up Senator Howard Baker. The Iowa Poll conducted by the *Des Moines Register and Tribune* gave Reagan 50 percent of the vote, and 14 percent to Bush in second place.

The Iowa precinct caucuses of January 21, 1980, were one of those wild cards that keep turning up in the American political deck just when it seems that everyone has mastered the game. They were supposed to be crucial for President Carter, who four years earlier had parlayed a better-than-expected showing in the Iowa caucuses to victory in the New Hampshire primary, and who in 1980 faced a challenge from Senator Edward Kennedy for the Democratic nomination. In comparison, the caucuses were expected to be of minor consequence in the Republican nominating process.

Events and the enterprise of the *Des Moines Register and Tribune* upped the ante for the Republicans. The newspaper, at the suggestion of editor James Gannon, decided to sponsor the first debates of the presidential campaign, scheduling the Republican event for January 5 and the Democratic debate two days later. But the Democratic contenders never met. On the first Sunday of November 1979, Iranian militants seized the U.S. embassy in Teheran and took fifty-two Americans hostage. The timing was fateful for Kennedy, who had announced his candidacy three days earlier. As Americans usually do in times of international crisis, they rallied behind their president. Carter surged ahead in the polls and stayed in the White House, where he said he was devoting his energies to the hostage crisis. He defeated Kennedy by a 2–1 margin in the Iowa caucuses.

The absence of a Democratic debate put the spotlight in Iowa on the Republican show. Six of the invited GOP candidates—Connally, Baker, Bush, Anderson, Crane, and Dole—accepted the debate invitation. Reagan rejected it, acceding to Sears' decision without a murmur. Sears left open the possibility of a New Hampshire debate, which Reagan booster William Loeb advocated, but did not think it necessary to expose the candidate in Iowa. In fairness to Sears, it is unlikely that Reagan would have reached a different decision on his own. He had avoided debating any opponents since his disastrous March 1966 joint appearance with George Christopher before the National Negro Republican Assembly during his first gubernatorial campaign. In the intervening years, Gaylord Parkinson's dictum about not speaking ill of fellow Republicans had served Reagan well, and he gave it one last fling in Iowa.

Only 22,000 Republicans had participated in the Iowa caucuses of 1976. The Reagan organizers in the state had no idea how many would participate in 1980. At least two political professionals, Eddie Mahe, for Connally, and Richard Redman, for Baker, thought the total could go as high as 100,000, but these forecasts seemed excessive to almost everyone else. The Reagan forces adopted what they believed was a prudent organizational course: They would try to turn out 30,000 certified Reaganites at the caucuses, leaving a hefty margin of error for their candidate in a seven-man field. Sears and Wirthlin agreed that it would be a waste to poll because of the difficulty of defining the electorate. "Who would you be polling?" Wirthlin said to me a few days before the election. "How do you know who's going to turn out?" But Wirthlin confessed that he was jittery about Iowa, and Black shared his concern. Early in the month, an observant Reagan field operative, Kenneth Klinge, had warned about the progress being made by Bush. The signs of trouble were there, but the Reagan campaign did not heed them.

Perhaps both Sears and Reagan would have reacted differently if they had spent more time in Iowa. The candidate made eight appearances in the state, but he flew in and out so quickly that Bush was able to boast he had spent more days in Iowa than Reagan had hours. Wirthlin called these trips "cameo appearances," and they did not fool Iowa Republicans into thinking that Reagan was campaigning. The Reagan visit that attracted the most attention was a fly-in to Davenport two days after the debate. Reagan held a short, confused press conference in the lobby of the Black Hawk Hotel, trying to explain why he had ducked the debate. Connally had said during the debate that he didn't know where Reagan stood on various issues, and a reporter asked Reagan about it. "He must have been living under a rock," Reagan said heatedly. "I've been saying what I believe for a long, long time, and I spent eight years as governor trying to implement what I believe. I haven't changed these views, and I have been speaking in specifics."

But at this very press conference, Reagan announced an important change in his views. The other Republican candidates, except for Anderson, had criticized President Carter for imposing a grain embargo against the Soviet Union in response to the invasion of Afghanistan. Reagan initially supported the embargo, but Sears and Wirthlin persuaded him that this was an unacceptable stance in Iowa, where grain exports were important to farmers. So in Davenport, asserting that the embargo punished American farmers without having any impact on the Soviets, Reagan promised to lift it if he became president. He would keep that promise, without ever acknowledging that it was made for blatant political reasons.

The Bush organization in Iowa sent out a million pieces of mail during the last week of the campaign, a discovery the Reagan team did not make until after the caucuses. Reagan spent most of the week before the caucuses with Sears at his side, cruising the campaign manager's chosen battleground, the Northeast. While Bush was spending every day in Iowa, Reagan traveled to New Hampshire, Vermont, Connecticut, and New York, wooing politicians in four states that had given Ford 204 delegates and Reagan only 23 at the 1976 convention. By now, Bush's surge had become evident, and my editors at *The Washington Post* wanted predictive estimates of the Iowa caucuses. Sears responded to my inquiries as if Iowa were on the moon. Instead of analyzing the caucuses, he provided me with a detailed and generally accurate forecast of where and how Reagan would win delegates in the Northeast. "Reflect on this," said Sears. "This time we don't have the support of Strom Thurmond who was backing Connally and we have the support of half the delegation from New York."[5] True enough, but what about Iowa? Sears gave an expressive shrug.

Reagan made a final appearance in Iowa, delivering a statewide television version of his basic speech the Saturday night before the Monday caucuses. Then he flew home to California. Bush stayed in Iowa, and won. After all his work, however, and all of Reagan's neglect, Bush's victory was by the narrow margin of 2,182 votes. The Reagan forces slightly exceeded their original target, winning 31,318 votes. But 110,000 Republicans participated in the caucuses, and Reagan's vote was slightly less than 30 percent of the total. Bush received 33,500 votes, almost 33 percent. The outcome finished off the front-runner strategy, and there were those in Iowa who thought it had taken the front-runner down with it. Wirthlin, the pollster who had not polled, had a sense of déjà vu. He remembered 1976, when Reagan had left New Hampshire the Sunday before the election and lost the primary narrowly to Gerald Ford. "It was like sitting through a rerun of a bad old movie you hadn't wanted to see the first time," he said.[6]

Reagan was watching a new movie the night the returns came in from Iowa. Relaxing while most of his rivals were still campaigning, Reagan had gone to the swank Bel Air home of producer Hal Wallis to see a preview of *Kramer vs. Kramer*. Informed during the movie about what was happening in Iowa, Reagan was shaken. "It was a jolt," he told me months later, remembering that night as the low point of the campaign. "There are going to be some changes made," Meese recalled Reagan saying to him that same evening.

The changes occurred immediately. Rather than ruining Reagan, Iowa freed him from the shrouds in which his managers had wrapped him, permitting him to campaign as a natural candidate drawing on the resources of his personality. "I sensed that weeks before that, psychologically, Ron felt trapped," Laxalt told me afterward. "He concurred in avoiding the Iowa debate but subconsciously he didn't feel right about it. When he changed, he was liberated and it enabled him to perform in New Hampshire."[7] Ever since Reagan's fiery performance in the 1976 North Carolina primary, Laxalt had believed the candidate was his own best asset. He reminded Reagan of this the next day, recalling the Super Bowl game of the week before, where the Pittsburgh Steelers had defeated Reagan's beloved Los Angeles Rams. "The Steelers wouldn't have won if [quarterback] Terry Bradshaw had been sitting on his ass for three quarters, and you were sitting on your ass in Iowa," Laxalt said.[8] Reagan promised that the world would see a different candidate in New Hampshire. Nofziger, still on the outs, summed up the unanimous attitude of Laxalt and the Californians: "If you're going to follow a Rose Garden strategy, you better be sure you have a Rose Garden."[9]

No one knew the need for change more than John Sears. He was a political professional who realized that a failed strategy must be discarded, the sooner the better. In a transformation as swift as any ever made at Central Casting, the high-flying and disengaged front-runner became the accessible, bus-bound underdog. During one stretch, Reagan campaigned for twenty-one consecutive days, mostly by bus, in New Hampshire, with a couple of quick flights to the early primary states of South Carolina and Florida thrown in. Before Iowa, reporters had swapped jokes about such innovations as the Ronald Reagan doll, which, when wound, ran for an hour before it had to take a nap. But the easy duty ended in New Hampshire, where a sign went up on the press bus saying, "Free the Reagan 44."

Reagan's days were longer, but his life was easier on the ground. He warmed up crowds and was warmed by them. He answered questions without consulting his strategists, bluntly expressing opposition to budget deficits, the Soviet Union, and permissive abortion laws. He went after Bush, too. In response to a question at the Franklin Rotary Club about differences between himself and Bush, Reagan said that Bush favored a liberalized abortion law, the Equal Rights Amendment, and a guaranteed-income welfare plan, all of which he opposed. Later in the evening, he told the Hookset Men's Club that he had "forgotten" to mention that Bush also favored gun control, an accusation dimly based on Bush's support of a 1968 law restricting mail-order sales of rifles and shotguns.

Reagan's greatest success in New Hampshire was in defusing the "age issue," which had come to the forefront in the wake of Iowa. Hearing that some of Reagan's opponents planned to celebrate his sixty-ninth birthday on February 6, less than three weeks before the primary, the Reagan team beat them to it. Acting on the suggestion of California Reagan activist Lorelei Kinder, Sears saw to it that birthday parties were organized up and down the eastern seaboard. There were balloons and birthday songs and signs and so many mammoth cakes that Reagan finally fell into one of them at a party in Greenville, South Carolina, on February 7. The press scored the birthday parties "Reagan 6, Cakes 1." Taken in their entirety, however, the parties turned a supposed liability into an asset. After New Hampshire, Reagan's age was no longer an issue in the campaign.

Reagan's breakthrough in New Hampshire was at a debate, but not the one in Nashua that is celebrated in American political lore. The Nashua debate was on February 23, the Saturday before the primary. Reagan's breakthrough came on February 20, when he joined the six Republican candidates he had eluded in Iowa for a joint appearance in Manchester sponsored by the League of Women Voters. Reagan was nervous at the outset. He fumbled some questions and offered the startling opinion that it is acceptable for U.S. corporations doing business abroad to bribe foreign governments if that is what is expected of them.

But Bush was uninspiring. He drew few differences with Reagan, and he took mild jabs from the other candidates, who now regarded him as the front-runner with the momentum that Bush called "Big Mo." This was a misperception that was widely shared in the press corps. Reagan's stature with Republican voters, and particularly with conservatives, had not been built in a day. He had been their hero since 1964, and he had campaigned for his principles and himself in two presidential elections. He stood with them on the gut issues. To conservatives in New Hampshire and the nation, the concerns about Reagan were his vitality and his age. Reagan fueled these doubts by absenting himself from Iowa; he answered them convincingly in New Hampshire with his vigorous campaigning. Reagan did not have to "win" the debate in Manchester, and a "draw" would not have been good enough for Bush. Reagan won just by showing up and being himself.

Wirthlin's polls demonstrated the decisiveness of Manchester. Thirty-seven percent of the Republicans intending to vote in the election watched, and most of these picked a winner. Reagan was first choice, with 33 percent, compared to 17 percent who thought that Bush had won. Even viewers who did not think that Reagan had won approved of his response to a question from the audience criticizing him for telling an ethnic joke to his staff.* Reagan said he had been "stiffed" by the press and was telling the joke as an example of jokes politicians shouldn't tell. This was an amazing lie, as reporters knew. Reagan got away with it because the joke was not especially offensive and because Reagan was sincere in saying that he was not a prejudiced person.[10] And he got away with it, also, because he had more credibility with the Republican electorate in New Hampshire than the national press did. Wirthlin's tracking polls showed Reagan moving from a point behind Bush to 20 points ahead on the strength of the Manchester debate. The pollster was back in the field when Reagan went to Nashua on Saturday for a face-to-face debate with Bush that would provide the most memorable moments of the 1980 election campaign.

In a way, what happened in Nashua was a fitting last hurrah for embattled John Sears, the master political tactician. In another way it was a demonstration of the most genuine qualities of Reagan and the most disquieting ones of the man he was to make his vice president. Seen without the informing comfort of hindsight, it was another stroke of the Reagan luck. And for an audience of 2,500, it was a splendid political show.

The Nashua debate was the proposal of Jerry Carmen, who believed that the way to cut Bush down to size was to put him one-on-one with Reagan. Bush's managers liked the idea because they believed that such

---

*The joke went like this: "How do you tell who the Polish fellow is at a cockfight? He's the one with the duck. How do you tell who the Italian is at the cockfight? He's the one who bets on the duck. How do you know the Mafia was there? The duck wins." News services carried an account of Reagan telling the joke, which was overheard by a reporter. The story prompted Ed Meese to quip, "There goes Connecticut," a reference to the prominent participation of Italian Americans in the Republican politics of that state.

a debate would demonstrate that the Republican race had become a two-man affair between Bush and Reagan. So, Hugh Gregg, the Reagan campaign manager in New Hampshire in 1976 who was in 1980 directing the Bush operation in the state, talked to the publisher of the *Nashua Telegraph*, who agreed to sponsor the debate.

Bob Dole then complained to the Federal Elections Commission that this sponsorship would be an illegal contribution to the Reagan and Bush campaigns if the other candidates were excluded. The commission agreed. To comply with the campaign law, Carmen and Sears proposed that Reagan and Bush split the costs of the debate. Had Bush accepted this reasonable offer, the so-called "ambush at Nashua" that was later blamed on Sears would not have occurred. But Gregg could be stiff-necked, and the Bush national strategists deferred to him, as Sears and Lake had done in 1976. Gregg refused to pick up any of the costs, and Sears agreed that the Reagan campaign would pay for the debate. Sears realized that this action gave the Reagan camp de facto control of the proceedings despite the *Nashua Telegraph*'s sponsorship. The campaign manager and Lake then called the other candidates, explaining to them that Reagan felt it was unfair to exclude them. If they came to Nashua, Sears said, there might be an opportunity for them to participate.[11] All of the candidates, except Connally, who was campaigning in South Carolina, agreed to come. Meanwhile, word was passed to reporters that Nashua was not going to be a cut-and-dried affair.

Reagan spent the afternoon resting and boning up on debate questions he thought might be raised by Bush. Although he did not know what Sears had arranged for the evening, Reagan had been told that the results of the Manchester debate were positive for him, which meant that he no longer needed to meet Bush in an isolated debate. In the car en route to the debate site at the Nashua High School gymnasium, Lake told Reagan that Anderson, Baker, Dole, and Crane would be there as well as Bush. "Fine," said Reagan, who afterward told me that he had never cared much for excluding the other candidates in the first place.

At the gymnasium, Reagan met with the four excluded candidates at one end of a long hall while Sears met in an adjoining room with Bush campaign manager James Baker and told him that Reagan wanted to open up the debate. Baker refused. After leaving Sears, he spotted the other candidates in the room with Reagan and went back to tell Bush that he was about to be "ambushed." Bush persisted in his opposition to an open debate, saying that the rules had been agreed upon in advance. Out in the hall, *Nashua Telegraph* editor Jon Breen was telling reporters that he would not change the ground rules. By now, Reagan had agreed with the four excluded candidates that he wouldn't debate if they weren't allowed to participate. Reagan's strategists argued, however, that he couldn't walk out, because that would make it look as if he were afraid to debate Bush.

Angrily, without his aides knowing what he was going to do, Reagan stalked to the hall followed by the Nashua Four. He took his seat at the podium, and the excluded candidates stood behind him at the back of the stage. Bush, stiff and unbending, stared straight ahead, looking, as William Loeb wrote afterward, "like a small boy who has been dropped off at the wrong birthday party." The gym was a tumult, and it was clear that even many of the Bush partisans favored a free-for-all debate. "Get them chairs," several people shouted. "Baker can stand on the table," cried a raucous voice, in reference to the senator's diminutive stature. When *Nashua Telegraph* publisher J. Herman Pouliot tried to quiet the crowd, he was booed. Reagan, his face flushed, waited his turn and tried to explain why he wanted the other candidates to participate.

"Turn Mr. Reagan's microphone off," said Breen, not knowing that the Reagan camp had seen to it that the sound technician was a Reagan loyalist. Reagan didn't know it, either, and he didn't need technical help.

"I paid for this microphone, Mr. Green," Reagan said with controlled fury, mangling the name of the editor but getting everything else right.*

Next to me, in a fourth-row seat in the gymnasium, David Broder said quietly, "Reagan is winning this primary right now." And much later, in a retrospective of the tumultuous event, *The Boston Globe* would sum up the moment in a resonant subhead: "At a high school in Nashua, the Gipper grabbed the brass ring."

Once, in a memo to my editors at *The Washington Post*, I compared Ronald Reagan to a big, lackadaisical tackle on my football team in high school. The "book" on this player, although it was not a word we used then, was to leave him alone, treat him politely, and pick him up if you happened to block him. He was a competent player, but of limited range, and no particular menace when left alone. But if he was blocked from behind or someone made him angry, he became aroused and dominated the field of play. Reagan was like that. He was no menace to his opponents sitting in a plane and working on his five-by-seven cards and taking his naps. But he was a terrific candidate when aroused, and he wiped out Bush in the debate that night. Bush's managers knew it, even if Bush didn't. Two days later, Bush's press secretary, Peter Teeley, gave his candidate an irreverent and accurate update: "The bad news is that

---

*To some, the line recalled the 1948 film *State of the Union*, when Spencer Tracy said, "Don't you shut me off! I'm paying for this broadcast."

the media is playing up the confrontation. The good news is that they're ignoring the debate, and you lost that, too."[12]

This time Reagan did not sit on his lead. He did not fly off to Peoria to campaign in another primary. He did not take Sunday off. He did not go home to Los Angeles to watch a movie. This time Reagan remembered his narrow loss in New Hampshire four years earlier and his defeat in Iowa the previous month. This time he stayed in New Hampshire and campaigned as the story of his big night in Nashua dominated network coverage and the local news. This time it was Bush who abandoned the field, acting on the same wrong advice that Reagan had been given in 1976—and from the same adviser. The price Bush paid for obtaining Hugh Gregg to run his campaign in New Hampshire had been turning over total control of his operation in that state to the former governor. Gregg, who had been governor in a day when organizational politics instead of television called the tune, had not learned the lessons of 1976. He sent Bush back to Houston for the same reasons he had rid himself of Reagan four years earlier: To give the campaign workers a chance to mobilize for election day. Tired and distraught, Bush went along with Gregg even though Teeley argued that he should stay in New Hampshire until the primary was over. Instead, Bush appeared on Sunday on television in the warm, pleasant surroundings of his Houston home while Reagan, also seen on television, met voters in subfreezing New Hampshire.

On Tuesday, February 26, Reagan won the New Hampshire primary. He received 54,897 votes (51 percent) to 23,777 (22 percent) for Bush. Baker was a badly beaten third, getting 13 percent. After his month of hard campaigning and his two debate victories, Reagan was back in the saddle again.

But Sears was not riding with him. On the afternoon of his big New Hampshire victory, Reagan summoned Sears, Black, and Lake to his hotel room and fired them with Nancy Reagan and William J. Casey, the new campaign manager, looking on. It was quickly done, on a single sheet of paper, which said that Sears was resigning to return to his law practice and that Black and Lake were quitting with him. The only reference in the statement to the differences that had prompted the action was a declaration that "the campaign requires a sharp reduction in expenses and restructuring of our organization to intensify the people-to-people campaigning I have been doing in New Hampshire." Sears took the news soberly, Black with a quip that he was resigning before he could be fired, and Lake with a blunt denunciation of Meese. "Governor, Ed Meese manipulates you, he manipulates you," Lake said. However, the decision, reached the Sunday before and presented as a fait accompli to Sears and his aides, was more complicated than that. And it was Nancy Reagan, not Meese, who had taken the lead role in making it.

After Iowa, Reagan's California cadre and movement conservatives had stepped up their campaign to oust Sears. Reagan had been unhappy with the campaign manager ever since the Deaver walkout, but he did not like to be pressured, even by his wife, to make personnel changes.

The shaky fiscal condition of the campaign, more than anything else, forced Reagan's hand. As early as January 5, campaign treasurer Bay Buchanan warned that the campaign would bump up against the federal spending limit of $17.6 million by the end of April. Publicly, Reagan said the limit was unrealistic because so many states had added primaries. Privately, he unsuccessfully prodded Sears to explain what was happening. Sears was unconcerned because he was convinced that Reagan would clinch the nomination early and go to ground. But even some Sears loyalists realized that he did not appreciate the campaign's fiscal plight. Probably, this was because Sears' frame of reference was the sky's-the-limit campaigns of Richard Nixon, who had spent $10 million to be nominated in nine primaries in 1968 and $20 million in the renomination effort of 1972. Under the new campaign financing law, Reagan was limited to $17.6 million in thirty-three primaries, and two-thirds of this money was used up by the end of the New Hampshire race. This made Reagan nervous. He was not a candidate who always read his briefing papers, but he was used to keeping an eye on the ledger books.

Early in February, Sears created the context for his inevitable fall. He complained to Nancy Reagan that, while in a washroom in an East Orange, New Jersey, motel, he had overheard Meese in an adjoining staff room saying over the telephone that Sears, Lake, and Black would be fired after the New Hampshire primary. Meese denied ever having such a conversation, but Nancy Reagan expressed sympathy to the indignant Sears. She saw his complaint as an opening for resolving the persistent problems of her husband's turmoil-ridden staff, and she discussed with Sears the possibility of bringing in an administrator to share the duties of the campaign. Nancy Reagan was not out to get Sears. Alone among the participants in the staff struggle, she acted always with her husband's interests in mind. Nancy Reagan knew how difficult it was to get him to make a painful decision but also realized that he could not operate indefinitely in an atmosphere of worry and tension. "I go out and have these good days and then I get these knots in my stomach when I come back here," Reagan confided to her one day when he had returned to his hotel in Andover, Massachusetts, where his campaign was headquartered to avoid having lodging costs charged to his New Hampshire spending limit. Nancy Reagan realized that something had to be done, and she was not hesitant in doing it.

She began by trying to get a handle on the fiscal situation. At Nancy Reagan's suggestion, Justin Dart of the Kitchen Cabinet was put in charge of a committee to examine the campaign's spending patterns. Then came the question of Sears, who was not easily replaceable. One possibility was to bring in an entire new team, but Reagan, after losing Deaver, was not about to give up Meese, the other California aide he trusted for information and advice. His preferred solution was to keep Sears as a strategist and Meese as chief of staff, an idea that Nancy Reagan broached with Sears. He didn't go for it, and Nancy Reagan decided that he had to be replaced.

It is doubtful, even if Sears had been willing to share his authority, that he and Meese could have run a campaign together for very long. Both were idea men, of vastly different sorts, and neither had displayed a flair for administration. Meese had a gift for defining issues for Reagan and for explaining to others what Reagan's positions were, or were likely to be, without adding the coloration of his own opinion. He was lawyer-like, affable, and thoughtful but had organizational problems and was often overcautious. His greatest value to Reagan, in government and politics, was that he made sure that his client heard a variety of viewpoints before he acted. Usually, these viewpoints were "round-tabled" in the cabinet style preferred by Reagan when he was governor. This approach was anathema to Sears, who played politics close to the vest and reserved tactical decisions to himself. Sears suffered, more than he realized, from contempt for his candidate's capacity. He also held a low opinion of Meese, whom he thought prepared Reagan poorly on issues and poached on political territory reserved for the campaign manager. Meese believed that Sears had become irrational in his drive for power and that he regarded anyone who had the ear of Reagan as a personal threat. These were strong perceptions by influential men, and they were not easily reconcilable within the framework of a presidential campaign. Someone else was needed.

The first "someone" was suggested by Sears and pursued by Nancy Reagan. He was William P. Clark, Reagan's onetime executive secretary and later his appointee to the California Supreme Court. Clark had good judgment and was trusted by Reagan. Sears said he wanted a buffer whom Reagan could rely upon, but the Reagans and most others in the campaign interpreted this as an ill-disguised roundabout strategy for getting rid of Meese. Still, Clark had the needed requirements of management skill and collegiality. Nancy Reagan telephoned him and asked if he would be interested in serving as Reagan's chief of staff.

"Doesn't the governor already have a chief of staff?" Clark asked.

"That's our problem," she replied. "We've got two of them."

On the second weekend of February, the Reagans' only California interlude of that tumultuous month, Clark made the two-and-a-half-hour drive from his ranch near Paso Robles to Rancho del Cielo to discuss the problem. Clark was loyal to Reagan and told him he would leave the court if Reagan needed him in another capacity. But the court was closely divided, and Reagan could see that Clark wanted to remain a justice.* Nor, as Clark told him, could he take a leave for political purposes. So the talk soon turned to other possibilities, and Nancy Reagan brought up the name of Casey, whom the Reagans had met during a New York fund-raising dinner. Surely someone who had been chairman of the Securities and Exchange Commission could straighten out the finances of a political campaign.

The idea appealed to Reagan and even more to Clark, who neither wanted to disappoint the Reagans nor leave the court. Nancy Reagan said she had Casey's phone number. Clark helped the Reagans outline some talking points on a yellow legal pad, and they called Casey at his Long Island home. It was now late in the evening New York time, and Casey was in bed. Still drowsy, he listened to the outline of a proposal by Reagan and Clark that called for him to join the campaign as its chief administrator. Before Casey could respond, Reagan said he didn't need an answer that night but wanted Casey, literally in this case, to sleep on his decision. A few days later, Casey met with Meese in New York and agreed to join the campaign, ostensibly to help with the upcoming debates. But the wheels were now in motion for the removal of Sears, who had made it clear to the Reagans that he would not accept a subordinate role.[13]

The Reagans announced their decision to the inner circle the Sunday after the candidate's stunning debate triumph at Nashua. Attending the meeting in their third-floor hotel room at Andover were the Reagans, Meese, Casey, and Peter Hannaford. Foreign policy adviser Richard V. Allen, a foe of Sears' and a friend of Casey's, arrived during the meeting. Reagan also consulted by phone with Deaver, telling him he wanted him back aboard. Midway through the discussion, Wirthlin called. "Are you sitting down, governor?" he asked. Wirthlin then told him the good news: The latest survey results showed Reagan leading Bush by 17 points and climbing. A cheer went up, but Wirthlin's report made the

---

*The California Supreme Court was then balanced between liberals and conservatives, and Clark didn't want to upset the balance by leaving. By 1981, when Clark accepted a post in the Reagan administration, the death of one justice and the resignation of another had changed the court's leanings in a liberal direction, and Clark's vote was no longer decisive.

timing of the Sears firing even more critical. Everyone agreed that it had to be done on primary day before the returns came in. "There was no other choice, really," Hannaford said. "If you won and fired him, you looked like an ingrate. If you lost and did it, you looked like a sore loser."[14]

As it turned out, the timing was perfect for the Reagans. The campaign shakeup, which seemed momentous to political reporters, was overshadowed by Reagan's landslide victory. The big win, the return of Deaver, and the newfound staff harmony relaxed Reagan, who had made his decision to fire Sears with a report before him from Justin Dart telling him that the financial situation was even worse than he had thought. Straightening out the finances was Casey's responsibility. Though Casey knew next to nothing about presidential politics and had been a loser in his one congressional race, he knew how to squeeze the value from a dollar. Aides were fired by the dozen, sometimes without a thank you. The cutbacks accomplished the dual purpose of trimming the payroll and purging anyone suspected of loyalty to Sears. Casey also discontinued, in mid-charter, the expensive campaign plane Reagan had used, leaving some reporters stranded in South Carolina. He pared office expenditures to the bone. Aided by Verne Orr, the former state finance director whom Meese had installed in the Los Angeles office, Casey restored the campaign to fiscal solvency. The Reagan campaign wound up with $500,000 reserved for contingencies at the national convention.

As it turned out, this money wasn't needed. Baker dropped out of the race after the March 4 round of primaries, which Bush won in Massachusetts and Reagan won in Vermont, with Anderson second in both races. Dole, never a factor, was soon gone. Connally, the boardroom barrister with the most experience and the highest negative ratings of any of the candidates, was swamped by Reagan in South Carolina and quit the following day. For all practical purposes, Reagan sewed up the nomination in the March 18 Illinois primary after a debate where his practiced one-liners were as effective as his spontaneous anger had been at Nashua. Only four contestants remained in the race, and one of them, Phil Crane, had never been more than a contingency candidate on the Right whose hopes were invested in the collapse of the Reagan campaign. In the Chicago debate on March 13, Reagan tried out the role of statesman while Bush and Crane verbally beat up Anderson, who had made the mistake of saying he would prefer Senator Kennedy as president to Reagan. That remark completed Anderson's uncontested cornering of the limited market of GOP liberalism as he moved toward becoming an independent candidate instead of a Republican one. No one who saw the Chicago debate is likely to forget Reagan turning to Anderson and saying, lightly and in mock astonishment, "John, would you *really* find Teddy Kennedy preferable to me?"

Wirthlin's polls showed Reagan winning the debate in a runaway. In the primary, Reagan won 48 percent of the vote, beating home state Congressman Anderson by more than 11 points with Crane far back. It was the first impressive demonstration of Reagan's drawing power among crossover Democratic voters in a major industrial state.

Now, Reagan's opposition was down to Bush. Nashua had reduced him to the perfect foil for Reagan, casting Bush as the uptight eastern elitist facing the down-to-earth conservative cowboy from the West, the traditional Republican of wealth and privilege matched against the self-made man. On the campaign stump, and especially on television, Bush came across as an out-of-focus picture in a vertical frame. His prep school and Ivy League background and senatorial good looks were undermined by a strange, almost boyish exuberance that made him seem, at fifty-five, not quite mature. And Bush compounded this impression with his campaign strategy. His comments, and his campaign advertising, stressed his wartime bravery and his athletic interests, especially a daily addiction to jogging. This self-portrait promoted Bush more as a candidate for the Olympics than the presidency and, if anything, distracted voters from the central question about Reagan, which concerned his intellectual qualifications, not his physical ones.

Certainly, on paper Bush was better prepared than Reagan to be president. He had been an overachiever at Andover and Yale, a star athlete and certified war hero, a congressman from Texas, ambassador to the United Nations, national Republican chairman, liaison to the People's Republic of China, and director of the Central Intelligence Agency. But in some ways, the very breadth of this career counted against Bush, for his resume was seen in party circles as reflecting not only a devotion to duty but an inability to say no. To many Republicans, the whole of Bush was less than the sum of the parts. He was not a focused candidate against Reagan after the New Hampshire debates, and he was never truly competitive for the nomination. In fact, he won only four of the thirty-three primaries in which he participated with Reagan, who finished first in the other twenty-nine.*

As the primaries wore on, however, Bush exhibited an unadvertised doggedness that gradually overcame the negative aftertaste of Nashua. As a winner, Bush had been enthused, excitable, and unimpressive. As a loser, he displayed true grit. "The amazing thing about Bush's candi-

---

*Bush defeated Reagan in Massachusetts, Connecticut, Pennsylvania, and Michigan. He also won the Puerto Rico primary, in which Reagan did not compete.

dacy," observed *The Washington Post*'s Bill Peterson, "was not that it failed but that it kept going as long as it did."[15] Battling uphill, Bush improved as a campaigner and as a public speaker. Ultimately, his determination did for him what his heritage and glittering resume had been unable to accomplish, making him the widespread party choice, even in the Reagan camp, for the vice presidency.

During this post-Sears period, the Reagan campaign resumed its California look. Deaver was once more the indispensable adjutant, always on the plane and at Reagan's side. Wirthlin became the strategist, and Meese the actual as well as titled chief of staff. Martin Anderson, a traditional conservative economist who had been exiled to his base at Stanford while Sears pursued Kemp and his supply-siders, returned as Reagan's domestic adviser. Eventually, Nofziger returned for still another stint as press secretary. The Reagan team also brought in Joe Canzeri, a popular longtime travel secretary for Nelson Rockefeller, and James S. Brady, who had gained plaudits from reporters as Connally's press secretary. Brady's mission was to beef up an issues research system that had failed to bridge the candidate's increasingly visible knowledge gap.

Reagan was always a better candidate in adversity than when running loose in the lead. With no one pressing him after Illinois, he again became the *Reader's Digest* of politics, using old speeches and still older statistics as he coasted to the convention. He picked up horror stories about federal programs at random, sometimes tearing stray articles out of newspapers as he had done in his General Electric days. He believed what he read in *Human Events* or in Republican newsletters. Working this way, Reagan cited a General Accounting Office report on waste and fraud that never existed, claimed that it cost the Department of Health, Education and Welfare $3 to deliver $1 worth of services (the actual amount was not $3 but 12 cents), and said that the "finest oil geologists in the world" had told him that U.S. reserves of oil exceeded Saudi Arabia's. Columnist Mark Shields spoofed the latter claim, writing that Reagan thought there was "more oil under second base at Yankee Stadium" than in the Middle East.

One of the problems, Martin Anderson creatively told Douglas E. Kneeland of *The New York Times*, was that Reagan used "hundreds of stories for examples" in his campaign speeches. "Ninety-nine times out of a hundred, things checked out," Anderson added, "but sometimes the source is wrong. As we all know, sometimes the written word is wrong."[16] And sometimes the spoken one. Even when Reagan was well briefed, he was apt to get his facts mixed up. In Grand Island, Nebraska, on April 9, Reagan said that Vietnam veterans were "not eligible for GI

Bill of Rights benefits with regard to education or anything." Reagan's mind had wandered during a Washington briefing by two high-ranking military officers, who had discussed the problems facing Vietnam veterans. During the same briefing, the officers also told him that peacetime veterans of the new volunteer Army received no educational benefits, and Reagan had confused the two issues. This kind of wool-gathering was a prescription for disaster and an augury of the troubles that would beset Reagan in August.

The candidate blamed the press and not himself for his shortcomings. When a series of reports in *Time*, Knight-Ridder newspapers, *The Washington Post*, and CBS News made similar points during the same time frame, Reagan acted as if they were collaborating against him. "What I think we're seeing in what's going on is a little journalistic incest," Reagan said. He explained that he was referring to what happens when "one person reads another story and it is accepted as gospel." It is true that "pack journalism" had its place in the Reagan campaign, as in all others. But what Reagan was really experiencing was a magnified version of his experience during the 1976 New Hampshire primary, when reporters began to realize that he could become president. A case can be made that the added scrutiny was belated in 1980, perhaps because there were many in the media who found it hard to believe that Reagan would be nominated. However, when Reagan clinched the nomination early and it was apparent that his opponent would be an unpopular incumbent nominated by a divided party, the prospect of "President Reagan" no longer seemed remote. The scrutiny came all at once, in April, during an anticlimactic period of the primaries. Subsequent events would demonstrate that Reagan did not learn as much from this experience as he should have.

If Reagan was unsuccessful in keeping his statistics straight, he remained an effective, practicing politician who understood the need for party unity. In terms of bringing himself up to speed on issues, Reagan wasted much of the valuable interim between May 26, when Bush finally dropped out, and the Republican National Convention in Detroit on July 13. But he healed party wounds during this period, when President Carter was still preoccupied with the Kennedy challenge. Defeated Republican candidates would have supported Reagan in any case. However, they became real enthusiasts after Reagan agreed to help them pay off nearly $3 million in campaign debts at a series of Republican unity dinners.

Reagan's penchant for unity, at least when he was the nominee, also saved him from endorsing the potentially divisive efforts of Senator Laxalt and Jerry Carmen to replace Republican National Chairman

William Brock with a doctrinaire conservative. Instead, Reagan opted for a course favored by Meese, which was to keep Brock as chairman while installing his own man as chief operational officer at the Republican National Committee. Carmen, who had written a report critical of Brock's performance and loyalty, wanted the job, but even Laxalt realized this wouldn't work. So the Reagan man at the committee turned out to be Sears recruit Drew Lewis, who had been Ford's man in Pennsylvania during the 1976 campaign but was now considered a Reagan loyalist. The compromise gave Reagan the best of both worlds. It avoided a shakeup that would have been seen as a swing to the right, and it put one of the few seasoned politicians in the Reagan camp into the strategic political post at the National Committee.

Reagan's most important unity effort was directed at Gerald Ford. The former president had been a brief threatening cloud in March, when Ford had finally realized that no other Republican had a chance of stopping Reagan. Ford toyed with getting into the race, but a group of Ford's friends met with him in Washington on March 12, at a time when the deadline for entering sufficient primaries to win had passed, and convinced him that Reagan had a lock on the nomination.

Reagan, realizing that even an abortive campaign by the former president would have revived party divisions, appreciated Ford's decision not to run. He expressed his gratitude to Ford during a June 5 visit to his office adjacent to the Rancho Mirage golf course near Palm Springs. This visit was more than a courtesy call. Only a few days earlier, Ford had reconfirmed in a private conversation his belief that Reagan's reluctant campaigning had cost him the election in 1976. The substance of this conversation was relayed to Reagan, who came armed with information about the number of campaign speeches he had made for Ford and an appeal for his support against President Carter. Petty politicians would not have been impressed with the self-serving version of history that Reagan presented, but no one in politics forgave a grudge as easily as Ford. Reagan, no grudge-holder himself, was hard to dislike, and Ford found himself strangely drawn to this old foe who shared with him a midwestern upbringing and a natural friendliness. Ford also thought that Carter had been a terrible president and wanted to help defeat him. It was in this atmosphere that Reagan suggested a supposed "dream ticket" in which Ford would be his running mate. Ford's response was negative, but he appreciated the gesture. In ninety minutes of private conversation together at Rancho Mirage, Ford became a supporter of the Reagan candidacy. He also very nearly became vice president.

The Ford boomlet that crested and broke at the Republican National Convention was, more than anything, the product of Reagan's reservations about Bush. When the primaries were over, Bush had won respect in the Reagan camp. He had the quiet but significant backing of fellow Yale graduate Ed Meese. He also had support from Drew Lewis. Party unity dictated the selection of a prominent Republican from outside the Reagan ranks, and there was never any serious thought in the inner circle to choosing a regional and ideological Reagan soul mate such as Laxalt, except by Laxalt himself. Senator Howard Baker had no champion within the Reagan inner circle and also suffered from the accurate perception that he would be more valuable to a Reagan presidency as Senate leader than as vice president. The choice of the insiders, except for Laxalt, was Bush. He brought instant unification to the party, and he almost certainly would have been selected, though not announced, in June except for the reservations of the Reagans.

Reagan's disrespect for Bush had been born at Nashua. He could not understand why Bush had sat in his chair staring straight ahead without speaking to him or the other candidates who filed onto the stage for the debate. Reagan later told an aide that Bush lacked "spunk." After Nashua, Reagan's doubts about Bush were ratified by a curious incident in the Texas primary campaign that went almost unnoticed in the national press. The incident was the outgrowth of Bush's irritation with right-wing leaflets that attributed a demonic aspect to his former membership in the Trilateral Commission, a private body of distinguished citizens in North America, Europe, and Japan that seeks to foster international economic cooperation. But to a few fringe activists on the Right and Left, the Trilateralists were a sinister one-world conspiracy headed by David Rockefeller, the North American regional chairman.

Reagan knew better. His former state finance director, Caspar Weinberger, had been a member of the commission. But Reagan also knew that some of his more strident supporters held a conspiracy view of the Trilateralists, and he had done nothing to dissuade them from harassing Bush. In Bush's mind, this made Reagan responsible for the leaflets, and he called upon his opponent to denounce them. "I have never seen any of the literature he's talking about," Reagan replied blandly. "The only person I've seen raise the Trilateral issue is George Bush and maybe he should tell us why he resigned."

Bush continued to blame Reagan for the leaflets. On May 2, in Houston, Reagan, asked during a televised interview on KTRK about Bush's charges, accused him of a "desperation gambit." In a resourceful effort to stage its own debate on this issue, KTRK had lined up Bush for an interview at his Houston home immediately following Reagan. Bush was informed that Reagan was on camera at another location and was asked to respond to him. But to the surprise of the Reagans, Bush backed down, telling his interviewer, "It's not a big deal, frankly." Nancy Reagan, watching on television, hooted. "If it's no big deal, then why does he keep raising it?" she said. Reagan said later that the interview reminded him of Bush's performance at Nashua. "He just melts under pressure," Reagan said, a point he would raise again when his aides told him that Bush was the best choice to unify the party.

It was the Reagans' low opinion of Bush that kept the Ford option alive. Wirthlin, who took the lead in pushing Ford, had a positive view of Bush but realized that Reagan didn't. The pollster-strategist was convinced that Reagan needed a prominent moderate as his running mate, and a nationwide poll taken by his firm, Decision Making Information, gave him plenty of data to use in his arguments. Bush was the first choice in this poll by a wide margin as the person whom voters thought Reagan should put on the ticket. Wirthlin made this point to the candidate, knowing that it would have an impact no matter what Reagan thought personally about Bush. Ford was the clear second choice, with Baker reduced to an outside possibility. Reagan, like Meese, realized it would be a mistake to choose someone who would have to become nationally known during the crucible of campaigning. This eliminated Laxalt and Kemp.[17] The only other well-known person on Wirthlin's list of twenty-one potential choices was John Connally, and he had high negatives.

By the time the Republican convention opened Monday night, July 14, the consensus within the Reagan camp was that the nominee-to-be would reluctantly choose Bush. Ford pollster Teeter had told Reagan pollster Wirthlin that Ford was not interested. Stuart Spencer, then aboard tenuously as a consultant to the Reagan campaign, had sounded out Ford at Deaver's behest and also found no interest. But Ford, in a fiery speech on the opening night of the convention, denounced Carter and seemed to be sending a different message. "Elder statesmen are supposed to sit quietly and smile wisely from the sidelines," Ford said. "I've never been much for sitting. I've never spent much time on the sidelines. Betty'll tell you that. This country means too much to me to comfortably park on the bench. So, when this convention fields the team for Governor Reagan, count me in."

Reagan loved Ford's speech, remarking to an aide what a fine campaigner he would be. He also interpreted his remarks as a sign that Ford was becoming receptive to the second spot on the ticket. The two men met privately the next afternoon in Reagan's suite, and Reagan urged Ford to reconsider. Ford said he didn't think he could do it, but he didn't firmly shut the door, either. And that night, Ford's crowd from the White House—led by Henry Kissinger, Alan Greenspan, and Jack

Marsh—were at him again. Like Reagan, they noticed that Ford stopped just short of firmly saying no.

From beginning to end, the consummation of this improbable political romance seemed unlikely to political veterans Teeter and Spencer and remote even to Wirthlin, who had pushed it more than anyone in the Reagan camp. Spencer and Teeter (and Meese, as well) realized that the "dream ticket" had the potential of turning into a nightmare in which Ford upstaged the presidential nominee and drew unwanted attention to Reagan's lack of experience in foreign policy. "The day after the convention Ford would have been 'Mr. President' and Reagan would have been 'Mr. Reagan,'" said Spencer. "How would that play? A vice president is supposed to be No. 2."[18] The prospective Ford entourage caused even more obstacles. Conservatives were appalled by the thought that Kissinger would again have a say in foreign policy. Some of the supply-siders were equally appalled by Greenspan, whose presence, to them, represented an "old economics" that was not receptive to massive tax cuts. Bush, with his description of supply-side ideas as "voodoo economics," was no favorite, but there was no question that he would be a discreet No. 2 man to Reagan. Of Ford and his team, there was no end of questions.

Ultimately, these questions sent the "dream ticket" back to the realm of fantasy from which it had come. Reagan allowed Meese, Casey, and Wirthlin to draw up ten talking points and discuss them with Kissinger, Greenspan, Marsh, and Ford's personal aide, Bob Barrett. But Reagan was by then having second thoughts that he might be dealing away constitutional powers of the presidency. Deaver, in the strongest terms, spoke for Reagan in telling Wirthlin, "Reagan is going to be the president and we do not want to create any constraining conditions on him." Wirthlin agreed, but the talking points included proposals for giving Ford an enhanced role in national security affairs and the federal budget. One negotiator said Ford would become "super director of the executive office of the president," a role never envisioned for the vice president by the founders. Nor was such a role envisioned by Reagan, who had worked hard for the nomination and did not want to share the prize he had won. Reagan flirted with the idea only because he realized that political logic dictated either Ford or Bush as his running mate, and he didn't want Bush.

In the end, Ford made the decision easy. By Wednesday, July 16, jokes were circulating in both camps about how Ford would be president before nine, after five, and on weekends. That night Ford was interviewed on CBS News. When Walter Cronkite asked him how he would respond to a draft from the convention floor, the former president used the question to give his view of the role he wanted to play. Ford said he would not go to Washington as "a figurehead vice president." If he accepted, Ford said, "I have to go there with the belief that I will play a meaningful role across the board in the basic and the crucial and the important decisions that have to be made in a four-year period." Reagan, watching this performance on television in his suite at the Detroit Plaza, could not believe what he was seeing. It had not occurred to him that Ford would publicly discuss what Reagan considered to be a private offer. "Is that Ford?" he asked incredulously when the unmistakable figure of the former president appeared on the screen. Reagan realized immediately that Ford's remarks would be interpreted as a sign that he had been offered the vice-presidential nomination and accepted it. He was right. Within moments, the dream ticket was being promulgated as a done deal by television commentators who filled in the gaps with their opinions.

The truth was that the negotiators had bogged down on the talking points, aware they were skating on thin constitutional ice in trying to define a role for Ford that did not infringe upon the duties and prerogatives of the president. Kissinger asked Meese to extend the informal Wednesday night deadline that the negotiators had agreed upon to Thursday morning. Meese opposed the extension and consulted with Reagan, who was even more strongly opposed. The networks had just nominated Ford, an aide remembered Reagan saying, and there would be "a terrible letdown" if he waited a day and then picked someone else. By now Reagan realized that too much would have to be given up to get Ford on the ticket. He called Ford shortly after 9:00 P.M. and said that he needed a decision that night. An hour and a half later, Ford called on Reagan in his suite and, in an emotional moment, turned down the offer. Then he expressed his affection for Reagan, gave him a hug, and promised he would do whatever he could to help him win the fall campaign. Reagan was moved. He had grown to like Ford, and he appreciated that the former president had taken him off the hook. "He was a gentleman," Reagan said afterward. "I feel we're friends now."

Within five minutes of Ford's departure from the suite, Reagan was on the telephone to George Bush. An hour and a half after that, Reagan was back at Joe Louis Arena, smoothly presenting the convention with the ticket that necessity had demanded. Reagan knew what he had to do to cut his losses, and he wanted no stories reflecting on his ability to act decisively. There were a few such stories anyway, but they were overshadowed by the news of Reagan's decision. At the last moment, the hero had ridden to the rescue of the girl he had tied to the tracks.

Reagan further dispelled the doubts he had created about his leadership on Thursday, the final night of the convention. His grace note was an acceptance speech that matched old themes of economy in government with old values of "family, work, neighborhood, peace and freedom." These values were intended to be the basis of a "new consensus" in which traditional Democrats would join with independents and Republicans to replace "the mediocre leadership" of Jimmy Carter with a president who would simultaneously balance the budget and reduce taxes and who would build up U.S. military capability while pursuing an objective of "lasting world peace." All this was roundly cheered by the convention. But the arena crowd fell quiet when Reagan started quoting from a past president about the need for governmental economy and reform. The words were those of Reagan's first political hero, Franklin Roosevelt, at his 1933 inaugural, and they seemed oddly out of place in the acceptance speech of a Republican nominee who was proposing to undo much of what FDR and his successors had done. Looking down at the silent crowd, David Broder observed, "They're saying, come on, Ronnie, don't give us any of that New Deal guff."

Reagan, however, was speaking to the country, not just the Republicans assembled in Joe Louis Arena. His audience was an electorate in which Democrats had been a majority for two generations because of what FDR had done. Reagan knew that this electorate had lost confidence in President Carter. To Americans in their living rooms, Reagan held up a mirror of the past that reflected the days when the White House was the source of effective national leadership. Reagan believed that most Americans yearned for such leadership again. Looking straight into the television cameras, that is what he promised to provide.

30

PRESIDENT

R EAGAN LEFT Detroit with a running mate, a unified party, a commanding lead in the polls, and a campaign plan that accurately anticipated the strategy of President Carter. He faced an opponent who was dogged by the captivity of hostages he could not free, an economy he could not improve, a brother he could not disown, and an opponent he could not shake. Reagan had the luxury of a month in which the last gasp of the Kennedy challenge prevented Carter from focusing on the fall campaign. For two weeks of that month, the media had focused on the revelation that Carter's brother, Billy, had accepted $220,000 from the Libyan government for lobbying efforts in the United States. The president was depicted as a man who could not control his brother, much less the country. Reagan had every imaginable advantage. And following a pattern that he and his team had established for doing worst when things were going best, Reagan then went out and almost blew the election before the campaign formally began.

The first sign of trouble came when Reagan insisted on stopping off in Mississippi en route to New York to make a speech to the convention of the National Urban League. It was Reagan's only speech to a predominantly black organization after his nomination, but his message was directed to a larger audience. Richard Wirthlin's polls showed that moderate Republicans and independents were skeptical that Reagan was sensitive to problems of minorities and the poor. Reagan was supposed to correct this impression as much as he could in his speech to the Urban League, but he sent a different message by stopping first at the Neshoba County Fair, in Philadelphia, Mississippi, where three civil rights workers had been murdered with the complicity of local police officials in 1964.

Wirthlin thought the symbolism of this stopover was appalling and tried to persuade Reagan to fly directly to New York. But Trent Lott had told Reagan that a visit to Mississippi, which Carter had carried in 1976, could make the difference between victory and defeat. (Lott was then a member of the House of Representatives and held a parochial view that more than two decades later would lead to his demise as Senate majority leader.) When Wirthlin suggested to Reagan that he ignore Lott and cancel the Mississippi appearance, Reagan replied that he had learned in show business that an actor should always appear once his billing has been announced. Wirthlin, normally deferential, persisted and said the Neshoba appearance would undermine the purpose of the Urban League speech. Reagan reddened and hurled his briefing papers at Wirthlin. "Well, I guess, governor, you're pretty well set on going," Wirthlin said.[1]

Go Reagan did. On August 3, he told a shirt-sleeved crowd in Neshoba that he "believed in state's rights" and as president would do everything he could to "restore to states and local governments the powers that properly belonged to them." When Reagan addressed the Urban League the next day, television reports included clips of this speech and showed a sea of white faces cheering him. As Wirthlin had predicted, these images overshadowed the address to the Urban League, in which Reagan compared himself to President Kennedy attempting to win Protestant votes in 1960 and urged his audience not to consider him "a caricature conservative" who was "anti-poor, anti-black and anti-disadvantaged."

After this speech, Reagan was whisked off to the South Bronx for a press conference on a rubble-strewn lot where candidate Carter, on October 5, 1977, had promised a new federally sponsored housing and job training center. His theme was that Carter had made promises he hadn't kept. In case anyone missed the point, the word "Decay" had been freshly painted in huge letters on a gutted building nearby. But Reagan's advance men had earned an "A" in art while flunking their major. For some reason, it never occurred to them that local residents might turn up in an area where so many people were unemployed. Soon the locals formed a shouting crowd that jeered at Reagan and alarmed the Secret Service. When he tried to hold the press conference, the crowd shouted, "Talk to the people, not to the press." When he tried to talk to the people, he was heckled unmercifully. Finally, in his most effective burst of emotion since Nashua, Reagan shouted back at a heckler, "I can't do a damn thing for you if I don't get elected."

The crowd then quieted down enough for Reagan to finish his presentation, although a few people still jeered when he left. Reagan's command presence had once more saved the day. The evening television news showed an angry but controlled candidate forcefully putting down a hostile black crowd in a manner that won the respect even of those who had been shouting at him. It was the perfect image for a candidate campaigning on the theme that his opponent was a failed leader. But the haphazard nature of Reagan's campaign was courting disaster, and disasters were not long in coming.

What Reagan really was doing, although he didn't realize it, was wasting the month of August. On paper he had a plan, drafted by Wirthlin, calling for him to speak to constituencies that were already solidly for or against him. The theory was that Reagan, after Labor Day, could then concentrate on key blocs of undecided voters. But Reagan's campaign lacked cohesion and leadership. Wirthlin's poll data were valuable and he was a strategic thinker, but he had neither the authority nor the standing with Reagan to run the campaign. Nor, for all his skills, was he an instinctive politician. The only person in the campaign who met this description was Reagan, and he was tugged this way and that, making too many speeches when he should have been boning up on issues, and being placed in too many situations where something could go wrong.

Many things did. Reagan in mid-August launched a "defense week" anchored by speeches to the Veterans of Foreign Wars and the American Legion. The idea, again, was to illustrate Carter's supposed broken promises, in this case to maintain a strong military and take good care of veterans. Before the VFW in Chicago on August 18, Reagan asserted that Carter had made a "shambles" of national defense while remaining "totally oblivious" to the Soviet Union's drive toward world domination. This prepared message was overshadowed by Reagan's ad hoc comments on the Vietnam War. First, Reagan repeated a line with which he had often roused audiences during his 1976 campaign: "Let us tell those who fought in that war that we will never again ask young men to fight and possibly die in a war our government is afraid to win." The VFW members rose to their feet in applause. Then, at a convention where neglect of Vietnam veterans was a central issue, Reagan said, "We dishonor the memory of 50,000 young Americans who died in that cause when we give way to feelings of guilt as if we were doing something shameful, and we have been shabby in our treatment of those who returned. It is time we recognized that ours, in truth, was a noble cause."

Reagan had written the last sentence into his copy of the speech text. It gave reporters an unexpected lead and provoked angry calls to talk shows and letters to the editors from opponents of the war, who accused Reagan of opening wounds that were just beginning to heal. Vietnam veterans wrote in, too. Some supported Reagan. Others pointed out that he had never seen combat. Writing for the op-ed page of the *Los Angeles Times*, former Marine Captain Frank McAdams recounted the bloody details of a battle on an August day at Cam Le a dozen years before. "A noble cause, Mr. Reagan?" wrote McAdams. "I would call it a horrible experience."[2] Wirthlin's polls, as busily recording Reagan's glitches as a seismograph charting a series of small earthquakes, found that "noble cause" hurt Reagan more with voters than anything else he said in August.

The voters, if they were paying attention, had plenty of glitches from which to choose. One was a decision, which no one in the campaign was willing to claim, to send George Bush on a fence-building mission to the People's Republic of China, where he had served as U.S. liaison after President Nixon's resumption of relations with the mainland government. The trip was supposed to advertise the competence of the Reagan-Bush ticket in dealing with world issues. Instead, it revealed Reagan's devotion to his old friends in Taiwan. Reagan had twice visited Taipeh, and the Deaver-Hannaford firm in Los Angeles, which represented Reagan before he became a candidate, counted the Taiwanese government as a client at the same time.* In a column drafted for him by Hannaford on May 5, 1978, Reagan had warned that establishing full relations with the mainland government at the expense of Taiwan could "start a chain of events that could prove disastrous, not only for Taiwan, but for the United States itself." When the Carter administration took this action late in 1978, Reagan was one of the loudest critics. And in the early months of 1979, Reagan used the phrase "no more Taiwans, no more Vietnams" as part of his campaign litany in calling for a U.S. government that kept its word to its traditional allies.

Reagan foreign policy adviser Richard V. Allen agreed with Reagan that Carter had received nothing in return for the de-recognition of Taiwan, but he was politically realistic. Allen assured reporters at the Republican National Convention that Reagan did not intend to "turn the clock back,"[3] and the Bush mission was interpreted as a sign that Reagan did, in fact, recognize that times had changed. But Reagan's personal reluctance to abandon Taiwan made it difficult for him to embrace the official policy of his campaign. At a joint press conference with Bush as he departed for China, Reagan startled both his running

---

*Hannaford landed the contract with Taiwan, which the firm began representing on November 19, 1977. After Don Oberdorfer wrote about it on June 6, 1980, in a page-1 story in *The Washington Post*, campaign aides recognized that Reagan was vulnerable to the charge of a conflict of interest. Meese discussed this with Deaver, who took a leave of absence from his firm for the duration of the campaign.

mate and Allen by saying that he intended to establish an official liaison office in Taipeh, an act prohibited by the Taiwan Relations Act of 1979. The Chinese government's official newspaper denounced this statement as a resurrection of the abandoned U.S. "two-China policy." Leonard Woodcock, the U.S. ambassador in Beijing, chimed in, calling Reagan's statement a menace to the "carefully crafted relationship" existing between China and the United States.[4]

Bush was in a tough spot. A few words from Reagan had turned a promising trip into a hand-holding mission in which Bush tried to reassure the Chinese government and overseas reporters that Reagan meant no change in the Sino-American relationship. But Reagan would not be quieted. After Bush returned, Reagan did it again, saying that he regarded the U.S.-funded American Institute on Taiwan as an act of Carter "hypocrisy" because it was really an embassy by another name. By now, however, Allen and negative press reaction had convinced Reagan that he needed to back off. Reluctantly, and in a manner that left little doubt about his true feelings, Reagan said he no longer favored the establishment of an official liaison office with Taiwan.

On the heels of the Taiwan muddle, Reagan traveled to Dallas on August 22 to address a national rally of evangelical Christians. He held a press conference at which a reporter for a religious publication asked Reagan his views about creationism. While his aides shifted uneasily, Reagan gave a longwinded answer in which he tried to please his questioner by suggesting that creationism be taught in schools as an alternative theory to Charles Darwin's theory of evolution. The answer, fortunately for Reagan, was a relatively minor story because the media was still preoccupied by Reagan's shifting statements on Taiwan. "The only good news for us at this time," an aide remarked afterward, "is that we were making so many blunders that reporters had to pick and choose which ones they would write about. 'Creationism' made Reagan look like an idiot, but he got away with it." Even so, he had blown most of a double-digit lead in the polls by Labor Day, when the campaign formally began.

Labor Day started well enough. Reagan gave an effective speech to an "ethnic picnic" in Liberty Park, New Jersey, where the Statue of Liberty provided a television backdrop and one of the featured participants was Stanislaw Walesa, the father of Lech Walesa, who was then leading a strike of Polish workers. Reagan praised the strikers. On the plane from Newark to Detroit, he observed that he was opening his campaign in the working-class "Democratic country" of New Jersey and Michigan, while Carter was protecting his base in the South. Then Lyn Nofziger chimed in, saying that Tuscumbia, Alabama, where Carter opened his campaign (and also praised the Polish workers), was a center of activity for the Ku Klux Klan. He didn't mention that the score or so robed KKK members who showed up at the Carter rally had been rebuked by the president as people who "do not understand that the South and all America must move forward."

As Reagan spoke that afternoon to a friendly crowd from a gazebo at the Michigan State Fair, he recalled fragments of Nofziger's comments. The day was hot and humid, and Reagan was tired after a long walk through the fairgrounds. It had begun to rain. In the front row Reagan noticed a woman heckler with a Carter mask. It reminded him of the president at Tuscumbia. "Now I'm happy to be here while he is opening his campaign down there in the city that gave birth to and is the parent body of the Ku Klux Klan," Reagan said. There was a gasp from the crowd. It sounded as if Reagan, who rarely attacked an opponent, was linking Carter to the Klan. Reagan knew immediately that he had misspoken. "I blew it," Reagan told his aides afterward. "I should never have said what I said."

Before the night was out, concerned southern Republican leaders were calling Reagan headquarters and the candidate found it necessary to apologize to the state of Alabama and the community of Tuscumbia, which was not in fact the birthplace of the Klan. By now, Reagan's confidence was shaken. The usually sure-handed Nofziger made matters worse, blaming the press for overplaying the story and declining to mention his own contribution to Reagan's blunder. On the campaign plane returning to Washington the next evening, Nofziger had an acrimonious exchange with reporters that ratified their growing view that Reagan was a shaky candidate with an even shakier campaign. Wirthlin's polls confirmed that Reagan, who was supposed to be making Carter's leadership the issue, was instead raising questions about his own competence. In a gaffe-filled run of seventeen days, he had forfeited much of his presumed advantage on the leadership issue.

Fortunately for Reagan, however, all of his mistakes, except the Labor Day mishap, had occurred in August, when the public was barely focused on the presidential campaign. The "creationism" statement had gone relatively unnoticed, and "Taiwan" was a bigger issue with the press than with the public. But "noble cause" and "Ku Klux Klan" had been big losers, and the accumulation of stumbles was creating an impression that Reagan was in over his head. "We were close, *that* close, to making Reagan rather than Carter the chief issue of the campaign," a Reagan aide later said, holding up a thumb and forefinger less than an inch apart. By the end of Reagan's first week on the general election campaign trail, the press was circling the candidate like hunters whose wounded prey was about to drop. When Stuart Spencer arrived in Washington soon afterward, a reporter asked him what he was doing in town. "I'm here to see old foot-in-the-mouth," Spencer grinned.[5] He didn't have to add that he was talking about Ronald Reagan.

Spencer was not in town by accident. He had been getting distress calls from Wexford, the Virginia hunt country estate near Middleburg that the Reagans had rented for the fall. Many of the Reagan senior staff members disliked Wexford, an inconvenient hour's drive from campaign headquarters in Arlington. But the aides were out in force at Wexford on September 3, Reagan's first day back from Detroit, and again for a long, sequestered session the following weekend. The top staff included Casey, Meese, Wirthlin, Deaver, Nofziger, Bill Timmons, and, later, James Baker. As the campaign wore on, David Stockman became a participant. All these advisers had something to offer, but, as Nancy Reagan realized, none had the experience or know-how to run a high-powered political campaign, deal with the press, and make the myriad gut decisions that make the difference between victory and defeat.

Casey, the campaign manager, was a particular problem. At sixty-seven, he looked and acted older than Reagan. His political experience, all before the age of modern media campaigns, was in losing—with Wendell Willkie, with Thomas E. Dewey, with himself as a congressional candidate. At the national convention, he dozed off while he and Meese were briefing the press. (Meese either failed to notice or pretended that he did not and continued the briefing.) Casey was so forgetful that he once invited two important Republicans from the East Coast to Los Angeles and then left town before they arrived. Behind his back, other senior staffers called him "Spacey." Campaign reporters, preparing an irreverent list of book titles supposedly appropriate for the Reagan team, invented a biography of Casey called *The Man Who Never Was*.[6] This was an unflattering and unfair portrait of a man who had done important work for his country in World War II intelligence and won respect for his performance as chairman of the Securities and Exchange Commission. But Casey was out of his league in national politics, and no one else in the Wexford cast was capable of taking over the campaign manager's role. Meese was preoccupied with the headquarters and Deaver with the campaign plane. Timmons, a capable and experienced Republican organizer, was not close to Reagan. Wirthlin, whose polls and campaign plan were the source of many useful themes and strategies, was not a tactician. "Where's Stu?" Nancy Reagan wanted to know. "Why isn't Stu here?"

Stuart Spencer was not the type of man whose presence was ordinarily sought by Nancy Reagan. He was combative, short, rumpled, profane, and blunt, almost a cartoonist's dream of a political operative. But he was a natural politician, with a feel for the strengths and weaknesses of others. To Spencer, every campaign was a psychological enterprise, a triumph of mind over matter. He understood that the key to Reagan's campaign in 1980 was restoring the candidate's self-confidence, and he had a knack for directing Reagan without pushing him. "Remember, Ron, don't talk about China," he would say, making his point in a light way but always making it. Unlike others in the entourage, Spencer had no ambition to serve in the White House or the cabinet and wanted nothing from the Reagans except an occasional favor for his clients. Nor was he stuck up; Spencer said his reputation was "based 50 percent on ability and 50 percent on bullshit."[7] But Spencer was intensely competitive, and he believed he could get Reagan elected president. On a staff that was short of politicians, he was just what the Reagans needed.

The question "Where's Stu?" that Nancy Reagan had asked at Wexford had been asked before by her husband and by Mike Deaver. During the period of Deaver's exile from the Sears-led campaign, Spencer and Deaver had buried the hatchet on old grudges extending from the first Reagan administration. Deaver wanted Spencer back. So did the candidate, but there were many in his entourage who blamed Spencer for preventing Reagan from securing the presidential nomination in 1976. Spencer agreed with this assessment and was rather proud of it. In the course of working for Ford, he had developed respect and affection for him and often said he would be remembered well in history. When Spencer was asked to serve as a consultant to the Reagan campaign at the Republican National Convention, he made a point of checking with Ford, knowing that Ford would approve but wanting to demonstrate his loyalty. Now that the Reagan campaign wanted him back on a full-time basis, Spencer insisted on knowing that Nancy Reagan did not bear any hard feelings from 1976. She didn't. Always practical, Nancy Reagan wanted whatever would help her husband get ahead. Deaver placed the call, and she told Spencer he was needed aboard the campaign plane. On September 4, when "LeaderShip '80" left Dulles International Airport bound for Jacksonville, Florida, Spencer was aboard. He stayed with the campaign for the duration.*

On that first Spencer trip, Reagan was noticeably more relaxed than at any time since the convention. "Ron needed to be shown, very sim-

---

*Casey originally suggested that Paul Laxalt be Reagan's "man on the plane," and Spencer had proposed this idea to Laxalt. The Nevada senator declined because he was up for reelection. Laxalt had lost a race by 84 votes in 1964 and won his Senate seat in 1974 by 624 votes. "Those are the kind of elections that make you not take anything for granted," he told me.

ply, that the level of campaigning he was now in was much greater, much different than anything he'd done in his life," Spencer said afterward. "He needed to know that he was talking to every audience at every stop, that he was talking to the whole nation every time he said something. Everything he said had to be viewed in that light. And everything he said had to be scrutinized ten times more than it ever was before. The rhetoric that brought everybody out of their seats in the primary wasn't going to do it in the general election. . . . Noble cause would have been a good issue in the primaries. . . . And he needed to know that if one of you [reporters] shouted a question at him, he didn't have an obligation to answer that question."[8] Reagan heeded all of Spencer's advice except the last. His natural inclination was to answer any question that was put to him, whether or not he knew the answer. In those rocky first days of September, Spencer and Deaver decided that they would have to keep their lip-shooting candidate away from the press.

While Spencer was settling down the candidate, Reagan's issues team at Arlington exploited a misstep by two Carter administration officials. On August 22, while Reagan was mired in "defense week," Defense Secretary Harold Brown and Pentagon research director William J. Perry had disclosed at a news conference the plans for the "Stealth" bomber, the administration's distant alternative to the B-1. It was a thinly disguised effort to take the edge off Reagan's charges that Carter had let the nation's defenses slide, but it alarmed General Richard B. Ellis, commander of the Strategic Air Command. Ellis believed that the administration had disclosed classified information for partisan political purposes and said so. The announcement, he said, gave the Soviets too much advance warning about an aircraft that should have been kept top secret. In Jacksonville, Reagan called the action "a cynical abuse of power and a clear abuse of the public trust," asserting that Brown and Perry had committed "a serious breach of national security secrets." Some Democrats agreed, notably Representative Samuel Stratton of New York. He wanted to know why the two high-ranking officials were "yielding up territory to the enemy" and headed up a subcommittee that investigated and criticized the disclosure. The issue temporarily put Carter on the defensive. Although Stealth did not persist as a major issue in the campaign, the incident took the spotlight off Reagan at a useful time for Spencer, who was focused on his No. 1 goal of restoring the candidate's confidence.

For the next ten days, Reagan became a more buttoned-up candidate than ever before. Reporters who had previously enjoyed access were kept at a distance, and Reagan was not allowed to stray close enough to any of them to indulge his habit of giving unrehearsed answers. The isolation of Reagan did not sit well with the campaign press corps, as Spencer had anticipated. Keeping Reagan away from the press was a tactic he used sparingly, realizing that to do so over a prolonged period would produce stories questioning the candidate's capability. In the long run, Spencer wanted a reasonably happy press corps; in the short run, he needed a confident candidate even more. When a reporter complained to him about Reagan's isolation, Spencer assured him it wouldn't continue and said he was just trying to get Reagan "over the bumps." And, in a few days, that is what he did.

By mid-September, Reagan's optimism had reasserted itself and he was free to move around naturally again. Spencer brought him back into contact with the press in stages, trying to avoid a bruising confrontation from which Reagan would emerge as a know-nothing. One afternoon, on LeaderShip '80, he had Nofziger announce a press conference a half hour before the airplane landed at Dulles. His intention was to limit the preparation of reporters and to prevent them, in those days before cellular telephones, from calling their desks ahead of time. The press conference produced little news, which is what Spencer wanted, but boosted the morale of Reagan, who believed that as governor he had turned most press encounters to his own advantage. Reagan was right about that, but there was an enormous gulf between the generally orderly news conferences in Sacramento and the hothouse exchanges of a presidential campaign, where Reagan's off-the-cuff style and tendency to say whatever came into his head was an invitation to trouble. Reagan's struggle was with himself more than the press. At nearly seventy years of age, he was forced to unlearn habits of a lifetime. This meant refraining from offering casual opinions on arms control or creationism or the myriad other subjects about which he had memorized dangerous scraps of information. It meant running the risk of displeasing his questioners, whether they were campaign supporters or reporters. In a sense far different from what Reagan had meant when he used the phrase in the primaries, it meant "no more Taiwans, no more Vietnams."

Reagan's reemergence as a confident candidate was accompanied by the stabilizing of his position in the polls. *The Washington Post* poll published on September 14, but taken when Reagan was recovering from his case of the staggers early in the month, showed him tied with Carter at 37 percent and independent candidate John Anderson far back at 13 percent. *The New York Times* poll a week later put Carter 3 points ahead, and a Gallup Poll taken September 12–14 gave Reagan a 2-point lead. The conventional wisdom was that it was a close race, with the Anderson vote possibly holding the key to the outcome. But Wirthlin's surveys in several key states suggested that the appearance of an even race was, in terms of electoral votes, an illusion. Behind the facade of a closely balanced contest, a Reagan electoral vote landslide was taking shape from the time the Reagan campaign stabilized in mid-September. This was because Reagan's base in the West was unassailable by Carter, while Carter's base in the South was threatened by Reagan. And among the "megastates"—the ten most populous and influential states in presidential elections—Reagan had secure leads in California, Texas, and Florida, while Carter could not take any state for granted. The knowledge that Reagan enjoyed this electoral vote cushion bolstered the mood of optimism in the Republican nominee's camp despite a public perception that President Carter had overcome Reagan's early lead and was still climbing. And at this pivotal moment in the campaign, Carter abruptly handed Reagan the initiative.

On September 16, a celebrated anniversary of Mexican independence, Reagan was campaigning in Texas on a "color day" designed for television. Reagan's short speeches, which featured words of praise for the "undocumented workers" so critical to Texas agriculture, were intentionally overshadowed by the visual images of the candidate wearing a sombrero, riding in a riverboat, or attending a mariachi musicale. Other than a brief lapse in Harlingen, where he referred to the Mexican patriot Miguel Hidalgo as "a brave American priest," Reagan avoided trouble.

But Carter did not. While Reagan was campaigning in Texas, the president spoke to a black audience at Ebenezer Baptist Church in Atlanta, which had been warmed up by Representative Parren J. Mitchell of Maryland describing Reagan as someone "who seeks the presidency of the United States with the endorsement of the Ku Klux Klan." Carter, after appearing momentarily discomfited, grinned and shook Mitchell's hand. Then the president launched into an attack on Reagan. Speaking in the church where Martin Luther King Sr., had preached for years, Carter said that if Reagan were elected, there would probably never be a national holiday for King's murdered son. He criticized Reagan for opposing the 1964 Civil Rights Act and said: "You've seen in this campaign the stirrings of hate and the rebirth of code words like 'state's rights' in a speech in Mississippi; in a campaign reference to the Ku Klux Klan relating to the South. This is a message that creates a cloud on the political horizon. Hatred has no place in this country."

The grounds for this attack were curious. Carter had no record of support for the 1964 Civil Rights Act, and Reagan was no bigot. The perception in Carter's camp, as in Reagan's, was that Reagan was vulnerable on foreign policy because some voters worried that he was un-informed and potentially trigger-happy. But most Americans outside the black community had a benign view of Reagan's motivations. By suggesting that Reagan was a racist, Carter devalued the currency of subsequent substantive criticisms of the Republican nominee on for-eign policy issues, which tended to be dismissed as personal attacks. Reagan supporters recognized that Carter had blundered. "Until last Tuesday, Jimmy Carter had contented himself with implying that Ronald Reagan is an equal opportunity warmonger who will incinerate everyone on earth, regardless of race, color or creed," wrote columnist George Will. "But Carter has decided that such moderation in pursuit of power is no virtue. Now he has said that Reagan is a racist."[9] Will re-called Carter's campaign record in Georgia, where his supporters in the 1970 primary distributed in segregationist regions a leaflet showing Governor Carl Sanders in the company of a black athlete. He con-trasted this tactic to Reagan's opposition to the 1964 Civil Rights Act "on constitutional grounds." Reagan, meanwhile, said that the civil rights law "had worked" and that he was satisfied with what it had ac-complished. He called Carter's accusation that he had injected race ha-tred into the campaign "shameful."

Did Carter mean to portray Reagan as a bigot? The president denied it, and there remains to this day some mystery about Carter's tactics, if not his larger strategy.* Carter, no less than Reagan, at times suffered from saying whatever popped into his head. His 1976 campaign against Ford also had survived a shaky early September, and a *Playboy* interview in which he famously said, "I've looked on a lot of women with lust. I've committed adultery in my heart many times." In 1980, the goal of the Carter campaign was to drive turnout among African Americans, who overwhelmingly preferred the president (or almost any Democrat) to Reagan. Black voter turnout, however, was problematic in a number of key states, and Democrats needed to energize their base. Race was one way to do it. The race issue was injected into the campaign by a Carter cabinet member, Patricia Harris, the secretary of health and human services, and an African American, who said the Reagan candidacy raised the "specter of white sheets." She ostensibly said this on the basis of an endorsement of Reagan by a small KKK faction but after Reagan repudiated the endorsement and the entire Klan. Carter was speaking

---

*Two days after the Atlanta speech, Carter held a press conference at which he repeatedly denied that he was accusing Reagan of injecting racism and hatred into the campaign. But, as Jack W. Germond and Jules Witcover observed, the Carter campaign the next day launched a major advertising campaign in black newspapers that said, in part: "Jimmy Carter named thirty-seven black judges, cracked down on job bias, and created one million jobs. That's why the Republicans are out to beat him."[10]

from notes in the Ebenezer Baptist Church, not off the cuff. The evidence suggests that the linking of Reagan and racial bigotry by the Carter team was deliberate.

Reagan's campaign team had been anticipating a personal attack of some sort and was waiting to cry "foul." "Even if Carter and Reagan were running neck and neck early this fall, we could still expect that a strong, negative and highly personal campaign would be directed against Ronald Reagan," Wirthlin had written in the June campaign plan. "Carter's record in office has denied him use of the traditional Democratic theme song of the economy and how Republicans would foul things up. . . . More than ever, the electorate questions Carter's very capacity to lead. So, to beat us in November, Carter's task seems to be clear: Reagan must be demonized." Wirthlin believed this strategy, if properly answered, would fail. So did Les Francis, the executive director of the Democratic National Committee, who knew from his California political experience how difficult it was to demonize Reagan. In a prophetic July 21 memorandum to Campaign Manager Hamilton Jordan, Francis warned that Carter risked forfeiting his reputation of being "a good and decent person who practiced good Christian charity in his dealings with others." Wrote Francis: "Quite frankly I hear more and more talk about Jimmy Carter having a 'mean streak' behind his smile; people cite his 'I'll whip his ass' statement vis-à-vis Kennedy last fall, his blast at Cy Vance after the latter's resignation, and our negative media ads during the primaries as grounds for their concern. A *particularly nasty* anti-Reagan campaign—either in our paid media or the President's rhetoric—will serve to play into this developing 'mean streak' concept."

Spencer and Wirthlin had discussed what they called this "meanness factor." Wirthlin's campaign plan raised many of the same issues as the Francis memo and included quotations from the commercials that media adviser Gerald Rafshoon had devoted to the denigration of Kennedy even after Carter was assured of the nomination. Wirthlin concluded: "We can expect Ronald Reagan to be pictured as a simplistic and untried lightweight (dumb), a person who consciously misuses facts to overblow his own record (deceptive) and, if President, one who would be too anxious to engage our country in a nuclear holocaust (dangerous)." It was an accurate forecast, except that Wirthlin expected the attack in the early stages of the campaign to come from surrogates and television commercials rather than from Carter himself. Spencer was less surprised at Carter's involvement. He had run a mean campaign of his own for Ford against Reagan in 1976, and he had been through the tough, losing battle against Carter that followed. Spencer knew how nasty presidential politics could get and realized that the candidates are apt to get caught up in the nastiness. Both Spencer and Wirthlin believed that Carter had a mean streak. "It's sure to surface someplace," Spencer had predicted to Deaver at the Republican National Convention. "And when it comes, it's going to hurt Carter."

In fairness to Carter, his options were limited. As Richard Harwood of *The Washington Post* wrote in a retrospective evaluation: "After only two years in the White House, Carter's competence had become something of an international joke, and by Labor Day, 1980, that perception had not changed."[11] Fifty-two Americans were still being held hostage in Iran, and a military attempt to rescue them had failed.[12] The economy was in free fall, and inflation was rising. As a candidate in 1976, Carter had promised inflation and unemployment rates of 4 percent, a balanced budget, and less reliance on oil imports. By September 1980, the inflation rate was 13 percent and rising and the unemployment rate was 8 percent. There was a $60 billion budget deficit, and oil imports were 24 percent higher than when Carter had taken office. Carter could not win on his record. His only hope of being reelected was to make Reagan the issue.

The precondition of doing this, however, was to recognize that Reagan was a formidable opponent. Carter came up short on this score. Following the trail of a long line of Reagan opponents, beginning with Pat Brown in 1966 and continuing through Gerald Ford in 1976, Carter underestimated his challenger. He had no excuse, for Carter, unlike Brown, had the advantage of advice from fellow Democrats who appreciated Reagan's political talents. At a June meeting in the Hay-Adams Hotel, across Lafayette Park from the White House, Les Francis brought in California Democrats Jesse Unruh and Bob Moretti to give what he called "some rough, tough, gruff unvarnished political advice" to the Democratic campaign team. Hamilton Jordan recalled after the election how Unruh had pointed his finger at him, warning him not to underestimate Reagan as a communicator. Moretti, in the course of a profane but respectful evaluation of Reagan, referred to him as "the Great Deflector."[13] His reference was to Reagan's skill in turning aside hard questions in ways that reflected on those who had raised them. In his subsequent memo, written after the Republican convention, Francis tried to reinforce Moretti's message, saying of Reagan: "He may not be an intellectual, but he is no dummy; and, the people around him are smart. No matter what doubts may reside in the minds of many American voters about a Reagan presidency, he will always enjoy a public perception that he is a 'nice guy.' To level an attack against a nice guy is certain to result in a backlash which could really hurt us."

This briefing had some effect upon Jordan, but the inoculation did not take with the campaign as a whole. Rafshoon and White House Press Secretary Jody Powell, who needed to hear it, did not attend. White House pollster Pat Cadell attended but continued to describe Reagan as a vulnerable challenger who could be overhauled by Carter. Despite the efforts of the Californians, Reagan remained underestimated until the end.

The ability of the Great Deflector to turn an issue back on his opponent was soon demonstrated. Carter, in a speech to the California AFL-CIO convention on September 23, said the election would decide "whether we have peace or war." Even Jody Powell characterized the remark to reporters as an "overstatement." But Carter stayed with the theme the following day, calling upon Reagan to explain his "repeated habit" of calling for the use of military force. As examples of this habit, Powell offered reporters comments drawn from various news clippings. They ranged from a Reagan statement in 1975 that the United States should send destroyers to accompany tuna fishing boats that were being seized by Ecuador to a suggestion Reagan had made during the 1980 primaries that blockade of Cuba would be an appropriate response to the Soviet invasion of Afghanistan. Unlike Carter's remarks on the race issue, this portrait of a warmonger had been fully expected, and Reagan was ready to react. Leaving the Marriott Hotel in Miami on September 23, Reagan stopped before the television cameras and was asked about Carter's statement to the AFL-CIO. Using language that had been discussed that morning with Spencer and Deaver, Reagan said, "I think it is inconceivable that anyone, and particularly a President of the United States, would imply, and this is another incident that he is implying and has several times, that anyone, any person, in this country would want war. And that's what he has been charging and I think it is unforgivable."

This prepared response was adequate. But as was so often the case when he came under fire, the issue worked inside Reagan and made him angry. By the time he arrived at the Pensacola Airport an hour and a half later, Reagan had received a full report of Carter's speech, and he was steaming. "First of all I think to accuse that anyone would deliberately want a war is beneath decency," Reagan emotionally told an airport rally. "I have two sons. I have a grandson. I have known four wars in my lifetime and I think like all of you that world peace has got to be the principal theme of this nation."[14] This was the Great Deflector playing the role of aggrieved candidate and playing it to perfection.

Carter was just warming up. On October 6, he began the day in a Milwaukee suburb with a detailed criticism of Reagan's old proposal to transfer federal programs to state and local governments. Later, in the Republican stronghold of DuPage County, outside Chicago, the president attacked Reagan's "very dangerous" position on nuclear arms control. "What was striking about the attack was its stridency and directness," wrote Edward Walsh the next day in *The Washington Post*. "Although Carter has made the 'war and peace' theme the centerpiece of his campaign, he has usually done so in a low-keyed manner, often not even mentioning Reagan by name."[15]

Carter continued in the strident style that night at a Democratic fund-raising dinner in Chicago, raising his voice as he declared it would be "a catastrophe" if Reagan were elected and telling his partisan audience: "You'll determine whether or not this America will be unified or, if I lose this election, whether Americans might be separated, black from white, Jew from Christian, North from South, rural from urban." Reagan, campaigning in Pennsylvania, issued a prepared response saying that he was "saddened" by the remarks and declaring that Carter owed the country an apology. His real feeling came through when a reporter asked him if Carter "fights dirty." "I think," said Reagan, "he's a badly misinformed and prejudiced man." The president's comments, said Reagan to an aide, convinced him that Carter knew he was losing the election.

Wirthlin's polls gave a more complex picture. They showed that Carter's attacks had surfaced latent doubts among voters about the dangers of putting Reagan in the White House. This was worrisome to the pollster, who realized that a Reagan misstep on the war-and-peace issue in the final weeks of the campaign had the potential for transferring the election from a referendum on Carter's competence to a question of whether Reagan's hand should be allowed on the nuclear trigger. At the same time, Carter had paid an expensive price for his success. The Wirthlin surveys found that even Carter supporters were disappointed at the way the president was conducting himself in the campaign. In trying to portray Reagan as both warmonger and bigot, Carter had undermined his carefully cultivated reputation as a decent man who followed a more moral code than other politicians. The gain was not worth the loss. The president's decision to lead the personal attack on Reagan had forfeited Carter's strongest asset with an electorate that had long since become disenchanted with his leadership.

Carter also had accomplished something for his opponent that the polls could not measure, and that Reagan may have been unable to accomplish for himself. By his personal attacks, Carter had roused within Reagan those competitive fires that had made him such an extraordinary candidate in the North Carolina primary of 1976 and the New

Hampshire primary of 1980. That keen competitive edge had been lacking as Reagan approached the fall campaign, and its absence may have contributed to the series of stumbles with which Reagan began it. He had not been distorted by the pursuit of the presidency, but he had not, since New Hampshire, been especially pushed by it, either. His approach combined a self-indulgent fatalism with a traditional patriotic respect for the office of the presidency. Inevitably, although Reagan was no fan of Carter, some of that respect rubbed off on the office-holder and made Reagan a more quiescent candidate than he should have been. Carter wiped away that respect with his personal attacks, particularly with the suggestion that a Reagan victory would also be a triumph for the forces of racial and religious prejudice. Unwittingly, Carter had collaborated with Spencer & Co. in restoring the confidence of a candidate who was shakier than he appeared from the outside.

On LeaderShip '80, Spencer and Deaver needed all the help they could get. While Carter floundered and Reagan recovered, the Reagan campaign evolved into a vast, multilayered bureaucracy headquartered in Arlington and beset by the myriad conflicts attendant to such enterprises. The Reagan campaign was particularly susceptible to layering because Casey's title of campaign director was largely a fiction. He knew a good deal about organization but little about the technical requirements of a political campaign, which meant that he had to rely on others for decisions that could have quickly been made by an experienced political professional.

Spencer, who met that description, tried to ignore Arlington as he made the numerous on-the-spot tactical decisions that any national campaign requires. Reagan trusted his judgment, and Spencer could count on help from Deaver and, in a pinch, from Nancy Reagan. Even so, there were daily struggles between the politicians on the plane and the technocrats at headquarters. From the vantage point of the campaign plane, Arlington was a behind-the-lines command post given to ponderous decision-making, multiple speech drafts, and frequent second-guessing. In the view of Arlington, LeaderShip '80 was a porous three-ring circus in which the press was allowed too much access to the candidate and his strategists and printed or aired too many inside stories. But Spencer saw these stories as part of an overall strategy to present Reagan as a better man than Carter. He had heard from political sources and from reporters switching campaigns that Carter's aides blamed the "meanness issue" on the press rather than on the president's inferences that Reagan was a warmonger and racist. As Spencer picked it up, the Carter line was that the president had to carry the attack to his opponent because the press was giving Reagan a free ride.* To reporters covering Reagan, this seemed a hollow and desperate claim. Reagan had criticized them in the primaries for "journalistic incest" when they focused on his many bloopers. Nofziger had claimed that this focus was partially responsible for Reagan's bad run in August and early September.

The issue of balanced news coverage was of no consequence to Spencer, who was running a campaign, not a journalism seminar. He knew from experience that sinking candidates and their staffs are apt to blame the media for their misfortunes. Spencer had benefited from this tendency when Pat Brown was losing in 1966, and he had been damaged by it a decade later after President Ford's mix-up on Poland in the debate with Carter. When the Carter team started whining about press coverage, Spencer knew he had the opposition on the ropes and pressed his advantage. Reagan was trotted out for "press availabilities" and interviews, and a relaxed, accessible campaign style was deliberately introduced aboard LeaderShip '80. Senior staff aides made themselves available. Nancy Reagan came back to the press section on every leg of every flight, passing out chocolates and chatting with reporters. When the plane took off, she rolled an orange down the aisle. The takeoffs were accompanied by a tape featuring Willie Nelson singing "On the Road Again" and a fragment of a Carter speech in which the president described glowingly to an interviewer how he and Rosalyn Carter read the Bible to each other in Spanish. Casey and Timmons objected to the looseness of the campaign plane and the "leaks" of strategy it inevitably produced. "This isn't Richard Nixon," Spencer would say in response. "This is Ronald Reagan. It gets a little bit trying at times, for me and everyone else, but we're going to reflect the nature of the candidate."[16]

Sometimes the nature of the candidate helped the Reagan campaign, and other times it did not. On August 27, before Spencer was aboard, Reagan spoke to a Teamsters luncheon in Columbus, Ohio, where he said that the lives of working people had "been shattered by a new Depression—the Carter Depression." Reporters hunted up Alan Greenspan, who had drafted the speech, and asked if he agreed with Reagan's description of the economy. Greenspan said candidly that Reagan had inserted the words. He added that the United States was "in one of the major economic contractions of the last fifty years," but that he would not have used Reagan's language.

*Albert R. Hunt, writing in *The Wall Street Journal*, contended that it was important to hold Reagan accountable for his misstatements but observed that the only reason Carter was aware of them was that they had been reported in the press. Hunt quoted one Carter operative as saying, "You all don't like Jimmy Carter so you've decided to give Reagan a free ride." This belief, added Hunt, was "a conspiratorial theory that would do Spiro Agnew proud."

This disavowal, coming at a time when Reagan was rediscovering the virtues of creationism, Taiwan, and the Vietnam War, was treated by some reporters as another Reagan goof. It wasn't. Reagan had inserted the word "Depression" deliberately, with a good politician's intuitive sense of the most effective phrase. After Greenspan's disavowal, he was forced to issue a correction but turned this into another effective political statement. "As far as I am concerned, the line between recession and depression cannot be measured in the strict economists' terms but must be measured in human terms," Reagan said. "When our working people —including those who are unemployed—must endure the worst misery since the 1930s, then I think we ought to recognize that they consider it a depression." Later, this answer evolved into a Reagan campaign litany that crowds sometimes chanted with him in cadenced unison: "If he wants a definition, I'll give him one. A recession is when your neighbor loses his job. A depression is when you lose yours. And recovery is when Jimmy Carter loses his."

By October, when Carter was focusing on foreign policy, Reagan was hitting hard at the president's economic policy in the steel towns of Pennsylvania and Ohio. On October 7, he traveled to Steubenville, Ohio, in the hard-pressed Ohio Valley, for a rally sponsored by the Save Our Steel Committee. Reagan noticed that hundreds of workingmen were in the crowd, even though the local Steelworkers Union had endorsed Carter and withdrawn from Save Our Steel—an organization of steel and coal company executives and community leaders—because of its sponsorship of the Reagan rally. After Reagan's speech, reporters were herded into a makeshift press room in the lobby of the Ohio Valley Towers while Reagan went to an upper floor of the building to address 150 members of Save Our Steel. He started out by listening to complaints about foreign "dumping" and "environmental regulatory overkill." One coal company president related his "sickening and discouraging" experience with the "faceless bureaucrats" of the Environmental Protection Agency in trying to work out a compromise that would permit burning of high-sulfur Ohio coal.

This was down Reagan's alley, and he did not disappoint his selective audience. "We are all today environmentalists," he said. "But we've got to realize that people are ecology, too." Some of those in Washington, he said, had gone beyond protecting the environment. "What they believe in is no growth," he said. "What they believe in is a return to a society in which there wouldn't be the need for the industrial concerns or more power plants and so forth. . . . I have flown twice over Mt. St. Helens out on our West Coast. I'm not a scientist and I don't know the figures, but I just have a suspicion that that one little mountain out there in these past several months has probably released more sulfur dioxide into the atmosphere of the world than has been released in the last ten years of automobile driving or things of that kind that people are so concerned about."

By now, Reagan was intent only on his enthusiastic audience. He was oblivious to the small press pool in the room and didn't know—and in his expansive mood may not have cared—that the entire speech was being piped by loudspeaker to the press room, where reporters, sensing that Reagan was on a roll, had begun to flip on their tape recorders. "Indeed," Reagan continued,

> there is a very eminent scientist associated with Texas A&M who has written about nature laughing at us and, according to his research, if we totally eliminated all the man-made sulfur dioxide in the air today, we would still have two-thirds as much as we have because that's how much nature is releasing. I know Teddy Kennedy had fun at the Democratic convention when he said that I had said that trees and vegetation cause 80 percent of the air pollution in this country. Well, now he was a little wrong about what I said. First of all, I didn't say 80 percent, I said 92 percent, 93 percent, pardon me. And I didn't say air pollution, I said oxides of nitrogen. And I am right.* Growing and decaying vegetation in this land are responsible for 93 percent of the oxides of nitrogen.

There was more. Reagan told his enthralled audience that the Great Smoky Mountains are so named because "that haze over those mountains are oxides of nitrogen. I think it's kind of interesting that there are some doctors that are lately investigating and experimenting [and] that they believe that that atmosphere up there in those mountains might be beneficial to tubercular patients." For some reason, this point reminded Reagan of a history he had read of Santa Barbara, California, "where we have some oil wells being drilled out in the harbor and a great organization formed to stop that." He went on:

> There have been sixteen permanent oil slicks in the Santa Barbara channel as long as the memory of man and far back beyond any development of oil or drilling of oil any place before we even knew about such things. And an English sea captain back in the 1700s anchored off that shore,

---

*He was right, but the statistic was irrelevant. Reagan apparently confused nitrous oxide, which growing plants emit, with nitrogen dioxide, which is emitted by smokestacks. And he wasn't even close to being right in his guess about the volcanic Mt. St. Helens, which at its peak activity was producing 2,000 tons of sulfur dioxide a day compared to 81,000 tons of sulfur dioxide produced each day by automobiles.

woke up in the morning and wrote in his log-book, "The sea was covered with a viscous material that when the waves moved it gave off iridescent hues." But around the turn of the century when we did know something about oil, Santa Barbara was a great health spa. . . . And one of their advertisements at that time said in addition to salubrious climate, that the southwesterly prevailing winds blowing across a large oil slick off the coast of Santa Barbara purified the air and prevented the spread of infectious diseases.

A new chapter in Reagan's singular history of pollution was added the following day in Youngstown, Ohio. While Reagan toured an abandoned steel mill, his aides handed out a report on regulatory reform that included the statement, "Air pollution has been substantially controlled." By now reporters had transcribed Reagan's rambling discourse at Steubenville. In the manner of many campaign stories, this one slowly gathered momentum as the transcript circulated, and Reagan was questioned about it at subsequent stops. The buildup was helped by the coincidence of a record smog siege in Los Angeles, Reagan's destination at the end of the week. When Reagan was asked in St. Louis whether what was happening in Los Angeles didn't contradict his stand in favor of relaxed air pollution controls, he said, "Fellas, I think all of this is, again, a little nitpicky trying to divert us from the real issues." He then went on to recount his support of strict air pollution laws as governor of California. But by the time Reagan reached Birmingham, Alabama, he was disowning the Youngstown statement that air pollution was "substantially controlled." A Reagan aide told reporter David Hoffman, covering the campaign for Knight-Ridder newspapers, that this statement may have been issued without the candidate's approval.

In California, the air was even murkier than Reagan's views of air pollution. Reagan was scheduled to address a homecoming Friday night rally in Burbank on October 11, but the smog was so thick that his plane was diverted from the Hollywood-Burbank Airport to Los Angeles International Airport. Reagan arrived late at the rally, where the musical accompaniment included Roy Rogers and the Sons of the Pioneers playing "Cool Clear Water" and other favorites of their western movie days. Despite this nostalgia and extensive advance work, the crowd was small. The smog was so heavy it had driven even pollution-toughened Los Angelenos indoors.

Reagan pushed on. The next day at Claremont College, demonstrators chanted "Smog, smog" and someone tacked a poster to a nearby tree that said, "Chop Me Down Before I Kill Again." But the smog began to lift as Reagan toured Southern California by helicopter, finishing the day with a visit to a Van Nuys synagogue, where he donned a white yarmulke and quipped, "In the business I used to be in, the good guys wore the white hats." Reagan's series of declarations on air pollution, reminiscent of his comments about redwoods in his 1966 campaign, had made him anything but a "white hat" with conservationist groups, but Wirthlin's polls showed the political damage was slight. He had lost a little ground in California, where his lead remained commanding, and dropped a few points in Oregon, where voters take their trees seriously. Briefly, Carter became a competitive candidate for Oregon's six electoral votes. Nationally, however, Reagan got away with Mt. St. Helens and the "substantial control" of air pollution, although the issue was a sensitive one at Arlington headquarters for the remainder of the campaign. On one flight of LeaderShip '80, speechwriter Ken Khachigian noticed a forest fire below and said softly, "Killer trees." The irreverent James Brady, who rarely said anything softly, repeated in a loud voice, "Killer trees." The phrase found its way into *The New York Times* with attribution to Brady, who was briefly grounded by Casey and his irate operatives at Arlington. Soon, however, Spencer and Deaver brought him back aboard.

Spencer believes there is a time in every campaign, no matter how well it is going, when it plunges into the doldrums and loses the ability to move forward. This had now happened to the Reagan campaign. Early in October, Carter's paid advertisements began to carry the brunt of the attack against Reagan. Carter acknowledged in an October 8 interview with Barbara Walters that he had made some mistakes in his comments about his opponent, although he continued to criticize the press coverage of Reagan. It was not quite an apology, but it was close, and Carter began to climb in the polls. On October 14, for the only time in the campaign, Wirthlin's trackings gave Carter a narrow lead. Adjusted for the undecided vote, the percentages were Carter 45.17, Reagan 43.43, and Anderson 11.35. "We were flat, flat, flat," Spencer said afterward. "We weren't moving and we had to do something."[17] The "something," everyone agreed, should be a new issue—and one that was aimed at a constituency where Reagan needed help.

Reagan's doldrums produced an announcement at an October 14 press conference in Los Angeles that he would name a woman to "one of the first Supreme Court vacancies in my administration." That promise would lead to the appointment of Justice Sandra Day O'Connor, although at the time Reagan's "one of the first" language seemed so carefully couched that it scarcely looked like a promise at all.[18] Both Spencer and Wirthlin were concerned about reaching out to women voters, who at this point in the campaign were decidedly less favorable to Reagan than were men. On the same day Reagan made his announcement, a poll in *The New York Times* showed the Republican nominee with an 11-point lead among male voters and a 9-point deficit among female voters in the key state of Illinois.

In part, what later was called the "gender gap" related to Reagan's opposition to the Equal Rights Amendment and to permissive abortion-rights laws. But the more significant reason, particularly among swing voters, was the concern of women voters that the military buildup advocated by Reagan increased the risk of war. Reagan had softened his opposition to the Strategic Arms Limitation Treaty known as SALT II by saying he would bargain willingly with the Soviets for a new treaty that would reduce nuclear armaments instead of merely slowing the pace of the arms race. But memories of Reagan's bristling anti-Soviet rhetoric lingered with voters, especially women. Spencer knew from long experience that these voters were more apt to be frightened by Reagan's words in print than they were by Reagan personally. The best way to deal with the issue of whether Reagan was warlike, Spencer believed, was to let voters see him side by side with President Carter. The doldrums that would produce Justice O'Connor also would lead to the only debate between Reagan and Carter in the 1980 campaign.

Personally, Reagan had always been inclined to debate. I had asked him about it in August at a time when the avowed campaign strategy was to insist that Anderson be involved in any debate format. This position, as well as Carter's insistence on Anderson's exclusion, was based on polling information that showed the independent candidate pulling votes from Carter as long as he stayed above 10 percent. Wirthlin did a series of projections, however, that showed Anderson hurting Reagan if he dropped to the 5 or 6 percent level.* Reagan realized that Anderson might sink out of sight in the polls if the two major candidates froze him out of a debate. Even so, it was clear to me that Reagan had learned the negative lesson of Iowa and the positive ones of Nashua and Chicago. When I asked Reagan if he looked forward to a one-on-one debate with Carter, he forgot about the strategy and said, "I do look forward to it, not because of any contrast of ability in debating, but because I think the president cannot deny the record. This would be the nature of a de-

---

*This was because Anderson's core vote contained a disproportionate number of liberal Republicans who were unlikely to vote for Carter under any circumstances. Overall, however, Anderson helped Reagan and hurt Carter because of the states in which he was a factor. Wirthlin's polls showed Anderson taking votes from Reagan in California and Texas, where Reagan's cushion was so large it didn't matter. But Anderson drew from Carter in northeastern states that Reagan could not have carried on his own. Anderson's 7.5 percent of the vote in New York probably cost Carter the state, and his 15.2 percent in Massachusetts certainly accounted for Carter's loss there.

bate, these would be the things that would be brought forth in a debate."[19]

Reagan also was aware that challengers Kennedy in 1960 and Carter in 1976 had been declared "winners" by the media for holding their own with incumbents. After Carter turned down a three-way debate, Reagan and Anderson conducted a debate of their own, under League of Women Voters auspices, on September 21 in Baltimore. The debate was no barn-burner, but Carter suffered in the public opinion polls and at the hands of editorial writers for avoiding it. The reviews of Reagan were mixed, but the prevailing opinion—again supported by the polls—was that he had held his own against a knowledgeable and quick-witted opponent. Reagan's showing further bolstered his confidence and contributed to his growing belief that he would not be overmatched against Carter. Paul Laxalt, influential with Reagan, encouraged him in that opinion. So Reagan was not surprised when Spencer approached him on a mid-October flight from Los Angeles to Idaho Falls and proposed that he debate Carter. "I think I'm going to have to debate him," Reagan said.

Reagan's confidence was bolstered again the following evening in New York City at the annual Alfred E. Smith Memorial Dinner, the one occasion on which Reagan and Carter were then scheduled to meet. The dinner is a tradition-hallowed event where speakers blend humor with homage to Smith, the onetime New York governor and 1928 Democratic presidential nominee. It was a made-to-order event for Reagan, and he took full advantage of it, winning the plaudits of the audience with a graceful, self-deprecating speech and a wisecrack that there wasn't any truth to the rumor "that I look younger because I keep riding older and older horses." The format was less kind to Carter, who heavy-handedly called attention to his Camp David achievements and to Reagan's support by fundamentalist Christian activists.

The next morning, in Reagan's Waldorf-Astoria suite, the candidate and his team debated whether to debate Carter. Key aides had flown up from Washington for the meeting, and not all of them were enthusiastic about the idea. Timmons thought the debate was a high-risk proposition; he preferred to rely on a superior field force that would turn out Reagan's supporters on election day. Wirthlin also opposed the debate. His poll on that morning of October 17 showed Reagan firmly back out in front, with 48.17 percent to 41.55 percent for Carter. Anderson was holding at 10.28 percent, and Wirthlin was concerned that a debate between Reagan and Carter would cause him to drop off the charts. If so, Wirthlin contended, this could cost Reagan both New York and Massachusetts. Wirthlin believed in his data, which had provided a reliable barometer to issues and personalities throughout the year. He considered the tiny lead that Carter had taken on October 14 to be an aberration.[20] Reagan had otherwise led throughout the campaign and he was leading now. Why take a chance on losing that lead by debating the trailing candidate?

Spencer always trusted his intuitions as much as the polls and his feelings more than his campaign plans. "Planning is indispensable; plans are worthless," he liked to say, attributing the quotation to Dwight Eisenhower. Spencer had found it unusually difficult to reach a settled feeling about the debate. He had learned in 1976, when Ford had said that the Soviets did not dominate Poland, how easily a candidate could destroy himself with a chance remark, and Reagan was always on the brink of some such calamity. But Spencer kept returning to the idea that the visual impression of a debate would undermine the portrait of Reagan as potentially dangerous. And Spencer was aware, along with everyone else in the suite, that a "tie" would be seen as a defeat for the president.

In the end, tactical considerations and Reagan's inclinations decided the issue. Nearly everyone in the Reagan campaign worried that Carter would come up with an "October surprise," which probably meant freeing the American hostages in Iran during the last weeks of the campaign. Wirthlin had raised this possibility in his campaign plan in June, and Casey and Meese had tried to defuse it in advance by mentioning it to reporters at the Republican convention. Both Spencer and Wirthlin believed until well into October that if Carter was able to bring back the hostages before the election, he could wash away much of the emotion and acrimony of the campaign and the concerns about his leadership and rally the voters to his side. Seen in this context, a 7-point lead didn't seem insurmountable. To Spencer, the debate loomed as a hedge against the October surprise and what might be Reagan's only opportunity to regain the attention of voters if the hostages were released.

Spencer also made another judgment. Reading Wirthlin's surveys, he reached a different conclusion than the pollster about the meaning of the data. As Spencer saw it, a late debate would help whoever was ahead by diminishing the events that came before it. "It froze the two candidates where they were, which meant it froze Reagan in the lead,"[21] Spencer said afterward, repeating a point he made at the Waldorf-Astoria that morning. These were persuasive arguments, and they carried the day. Deaver, Casey, and Nofziger favored the debate. So did advertising specialist Peter Dailey, originally a doubter. Meese played his usual collegial role and saw to it that the dissenting views of Wirthlin and Timmons were heard, but in the end, he, too, favored the debate.

There was another dissenter who did not speak that morning, but had already made her views known to the candidate. Nancy Reagan was skeptical of a debate from the start, out of concern that her husband would make a mistake that would cost the election. But she valued Spencer's judgments, and she knew that her husband wanted to debate. A participant in the meeting remembered Nancy Reagan sitting and watching in her bathrobe, silent as the decision was ratified. She had been influential in the past, and she would be again. But on this day, on this big decision, Reagan acted without her approval. He followed instead the advice of his most experienced strategist and the sure guide of his own political instincts.

The job of translating this decision into an actual debate was entrusted to James Baker. The ticklish point for Reagan was to change positions without appearing to abandon his stand that Anderson deserved to be included. The League of Women Voters, which earlier had set a 15 percent standing in the polls as the threshold entitling a candidate to participation in a presidential debate, gave Reagan a way out when Anderson dropped to 8 percent in the Gallup Poll. The League promptly issued a new invitation for a two-way debate. Carter was in no position to refuse. He had consistently turned down the three-way debate, calling Reagan and Anderson "two Republicans," and he had taken a battering in both the press and the polls because of it. Carter campaign strategist Robert Strauss had accepted a number of alternative two-way debates, all of them rejected by Baker. A Carter refusal to debate at this point would have seemed a sign of weakness. Also, as Baker reported back to the Reagan campaign team, Carter's strategists were not convinced that Reagan really wanted to debate.

Baker started his negotiations with what seemed like an absurd proposal—an election eve debate designed to give Reagan total protection against a November variant of the "October surprise" and to freeze the lead for the longest possible moment. The Carter counteroffer to debate on October 28, the Tuesday before the election, delighted the Reagan camp and was accepted after a bit of play-acting by the skillful Baker. The debate was close enough to the election to suit Spencer. If anything happened after that, he reasoned, it could produce a backlash against Carter because voters would believe the president was deliberately contriving an eleventh-hour event.

As it turned out, Spencer's belief that Reagan would be frozen into his lead proved accurate. Once the debate was agreed upon, the press coverage and the candidates' speeches became perfunctory, with everyone waiting for the big event. Reagan was the beneficiary of this hiatus. From October 17 until the day of the debate in Cleveland, on October

28, he held a consistent lead in Wirthlin's daily polls, never less than 5 points and never more than 8. Reagan took it easy, boning up for his debate at Wexford with such questioners as Jeane Kirkpatrick and George Will impersonating members of the press panel. David Stockman, who had successfully impersonated his onetime mentor John Anderson in preparation for the earlier debate, played the Carter role. "After Stockman," Reagan said afterward, "both Anderson and Carter were easy."

Easy was too strong a word for it, but it wasn't that difficult either. It was often said of Reagan, from his first campaign to his last, that he was an actor who knew how to deliver his lines. This was true, but Reagan also was an experienced politician with convictions and a plan of action that he believed would rescue a nation in need of leadership. Reagan favored tax cuts that he assumed would jumpstart a lagging economy. He favored a military buildup that he said would enable the United States to deal with the Soviet Union from a position of strength.* On economic issues, Reagan had a clear advantage. Even Americans who didn't share his passion for tax cuts had decided he could do better with the economy than Carter, in whom they had lost confidence. Reagan was vulnerable in the debate only if his advocacy of a military buildup came across as trigger-happy and likely to lead the nation into war.

This issue was joined in the first question of the debate at the Cleveland Public Music Hall, in which Reagan was asked about the perception that he was "all too quick to advocate the use of lots of muscle, military action, to deal with foreign crises." Reagan set the tone of the debate with his response: "I'm only here to tell you that I believe with all my heart that our first priority must be world peace, and that use of force is always and only a last resort when everything else has failed. . . . To maintain that peace requires strength. America has never gotten into a war because we were too strong."

Reagan was nervous at the outset of the debate, as performers often are, but the success of his first answer settled him down. To the audience, it seemed that Carter was the nervous one. Reagan had put him on the defensive before the debate began by walking over and extending his hand. Carter took it but seemed surprised. It was Reagan's way of saying he was the peer of the president, over whom he towered. And it reinforced Spencer's notion that all the "visuals" of the encounter favored Reagan.

Reagan had a clear understanding of what he needed to accomplish in the debate. He used the word "peace" so often it sounded as if he had

*Reagan, like his icon Franklin D. Roosevelt in 1932, also promised a balanced budget. John Anderson said the only way Reagan could accomplish this while carrying out his other promises was "with mirrors."[22]

invented it. Concluding his answer to the first question, which called upon him to draw differences between himself and Carter over use of military power, Reagan said, in words similar to those he had used in rebuttal to Carter's attacks: "I have seen four wars in my lifetime. I am a father of sons; I have a grandson. I don't ever want to see another generation of young Americans bleed their lives into sandy beachheads in the Pacific or rice paddies and jungles of Asia or the muddy battlefields of Europe."

Carter was less successful than Reagan at using his parenthood to bolster his credentials as a man of peace. He did well on nuclear proliferation, reminding viewers that Reagan had said that the spread of such weapons was "none of our business." But when Carter summed up his position on arms control, he said: "I think to close out this discussion, it would be better to put into perspective what we're talking about. I had a discussion with my daughter Amy the other day before I came here to ask her what the most important issue was. She said she thought nuclear weaponry and the control of nuclear arms." The crowd groaned. (Hamilton Jordan, watching the debate on television, groaned, too, according to Jack Germond and Jules Witcover.[23]) The remark seemed patronizing to Reagan and to viewers, and everyone on both sides knew it. As Deaver observed afterward, "People may not understand the intricacies of arms control, but they know you don't ask your twelve-year-old for the solution."[24] Of course, Carter had not said that he was using his daughter as a nuclear weapons consultant. He apparently was trying to find an acceptable way to say that he was less likely than Reagan to lead the nation into nuclear war. If this was his intent, he failed. Post-debate polls found that voters linked the Amy reference to Carter's earlier depiction of Reagan as a warmonger and were not impressed by it. It was another self-inflicted wound, coming at a time when Carter could not afford mistakes. In the final week of the campaign, "Amy" became a staple for television comedians, and "Ask Amy" signs proliferated at Republican rallies.

As the debate unfolded, Reagan became aware that his opponent was pressing. This added to Reagan's confidence. One of the signs of Reagan's professionalism as a performer was that he always knew how he looked on the screen. Carter did not. The cameras showed a serious challenger who was nonetheless not afraid to smile, and an intense president who looked daggers at his opponent whenever he disagreed with him. Near the end of the debate, after both Carter and Reagan had bobbled statistics on Social Security and health care, the president said, "Governor Reagan, as a matter of fact, began his political career campaigning around this nation against Medicare." Carter then launched into a defense of national health insurance, pointing out that Reagan opposed this proposal. Reagan ignored this accurate description of his position and instead jumped at the Medicare remark.

"There you go again," said Reagan almost sorrowfully, like an uncle rebuking a none-too-favorite nephew who was known to tell tall tales.

He went on to say that he had supported an alternative to Medicare sponsored by the American Medical Association, an action that certainly merited Carter's description of "campaigning against Medicare." But "there you go again" finished off Carter. The reply was the Great Deflector's high point of the debate and perhaps of the entire campaign. It seemed such a wonderful, natural summation of political excess that overnight it became part of the language. After Reagan became president, the phrase lived on in the White House, where people would say to one another in correction of some habitual behavior, "There you go again."

The phrase, however, had not just popped into Reagan's head. During the debate preparation, issues specialists had given Reagan a cram course on the various arguments they thought Carter might use. Defense adviser William Van Cleave, especially, wanted Reagan to master the intricacies of strategic weapons deployment, on which Carter was well-informed. Reagan listened politely but spent his time practicing one-liners in the belief that viewers would be more apt to remember a deft phrase than a technical argument. In one rehearsal, Stockman, the Carter impersonator, whaled away at Reagan on nuclear proliferation. After the rehearsal, Reagan assembled his closest aides to review what he had done. None of his answers had been fully satisfactory, and Reagan, commenting on his responses, said: "I was about ready to say, 'There you go again.' I may save it for the debate." And so he did.

The immediate verdict of the press about the debate was not unanimous. When some of us closed a hotel bar that night after filing our various accounts, several reporters thought Carter the winner. Many more agreed with the opinion expressed in the subhead of the *Cleveland Plain Dealer* story the next day: "Each candidate leaves the ring without errors." But another story on page one of the same edition reported that an ABC poll of viewers found Reagan the winner by a 2–1 margin. Other polls were closer but also showed Reagan a winner. CBS put Reagan ahead by only 44–36 but found that the number of voters who thought Reagan would "lead the country into war" had declined from 43 to 35 percent. This was the statistical expression of a point made in a post-debate analysis by David Broder, who wrote that Carter had "accomplished almost every objective except the most important one: The destruction of Reagan's credibility as a president."

Wirthlin's rolling polls recorded a surge to Reagan that continued unabated until election day. On October 29, the day after the debate, Reagan led by 5.5 percentage points. The number increased steadily each day after that as more and more debate viewers were added to the averages. On October 31, when the data included three post-debate days, Reagan's lead stood at 9 points. It crested on November 2, the Sunday before the election, at nearly 11 points. Adjusted for undecided voters, the figures were Reagan 51.30, Carter 39.33, and Anderson 9.32.

A winner's feeling of exhilaration crept over LeaderShip '80 in the days following the debate. It was difficult to resist, but Reagan resisted it because he was mindful of what had happened to him in the 1976 New Hampshire primary and the 1980 Iowa caucuses. His superstition about overconfidence was appreciated by comedian Bob Hope, who had joined the campaign in its last days. "He remembers how Dewey fell off the wedding cake," Hope said to me as LeaderShip '80 made its final flight to the West Coast.

Nonetheless, the good feeling in the Reagan camp found expression in the candidate's speeches. For the first time since the birth of Carter's attack strategy, Reagan no longer seemed concerned about being cast as the mad bomber. He had taken over the orange-rolling-down-the-aisle chores from his wife, and when photographer Michael Evans jokingly warned him about the number of pictures he would have to autograph, Reagan replied, "You know, after you've canceled Social Security and started the war, what else is there for you to do?" On the stump, Reagan had returned to his original theme—that Carter was a failed and incompetent president. "In place of competence, he has given us ineptitude," Reagan said at airport rallies in New Orleans and Texarkana two days after the debate. "Instead of steadiness, we have gotten vacillation. While America looks for confidence, he gives us fear. His multitude of promises so richly pledged in 1976 have fallen by the wayside in the shambles of this administration." These were strong words from a candidate who had complained about his opponent's harshness. But Reagan expressed himself with a winner's warmth and conviction that made these words sound less strident than they appear on paper. He was not about to claim victory, but he was a happy man.

The euphoria was marred only by the news from Iran, where, on the Saturday before the election, the Iranian parliament began debating conditions for release of the Americans held captive for a year. The consensus of Reagan's strategists was that it was too late for any November version of the October surprise to turn things around, but the volatility of the hostage situation introduced an element of risk into what seemed an assured election. By Sunday morning, the hostage story dominated the news, sweeping aside domestic political issues. Every network ran a special program commemorating the anniversary of the hostages' capture. The front page of *The Washington Post* that day contained nine stories—eight of them about the hostages and the other an analysis by Broder of the effect a hostage release might have on the election.

Reagan and his entourage had spent the night at Neal House in Columbus, Ohio. At 6 A.M., Ed Meese was awakened by a call from Arlington headquarters telling him that the State Department was trying to reach him. At 6:15 A.M., Meese talked to Harold Saunders, Carter's assistant secretary of state for Near Eastern and South Asian affairs, who informed him that the Iranian special commission on the hostages had issued four conditions for release of the Americans. Later that morning, this briefing became the basis for a strategy session on the hostage issue in which the unanimous view was that Reagan should do nothing that could be construed as trying to take political advantage of the situation. Reagan, Meese, and Spencer were aware that their own frequent warnings of "an October surprise" had heightened the consciousness of voters to political exploitation of the hostage issue. They knew this strategy could backfire on Reagan if he appeared to be trying to draw political benefit from what literally could be a life-or-death situation for the Americans in Iran. The session at Neal House broke up with Reagan and his aides agreeing to keep their mouths shut. "All I can tell you is I think this is too sensitive to make any comment on it at all," Reagan told reporters on the sidewalk outside the hotel. "I won't make any more comment about it."

But Meese did comment, to the surprise of colleagues in the front compartment of LeaderShip '80. Responding to the requests of reporters, he went back on the plane and held a mini–press conference in which he discounted the impact of the news upon the election. Casey discounted it, too, telling Broder in Washington, "The campaign is over. We're just playing it out."[25] From a campaign manager who had complained about the "leaks" on LeaderShip '80, this was a startling public expression of the private view that the Reagan aides at Neal House had agreed to keep to themselves.

For weeks, the Reagan team had feared that a secret deal had been struck to free the fifty-two American hostages around election day. When the nonexistent "deal" appeared at hand, Carter played it straight, canceling his campaign appearances and flying back to the White House for a day of meetings with his foreign policy advisers. That evening he issued a careful televised statement saying that the Iranian proposals "appear to offer a positive basis" for a solution. "We are within two days of an important national election," the president said. "Let me assure you that my decisions on this crucial matter will not be affected by the calendar." Reagan heard this statement on television en route from Dayton to Cincinnati, and he believed it. But he also believed, as Spencer had told him, that voters would remember the convenient timing of a past announcement about the hostages that had helped Carter win the crucial Wisconsin primary against Senator Kennedy. As Reagan headed for rallies in his two home states of Illinois and California on the final day of the election, he was, as Casey had said, "just playing it out."

And then, after all of Reagan's primaries and promises, after all his struggles to find the right themes and the right words and a balance between isolation and accessibility, after Bush and Nashua and "noble cause" and "meanness" and "there you go again"—after all this, the long campaign for the presidency was coming to an end. The crowd in Peoria, where a sprinkling of old-timers remembered Reagan from his Illinois days, welcomed the finish because they sensed victory. Assembled under a banner of "Reagan Plays Well In Peoria," this happy crowd bantered with reporters and laughed at Bob Hope's warm-up jokes. Amy Carter, said Hope, had developed an interest in nuclear weapons because "Uncle Billy gave her a Raggedy Ann doll with a nuclear warhead." The difference between Jimmy Carter and his brother was that Billy had a foreign policy. And, with Jerry Ford alongside him, Hope said that Ford had told him he would "pardon Carter" if he ever returned to the White House.

Those of us who talked to Ford had our doubts. The previous Saturday, Ford had led the Republican campaign triumphantly through his home state of Michigan while Reagan played the role of devoted admirer and said that Carter had failed because of his "total inability to fill Jerry Ford's shoes." On the plane to Oregon and California that Monday, I asked Ford what would happen in the election. "The voters are going to correct a mistake they made four years ago," he said firmly. In their campaigning together, Ford had grown fond of Reagan, burying his grievances from the 1976 campaign. But his dislike of Carter, whom Ford considered a failure as a president, burned brightly.

The last public event of the campaign took place in San Diego, where a patriotic rally awaited Reagan when he arrived late after a stop in Portland. The candidate was jubilant but tired. Curiously, the campaign ended as it had begun, with Reagan responding to a heckler. This time, it was not a woman with a Carter mask but a man in a black coat and stovepipe hat who hollered "ERA" and "equality" intermittently throughout the Reagan speech. "Aw, shut up," Reagan finally said. The crowd cheered. The evening ended with a fireworks display and the lighting of a gigantic American flag. The Reagans joined the crowd in singing "God Bless America."

Most Americans did not see this last event. What they saw instead, interspersed between news programs about the plight of the hostages, was one of the best speeches Reagan has ever given on television. Reagan called it a vision for America, which is what presidential candidates always talk about on election eve, but it really was Reagan's vision, and it had brought tears to Jim Brady's eyes when he watched the taping of the speech earlier that day in Peoria. True to the candidate, the speech was a vision of the past, of Pilgrims landing in New England, of American prisoners of war returning home from Vietnam, of astronauts landing on the moon. "Does history still have a place for America, for her people, for her great ideals?" said Reagan. "There are some who answer 'no,' [who say] that our energy is spent, our days of greatness at an end, that a great national malaise is upon us." Reagan gave his own answer later in the speech, taking issue with a famous speech that Carter had given in July 1979 without ever mentioning it.* "I find no national malaise," Reagan said. "I find nothing wrong with the American people." Foreshadowing what he would say in his inaugural address, Reagan addressed ordinary Americans as "heroes" who had not shirked history's call. "Any nation that sees softness in our prosperity or disunity . . . let them understand that we will put aside in a moment the fruits of our prosperity and the luxury of our disagreements if the cause is a safe and peaceful future for our children."

Concluding his debate with Carter in Cleveland a week earlier, Reagan had asked a series of questions that were intended to make voters measure their president against their own expectations of America. He repeated these questions in extended form in this final campaign speech, saying first that President Carter would be reelected "if he instills in you pride for your country and a sense of optimism about our future."

"But consider these questions as well when you finally make your decision:

"Are you more confident that our economy will create productive work for our society or are you less confident? Do you feel you can keep the job you have or gain a job if you don't have one?

"Are you satisfied that inflation at the highest rates in thirty-three years were the best that we could do? Are interest rates at 14 1/2 percent something you are prepared to live with?

---

*Carter never actually used the word "malaise" in this speech. What he did say, in a nationally televised address on July 15, 1979, was that Americans were suffering from "a crisis of confidence . . . that strikes at the very heart and soul and spirit of our national will."

"Are you pleased with the ability of young people to buy a home; of the elderly to live their remaining lives in happiness; of our youngsters to take pride in the world we have built for them?

"Is our nation stronger and more capable of leading the world toward peace and freedom or is it weaker?

"Is there more stability in the world or less?

"Are you convinced that we have earned the respect of the world and our allies, or has America's position across the globe diminished?

"Are you personally more secure in your life? Is your family more secure? Is America safer in the world?

"And most importantly—quite simply—the basic question of our lives: Are you happier today than when Mr. Carter became president of the United States?"[26]

Later the next morning, the Reagans voted at the Pacific Palisades home owned by Robert and Sally Gulick. He was a retired Marine Corps officer and a stockbroker. She was a Reagan fan. The table where the voters signed in was decorated with a papier-mâché elephant and black licorice jellybeans. The poll workers had brought books and pictures for the Reagans to sign. In their eyes, he was already president. The precinct where the Reagans voted was home to celebrities, including Sylvester Stallone, Lawrence Welk, and Vince Scully. But Reagan from this day forward was the biggest celebrity of all. He posed for pictures and quipped with reporters and said that he had voted for Nancy. He left to get a haircut. He refused to claim victory. When a reporter asked if he had won, Reagan said, "You know me, I'm too superstitious to answer anything like that." Another reporter told him that George Bush had said the ticket was "in like a burglar." Reagan laughed. "I think he was using a figure of speech," he said.

But Reagan was "in," carrying the Republicans to control of the Senate with him, and by a margin as great as Wirthlin's surveys of the last four days had shown.* He was showering before dinner in his Pacific Palisades home and Nancy Reagan was taking a bath when network news carried reports of Reagan victories in the South and East, and then, at 5:15 P.M. Pacific time, projected the landslide victory. Wrapped in towels and bathrobes, the Reagans watched the report, which was interrupted by a telephone call. It was President Carter calling to concede.

---

*Reagan won by a plurality of 8,417,992 votes. He received 43,901,812 votes (50.7 percent) to 35,483,820 votes (41 percent) for Carter and 5,719,722 (6.6 percent) for Anderson. The electoral vote margin was even wider—489 for Reagan and 44 for Carter. The president carried his home state of Georgia plus Hawaii, Maryland, Minnesota, Rhode Island, West Virginia, and the District of Columbia.[27]

That evening, at dinner with his closest friends and aides at the Bel Air home of Earle Jorgenson, and later in the top-floor suite of the Century Plaza Hotel, Reagan acted like a man who had been happily surprised by unexpected good fortune. Nancy Reagan was visibly excited, hugging Mike Deaver and others who streamed in with their congratulations. Reagan talked patiently on the telephone, thanking politicians who had helped him and congressmen whose support he would need as president. He seemed more contented than excited. When a caller told him that independent candidate John Anderson had reached the 5 percent threshold he needed to qualify for federal funds, Reagan said, "Good, good." He knew that Anderson's candidacy had helped him, and he did not want him saddled with campaign debts.

Soon afterward, Neil Reagan came by, shook his brother's hand, and talked to him through the din.

"I bet there's a hot time in Dixon tonight," Neil said.

"I'd like to be there off in a corner just listening," said Ronald Reagan, the small-town boy and former governor of California who had just been elected president of the United States.

NOTES

Governor Reagan: His Rise to Power is based upon manifold source material. These sources include my accumulated writings about Ronald Reagan, thirty formal interviews and numerous other conversations with him in the pre-presidential years, interviews with members of his cabinet, staff, and family, and the historical record of his governorship.

The most important of these written records are the cabinet minutes, which have been examined in their entirety for the first time for this book. Of particular value are the early cabinet minutes taken by Helene von Damm at the direction of William P. Clark, an important figure in the Reagan era, who has custody of the minutes for the first two years of Reagan's governorship. Later minutes are in the Ronald Reagan Presidential Library at Simi Valley, California. All citations to these minutes, a few of which were technically sub-cabinet meetings, are cited in these notes as "cabinet minutes."

Thomas C. Reed and Norman ("Ike") Livermore, two other important figures in the Reagan governorship, kept a contemporaneous record. Many of Reed's notations were incorporated into unpublished book chapters, which he made available for this book. I have attributed information provided by Reed and Livermore to their interviews or records, as appropriate.

Some passages about Reagan's early governorship were taken from *Ronnie and Jesse: A Political Odyssey*, my 1969 biography of Reagan and Jesse Unruh. The book is abbreviated in the notes as R&J. Some passages, particularly in the third section of this book, were taken from my 1982 biography, *Reagan*. In most cases, they are cited to their original sources.

Reagan's useful first autobiography, *Where's the Rest of Me?*, is abbreviated in the notes as WTROM.

I have identified sources whenever possible. On those occasions when sources insisted on confidentiality, I have followed my past practice, as a reporter for the *San Jose Mercury-News* and *The Washington Post*, and as a Reagan biographer, of holding anonymous information to a higher standard of verification. Some persons who provided information anonymously for earlier books have allowed themselves to be identified for this one. Holmes Tuttle, who is deceased, told me in interviews for earlier books that he wished to be anonymous on several matters while Reagan was in office but could be identified after Reagan retired from public life. I have followed these ground rules.

Quotations from Reagan's speeches during his presidency are from the *Public Papers of the Presidents*. Where sources are identified in the text, I have tried to avoid duplicating the information in the notes.

Lou Cannon

Chapter 1: California

1. William Faulkner, "On Privacy," *Harper's*, July 1955.
2. Carey McWilliams, quoted in *The Pacific States of America: People, Politics, and Power in the Five Pacific Basin States*, by Neal R. Peirce, W. W. Norton, 1972, page 24.
3. This was a favorite reference of California Water Resources Director William E. Warne, and sometimes of Brown himself. "By the time our astronauts reach the moon, the California Aqueduct of the State Water Project will take its place with the Great Wall of China and become one of only two man-made things on earth that moon visitors are expected to be able to see with the naked eye," Warne once declared in a burst of enthusiasm. This prompted Harry Farrell of the *San Jose Mercury-News* to write that the only other manmade thing that would be visible from the moon was the building that the Department of Water Resources would construct to house all its press releases on the glory of the Water Project. See my book *Ronnie and Jesse: A Political Odyssey* (hereinafter R&J), Doubleday, 1969, page 217.
4. Champion miscalculated. "It's not an issue; people don't understand it," he said. But the difficulty of understanding it made it easier for Republicans to convince voters that the accounting change was flim-flam. On balance, it may have damaged Brown more than a modest tax increase would have. See R&J, page 78.
5. The student revolt, and especially the occupation of Sproul Hall, cost the university dearly in alumni support. See R&J, pages 229–230. For a more extended reconstruction of the Sproul Hall occupation, see *The Right Moment: Ronald Reagan's First Victory and the Decisive Turning Point in American Politics*, by Matthew Dallek, The Free Press, 2000, chapter 5.
6. The best account of this historic meeting, albeit from a pro-Chavez point of view, is in chapter 6 of *Cesar Chavez: Autobiography of La Causa*, by Jacques Levy, W. W. Norton, 1975.
7. The comment was made by Assembly Speaker Bob Moretti in "Reagan's Quixotic Reign, 1967–1974," *Los Angeles Times*, September 29, 1974. Moretti's negotiations with Reagan during his governorship are discussed extensively later in this book. See especially chapter 23.

Chapter 2: Optimist

1. *The Films of Ronald Reagan*, by Tony Thomas, Citadel Press, 1980, page 224. Reagan also told me on several occasions that he regretted making *The Killers*.
2. I was interviewing Reagan for *Ronnie and Jesse*, the first of my five books about him. He had repeated so many passages of his autobiography verbatim that I was becoming frustrated and told him so. Reagan cocked his head and said, "You want something new?" I nodded. Thereafter, in every interview over the next thirty years, he always gave me "something new," often a tidbit but occasionally a revelation.
3. Garry Wills said there were four doctors in Tampico when Ronald Reagan was born. See

Reagan's America: Innocents at Home, by Garry Wills, Doubleday, 1985, page 79.

4. Interview with Neil Reagan, October 1968, R&J, page 3.
5. Interview with Nancy Reagan, May 5, 1989.
6. Interview with Neil Reagan, October 1968, R&J, page 4.
7. *Where's the Rest of Me?* by Ronald Reagan and Richard C. Hubler, Dell, 1965, hereinafter WTROM, page 18.
8. WTROM, pages 12–13.
9. Ibid.
10. Interview with Neil Reagan, June 19, 1989.
11. WTROM, page 14.
12. *Reagan's America*, pages 16–17.
13. Ibid., page 21.
14. *An American Life*, by Ronald Reagan, Simon and Schuster, 1990, page 20.
15. Ibid., page 21.
16. The explosion killed ten persons, injured forty others, and led to one of the most celebrated legal cases in the annals of the American labor movement. In 1917, labor agitator Thomas J. Mooney was convicted of murder in connection with this bombing and sentenced to hang. His supporters said the evidence was rigged. After an investigation, Mooney's sentence was commuted to life imprisonment. Several years later, he was offered release from prison but asserted his complete innocence and declined to accept anything less than a full pardon. He was eventually pardoned on January 7, 1939, by Governor Culbert Olson, who said Mooney had been convicted on perjured testimony and was the innocent victim of a frame-up.

CHAPTER 3: LIFEGUARD

1. Reply to O. Dallas Baillio, director of the Public Library of Mobile, Alabama, 1977. Cited in "Young Reagan's Reading," by Jerry Griswold, *The New York Times Book Review*, August 30, 1981.
2. WTROM, page 23.
3. Interview with David S. Broder, June 12, 2002.
4. Interview with Dan Balz, March 1981.
5. Interview with George F. Will, June 12, 2002. Will also wrote about the impact of Illinois on Reagan for the 1981 Inaugural Program when Reagan was sworn in as the fortieth president of the United States. The reference to Reagan's "talent for happiness" in this paragraph is taken from Will's essay in the program.
6. The best list of Reagan's early reading is in *Ronald Reagan in Hollywood: Movies and Politics*, by Stephen Vaughn, Cambridge University Press, 1994, pages 5–6. Reagan mentioned all of these authors to me in one or another of my interviews with him, but he often forgot the names of the books, which was also true of books he read as an adult. *The White Company* is not included in Vaughn's list, but Reagan recounted the plot vividly to me in a 1968 conversation. I recognized the book he was describing since it was also one of my boyhood favorites.
7. Griswold, "Young Reagan's Reading," op. cit.
8. WTROM, page 22.
9. *Reagan's America*, page 30.
10. The exception to "most biographers" is Garry Wills, who in chapter 3 of *Reagan's America* extensively discusses Reagan's many responsibilities at Lowell Park.
11. Interview with Ronald Reagan, July 30, 1981.

CHAPTER 4: STORYTELLER

1. Reagan's arrival at Eureka is described in WTROM, pages 30–31 and 38–41; in *Early Reagan: The Rise to Power*, by Anne Edwards, William Morrow, 1987, pages 82–84; and in my

book, *Reagan*, G. P. Putnam's Sons, 1982, pages 34–35. The accounts are similar. McKinzie was reluctant to recommend Reagan for the scholarship because he had a low opinion of his high school credentials as a football player.

2. WTROM, page 33.
3. Ibid.
4. Ibid., pages 34–35.
5. Ibid., pages 36–37.
6. Ibid., page 38.
7. *Reagan's America*, pages 43–52.
8. Ibid., page 35.
9. Reagan's speech at Eureka, October 17, 1980.
10. Interview with Ronald Reagan, July 31, 1981. Reagan discussed his reaction to seeing *Journey's End* in WTROM, page 37.
11. Interview with Ronald Reagan, July 31, 1981.
12. "The Saga of Burky and Dutch," by Henry Allen, *The Washington Post*, March 7, 1981. I talked to Burghardt by phone soon afterward and also discussed this story with Mark Shields, who had interviewed Burghardt for an article in *Inside Sports*. Most of the quotes are from the Allen story.
13. Interview with Neil Reagan, 1968. Quoted in R&J, page 8, and in *Reagan*, page 39.
14. Ibid.
15. Quoted by Myron Waldman, "Ronald Reagan's America," *Newsday*, January 18, 1981.
16. *Ronald Reagan in Hollywood*, page 21. Vaughn mistakenly called him "Alexander" Gray.
17. *Reagan's America*, pages 60–61.
18. *Dixon Evening Telegraph*, February 28, 1981. Reagan also recounted this story on several occasions.
19. Interview with Ronald Reagan, 1968. Also recounted in WTROM, pages 55–57.
20. WTROM, page 58.

Chapter 5: Announcer

1. In WTROM, page 66, Reagan says his mother taught him that "the Lord's share was a tenth." As a result, said Reagan, "Moon got ten dollars a month," a tenth of Reagan's salary. When I asked Neil about this in 1968, he said he did not remember the amount but that his brother sent him money "regularly."
2. "Out of the Past, Fresh Choices for the Future," by Roger Rosenblatt, with Laurence I. Barrett, *Time*, January 5, 1981, pages 13–14.
3. WTROM, page 67.
4. WTROM, pages 68–69.
5. *Reagan's America*, page 100.
6. Ibid., page 62.
7. WTROM, page 55.
8. Interview with Neil Reagan, October 14, 1981.
9. Interview with Suzanne Hanney, November 19, 1981.
10. Interview with Myrtle Moon, by Robin Gradison, August 25, 1981.
11. Ibid.
12. *The Rise of Ronald Reagan*, by Bill Boyarsky, Random House, 1968, page 20.
13. *President Reagan: The Role of a Lifetime*, by Lou Cannon, Simon and Schuster, 1991. Second edition, revised and updated, published by PublicAffairs in 2000. This story is recounted on page 174 of the updated book.
14. Interview with Harold Rissler, by Robin Gradison, August 23, 1981.
15. "Growing Up in the Midwest," by Myron S. Waldman, *Newsday*, January 18, 1981.
16. Interview with Ronald Reagan, 1968. He discusses his experiences in the reserves on pages 79–82 in WTROM.
17. Waldman, "Growing Up in the Midwest."
18. These stories of Myrtle Moon's are from Gradison's interview of her, from Waldman's

"Growing Up in the Midwest," and from portions of Waldman's interview with Moon that were not published but which he graciously let me use.

19. *Early Reagan*, page 151.
20. WTROM, page 86.
21. WTROM, page 87.
22. *Early Reagan*, pages 156–157.
23. Interview with Ronald Reagan, 1968.

Chapter 6: Actor

1. *California: The Great Exception*, by Carey McWilliams, Peregrine Smith, 1976, page 25.
2. WTROM, page 93; *Early Reagan*, page 167.
3. Myron S. Waldman, "Growing Up in the Midwest" *Newsday*, January 18, 1981.
4. *Reagan's America*, page 179.
5. Interview with Pat O'Brien, June 29, 1981.
6. Interview with Ronald Reagan, 1968. Quoted in R&J, page 32.
7. Warner's letter is quoted extensively in *Reagan*, pages 66–67. It is in the Warner Brothers Archives Collection at the University of Southern California.
8. "Scorecard/Bob Lemon, 1920–2000," by Ron Fimrite, *Sports Illustrated*, January 24, 2000, page 32.
9. *Reagan's America*, page 178.
10. *The Reagan Wit*, edited by Bill Adler with Bill Adler Jr., Caroline House Publishers, 1981, page 30. Bill Roberts told me that Reagan used this line in speeches to Republican groups during this period in a characteristic attempt to defuse criticism, in this case about his inexperience in government, with self-deprecating humor.
11. Reagan often said this privately in the final years of his presidency. He said it publicly in a "farewell interview" with David Brinkley on ABC News, December 22, 1988.
12. Interview with Ronald Reagan, 1968.

Chapter 7: Family Man

1. *Early Reagan*, page 193.
2. Ibid., page 197.
3. *Reagan's America*, pages 144–145.
4. There is an enduring mystery about Sarah Jane's birth date. The accepted date is January 4, 1914. However, when her mother, Emma Fulks, enrolled her in first grade in St. Joseph, she gave Sarah Jane's birth date as January 28, 1917. Jane Wyman later said she was born in 1914, but as Anne Edwards observed in *Early Reagan*, page 188, "It is unlikely that a child would enter the first grade at age nine." On grounds that her mother was the most reliable guide, I have used the 1917 date in references to Wyman's age.
5. Quoted in *The Forties Gals*, by James Robert Parish and Don E. Stanke, Arlington House, 1980, page 374.
6. Ibid.
7. *Southern California: An Island on the Land*, by Carey McWilliams, Peregrine Smith, 1973, page 343.
8. "Making a Double Go of It," by Mary Jane Manners, *Silver Screen*, August 1941.
9. *The Films of Ronald Reagan*, page 138.
10. Quoted in *Ronald Reagan in Hollywood*, page 107, from *The New York Times*, February 9, 1942, page 1.
11. Ibid. There were approximately 700 movie industry employees on active duty.
12. "How to Make Yourself Important," by Ronald Reagan, *Photoplay*, August 1942.
13. Ibid.
14. Quoted by Vaughn, *Ronald Reagan in Hollywood*, page 113, from *My First Hundred Years in Hollywood*, by Jack L. Warner, with Dean Jennings, Random House, 1965.

15. Quoted by Vaughn, *Ronald Reagan in Hollywood*, page 104, from *Winged Warfare*, by H. H. Arnold and Ira C. Eaker, Funk and Wagnalls, 1943.

16. Interview with Ronald Reagan, 1968.

17. In his State of the Union Address to a joint session of Congress on February 6, 1985, defending his requests for an increase in military spending, Reagan said: "You know, we only have a military-industrial complex until a time of danger, and then it becomes the arsenal of democracy." Reagan did not credit FDR for the phrase "arsenal of democracy" in his speeches until 1988, when, while campaigning for the election of George Bush, he repeatedly identified Roosevelt as its author.

18. *Speaking My Mind*, by Ronald Reagan, Simon and Schuster, 1989, page 127. The book is a compilation of selected speeches; the comment was made by Reagan to Landon Parvin, a White House speechwriter who edited the book.

19. Reagan told this story on at least two occasions in the Oval Office: on November 29, 1983, in a meeting with Prime Minister Yitzhak Shamir of Israel, and on February 16, 1984, in a meeting with Nazi-hunter Simon Wiesenthal and Rabbi Marvin Hier of Los Angeles. For an account of these meetings, see *President Reagan: The Role of a Lifetime* (2000), pages 428–431, and also *Reagan's America*, pages 168–169.

20. For Reagan's account, see WTROM, pages 136–139. For the impact of the bombing of the Peenemunde site, see *A World at Arms: A Global History of World War II*, by Gerhard L. Weinberg, Cambridge University Press, 1994, page 465.

21. Reagan told me this in a conversation on the plane from Washington, D.C., to Los Angeles the day he left the presidency, January 20, 1989. Reagan told this story, possibly apocryphal, in WTROM, page 125: Two doctors examine his eyesight after he was called to active duty and one says, "If we sent you overseas, you'd shoot a general." The other doctor says, "Yes, and you'd miss him."

22. *Early Reagan*, page 279.

23. *First Father, First Daughter: A Memoir*, by Maureen Reagan, Little, Brown, 1989, page 44.

24. WTROM, page 223.

25. "Last Call for Happiness," by Louella O. Parsons, *Photoplay*, April 1948.

26. *Modern Screen*, February 1948. Reagan often used this line. He repeated it to me in a 1968 interview.

27. *People*, August 10, 1981.

28. Interview with Nancy Reagan, May 5, 1989.

29. *First Father*, page 70.

30. *They Call Me the Showbiz Priest*, by Robert Perrella, Trident Press, 1973, pages 130–131.

31. *People*, December 29, 1980.

32. Interview by Hugh Sidey for *Time* magazine, July 25, 1985.

33. *An American Life*, page 502.

34. Interview with Ronald Reagan, July 30, 1981.

35. *Reagan's America*, page 183.

36. *Early Reagan*, page 394.

37. R&J, page 41.

38. *My Turn: The Memoirs of Nancy Reagan*, by Nancy Reagan, with William Novak, Random House, 1989, page 97.

39. *Nancy*, by Nancy Reagan, with Bill Libby, William Morrow, 1980, page 125.

40. *I Love You, Ronnie: The Letters of Ronald Reagan to Nancy Reagan*, Random House, 2000, page 22.

41. Ibid., page 36.

42. Interview with Nancy Reagan, May 5, 1989.

43. "Interview: Ron Reagan," *fathers*, July–August 1986.

44. *First Father*, page 69.

45. *On the Outside Looking In*, by Michael Reagan, with Joe Hyams, Zebra Books, 1988, page 54.

46. Interview with Patti Davis, October 19, 1989.

47. "Interview: Ron Reagan," op. cit.

48. *On the Outside Looking In*, page 10.

49. Interview with Patti Davis, October 19, 1989.
50. Interview with Nancy Reagan, May 5, 1989.
51. *My Turn*, page 106.
52. Interview with Martin Anderson, April 4, 1989.
53. Quoted by Samuel Johnson in an April 17, 1778, letter: "As the Spanish proverb says, 'He, who would bring home the wealth of the Indies, must carry the wealth of the Indies with him,' so it is in traveling, a man must carry knowledge with him if he would bring home knowledge."

Chapter 8: Politician

1. *The Washington Post*, May 31, 1981.
2. Interview of Ronald Reagan by Dan Blackburn, NBC Radio, October 31, 1980.
3. Even the nomenclature of this committee was disputed. Opponents called it "HUAC," for House Un-American Activities Committee. Its supporters insisted on the formal name, the House Committee on Un-American Activities, which had the less euphonious abbreviation, "HCUA." I have used the first version, not as a political statement, but because it is the common journalistic shorthand for all committees, e.g. "House Labor Committee," which is also used in this chapter.
4. This is from a speech in the House of Representatives by Lincoln on January 11, 1837. It is quoted in *Lincoln's Virtues: An Ethical Biography*, by William Lee Miller, Alfred A. Knopf, 2002, page 103, as part of a discussion of Lincoln's view of politicians. Miller called this a "half-joshing comment."
5. Interview with Paul Laxalt, May 22, 1989.
6. WTROM, page 154.
7. *An American Life*, page 90.
8. WTROM, page 153.
9. Ibid., page 154.
10. Interview with Jack Dales, August 18, 2002.
11. Minutes of the board of directors of the Screen Actors Guild, March 10, 1947. After Montgomery, Tone, Powell, and Cagney resigned, John Garfield, Harpo Marx, and Dennis O'Keefe said they "were in approximately the same position" and also resigned from the board and left the meeting. In resigning, Montgomery and the other actors said their "primary interest will always be that of actors, they do not feel that they should hold office in the Guild while their present status in the industry continues, particularly in view of the fact that the Guild will soon be going into negotiations for its new contract."
12. *King's Pawn: The Memoirs of George H. Dunne, S.J.*, Loyola University Press, 1990, page 148.
13. Ibid.
14. *Hollywood Citizen News*, January 14, 1954.
15. Interview with Ronald Reagan, 1968.
16. WTROM, page 175.
17. *Los Angeles Examiner*, January 14, 1954. The lawsuit was a $200,000 action filed by Michael Jeffers against the Screen Actors Guild.
18. For Dunne's account, see *King's Pawn*, pages 147–166. For Wills' account, see *Reagan's America*, pages 224–240.
19. *King's Pawn*, page 156.
20. Freedom of Information Act records. Reagan was given a number, T–10. Wyman, who seems to have been less involved as an informant, was not given a number.
21. *Ronald Reagan in Hollywood*, page 94.
22. *Southern California: An Island on the Land*, page 335.
23. Interview with Neil Reagan, 1968, for R&J.
24. Interview with Ronald Reagan, 1974.
25. Interview with Neil Reagan, 1968.
26. WTROM, page 160.

27. Interview with Jack Dales, August 18, 2002.
28. WTROM, page 193.
29. Testimony before House Un-American Activities Committee, hereinafter HUAC, April 10, 1951.
30. For a detailed account of this incident, see *The Inquisition in Hollywood,* by Larry Ceplair and Steven Englund, Anchor Press, 1980, pages 225–239.
31. Interview with Ronald Reagan, July 31, 1981.
32. Testimony before HUAC, October 23, 1947.
33. *Time,* November 3, 1947.
34. Testimony before HUAC by Reagan, op. cit.
35. Ibid.
36. *Take Two,* by Philip Dunne, McGraw-Hill, 1980, page 206.
37. Testimony before HUAC, October 30, 1947.
38. *The Committee,* by Walter Goodman, Farrar, Straus and Giroux, New York, 1964, page 300. The official record of the Screen Actors Guild showed Reagan's view conveyed in a letter to Sondergaard by Jack Dales.
39. Interview with Ronald Reagan, July 31, 1981.

CHAPTER 9: COMPANY MAN

1. Reagan testimony to federal grand jury, February 5, 1962, page 55.
2. "Pragmatic Leadership: Ronald Reagan as President of the Screen Actors Guild," an interview of Jack Dales conducted by Mitch Tuchman on June 2, 1981 for the California Oral History Project, UCLA special collections, page 46. Dales also made this point to me in an interview on August 18, 2002.
3. Reagan testimony to grand jury, op. cit.
4. *Reagan's America,* page 265.
5. *Early Reagan,* page 440, but Edwards also says on 478, "Reagan testified for nearly two hours without a break and acquitted himself well."
6. Reagan testimony to grand jury, op. cit.
7. Interview with Peter Wallison, July 5, 1989.
8. Interview with Jack Dales, August 18, 2002. Dales told me he thought it would have taken "seven or eight years" before Hollywood became the production center for television.
9. WTROM, page 285.
10. *I Love You, Ronnie,* page 43.
11. Interview with Ronald Reagan, July 30, 1981.
12. Ibid.
13. Interview with Edward Langley, July 8, 1981.
14. Ibid.
15. *Reagan's America,* page 268.
16. Interview with Ronald Reagan, 1968. Quoted in R&J, page 68.
17. Interview with Ronald Reagan, July 30, 1981.
18. Ibid.
19. Ibid.
20. Ibid.
21. *I Love You, Ronnie,* page 63.
22. *Confessions of a Hollywood Columnist,* by Sheila Graham, William Morrow, 1969, pages 258–259. Graham was hostile to Reagan after he became an avowed conservative. The chapter on him in her book is entitled, "Ronald Reagan—Progress Is His Least Important Product."
23. *Early Reagan,* page 465.
24. WTROM, pages 313–314. Reagan said he was confident that Wasserman would agree with him that his film career had suffered because of his Guild activity, which would allow him to turn down the job with "a clear conscience." Instead, Wasserman told him he should take the job, and Reagan did.
25. Interview with Ronald Reagan, July 30, 1981.

26. Ibid.
27. *Reagan's America*, page 284.
28. After the publication of *Reagan's America*, Wassmansdorf wrote Wills a letter on September 21, 1987, relating his version of the events that led to the cancellation of General Electric Theater. Wills, with typical generosity, passed the letter on to me after telling Wassmansdorf that he was not planning to write additional books on Reagan but that I was. On January 30, 1988, I interviewed Wassmansdorf at his home in La Jolla, California. The information quoted here is from both the letter and the interview.
29. Ibid.
30. Ibid.
31. Interview with Ronald Reagan, July 30, 1981.
32. Wassmansdorf letter and interview, op. cit.

CHAPTER 10: VISIONARY

1. Interview with Michael Deaver, July 1, 2002.
2. See *President Reagan: The Role of a Lifetime* (2000), pages 110–112, and *Frames of Mind: The Theory of Multiple Intelligences*, by Howard Gardner, Basic Books, 1985. When I interviewed Gardner about Reagan on July 11, 1989, he said, "Reagan's good with language but not logically. He makes sense of the world narratively."
3. Interview with Annelise Anderson, April 6, 1989.
4. Interview with Martin Anderson, April 4, 1989.
5. Interview with William F. Buckley, May 16, 1989.
6. *In the Arena: A Memoir of the 20ᵗʰ Century*, by Caspar W. Weinberger, with Gretchen Roberts, Regnery Gateway, 2001, page 147.
7. "Ronald Reagan and the American Public Philosophy," a paper presented to the Conference on the Reagan Presidency at the University of California at Santa Barbara, May 27–30, 2002, by Hugh Heclo, Robinson Professor of Public Affairs, George Mason University, page 3.
8. Conversation with Frank Mankiewicz, January 1990. In *President Reagan: The Role of a Lifetime*, page 286 in the 1991 edition, page 246 of the 2000 edition, I quoted Mankiewicz as saying he believed Reagan would have run for Congress in 1952 if he had received the Democratic Party endorsement.
9. FDR campaign speech in Boston, November 4, 1944.
10. The North American accord was the only discernible new idea in a speech on November 11, 1979, in New York City in which Reagan formally announced his 1980 presidential candidacy. Domestic conservatives were cool to the proposal, which rankled nationalist sensibilities in Canada and Mexico and was largely dismissed by the media as a campaign gimmick. But Reagan was serious about the idea. He pursued and obtained a U.S.-Canadian free trade agreement and signed a "framework" agreement with Mexico that presaged the 1992 North American Free Trade Agreement.
11. Reagan often told this story in the latter years of his presidency, sometimes attributing the sentiments to a letter and sometimes not. The quotation cited here is from remarks to students at Moscow State University on May 31, 1988.
12. Reagan's remarks at Fudan University, Shanghai, April 30, 1984. The Chinese government deleted this passage from a televised speech Reagan made to the people of China three days earlier, breaking a promise that Reagan's speech would not be censored. Reagan then used the same words in a question-and-answer session with students at Fudan University. His comments were locally but not nationally televised.
13. Heclo, "Ronald Reagan and the American Public Philosophy," op. cit., pages 4–5.
14. Remarks at a Reagan-Bush rally in Cupertino, California, September 3, 1984.
15. Heclo, "Ronald Reagan and the American Public Philosophy," op. cit., page 6.
16. Reagan speech, "Business, Ballots, and Bullets," May 1959, quoted in *Actor, Ideologue, Politician: The Public Speeches of Ronald Reagan*, edited by Davis W. Houck and Amos Kiewe, Greenwood Press, 1993.

17. *A Necessary Evil: A History of American Distrust of Government,* by Garry Wills, Simon and Schuster, 1999, pages 297–298.
18. Interview with Stuart Spencer, June 7, 2002.
19. In some versions of this widely reproduced speech, Reagan said "$350 a month" instead of $330. I have used the latter figure because it is the correct addition.
20. Reagan speech, "Business, Ballots, and Bullets," op. cit.
21. See "The Real Computer Virus," by Carl Cannon, *American Journalism Review,* April 2001, and "Perot's Familiar Misquotations," by John J. Pitney Jr., *The Weekly Standard,* September 16, 1996.

CHAPTER 11: CANDIDATE

1. *The Making of the President: 1964,* by Theodore H. White, Atheneum, 1965, pages 405–407.
2. "The Republican Party and the Conservative Movement," *National Review,* December 1, 1964. The italics are Reagan's.
3. Interview with Holmes Tuttle, 1968.
4. This is the account of Stephen Shadegg in *What Happened to Goldwater? The Inside Story of the 1964 Republican Campaign,* Holt, Rinehart, and Winston, 1965, pages 252–253. When I interviewed Kitchel on November 2, 1981, he confirmed that he had objected to the Reagan speech but said that Baroody thought it was "fine."
5. Interview with Maureen Reagan, August 31, 1981. She had saved the letter and showed it to me—the italicized word was underlined by Ronald Reagan.
6. Ibid.
7. Interview with Holmes Tuttle, 1968.
8. Ibid.
9. Interview with Stuart Spencer, June 7, 2002.
10. Interview with Bill Roberts, 1968.
11. Ibid.
12. Interview with Stuart Spencer, June 7, 2002.
13. Ibid.
14. Interview with Bill Roberts, 1968.
15. Interview with Lyn Nofziger, April 19, 2002.
16. Interview with Stuart Spencer, June 7, 2002.
17. The editor was the late Art Stokes of the *San Jose News.*
18. Interview with Stuart Spencer, June 7, 2002.
19. *The Republican Establishment,* by David S. Broder and Stephen Hess, Harper and Row, 1967, page 274.
20. Interview with Stuart Spencer, June 7, 2002.
21. The description of the movie is from a Columbia Pictures release promoting the film.
22. Remarks to the National Conference of State Legislators, Washington, D.C., January 29, 1988.
23. The book is *The Last Jeffersonian: Ronald Reagan's Dreams of America,* by Steven Greffenius, TechWrite Publishing, 2002. The author contended that Reagan was the logical heir of Jefferson and his beliefs in limited government.
24. Bill Boyarsky, who reported on Reagan for the Associated Press and the *Los Angeles Times* and wrote the first book about his entry into politics, has often made this point in conversation, in this case on October 3, 2002.
25. "More Than Just an Actor: The Early Campaigns of Ronald Reagan," interview of Stanley Plog, 1981, by Stanley Stern, UCLA Oral History program, UCLA special collections.
26. Interview with Lyn Nofziger, April 19, 2002; "Reagan Walkout Laid to Ire at Christopher," by Carl Greenberg, *Los Angeles Times,* March 10, 1966.
27. *The Rise of Ronald Reagan,* page 151.
28. Interview with Harry Farrell, 1968.
29. Conversation with George Christopher, May 12, 2000.

CHAPTER 12: WINNER

1. Interview with Lyn Nofziger, April 19, 2002.
2. Interview with Edmund G. ("Pat") Brown, 1968.
3. Interview with Frederick Dutton, September 2, 1981.
4. R&J, page 116.
5. Ibid., page 117.
6. Roberts told me in 1968 that he and Spencer were concerned that slight variations in Reagan's answers would have produced numerous stories and over time created an opening for reporters to "corner" him on the Birch issue. Spencer had a similar recollection when I interviewed him on June 7, 2002. While Reagan did refer reporters who asked him about Birch Society support to his written statement, he continued to denounce Welch for his description of Eisenhower as a Communist.
7. Spencer was disappointed as well as shocked. He considered Rousselot an exceptional candidate with the potential to become a U.S. senator if he renounced his Birch ties. Spencer believed that Rousselot was motivated to remain a Bircher because of loyalty to friends who were JBS members. In 1970, with the Birch Society a much diminished issue, Rousselot was elected to the House from a Pasadena–San Marino district. He served six terms. In 1972, he was asked by White House aides to oppose Representative Paul ("Pete") McCloskey, a boyhood friend, who was challenging President Nixon for the Republican presidential nomination because Nixon had not withdrawn U.S. military forces from Vietnam. Rousselot, always loyal to friends, refused.
8. Reagan commented on Rousselot's "offer" to a meeting of the California Republican Assembly, a volunteer and conservative GOP group, in San Francisco on July 21, 1965. He joked that Rousselot had offered to publicly denounce him. In retrospect (June 7, 2002), Spencer believed that Reagan's relaxed view was justified and that the Birch Society was less potent as a force and a political issue than he and Roberts believed at the time.
9. Reagan and Wyman applied for membership in the Lakeside Country Club in North Hollywood near the Warner Brothers studio. They were accepted, but Jack Warner was rejected because he was Jewish. As soon as Reagan learned about Warner's rejection, he accused the club of anti-Semitism and resigned, as did Wyman. The best account of this incident is in *Early Reagan*, pages 203–204.
10. Letter from Reagan to John Rothman, August 24, 1966, provided to me by Rothman.
11. Transcript of *Meet the Press*, September 11, 1966, provided by Tim Russert.
12. Ibid.
13. Interview with Bill Roberts, 1968.
14. Interview with Frederick Dutton, September 2, 1981.

CHAPTER 13: ADVERSARY

1. The population of California was 19.2 million in July 1966 and 19.7 million in July 1967, according to estimates by the State Department of Finance. In other words, California added 500,000 new residents during the last six months of Pat Brown's administration and the first six months of Ronald Reagan's. This continued a trend of constant growth in California in the middle decades of the twentieth century. The state's population was 10,643,000 in the 1950 census; 15,863,000 in 1960, and 20,039,000 in 1970 at the end of Reagan's first term as governor.
2. Interview with Jesse Unruh, 1968.
3. Samish was a legendary lobbyist who, after the repeal of Prohibition, wrote a liquor-control law that was passed by the Legislature and became a source of corruption. He survived various investigations but over time became boastful and careless. The proximate cause of Samish's downfall was a magazine article, "The Secret Boss of California," written by investigative journalist Lester Velie, which appeared in *Collier's* in two installments, August 13 and August 20, 1949. In this article, Samish candidly described the greed of

various legislators and allowed his picture to be taken with a ventriloquist's dummy representing the Legislature. See also R&J, pages 50–51.

4. The Samish replacement was Daniel Creedon, who became one of the most successful lobbyists in Sacramento. Unlike Samish, he was consistently discreet.

5. "Money, Power, Politics," a series by Harry Farrell, *San Jose Mercury-News*, May 5–16, 1963. This was a trailblazing series describing how money was raised and distributed in Sacramento and exposing the Unruh-Ahmanson relationship. Unruh and Ahmanson were alarmed by the stories and persuaded Herman Ridder, publisher of the *Long Beach Press-Telegram*, to pressure his half-brother, Joseph B. Ridder, publisher of the *San Jose Mercury-News*, to tone down the conclusions of Farrell's series. It was a power play that reflected poorly on Unruh, Ahmanson, and the Ridders, but Farrell had already made his point.

6. Ibid.

7. R&J, pages 99–100. Finch and Unruh respected each other and, on many issues, had similar moderate views. They talked privately on at least two occasions of which I am aware during the early months of the Reagan administration in Sacramento.

8. A bowdlerized version of this quote appears in "This Is How Payola Works in Politics (by Assemblyman X as told to Lester Velie)," *Reader's Digest*, August 1960. Unruh was Assemblyman X.

9. Interview with Pat Brown, 1968.

10. The best account of Brown and the Chessman case is given in *Jerry Brown: The Philosopher Prince*, by Robert Pack, Stein and Day, 1968, pages 131–134. Pack erred in saying that the "most that Brown could do" was grant Chessman a temporary reprieve, but his account of Jerry Brown's role and his father's response to it is firsthand and accurate.

11. Unruh declared his support for the bill banning capital punishment that was introduced in the Assembly in 1959 by Assemblyman Lester McMillan, a perennial liberal foe of the death penalty. "I don't think they'll ever use the death penalty on me, but I'll give Les a vote," he told a friend. But Unruh did nothing to promote the bill, which died in committee.

12. For a more extended discussion of this meeting, see R&J, pages 121–122. I concluded then that Unruh and Brown remembered the meeting as they wanted to remember it, but I think now that the weight of the evidence favors Unruh. Brown was notorious for making promises that he failed to remember. Crown, in my view the most objective witness of the three, was no longer an Unruh ally when he told me his version of the meeting.

13. Unruh's family, staff, friends, and adversaries gave various estimates of his weight loss, and Unruh himself used different figures. He told me that he had weighed 280 pounds when he began his diet and "less than 200" pounds when it ended.

Chapter 14: Novice

1. In WTROM, page 283, Reagan said, "One of our good friends is Carroll Righter, who has a syndicated column on astrology. Every morning Nancy and I turn to see what he has to say about people of our respective birth signs." Reagan related this in the context of his reluctant acceptance of a 1954 Las Vegas nightclub booking, which his agents had advised him to take. His horoscope that day told him to "listen to the advice of experts."

2. R&J, page 77, and *The Rise of Ronald Reagan*, pages 108–110.

3. "Reaction Split on Address," by Lou Cannon, *San Jose Mercury*, January 6, 1967.

4. Rubel died in June 1967.

5. Interviews with Lyn Nofziger, 1968, and April 19, 2002.

6. Interview with Holmes Tuttle, 1968.

7. "Ex-Reagan Aide Shunned 'Bought For Lunch Bunch,'" by Lou Cannon, *San Jose Mercury*, April 21, 1967.

8. Interview with Tom Reed, April 14, 2002.

9. Cannon, "Ex-Reagan Aide Shunned 'Bought For Lunch Bunch,'" op. cit.; see also R&J, pages 135–137.

10. Interview with Tom Reed, April 14, 2002, and conversation with Reed, November 13, 2002.
11. Interview with Gordon Luce, August 13, 2002.
12. Interview with Caspar Weinberger, 1968. The gist of this conversation was confirmed in a 1968 letter to me from Champion, who said he briefed Weinberger, Battaglia, and Clark in a two-hour session during the transition. "I think it was at that meeting that for the first time they got any real view of the large fiscal questions facing the state," Champion wrote. Also see R&J, pages 134–135.
13. Interview with Alan Post, February 28, 2002.
14. *In the Arena*, page 151.
15. R&J, page 133.
16. Interview of Edwin W. Beach, August 16, 1984, by Gabrielle Morris, The Bancroft Library Oral History Office, University of California.
17. Interview with Verne Orr, February 9, 2002. Orr was invited by Holmes Tuttle to hear Reagan. He was impressed with the thrust of Reagan's speech but disagreed with his proposal for an across-the-board budget cut. As a protégé of Tuttle's, Orr became director of motor vehicles in the Reagan administration and subsequently the director of finance.
18. "Time too Short for Enactment, Burns Declares," by Jerry Gillam, *Los Angeles Times*, February 1, 1967.
19. "The Transition from Pat Brown to Ronald Reagan," a master's thesis by F. Alex Crowley of Princeton University, 1967.
20. Interview with Lyn Nofziger, 1968.

CHAPTER 15: PRAGMATIST

1. Cabinet minutes, June 16, 1967.
2. Cabinet minutes, February 23, 1967.
3. Ibid.
4. R&J, page 138.
5. Interview of Roy M. Bell, August 29, 1984, by Gabrielle Morris, The Bancroft Library Oral History Office, University of California.
6. "Reagan Aides Are at Odds on State Budget Reductions," by Tom Arden, *The Sacramento Bee*, March 2, 1967.
7. R&J, pages 145–146.
8. "Inside Agnews—A Sneak Peek," by Lou Cannon, *San Jose Mercury-News*, April 2, 1967. The senator who staged the drop-in visit, and is quoted here, was Alfred Alquist of San Jose.
9. Cabinet minutes, March 7, 1967.
10. "Mental Care Staff Cutbacks Stir Storm of Protests for Reagan," by Martin Smith, *The Sacramento Bee*, March 16, 1967.
11. "Reagan Denies Program Would Cut Care Quality," Associated Press story in *The Sacramento Bee*, March 16, 1967.
12. The lobbyist was Dan Trolio of the California State Employees Association, quoted in Crowley, "The Transition from Pat Brown to Ronald Reagan."
13. Cabinet minutes, March 14, 1967.
14. "Reagan's Cutbacks Are Dubious as Economies," editorial in *The Sacramento Bee*, March 8, 1967.
15. "Physicians Warn Staff Cuts Imperil Mental Hospitals," by Peter Weisser, *The Sacramento Bee*, March 28, 1967.
16. Cabinet minutes, March 15, 1967.
17. R&J, page 148.
18. Interview with Ronald Reagan, October 1968.
19. Interview with Bob Monagan, September 11, 2001.
20. Interview with Jack Lindsey, June 30, 2002. The reference is to a gift given by textile manufacturer Bernard Goldfine to Adams, a longtime friend. Adams was accused by a

House committee in 1958 of bringing pressure on federal regulatory agencies on Goldfine's behalf. He denied doing so. Although no impropriety was proved, and Eisenhower said that he needed Adams as his chief of staff, Adams resigned.

21. Ibid.

22. "Reagan Will Reveal Tax Plans Today," by Ray Zeman, *Los Angeles Times*, March 8, 1967.

23. Reagan often used this phrase, which was intended to show his determination to resist withholding. In the cabinet meeting of April 12, 1967, according to the cabinet minutes, Reagan related a discussion with Veneman, who warned him that the Assembly version of the tax bill would include withholding. Reagan told Veneman "that when the bill comes down here [to the governor's office] my feet will be in concrete."

24. Interview with George Deukmejian, July 27, 2002.

25. Ibid.

26. *California's Tax Machine: A History of Taxing and Spending in the Golden State*, by David R. Doerr, California Taxpayers' Association, 2000. Doerr, the chief tax consultant for the association, formerly worked for the Assembly and coauthored the study demonstrating the regressive nature of the property tax.

27. The senator who benefited from the trade for judges was Alfred Alquist, one of the legislators who had challenged Reagan on the budget cuts in the mental hospitals.

28. Interview with George Deukmejian, July 27, 2002.

29. *Here's the Rest of Him*, by Kent Steffgen, Foresight Books, 1968.

30. Interview with Ronald Reagan, October 1968.

31. The cabinet minutes of February 28, 1967, show that Reagan was advised to take this course of action by Bill Clark. Clark said Reagan's "house legal counsel," in which he included himself, Battaglia, Spencer Williams, and clemency secretary Edwin Meese, agreed that Lynch should "at least remain silent and file nothing" in the appeal. "That sounds fine," Reagan said.

32. Interview with William Bagley, June 18, 2002.

33. Ibid.

34. I twice heard Burns use this line in speeches to political groups. As he said "wave the American flag," he moved his hand in a circular motion above his head and twirled around.

35. "Senate Axes Rumford Act," by Lou Cannon, *San Jose Mercury*, April 14, 1967. Interview with William Bagley, June 18, 2002.

36. "Rumford Act Is Set Back By Committee," by Richard Rodda, *The Sacramento Bee*, August 5, 1967.

37. "State Senate Waters Down Housing," by Lou Cannon, *San Jose Mercury*, August 3, 1967.

38. The operation was announced at the time by Reagan's press office as a procedure to correct a bladder-stone constriction. This was true, but the surgery involved more than that. Lyn Nofziger provided a detailed description of Reagan's physical condition and the operation in *Nofziger*, Regnery Gateway, 1992, page 84.

39. This was Bagley's recollection in 2002. Bagley misremembered several details of various issues we discussed, although his recollection about the basic points was usually accurate. Several contemporary news stories, including one of mine, reported that the negotiators met at least once. But the "meeting," if it took place, was probably pro forma. Divisions between the conservative Senate members of the committee and the liberal Assembly members were so immense that no serious negotiation was possible, especially in the waning hours of a session when legislators were exhausted and focused on other legislation of more direct importance to their districts.

40. Interview with William Bagley, June 18, 2002.

41. "Governor Says He'd Veto Rumford Act Repeal Bill," by Lou Cannon, *San Jose Mercury*, April 3, 1968.

42. Cabinet minutes, April 4, 1968.

43. Reagan struggled to reconcile his beliefs that discrimination is morally wrong but that individuals nonetheless have a right to discriminate as long as government does not assist them. The cabinet minutes are sprinkled with statements reflecting one or the other of these views. At a cabinet meeting on February 9, 1968, Reagan objected to a draft pro-

posal by the California Real Estate Association that would have allowed discrimination in the sale of new subdivisions. "It bothers me—it seems to me that a man with a whole tract—it seems to me you are getting into the area of restrictive covenant. I would have no quarrel to have this [discrimination in housing sales] included as a violation of restrictive covenant. I want it more for the man with private property," Reagan said. The day before, at a staff meeting, Gordon Luce had put the political dimension of the issue succinctly: "[The] governor doesn't want to get out on a limb."

CHAPTER 16: CONSERVATIVE

1. "A Warning to the Viet Cong—Keep New Year's Truce or Else," by John Steinbeck, *Los Angeles Times*, January 1, 1967.
2. *The Age of Reagan: The Fall of the Old Liberal Order, 1964–1980*, by Steven F. Hayward, Forum, 2002, page 153.
3. *Our Country: The Shaping of America from Roosevelt to Reagan*, by Michael Barone, The Free Press, 1990, page 421.
4. *Life So Far: A Memoir*, by Betty Friedan, Simon and Schuster, 2000, pages 175–176.
5. "Gals for CHP? 'Why Not?' Asks One," *The Sacramento Bee*, March 16, 1967.
6. Interview with Anthony Beilenson, May 17, 2002.
7. *San Francisco Examiner*, by Jack S. McDowell, April 23, 1967.
8. R&J, page 181.
9. Interview with Ronald Reagan, 1968.
10. Moretti was observed by George Skelton of the *Los Angeles Times*.
11. Interview with Ronald Reagan, 1968.
12. General Report, State of California, Department of Health Services, Center for Health Statistics Abortion Report, 1967–1980.
13. Interview with Anthony Beilenson, May 17, 2002.
14. *Reagan, In His Own Hand: The Writings of Ronald Reagan That Reveal His Revolutionary Vision for America*, edited by Kiron K. Skinner, Annelise Anderson, and Martin Anderson, The Free Press, 2001, page 222.
15. Reagan speech to the National Sheriffs Association, Las Vegas, Nevada, June 19, 1967.
16. R&J, pages 177–178.
17. Interview with Nancy Reagan, 1968.
18. Meese told me he had presented this information to Reagan and that the governor agreed with him that Thomas should be spared. The language quoted here was used in a press release issued by Lyn Nofziger on June 29, 1967.
19. Conversation with Steve Merksamer, 2000.
20. Interview with Paul Haerle, July 12, 2002.
21. Interview with Paul Haerle, 1968. Quoted in R&J, pages 304–305.
22. Ibid.
23. Interview with Paul Haerle, July 12, 2002. Haerle's successor, the late Ned Hutchinson, made a similar observation to me in 1968 although I no longer have notes of that conversation.
24. R&J, page 305.
25. Ibid.
26. Republicans emerged from the 1968 elections with a two-vote majority in the Assembly, but one Republican seat was vacant because of a death and another by the departure of John Veneman for a post in the Nixon administration. Republican strategists believed they were likely to lose one of the special elections to fill these vacancies. Among the Democratic-held seats, Harvey Johnson's was believed to be the most vulnerable—but only if the popular Johnson was not a candidate. As it turned out, Republicans won special elections to fill both of the vacancies, holding onto the Veneman seat by 57 votes and preserving their 41–39 majority in the Assembly.
27. *Judging Judges: The Investigation of Rose Bird and the California Supreme Court*, by Preble Stolz, The Free Press, 1981, page 100.

28. Charles Cahan was convicted of bookmaking on the basis of evidence obtained by microphones secretly planted by the Los Angeles Police Department. The California Supreme Court, in a 1955 opinion written by Chief Justice Roger Traynor, overturned the conviction on a 4–3 decision, which held that the evidence violated the Fourth Amendment's protection against illegal searches, the so-called exclusionary rule. The ruling reversed a 1922 ruling exempting municipal peace officers in California from Fourth Amendment restrictions.

29. In all, the *Anderson* ruling overturned 106 death penalty convictions. Four of the condemned were not yet on Death Row. For a cogent summary of the decision, see "State Supreme Court Rules Death Penalty Unconstitutional in California," *California Journal*, February 1972, page 51.

30. Interview with Edwin Meese, April 4, 2002, and subsequent telephone conversations, December 14, 2002, and April 29, 2003. Meese is firm in his recollection that at the meeting with the governor Wright said he believed that capital punishment was an "appropriate" penalty. Meese does not remember who raised the issue. Reagan told me once that Wright had "volunteered" that he favored the death penalty. Bill Clark, then a Superior Court judge, said he was also told this soon after the meeting; he doesn't remember who told him. It is unlikely that Reagan would have raised the issue, for he made it a practice not to ask prospective judicial nominees of their opinions on specific issues. Wright told me in a telephone conversation, that he had no recollection of discussing the death penalty with Reagan. In *Ronald Reagan: His Life and Rise to the Presidency*, Random House, 1981, pages 181–184, author Bill Boyarsky reported that Wright told him he was not asked his views on the death penalty by Reagan, Meese, Appointments Secretary Ned Hutchinson, or Legal Affairs Secretary Herbert Ellingwood, who met with him in San Francisco to discuss his appointment before the meeting in the governor's office. Reagan, Wright, Meese, and Ellingwood were present at the latter meeting.

31. "6 to 1 Decision Affects 106 Facing Execution; Only McComb Dissents," by Dennis Campbell, *The Sacramento Bee*, February 18, 1972.

32. *Judging Judges*, page 82.

33. "Death Penalty Ban Assailed by Reagan; State to Appeal," by Ed Meagher, *Los Angeles Times*, February 19, 1972.

34. "Death Penalty and the Court," *San Francisco Examiner*, February 20, 1972.

CHAPTER 17: LEADER

1. Reagan often had given this answer of necessity during the early stages of his 1966 campaign. Lyn Nofziger encouraged Reagan to continue this practice after he was elected governor when he didn't know the answer to a question. Nofziger believed that it was more damaging for Reagan to give inaccurate statements than to acknowledge he didn't know the answers.

2. Interview with George Steffes, September 11, 2001.

3. "Charlie Rose Show," KXAS, Fort Worth, Texas, May 1, 1980.

4. Interview with George Steffes, September 11, 2001.

5. Ibid.

6. *Roosevelt: The Lion and the Fox*, by James MacGregor Burns, Harcourt, Brace, 1956, page 402.

7. "Reagan Steals Show in Capitol," by Tom Arden, *The Sacramento Bee*, August 6, 1967.

8. Ibid.

9. Jack Lindsey and George Steffes, in separate interviews, told me of occasions on major legislation where Reagan appealed directly to industry and business leaders over the heads of their Sacramento lobbyists.

10. *Reagan*, page 140.

11. Ibid.

12. Ibid.

13. "Reagan Outpoints Romney at Dinner," by Warren Weaver Jr., *The New York Times*, March 3, 1967. Weaver gave this example of a Romney joke that bombed with the audience: "I found out how the West was won: Blood, sweat, and avoiding press conferences."

14. "Reagan Steals Play in National Debut," by Leo Rennert, *The Sacramento Bee*, March 2, 1967.

15. "Reagan Says He Will Be Favorite Son Only," by James Wrightson, *The Sacramento Bee*, March 2, 1967.

16. Interview with Ronald Reagan, 1968. For more detail on Reagan and wine, see R&J, page 140.

17. "Ronald Reagan: The First Year," an unpublished compilation of recollections by Jack B. Lindsey, June 7, 2002.

18. Reporters were not allowed at the dinner. This passage is based on the account of Judson Clark, then an Assembly staff member and a personal friend, who was present at the dinner. The Reagan-Flournoy exchange was reported by *The Sacramento Bee*. ("Reagan, Flournoy Trade Harsh Words," March 17, 1967.) The story lacks the context of Reagan's reference to Cranston chasing him from airport to airport. As a result, the exchange with Flournoy comes out as "harsh words." Clark suspected that either the reporter or the source of the story, which has no byline, missed the point of the joke.

19. The last governor with children to live in the executive mansion was Earl Warren, who was appointed Chief Justice of the United States by President Eisenhower in 1953. The children of Warren's successors, Goodwin Knight and Pat Brown, were no longer living at home when their fathers became governor.

20. Nancy Reagan often told this story to reporters, including me. This version is from "What Is Nancy Reagan Really, Really Like?" by Eleanor Harris, *Look* magazine, October 31, 1967.

21. The Reagans paid $1,250 monthly in rent for the Sacramento house, according to contemporaneous accounts. Harris used the figure of $2,500, which would have been well above the going rate for Sacramento rentals in this area at the time. For more detail on the Reagan's move from the mansion, see R&J, page 139.

22. Interview with Paul Haerle, July 12, 2002.

23. Interview with Nancy Reagan, 1968.

24. Interview with Ronald Reagan, 1968.

25. The Reagans subscribed to the *Los Angles Times*, the *San Francisco Chronicle*, *The Wall Street Journal*, and the *Sacramento Union* in the mornings and the *Los Angeles Herald-Examiner*, the *Oakland Tribune*, and the *San Francisco Examiner* in the afternoons.

26. "Pretty Nancy," by Joan Didion and John Gregory Dunne, *The Saturday Evening Post*, June 1, 1968.

27. Interview with Nancy Skelton, August 11, 1981.

28. Ibid.

29. *My Turn: The Memoirs of Nancy Reagan*, page 37.

30. "Nancy Reagan: A Model First Lady," by Lynn Lilliston, *Los Angeles Times*, December 13, 1968.

31. Harris, "What Is Nancy Reagan Really, Really Like?" op. cit.

32. Ibid.

33. R&J, pages 158–159.

34. Interview with Ronald Reagan, 1968.

35. Interview with Lou Papan, May 22, 2002.

CHAPTER 18: SURVIVOR

1. *The Pacific States of America*, page 180.

2. Interview with Norman Livermore, March 1, 2002.

3. Interview with William Clark, January 8, 2003.

4. Ibid.

5. Interview of Edgar Gillenwaters, February 13, 1983, by Sarah Sharp, for the State Gov-

ernment History Documentation Project, Bancroft Library, University of California, page 12.

6. Interviews of Leland L. Nichols, November 12, 14, 19 and December 3, 1991, by Donald B. Seney, California State University, Sacramento, for the California State Archives, State Government Oral History Program, page 340.

7. Ibid.

8. *Nofziger,* page 74.

9. Interview with Tom Reed, January 9, 2002.

10. Interview with William Clark, January 8, 2003.

11. Interview with Tom Reed, April 14, 2002.

12. Interview with Tom Reed, January 9, 2002.

13. *Nofziger,* page 77.

14. Interview with William Clark, January 8, 2003.

15. Interview with Tom Reed, January 9, 2002.

16. *The Making of the President: 1964,* page 388.

17. *Counsel to the President: A Memoir,* Clark Clifford, with Richard Holbrooke, Random House, 1991, pages 399–402.

18. Interview with Tom Reed, January 9, 2002. Reagan's remark, "My God, has government failed?" appears, without attribution, in R&J, page 183. According to this account, Reagan then said that the action he needed to take was obvious. The problem with this account is that none of those present—and I talked to eight of those who were, in addition to Reagan—recalled his precise words, although all of them said it was clear he was shocked by the report. Based on subsequent knowledge of the way Reagan communicated in crises, I think it likely that he indicated acceptance of the report to the coup plotters more by his demeanor and body language than by anything he said.

19. Interview with Paul Haerle, July 12, 2002.

20. Interview with Tom Reed, January 9, 2002.

21. Interview with Paul Haerle, July 12, 2002; *Nofziger,* page 78. Reed and three other members of the group also told me that they drank liberally at the airport.

22. Tuttle declined to discuss the incident in detail. But he told me that he had spoken "plainly" to Battaglia, who acknowledged nothing.

23. "Friends Say Battaglia Always Meant to Serve Only for Year," by Carl Greenberg, *Los Angeles Times,* August 29, 1967.

24. "Governor Warns Ex Top Aide," by Lou Cannon, *San Jose Mercury,* October 16, 1967.

25. *Nofziger,* pages 79–80.

26. Ibid.

27. Ibid., pages 80–81.

28. R&J, page 186. When another aide talked to Reagan about family members of one of the deposed aides, the governor snapped, "You don't have to give me a lecture. I'm well aware of it." Reagan was under stress. He was sensitive to the plight of Battaglia and also realized that the story could harm his own reputation for truthfulness. His aides, for the most part, shared both concerns. My files contain an undated handwritten memo of advice from the politically savvy Gordon Luce that begins, "Governor should never admit any knowledge of Phil's 'personal problems.'"

29. "Reagan Did Demand Resignations," by Jack S. McDowell, *San Francisco Examiner,* November 1, 1967. Also see, "Inside Story of Scandal Fuss," by Lou Cannon, *San Jose Mercury-News,* November 12, 1967.

30. "Pearson's Office Defends Report," an Associated Press story in *The Sacramento Bee,* November 1, 1967. These comments, which, according to the story, were issued by "Pearson's office," were widely printed in many papers.

31. Interview with Ronald Reagan, 1968.

32. Interview with Stuart Spencer, June 7, 2002.

33. *Nofziger,* page 78.

34. George Price cartoon in *The New Yorker,* April 8, 1944, page 19.

35. R&J, page 184.

36. "Turn Back the Tide of Bigness," by Lou Cannon, *San Jose Mercury,* August 29, 1967.

37. "Lawyer Revamps Reagan's Regime," by Gladwin Hill, *The New York Times*, September 10, 1967.
38. "State Finance Chief Quits," by Lou Cannon, *San Jose Mercury*, February 2, 1968. The story briefly recounts the controversy over the Medi-Cal cuts and Unruh's offer to bet that Smith would be fired.
39. Cabinet minutes, February 1, 1968.

Chapter 19: Noncandidate

1. *The Making of the President: 1968*, by Theodore H. White, Atheneum, 1969, pages 66–70.
2. Ibid., pages 40–41.
3. Interview with Lyn Nofziger, April 19, 2002.
4. The date of the dinner is from Tom Reed's diary. Rusher, without mentioning a date, also told me that he had recommended White to the Reagan campaign.
5. Interview with Stuart Spencer, June 7, 2002.
6. Interview with Tom Reed, January 8, 2003.
7. "Reagan Turns Back Prairie Fire," by David S. Broder, *The Washington Post*, January 14, 1968. Nofziger had often predicted that Reagan would "light a prairie fire" across the country. In response, Democrat Hale Champion derisively called Reagan the "pyromaniac of the prairies." See R&J, page 265.
8. This became Reagan's standard response when he was asked if he would rule out becoming a candidate. He sometimes attributed this comment to Dwight Eisenhower.
9. "Where's the Rest of Ronald Reagan?" by Jules Witcover and Richard M. Cohen, *Esquire*, March 1976. Kennedy was at a disadvantage because the students, except for Rhodes scholar and future U.S. senator Bill Bradley, were hostile to the United States and sympathetic to North Vietnam. In *The Age of Reagan*, page 168, Steven Hayward said the tone of the questions "was so insulting that CBS edited out 30 minutes of the taped program."
10. R&J, page 267.
11. Ibid., page 268.
12. *The Making of the President: 1968*, page 213.
13. These meetings, as far as I have been able to determine, were not transcribed. Rus Walton briefed me on them afterward and arranged meetings for me with some of the participants under a ground rule that I would not identify them or quote them directly.
14. McClellan bought a small paint company in Los Angeles in 1927 and turned it into a profitable business before selling it in 1962. After the 1965 Watts riot, he worked with the Los Angeles Chamber of Commerce and the Pat Brown administration to increase employment in the riot-torn area. Partly because of Reagan's support, his efforts intensified in the late 1960s. In *The Rise of Ronald Reagan*, pages 207–209, Bill Boyarsky discussed McClellan's efforts and quoted writer Budd Schulberg as questioning his claim to have provided 18,000 new jobs.
15. *Our Country*, page 435.
16. Reagan showed me the letter after Richard Nixon had been nominated for president.
17. R&J, page 272.
18. Interview with Ronald Reagan, July 1968.
19. Ibid.
20. "Reagan Likes Wallace Views," by Lou Cannon, *San Jose Mercury*, July 17, 1968.
21. *The Making of the President: 1968*, page 280.
22. Nofziger and Reagan recounted this story to me in separate 1968 interviews. In *Nofziger*, pages 73–74, Nofziger said it was "dumb of me to take Knowland to Reagan without bringing in White or Reed or any of the others." According to Nofziger, Holmes Tuttle was angry with Reagan for becoming a declared candidate and told him so. Reagan, not wanting to alienate Tuttle, let him have his say.
23. Interview with Ronald Reagan, October 1968. Harold Stassen, the onetime "boy wonder" governor of Minnesota, ran nine times for president of the United States.
24. Interview with Nancy Reagan, November 1968.

25. Interview with Ronald Reagan, October 1968.
26. Interview with Tom Reed, October 1968.
27. Interview with Robert Finch, 1968.
28. This was a post-convention syndicated column by Buckley. Quoted in R&J, pages 275–276.
29. Ibid.
30. Interview with Ronald Reagan, October 1968.
31. Ibid.
32. Interview with Tom Reed, January 8, 2003.

CHAPTER 20: REGENT

1. Interview of H. R. Haldeman, June 18 and 25, 1981, by Dale E. Treleven, for the UCLA California State Archives State Government Oral History Program, pages 226–230.
2. Salvatori told me about the message from the "Nixon people" in 1976, five years before Haldeman's interview. He didn't mention anyone by name. At the time I discounted Salvatori's statement because he was then highly critical of Reagan for challenging President Gerald Ford for the Republican presidential nomination. (Salvatori backed Ford.) It seems likely, however, that Salvatori was referring to Haldeman's communication.
3. *Time*, October 6, 1947.
4. *The Pacific States of America*, page 67.
5. R&J, page 232.
6. Haldeman oral history, op. cit., pages 242–243.
7. R&J, page 232.
8. *The Gold and the Blue: A Personal Memoir of the University of California, 1949–1967*, vol. 2, *Political Turmoil*, by Clark Kerr, with the assistance of Marian L. Gade and Maureen Kawaoka, University of California Press, 2003, pages 294–295. Kerr said that Chandler praised him as an "outstanding president" and that he "greatly appreciated her candor and consideration."
9. Interview with Ronald Reagan, October 1968.
10. "Veil of Confusion over Dismissal of Kerr Lifts," by Peter Weisser, *The Sacramento Bee*, January 22, 1967. Weisser quoted Kerr as saying: "I have never asked for a vote of confidence, and I didn't yesterday. I would have been stupid to call for a vote of confidence with that board." In *The Gold and the Blue*, page 301, Kerr said the issue was whether he would "take the easy route out for the governor and the regents and resign" or accept dismissal. He said he opted for a vote on dismissal. "The Board of Regents had an obligation and an opportunity to justify its constitutional independence by not instantly and abjectly following the orders of a new governor who had vilified the university in his political campaign, and by not acting with a narrow majority vote of 14–8 when the last 4 votes came from new regents totally unfamiliar with the university and with my presidency."
11. Interview with Ronald Reagan, 1968. Kerr's supporters also realized that it would be more difficult to fire him later if the board expressed confidence in him at the first regents' meeting of the Reagan governorship. William Roth, who backed Kerr, made a motion during the meeting to postpone any decision on Kerr until July. It was defeated.
12. *Nofziger*, page 64.
13. Haldeman oral history, op. cit., page 240. "The way to look at it . . . is that a number of regents set out to sack Kerr and took advantage of the Reagan-Finch votes to change the balance," Haldeman said. "As it turns out, they didn't need them." Haldeman was wrong on the latter point. The eight pro-Kerr regents were solid, and Kerr, even if he had been allowed to do so, would not have voted to oust himself. The anti-Kerr forces would not have reached the required minimum of thirteen votes without Reagan, Finch, and Grant.
14. "Dismissal Angers Students at UC; Leftists Rejoice," *The Sacramento Bee*, January 21, 1967. Savio subsequently apologized in a letter to the UC student newspaper, *The Daily Californian*, for referring to Kerr as "rubbish."
15. "Governor Shelves UC Probe," United Press International story in *San Jose Mercury*, Jan-

uary 27, 1967. Reagan said he was postponing the investigation indefinitely "because it would be unfair to ask a new university president to take office in the midst of such an inquiry." He never raised the issue again. A few hours after Reagan's announcement, a joint Senate-Assembly committee shelved an Unruh proposal for a legislative investigation of the university. An Unruh ally on the committee made a motion to conduct the inquiry, but it died for lack of a second.

16. Champion speech cited in R&J, pages 237–238.

17. "UC Students Take Gripes to Reagan," *The Sacramento Bee*, February 9, 1967. The students assembled at UC Davis, west of Sacramento, where they changed clothes for the march. Annabelle Morgan, an eighteen-year-old sophomore from UCSB, said to a photographer: "Don't take our picture in capris. We're going to wear suits and dresses at the parade. It just presents a better image."

18. Interview with William Clark, December 27, 2001.

19. Interview with Jesse Unruh, September 1968.

20. "The Transition from Pat Brown to Ronald Reagan," a master's thesis by F. Alex Crowley of Princeton University, 1967.

21. This account is based on my conversations with seven regents: Reagan, Unruh, Chandler, Haldeman, Pauley, Roth, and Dutton.

22. Interview with Ronald Reagan, October 1968.

23. In 1985, when President Reagan launched his series of meetings with Soviet leader Mikhail Gorbachev, he reminisced about negotiating with movie producers when he was president of the Screen Actors Guild. I asked Reagan what he had learned from this experience. "That the purpose of a negotiation is to get an agreement," he replied.

24. *Our Country*, page 437.

25. *Nofziger*, page 64.

26. "People and Politics: Spencer Williams Off to Washington," by Harry Farrell, *San Jose Mercury-News*, January 2, 1969.

27. Reagan used variants on this line. Sometimes the "hippie" was a "picket" and sometimes he "looked like Tarzan." In a Milwaukee speech on September 30, 1967, Reagan said "this fellow . . . had a haircut like Tarzan. He walked like Jane and smelled like Cheetah." According to Kurt Ritter, professor of speech communication at Texas A&M University, the line did not appear in any Reagan speech text. This was typical of Reagan, who wrote a word or two of shorthand on his speech cards to remind him of an anecdote.

28. Interview with Ronald Reagan, October 1968.

29. Cabinet minutes, December 12, 1967. Reagan added: "I was sitting in Dwight Dining Hall [and] thought it was a gag at first, but there they were—blue jeans, beads, bells, the works. I thought, 'Whatever happened to Frank Merriwell?'" Merriwell is a fictional Yale sports hero.

30. Interview with Ronald Reagan, October 1968.

31. R&J, page 253.

32. Cited in R&J, pages 253–254. The *Sacramento Union* is defunct.

33. Reagan's press secretary, Paul Beck, showed me a copy of the Huntley letter.

34. Interview with Paul Beck, October 1968. Quoted in R&J, page 257.

35. Reagan speech to the Commonwealth Club in San Francisco, July 13, 1969.

36. "The Student Revolution Breaks New Ground—Bank Burned," by Leroy F. Aarons, *The Washington Post*, May 3, 1970. This story is a thorough and balanced examination of why the students at Isla Vista acted as they did.

37. "Violence, Arson, Hit UC Santa Barbara for 2nd Night," by Doug Shuit and William Drummond, *Los Angeles Times*, February 26, 1970.

38. "'Silent Majority' of Students Urged to Act," Associated Press story in the *Santa Barbara News-Press*, April 21, 1970.

39. "The Isla Vista War: Campus Violence in a Class by Itself," by Winthrop Griffith, *The New York Times Magazine*, August 30, 1970, described police activity in Isla Vista as a lawless rampage. Two stories giving a more mixed picture of police conduct were written by Tim O'Brien of the *Santa Barbara News-Press*. They are "Supervisors Ask Governor to Send Guard into I.V.," June 11, 1970, and "I.V. Again Peaceful; Curfew Off," June 12, 1970.

40. *The Pacific States of America*, page 187.

41. The plaque was donated by an admirer of Reagan's, according to the governor and Paul Beck, but a search of letters and gift records initiated by Beck at my request failed to turn up the name of the donor.

42. Interview with Paul Beck, October 1968.

43. "Governor and Academia Never Came to Terms," by William Trombley, *Los Angeles Times*, September 29, 1974. Trombley also said that UC maintenance and library cataloging had suffered because of the "budget cuts," a reference to reductions from university requests since the budget had risen significantly.

44. "Reagan on Reagan Plus Some Other Views," *Los Angeles Times*, September 29, 1974. Hitch acknowledged that UC maintenance and libraries had declined under Reagan but added, "I don't think it's going to be a matter of serious, lasting damage."

45. *Reagan*, page 154.

Chapter 21: Conservationist

1. Early in his governorship, Reagan tended to use the word "environmentalist" in a pejorative context and "conservationist" in positive connotations. This distinction largely vanished after the environmental movement became more prominent in 1970.

2. "It Takes a Lot of Energy to Keep Up with Interior's Jim Watt," by Bill Hosokawa, *Denver Post*, March 1, 1981.

3. *Ronald Reagan: His Life and Rise to the Presidency*, page 169.

4. The Sierra Club contracted with the regional oral history office of the Bancroft Library to interview Sierra Club leaders and other environmental activists of the 1960s and 1970s. These interviews became part of the Government History Documentation Project of the Ronald Reagan gubernatorial era and are stored at the Bancroft Library in Berkeley. The 285-page Livermore oral history is especially useful. "Man in the Middle: High Sierra Packer, Timberman, Conservationist, and California Resources Secretary," conducted by Ann Lage and Gabrielle Morris for the Sierra Club History Series of the Bancroft Library, University of California. Livermore covered much of the same ground in my interviews with him for *Ronnie and Jesse* and *Reagan*, an interview for this book on March 2, 2002, and in subsequent telephone conversations and correspondence.

5. Shultz succeeded Al Haig as Reagan's secretary of state on June 25, 1982. As recounted in *President Reagan: The Role of a Lifetime*, Shultz on at least three occasions hinted at resignation because of differences with administration policies. This tactic rarely worked with Reagan, who was usually quick to accept resignations, as he had done with Haig. But Shultz had more leeway, for he knew that Reagan didn't want a third secretary of state. Livermore had leeway, too, because Reagan knew he was an effective buffer against criticism from environmental groups.

6. This quotation, in fuller form, was cited in Chapter 14. It is from a speech Reagan gave to the Western Wood Products Association in San Francisco on March 12, 1966.

7. Cabinet minutes, February 20, 1967.

8. Cabinet minutes, March 7, 1967. When Bill Clark announced at this meeting that there would be a discussion of the redwoods, Reagan quipped, "Haven't we cut them all down yet?"

9. Cabinet minutes, March 29, 1967.

10. For Livermore's comment, see "Reagan, Aide Like Park Plan Proviso," *The Sacramento Bee*, September 11, 1968. Also see "Conservationists Laud Redwoods Bill," *The Sacramento Bee*, September 10, 1968.

11. Jacobs said that Burton opposed the 1968 bill creating Redwood National Park (page 333). Burton voted against the House version of the bill. But he supported the conference report creating the park that was patterned after the Senate version of the measure.

12. *I Love You, Ronnie*, page 45.

13. Cabinet minutes, January 26, 1968.

14. "After fourteen years in the movies, Ronald Reagan finally got to make a real western,"

wrote Tony Thomas in *The Films of Ronald Reagan*, page 183. *The Last Outpost* was released in 1951. Reagan had ridden a horse in *Santa Fe Trail* (1940), in which he was cast as a cavalry officer, but neither he nor Thomas considered this a "real western."

15. Interview with Ronald Reagan, October 1968. Garry Wills pointed out in *Reagan's America*, page 269, that the sale was not made until December 13, 1966, and suggested that Reagan misremembered the sequence of events, as he often did. I'm convinced on the basis of my reporting that Reagan had decided before the election to sell the ranch, for whatever reason. By waiting until after he was elected to consummate the deal, Reagan avoided any possibility that questions about his profits from the sale would become a campaign issue.

16. At William Penn Mott's direction, the State Parks and Recreation Department was at the time aggressively buying land in the Santa Monica Mountains, a large and picturesque open space in the midst of a congested metropolitan area. Since the state paid only $1,800 per acre for land that 20th Century-Fox had bought from Reagan for $8,000 an acre, it raised a question of whether the original transaction between Reagan and the studio was a disguised contribution. State officials said the land they purchased from 20th Century-Fox included extensive mountain acreage of less value than the Reagan acreage. After conducting my own review of comparable sales in the area at the time Reagan sold his land, I concluded that he did get a "good deal," but not one that was outlandishly out of line with prevailing market values. The land that Fox bought from Reagan was strategically located in relation to the property the studio already owned, which may have made it more valuable to the studio.

17. *Reagan*, page 354.

18. Reagan letter to Jane Ashman, September 14, 1966.

19. Cited by Steven Hayward, *The Age of Reagan*, page 249.

20. "Losing the Water Battle," by Frank Stead, *Cry California*, Summer 1968.

21. "What Price Environment?" a speech by Livermore to the Commonwealth Club, San Francisco, May 22, 1970.

22. *The River Stops Here: How One Man's Battle to Save His Valley Changed the Fate of California*, by Ted Simon, Random House, 1994, page 296. Simon said Livermore made contemporaneous handwritten notes of the conversation. Livermore confirmed this in my interview with him on March 2, 2002.

23. Ibid.

24. *The River Stops Here*, page 314.

25. Interview with William Clark, 1969.

26. "Environmental Lobby Suffers Second Year of Defeat for Its Major Proposals," *California Journal*, November 1971, page 298.

27. "Reagan OKs Tough Bill on Rivers," by Richard Rodda, *The Sacramento Bee*, December 21, 1972.

28. "Managing the State Park System, 1967–74," an interview of William Penn Mott conducted by Ann Lage in 1984 for the State Government History Documentation Project, Bancroft Library, University of California, pages 3–4.

29. Ibid., page 9.

30. Ibid., page 32.

31. "The Man Who Saved the Sierra," by George Skelton, *Los Angeles Times*, July 28, 1997.

32. Conversation with George Skelton, February 21, 2003.

33. "Project Halted: Nixon Stops Sierra Meadow Road Plans," by Wilson K. Lythgoe, *The Sacramento Bee*, June 29, 1972.

34. A copy of the letter is in Ronald Reagan's Governor's papers: Governor's office files, box 150, Business and Transportation, at the Ronald Reagan Presidential Library, Simi Valley, California.

35. Skelton, "The Man Who Saved the Sierra," op. cit.

36. When some oil company executives complained that Watt wanted to open too much land for drilling, he said, "Boys, do you want to compete or don't you?" Interview of Watt by editors and reporters of *The Washington Post*, May 29, 1981.

37. *The River Stops Here*, page 354.

38. Financial disclosure rules would have required Hansen to have his family ranch at Jackson Hole, Wyoming, appraised at its "highest and best use," which would have resulted in an increase in his property taxes. He also owned grazing leases in Grand Teton National Park in the names of his wife and daughter that had been "grandfathered" in when the park was expanded to include this land. Hansen was concerned that the leases would constitute a conflict of interest if he became the secretary of the interior. There was, however, never any question about Hansen's honesty. Watt was indicted on twenty-five felony counts for contacting political appointees at the Department of Housing and Urban Development after he left the Reagan administration. He pleaded guilty to a single misdemeanor and was fined $5,000.

39. *President Reagan: The Role of a Lifetime* (2000), pages 256–258.

40. Interview of Doug Scott by Tom Kizzia, July 16, 1981, for *Reagan*.

CHAPTER 22: INCUMBENT

1. Beck was hired by Lyn Nofziger, who respected his hard-edged political coverage for the *Los Angeles Times* during the 1966 campaign. But the skepticism that served Beck well as a reporter did not help him in the press office. Many reporters, including me, found him suspicious and reluctant to provide information. This incident marked a turning point in our professional relationship. From then on, Beck was consistently helpful.

2. *California's Tax Machine*, page 90.

3. Kuchel may have lost the primary because of inattention to constituents at home. He at first took Rafferty so lightly that he ignored many of the rural counties in northern California that he had visited in previous campaigns. Kuchel carried all but one of the counties in which he made an appearance and lost most of those he did not visit. He lost by only 69,632 votes out of 2,223,782 votes cast in the Republican primary.

4. *Nofziger*, page 89.

5. Interview with Tom Reed, April 14, 2002.

6. Interview with George Steffes, September 10, 2001.

7. Meese did, however, emphasize particular issues in which he was interested. This was often a help to Reagan. Ike Livermore, the resources director, and William Penn Mott, the state parks director, considered Meese an ally on most environmental issues.

8. Way made the allegations on the basis of stories written by Robert Fairbanks in the *Los Angeles Times*. They disclosed that Burns, an insurance lobbyist, and another associate had divided a $500,000 profit from the legislation.

9. "Schrade Beats Way to Take Top Senate Post," by Richard Rodda, *The Sacramento Bee*, February 10, 1970.

10. Interview with George Steffes, September 10, 2001.

11. "Governor Saves Tot," by Lou Cannon, *San Jose Mercury*, June 17, 1969.

12. Interview with Verne Orr, February 9, 2002.

13. Ibid.; also interview with George Steffes, September 10, 2001. I talked to four people who attended this meeting: Orr, Steffes, Kirk West, and Ed Meese. Their accounts differed only in minor details.

14. Interview with George Steffes, September 10, 2001.

15. Ibid.

16. Interview with Edwin Meese, April 4, 2002.

17. Meese and Bagley told me about the calls to Carrell's wife and physician. "Senate Defeats Governor's Tax Program," on page 222 of the August 1970 *California Journal*, provides a detailed recap of the maneuvering that led to defeat of the tax bill.

18. John Van de Kamp, who was helping Unruh organize his campaign, told me (on March 25, 2003) that he and Unruh were at the time far more concerned about Alioto than they were about Yorty, since it was obvious that Yorty could not win the Democratic nomination. Tom Reed (on March 28, 2003) told me that Alioto was also considered by the Reagan camp to be a potentially formidable opponent. Alioto ran for governor in 1974 but lost to Jerry Brown in the Democratic primary.

19. "Reagan Starts Campaign Trail in Riverside, San Bernardino," by Martin Smith, *The Sacramento Bee*, March 11, 1970.
20. Interview with Stuart Spencer, June 7, 2002. Roberts also told me about his difficulties with the Reagan staff on several occasions.
21. Interview with Tom Reed, March 28, 2003.
22. Interview with Stuart Spencer, June 7, 2002.
23. This account is based on the above-cited interviews with Spencer and Reed and on a chapter in an unpublished narrative of the campaign that Reed made available to me for this book. In the chapter, Reed asserted that Roberts was not meeting his contractual commitment to the campaign but also acknowledged that his "micro-managing" may have bothered Roberts.
24. Interview with Stuart Spencer, June 7, 2002.
25. This paragraph draws upon an account in *Our Country*, page 476.
26. Interview with Tom Reed, March 28, 2003.
27. Ibid.
28. "Reagan-Unruh-Yorty Battle Royal," *California Journal*, April 1970, page 110.
29. Interview with Tom Reed, March 28, 2003.
30. Interview with John Van de Kamp, March 25, 2003.
31. "Unruh, Salvatori Meet in Angry Confrontation," by Richard Bergholz, *Los Angeles Times*, September 8, 1970, and "Unruh Visits Reagan backer to Open Governorship Drive," by Leroy F. Aarons, *The Washington Post*, September 8, 1970. My account is based on these stories and an extended conversation with Katharine Macdonald, who in 1970 was a young aide on the Unruh campaign staff. She subsequently worked as a news aide in the Los Angeles bureau of *The Washington Post* when I was bureau chief there and later as a reporter for the *San Francisco Examiner*.
32. Interview with Phil Schott, March 26, 2003.
33. Ibid.
34. Quoted in *Reagan*, page 174.
35. "Both Unruh, Reagan Glad of Slug Out," by Lou Cannon, *Pasadena Star-News*, November 2, 1970.
36. Interview with Tom Reed, March 28, 2003. Spencer also confirmed the essentials of this account.
37. Cannon, "Both Unruh, Reagan Glad of Slug Out," op. cit. Slightly different versions of this story appeared in other Ridder publications in California, the *San Jose Mercury* and the *Independent Press-Telegram* in Long Beach.
38. "Barrage of Bottles and Eggs Greets President After Rally," by William Endicott and Stuart H. Loory, *Los Angeles Times*, October 30, 1970.
39. *Before the Fall*, by William Safire, Doubleday, 1975. See also the account in *Nixon: The Triumph of a Politician, 1969–1972*, by Stephen Ambrose, Simon and Schuster, 1989, pages 394–396.
40. Endicott and Loory, "Barrage of Bottles," op. cit. "S.J. Police Poised, Praised," by Jim Larimore, in the *San Jose Mercury*, October 30, said, "An egg fell near the President, splattering the trousers of a Secret Service man."
41. "Stand and Be Counted," By Lou Cannon, *San Jose Mercury*, October 30, 1970.
42. This comment appeared in a press pool report. Reagan was notably more composed than either Murphy or Nixon in television appearances after the incident. A Reagan aide explained this by saying that the governor was accustomed to demonstrations because of his experience with campus disorders. Reagan described the incident dramatically in a speech to a Republican fund-raising dinner in Los Angeles on October 30. Reagan said he was sure that if the demonstrators "could have encountered one lone unarmed human being, they would have torn him to pieces." See "Murphy, Reagan Hit Mob," by Bob Houser, *Independent Press-Telegram*, October 31, 1970.
43. Twenty percent is a conservative estimate. A postelection DMI poll found that Reagan had won 26 percent of the Democratic vote. This estimate was based on a small sample with an error margin of 7 percent. In his final preelection poll published the weekend before the election, Mervin Field found that Reagan was winning 25 percent of the Demo-

cratic vote. But Field's poll projected Reagan winning by 12 percent; his margin of victory was 7.8 percent. How well Reagan did among Democrats cannot be determined precisely. However, since Republicans constituted only 40 percent of registered voters, it is clear that he received a significant percentage of Democratic votes.

44. Interview with Wilson Riles, September 25, 1981.

45. Murphy had been paid $20,000 a year as a consultant to Technicolor since 1965. He maintained there was nothing wrong with these payments but severed his relationship with Technicolor after Tunney made it an issue. Murphy could never explain why he had stopped accepting the payments if they were proper and on several occasions became angry when reporters pressed him on this point.

46. "Highlights of Post-Election DMI Statewide California Survey," a private report to Reagan and his top aides prepared by Tom Reed on the basis of Richard Wirthlin's polling a week after the campaign. Reed supplied me with a copy of the report. The polling found that Reagan received 43 percent of the vote from union families, that is, families with at least one person who belonged to a labor union. The poll's most remarkable finding was that not a single voter cited Unruh's record as a reason for voting for him. Reed believes that some credit for Unruh's defeat should go to Bob Monagan, who waged a campaign devoted to the proposition that Unruh's reign as Assembly speaker had been harmful to California. However effective this may have been against Unruh, it had no impact on key legislative races, which were won by Democrats.

CHAPTER 23: REFORMER

1. Edwin Meese papers at Hoover Institution on War, Revolution and Peace, Stanford University. Hereinafter, Meese papers.

2. Ibid.

3. Republicans controlled the Assembly in 1957. The Senate, while under nominal Democratic control, was predominantly rural and conservative. Republican Goodwin Knight was the governor.

4. "Governor's Welfare Proposals Scored by Democratic Leaders," by Robert Fairbanks, *Los Angeles Times*, March 4, 1971.

5. *The Age of Reagan*, page 237.

6. "The Advocates," PBS Television, December 1, 1970, page 11 of transcript.

7. Conversation with Marie Moretti, April 7, 2003.

8. Interview of Bob Moretti, February 2, 1983, by Sherry Bebitch Jeffe, for Oral History of the Modern Speakership of the California State Assembly, Institute of Politics and Government, University of Southern California, pages 10–11. Moretti told Larry Margolis, the chief of staff, that if he could break his word, he could also go back on a written pledge. "Either you trust me and believe me or you don't," Moretti said.

9. *Dictionnaire Philosophique*, Dramatic Art.

10. Interview with Bill Hauck, August 5, 1981.

11. Meese papers, op. cit.

12. Interview with George Steffes, September 10, 2001. I also discussed this with Steffes in 1981 and again in a conversation on March 27, 2003.

13. Interview with Bill Hauck, August 5, 1981.

14. Interview with Bob Moretti, August 5, 1981.

15. Interview with George Steffes, September 10, 2001.

16. Interview with Bob Moretti, August 5, 1981.

17. Conversation with Edwin Meese, April 2, 2003.

18. Interview with Ronald Reagan, September 1974. In the oral history interview with Jeffe on February 22, 1983, page 3, Moretti made a similar point about Reagan. Moretti said that Governor Pat Brown had "a very bad habit of breaking his word—or, let's put it this way: He was always convinced by the last person with whom he spoke. In that regard, Reagan was a much stronger governor; if he gave his word, he kept it."

19. Interview with Bob Moretti, August 5, 1981.

20. Interview with Anthony Beilenson, May 17, 2002.
21. Ibid.
22. Interview with Bob Moretti, August 5, 1981.
23. Conversation with George Steffes, March 27, 2003; interview with Anthony Beilenson, May 17, 2002. Also, in an interview with Steven Edgington in 1982 for the Oral History Program of the Ronald Reagan Era at the University of California at Los Angeles, Beilenson said that Carleson was "one of the most offensive people I've met in my life" (page 54).
24. Interview with Bob Moretti, August 5, 1981.
25. Meese papers, op. cit.
26. "California Population, 1971," a report by the State Department of Finance, May 1972, from the *California Journal* archives, California State Library, Sacramento.
27. "What Ronald Reagan Can Teach the U.S. About Welfare Reform," by Frank Levy, The Urban Institute, 1977.
28. "No-Tax Story Jolts Capitol," by Richard Rodda, *The Sacramento Bee*, May 7, 1971. The lead of the story read: "The Ronald Reagan tax-free episode is going down in California history for its political impact along with the Nixon fund of 1952, the Knowland-Knight switcheroo of 1958 and the Max Rafferty cane incident of 1968." The "cane incident" is a reference to an allegation that Rafferty, who had a medical deferment from the draft, threw away his cane the day World War II ended.
29. "Demos Feel Reagan's Example Proves Need," *The Sacramento Bee*, May 5, 1971.
30. "Governor Terms Tax Tip 'Illegal,'" *The Sacramento Bee*, May 5, 1971.
31. When William French Smith was attorney general, he lived at the Jefferson Hotel in Washington, D.C., diagonally across the street from *The Washington Post*. We occasionally had a drink at the hotel bar. Smith was friendly but usually cautious and circumspect. Once, after two drinks, I asked him if Reagan had ever become angry with him. Rarely, he said, and went on to tell me about Reagan's reaction when he had advised the governor that he didn't need to pay taxes if he didn't owe them. "You don't get it, Bill," he said in a passable imitation of Reagan. Smith's point was that Reagan was being smart politically and that he (Smith) was being dense. But Smith never forgot the conversation and saw to it that Reagan paid state income taxes during all his subsequent years in office.
32. "School Finance Ruling Evokes Wide Reaction," by Richard Rodda, *The Sacramento Bee*, August 31, 1971. According to Rodda, "The court noted property tax bases supporting local schools range throughout the state from $103 per child to $952,156—a ratio of nearly 10,000 to 1."
33. "The 1971 Tax Law Eases State's Fiscal Crisis, Postpones Major Tax Restructuring," *California Journal*, December 1971, page 339.
34. To dramatize the situation, Assemblyman Bagley at one point introduced legislation that would have required putting Moretti's picture on the IOUs, known as registered warrants, that the state would have to issue if it did not balance the budget. *California's Tax Machine*, page 106.
35. "Governor Reagan Submits Fiscal Plan for 72–73," *California Journal*, January 1972, page 4.
36. *California Journal* analysis of Proposition 14, October 1972, page 307. The legislator was Assemblyman Bagley.
37. Senate Bill 90 was a minor bill authored by Senator Ralph Dills that was transformed when the entire Reagan-Moretti tax package was amended into it. The legislation continued to bear Dills' name, but the governor, legislators, and the media usually referred to it as "SB 90."
38. "Legislators, Governor Hail 11th Hour Victory for Property Tax Relief–School Finance Bill," *California Journal*, December 1972, page 368. Reagan was an inveterate reader of popular history and picked up phrases that he used in his speeches, usually without recalling the source. His remark here is reminiscent of a famous phrase by President Woodrow Wilson, who on March 4, 1917, denounced the "little group of willful men" who had led a successful Senate filibuster against the arming of U.S. merchant ships. Wilson later applied the same phrase to these determined isolationists when they opposed U.S. entry into the League of Nations.

39. Marks said he voted for the bill because it offered "meaningful renter relief" and an additional $5 million in special financing for San Francisco schools. "Senate Tax Vote Is Decisive," *San Francisco Chronicle*, December 2, 1972. The money for San Francisco schools was one of the last concessions that Reagan made to win approval of the measure.

40. Interview with David Roberti, April 6, 2003.

41. The Democratic senators who joined Roberti in voting for the bill were James Mills and Walter Stiern. See "Senate Ranks Break, Tax Revision Passes," by Richard Rodda, *The Sacramento Bee*, December 1, 1972.

42. Reagan and Moretti thought Senate Bill 90 had resolved *Serrano*. But in 1974, a Superior Court judge in Los Angeles ruled that the legislation had not cured the inequities in school financing caused by the variations in the local property tax. Subsequently, the U.S. Supreme Court took up the issue in a Texas case and found that reliance on the property tax was constitutional. But the California Supreme Court, in 1977, affirmed the Los Angeles judge's ruling, saying that school financing based on variable property taxes violated the state constitution. So California was stuck with *Serrano* even though the nation was not. In 1977, the Legislature and Governor Jerry Brown provided $4 billion over five years to equalize school financing. Before this formula could be tested in the courts, voters in 1978 passed the Proposition 13 initiative, which equalized local property taxes at 1 percent of assessed value and effectively laid *Serrano* to rest.

43. Interview with Bob Moretti, August 5, 1981.

44. Ibid.

CHAPTER 24: SALESMAN

1. *Ronald Reagan: His Life and Rise to the Presidency*, page 161.

2. In his book *With Reagan: The Inside Story*, Regnery Gateway, 1992, page 36, Meese identified Uhler as leader of the task force that "came up with a proposal for holding state taxes and expenditure increases to corresponding increases in the economy." For a more extensive look at Uhler, see Boyarsky's *Ronald Reagan: His Life and Rise to the Presidency*, pages 160–163.

3. "The Surplus: Where It Came from and What Can Be Done with It," *California Journal*, February 1973, page 47.

4. Conversation with Mervin Field, April 10, 2003.

5. *Ronald Reagan's Call to Action*, by Charles D. Hobbs, Thomas Nelson, 1976, page 184. This quotation originally was part of an article "How Reagan Governs California," in the January 17, 1975, issue of *National Review*. Hobbs served as an assistant to Uhler on the Tax Reduction Task Force.

6. Interview with Edwin Meese, April, 4, 2002. On page 108 of *Ronald Reagan: His Life and Rise to the Presidency*, Boyarsky quoted Meese as saying that Reagan "originated a lot of ideas himself" but that he couldn't recall any specific ideas.

7. Interview with Verne Orr, April 13, 2003.

8. Ibid.

9. Interview with Michael Deaver, July 1, 2002.

10. Spencer and Roberts, in separate conversations, told me years ago that they were convinced that Meese and others in the Reagan administration were undermining them. This comment is from a conversation with Spencer on April 6, 2003. Meese's comment is from a conversation on April 28, 2003.

11. Interview with Bob Moretti, August 5, 1981.

12. "Measure shifts burden to local taxpayers," by Alan Post, *California Journal*, special section on Proposition 1, September 1973, page 4. Post's remarks were excerpted from a paper he presented on the measure at UCLA.

13. Interview with Wilson Riles, September 25, 1981.

14. "Blank-check state spending must be halted," by Ronald Reagan, *California Journal*, special section on Proposition 1, September 1973, pages 2–3. The article, prepared for the

magazine by Reagan, closely followed the text of his many speeches in behalf of the measure.

15. Post, "Measure shifts burden," op. cit.
16. The professor was Neil H. Jacoby of the UCLA Graduate School of Management. His comments appeared on page 7 of the *California Journal* special section on Proposition 1, op. cit. Reagan considered such arguments demagogic attempts to confuse the voters. Both the governor and Moretti knew from experience that state spending was unlikely to decline.
17. "Public Opinion Fluid in Closing Days of Campaign, Survey Shows Trend Running Against the Measure," survey by Mervin D. Field, completed November 1, 1973. Provided by the Field Research Corporation, San Francisco.
18. "Voters Reject Proposition 1; Reagan's First Major Defeat," by Tom Goff, *Los Angeles Times*, November 4, 1973.
19. "An Offer Californians Did Refuse," by Bruce Keppel, *California Journal*, December 1973, page 403.
20. Interview with Michael Deaver, July 1, 2002.

CHAPTER 25: ACHIEVER

1. "Reflections on the Failure of Proposition #1," by Ronald Reagan, *National Review*, December 7, 1973, page 1370.
2. Interview with Michael Deaver, July 1, 2002. "I was devastated," Deaver said. His "two failures for Reagan," he said, were the loss of Proposition 1 and his advance work in scheduling a trip for President Reagan in 1985 to a cemetery in Bitburg, Germany, where members of the SS are buried. The latter incident is described in the "Turning Point" chapter in *President Reagan: The Role of a Lifetime*.
3. "An Offer Californians Did Refuse," by Bruce Keppel, *California Journal*, December 1973, page 402.
4. "Lenny Bruce on Thin Ice," by George F. Will, *National Review*, December 7, 1973, page 1345.
5. *Paradise Lost: California's Experience, America's Future*, by Peter Schrag, The New Press, 1998, page 132.
6. Reagan took himself out of the Senate race in the spring of 1973. This early decision was meant to help Republicans develop an effective candidate against Cranston, but it didn't work out that way. H. L. Richardson, a member of the John Birch Society, won the GOP primary and was routed by Cranston in the general election.
7. Reagan's comment is quoted in *Reagan*, page 191, without mention of Tuttle. Reagan was president at the time; Tuttle said he wished to remain anonymous as long as Reagan was in the White House.
8. "State Unit to Evaluate Appointment of Clark," *Sacramento Union*, February 18, 1973.
9. "Clark Confirmed to High Court Despite Wright's Objection," by Philip Hager, *Los Angeles Times*, March 4, 1973.
10. Reagan was able to block the bill, which had been authored by Assemblyman (and Democratic State Chairman) John Burton, because of the California constitutional provision requiring a two-thirds vote for bills with a fiscal impact. The Democrats fell two votes short of the twenty-seven needed for passage in the State Senate. The comment about "bad staff advice" was made by Deaver to George Skelton of the *Los Angeles Times* and quoted in the February 5, 1974, story "Reagan Setbacks: Is Political Grip Failing?" For a concise overview of the controversy, see "Welfare showdown: Reagan over a barrel," by Bruce Keppel, in *California Journal*, January 1974, page 4.
11. Skelton, "Reagan Setbacks," op. cit.
12. My evaluation, "The Reagan Years," was the cover story in the November 1974 *California Journal*.
13. United Press International dispatch, May 1, 1973.
14. Reagan press conference transcript, August 27, 1974.

15. Conversation with Robert Teeter, May 1973. Quoted in *Reagan*, page 188.
16. "Legacy for State: Footprints, but No Permanent Monuments or Scars," by Tom Goff, *Los Angeles Times*, September 29, 1974.
17. Conversation with Judson Clark, 1981. Quoted in *Reagan*, page 185. Clark, the chief executive officer of a Sacramento-based legislative information company, was formerly an aide to speakers Jesse Unruh and Bob Monagan.
18. Interview with Wilson Riles, September 25, 1981.
19. "Reagan Will Be a Hard Act to Follow," an analysis by Sydney Kossen, political editor, *San Francisco Sunday Examiner & Chronicle*, December 22, 1974.
20. "The Reagan Years," editorial in *The Sacramento Bee*, December 8, 1974.
21. Field's poll found that 35 percent of voters rated Reagan's performance as good or excellent and that 24 percent gave him a poor mark. Thirty-six percent rated his performance as fair. Surveys measuring the approval ratings of public officials other than the president were relatively infrequent in this era. Field measured Pat Brown's approval ratings only four times during his eight years as governor and Reagan's ratings only five times in the eight successive years.

CHAPTER 26: CHALLENGER

1. *A Time to Heal: The Autobiography of Gerald R. Ford*, Harper and Row, 1979, page 161. On pages 157–181, Ford gives an extensive discussion of his reasons for granting the pardon and the negotiations leading up to it.
2. "GOP Image Fares Badly in New Poll," by Lou Cannon, *The Washington Post*, January 26, 1975.
3. My account of this meeting is based on conversations in 1981 with Deaver, Lake, Tuttle, and Jenkins.
4. *Marathon: The Pursuit of the Presidency, 1972–1976*, by Jules Witcover, The Viking Press, 1977, page 67.
5. Interview with Lyn Nofziger, April 19, 2002.
6. "Reagan Checks His Options for '76 White House Drive," by Larry Stammer, *San Jose Mercury-News*, December 16, 1973.
7. "Reagan Future: Which Office to Aim For?", by Richard Bergholz, *Los Angeles Times*, August 13, 1974.
8. In a conversation on May 22, 2003, Luce told me he could not recall if he had discussed the telegram with Reagan but said he would not have sent it unless he believed the governor approved.
9. *A Time to Heal*, pages 142–145. Ford said he started with a sixteen-person list. Bryce Harlow, who advised Ford and many other presidents, reduced the list to five. In addition to Rockefeller, the short list included George H.W. Bush, then the Republican Party national chairman, plus Rogers Morton, House minority leader John Rhodes, and Tennessee Senator Bill Brock. Ford did not provide the names of others on the longer list.
10. Reagan press conference, August 27, 1974.
11. Interview with Ronald Reagan, October 1974.
12. *A Time to Heal*, pages 294–295.
13. Interview with Ronald Reagan, October 1974.
14. Ibid.
15. Interview with Michael Deaver, July 1, 2002.
16. Memo from Tom Reed, April 11, 2003.
17. *Marathon*, page 373.
18. Interview with Peter Hannaford, October 14, 1981.
19. Interview with Martin Anderson, April 4, 1989.
20. Interview with Stuart Spencer, November 18, 1980.
21. Interview with Peter Hannaford, October 14, 1981.
22. Reagan's remarks were made at a news conference in Charlotte, North Carolina, on November 21, 1975. His comment to me was in an airplane interview the next day.

23. "Those Other Pearl Harbor Heroes . . . Tell Me," *Honolulu Advertiser*, December 6, 1998.
24. Interview with James Lake, October 12, 1981.
25. Ibid., October 13, 1981.
26. Wirthlin told me about these surveys in a series of interviews in May 1980.
27. Ibid.

Chapter 27: Contender

1. Jules Witcover, then a colleague at *The Washington Post*, called Spencer from New Hampshire to discuss the impact of the Nixon trip. "He was livid," Witcover wrote in *Marathon*, page 395. "If we lose, it will be because of Nixon," he quoted Spencer as saying.
2. Wirthlin's projection in the last of his four polls put Ford ahead 50.7 to 49.3 percent. The official tally from New Hampshire gave Ford 54,824 votes and Reagan 53,507. The actual result may have been even closer. New Hampshire law allowed delegates who were not on a candidate's official slate to run as pledged to him. Three such delegates pledged to Reagan were on the ballot and refused to withdraw. Ballots in which voters chose a mix of official Reagan delegates and nonofficial delegates were invalidated. Governor Thomson, and subsequently Reagan, believed enough such ballots were cast to cost Reagan the election. State election officials disputed this claim. It cannot be proved one way or the other because the invalidated ballots were destroyed without a count being made of them.
3. I witnessed this scene. The campaign worker seemed uncomfortable with Deaver's order but did as he was told.
4. Interview with Paul Laxalt, 1976.
5. "Reagan Virtually Concedes Defeat in North Carolina," by James M. Naughton, *The New York Times*, March 22, 1976.
6. Nofziger behaved professionally and continued to return my telephone calls. Many other members of the Reagan team did not. Sears would not talk to me until Reagan renewed his quest for the presidency in 1979 and I was again assigned to the campaign by my editors at *The Washington Post*. In our first conversation, Sears acknowledged matter-of-factly that he had helped try to freeze me out after the July 19, 1976, story, which he said "hurt us very much." Reagan never mentioned the story to me at any time. My most vivid memory of this period is of Ben Bradlee, the executive editor of *The Post*, coming up to me in the newsroom, putting his arm around my shoulder, and loudly praising my story in view of editors and other reporters. Then, lowering his voice so I alone could hear, he warned me to "be careful" because the Reagan team would try to discredit me. This was typical of Bradlee, who backed up his reporters and showed concern for our well-being. When I later told him that I was missing some stories because Sears and Deaver weren't getting back to me, Bradlee waved me off, saying, "That's their problem."
7. Ruckelshaus subsequently told me he thought that Sears was offering him a spot on the ticket. Witcover, in *Marathon*, page 457, quoted Sears as denying that he made Ruckelshaus a firm offer or considered anyone other than Schweiker.
8. This was Reagan's account to me in a 1977 interview. In *Marathon*, page 461, Witcover presented a slightly different version of the conversation, making the same point and quoting Reagan's reply to Schweiker as "And I'm no knee-jerk extremist."
9. Interview with Michael Deaver, October 13, 1981.
10. Interview with Stuart Spencer, June 7, 2002.
11. *A Time to Heal*, page 398.
12. Interview with Ronald Reagan, 1977.
13. In his speech, Reagan told about being asked to write a letter for a time capsule that would be opened in Los Angeles in a hundred years. He said he thought about what he would say as he rode down the Pacific Coast in an automobile and that his thoughts turned to the prospects of nuclear destruction. "And suddenly it dawned on me," Reagan said. "Those who would read this letter a hundred years from now will know whether those missiles were fired. They will know whether we met our challenge." This was the story President Reagan tried to tell in the closing remarks of his debate with Democratic nomi-

nee Walter F. Mondale on October 21, 1984, also in Kansas City. He never finished it on this occasion because his remarks ran over the allotted time and he was cut off by the moderator.

14. Both Reagan and Ford subsequently told me that Reagan responded approvingly at the mention of Dole, whom Ford chose as his running mate.

15. Interview with Richard Wirthlin, May 1980.

16. Carter led Ford by a 62–29 percentage margin in a Gallup Poll after the Democratic convention in mid-July. This was, said Michael Barone in *Our Country*, page 552, a lead that was "far larger, quite possibly, than the lead Franklin Roosevelt would have held over Herbert Hoover had polls been conducted in 1932."

17. I was interviewing Ford for his obituary, which I was preparing for *The Washington Post*. Before the interview, we chatted about the Reagan challenge. Without displaying rancor against Reagan, Ford said his challenge had cost him the presidency.

18. *A Time to Heal*, page 333.

19. Interview with James Lake, October 13, 1981.

20. *Our Country*, page 555.

21. Interview with Michael Deaver, October 13, 1981.

22. Interview with Peter Hannaford, October 14, 1981.

23. Interview with Stuart Spencer, June 7, 2002.

24. Conversation with Michael Barone, May 28, 2003. His data show almost a dead heat between Ford and Carter among white voters in the South, which in Barone's definition includes West Virginia and Kentucky (carried by Carter) and Oklahoma (carried by Ford), as well as the eleven states of the former Confederacy. Carter won most southern states decisively because of his huge margin among African Americans. Carter also did well among a category that was new to most pollsters: evangelical Christians. In Barone's view, Reagan would not have done as well among these voters against Carter as he did in 1980 after the Internal Revenue Service had questioned tax exemptions for a number of Christian schools on grounds they practiced segregationist admissions policies.

25. *Our Country*, page 558.

Chapter 28: Heir Apparent

1. Reagan's weekly radio commentaries were produced by Harry O'Connor. He began taping them on January 23, 1975, at O'Connor's recording studios in Hollywood, recording fifteen commentaries at a time. They were discontinued on November 20 when he declared his presidential candidacy and resumed on September 1. Reagan continued the commentaries (and the columns) until November 13, 1979, when he again announced he was seeking the presidency. As president, Reagan gave weekly Saturday radio speeches, many of which he wrote himself.

2. Reagan's assets were held in trust throughout his governorship. The trustees were William French Smith, Justin Dart, and Wilson, who during the Reagan presidency became Reagan's personal emissary and later U.S. ambassador to the Vatican. Reagan spent all or part of 345 days at Rancho del Cielo during his presidency, using the ranch both as a vacation retreat and as a place to host dignitaries such as Mikhail Gorbachev and Queen Elizabeth. In 1998, when Reagan was no longer able to use the ranch because of Alzheimer's disease, it was sold for $4.5 million to Young America's Foundation, a conservative outreach group that has maintained and improved the ranch house and other buildings on the property.

3. "Reagan: More Serious Than Ever," by Marquis Childs, *The Washington Post*, May 16, 1978.

4. "Reaganites Quietly Build for Future," by Richard Bergholz, *Los Angeles Times*, April 9, 1977.

5. Interview with Robert Teeter, October 14, 1981.

6. Interview with Stuart Spencer, June 7, 2002.

7. Interview with Michael Deaver, July 21, 1981.

8. Interview with Robert Teeter, October 14, 1981.
9. "Intimates Doubt Ford Will Run," by David S. Broder, *The Washington Post*, September 29, 1978.
10. *Our Country*, page 571.
11. "'Sears Factor' Is Troubling Conservatives," by M. Stanton Evans, *Human Events*, October 27, 1979.
12. Interview with Paul Laxalt, May 27, 1980.
13. Interview with James Lake, October 12, 1981.
14. Ibid.
15. Interview with Nancy Reynolds, July 14, 1981.
16. The account of this meeting is based upon interviews with Ronald Reagan, Nancy Reagan, Deaver, Black, and Lake.

CHAPTER 29: DEBATER

1. "Reagan's Latest Campaign Brings Same Message, but New Audience," by Martin Smith, *The Sacramento Bee*, November 18, 1979.
2. "Reagan Declares He's Not Moving Toward Center," by Richard Bergholz, *Los Angeles Times*, September 30, 1979.
3. "Reagan Displays Vitality but Bobbles a Few on Opening Tour," by Lou Cannon, *The Washington Post*, November 19, 1979.
4. Ibid.
5. "Reagan Woos Northeast, the Key to His Nomination Strategy," by Lou Cannon, *The Washington Post*, January 20, 1980.
6. Interview with Richard Wirthlin, May 1980.
7. Interview with Paul Laxalt, May 27, 1980.
8. Ibid.
9. This was a frequent quip of Nofziger's, who had not yet rejoined the Reagan staff after the Iowa caucuses. It is jotted down in my notes from an undated conversation, probably in February 1980.
10. Italian Americans would doubtless have been more offended had they known of a joke that Reagan had been telling off-the-record since his days as governor of California: A man who was prejudiced against Italians walked down a street with a friend, encountered an Italian organ-grinder with a monkey, and put five dollars in the monkey's hat. His friend was astounded. "You've been telling me for years how much you hated Italians, and here you do that," he said. The prejudiced man replied, "They're so cute when they're little."
11. I was having lunch that day in a shopping mall with John Anderson and an aide plus two or three reporters from Illinois newspapers and some youthful Anderson supporters. Anderson was scheduled to speak in Concord that night. During lunch, he left to take a telephone call from Sears urging him to come to Nashua that evening. When he returned, Anderson, with typical openness, told everyone what Sears had said and asked our opinion on what he should do. The aide reminded him of the Concord engagement. The reporters said they were going to the debate. Anderson observed that Sears wouldn't have called him unless it was important. "I think I'll go to Nashua and have a look," he said.
12. "Reagan: The Iowa Loss Allowed Him to Campaign His Way," by Lou Cannon, *The Washington Post*, June 11, 1980.
13. This account of the telephone exchange between Nancy Reagan and Clark and the subsequent meeting is based upon conversations with each of them. Their stories differed only in minor details.
14. Interview with Peter Hannaford, October 14, 1981.
15. *The Pursuit of the Presidency, 1980*, by David Broder, Lou Cannon, Haynes Johnson, Martin Schram, Richard Harwood, and the staff of *The Washington Post*, Berkley Books, 1980, page 152.
16. "Challenges to Statements Putting Reagan on the Defensive," by Douglas E. Kneeland,

The New York Times, April 13, 1980.

17. Kemp was known by 12 percent of the voters and Laxalt by only 6 percent. For a more detailed analysis of this poll, see *Reagan,* page 264.

18. Interview with Stuart Spencer, November 18, 1980.

Chapter 30: President

1. Interview with Richard Wirthlin, March 3, 1989.

2. "What Price Glory, Captain Reagan?" by Frank McAdams, *Los Angeles Times,* August 27, 1980.

3. "Reagan to Keep Status Quo on China, Aide Says," by Larry Green, *Los Angeles Times,* July 11, 1980.

4. "Woodcock Warns Reagan Stand Perils Ties to China," by Linda Mathews, *Los Angeles Times,* August 27, 1980.

5. I was the reporter. A friend had tipped me off that Spencer was coming to Washington, and we talked after he arrived and before he went to Wexford. At the time, Spencer expressed confidence about his ability to help Reagan but said he didn't want to commit himself until he knew more about the staff situation.

6. Some other mythical books attributed to campaign figures by the Reagan press corps were: *Beyond Reason: The Collected Speeches and Press Conferences of Ronald Reagan; The Return of Frankenstein,* by Henry Kissinger; *With All Deliberate Speed: The Memoirs of Edwin Meese; The Case for Chiang Kai-shek,* by Michael Deaver, with an introduction on Taiwan by Peter Hannaford; *Second Choice: My Years with Reagan,* by Stuart Spencer; and *Lies, Damn Lies and Statistics: An Unauthorized Biography of Richard Wirthlin,* by Pat Caddell.

7. "The Campaign Chieftains," by Myra MacPherson, *The Washington Post,* January 18, 1976.

8. Interview with Stuart Spencer, November 18, 1980.

9. "The Smear," by George F. Will, *The Washington Post,* September 21, 1980.

10. *Blue Smoke and Mirrors: How Reagan Won and Why Carter Lost the Election of 1980,* Jack W. Germond and Jules Witcover, The Viking Press, 1981, page 246.

11. *The Pursuit of the Presidency, 1980,* page 279.

12. The attempt to rescue the hostages, known as Operation Eagle Claw, failed on April 24, 1980, when a helicopter developed engine trouble in a staging area of the Iranian desert. As U.S. forces withdrew, two planes collided, killing eight of the would-be rescuers. Secretary of State Cy Vance opposed using force to free the hostages and told President Carter he would resign after it was over, no matter what the outcome. He did and was sharply criticized by Carter.

13. "The Campaign Carter Couldn't Win," by Hamilton Jordan, *Life* magazine, January 1981. Moretti told me in August of that year that he and Unruh had wasted their time in Washington because the Carter people were not receptive to their warnings about Reagan.

14. "Carter Assailed For Depicting a Warlike Reagan," by Edward Walsh and Lou Cannon, *The Washington Post,* September 24, 1980.

15. "Carter Criticizes Reagan on Arms Control," by Edward Walsh, *The Washington Post,* October 7, 1980.

16. Interview with Stuart Spencer, November 18, 1980.

17. Ibid.

18. Reagan remembered his promise as a commitment to appoint a woman to the first vacancy on the court. For a discussion of her appointment, see *President Reagan: The Role of a Lifetime,* pages 804–805 in the 1991 edition and pages 722–723 in the 2000 edition.

19. Interview with Ronald Reagan, August 19, 1980.

20. Wirthlin's theory about why Carter was ahead in the October 14 survey is that there was a lag between the impact of Carter's attacks on Reagan and the backlash effect of these attacks on Carter. This was particularly true, Wirthlin said, with the October 6 speech in Chicago, where Carter talked about the election determining "whether Americans might

be separated, black from white, Jew from Christian," and so on. As that statement made the rounds and was repeated, it continued to show up in voter responses well into the final month of the campaign.

21. Interview with Stuart Spencer, November 18, 1980.

22. Anderson first made this statement, which he afterward repeated on several occasions, at the forum of six Republican presidential candidates in Des Moines, Iowa, on January 6, 1980. This was the forum before the Iowa caucuses in which Reagan did not participate.

23. *Blue Smoke and Mirrors*, page 280.

24. Interview with Michael Deaver, October 13, 1981.

25. "The Unfolding Hostage Drama Adds New Volatility to Election," by David S. Broder, *The Washington Post*, November 3, 1980.

26. Reagan's more familiar summary of these questions was: "Are you better off than you were four years ago?" Michael Barone traced this rhetorical question to a June 1934 fireside chat by Franklin D. Roosevelt, who was campaigning for Democrats in the first midterm election of the New Deal. For more details, see *Our Country*, page 595.

27. Carter's percentage of the vote was the lowest for an incumbent president since Herbert Hoover's in 1932. Republicans also gained thirteen Senate seats and won control of the Senate for the first time since 1952. The GOP gained thirty-three seats in the House, where the Democrats remained in control.

BIBLIOGRAPHY

BOOKS AND MANUSCRIPTS

Adler, Bill, and Bill Adler Jr., editors. *The Reagan Wit*. Caroline House Publishers, 1981.

Ambrose, Stephen. *Nixon: The Triumph of a Politician, 1969–1972*. New York: Simon and Schuster, 1989.

Anderson, Martin. *Revolution*. New York: Harcourt Brace Jovanovich, 1988.

Barone, Michael. *Our Country: The Shaping of America from Roosevelt to Reagan*. New York: The Free Press, 1990.

Boyarsky, Bill. *The Rise of Ronald Reagan*. New York: Random House, 1968.

———. *Ronald Reagan: His Life and Rise to the Presidency*. New York: Random House, 1981.

Broder, David S., and Stephen Hess. *The Republican Establishment*. New York: Harper and Row, 1967.

Bronson, William. *How to Kill a Golden State*. Garden City, N.Y.: Doubleday, 1968.

Burns, James MacGregor. *Roosevelt: The Lion and the Fox*. New York: Harcourt, Brace and Company, 1956.

Cannon, Lou. *President Reagan: The Role of a Lifetime*. New York: Simon and Schuster, 1991; 2d ed., New York: PublicAffairs, 2000.

———. *Reagan*. New York: G. P. Putnam's Sons, 1982.

———. *Ronnie and Jesse: A Political Odyssey*. Garden City, N.Y.: Doubleday, 1969.

Ceplair, Larry, and Steven Englund. *The Inquisition in Hollywood*. New York: Anchor Press, 1980.

Clifford, Clark, with Richard Holbrooke. *Counsel to the President: A Memoir*. New York: Random House, 1991.

Cresap, Dean R. *Party Politics in the Golden State*. Los Angeles: The Haynes Foundation, 1954.

Crowley, F. Alex. "The Transition from Pat Brown to Ronald Reagan." Unpublished master's thesis, Princeton University, 1968.

Dallek, Matthew. *The Right Moment: Ronald Reagan's First Victory and the Decisive Turning Point in American Politics*. New York: The Free Press, 2000.

Deaver, Michael K., with Mickey Herskowitz. *Behind the Scenes*. New York: William Morrow, 1987.

Doerr, David R. *California's Tax Machine: A History of Taxing and Spending in the Golden State*. Sacramento: California Taxpayers' Association, 2000.

Dunne, George H., S. J. *King's Pawn: The Memoirs of George H. Dunne, S. J.* Chicago: Loyola University Press, 1990.

Dunne, Philip. *Take Two*. New York: McGraw-Hill, 1980.

Edwards, Anne. *Early Reagan: The Rise to Power*. New York: William Morrow, 1987.

Edwards, Lee. *Reagan: A Political Biography*. San Diego, Calif.: Viewpoint Books, 1967.

Evans, Rowland, and Robert Novak. *The Reagan Revolution*. New York: E. P. Dutton, 1980.

Ford, Gerald R. *A Time to Heal: The Autobiography of Gerald R. Ford*. New York: Harper and Row, 1979.

Friedan, Betty. *Life So Far: A Memoir*. New York: Simon and Schuster, 2000.

Gardner, Howard. *Frames of Mind: The Theory of Multiple Intelligences*. New York: Basic Books, 1985.

Germond, Jack W., and Jules Witcover. *Blue Smoke and Mirrors: How Reagan Won and Why Carter Lost the Election of 1980*. New York: Viking Press, 1981.

Goodman, Walter. *The Committee.* New York: Farrar, Straus and Giroux, 1964.

Graham, Sheila. *Confessions of a Hollywood Columnist.* New York: William Morrow, 1969.

Greffenius, Steven. *The Last Jeffersonian: Ronald Reagan's Dreams of America.* Westwood, Mass.: Tech-Write Press, 2002.

Hannaford, Peter. *The Reagans: A Political Portrait.* New York: Coward-McCann, 1983.

———. *Ronald Reagan and His Ranch: The Western White House, 1981–1989.* Bennington, Vt.: Torgis Ilg Isselhardt, 2002.

Hayward, Steven F. *The Age of Reagan: The Fall of the Old Liberal Order, 1964–1980,* Roseville, Calif.: Forum, 2002.

Heclo, Hugh. "Ronald Reagan and the American Public Philosophy," a paper presented to the Conference on the Reagan Presidency at the University of California at Santa Barbara, May 27–30, 2002.

Higham, Charles. *Warner Brothers.* New York: Charles Scribner's Sons, 1975.

Hobbs, Charles D. *Ronald Reagan's Call to Action.* Nashville: Thomas Nelson, 1976.

Houck, Davis W., and Amos Kiewe, editors. *Actor, Ideologue, Politician: The Public Speeches of Ronald Reagan.* Westport, Conn.: Greenwood Press, 1993.

Jacobs, John. *A Rage for Justice: The Passion and Politics of Phillip Burton.* Berkeley: University of California Press, 1995.

Kerr, Clark, with the assistance of Marian L. Gade and Maureen Kawaoka. *The Gold and the Blue: A Personal Memoir of the University of California, 1949–1967,* vol. 2, *Political Turmoil.* Berkeley: University of California Press, 2003.

Lavender, David. *California: Land of New Beginnings.* New York: Harper and Row, 1972.

Levy, Frank. "What Ronald Reagan Can Teach the U.S. About Welfare Reform." Washington, D.C.: Urban Institute, 1977.

Levy, Jacques. *Cesar Chavez: Autobiography of La Causa.* New York: W. W. Norton, 1975.

Lewis, Joseph. *What Makes Reagan Run.* New York: McGraw-Hill, 1968.

Lewis, Sinclair. *Main Street.* New York: Grosset and Dunlap, 1921.

Lindsey, Jack B. "Ronald Reagan: The First Year." Unpublished manuscript, June 7, 2002.

McWilliams, Carey. *California: The Great Exception.* New York: A. A. Wyn, 1949, Peregrine Smith, 1976, 1979.

———. *The Education of Carey McWilliams.* New York: Simon and Schuster, 1978.

———. *Southern California: An Island on the Land.* New York: Peregrine Smith, 1973.

Meese, Edwin, III. *With Reagan: The Inside Story.* Washington, D.C.: Regnery Gateway, 1992.

Miller, William Lee. *Lincoln's Virtues: An Ethical Biography.* New York: Alfred A. Knopf, 2002.

Neustadt, Richard E. *Presidential Power: The Politics of Leadership.* New York: John Wiley and Sons, 1976.

Nofziger, Lyn. *Nofziger.* Washington, D.C.: Regnery Gateway, 1992.

Pack, Robert. *Jerry Brown: The Philosopher Prince.* New York: Stein and Day, 1968.

Parish, James Robert, and Don E. Stanke. *The Forties Gals.* Westport, Conn.: Arlington House, 1980.

Peirce, Neal R. *The Pacific States of America: People, Politics, and Power in the Five Pacific Basin States.* New York: W. W. Norton, 1972.

Perrella, Robert. *They Call Me the Showbiz Priest.* New York: Trident Press, 1973.

Phillips, Herbert L. *Big Wayward Girl.* Garden City, N.Y.: Doubleday, 1968.

Reagan, Maureen. *First Father, First Daughter: A Memoir.* Boston: Little, Brown, 1989.

Reagan, Michael, with Joe Hyams. *On the Outside Looking In.* New York: Zebra Books, 1988.

Reagan, Nancy. *I Love You, Ronnie: The Letters of Ronald Reagan to Nancy Reagan.* New York: Random House, 2000.

Reagan, Nancy, and Bill Libby. *Nancy.* New York: William Morrow, 1980.

Reagan, Nancy, with William Novak. *My Turn: The Memoirs of Nancy Reagan.* New York: Random House, 1989.

Reagan, In His Own Hand: The Writings of Ronald Reagan That Reveal His Revolutionary Vision for America, edited by Kiron K. Skinner, Annelise Anderson, and Martin Anderson. New York: The Free Press, 2001.

Reagan, Ronald. *An American Life.* New York: Simon and Schuster, 1990.

———. *The Creative Society.* New York: The Devin-Adair Company, 1968.

———. *Speaking My Mind.* New York: Simon and Schuster, 1989.

Reagan, Ronald, and Richard C. Hubler. *Where's the Rest of Me?* New York: Dell, 1965.

Regan, Donald T. *For the Record: From Wall Street to Washington.* New York: Harcourt Brace Jovanovich, 1988.

Safire, William. *Safire's Political Dictionary.* New York: Ballantine Books, 1978.

Schlesinger, Arthur M., Jr. *The Coming of the New Deal.* Boston: Houghton Mifflin, 1958.

———. *The Crisis of the Old Order.* Boston: Houghton Mifflin, 1957.

Schrag, Peter. *Paradise Lost: California's Experience, America's Future.* New York: The New Press, 1998.

Shadegg, Stephen. *What Happened to Goldwater? The Inside Story of the 1964 Republican Campaign.* New York: Holt, Rinehart, and Winston, 1965.

Simon, Ted. *The River Stops Here: How One Man's Battle to Save His Valley Changed the Fate of California.* New York: Random House, 1994.

Steffgen, Kent H. *Here's the Rest of Him.* Reno, Nev.: Foresight Books, 1968.

Stolz, Preble. *Judging Judges: The Investigation of Rose Bird and the California Supreme Court.* New York: The Free Press, 1981.

Thomas, Tony. *The Films of Ronald Reagan.* Secaucus, N.J.: Citadel Press, 1980.

Thompson, Warren S. *Growth and Changes in California's Population.* Los Angeles: The Haynes Foundation, 1955.

Van Voris, Jacqueline. *College: A Smith Mosaic.* West Springfield, Mass.: Smith College, 1975.

Vaughn, Stephen. *Ronald Reagan in Hollywood: Movies and Politics.* Cambridge: Cambridge University Press, 1994.

Von Damm, Helene. *At Reagan's Side: Twenty Years in the Political Mainstream.* New York: Doubleday, 1985.

Wanniski, Jude. *The Way the World Works.* New York: Simon and Schuster, 1978.

Washington Post, The. National staff of. *The Pursuit of the Presidency.* New York: Berkley Books, 1980.

Weinberg, Gerhard L. *A World at Arms: A Global History of World War II.* Cambridge: Cambridge University Press, 1991.

Weinberger, Caspar W., with Gretchen Roberts. *In the Arena: A Memoir of the 20ᵗʰ Century.* Washington, D.C.: Regnery Gateway, 2001.

White, Theodore H. *The Making of the President: 1964.* New York: Atheneum, 1965.

———. *The Making of the President: 1968.* New York: Atheneum, 1969.

Wills, Garry. *A Necessary Evil: A History of American Distrust of Government.* New York: Simon and Schuster, 1999.

———. *Reagan's America: Innocents at Home.* Garden City, N.Y.: Doubleday, 1985.

Witcover, Jules. *Marathon: The Pursuit of the Presidency, 1972–1976.* New York: Viking Press, 1977.

Wright, Harold Bell. *That Printer of Udell's: A Story of the Middle West.* Chicago: The Book Supply Company, 1903.

Articles and Documents

Aarons, Leroy F. "The Student Revolution Breaks New Ground—Bank Burned," *The Washington Post,* May 3, 1970.

———. "Unruh Visits Reagan Backer to Open Governorship Drive," *The Washington Post,* September 8, 1970.

Adams, Harold. "Reagan's College Years Recalled by Fellow Students," *Woodford County Journal,* October 16, 1980.

Allen, Henry. "The Saga of Burgie and Dutch," *The Washington Post,* March 7, 1981.

Arden, Tom. "Reagan Aides Are at Odds on State Budget Reductions," *The Sacramento Bee,* March 2, 1967.

———. "Reagan Steals Show in Capitol," *The Sacramento Bee,* August 6, 1967.

Associated Press. "Reagan Denies Program Would Cut Care Quality," March 16, 1967.

Balz, Daniel J. "'Reagan,' The Citizen's Guide to the 1976 Presidential Candidates," Capitol Hill News Service, 1976.

Beilenson, Anthony, and Larry Agran. "The Welfare Reform Act of 1971," *Pacific Law Journal*, July 1972.

Bergholz, Richard. "Reagan Declares He's Not Moving Toward Center," *Los Angeles Times*, September 30, 1979.

———. "Reagan Future: Which Office to Aim for," *Los Angeles Times*, August 13, 1974.

———. "Reaganites Quietly Build for Future," *Los Angeles Times*, April 9, 1977.

———. "Unruh, Salvatori Meet in Angry Confrontation," *Los Angeles Times*, September 8, 1970.

Blubaugh, Ronald. "Evidence of a Double Standard for Education," *The Sacramento Bee*, March 2, 1969.

Boyarsky, Bill. "Another Democrat Contributor, Foe of Unruh, to Back Reagan," *Los Angeles Times*, August 11, 1970.

———. "Reagan, Unruh: The Final Week," *Los Angeles Times*, October 28, 1970.

Broder, David S. "Conservatives Eye Third-Party Option," *The Washington Post*, February 15, 1975.

———. "Intimates Doubt Ford Will Run," *The Washington Post*, September 29, 1978.

———. "Reagan Banks Prairie Fire," *The Washington Post*, January 14, 1968.

———. "Tax Turnback to States Is Done, Aide Says," *The Washington Post*, October 23, 1981.

———. "The Unfolding Hostage Drama Adds New Volatility to Election," *The Washington Post*, November 3, 1980.

Buckley, William F., Jr. "Reagan: A Relaxing View," *West*, October 1, 1967.

Bumiller, Elisabeth. "Michael Deaver: The Man Who Looks After the Man," *The Washington Post*, March 8, 1981.

California, State of. General Report. Department of Health Services, Abortion Report, 1967–1979.

California Cabinet Minutes, 1967–1974.

California Journal. Analysis of Proposition 14, October 1972.

———. Election reports, June 1970, December 1970, July 1974, December 1974.

———. "Environmental Lobby Suffers Second Year of Defeat for Its Major Proposals," November 1971.

———. Final Summary of the 1972 Legislative Session, January 1973.

———. "Governor Reagan Submits Fiscal Plan for 72–73," January 1972.

———. "Legislators, Governor Hail 11th Hour Victory for Property Tax Relief–School Finance Bill," December 1972.

———. "The 1971 Tax Law Eases State's Fiscal Crisis, Postpones Major Tax Restructuring," December 1971.

———. "The Reagan Tax Initiative," September 1973.

———. "Reagan-Unruh-Yorty Battle Royal," April 1970.

———. "Senate Defeats Governor's Tax Program," August 1970.

———. "The Surplus: Where It Came From and What Can Be Done with It," February 1973.

California Migration: 1955–1960. California Department of Finance, Sacramento, 1964.

California Population, 1967. California Department of Finance, Sacramento, October 1967.

California Population, 1971. California Department of Finance, Sacramento, May 1972.

California Statement of Vote: 1950–1976. California Secretary of State, Sacramento.

Campbell, Dennis. "6 to 1 Decision Affects 106 Facing Execution; Only McComb Dissents," *The Sacramento Bee*, February 18, 1972.

Cannon, Carl. "The Real Computer Virus," *American Journalism Review*, April 2001.

Cannon, Lou. "Appointments by White House Take Right Turn," *The Washington Post*, June 18, 1981.

———. "Both Unruh, Reagan Glad of Slug Out," *Pasadena Star-News*, November 2, 1970.

———. "GOP Fares Badly in New Poll," *The Washington Post*, January 26, 1975.

———. "Governor Saves Tot," *San Jose Mercury*, June 17, 1969.

———. "Governor Says He'd Veto Rumford Act Repeal Bill," *San Jose Mercury*, April 3, 1968.

———. "Governor Warns Ex Top Aide," *San Jose Mercury*, October 16, 1967.

———. "High Dam in the Valley of the Tall Grass," *Cry California*, Summer 1968.

———. "Inside Agnews—A Sneak Peek," *San Jose Mercury-News*, April 2, 1967.

———. "Inside Story of Scandal Fuss," *San Jose Mercury-News*, November 12, 1967.

———. "Reaction Split on Address," *San Jose Mercury*, January 6, 1967.

———. "Reagan: The Iowa Loss Allowed Him to Campaign His Way," *The Washington Post*, June 11, 1980.

———. "Reagan As the Savior of American Liberalism," *The Washington Post*, March 8, 1981.

———. "Reagan Displays Vitality but Bobbles a Few on Opening Tour," *The Washington Post*, November 19, 1979.

———. "Reagan Likes Wallace Views," *San Jose Mercury*, July 17, 1968.

———. "Reagan Woos Northeast, the Key to His Nomination Strategy," *The Washington Post*, January 20, 1980.

———. "The Reagan Years," *California Journal*, November 1974.

———. "Reagan's Camp: Air of Resignation," *The Washington Post*, July 19, 1976.

———. "Reagan's Ranch a Retreat, Tax Shelter—and Security Risk," *The Washington Post*, July 5, 1980.

———. "Ronald Reagan," *Political Profiles*, 1980.

———. "Senate Axes Rumford Act," *San Jose Mercury*, April 14, 1967.

———. "Stand and Be Counted," *San Jose Mercury*, October 30, 1970.

———. "State Finance Chief Quits," *San Jose Mercury*, February 2, 1968.

———. "State Senate Waters Down Housing," *San Jose Mercury*, August 3, 1967.

———. "Turn Back the Tide of Bigness," *San Jose Mercury*, August 29, 1967.

Cannon, Lou, and Joel Kotkin. "The Embattled West," *The Washington Post*, June 17, 1979.

Champion, Hale. "The First 100 Days: A Democratic Appraisal," *West*, April 23, 1967.

Childs, Marquis. "Reagan: More Serious Than Ever," *The Washington Post*, March 16, 1978.

Congressional Quarterly Almanac. Washington, D.C., 1960–1980.

Crowther, Bosley. Film reviews: "The Hasty Heart," January 21, 1950; "Kings Row," February 3, 1942; "Knute Rockne—All American," October 19, 1940, *The New York Times*.

Didion, Joan, and John Gregory Dunne. "Pretty Nancy," *The Saturday Evening Post*, June 1, 1968.

Endicott, William, and Stuart H. Loory. "Barrage of Bottles and Eggs Greets President After Rally," *Los Angeles Times*, October 30, 1970.

Evans, M. Stanton. "Sears Factor Is Troubling Conservatives," *Human Events*, October 27, 1979.

Fairbanks, Robert. "Governor's Welfare Proposals Scored by Democratic Leaders," *Los Angeles Times*, March 4, 1971.

Farrell, Harry. "Money, Power, Politics," *San Jose Mercury-News*, May 5–16, 1963.

———. "People and Politics: Spencer Williams Off to Washington," *San Jose Mercury-News*, January 2, 1969.

———. "Reagan Blasts Unruh Tactics," *San Jose Mercury-News*, September 14, 1970.

fathers. "Interview: Ron Reagan," July–August 1986.

Faulkner, William. "On Privacy," *Harper's*, July 1955.

Fimrite, Ron. "Scorecard/Bob Lemon, 1920–2000," *Sports Illustrated*, January 24, 2000.

Fremstad, Lee. "Three-Man Panel Hears Praise, Criticism of Controversial Judge Nominee Clark," *The Sacramento Bee*, March 3, 1973.

Gillam, Jerry. "Time too Short for Enactment Burns Declares," *Los Angeles Times*, February 1, 1967.

Goff, Tom. "Legacy for State: Footprints, but No Permanent Monuments or Scars," *Los Angeles Times*, September 29, 1974.

———. "Looking Back: His Bark Has Exceeded His Bite," *Los Angeles Times*, July 20, 1970.

———. "Voters Reject Proposition 1; Reagan's First Major Defeat," *Los Angeles Times*, November 4, 1973.

Gold, Mike. *The Daily Worker*, February 12, February 23, March 2, March 16, 1946.

Green, Larry. "Reagan to Keep Status Quo on China, Aide Says," *Los Angeles Times*, July 11, 1980.

Greenberg, Carl. "Friends Say Battaglia Always Meant to Serve Only for Year," *Los Angeles Times*, August 29, 1967.

————. "Reagan Walkout Laid to Ire at Christopher," *Los Angeles Times*, March 10, 1966.

Gregg, James E. "Educator Probes Causes of State College Crisis," *The Sacramento Bee*, January 19, 1969.

Griffith, Winthrop. "The Isla Vista War: Campus Violence in a Class by Itself," *The New York Times Magazine*, August 30, 1970.

Griswold, Jerry. "Young Reagan's Reading," *The New York Times Book Review*, August 30, 1981.

Hager, Philip. "Clark Confirmed to High Court Despite Wright's Objection," *Los Angeles Times*, March 4, 1973.

Hall, Gladys. "Those Fightin' Reagans," *Photoplay*, February 1948.

Harris, Eleanor. "What Is Nancy Reagan Really, Really Like," *Look*, October 31, 1967.

Hill, Gladwin. "Lawyer Revamps Reagan's Regime," *The New York Times*, September 10, 1967.

Hollander, Anne. "The Reagan Style—What Is It?" *The Washington Post*, February 2, 1981.

Honolulu Advertiser. "Those Other Pearl Harbor Heroes . . . Tell Me," December 6, 1998.

Hoppe, Art. "Sir Ronald Meets the Pearson-Person," *San Francisco Chronicle*, November 20, 1967.

Hornblower, Margot. "Reagan: 'Though I Am Wounded, I Am Not Slain,'" *The Washington Post*, August 22, 1976.

Hosokawa, Bill. "It Takes a Lot of Energy to Keep up With Interior's Jim Watt," *Denver Post*, March 1, 1981.

House Committee on Un-American Activities. Testimony from October 23, 1947, October 30, 1947, and April 10, 1951.

Houser, Bob. "Murphy, Reagan Hit Mob," *Independent Press-Telegram*, October 31, 1970.

Hunt, Albert R. "The Inner Reagan," *The Wall Street Journal*, May 22, 1980.

————. "Shaky Start," *The Wall Street Journal*, September 4, 1980.

Joint Committee on Higher Education of the California Legislature. *The Academic State*, 1968.

————. *The Challenge of Achievement*, 1968.

Jordan, Hamilton. "The Campaign Carter Couldn't Win," *Life*, January 1981.

Keppel, Bruce. "An Offer Californians Did Refuse," *California Journal*, December 1973.

————. "Welfare Showdown: Reagan over a barrel," *California Journal*, January 1974.

Klurfeld, Jan. "The MX Debate: U.S. Rethinking the Unthinkable," *Newsday*, February, 3, 4, and 5, 1980.

Kneeland, Douglas E. "Challenges to Statements Putting Reagan on the Defensive," *The New York Times*, April 13, 1980.

Kossen, Sydney. "Reagan will be a hard act to follow," *San Francisco Sunday Examiner & Chronicle*, December 22, 1974.

Larimore, Jim. "S.J. Police Poised, Praised," *San Jose Mercury*, October 30, 1970.

Lilliston, Lynn. "Nancy Reagan: A Model First Lady," *Los Angeles Times*, December 13, 1968.

Los Angeles Times, Staff of. "Reagan's Quixotic Reign, 1967–1974," September 29, 1974.

Lucier, James P. "Panama Canal: Focus of Power Politics," *Strategic Review*, Spring 1974.

Lythgoe, Wilson. "Project Halted: Nixon Stops Sierra Meadow Road Plans," *The Sacramento Bee*, June 29, 1972.

MacPherson, Myra. "The Campaign Chieftains," *The Washington Post, Potomac Magazine*, September 5, 1980.

Maltz, Albert. "Moving Forward," *New Masses*, April 9, 1946.

————. "What Shall We Ask of Writers," *New Masses*, February 12, 1946.

Manners, Mary Jane. "Making a Double Go of It," *Silver Screen*, August 1941.

Mathews, Linda. "Woodcock Warns Reagan Stand Perils Ties to China," *Los Angeles Times*, August 27, 1980.

McAdams, Frank. "What Price Glory, Capt. Reagan?" *Los Angeles Times*, August 27, 1980.

McDaniel, Wanda. "Nancy Reagan, Behind the Mask," *The Washington Post*, November 11, 1980.

McDowell, Jack S. *San Francisco Examiner*, April 23, 1967.

Meagher, Ed. "Death Penalty Ban Assailed by Reagan; State to Appeal," *Los Angeles Times*, February 19, 1972.

National Review. "The Republican Party and the Conservative Movement," December 1, 1964.

Naughton, James M. "Reagan Virtually Concedes Defeat in North Carolina," *The New York Times*, March 22, 1976.

Newsweek. "A Grand Old Man of Parts," March 14, 1980.

———. "Reagan Is Back in the Saddle," March 10, 1980.

———. "Reds: Star Witnesses," November 3, 1947.

———. "Ronald Reagan Up Close," July 21, 1980.

Nugent, Frank S. "'Brother Rat,'" *The New York Times*, November 5, 1938.

Nyhan, David. "A Golden Night for Reagan," *Boston Globe*, June 1, 1980.

———. "Yessir, He's Quite a Guy," *Boston Globe*, August 7, 1980.

O'Brien, Tim. "I.V. Again Peaceful; Curfew Off," *Santa Barbara News-Press*, June 12, 1970.

———. "Supervisors Ask Governor to Send Guard into I.V.," *Santa Barbara News-Press*, June 11, 1970.

Parsons, Louella O. "Last Call for Happiness," *Photoplay*, April 1948.

People magazine. "Five Former Co-Stars Rate Reagan as a Leading—and Sometimes Misleading—Man," August 10, 1981.

———. "The President-Elect Talks About His Health, His Children and His Divorce," December 29, 1980.

Peoria Journal-Star, October 17, 1980.

Perry, James M. "Reagan's Roots," *The Wall Street Journal*, October 8, 1980.

Pitney, John J., Jr. "Perot's Familiar Misquotations," *The Weekly Standard*, September 16, 1996.

Post, Alan. "Measure shifts burden to local taxpayers," *California Journal*, September 1973.

Quinn, Sally. "A One-Man Woman, A One-Woman Man," *The Washington Post*, June 10, 1976.

Raines, Howell. "Carter and Reagan Open Fall Race With Praise for the Polish Workers, Republican Stresses Economy," *The New York Times*, September 2, 1980.

Rankin, Jerry. "Reagan Ranch: Next Western White House?" *Santa Barbara News-Press*, June 22, 1980.

Reagan Campaign Plan, Decision Making Information. Santa Ana, California, June 1980.

Reagan, Collection of State Papers. Ronald Reagan Presidential Library, Simi Valley, California.

Reagan, Ronald ("Dutch"). "Dutch Reagan's Own Story," *Des Moines Register and Tribune*, June 13, 1937, with occasional articles until October 28, 1937.

Reagan, Ronald. "Blank-check state spending must be halted," *California Journal*, September 1973.

———. "How Do You Fight Communism," *Fortnight*, January 22, 1951.

———. "How to Make Yourself Important," *Photoplay*, August 1942.

———. "Reflections on the Failure of Proposition #1," *National Review*, December 7, 1973.

Reid, T. R. "Reagan's Register Totals 25 Percent Less," *The Washington Post*, January 1, 1982.

Rennert, Leo. "Reagan Steals Play in National Debut," *The Sacramento Bee*, March 2, 1967.

Rodda, Richard, "No-Tax Story Jolts Capitol," *The Sacramento Bee*, May 7, 1971.

———. "Reagan OKs Tough Bill On Rivers," *The Sacramento Bee*, December 21, 1972.

———. "Schrade Beats Way To Take Top Senate Post," *The Sacramento Bee*, February 10, 1970.

———. "Senate Ranks Break, Tax Revision Passes," *The Sacramento Bee*, December 1, 1972.

Rosenblatt, Roger, with Laurence I. Barrett. "Out of the Past, Fresh Choices for the Future," *Time*, January 5, 1981.

Sacramento Bee, The. "Conservationists Laud Redwoods Bill," September 10, 1968.

———. "Demos Feel Reagan's Example Proves Need," May 5, 1971.

———. "Dismissal Angers Students at UC; Leftists Rejoice," January 21, 1967.

———. "Gals for CHP? 'Why Not?' Asks One," March 16, 1967.

———. "Governor Terms Tax Tip 'Illegal,'" May 5, 1971.

———. "Reagan, Aide Like Park Plan Proviso," September 11, 1968.

———. "Reagan, Flournoy Trade Harsh Words," March 17, 1967.

———. "The Reagan Years," December 8, 1974.

———. "Reagan's Cutbacks Are Dubious as Economies," March 8, 1967.

———. "2–1 Vote Confirms Clark's Appointment by Gov. Reagan to State Supreme Court," March 4, 1973.

———. "UC Students Take Gripes to Reagan," February 9, 1967.

Sacramento Union. "State Unit to Evaluate Appointment of Clark," February 18, 1973.

Salditch, Martin. "Style Triumphs over Knowledge When Reagan Meets the Press," *Riverside Press-Enterprise*, March 19, 1967.

San Francisco Chronicle. "Senate Tax Vote Is Decisive," December 2, 1972.

San Francisco Examiner. "Death Penalty And the Court," February 20, 1972.

San Jose Mercury. "Governor Shelves UC Probe," United Press International, January 27, 1967.

Santa Barbara News-Press. "'Silent Majority' of Students Urged to Act," Associated Press, April 21, 1970.

Sherwood, John. "The Real Life, Inside, Movie Mag Scoops About Ronnie and Jane," *The Washington Post*, November 23, 1980.

Shields, Mark. "President Reagan's Wide World of Sports," *Inside Sports*, March 31, 1981.

Shogan, Robert. "Bush Ends His Waiting Game," *Los Angeles Times*, April 14, 1980.

Shuit, Doug, and William Drummond. "Violence, Arson, Hit UC Santa Barbara for 2nd Night," *Los Angeles Times*, February 26, 1970.

Sidey, Hugh. Interview with President Reagan, *Time*, July 25, 1985.

Skelton, George. "The Man Who Saved the Sierra," *Los Angeles Times*, July 28, 1997.

———. "Reagan Calls CHP to Protect UC Campus," *Sacramento Union*, February 6, 1969.

———. "Reagan Setbacks: Is Political Grip Failing?" *Los Angeles Times*, February 5, 1974.

Skelton, Nancy. "An Hour with Nancy," *The Sacramento Bee*, May 5, 1974.

———. "Nancy Reagan—Does She Run the State or the Home?" *The Sacramento Bee*, July 10, 1968.

Smith, Martin. "Mental Care Staff Cutbacks Stir Storm of Protests for Reagan," *The Sacramento Bee*, March 16, 1967.

———. "Reagan Starts Campaign Trail in Riverside, San Bernardino," *The Sacramento Bee*, March 11, 1970.

———. "Reagan's Latest Campaign Brings Same Message, but New Audience," *The Sacramento Bee*, November 18, 1979.

Snyder, Camilla. "A Reagan at Large," *Washington Star*, November 9, 1975.

Stammer, Larry. "Reagan Checks His Options for '76 White House Drive," *San Jose Mercury-News*, December 16, 1973.

Stead, Frank. "Losing the Water Battle," *Cry California*, Summer 1968.

Steinbeck, John. "A Warning to the Viet Cong—Keep New Year's Truce or Else," *Los Angeles Times*, January 1, 1967.

Stockman, David A. "The Social Pork Barrel," *Public Interest*, Spring 1975.

Time. "Reagan's Rousing Return," March 10, 1980.

———. October 6, 1947.

———. October 7, 1966.

———. August 16, 1968.

———. September 6, 1968.

Trombley, William. "Governor and Academia Never Came to Terms," *Los Angeles Times*, September 29, 1974.

Velie, Lester. "The Secret Boss of California," *Collier's*, August 13 and August 20, 1949.

———. "This Is How Payola Works in Politics (by Assemblyman X as told to Lester Velie)," *Reader's Digest*, August 1960.

Waldman, Myron S. "Growing Up in the Midwest," *Newsday Sunday Magazine*, January 18, 1981.

Walsh, Edward. "Carter Criticizes Reagan on Arms Control," *The Washington Post*, October 7, 1980.

Walsh, Edward, and Lou Cannon. "Carter Assailed For Depicting a Warlike Reagan," *The Washington Post*, September 24, 1980.

Weaver, Warren, Jr. "Reagan Outpoints Romney at Dinner," *The New York Times*, March 3, 1967.

Weisman, Steven R. "Carter and Reagan Open Fall Race With Praise for the Polish Workers, President Denounced the Klan," *The New York Times*, September 2, 1980.

Weisser, Peter. "Physicians Warn Staff Cuts Imperil Mental Hospitals," *The Sacramento Bee*, March 28, 1967.

———. "Veil of Confusion over Dismissal of Kerr Lifts," *The Sacramento Bee*, January 22, 1967.

Whalen, Richard J. "Why Ronald Reagan Will Be the Next President," *The Washington Post*, March 23, 1980.

Will, George F. "Lenny Bruce on Thin Ice," *National Review*, December 7, 1973.

———. "The Smear," *The Washington Post*, September 5, 1980.

Wilson, George C. "Brown Denies Politicking," *The Washington Post*, September 5, 1980.

Witcover, Jules, and Richard M. Cohen. "Where's the Rest of Ronald Reagan?" *Esquire*, March 1976.

Woods, Tom. "Phil Battaglia, Chief of Staff," Pacific Coast News Service, February 2, 1967.

Wrightson, James. "Reagan Says He Will Be Favorite Son Only," *The Sacramento Bee*, March 2, 1967.

Zumbrun, Ronald A., Raymond H. Momboisse, and John H. Findley. "Welfare Reform: California Meets the Challenge," *Pacific Law Journal*, July 1973.

Index

PUBLICAFFAIRS is a publishing house founded in 1997. It is a tribute to the standards, values, and flair of three persons who have served as mentors to countless reporters, writers, editors, and book people of all kinds, including me.

I. F. STONE, proprietor of *I. F. Stone's Weekly*, combined a commitment to the First Amendment with entrepreneurial zeal and reporting skill and became one of the great independent journalists in American history. At the age of eighty, Izzy published *The Trial of Socrates*, which was a national bestseller. He wrote the book after he taught himself ancient Greek.

BENJAMIN C. BRADLEE was for nearly thirty years the charismatic editorial leader of *The Washington Post*. It was Ben who gave the *Post* the range and courage to pursue such historic issues as Watergate. He supported his reporters with a tenacity that made them fearless, and it is no accident that so many became authors of influential, best-selling books.

ROBERT L. BERNSTEIN, the chief executive of Random House for more than a quarter century, guided one of the nation's premier publishing houses. Bob was personally responsible for many books of political dissent and argument that challenged tyranny around the globe. He is also the founder and was the longtime chair of Human Rights Watch, one of the most respected human rights organizations in the world.

· · ·

For fifty years, the banner of Public Affairs Press was carried by its owner Morris B. Schnapper, who published Gandhi, Nasser, Toynbee, Truman, and about 1,500 other authors. In 1983 Schnapper was described by *The Washington Post* as "a redoubtable gadfly." His legacy will endure in the books to come.

Peter Osnos, *Publisher*